Romania
& Moldova

Nicola Williams

D1048600

Romania & Moldova

1st edition

Published by
Lonely Planet Publications
Head Office: PO Box 617, Hawthorn, Vic 3122, Australia
Branches: 150 Linden St, Oakland, CA 94607, USA
10a Spring Place, London NW5 3BH, UK
1 rue du Dahomey, 75011 Paris, France

Printed by
The Bookmaker Pty Ltd
Printed in China

Photographs by
Mark Daffey   Matthias Lüfkens   Colin D Shaw   Nicola Williams

Front cover: Folk Dancers, Moldova (Grant V. Faint, The Image Bank)

First Published
May 1998

National Library of Australia Cataloguing in Publication Data

Williams, Nicola, 1971-
Romania & Moldova.

1st ed.
Includes index.
ISBN 0 86442 329 2.

1. Romania – Guidebooks. 2. Moldova – Guidebooks. I. Title

914.7604

Nicola Williams

Nicola's first trip to Romania was in 1991 when she trucked it to Transylvania with 10 Welsh policemen as part of an international aid convoy. Within months of her return, she had quit her job as a journalist at the *North Wales Weekly News* and, on the strength of a five minute telephone interview, flown back east to Latvia to take up a post as features editor for the English-language newspaper *The Baltic Observer*. Following a one year stint in Riga, Nicola moved to neighbouring Vilnius where she spent a happy 12 months travelling the length and breadth of the region as Editor-in-Chief of the Lithuanian-based *In Your Pocket* Baltic and Russian city guide series.

Nicola grew up in Wales, graduated from Kent, then did an MA in Islamic Societies & Cultures at London's School of Oriental & African Studies. She updated the Baltic chapters of Lonely Planet's *Scandinavian & Baltic Europe* and updated *Estonia, Latvia & Lithuania*. Nicola lives in France with Matthias.

Dedication

To Matthias Lüfkens for his professional advice, criticism and nit-picking proof readings. Sweet thank-yous for your *caşcaval pâine* fetish which led you a quarter of the way around Romania with me; for arranging our wedding while I was gone; and for good-humouredly travelling back to Romania with me two days after we married.

From the Author

In Bucharest, biggest thanks to Mishy and Max; Diana Pop and David; Denise from the Eastern European Partnership; the VSO gang; Reuters' Adrian Dascale; Liviu Plop from the Ministry of Tourism; Hannes Schwaiger, Roberto and all the guys from the Vila Helga hostel; and Dr Enyati for telling me where Lenin is and giving me a rabies jab.

Further afield, thank you to Jolanda Beldiman; Ana Oniceă; Maricica Văcaru; Cristian Lanoş; Tudor Rusu; Carmen Atiţoaei for her off-road driving skills; Daniela Munteanu for the best *mămăligă* in town; Andrei Munteanu for his piano recital; Ioan & Ioanid Bilius for their home-made cheese and wine; SALVAMONT's Dan Trif; Colin Shaw of Roving Romania; Manuela Zăneascu; Marcel Giurgiulescu; Avram Narcis; Emil Silvestu from the Institute of Speleology; Professor Ioan Piso from the National History Museum in Cluj-Napoca; Grigore Gherman for his strawberries and *pălincă*; Ceauşescu's sister for being grouchy; Dorothy; the Mini-Hotel in Giurgiu for screening Diana's funeral; Denisa Covrig and everyone at Agro-Tur in Vadu Izei; Dan Antal; Marilene & Maria Stoian; the ANTREC crew in Bran; Ciprian Vişan; Sorin Bibicioiu; Laura Vesa in Braşov; and Christoph Promberger of the Carpathian Wolf Project. Big smiles to the masses I don't mention.

In Moldova, thanks to Mark Horton from the IMF; the OCSE in Chişinău, and Sergei Liubovetsky from the OCSE in Tiraspol.

In the UK, eternal gratitude to Neil Taylor; Chris Cross; Dan Mihai; Drago Voirel Tigau; Evelyn Rodrigues of the Eastern European Partnership; Claire Jarvis of the Romanian Orphanage Trust; the Romanian Information

Centre's Michelle Bonnel; Janet Matthew; Tony Shaw; and of course to the dedicated Mark Shipperley of LINK Romania. Elsewhere on the globe, thank you Vladimir Ivanov, Reine d'Hanens and Nomeda Navickaité.

From the Publisher

This book was edited at the Lonely Planet office in Melbourne by Liz Filleul, Wendy Owen and Lou Callan. It was proofed by Liz, Lou, Anne Mulvaney and Mary Neighbour. Mapping was coordinated by Anthony Phelan, with help from Tony Fankhauser, Jenny Jones, Mark Griffiths, Lyndell Taylor and Michelle Lewis. Ann Jeffree and Tamsin Wilson drew the illustrations, and Adam McCrow designed the cover and drew the back cover map. Mary Neighbour, Marcel Gaston, Steve Womersley and Suzi Petkovski helped out at layout.

Warning & Request

Things change – prices go up, schedules change, good places go bad and bad places go bankrupt – nothing stays the same. So, if you find things better or worse, recently opened or long since closed, please tell us and help make the next edition even more accurate and useful.

We value all the feedback we receive from travellers. Julie Young coordinates a small team who read and acknowledge every letter, postcard and email, and ensure that every morsel of information finds its way to the appropriate authors, editors and publishers.

Everyone who writes to us will find their name in the next edition of the appropriate guide and will also receive a free subscription to our quarterly newsletter, *Planet Talk*. The very best contributions will be rewarded with a free Lonely Planet guide.

Excerpts from your correspondence may appear in new editions of this guide; in our newsletter, *Planet Talk*; or in updates on our Web site – so please let us know if you don't want your letter published or your name acknowledged.

Contents

GLOSSARY 481

LANGUAGE GUIDE 482

INDEX 485

Boxed Asides

Map Legend

BOUNDARIES

................International Boundary
................Provincial Boundary
................Disputed Boundary

ROUTES

..... Freeway, with Route Number
.... Major Road
.... Minor Road
.... Minor Road - Unsealed
................City Road
................City Street
.... City Lane
........Train Route, with Station
........Metro Route, with Station
.... Cable Car or Chairlift
................Ferry Route
.... Walking Track

AREA FEATURES

................Building
................Cemetery
................Beach
.... Market
................Park, Gardens
................Pedestrian Mall
.... Reef
.... Urban Area

HYDROGRAPHIC FEATURES

................Canal
................Coastline
.... Creek, River
................Lake, Intermittent Lake
................Rapids, Waterfalls
................Salt Lake
.... Swamp

SYMBOLS

✪ **CAPITAL** ....National Capital	✈ ....Airport	← ....One Way Street
◉ **CAPITAL** ....Provincial Capital	～ ...Ancient or City Wall	P ....Parking
● **CITY** ....City	✪ Bank, Foreign Exchange	)(................Pass
● **Town** .... Town	☂ ....Beach	⛽ ....Petrol Station
● Village ....Village	⌒ ....Cave	★ ....Police Station
	➕ ☗ ....Church	☒ .... Post Office
■ ....Place to Stay	～～ ...Cliff or Escarpment	⁂ ....Ruins
⅄ ....Camping Ground	⬔ ....Dive Site	❖ ....Shopping Centre
⌂ ....Caravan Park	⊘ ....Embassy	⚘ ....Ski Field
⌂ ....Hut or Chalet	⌐ ....Golf Course	◎ ....Spring
	✛ ....Hospital	🏛 ....Stately Home
▼ ....Place to Eat	❈ ....Lookout	▭ ....Swimming Pool
⛾ ....Pub or Bar	⚑ ....Monument, Statue	⬚ ....Synagogue
	▣ ....Mosque	☎ ....Telephone
○ ....Point of Interest	▲ ....Mountain or Hill	❶ .....Tourist Information
	⛩ Museum, Art Gallery	◒ ....Transport
	⚓ ....National Park	🐾 ....Zoo

Note: not all symbols displayed above appear in this book

Map Index

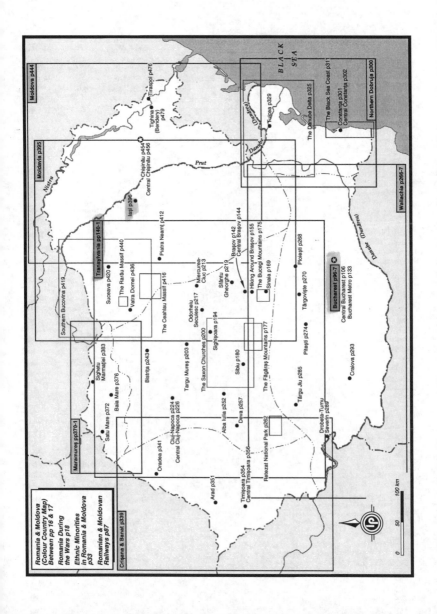

Romania & Moldova
(Colour Country Map)
Between pp 16 & 17

Romania During
the Wars p18

Ethnic Minorities
in Romania & Moldova
p33

Romanian & Moldovan
Railways p87

Crişana & Banat p339

Maramureş pp370-1

Satu Mare p372

Sighetu
Marmaţiei p383

Baia Mare p376

Oradea p341

Cluj-Napoca p224
Central Cluj-Napoca p226

Bistriţa p243

Targu Mureş p203

Arad p351

Timişoara p354
Central Timişoara p356

Alba Iulia p252

Deva p257

The Saxon Churches p200

Sighişoara p194

Sibiu p180

Retezat National Park p262

The Făgăraş Mountains p177

Targu Jiu p285

Drobeta-Turnu
Severin p289

Craiova p293

BLACK
SEA

Moldova p444

Moldavia p395

Iaşi p395

Transylvania pp140-1

Southern Bucovina p419

Suceava p420

The Rarău Massif p440

Vatra Dornei p436

The Ceahlău Massif p416

Piatra Neamţ p412

Miercurea-
Ciuc p213

Odorheiu
Secuiesc p217

Sfântu
Gheorghe p219

Braşov p142
Central Braşov p144

Hiking Around Braşov p155

The Bucegi Mountains p175

Sinaia p169

Ploieşti p268

Piteşti p274

Targovişte p270

Wallachia p266-7

Chişinău p454
Central Chişinău p456

Prut

Nistru

Tighina
(Bendery)
p479

Tiraspol p476

Dunărea

Danube (Dunărea)

Northern Dobruja p300

The Black Sea Coast p311

Constanţa p301
Central Constanţa p302

The Danube Delta p325

Tulcea p329

Bucharest p96-7

Central Bucharest p106
Bucharest Metro p133

0   50   100 km

Introduction

Romania is a country of crazy superstitions and fantastic legends. With its dramatic castles and medieval towns where mass tourism means you, a horse and cart and a handful of farmers, Romania *is* the Wild West of eastern Europe.

Dracula fiends flock to this land of alpine peaks, Black Sea beaches, and fantastic castles in the Carpathian mountains. Ghoulish appetites feed on Romania's rich pageant of medieval princes, about whom heroic and horror stories abound (Bram Stoker's *Dracula* novel included). These noble spirits live in the country's abundant ruined palaces and restored monasteries.

Few eastern European nations feature such a kaleidoscope of cultures: Transylvania's towns are straight out of medieval Hungary or Germany while the exotic Orthodox monasteries of Moldavia and Bucovina evoke Byzantium. Western Romania bears the imprint of the Austro-Hungarian empire, while Roman and Turkish influences colour Constanţa and Dobruja. Bucharest, dubbed

by travellers as 'the Paris of the East' or 'Hell on Earth', has a Franco-Romanian character all its own.

Romania's recent past is equally legendary. During Christmas 1989 the world watched with bated breath as revolutionaries rid themselves of one of the most ruthless dictators Europe has seen this century. On 26 December, the first TV pictures of the executed communist leader Nicolae Ceauşescu and his wife-in-crime Elena flashed across the globe: Romania's 20th century Dracula was finally dead.

In 1996 Romania staged a Velvet Revolution. In a last-ditch attempt to rid itself of Ceauşescu's communist leftovers, voters kicked out its neocommunist government and rolled out the carpet for a more liberal one instead. This new reform-minded government has sped along the road to a western market economy, bringing new hope to a people haunted by modern-day Draculas for far too long.

Next door to Romania is Moldova, a

former Soviet republic sharing roughly the same history and language with Romania. This country comprises part of historic Bessarabia and has been heavily Russified and sovietised over the past century. Since it gained independence in 1991, the question of reunification with Romania has cropped up. By 1997, however, this young country, sandwiched between Romania and Ukraine, was charting an arduous independent course towards market reform.

Moldova's bloody inter-ethnic conflict in 1992 briefly made international headlines but the country remains unexplored. Within Moldova, Russian-speaking separatists have created the self-styled Transdniestr republic, probably the last bastion of Soviet socialism in Europe.

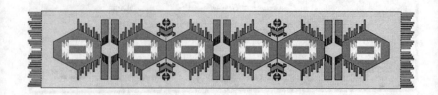

Facts about Romania

HISTORY
Antiquity

Ancient Romania was inhabited by Thracian tribes. The Greeks called them the Getae, the Romans called them Dacians, but they were actually a single Geto-Dacian people. Their principal religion was the cult of Zalmoxis, based on the fundamental belief that believers did not die but went to the god Zalmoxis. The Geto-Dacians communicated with their god by means of meditation and ritual sacrifice. The ultimate communion with Zalmoxis could only be achieved through shunning all bodily desires.

From the 7th century BC the Greeks established trading colonies along the Black Sea at Callatis (Mangalia), Tomis (Constanţa) and Histria. In the 1st century BC, a Dacian state was established by King Burebista to counter the Roman threat. During the Roman civil wars, Burebista lent his backing to Pompey in his struggle against Julius Caesar, prompting Caesar to plot an attack against the Dacians. Caesar was murdered before he could carry out his plans.

The last Dacian king, Decebal (87-106 AD), consolidated this state but was unable to stave off attacks led by the Roman emperor Trajan in 101-102 AD. Further attacks ensued in 105-106 AD, leading to the Roman victory at the Dacian capital of Sarmizegetusa which led to the final Roman conquest of the region. Rather than fall captive to Trajan's army, King Decebal committed suicide. Dacia thus became a province of the Roman Empire.

The Romans recorded their expansion north of the Danube (most of present Romania, including the Transylvanian plateau, came under their rule) on two famous monuments: Trajan's Column in Rome, and the 'Tropaeum Trajani' at Adamclisi, on the site of their victory in Dobruja. The slave-owning Romans brought with them a superior civilisation and mixed with the conquered tribes to form a Daco-Roman people speaking Latin. A noted visitor during the Roman period was the Latin poet Ovid, who was exiled to Tomis (Constanţa) on the Black Sea by the Roman emperor, Augustus, in 9 AD. In the works that he wrote during his banishment, Ovid complained of barbarians who attacked Tomis inhabitants with poisoned arrows, of wild tribes whose hairy faces were covered with icicles in winter, of regular sword fights between neighbours in the city forum, and of the horrific human sacrifices that the Tomisans practised.

Little is known of what became of the traditional Geto-Dacian god Zalmoxis. The Romans destroyed all the Dacian sanctuaries, replacing them with temples to their own deities. Any elements of Zalmoxian beliefs surviving the Roman occupation were rapidly absorbed by the spread of Christianity in the Roman province in the 2nd and 3rd centuries.

Faced with Goth attacks in 271 AD, Emperor Aurelian (270-275 AD) decided to withdraw the Roman legions south of the Danube. But the Romanised Vlach peasants remained in Dacia – hence the formation of a Romanian people.

The Middle Ages

Waves of migrating peoples, including the Goths, Huns, Avars, Slavs, Bulgars and Magyars (Hungarians), swept across this territory from the 4th to the 10th centuries. The Romanians survived in village communities and gradually assimilated the Slavs and other peoples who settled there. By the 10th century a fragmented feudal system ruled by a military class had appeared. Small Romanian state formations emerged, developing first as *cnezats* (clusters of villages) and later evolving as *voievodats* (princely states) and *ţări* (literally 'land'). The eventual consolidation of these *ţări* led to the formation of the principalities of Moldavia, Wallachia and Transylvania.

From the 10th century the Magyars expanded into Transylvania, north and west of the Carpathian mountains, and by the 13th century all of Transylvania was an autonomous principality under the Hungarian crown (although Romanians formed a majority of the population). This marked the first division of the Romanian population, thus preventing the formation of a united medieval Romanian state.

Following devastating Tartar raids on Transylvania in 1241 and 1242, King Bela IV of Hungary invited German Saxons to Transylvania to defend the crown's southeastern flank. He offered the Saxons free lands and tax incentives to persuade them to settle in the region. The Hungarian king also coerced the Székelys – a Hungarian ethnic group who had earlier migrated to the region with the Magyars – into a defensive role. The Székelys were renowned for their remarkable warrior qualities and were granted autonomy by the crown in return for services rendered.

In the 14th century, Prince Basarab I (1310-52) succeeded in uniting the various political formations in the region south of the Carpathians to create the first Romanian principality – Wallachia. Hungarian forces almost immediately attacked the newly created principality in an attempt to force it to accept the suzerainty of the Hungarian crown. From 9 to 12 November 1330, Basarab's forces won an outstanding victory at the Battle of Posada, thus confirming Wallachian independence. The principality was dubbed Ţara Româneasca (Romanian Land).

The small state formations led by dukes and princes in the region east of the Carpathians were united into the principality of Moldavia by Bogdan of Cuhea in 1359. Hungarian king Louis I likewise sent an army to force Romania's second independent land into submission. But again, his forces were defeated.

Peasants dominated the populations of these medieval principalities. In Wallachia and Moldavia peasants were subjugated as serfs to the landed aristocracy (boyars), a hereditary class. There were some free, landowning peasants (moşneni) too. The two principalities were ruled by a prince (voievod) who was also the military leader of the principality.

The feudal set-up in Transylvania differed to the extent that feudal lords – noblemen – could only be recognised by the Hungarian crown. Most noblemen were Hungarian. The peasants were Romanians. In 1437 Transylvanian peasants staged an uprising against the nobles which was quickly crushed. Afterwards the Transylvanian nobles formed a political alliance with the Székely and Saxon leaders. This Union of the Three Nations became the constitutional basis for government in Transylvania in the 16th century.

Ottoman Expansion

Throughout the 14th and 15th centuries the Romanian-speaking principalities of Wallachia and Moldavia offered strong resistance to the Ottoman's northward expansion. Mircea cel Bătrân (Mircea the Old, 1386-1418), Vlad Ţepeş ('The Impaler'; 1448, 1456-62, 1476), and Ştefan cel Mare (Stephen the Great, 1457-1504) became legendary figures in this struggle.

When the Turks conquered Hungary in the 16th century, Transylvania became a vassal of the Ottoman Empire, retaining its autonomy by paying tribute to the sultan. The threefold medieval nation which embraced the Hungarian nobility, the Saxons and the Székelys – and discounted the Romanians – was immediately reinforced by the new Transylvanian Diet. Semi-independence also meant that Hungarians and Saxons in Transylvania were able to convert from Catholicism – formerly imposed on them by medieval Hungary – to Protestantism. The Diet consequently recognised the Catholic and Protestant faiths as official state religions. The Orthodox faith of many Romanians by this time remained an unofficial, 'non-national' religion.

After the Ottoman victory in Transylvania, Wallachia and Moldavia also paid tribute to the Turks but maintained their autonomy (this indirect control explains why the only Ottoman buildings seen in Romania today are in Dobruja, the area between the Danube and the Black Sea).

In 1600 the three Romanian states were briefly united under Mihai Viteazul (Michael the Brave, 1593-1601) at Alba Iulia. Viteazul came to the Wallachian throne in 1593 and pursued a staunchly anti-Ottoman policy. In November 1594 he joined forces with the ruling princes of Moldavia and Transylvania against the Turks, attacking Ottoman strongholds on the Danube and ordering the massacre of all Turks in Wallachia. In Giurgiu on 28 October 1595 the three Romanian armies launched a devastating attack on Turkish troops, after which the Turks called a truce with Viteazul.

The Transylvanian prince, Andrew Báthory, consequently turned against the Wallachian prince and, on 28 October 1599, Mihai Viteazul defeated Báthory's troops near Sibiu. Báthory fled the battle scene only to be captured by Székely troops who beheaded him and presented his head on a plate to Viteazul. To show disapproval for the Székelys' ruthlessness, Viteazul staged an elaborate funeral for Báthory and then marched straight to Alba Iulia to declare himself the new prince of Transylvania. In spring 1600 he invaded Moldavia and within three weeks was crowned prince of Moldavia too. This first political union of the three Romanian principalities lasted but a year: Viteazul was defeated by a joint Habsburg-Transylvanian noble army just months later and in August 1601 was captured and beheaded on the orders of Habsburg general George Basta.

In 1683 the Turks were defeated at the gates of Vienna and in 1687 Transylvania came under Habsburg rule. Great attempts were made during this period to convert Orthodox Romanians – whose faith still remained unrecognised – to Catholicism, and between 1703 and 1711 the Austrian Habsburgs suppressed an independence struggle led by the Transylvanian prince, Francis (Ferenc) Rákóczi II.

The 18th century in Transylvania marked the start of Transylvanian Romanians' fight for political emancipation. Romanian peasants constituted 60% of the population at this time yet continued to be excluded from political life. In 1784 three serfs called Horea, Cloşca and Crişan led a peasant uprising. It was squashed, and its leaders were imprisoned and crushed to death (Crişan killed himself in prison). But on 22 August 1785 the Habsburg emperor, Joseph II, abolished serfdom in Transylvania.

Turkish suzerainty persisted in Wallachia and the rest of Moldavia well into the 19th century. The 17th century in Wallachia was marked by the lengthy reign of Constantin Brâncoveanu (1688-1714), a period of relative peace and prosperity characterised by a great cultural and artistic renaissance. The Turks called Brâncoveanu *Altân-bey* (Golden Prince) and his reign went down in history as the golden age of Romanian art and literature. The 18th century saw the imposition of a Phanoriot regime in both Wallachia and Moldavia. Moreover, in 1775 part of Moldavia's northern territory – Bucovina – was annexed by Austria-Hungary. This was followed in 1812 by the

Constantin Brâncoveanu presided over one of Wallachia's rare periods of prosperity.

Rural life in Romania

Romania & Moldova

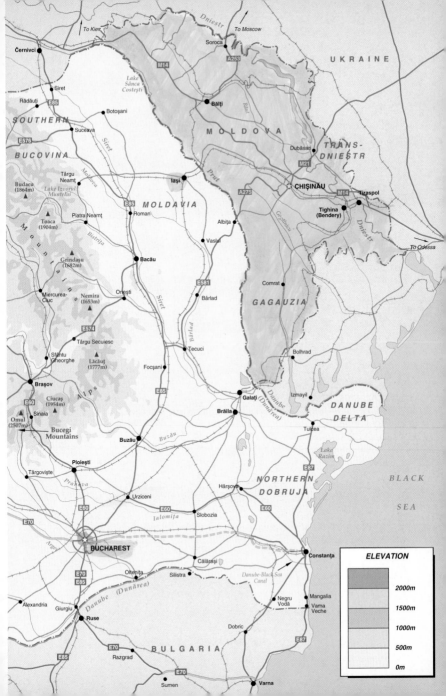

Romanians at work (and play)

loss of its eastern territory – Bessarabia – to Russia.

Following the national uprising led by Tudor Vladimirescu in 1821, native princes were returned to the Wallachian and Moldavian thrones. After the Russo-Turkish War of 1828-9 Ottoman domination over the principalities finally came to an end.

Nationalism

The year 1848 was one of revolutions in Wallachia, Moldavia and Transylvania as well as the rest of Europe. The uprisings in all three principalities were unsuccessful but they gave impetus to a growing national movement which culminated in the creation of the national state of Romania in 1862.

Severe droughts in Wallachia and Moldavia followed by a cholera epidemic pre-empted the revolutions in these two principalities. The Wallachian nationalist movement's manifesto called for the abolition of serfdom and boyar privileges, freedom of the press and a democratically elected assembly. Russian troops intervened to squash revolutionary troops. In Moldavia ruling prince Mihai Sturdza initially conducted talks with the revolutionaries demanding reforms. Fearing Tsarist intervention however, he almost immediately arrested revolutionary leaders.

In Transylvania the revolution was entangled with the Hungarian revolution which was led in Transylvania by Hungarian poet Petőfi Sándor. Hungarian revolutionaries sought an end to Habsburg domination of Hungary. Romanian revolutionaries demanded their political emancipation, equality and the abolition of serfdom.

Meanwhile in Budapest Hungarian revolutionaries had succeeded in briefly overthrowing the government, but in October 1848 Austrian rule was restored. The Austrian authorities then struck a deal with Transylvania's Romanians, promising them national recognition in return for joining forces with them against the Hungarian revolutionaries in Transylvania. Thus, in a twist of fate, Transylvanian Romanians fought against Transylvanian Hungarians.

Russian intervention finally squashed the Hungarian revolutionaries, ending a revolution that had shocked all sides by its escalation into civil war.

In its aftermath the Transylvanian Diet was abolished and the region fell under direct rule of Austria-Hungary from Budapest. Any remnants of Romanian nationalism were rapidly absorbed in the ruthless Magyarisation that followed. Hungarian was established as the official language and any Romanians – such as the Memorandumists of 1892 – who dared oppose the regime were severely punished.

By contrast Wallachia and Moldavia prospered in the years that followed. Romanian nationalism was accelerated further by Russian defeat in the Crimean War (1853-56), and in 1859, with French support, Alexandru Ioan Cuza was elected to the thrones of Moldavia and Wallachia, creating a national state that came into force as the United Romanian Principalities on 11 December 1861 (renamed Romania in 1862).

The reform-minded Cuza was forced to abdicate in 1866 and his place was taken by the Prussian prince Carol I. With Russian assistance, Romania declared independence from the Ottoman Empire in 1877. After the 1877-8 War of Independence, Dobruja – up to now part of the Ottoman Empire – became part of Romania. Under the consequent Treaty of San Stefano and the Congress of Berlin in 1878, Romanian independence was recognised. In 1881 it was declared a kingdom and on 22 May 1881 Carol I was crowned king of Romania.

WWI

Despite Romania forming a secret alliance with the Triple Entente (Britain, France and Russia) in 1883, Romania did not enter WWI immediately. In an equally secret agreement made with the Central Powers (Germany and Austria-Hungary), Carol I traded Romania's neutrality for recognition of part of Transylvania and Bucovina. However the king died in 1914. He was succeeded by his nephew Ferdinand I who, in 1916, gave his blessing for Romania to join WWI on the side of the

Triple Entente. Its objective was to liberate Transylvania – where 60% of the population was Romanian – from Austria-Hungary. During the fighting, the Central Powers occupied Wallachia, but Moldavia was staunchly defended by Romanian and Russian troops.

The defeat of Austria-Hungary in 1918 paved the way for the formation of modern Romania. Bessarabia, the area east of the Prut River which had been part of Moldavia until 1812 when it was taken by the Russians, was joined to Romania. Likewise Bucovina which had been in Austrian-Hungarian hands since 1775, was also reunited with Romania. Part of the Austrian-Hungarian Banat which had been incorporated in Romania, was also handed over. Furthermore, Transylvania was finally united with Romania. Hence, at the end of WWI Romania – now known as Greater Romania – more than doubled its territory (from 120,000sq km to 295,000sq km) and its pop-

ulation (from 7.5 to 16 million). The acquisition of this new territory was ratified by the Triple Entente powers in 1920 under the Treaty of Trianon.

WWII

In the years leading up to WWII, Romania, under the able guidance of foreign minister Nicolae Titulescu, sought security in an alliance with France and Britain, and joined Yugoslavia and Czechoslovakia in the Little Entente. Romania also signed a Balkan Pact with Yugoslavia, Turkey and Greece, and later established diplomatic relations with the USSR. These efforts were weakened by the western powers' appeasement of Hitler and by Romania's own King Carol II.

Carol II succeeded his father Ferdinand I to the throne. Under Ferdinand I, numerous political parties had emerged, of which the National Liberal Party led initially by Ion C Brătianu (1909-27) and the National Peasant Party headed by Iuliu Maniu (1926-33) played key roles in governing the country. Extreme right-wing parties opposed to a democratic regime also emerged, notably the anti-Semitic League of the National Christian Defence which consequently gave birth to the Legion of the Archangel Michael in 1927. This notorious breakaway faction, better known as the fascist Iron Guard was led by Corneliu Codreanu and by 1935 dominated the political scene.

Finding himself unable to manipulate the political parties, Carol II declared a royal dictatorship in February 1938. The following month all political parties were dissolved and in May 1939 electoral laws were passed which halved the size of the electorate. Carol II had the right to dissolve parliament. Between 1939 and 1940 alone, Romania had no less than nine different governments.

In 1939 Carol II clamped down on the anti-Semitic Iron Guard, which until 1937 he had actively supported. He had Codreanu and 13 other legionaries arrested and sentenced to 10 years imprisonment. Then he ordered their assassination. In revenge for their leader's death, Iron Guard members murdered Carol II's prime minister, Armand

GREATER ROMANIA (After WWI)

POLAND

HUNGARY

Bucovina

Bessarabia

Moldavia

Iași

Transylvania

USSR

Wallachia

YUGO-SLAVIA

⊕ Bucharest

BLACK SEA

■ Acquired by Romania (1918-1920)

Southern Dobruja

BULGARIA

ROMANIA (During WWII)

Northern Bucovina (to USSR)

HUNGARY

Transylvania (to Hungary)

Iași

USSR

Bessarabia (to USSR)

Timișoara

Brașov

YUGO-SLAVIA

⊕ Bucharest

BLACK SEA

■ Ceded from Romania (1940)

Southern Dobruja (to Bulgaria)

BULGARIA

Călinescu, leading to the bloody murder of 252 Iron Guard members by Carol II. In accordance with the king's wishes, the corpses were strung up in public squares.

Romania was isolated after the fall of France in May 1940, and in June 1940 Greater Romania collapsed in accordance with the Molotov-Ribbentrop Pact. The USSR occupied Bessarabia (which had been taken from Russia after WWI). On 30 August 1940 Romania was forced to cede northern Transylvania (which covers 43,493sq km) and its 2.6 million inhabitants to Hungary by order of Nazi Germany and Fascist Italy. In September 1940 southern Dobruja was given to Bulgaria.

Not surprisingly, these setbacks sparked widespread popular demonstrations. Even Carol II realised he could not squash the increasing mass hysteria and on the advice of one of his councillors, the king called in General Marshall Ion Antonescu. To defend the interests of the ruling classes, Ion Antonescu forced King Carol II to abdicate in favour of the king's 19-year-old son Michael. Antonescu then imposed a fascist dictatorship with himself as *conducător* (supreme leader). German troops were allowed to enter Romania in October 1940, and in June 1941 Antonescu joined Hitler's anti-Soviet war. One of Antonescu's aims in joining forces with Hitler was to recover Bessarabia and this was achieved in August 1941. The results of this Romanian-Nazi alliance were gruesome, with at least 400,000 Romanian Jews – mainly from newly regained Bessarabia – and 40,000 Roma deported to transit camps in Transdniestr and murdered in Auschwitz. After the war, Antonescu was tried as a war criminal: King Michael ordered his arrest on 23 August 1944 then turned him over to the Soviet authorities who condemned him to death in a show trial in Moscow two years later. Following the war, Bessarabia fell back into the hands of the USSR.

Throughout WWII, anti-Nazi resentment smouldered among the Romanian soldiers and people. As the war went badly and the Soviet army approached Romania's borders,

a rare national consensus was achieved. On 23 August 1944 Romania suddenly changed sides, captured 53,159 German soldiers who were in Romania at the time, and declared war on Nazi Germany. By this dramatic act, Romania salvaged its independence and shortened the war. By 25 October the Romanian and Soviet armies had driven the Hungarian and German forces from Transylvania. The Romanian army went on to fight in Hungary and Czechoslovakia. The costs, however, were appalling: 500,000 Romanian soldiers died fighting for the Axis powers, and another 170,000 died after Romania joined the Allies.

The Communist Era

Prior to 1945 Romania's Communist Party had no more than 1000 members and had little influence. Its post-war ascendancy, which saw membership soar to over one million, was a consequence of backing from Moscow. The Soviet-engineered return of Transylvania greatly enhanced the prestige of the left-wing parties, which won the parliamentary elections in November 1946. A year later Prime Minister Petru Groza forced King Michael to abdicate (allegedly by holding the queen mother at gun-point), the monarchy was abolished, and a Romanian People's Republic proclaimed.

A period of state terror then ensued in which all the pre-war leaders, prominent intellectuals and suspected dissidents were rounded up and imprisoned or interned in hard-labour camps. Peasants who opposed collectivisation of agriculture – integral to communist plans for a national economy – were also imprisoned. The most notorious prisons were in Pitești, Gherla, Sighetu Marmațtiei and Aiud where some of the worst abuses in the Soviet bloc occurred. Psychiatric hospitals were used for political purposes too.

In 1948 the Communist and Social Democratic parties united as the Romanian Workers' Party (in 1965 the name was changed back to the Romanian Communist Party). On 11 June 1948 a law on nationalisation was passed, paving the way for the state control of the country's industrial factories, mines and businesses – representing 90% of the country's production – by 1950. A new constitution based on the USSR model was introduced, pre-empting the intense period of the Russification of Romania. In 1953 a new Slavicised orthography was introduced to obliterate all Latin roots of the Romanian language, while street and town names were changed to honour Soviet figures. The town of Braşov was renamed Staline.

Romania's loyalty to Moscow continued until the late 1950s. It then started to distance itself from the Soviet Union. Soviet troops were withdrawn from Romania in 1958, and street and town names were changed once more to emphasise the country's Roman heritage. After 1960 Romania adopted an independent foreign policy under two 'national' communist leaders, Gheorghe Gheorghiu-Dej (1952-65) and his protégé Nicolae Ceauşescu (1965-89), both of whom had been imprisoned during WWII. Under these figures the concept of a great Romanian Socialist state was flaunted. Ceauşescu's first move was to change the Stalinist Romînia back to România.

Unlike other Warsaw Pact countries, Romania was allowed to deviate from the official Soviet line. While it remained a member of the Warsaw Pact, Romania did not participate in joint military manoeuvres after 1962. Romania never broke with the USSR, as did Tito's Yugoslavia and Mao's China, but Ceauşescu did refuse to assist the Soviets in their 1968 'intervention' in Czechoslovakia. He even condemned the invasion publicly as a 'shameful moment in the history of the revolutionary movement', earning him praise and economic aid from the west and turning him into an international hero. In the late 1960s Ceauşescu received British prime minister Harold Wilson, US president Richard Nixon, and French president Charles de Gaulle. In 1975 Romania was granted 'most favoured nation' status by the US which yielded more than US$1 billion in US-backed credits in the decade that followed. And when Romania condemned the Soviet invasion in Afghani-

stan and participated in the 1984 Los Angeles Olympic Games despite a Soviet-bloc boycott, Ceauşescu was officially decorated by Britain's Queen Elizabeth II. Abroad, western publishing houses such as Robert Maxwell's Pergamon Press reprinted books written by Ceauşescu.

In contrast to its skilful foreign policy, Romania suffered from increasingly inept government at home during the 25-year reign of Nicolae Ceauşescu. In 1974 the post of president was created for Ceauşescu, who went on to place members of his immediate family in high office during the 1980s. Thus his wife, Elena, became first deputy prime minister; his son, Nicu, became head of a communist youth organisation and later political boss of Transylvania; and three brothers were assigned to key posts in Bucharest.

Ceauşescu's domestic policy was chaotic at best, megalomaniacal at worst. Of the many grandiose projects he conceived, only two can be considered successes: the Trans-Făgăraşan Highway and the Bucharest Metro (which opened in 1985). Others were expensive failures.

Ordinary Romanians were kept in check by the Ministry of Interior's security police, better known as the Securitate. The Securitate was an offspring of the secret police organisation, Siguranţa, set up in 1924 and responsible for Corneliu Codreanu's assassination under the orders of Carol II in 1939. The Siguranţa was renamed the General Direction of Popular Security (Direcţia Generală a Securităţii Poporuliu, DGSP) – Securitate in short – in 1948. Its terror lay in its vast network of informers, recruited from the ordinary population. Phone lines were tapped, mail intercepted, all conversations reported. Teenagers who dared grow their hair long or sing Bob Dylan songs were 'called in' for interrogation by the Securitate. There were eyes and ears everywhere.

The Securitate (estimated to number 20,000 full-time personnel by the 1980s and over one million informers) was backed up by militia forces responsible for keeping tabs on people's whereabouts: no one was allowed to change dwellings without gaining permission from the militia and anyone who visited a town where they did not live for more than 24 hours had to report to the militia forces.

The personal liberty of Romanians was further infringed on by a 1966 law which made abortion illegal. Childbirth became nothing more than another of the nation's great industries. Women were required to have at least four or five children and the use of contraceptives was forbidden. Routine gynaecological checks were carried out on women in an attempt to stop illegal abortions.

By the late 1980s, with the Soviet bloc quickly disintegrating, the United States no longer required an independent Romania and withdrew Romania's 'most favoured nation' trading status. Undaunted, Ceauşescu continued spending millions of dollars to build the House of the People and transform Bucharest into a showcase socialist capital. But his greatest blunder was the decision in the 1980s to export Romania's food to help pay off the country's mounting debt.

Bread rationing was introduced in 1981. Rationing on eggs, four, oil, salt, sugar, beef, flour and even potatoes quickly followed. By the mid-1980s meat was completely unobtainable.

When Ceauşescu arranged lavish public celebrations in March 1989 to mark the final payment of Romania's US$10 billion foreign debt, few Romanians were in the mood to celebrate. In November 1987 a few thousand workers had rioted in Braşov to demand better conditions, and during the winter of 1988-9 the country suffered its worst food shortages in decades. Ethnic tensions simmered as the population endured prolonged scarcities of almost everything.

In late 1989, as the world watched the collapse of one communist regime after another, it seemed a matter of time before Romania's turn would come. However, on 20 November 1989, during a six hour address to the 14th Congress of the Romanian Communist Party, Ceauşescu denounced the political changes sweeping across eastern Europe and vowed to resist them. His speech was interrupted by 60 standing ovations. The Congress went on to re-elect Ceauşescu as general secretary.

The 1989 Revolution

The Romanian revolution was carried out with Latin passion and intensity. The spark that ignited Romania came on 15 December 1989, when Father Lászlo Tökés spoke out publicly against the dictator from his small Hungarian church in Timişoara. The following evening people gathered outside Father Tökés' home to protest against the decision of the Reformed Church of Romania to remove him from his post, and by 9 pm it had turned into a noisy demonstration. When the police began to make arrests, the unrest spread to other parts of the city and armoured cars began patrolling the streets.

On 17 December a huge crowd on

During the Cold War, Ceauşescu's foreign policy earned him hero status in the west.

Timișoara's Blvd 30 Decembrie (now Piața Victoriei) was confronted by the Securitate and regular army troops. When demonstrators broke into the Communist Party's district headquarters and threw portraits of Ceaușescu out of the windows, the army used tanks and armoured cars to clear the vast square. Despite this, further clashes took place in nearby Piața Libertății.

Back in Bucharest later that afternoon, the Executive Political Committee condemned the 'mild' action taken by the army and ordered that real bullets be used; this was the start of civilian casualties. The Securitate continued mopping-up operations all night, and the dead were collected and buried or allegedly sent to Bucharest to be cremated. The turning point came on 19 December, when the army in Timișoara went over to the side of the demonstrators.

On 20 December negotiators from Bucharest arrived in Timișoara to buy time until fresh troops could be sent to the city, while newly arrived Securitate units began firing on the demonstrators. At 6 pm Ceaușescu arrived back in Romania from a state visit to Iran and proclaimed martial law in Timiș County. Trainloads of elite troops were dispatched to the city with orders to crush the rebellion.

On 21 December Ceaușescu decided to address a mass rally in front of the Central Committee building in Bucharest, to show the world that the workers of Romania approved of the military action against the 'hooligan' demonstrators in Timișoara. Factories around Bucharest dutifully sent their most trusted cadres to applaud Ceaușescu's speech, as they had done so many times before. But upon their arrival early in the morning at Piața Gheorghe Gheorghiu-Dej (now Piața Revoluției), these people were told that Ceaușescu had changed his mind about the speech and that they could now go home. What went on behind the scenes may never be known, but one popular explanation is that Ceaușescu was set up by conspirators within the Communist Party. It's argued that men such as Ion Iliescu (Ceaușescu's successor as president, and a former Communist Party member) saw a need for *mild* political change, and were thus willing to sacrifice the Ceaușescus in order to maintain control of the government.

Whatever the case, a few hours later the word went out again that the speech would be held at noon and that workers should reassemble. However, the reliable party supporters had already left and factory bosses were forced to be less selective as they scrambled to send the required number of people to the square.

At 12.30 pm, as Ceaușescu began addressing the crowd of 100,000 from the balcony of the Central Committee building, youths who were being held back by three cordons of police started booing. Tension mounted in the silent crowd and suddenly Ceaușescu was cut off in mid-sentence by shouts of disapproval such as 'Murderer' and 'Timișoara'. For a second the dictator faltered, amazement at being directly challenged written across his face (as recorded on live TV). Pandemonium erupted as the youths attempted to break through the police lines while the assembled workers tried to escape. Urged on by his wife, Ceaușescu attempted to continue his speech even as police cleared the square, finally ending as the tape with pre-recorded applause and cheers was switched off.

Meanwhile the anti-Ceaușescu demonstrators retreated to the wide boulevard between Piața Universității and Piața Romană. At about 2.30 pm riot police with clubs and shields were deployed along Calea Victoriei, and plain-clothes police began making arrests. As more police and armoured cars arrived, the growing number of demonstrators became concentrated in these two piațas (squares). Posters of Ceaușescu were defaced and slogans such as 'Today Timișoara, tomorrow the whole country' were scrawled across most available walls. At about 5 pm, when the crowds still refused to disperse, the police at Piața Romană fired warning shots and then used gunfire and armoured cars to brutally crush the demonstrators.

Armoured cars also drove into the crowd

in front of the Inter-Continental Hotel on Piaţa Universităţii. Drenched by ice-cold water from fire hoses, the demonstrators refused to submit and began erecting barricades under the eyes of western journalists in the adjacent hotel. At 11 pm the police began their assault on Piaţa Universităţii, using a tank to smash the barricades. By dawn the square had been cleared and the bodies of those killed removed.

At 7 am on 22 December demonstrators began reassembling in Piaţa Romană and Piaţa Universităţii. By 11 am huge crowds faced a phalanx of army troops, tanks and Securitate units, all blocking the way to the Central Committee building where Ceauşescu was believed to be hiding. Rumours then began circulating about General Milea, the minister of defence, who allegedly had been forced to commit suicide for refusing to order his troops to fire on the people. (He was allegedly shot by Ceauşescu's bodyguards on the president's orders). Gradually the crowd began to chant 'The army is with us!' and to mix with the troops arrayed against them, offering the soldiers flowers and cigarettes.

At 11.30 am Bucharest Radio announced the 'suicide' of the 'traitor' Milea and the proclamation of a state of emergency. As thousands of people moved towards the Central Committee building, the Securitate drew back. At around noon Ceauşescu again appeared on the balcony and attempted to speak, but people began booing and throwing objects at him, forcing him to duck back quickly inside the building. At this point the crowd surged in through the main doors past unresisting police. Ceauşescu, his wife and several others managed to escape by helicopter from the roof. Soon after, the radio and TV stations were taken by the rebels who did not meet any resistance.

The helicopter took the Ceauşescus to their villa at Snagov, north of Bucharest. The plan was to proceed to an air base near Piteşti, where a waiting jet would take them into exile. Halfway to Piteşti, however, the helicopter pilot feigned engine trouble and set the chopper down beside a highway, where the two Securitate officers present commandeered a passing private car. The party then drove on to Târgovişte, where the Ceauşescus were arrested and taken to the local military base.

Other members of the Ceauşescu family were also rounded up. Nicolae's son, Nicu, was arrested in Sibiu and exhibited on the now free Romanian Television, while Zoia and Valentin, his sister and stepbrother, were later taken in too. TV cameras were allowed to tour the Ceauşescu family's luxury apartments, shots of which were later broadcast. Romanians living in squalor saw pure gold food scales in the Ceauşescus' kitchen and rows of diamond-studded shoes in Elena's bedroom. No wonder Romanians were prepared to believe unsubstantiated rumours that their 'great' leader renourished his bloodstream once a year with the blood of children.

On 24 December Nicolae and Elena Ceauşescu were tried by an anonymous court, condemned and summarily executed by a firing squad. (The army general who presided over the court committed suicide two months later.) Two days later an edited tape of the trial was shown on TV, allegedly to stifle resistance by die-hard Securitate units attempting to rescue them. News reports told of fierce resistance by the Securitate, but virtually all the buildings pockmarked with bullet holes were Securitate strongholds. This indicates that they were mostly on the receiving end of fire from army conscripts fighting on the side of the demonstrators. With their modern weapons, the Securitate could have caused tens of thousands of casualties had they so desired.

The general consensus now is that the Ceauşescus' speedy trial had much more to do with controlling the revolution and saving former Communist Party members than in stopping the Securitate from striking back at demonstrators. Clearly, Nicolae and Elena knew too much to be given an open trial, and there's little doubt that many of Romania's current politicians would not have been elected in 1990 and 1992 had the Ceauşescus spoken in their own defence at a public trial.

Reports of casualties in the revolution were wildly exaggerated. At the Ceauşescus' trial it was claimed that 64,000 people died in the revolution (alleged genocide); a few days later it was changed to 64,000 deaths in the entire 25-year Ceauşescu era. After a week the number of victims had been reduced to 7000 and the final count was 1033. In Timişoara, 115 people died, not the 70,000 first reported.

Democracy or Neocommunism?

Evidently, reformers in the Communist Party had been preparing a *coup d'état* against Ceauşescu and his family for at least six months when the December 1989 demonstrations forced them to move their schedule forward. When Ceauşescu fell, the National Salvation Front (FSN) was ready to take over.

Assuming power in December 1989, the FSN claimed to be a caretaker government until elections could be held. It also claimed that it would not field any candidates. However, on 25 January 1990 the FSN announced that it would in fact run. This prompted mass demonstrations both for and against the FSN amid charges of neocommunism.

The 20 May 1990 elections were contested by 88 political parties. In the presidential race Ion Iliescu of the FSN won 85% of the vote, Radu Câmpeanu of the National Liberal Party won 10.6% and Ion Ratiu of the National Peasant Party won 4.3%. The FSN also won control of the National Assembly and Senate.

In the meantime students had occupied Piaţa Universităţii to protest against the FSN's ex-Communist Party leadership. On 13 June 1990, after police cleared demonstrators from the square, protesters burned police headquarters and attacked the Ministry of the Interior in what the government called a 'fascist coup attempt'. This prompted 20,000 coal miners from the Jiu Valley near Târgu Jiu to travel to Bucharest for a counter-riot. Many injuries were sustained, and it was later revealed that secret police had infiltrated the miners and provoked the worst violence.

In September 1991 the miners returned to Bucharest to force the resignation of Prime Minister Petre Roman, whose free-market economic reforms had led to worsening living conditions. Roman's departure was a serious setback for the whole reform process. Once again, ex-Securitate elements were involved in the rioting that ensued.

In 1992 a new constitution was ratified establishing a semi-presidential system; elections that year were won by the Democratic National Salvation Front (DFSN), successor to the FSN), which formed a coalition government with smaller ex-communist or ultra-nationalist parties and promised to slow down economic reforms.

In October 1992 Iliescu was re-elected president, leading a coalition government under the banner of the Party of Social Democracy (PDSR, successor of the DFSN). Iliescu pursued Romania's slow, turbulent integration with the free-market west. Romania was the first to join the North Atlantic Treaty Organisation's (NATO's) Partnership for Peace program, and in April 1996 Romania applied (in vain) for full NATO membership. It has also signed associate-member agreements with the European Union (EU) and World Trade Organisation (WTO).

In early 1996 Romania met with its historic rival, Hungary, to negotiate trade, border regulations, and the rights of Transylvania's 1.8 million-strong Hungarian minority. This was followed in September 1996 by a landmark agreement in which Hungary relinquished all territorial claims on Transylvania. In exchange, Romania agreed to respect the rights of ethnic Hungarians in Romania.

Despite a period of relative political stability under Iliescu, most Romanians remained disillusioned by the lack of progress. Admittedly abortions had been relegalised in 1990, and freedom of speech and travel reinstated, but this served as little compensation to the vast majority. In 1993 subsidies on food, transportation and energy were scrapped prompting prices to jump four or five times. A retired professor's monthly pension could buy no more than 100 bunches of parsley a month it was argued. Declining living standards, rampant inflation, high unemployment, and corruption in a government perceived by most as a neocommunist bureaucracy, was the primary angst of these people who had expected their daily lives to improve after the revolution.

In the 1996 presidential elections, it was an embittered and impoverished electorate desperate for change that went to the polls. In a last-ditch attempt to win a democracy they had sought, and not got, in 1989, they voted overwhelmingly for a new government; Emil Constantinescu, leader of the reform-minded Democratic Convention of Romania (CDR), stepped into the presidential seat in November 1996,, marking the start of what has been dubbed Romania's Velvet Revolution.

Romania Today

Since early 1997 Romania has been a country on the move. Romanians have been hurled through a whirlwind of economic and social reforms, the majority of which have not made any mind-blowing improvement to most people's lives: poverty is still a major gripe, over 1000 street children squat in Bucharest's train stations, the number of children infected with the HIV virus continues to rise, prostitution is yet to be curbed, and the average monthly salary remains at no more than US$80.

But for most Romanians, President Emil Constantinescu has given back their most precious commodity – hope. Two years ago most young Romanians could not run to the west quickly enough. Today the vast majority are staunchly proud of their homeland, determined to stay put and reap the rewards a better future promises. Monthly inflation has been curbed, while food and transport prices, following an initial hefty increase by the new government, look set to stay. Century-old grievances between ethnic minorities appear to have finally been shelved as the government lives up to its

Emil Constantinescu was elected president on a promise of economic reform.

promise of respecting their rights, while steps are being made to improve social benefits. In March 1997 single women earning less than US$50 a month were exempted from paying the official US$9 abortion fee, while new benefits were credited to families with children.

Naturally there's a darker side to Romania's recovery from five decades of communist rule. The government's decision to clean up Romania's state industry sector by closing down loss-making factories and coal mines will inevitably create mass unemployment in some regions. Meanwhile, the lucrative redundancy packages paid by the government to Jiu Valley miners – the traditional militant voice of Romania's manual workforce – can only support unemployed miners and their families for so long.

More chilling is Prime Minister Victor Ciorbea's decision in October 1997, approved by parliament, to make public the country's Securitate files. This will enable ordinary people to see how their lives were sinisterly monitored by the secret police. Names of informers will not be revealed unless a person can prove they suffered as a result of a particular informer.

Equally sensitive is the government's decision, also announced in October 1997, to cut the number of certified revolutionaries receiving state benefits from 30,000 to 3000. In the immediate aftermath of the 1989 events, Iliescu issued certificates to *anyone* who submitted a claim that they had fought in the revolution, thereby granting them free public transport passes, a free hectare of land, exemptions from corporate tax and other generous benefits. Under the new government's proposed legislation, revolutionary records would be resorted to weed out those who laid false claims. Many Romanians see the move as a welcome attempt to curb corruption; others, strongly opposed to it, chained themselves to fences in Piaţa Victoriei and went on hunger strike. One protester set himself on fire.

GEOGRAPHY
Covering 237,500sq km, oval-shaped Romania is the largest eastern European country apart from Russia and Ukraine. The Danube River drains the whole of Romania (except the Black Sea coast) and completes its 2850km course through nine countries in Romania's Danube Delta. Romania's rivers are mainly tributaries of the Danube.

Most of central and northern Romania is taken up by the U-shaped Carpathian mountains which hoop north from Romania into western Ukraine, southern Poland, and Slovakia, ending in Bratislava. The highest point in the Romanian Carpathians is Mount Moldoveanu (2544m), part of the Făgăraş mountains south-east of Sibiu. The Transylvanian plain (Câmpia Transilvaniei), an eroded plateau with hills and valleys, occupies the centre of the U, while the Moldavian plateau lies to the east. Earthquakes are common in the south and south-west.

Traditionally the Carpathians are divided into the Southern Carpathians, also known as the 'Transylvanian Alps'; the western Carpathians which essentially comprise the Apuseni mountains; and the eastern Carpathians dubbed the 'Oriental Carpathians'. Forty per cent of Romania's forests grow in the eastern Carpathians.

The Carpathians account for about a third of the country's area, with alpine pastures above and thick beech, fir, spruce and oak forests below. Another third of Romania is covered by hills and tablelands full of orchards and vineyards. The final third is a fertile plain where cereals, vegetables, herbs and other crops are grown.

CLIMATE
The average annual temperature is 11°C in the south and on the coast, but only 2°C in the mountains. Romanian winters can be extremely cold and foggy with lots of snow

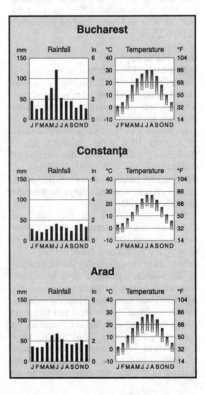

from mid-December to mid-April. In summer there's usually hot, sunny weather on the Black Sea coast. Annual rainfall is 600 to 700mm, much of it in spring. The mountains get the most rain and the Danube Delta the least.

ECOLOGY & ENVIRONMENT

Romania has an appalling environmental track record. This is a legacy of five decades of communist rule when a policy of reckless industrial expansion was pursued whatever the cost to the environment.

In 1987 Ceauşescu approved a chemical and nuclear waste-pit to be built at Sulina, inviting European countries to dump pollutive waste on the Romanian Black Sea coast in exchange for hard currency. In the Sibiu area industrial wastes were dumped by German companies which were heavily involved in toxic waste exports to eastern Europe. Following Poland's ban on this trade in 1990 Romania became even more of a dumping ground.

Pollution hot spots inland included Copşa Mică, a town blackened by thousands of tons of soot pumped out annually from its carbon-processing plant; Baia Mare where a permanent sulphur-dioxide smog discharged from heavy-metal plants smothered the town; and Zlatna, victim of an aluminium smelter. In Suceava pulp and paper works emitted 20 tonnes of cellulose and fibre waste daily. Târgu Mureş was plagued by toxic gases released by the Azomureş fertiliser plant, while residents in Giurgiu and neighbouring Ruse in Bulgaria were subjected to chlorine gas emissions from a chemical plant which led to a dramatic increase in chronic lung disease.

In 1988 international pressure forced the Romanian government to spend millions of US$ cleaning up the waste-pit at Sulina. In 1992 the environmental organisation Greenpeace mounted a campaign to force the German government to reclaim 500 tonnes of obsolete pesticides and industrial wastes it had deposited around Sibiu.

In the early 1990s new smoke stacks were built at Baia Mare – Romania's largest non-

ferrous metal centre – to help alleviate air pollution. The Giurgiu chemical plant was closed in 1991 in response to pressure from the Bulgarian authorities who feared for the future health of its Ruse inhabitants. In 1993, Copşa Mică's carbon-black processing plant was shut. The use of fertilisers, insecticides and pesticides has likewise been reduced dramatically. Despite all this, the communist legacy lives on.

Romania's health record speaks volumes; average life expectancy has dropped markedly since 1990. High levels of carcinogenic substances have been traced in the water supply of 32 of Romania's 41 counties, and nitrate levels exceed safety levels in 14 counties' water supply. Not surprisingly, Romania has the highest infant mortality rate in Europe after Albania.

The ecological ills of the Black Sea and Danube Delta have attracted most attention since communism's collapse. Large areas of land in the Delta are being 'ecologically reconstructed' by the Danube Delta Biosphere Reserve (DDBR) set up in 1991 to act as a watchdog for the region and prevent its further destruction.

In 1992 Romania signed the Bucharest Convention on the Protection of the Black Sea Against Pollution. Since 1992 the Romanian Ministry of Environment has been involved in various joint projects with the World Bank and has played an active role in the Black Sea Environmental Programme (BSEP) launched by the sea's coastal countries in 1993 to salvage 'an ecosystem in crisis'. A telltale sign was the collapse of the Black Sea fishing industry. Only six of the 26 Black Sea fish species caught for commercial purposes in the 1960s are exploitable today.

Green issues are raised in parliament by a handful of ecological political parties formed after 1989. On a local scale, some 50 environmental groups have been set up in Romania but resources are as limited as those on a state level and efforts have little impact on the damaged environment. With the aid of the UK-based environmental charity, Powerful Information, proposed recycling schemes have been submitted to local authorities in some towns.

Romania's only nuclear power plant is at Cernavodă in Dobruja. It was the first plant in eastern Europe to be built with western technology. Despite this plant being built in a known earthquake zone, it is the nuclear power plant 60km south of Craiova at Kozloduy in Bulgaria that poses a greater threat to Romania. This Soviet-built plant has been tagged the 'time-bomb of Europe' and 'the next Chernobyl disaster waiting to happen'. Between 1974 and 1990, more than 260 accidents were recorded at the plant. In 1996 the cost of upgrading four of its six reactors to meet safety standards was estimated at US$4.35 billion. The plant generates more than 50% of Bulgaria's electricity.

FLORA & FAUNA

Pre-WWII Romania was a predominantly agrarian society with 85% of its population leading a rural, peasant existence. Despite the environmental catastrophe that ensued, much of the country's rich natural heritage was untouched.

The Carpathians are among the least spoilt mountains in Europe. Beech trees cover the northern foothills of the southern Carpathians and fir and common spruce trees dress the slopes above 1000m. Alpine forests rich in sycamore, maple, poplar and birch can be found between 1200m and 1500m. Juniper tree, little willow and bilberry bush are dominant in the sub-alpine forests above 1700m. Less fertile zones in this region are home to common spruce forests.

About 1350 floral species have been recorded in the Carpathians, many common to Europe's alps too. Alpine species typical to this range include the yellow poppy, Transylvanian columbine, saxifrage and, in the southern Carpathians, the protected edelweiss – *floare de colt* (literally 'flower of stone').

Most fauna dwells in the lower mountain forests. Beech forests shield over 100 bird species including the green woodpecker, ring dove, grey owl and jay. The mountain cock, hazel hen, black woodpecker and golden pheasant live in the common spruce forests. Romania's thriving chamois population inhabits the rocky kingdom, bare of vegetation, above the forests. Other animals found throughout the Carpathian forests include the stag, wild boar, badger, deer and fox.

About 35% of Europe's lynx population lives in the Romanian Carpathians – estimated at 1500. Some 2500 wolves roam here (amounting to 40% of Europe's wolf population), along with 5500 brown bears (60% of Europe's bears). They live in the forested areas but it is not uncommon for tamer wolves and bears to prowl around the suburbs of Braşov and Poiana Braşov at night to rummage for food in waste bins. Despite this, bears and wolves pose little threat to tourists: bears are generally fearful of humans and keep well away.

Birdlife in the Danube Delta is unmatched. It is a major migration hub for numerous bird species and is home to 60% of the world's small pygmy cormorant population. Half the world's red-breasted goose population winters here. Protected species typical to the Delta include the great white egret, bee-eater and white-tailed eagle. This region also shelters Europe's largest white pelican and Dalmatian pelican colonies, and constitutes the largest unbroken reedbed in the world.

Cruelty to Animals

Between 1976 and 1989 brown bears were protected for only one reason – so Ceauşescu could hunt them.

Since Ceauşescu's fall, trophy hunting has become a big business. A bear yields up to US$20,000 for the Romanian forest administration authorities which encourage foreign trophy hunters to stalk prey in their forests. Hunters who wound a bear without killing it are obliged to pay a US$1580 fine. Since 1989 Romania's brown bear population has dropped by 30%. On average, 300 bears are killed by hunters each year.

Wolves and lynx are hunted too. Since 1996 wolves have been protected by law but the forest administration authorities are still allowed to issue permits to hunt them. Romania's wolf population has been depleted by almost 50% since WWII. Until 1987 when it's use was outlawed, poison was a popular means of killing wolves as well as brown bears, birds of prey and wild boar. Up until 1990 the government offered a bounty of up to 40% of the average monthly salary for an adult wolf and 20% for a cub. Even when the bounty was dropped, wolves remained a prime target for hunters who could sell a wolf fur to foreign tourists for double his own monthly salary.

Romania was a co-founder of the International Council for Hunting & Game Protection.

National Parks

Romania has 11 national parks. The first was created in 1935 in the Retezat mountains in the Southern Carpathians. Others have been designated more recently. There are also more than 500 nature reserves embracing 4.8% of Romania.

The Retezat and Rodna mountains and the entire Danube Delta are protected under biosphere reserves incorporated under the UNESCO umbrella. In the Danube Delta Biosphere Reserve (DDBR) there are 18 strictly protected zones. These, coupled with the large buffer zones surrounding them, cover an area of 273,300 hectares and are strictly off-limits to tourists and locals alike. These zones shelter a 500-year-old virgin forest and Europe's largest pelican colony.

Except for the DDBR, none of the reserves or national parks have organised visitor facilities. Some are accessible by public transport; others painfully not. Many reserves can only be accessed on foot or boat. Detailed information on the more noteworthy reserves and parks are included in the relevant regional chapters.

GOVERNMENT & POLITICS

In November 1996, seven years after communism's supposed collapse, Romanians staged what one international observer dubbed a 'Velvet Revolution'. In the 1996

Romania's coat of arms

general elections the former Communist Party of Social Democracy (PDSR) which had dominated the political scene since 1989 was ousted. In the run-off presidential elections that immediately followed, incumbent president Ion Iliescu was defeated by former geology professor Emil Constantinescu.

Constantinescu, leader of the right-of-centre election alliance Democratic Convention of Romania (CDR), appointed his running-mate Victor Ciorbea as prime minister. Ciorbea, a former trade union leader and Bucharest mayor, belongs to the National Peasant-Christian Democratic Party (NP-CDP), the main party of the CDR. The CDR (which holds 122 seats) patched together an unlikely and heterogeneous coalition government with the Social Democratic Union (USD) led by former prime minister Petre Roman and the Hungarian Democratic Union of Romania (UDMR), representing Romania's 1.8 million-strong Hungarian minority.

The reform-minded government made entry into NATO and the EU, fast-paced structural economic reform and the fight against corruption, its top priorities. Petre Roman of the USD was awarded with the presidency of the Senate (Upper House). Despite frequent rumours about a cabinet reshuffle because of political bickering over the pace of reforms and education reform, the disparate alliance has remained stable, easily surviving two no-confidence votes in June 1997.

The entry of the Hungarian minority into government (for the first time since 1918), the appointment of a member of the Hungarian minority as Minister of Tourism, and the decision to grant more rights to the Hungarian minority markedly improved relations with Hungary. While the previous government had already signed a basic treaty with Hungary in 1996, burying centuries of mistrust, relations were further improved under the new Romanian government – despite protests from Romanian nationalists who accused the Hungarian community of plotting secession.

On his historic visit to Romania in May 1997 Hungarian president Arpad Göncz in turn pledged Budapest's support for Bucharest's bid to join NATO. Despite vociferous opposition from Romanian nationalists to their country's improved relations with Hungary, the Council of Europe recognised that ethnic relations had improved sufficiently for them to lift council monitoring. Both governments subsequently planned to open two more border crossings between the two countries and to construct a highway linking Budapest and Bucharest.

An equally historic treaty was signed with Ukraine on 2 June 1997. Romania gave up its claims to northern Bucovina and southern Bessarabia in exchange for respect of minority rights of Romanians in Ukraine. A similar treaty with the republic of Moldova was in the making at the end of 1997.

Since Constantinescu's government has come into power, relations with Bulgaria – where an equally centre-right reform-minded government was elected in early 1997 – have likewise improved. At a summit meeting in Sofia the two presidents pledged

to fight cross-border crime and to revive talks on the construction of a new US\$400 million bridge over the Danube following years of disagreements about its location. Interestingly, Romania has always had friendly relations with Yugoslavia, and there are parallels between the personality cults of Ceauşescu and Marshal Tito, and the consequent dominance of neocommunists such as Ion Iliescu and Slobodan Milošević.

In February 1997 French president Jacques Chirac, the first foreign head of state to visit Romania since the victory of the centre-right coalition, solemnly reiterated Paris' backing for Romania's integration into NATO in the first wave. According to opinion polls, over 90% of Romanians yearn for NATO membership. In July 1997 when the Madrid Summit met to consider the first wave of NATO hopefuls, Bucharest had already made considerable efforts to streamline its 203,000-strong armed forces which participated in peacekeeping

---

Pro-NATO

Pro-NATO was a cunning feat of modern marketing conjured up by private TV channel, Pro-TV, to stir up popular support for Romania's bid to join NATO.

Each week TV presenter Florin Calinescu paddled in a sea of postcards sent in by viewers and picked out a winner. The postcards, emblazoned with the slogan Pro-NATO, mimicking the regular Pro-TV logo, could be picked up from post offices nationwide. The winner of the week's lucky dip won 10 million lei (US\$1400) – a year's salary or more for most.

Romania's dip in the NATO stakes was less fruitful. Romania has always been a wild card in the race to be among the first former Eastern-bloc countries to be admitted into the military alliance. From the start, the US made it clear it did not favour such rapid expansion and, at the Madrid Summit in July 1997, Romania's bid was turned down. Neighbouring Hungary, Poland and the Czech Republic were all admitted.

Pro-TV's Pro-NATO will no doubt take on a new twist when it's reworked for NATO's promised renewal of talks with Romania in 1999. ■

operations in Somalia, Angola, Bosnia and Albania.

Despite strong support from France, Italy and most countries on NATO's southern flank (Turkey, Greece and Spain), Romania's bid for NATO membership was rejected. Despite diplomatic setbacks, Emil Constantinescu and Victor Ciorbea put on a brave face and vowed to continue the reform process.

On an eight hour visit to Romania in 1997 US president Bill Clinton encouraged Romanians to press on with economic and political reforms. Standing in historic Piaţa Universităţii where many were killed during the 1989 revolution, Clinton said: 'Stay the course and Romania will cross the milestone', adding that Romania was 'one of the strongest candidates' for NATO membership in two years time. His speech was greeted by a 100,000-strong cheering crowd that was treated to free Coca-Cola and popcorn.

ECONOMY

In early 1997 Prime Minister Victor Ciorbea's government launched an ambitious 'shock-therapy programme' to overhaul an economy which was mired in post-communist stagnation. While other eastern European countries had rapidly moved towards a market economy from 1990 onwards, Romania had barely budged from the days of a centrally planned economy. Sluggish reforms and pre-election spending in late 1996 by Iliescu's neocommunist brigade had led to the halt of the International Monetary Fund (IMF) and World Bank lending programmes.

To secure the resumption of IMF credits of US$430 million in 1997, Ciorbea's government relaxed price control in early 1997. Prices for fuel, electricity and staple goods immediately doubled. Heating prices tripled and gas prices quintupled leading to a record 30.7% inflation in March 1997, putting a further strain on consumers struggling to survive on an average monthly salary of US$80.

In a bid to attract foreign investments,

parliament lifted restrictions on the sale of land to foreigners in March 1997. During the seven years Iliescu was in power following Ceauşescu's fall, foreign investment in Romania remained thinner than in any other eastern European country – attracting just over US$2.5 billion in seven years.

The old leftist government, dogged by entrenched bureaucrats and official corruption, resisted privatisation. By contrast, Ciorbea's centrist government slated some 3,600 companies for privatisation by the end of 1997, among them three major banks.

Ciorbea then went one step further, in April 1997 publishing an initial list of 10 state-owned companies shortlisted for closure. In August a second list was published, earmarking a further 17 industrial giants for closure. Not surprisingly, this controversial move did provoke sporadic labour unrest and protests in major cities which the government successfully quelled with promises of generous pay-offs. Trade unions consequently accepted the government's reform programme and refrained from work stoppages.

Just months later, these austerity measures yielded their first results: The monthly inflation rate fell from a record 30.7% in March 1997 to a stable 3.3% from September 1997. Despite this, the approval rating of the governing coalition dropped below the 50% benchmark for the first time since their coming into office.

For 1997 the IMF forecasts a 1.5% drop of the GDP after a 4.1% growth of the economy in 1996. Many analysts believe that the fall in industrial output of 16.3% registered in August 1997 compared to the previous year, would have been stronger if the government had rigorously implemented the closure of loss-making companies. The closure and sell-off of industrial giants is seen as vital for the pursuit of economic reforms in Romania. It will inevitably lead to further unemployment however.

Romania's capital market has seen a large inflow of foreign capital, encouraged by the government's commitment to push ahead with stalled market reforms. The biggest privatisation deal in 1997 was the sale of a 51% stake in Romania's largest cement maker Romcim to France's Lafarge for over US$400 million. The State Ownership Fund, which was in charge of privatisation, also sold Romania's only stainless steel maker, Otelinox in Târgovişte, to the Korean Samsung for US$40 million.

In autumn 1997 the oil sector was undergoing major restructuring with the creation of the new Societatea Nationala a Petrolului (Petrom SA) to replace the oversized National Oil Company set up by the previous government. Petrom's restructuring plan involves the cutting of extraction units from 61 to 11. The company would keep only 39,000 of its 60,000 staff. In 1996 Petrom extracted 6.4 billions cubic metres of gas, roughly a third of Romania's gas production. Its 25 on-shore and one off-shore platform extracted 6.6 million tonnes of crude oil (60% of Romania's domestic consumption), well below the frenzied exploitation of 14.6 million tonnes in 1976 when it had to pay its debts towards the former Soviet Union. Up to 20% of the company which posted gross profits of US$38 million in 1996 could be up for sale in 1998.

The largest foreign companies in Romania include Daewoo Heavy Industries, Shell, Coca-Cola and Colgate-Palmolive. Daewoo, the largest single investor in Romania, has taken a controlling share in Romania's car maker, Oltcit, in Craiova and plans to inject about US$1 billion into the Rodae car factory by the year 2000. Royal Dutch Shell, Romania's second biggest investor which operates numerous filling stations around the country pulled out of oil exploration in Romania after test drills proved unsuccessful. Shell, which also operates three LPG filling plants, announced however that it would complete a liquefied petroleum gas terminal in 1997 and start building a second US$150 million terminal on the Black Sea. Before WWII Shell held the biggest oil and gas concessions in Romania, which was the largest oil producer in eastern Europe after Russia.

Military enterprises have been severely hit by cuts in defence spending. Workers at the Avione SA in Craiova even blocked a highway with a jet fighter, angry at the lack of orders. The US$2 billion Romanian-American 'Dracula helicopter' project (a Romanian assembled version of the US Supercobra) didn't take off due to lack of funding by the defence ministry.

POPULATION & PEOPLE

Romania has a population of 23 million, 53% of whom live in towns and cities. Population density is 98 people per sq km. Bucharest (two million) is by far the largest city, followed by Constanţa, Braşov, Timişoara and Iaşi.

Romania's population is 89.7% Romanian, 6.9% Hungarian, 1.8% Roma, 0.4% German, 0.3% Ukrainian. Other nationalities, including Croats, Serbs and Turks, account for 0.8%. Romania's multiethnicity is most obvious in Transylvania which historically was dominated by Hungarians and Saxons (Germans).

Romanians consider themselves the direct heirs of ancient Rome and thus on a higher plain than the descendants of barbaric Slav and Hungarian tribes.

Many Romanians bear a fierce hatred towards Russians, who they blame for Romania's economic situation. Many believe if it were not for the former Soviet Union's interference during WWII, Romania would still be the economic superpower it was before 1940. Russia's reluctance to see NATO expand is perceived by Romanians as a Russian conspiracy aimed at stalling their economic growth and so maintaining Romania as a buffer zone.

Twelve per cent of the population is over 65. One of the oldest people in the world lives in Romania. Anicuta Butariu is 115 years old. She was born deaf and dumb, never learnt sign language, never married, and earned a living as a housekeeper then as a milkmaid on a Banat farm until the age of 82 when she retired to an old people's home.

Germans

The German population in Romania peaked

Ethnic Minorities in Romania & Moldova

in the 1930s when there were 800,000 Saxons in Transylvania. Numbers have since steadily dwindled to no more than 65,000 today. Their future looks equally gloomy: the remaining German population is elderly and most yearn for a better life in Germany.

Saxons from Rheinfranken settled in Romania between 1141 and 1181 upon the invitation of the Hungarian king, Geza II, who appointed them as guardians of Transylvania's mountain passes. After the Banat became an Austrian colony in 1718, Swabians from different parts of Germany colonised towns in the Banat while others from Würtemberg in Germany settled in Bucovina. Only the Saxons had a political voice in Romania, making up a quarter of Transylvania's population by the 18th century and contributing more than 60% of total taxes paid to the state.

During WWII, 175,000 Romanian Germans were killed or left the country. After Romania switched sides to join the Allies against Hitler's Nazi Germany, 70,000 Germans were accused of Nazi collaboration and sentenced to five years hard labour in the Soviet Union. The survivors· returned to find their land and properties confiscated by the newly installed communist regime.

Under Ceauşescu, Germans, like all other inhabitants, were not allowed to freely leave Romania. Instead Ceauşescu granted them exit permits in exchange for vast amounts of cash from the West German government. In the 1980s, West Germany 'bought' exit permits for some 70,000 people. One exit permit was alleged to have cost around US$8000. Not surprisingly, between 1989 and 1995 an estimated 100,000 Germans left the country.

More recently the German government has spent over US$67.7 million in aid to Romania's remaining Germans in a bid to curb their emigration. The Saxon community in Transylvania totals around 20,000 today. It is served by state-run German schools and represented politically by the German Democratic Forum (Demokratisches Forum der Deutschen).

Roma

The government estimates that only 400,000 Roma (gypsies) live in Romania, but a more accurate figure would be 2.3 million, making it the largest Roma community in the world.

During WWII 40,000 Roma were deported from Romania to Auschwitz, and under communism they remained persecuted.

This anti-Roma sentiment has only deepened since communism's fall. Roma provide a convenient scapegoat for Romania's economic problems. They are seen as the scum of society. Roma villages have been burned by Romanian nationalists with official complicity.

Roma families tend to be large. Eight or 10 children in a family is not unusual. Over 40% of Romania's Roma are children under 14. Many are considered 'problem children' by local authorities and hence forced out of state school. A quarter of Roma between 12 and 20 are estimated to be illiterate. In 1994 a charity school was set up in a mud-brick hut in Bucharest's suburbs for illiterate Roma children.

One bright spot was the success of the Roma Party in the 1996 parliamentary elections. The Roma political party, one of three in Romania, won a seat in parliament. Madalin Voicu, son of one of Romania's top violin virtuosos and a symphony orchestra conductor himself, heads the party. Romania's few remaining nomadic Roma – estimated to be 2000 – look to Roma king Florin Cioaba and rival Roma emperor Iulian Radulescu for support (see boxed aside in the Transylvania chapter).

The Ethnic Foundation of the Roma, Young Generation's Roma Society, Roma Centre for Social Intervention, and the Cultural Foundation for the Emancipation of the Roma all campaign for Roma rights.

Hungarians

In the past, the situation of the 1.8 million Hungarians in Romania has soured relations with Hungary. Under Ceauşescu, all Hungarian-language newspapers and magazines in Romania were closed down, and official plans to systemise some 8000 villages, many of them in Transylvania, threatened Romania's Hungarians with cultural assimilation.

Since 1989 – and especially since 1997 – things have improved. The 1991 constitution guarantees minority rights, and the Democratic Union of Hungarians (UDMR) is represented in both the Senate and House of Representatives, and since late 1996 has been part of the governing coalition. Hungarian-language secondary and university education is provided by the state and in October 1997 the centrist government agreed to set up a Hungarian university in Cluj-Napoca.

Most accounts of ethnic conflicts in Romania published in the West showed quite justified concern for the Hungarian minority, yet tended to ignore the fact that the Romanian majority in Transylvania was subjected to forced 'Magyarisation' under Hungarian rule prior to WWI. For more details on Hungarians in Romania see the Transylvania chapter.

EDUCATION

Education in Romania is free from preschool to university graduation. Some private secondary schools and universities have opened since 1989. A separate state education is theoretically organised for children with disabilities and special needs.

Legally children have to go to school from the age of seven. In reality, only those whose parents can afford to send them do. In rural villages particularly, parents need their children to help them work the fields. Illiteracy in these regions is common.

English and French are the first foreign languages taught in all Romanian schools. This, coupled with the fact that most films at cinemas and on TV are screened in their original language with subtitles in Romanian, means most younger Romanians are practically fluent in one, if not two, foreign languages.

Hungarian, German, Serbian and Ukrainian is also taught in some schools. Where minority groups comprise a class, they can be taught in their mother tongue. In Transylvania there are over 50 state-run German schools: there are five exclusively German secondary schools in Sibiu alone. There are Hungarian schools too. Romania's leading universities are Bucharest, Iaşi, Cluj-Napoca and Timişoara.

Under Ceauşescu, western teaching materials, including all literature by western authors, were banned in schools. Pupils had to learn lengthy patriotic poems and were taught with text books written by Ceauşescu. All books published during this period had to acknowledge in print Ceauşescu's 'intellectual guidance'. Schools serving ethnic minorities were closed.

ARTS

Folk & Roma Music

Traditional Romanian folk instruments include the *bucium* (alphorn), the *cimpoi* (bagpipes), the *cobză* (a pear-shaped lute) and the *nai* (a panpipe of about 20 cane tubes). Many kinds of flute are used, including the *ocarina* (a ceramic flute) and the *tilinca* (a flute without finger holes). The violin, which is of more recent origin, is today the most common folk instrument. Romania's best known composer George Enescu (1881-1955) was a virtuoso violinist and used Romanian folk themes in his work.

The *doină* is an individual, improvised love song, a sort of Romanian blues with a social or romantic theme. The *baladă* (ballad), on the other hand, is a collective narrative song steeped with feeling.

Couples may dance in a circle, a semicircle or a line. In the *sârbă* males and females dance quickly in a closed circle with their hands on each other's shoulders. The *hora* is another fast circle dance, and in the *brâu* (belt dance) the dancers form a chain by grasping their neighbour's belt.

Modern Roma or 'Tzigane' (gypsy) music has absorbed many influences, and professional Roma musicians play whatever their village clients desire. The *lăutari* (musicians) circulate through the village inviting neighbours to join in weddings, births, baptisms, funerals and harvest festivals. Improvised songs *(cântec)* are often directed at a specific individual and are designed to elicit an emotional response (and a tip). To appeal to older people, the lăutari sing traditional baladă or epic songs *(cântece epice)* in

verse, often recounting the exploits of Robin Hood-style *haiducs* (outlaws) who apply justice through their actions. Violin players are known as *ceteraşi*, their music inspiring villagers to leap up and dance *cingăresc* which involves much hip and body shaking with the hands raised above the head.

Professional Roma ensembles or *tarafs*, such as the famous *Taraf de Haiducs* (The Outlaws' Ensemble) from Clejani village south-west of Bucharest, use the violin, accordion, guitar, double bass, *ţambal* (hammered dulcimer), *fluier* (flute) and other instruments.

Under communism, an urbanised folk music was promoted by the state to bolster Romanian national identity. In this genre virtuoso *nai* and *ţambal mare* (concert cymbalum or dulcimer) players are backed by large orchestras seldom seen in Romanian villages. You'll love or hate the music of Gheorghe Zamfir, self-proclaimed 'Master of the Panpipe'.

Classical Music & Opera

The Romanian Philharmonic orchestra was established in Bucharest in 1868 and in the 1880s the Ateneul Român was built. It was here that the 'great genius' of Romanian music, George Enescu made his debut in 1898. His first major work *Oedip*, performed in Paris in 1936, evoked the soul and passion of the Romanian people through elements of Romanian folk music.

Romania's first opera *Crai Nou (New Prince)* was composed by Moldavian-born Ciprian Porumbescu (1853-83). It made its debut in Braşov in 1882. Porumbescu's best known love-ballad *Ballad of Ciprian*, was inspired by his thwarted love for a rich vicar's daughter who he was considered too poor to marry. He spent several years in prison for alleged anti-state activities and died in Braşov at the age of 30.

Romania's best-known contemporary opera star is soprano Angela Gheorghiu, daughter of a train conductor and a graduate of the Bucharest Conservatory. She has made recordings with tenor Placido Domingo among others.

Literature

Romanian literature draws heavily on the country's rich folklore heritage coupled with its turbulent history as an occupied country inhabited by a persecuted people. In 15th century medieval society, when writings were still scripted in Slavonic, an oral epic folk literature emerged. These fairy tales, legends and ballads were firmly rooted in traditional pastoral life and lamented on the great themes of birth, marriage and death. It was in this way that the Romanian *miorița* emerged, originally spread orally and later written down. The *miorița* was a simple folk tale featuring life in the fields or on the mountainside. Behind its colourful images of nature and folk culture, there would be a sting in the tale. Every region created its own version, adapted to the local philosophy of life. An oral literature also developed in the courts, in which the heroics of the great medieval princes and warriors were recounted.

Writings in the Romanian language, initially religious, took shape around 1420. Modern literature emerged in the mid-19th century in the shape of Romantic poet Mihai Eminescu (1850-89) who captured the spirituality of the Romanian people in his work. Only one volume of his work, *Poesii (Poems)*, was published during his lifetime (1883) but it served to create a new language in literature. Eminescu's grand disillusionment with love, interwoven with folk myths and historical elements, chararcterised his major works. Many of Eminescu's poems have been translated into English, including his most famous work *Luceafărul* (Evening Star), which appeared in *Poesii*.

During this period the influential Junimea literary society (1863), of which Eminescu was a member, was founded by Titu Maiorescu (1840-1917) in Iaşi. Maiorescu was a literary critic who condemned the growing influence of foreign literature on Romanian writers. The upshot of this in the period that followed was the emergence of a more realist genre in which daily life in Romania was depicted. In his plays, satirist Ion Luca Caragiale (1852-1912) decried the

impact of precipitous modernisation on city life and showed the comic irony of social and political change. His first play *O noapte furtunoasă (Stormy Night)* was a comedy based on his observations of middle-class life in Bucharest. Perhaps the Romanian writer best known internationally is playwright Eugene Ionesco (1912-94), a leading exponent of the 'theatre of the absurd', who lived in France after 1938.

The quest for 'national values' ensued in the pre-war period. Novelists Cezar Petrescu (1892-1961), Liviu Rebreanu (1885-1944), and Mihail Sadoveanu (1880-1961) all produced their best works during this period. The traditional lives of Carpathian shepherds are unravelled in a Moldavian dialect, distinctive of Sadoveanu's novels, in *Baltagul (The Hatchet)* published in 1930.

Romanian literature became a tool of the Communist Party from 1947 onwards, with few works of note emerging. In 1971 Ceauşescu passed a law forbidding the publication abroad of Romanian works prejudicing the state, thereby removing many writers' only means of expression. Paul Goma, born in 1935, was one of a handful of dissident writers who dared express his thoughts publicly in the 1970s. Goma had already spent two years in prison and fours years in solitary confinement in the 1950s for his outspoken views. In 1977 he was exiled to France where all his major works, including his 10th novel *My Childhood at the Gate of Unrest* (the first to be translated in English), were published.

Feminist poet Nina Cassian, whose works were also published abroad, sought political asylum in the US in 1985 after her poems were discovered in a friend's diary by the Securitate. Her volumes *Cheerleader for a Funeral* and *Call Yourself Alive?* are both available in English, as is *Silent Voices: An Anthology of Romanian Women Poets*, which also features her work.

Since 1989, numerous works have been published attesting to the horrors of the communist period, almost all of them translated into English. The story of Lena Constante – arrested in 1950 for her friendship with the wife of Lucreţiu Pătrăscanu, a communist leader purged in one of the period's 'show trials' – unfolds in her autobiography *The Silent Escape – 3000 Days in Romanian Prisons*.

Don't Harm Thy Neighbour by Nicholas Radoui is an autobiographical account of a Transylvanian doctor arrested by the Securitate in 1948. He escaped, sought refuge for three months in the mountains, then fled to Yugoslavia submerged in the water tank of a train, only to be arrested again. The author of *Hell Moved its Border*, Dumitru Nimigeanu, was a peasant farmer until he was deported to Siberia in 1939.

On Clowns – the Dictator and the Artist by Norman Manea is a cutting, philosophical rampage on Romanian dictatorship as seen through the eyes of an author who was deported to a Transdniestr concentration camp when he was five years old.

Equally angst-ridden is *On the Heights of Despair*, a musing on the Romanian struggle by Romanian-born Emil Cioran 'under the constraints of suicidal insomnia'. The giant autobiography of US-exiled Romanian writer Mircea Eliade – published in two volumes entitled *Journey East, Journey West 1907-1037* and *Exile's Odyssey 1937-1960* – has been translated into English.

Volumes of poems available in English translation include *Demon in Brackets* by Romanian poet Maria Banuş; *The Error of Being* by deportee Ion Caraion; *Let's Talk About the Weather* by satirist Marin Sorescu; and the savage *Exile on a Peppercorn* by Mircea Dinescu, today's president of the Bucharest Writers' Union and a leading light in the 1989 revolution. The poems in *A Jucier Way* were written in English in the 1960s by Romanian poet Mihai Radoi, but were not published until after the revolution.

Contemporary Romanian literature looks to the future as much as its past. The energy of today's generation of writers is epitomised in the two poetry volumes, *Young Poets of a New Romania* translated by Brenda Walker, and *An Anthology of Contemporary Romanian Poetry* translated by Andrea Deletant. The voice of Romania's minorities is also slowly being heard in this genre: *Pied Poets – A German Minority of Romanian Poets*, translated by Robert Elsie, features contemporary verse by Transylvanian Saxons and German-Danube poets.

Film

Romanian cinema has blossomed since the revolution. In 1994 Lucian Pintilie's *O Vara de Neuiţat (Unforgettable Summer)* made a small splash at Cannes. Other films to look out for are Mircea Daneliuc's *Senatorul Melcilor (Senator of the Snails)* and Radu Gabrea's *Rosenemil, o Tragica Lubire (The Tragic Love Story of Rosenemil)*. In 1996 Fox Studios paid US$1.5 million for film rights to *Almost Adam*, a novel by Petru Popescu, who was born in Romania.

Folk Art

Painting on glass and wood remains a popular folk art today. Considered to be of Byzantine origin, this traditional peasant art was widespread in Romania from the 17th century onwards.

Superstition and strong religious beliefs surrounded these icons which were painted, not for decorative reasons but to protect a

Romania Trivia

Romanians adore big-nosed French actor Gérard Depardieu as much as he adores Romania. Since visiting Romania with President Jacques Chirac in 1997, Depardieu has returned several times to set up a business there.

Romanians love big basketball player Gheorghe Mureşan even more; the 2.34m-tall Romanian player, centre for the Washington Bullets, co-stars with Billy Crystal in the film *My Giant*, released in mid-1998. Mureşan plays a simple Romanian monastery caretaker with a gift for Shakespeare who is discovered by a theatre agent and whisked to the US to star in the movies. Gheorghe Mureşan, 27 years old, was born in Triteni near Turda, studied in Cluj-Napoca, played basketball for France, and left Romania in 1993 to play for the Bullets. He's the tallest player in the NBA. ∎

household from evil spirits – St Dimitru protected the cattle from wolves, St Peter held the keys to heaven, while the archangels Michael and Gabriel cared for the souls of the deceased.

Well-known 19th century icon painters include Dionisie Iuga, Maria Chifor and Tudor Tocariu. The glass icons of contemporary artist Georgeta Maria Uiga from Baia Mare are exhibited worldwide.

Painting

Medieval painting was marked by a strong Byzantine influence. It expressed itself through frescoes depicting scenes from the Bible on outside walls as a means of educating peasants, on the iconstasis inside churches, and in miniature form as a decorative frame for religious manuscripts.

The reign of Ştefan cel Mare in Moldavia in the 16th century marked a watershed in Romanian art. The outside walls of churches and monasteries were adorned with frescoes. These churches, famed today as the painted monasteries of Bucovina, were not only the first in the world to be painted in this way – the frescoes tattooed on their walls also went beyond the confines of traditional religious art, conveying political as well as religious messages. A definite anti-Ottoman message dominated many.

The paintings of Nicolae Grigorescu (1838-1907) absorbed French impressionism and created canvases alive with the colour of the Romanian peasantry. He broke the prevailing strict academic mould, heralding the emergence of modern Romanian painting. Grigorescu's work is exhibited in art galleries in Bucharest, Iaşi raiova and Constanţa, and the Nicolae Grigorescu Museum is in Cîmpina.

Modernism was further embraced by Gheorghe Petraşcu (1872-1949) whose paintings also drew on the world around him.

The symbolist movement was represented by Ion Ţuculescu (1910-1962) who incorporated elements of Romanian folk art such as the decorative motifs of Moldavian carpets in his work.

Sculpture

Although primarily a resident of France after 1904, abstract sculptor Constantin Brâncuşi (1876-1957) endowed his native Târgu Jiu with some of his finest works in 1937. Brâncuşi revolutionised sculpture by emphasising essential forms and the beauty of the material itself.

SOCIETY & CONDUCT

Post-communist Romania is a jigsaw of economics and attitude as much as of ethnicity. While politicians refuse to play the game in fixing ethnic relations, the nationality of one's neighbour no longer matters for most people who find themselves united in a common battle for survival. Many of the older generation hark back with fondness to the 'great' days of communism when prices were low, pensions comparatively high and state benefits abundant. By contrast, Romania's younger generation is full of beans. A small chunk of it already drives big fast cars and sports mobile phones: the remaining chunk is driven by the dream.

Romanians are typically strong-minded and stubbornly proud – characteristics that have stood them in good stead since the collapse of communism. Despite an insatiable appetite for 'all things western', Romanians are staunchly aware of their roots and take great pride in their country's rich natural heritage and folk culture. Befriend any Romanian and within hours an expedition to the mountains will be mapped out for you.

Romanian hospitality is formidable. These people spill their hearts to you, welcome you with open arms into their modest homes, feed you until you burst, and expect *nothing* in return except simple friendship. Don't rebuff it.

Dos & Don'ts

Romanians are generally tactile. Men and women both greet each other with a kiss. Women walk down the street linking arms or holding hands, while menfolk offer a hearty handshake to practically every man they meet, regardless of whether they're only vaguely acquainted or saw each other just five minutes previously. Wild gesticulations in conversation are common.

Superstitions abound. The arrival of a guest is signified by a spider in the home. The bigger the spider, the more important the guest. If you happen to be that lucky guest, take a small gift for your host – flowers, a watermelon, but never money. Don't kiss or shake hands across the threshold and take your shoes off when you enter the house. Your host will usually offer you a pair of oversized slippers or beach shoes to wear. Don't expect your glass to be topped up during dinner until you have drained the last drop: if you do have the misfortune to have your glass filled by your host while it is half-full, it means she/he wants to kill you. Traditionally, your inner power and strength is derived from alcohol. Maybe this is the reason why most Romanians drink a lot, at any time of day.

On the streets, expect good luck if someone crosses your path with a pail of water (it does happen!).

In Bucharest prostitution is rife. So is child prostitution – and the HIV virus. For your own safety and the sake of the young girls at hand, restrain yourself. Don't even dabble in this activity.

Carrying your belongings in a tatty plastic bag is the first sign of adapting to local life (some expats in Bucharest carry their wallet in a plastic bag because they know that way no one will steal it). When you go shopping always take a bag with you. Take an egg box too if you don't want your eggs scrambled.

RELIGION

Romania is the only country with a Romance language that does not have a Roman Catholic background. Its ethnic diversity is reflected in its religious mix – 86% of the population is Romanian Orthodox, 5% Roman Catholic, 3.5% Protestant, 1% Greco-Catholic, 0.3% Muslim and 0.2% Jewish.

Romania's ethnic Saxon and Hungarian communities form the mainstay of Romania's Protestant church today. Tradi-tionally, Transylvanian Saxons are Luther-ans and many Hungarians belong to the Hungarian Reformed Church (also known as Calvinist). The Roman Catholic church was brought to Romania by the Habsburgs. Today it comprises Hungarians and Romani-ans whose ancestors converted during the great Habsburg drive to Catholicise Transyl-vania in the 17th century.

Most Muslim mosques are in Dobruja, serving small Turkish communities centred in Constanţa and Mangalia. The few Jewish synagogues still in use today serve an elderly congregation of around 14,000. The average age of the congregation is 60. A government ruling in mid-1997 paved the way for the synagogues confiscated by the communists to be returned to local Jewish communities.

Romanian Orthodoxy

Unlike other ex-communist countries where the church was a leading opposition voice to the dictatorial regime, Romania's leading Orthodox Church remained subservient to, and a tool of, the Romanian communist gov-ernment. In early 1997 the head of the Orthodox Church in Timişoara, Nicolae Corneanu, publicly admitted collaborating with the Securitate; in 1981 he had refused to ordain five Orthodox priests after they accused church leaders of 'prostituting' the Orthodox faith to communism. Yet immediately after the collapse of the Ceauşescu regime, Orthodox heads offi-cially asked forgiveness for sinning against the church through their 'compromises'.

The Romanian Orthodox Church fell under the patriarchy of Constantinople until 1864 when a free Romanian church was established. During the Habsburg domina-tion of Transylvania, the Orthodox Church was not recognised in the region. Its faithful suffered further persecution during the Hungarian occupation of northern Transyl-vania in 1940-44: Orthodox churches were burnt, destroyed and congregations forced to adopt the Habsburgs' Roman Catholic faith.

Today Romania's leading church is hier-archical, dogmatic and wealthy. It condemns abortion and homosexuality, warning against 'baby-murdering mothers' and 'unnatural sins'. New churches are being built in even the poorest of villages to accommodate its growing flock, while in Bucharest church leaders announced plans to build a vast 'Cathedral of the Nation's Salvation' estimated to cost US$130 million.

Greco Catholicsm

Unlike Romanian Orthodoxy, Greco Catholicism (also known as Uniate or the Catholic Church of the Eastern Rite) allows its congregation freedom of thought. The church, legally established in Romania in 1699, was seen as dangerous by the post-war government and in 1948 the Greco Catholic Church was outlawed. Its confiscated properties were turned over to the Orthodox Church, and its priests were among the tens of thousands imprisoned or interned in hard-labour camps by the communists from the late 1940s onwards for alleged 'anti-state' activities. Greco Catholics remained a persecuted minority until 1990 when the post-communist Romanian government finally relegalised the church. The government has yet to tackle the thorny issue of returning 2500 confiscated Greco Catholic churches and other assets to the church.

The Greco Catholic Church is an offspring of Orthodoxy. It established itself in Romania from the 17th century when Romanian Orthodox believers were persuaded to accept the authority of the Vatican as opposed to that of Constantinople. It adheres to the same Byzantine rite as the Romanian Orthodox Church but looks to the Pope for authority. Unlike in Roman-Catholicism,

priests are allowed to marry. Today the Greco Catholic church is strongest in Maramureş.

LANGUAGE

English and French are the first foreign languages taught in Romanian schools, and Hungarian is useful in Transylvania.

Romanian is much closer to classical Latin than it is to other Romance languages, and the grammatical structure and basic word stock of the mother tongue are well preserved. Some Slavic words were incorporated in the 7th to 10th centuries as the Romanian language took definite shape. Speakers of Italian, Spanish and French won't be able to understand much spoken Romanian but will find written Romanian more or less comprehensible.

Slavonic was the traditional language of scriptures and religious texts in the medieval principalities. Latin and Greek were the languages of culture while Romanian was oral.

During the communist purges of the late 1940s and consequent Russification of Romania, a new Slavicised orthography was enforced in an attempt to play down the Latin origins of the Romanian language. The letter *â* was replaced with the more Slavic *î*. It was not until 1994 however that the Romanian Academy ruled out the Stalinist *î* and reverted to the original Latin orthography. Old spellings such as Tîrgu Mures instead of Târgu Mureş and Tîrgovişte instead of Târgovişte are still found on many maps available in Romania. This book uses the correct *â* spellings.

See the Glossary and Language sections at the back of this book for handy words and phrases.

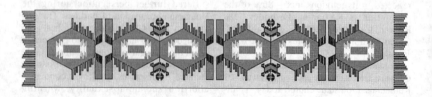

Facts for the Visitor

PLANNING

When to Go

May and June are by far the best months to visit, followed by September and early October. Spring in Romania is a pastiche of wildflowers, melting snow and melodious bird song. At higher elevations snow lingers as late as mid-May, and the hiking season doesn't begin in earnest until mid-June. The resorts along the Black Sea coast start filling up in late June and stay packed until mid-August. Romania is famous for its harsh winters, when tourism is focused on ski resorts such as Poiana Braşov and Sinaia.

Visiting southern Bucovina's monasteries off-season invariably proves more rewarding than joining the tour group pack in July and August. In early spring and autumn you will have these medieval works of art all to yourself; you also have more chances of being offered shelter at this time of year, providing a unique opportunity to see these world-famed monasteries from the 'inside'.

Birdwatchers flock to the Danube Delta in spring and autumn.

Maps

Maps are no longer deliberately distorted as they were under communism, but are still not that great. Sometimes minor roads and smaller villages are not marked on maps and it is not unusual for a forest road to be depicted as paved when it is downright rocky.

Romanian maps printed before 1989 include communist names for towns, villages and streets that have since been changed. Maps printed before 1994 feature the Russified spellings of towns and streets which have subsequently been changed back to pre-communist 'latinised' spellings. Even today, street names change. Come a state visit and a square will be renamed in honour of the visiting dignitary.

The only map you need before arriving is a country map. Romanian tourist offices and embassies abroad distribute free country maps and city maps of Bucharest which will tide you over until you find better ones in Romania.

Country Maps The best map of the region available abroad is Kümmerly & Frey's (Bern) 1996/7 edition of *Romania-Bulgaria* (1:750,000). The beauty of this map is that it includes Moldova as well as Romania. It also features decent-sized areas of Ukraine and Hungary as well as all of Bulgaria. The map costs US$8.

The only other map covering Romania and Moldova is the *Romania-Moldavia* map, which was published in 1997 by Geocenter (Stuttgart). Despite its recent publication, town names still bear pre-1994 spellings. *Roumanie & Moldavie* (Marco Polo & Institut Geographique National, Paris, 1994) is not bad either despite outdated spellings. Both maps are at a scale of 1:750,000 and cost around US$7.50. *Romania* (Cartographia, Budapest, 1995) is similarly scaled and priced.

One map of the region is truly outstanding – the Budapest-published *Erdély-Ardeal-Siebenbürgen-Transylvania* (1:500,000) covers Transylvania, Crişan and Banat, and Maramureş. It features almost every forest road, passable dirt track and village, showing their Romanian, Hungarian and old German names. It is sold in selected Hungarian-language bookshops in Cluj-Napoca for US$3.50. You can also contact the map distributors, Apex SRL (☎ 064-196 213, 064-195 981; fax 064-190 316), Str Inocenţui Micu Klein 11, RO-3400 Cluj-Napoca. Abroad, contact the publishers, DIMAP (☎ 1-177 7908), Báthory út 104, H-1196 Budapest; or try Stanfords (☎ 0171-836 1321), 12-14 Long Acre, London WC2.

The other top map, invaluable to anyone spending any length of time in central Romania is the *Ţara Secuilor-Székelyföld-Szeklerland*, published by Cartographia

(☎ 1-222 67227; fax 1-222 6728), Szabács út 4, H-1149 Budapest. It is at a scale of 1:250,000 and includes the entire Transylvanian region of the 'land of the settlers' with the Romanian, Hungarian and German names for most destinations. It is sold for US$3.50 in some bookshops in the Székely region, Transylvania.

The *Harta şi Ghidul Schiturilor, Mănăstirilor aşezămintelor cu moaşte şi icoane făcătoare de min uni*, published by Anastasia Editura (☎ 01-210 9530), Str Veneri 13, RO-70261 Bucharest, is a detailed country map of Romania on which all churches and monasteries are marked. It costs US$2.

Once you stray off the beaten tourist track, maps degenerate into outrageously outdated, Soviet-style efforts which are only 10 years old if you're lucky. Hopefully these maps will be eradicated within a couple of years as the last of the print-run finally gets shifted.

Details of maps available in each city and town are listed in the regional chapters of this book.

What to Bring
Don't bring too much. Most forgotten items can easily be picked up in Bucharest or other larger cities. Bring your own gear if you plan to hike or camp. If you intend travelling around, take a backpack – the grottier the better so you don't look like a 'rich foreigner'. A light day-pack is handy.

Basic necessities everyone should bring include a water bottle, small first-aid kit, a Swiss army knife, and a small torch (flashlight). A universal sink plug is also useful as is an adaptor plug for electrical appliances. Always carry a good wad of tissues or toilet paper in your pocket. If you intend visiting caves, bring a larger torch, and if you intend visiting the Danube Delta binoculars and vast amounts of insect repellent come in handy.

In early and late summer, bring a light waterproof garment. In spring and autumn there are cold snaps so bring warm headgear, gloves and a coat. In winter, bring thermals and snow gear. In the mountains it can be nippy year-round. Indestructible footwear is also recommended for all seasons.

Bring spare tapes for your camcorder, contact lens solution and any special medicines you need. Condoms are scarce; durability is not guaranteed on those that are available. In Bucharest and larger cities tampons and sanitary towels are available; elsewhere not.

HIGHLIGHTS
Scale mountain peaks. Share fresh cheese and milk with a local shepherd. Slam shots of fiery *ţiucă* with new-found friends. Shiver in an ice cave. Explore the Danube Delta's wild waterways. Climb 1480 steps to Dracula's castle in Poienari. Visit the mighty fortified churches of the Saxons. Snowboard in Poiana Braşov. Watch brown bears in the Carpathians. Join troops of tourists at Bran Castle. Boogie the night away on the Black Sea coast...

Romania's most valuable asset is its diversity, offering as much to do and see to tourists who want to stray off the beaten tourist track as those who want to stay well and truly on it.

Most people's 'must-see' list includes Bucharest's House of People (staggering) and Village Museum (also staggering); Bran Castle near Braşov (Count Dracula never slept there and it's full of British-made furniture); Peleş Castle in Sinaia (ranked as one of the finest royal pads in eastern Europe); the Gothic Hunedoara Castle (shame about the steel mill next door...); and the medieval old towns of Cluj-Napoca, Braşov, Sighişoara and Sibiu.

Things not on most people's 'must-see' list but should be include: Bucharest's Belu and Ghencea Cemeteries (see Eminescu's and the Ceauşescus' graves); a few nights in a rural Romanian home around Bran (the more remote the better); a mountain hike to 2000m in Sinaia (there is a cable-car); the ancient Greek and Roman remains at Histria; Maramureş' villages (homemade cheese); and the Danube Delta (birdwatching and fish).

For those following in the footsteps of

Dracula (tons do), Curtea de Argeş, Sighişoara, Bran, Bistriţa, Poienari, Arefu, and Târgovişte are all key points. Those more interested in tracking the 1989 revolution should spend time in Bucharest, Timişoara, Scorniceşti and Târgovişte. If you want to sleep in Ceauşescu's bed head for Sfântu Gheorghe or Lacul Roşu in Transylvania.

More highlights are listed at the top of each regional chapter.

TOURIST OFFICES
Local Tourist Offices
Romania has no tourist office network. The former ONT Carpaţi government agency that controlled tourism under communism is defunct today, although a handful of these state-run offices are still open. Others have been privatised but still trade under their former ONT title in the naive belief it attracts clients.

There are numerous private travel agencies in every town and city, many of which double as tourist offices and offer a range of services. The quality, usefulness and attitude of these agencies varies drastically. The better ones are listed in this guide but remember there are hundreds more.

Romania's student travel organisation, the Biroul de Turism Pentru Tîneret (BTT), is the national student and youth travel agency with offices in most towns and cities. Service is a hit and miss affair. Staff in more forward-thinking agencies welcome foreign tourists with open arms and are a mine of information. Others persist in adhering to old regime policies – ignoring foreign tourists at all costs. Occasionally BTT offices arrange private rooms.

Touring ACR, the travel agency of the Automobil Clubul Român (ACR), has desks in several hotels around Romania. These are useful for reserving accommodation at upmarket hotels and providing general information for visiting motorists.

Tourist Offices Abroad
The Romanian Ministry of Tourism runs an excellent network of tourist offices world-wide, most of which take accommodation bookings and dish out free maps. They include:

France
  12 rue des Pyramides, F-75001 Paris
  (☎ 01 40 20 99 33; fax 01 40 20 99 43)
Germany
  Zeil 13, D-60313 Frankfurt/Main
  (☎ 069-295 278/79; fax 069-292 947);
Frankfurter Tor 5, D-10243 Berlin
  (☎ & fax 030-589 2684)
Moldova
  Blvd Ştefan cel Mare 151-153, Chişinău
  (☎ 2-222 354; fax 2-261 992)
Russia
  ulitza Dimitria Ulianova 16/2, Moscow
  (☎ & fax 095-124 2473)
Turkey
  7 Lamartin Cad. Kat 1, TR-8090 Taksim, Istanbul (☎ 212-256 8417)
UK
  83a Marylebone High St, London, W1M 3DE
  (☎ & fax 0171-224 3692)
USA
  14 E 38th St, 12th Floor, New York, NY-10016
  (☎ 212-545 8484; fax 212-251 0429)

VISAS & DOCUMENTS
Entering Romania, everyone except Romanian citizens has to fill in a *talon de intrare* (entry card) which you present with your passport to be stamped. State your name, date of birth, passport details, your destination (Bucharest is sufficient), and the reason for your visit. Occasionally you will be asked where you intend staying. The name of any hotel in Bucharest will suffice. Attached to the bottom of this entry form is a *talon de ieşire* which is detached and given to you. Don't lose this as you will need it when you leave the country (see Getting There & Away – Leaving the Region for details).

Passport
Your number one document is your passport. Ensure its validity extends to at least six months beyond the date you enter the country. This is a requirement for obtaining a visa for Romania.

Visas
American citizens with valid passports have

the luxury of travelling visa-free for 30 days in Romania. All other western visitors need a visa to enter the country.

Romania issues three main types of visa: transit, single entry and multiple entry. To apply for a visa you need a passport, one recent passport photograph and the completed visa application form accompanied by the appropriate fee. If you are applying for a visa by post you have to enclose a stamped, self-addressed envelope too.

You can apply for a single transit visa which is valid for three days (one entry), or for a double transit visa which is valid for three days each time you enter the country (maximum two entries). These visas are issued the same day or, at the most, within 24 hours by most embassies. They cost US$39/50 and have to be used within one month of the issue date.

Single entry visas are valid for 30 days. If you are an independent traveller (ie not travelling as part of a tour group or with a charity), this costs around US$50 but note that prices do fluctuate between embassies. Single entry visas for package-holiday travellers are cheaper. These only cost US$10 and are usually incorporated in the price of the package deal.

Cut-price single entry visas are also issued to people travelling to Romania under the umbrella of an officially registered charity. At the time of writing, charity visas cost around US$20 but it is likely that this fee will be scrapped altogether in the near future. To obtain a charity visa you need all the documents listed above plus a letter from your home organisation confirming the purpose and role of your visit. You also need an official letter of invitation from the relevant charity in Romania. Individuals not linked with a home charity who are taking aid to a church group, school or non-governmental organisation in Romania, need a letter of invitation from the local mayor or from the state secretariat for religious affairs in Bucharest. Charity visas have to be used within three months of the issue date.

Multiple entry visas are generally valid for three or six months. Multiple entry visas cost US$94. They are usually issued to business travellers, who will need a letter from their company or some other authority outlining the reasons why they need one. Multiple entry charity visas are *not* issued.

Single entry transit and single entry tourist visas valid for 30 days are issued at the border. At Otopeni airport in Bucharest there is a 24 hour visa counter immediately on the right inside the arrival hall before passport control. The office is actually inside the Columna Bank, enabling you to change money and purchase a visa at the same time. In mid-1997 a three day transit visa cost US$21 and a single entry tourist visa was US$31. You can pay for visas in any convertible currency. At all other borders you are liable to get ripped off and it is better to get a visa before leaving home.

If you stay in the country longer than the validity of your visa, you will be charged for a new 30 day visa.

Visa Extensions Once inside Romania, extend your stay by reporting to a passport office – any local tourist office will have the address. The Bucharest office is at Str Nicolae Iorga 7 near Piaţa Romană. You must apply before your current visa expires.

Visas for Neighbouring Countries All westerners need a visa to enter Moldova. Visas are not issued at any borders (see the Moldova chapter for details). You need one for Yugoslavia too. These are issued promptly and usually free of charge at the Yugoslav embassy in Bucharest. You cannot obtain visas at the border.

EU nationals don't need a visa for Hungary. Since mid-1997 most won't need one for Bulgaria but double check with the Bulgarian embassy in Bucharest. Visa requirements change.

Everyone needs a visa for Ukraine. If you are taking the Bucharest-St Petersburg train you need Ukrainian, Belarusian and Baltic transit visas on top of the Russian visa. Some Europeans do not need a Baltic transit visa.

Travel Insurance

A fully comprehensive travel insurance policy to cover theft, loss and medical problems in all situations is strongly advisable, especially if you intend to do a lot of travelling. A policy which covers the costs of being flown out of the country for treatment is a definite bonus, given the still limited in-country facilities.

Driving Licence & Permits

If you are planning to drive in the region, an International Driving Permit (IDP) will be useful, though if you don't have one, your own national licence (if from a EU country) should suffice. It's obtainable, usually cheaply, from your local automobile association. British driving licence holders should note that licences not bearing a photograph of the holder have been known to upset traffic police: get an IDP before you arrive. You also need your vehicle's registration document. In Romania accident insurance is compulsory.

Hostel Card

With the hostel scene still in its infancy (three in Romania), International Hostel Federation (IHF) cards are yet to bring any discounts to hostellers. This could change in the future as hostels become affiliated with the IHF and spread their wings to other cities.

Student & Youth Cards

Student and youth cards don't yield any staggering bargains but, as with hostels in Romania, the concept is making headway fast. Of use so far are the International Student Identity Card (ISIC) and the Euro 26 card (the International Youth Card of the Federation of International Youth Travel Organisation; FIYTO), available to people who are 26 or under but not a student. These cards are issued at special student and youth travel agencies; you'll need your passport and two photos.

These cards are not officially recognised anywhere in Romania but flashing one often gets you into museums, cinemas and theatres at reduced rates. They can also come in handy if you are booking an international flight from Bucharest with airlines who offer student or youth discounts – see Getting There & Away.

Senior Cards

Few discounts are available for elderly foreigners.

EMBASSIES

Romania has embassies and consulates worldwide. Diplomatic missions in Romania are listed in the Information section of the relevant chapters, mainly in Bucharest.

Romanian missions abroad include:

Australia
    Embassy: 4 Dalman Crescent, O'Malley, ACT 2606 (☎ 02-6286 2343, 6290 2442, fax 02-6286 2433)
Bulgaria
    Embassy: Sitnjakovo 4, Sofia (☎ 02-70 70 46, 02-70 70 67; fax 02-70 21 74)
Canada
    Embassy: 655 Rideau St, Ottawa K1N 6A3 (☎ 613-789 5345; fax 613-789 4365)
    Consulates: 111 Peter St, Suite 530, Toronto M5V 2H1 (☎ 416-585 5802, 585 9177; fax 416-585 4798); 1111 St Urbain, Suite M 01, Montreal, QUE H2Z 1Y6 (☎ 514-876 1792, 876 1793; fax 514-876 1797)
France
    Embassy: 3-5 rue de l'exposition, F-75007 Paris (☎ 01-40 62 22 35, 40 62 22 07)
    Consulate: 6 rue Gustave Klotz, F-67000 Strasbourg (☎ 03-88 25 15 94, fax 03-88 37 16 70)
    157 blvd Michelet, F-13009 Marseille (☎ 04-91 22 17 34, 91 22 17 41; fax 04-91 22 17 87)
Germany
    Embassy: Legionsweg 14, D-53117 Bonn (☎ 0228-555 8633, 0228-555 8632)
    Consulate: Matterhorn Strasse 79/4129, Berlin (☎ 030-803 3018, 803 3019; fax 030-803 1684)
Hungary
    Embassy: Thököly út 72, H-1146 Budapest XIV (☎ 1-268 0271, 142 8394; fax 1-268 0269)
Ireland
    Embassy: 60 Merrion Rd, Ballsbridge, Dublin 4 (☎ 031-668 13 36, 668 14 47; fax 031-668 15 82)
Moldova
    Embassy: Str Bucureşti 66/1, Chişinău (☎ 0422-233 434, 224 118; fax 0422-233 469)
    Consular Section: Str Vlaicu Parcalab 39, Chişinău (☎ 0422-237 622)

Russia
> Embassy: ul Mosfilmovskaia 64, RUS-101000 Moscow (☎ 095-147 44 52, 143 04 24; fax 095-143 04 49)

UK
> Embassy: Arundel House, 4 Palace Green, London W8 4QD (☎ 0171-937 9666; ☎ & fax 0171-937 4675; fax 0171-937 8069; email consul@roemb.demon.co.uk; www.embassy.org/romania)

Ukraine
> Embassy: Kotziubinskogo 8, UA-252030 Kiev (☎ 044-224 52 61, 225 20 25; fax 044-224 52 61)

USA
> Embassy: 1607 23rd St NW, Washington DC-20008 (☎ 202-232 4829, 232 4747; fax 202-232 4748; email romania@embassy.org; www.embassy.org/romania); 200 E 38th St, New York, NY-10016 (☎ 212-682 9120; fax 212-972 8463)
> Consulate: 11766 Wilshire Blvd, Suite 560, Los Angeles, CA-90025 (☎ 310-444 0043; fax 310-445 0043)

Yugoslavia
> Consulate: Kneza Milosšua 38, YU-11000 Belgrade (☎ 011-645 685; ☎ & fax 011-646 071)

CUSTOMS

Romanian customs regulations are complicated but not often enforced. Gifts worth up to a total of US$100 may be imported duty free. For foreigners duty-free allowances are 4L of wine, 1L of spirits and 200 cigarettes.

Officially, you're allowed to import hard currency up to a maximum of US$50,000. Amounts over US$1000 in cash are supposed to be declared upon arrival although travellers' money belts are rarely *legally* searched (see the Money section for more on illegal searches).

Still, if you're carrying more than US$1000 in cash upon departure (and didn't declare it upon arrival), keep it out of sight to be on the safe side.

MONEY

The currency in Romania is the leu (plural lei). With the collapse of the Romanian leu, which was officially valued at nine to US$1 in 1989, Romania has become an inexpensive country for foreigners. Since the new government's implementation of tight fiscal policies since early 1997, the leu has remained remarkably stable and is expected to remain so. During the seven months it took to research this book the exchange rate for US$1 fluctuated between 6800 and 7700 lei. This *is* stable compared to times gone past. Romanians have still to adapt to the concept of a stable currency and many hotels and restaurants still quote prices in US$. For ease of comparison prices in this book are listed in US$ too (converted from lei at the official rate).

Costs

Romania is cheap for western travellers. However it is getting increasingly expensive for Romanians, for whom the average salary is no more than US$80. When discussing prices with Romanians be tactful. Express sympathy with their situation rather than raving about the bargains you've found. To do otherwise is to breed resentment and encourage overcharging of foreigners.

A handful of hotels, museums and TAROM domestic flights charge different prices for Romanians and foreigners. In these cases Romanians usually pay about 50% less.

Accommodation will be your biggest expense. In Bucharest cheap accommodation is scarce. Rockbottom rates for a shared room with communal bath in the train station area start at US$6 per person a night, without breakfast. For a bed in a dormitory in a city-centre hostel you pay US$12 a night, including breakfast. Expect to pay at least US$25 for a double room with shared bath in any hotel within walking distance of the centre. This is the average price for most hotels in other Romanian cities and towns. Accommodation in private homes in the countryside starts at US$10 a night, including a giant-sized, home-cooked breakfast.

The cost of dining is on the rise. Romanians cannot afford to eat out which means most restaurants are geared to 'rich foreigners'. In Bucharest it is tough to eat for less than US$5 a head, not including alcohol. Elsewhere feeding your tummy is cheaper while a bottle of fine Romanian wine can cost as little as US$1.50. You pay no more than US$1 for a ticket to see a film or play, while entrance fees to museums average US$0.20. The most expensive museums in the entire country are Ceauşescu's House of the People (US$2) and Peleş castle in Sinaia (US$4.50). In both places, and in the Bucovina monasteries, visitors are charged a fee for taking in a camera/camcorder. This photo fee is usually more than the entrance fee.

Public transport is dirt cheap by western standards. A ticket good for two journeys costs no more than US$0.20. Tickets for trains and buses have increased dramatically in recent months (by 70% in February 1997) but are still affordable for foreigners. US$1.70 will take you approximately 100km by bus or comfortable express train. Petrol is around US$0.40 a litre.

Carrying Money

As a westerner you will stick out like a sore thumb. And for Bucharest's skilled pickpockets that bulging wallet in your back pocket will stick out even more. Of all eastern Europe's capitals, Bucharest suffers the worst reputation for petty theft against foreigners (all westerners are wealthy as far as Romanians are concerned). *Always* store the bulk of your cash and all other important travel documents in a moneybelt beneath your clothing. Keep sufficient cash for the day in a separate, easily accessible (to you) wallet. Leaving a secret stash of cash in your hotel room is not a good idea.

Cash

Marked, torn or very used banknotes will often be refused at exchanges. Ensure whatever currency you bring is in good condition. US dollar notes issued before 1900 are generally not accepted either.

Travellers Cheques

Travellers cheques are useful because they offer protection against theft. It is easy to exchange them in most towns and cities in Romania, but not so easy to replace them if your originals are stolen. American Express only has an office that issues replacements in Bucharest. Banks usually charge 2 to 5 % to cash cheques in either US$ or lei. You need your passport to cash cheques.

ATMs

ATMs are becoming increasingly widespread in Romania, enabling you to get out Romanian lei on Visa/MasterCard 24 hours a day. The maximum transaction (in lei) per withdrawal is usually US$70.

Credit Cards

Credit cards are widely accepted in hotels, restaurants and shops, especially at the upper end of the market, in most towns and cities. You usually have to show your passport. In rural areas, plastic is useless. Credit cards are essential for hiring a car, unless of course you are willing to pay in cash up front.

You can get a cash advance on Visa/MasterCard from banks in most towns. They all usually charge 2 to 5%. In some banks you can get cash advance in US$; most only give lei. Most banks are only open on weekday mornings – see Business Hours later in this chapter.

International Transfers

Direct bank-to-bank transfer is possible – but it is painfully slow. Commission (usually 5%) is charged on the amount you transfer; the service takes at least five days.

Currency

Romania's currency is the leu (plural 'lei'). There are coins of one, three, five, 10, 20, 50 and 100 lei and notes of 200, 500, 1000, 5000, 10,000 and 50,000 lei. However, one, three and five lei coins as well as 200-lei notes have become extremely rare. The 500-lei bill features 19th century Romanian sculptor Constantin Brâncuşi, national poet Mihai Eminescu stares out of the 1000-lei banknote, historian Nicolae Iorga is on the 10,000-lei bill, and the smaller 50,000 lei note features 19th century composer George Enescu.

Currency Exchange

The following list shows approximate currency exchange rates for the Romanian leu which were correct at the time of going to press:

Australia	A$1	=	L5459
Bulgaria	BGL1	=	L4.65
Canada	C$1	=	L5927
France	1FF	=	L1389
Germany	DM1	=	L4650
Hungary	HUF1	=	L41
Japan	¥100	=	L64
UK	UK£1	=	L13,666
USA	US$1	=	L8475

Changing Money

You can change money in banks, in some major hotels, and in the numerous private exchange houses that abound in most towns. All major currencies are widely accepted. Compare rates as they do vary.

You always need your passport to change money. Keep receipts to prove you obtained lei legally. You can change excess lei back into hard currency at main branches of the banks listed earlier and at the exchange desk at Bucharest's Otopeni airport.

When changing more than US$20, ask if you can have 50,000 lei notes. If not you will end up with inches of banknotes.

Black Market

There is a black market offering 10 to 25% above the official bank rate for cash US dollars, British pounds and Deutschmarks. *Don't* risk it. People who change money on the street are usually professional thieves just waiting to trick you out of your cash. The most common scam is to switch the correct wad of money counted out in front of you with a dud roll at the last second. However smart you think you are, it's guaranteed these illegal moneychangers are smarter. Despite warnings, numerous travellers think they know what they are doing and end up cheated. For more information on scams, see the Dangers & Annoyances section.

Tipping & Bargaining

Tipping is not common in Romania, though you should always round up the bill to the nearest 500 lei (some waiters and taxi drivers do this automatically). While working wonders with service industry personnel, tips should not be offered to officials, including train conductors. Some bargaining, but not much, goes on in flea markets. Taxi drivers drive a hard bargain. *Always* haggle.

POST & COMMUNICATIONS
Postal Rates

Sending mail is comparatively cheap although no two postcards seem to cost the same to send. Expect to pay US$0.50 to send a postcard/letter under 20g to western Europe, and US$1 to Australia and the USA.

Sending Mail

Mail in and out of Romania is rapidly approaching western norms. Letters and postcards take four to six days to western Europe and seven to 10 days to North America.

Post offices *(poştă)* are often signposted with the letters PTTR. This is an abbreviation for Poştă-Telegraf-Telefon-Radio. All post offices sell stamps *(timbre)*. Mail boxes in Bucharest are red, elsewhere they are usually yellow. The slot marked *Pentru Bucureşti* is for letters for Bucharest. Mail for other destinations in Romania and abroad has to be posted in the slot marked *alte localitati* (other localities).

Within Romania, you can ensure a letter or parcel reaches its final destination by sending it by recommended post *(poştal recommandată)*. This means that the recipient has to sign a *confirmare de primire* confirming that they have received it. You can send mail by recommended mail from any post office. You also have to provide an address in Romania where the post office can send the confirmation slip. A post restante address suffices – see Receiving Mail.

A 1kg air-mail parcel costs about US$10 to anywhere in the world from Romania. Costly international express-mail services for letters and parcels are available in Bucharest and some larger cities.

Receiving Mail

The delivery time for inward-bound mail is

similar to that for outward-bound mail. Written addresses in Romania conform to western norms:

Mihai Eminecsu
Strada Ştefan cel Mare 62, Bl. 5, Sc. C, Et 2, Ap. 16
RO-5600 Piatra Neamţ
Romania

Strada Ştefan cel Mare 62 means No 62 Ştefan cel Mare Street, block No 5, stairway *(scară)* C, floor *(etage)* No 2, apartment No 16. In this book we have abbreviated Strada to Str and Bulevardul to Blvd. *Aleea* means drive or avenue and *Şoseaua* means highway.

There is a poste-restante mail service in the central post office in Bucharest and most major cities. Mail is kept for one month. Letters have to be addressed with the full name of the recipient plus:

Postă Româna Oficiul Bucureşti 1
Str Mateo Millo 10
RO-70700 Bucharest
Romania

You can collect your mail weekdays between 7.30 am and 8 pm, Saturday from 7.30 am to 2 pm.

Telephone
Making or receiving a telephone call in Romania is the same as anywhere else in the world. Direct international calls can be made/received from most private phones and public cardphones.

All calls can be made from bright orange cardphones. Only national and local calls can be made from blue phones which accept 50 and 100 lei coins as well as cards. Both types

of phone, installed by Romtelecom (the state-owned phone monopoly), are abundant in most towns and cities: on the street, at train and bus stations, in major hotels, and inside telephone offices.

Telephone calls can also be received on these phones. The telephone number flashes in the window at the top of the phone before you lift the handset. Note however that incoming calls are limited to three minutes following which you will be cut off.

Magnetic phonecards *(cartela telefonică)* costing US$3 (20,000 lei) or US$6 (40,000 lei) are sold at telephone offices in every city. Some hotels sell them too but charge a small commission.

To call an English-speaking operator abroad call ☎ 01-800 4444 (British Telecom), ☎ 01-800 4288 (AT&T USA Direct), ☎ 01-800 1800 (MCI Worldwide) and ☎ 01-800 0877 (Sprint). Dialling these services is ostensibly free although if you are calling from a hotel room, you will be charged for the service. If you speak basic Romanian there's a host of three-digit, free-phone information services available: train enquiries (☎ 952), taxis (☎ 953), directory enquiries (☎ 930), road & traffic information (☎ 954).

To call other cities in Romania, dial the city code (listed in the relevant chapters) followed by the recipient's telephone number. To call abroad dial 00 followed by the country and city code. To call Romania from abroad dial the international access code, Romania's country code (40), then the city code (minus the first 0) and the recipient's number.

In some rural areas, particularly in

Telephone Call Charges (per minute)					
	National Calls	*To Moldova/ Romania*	*To Western Europe*	*To Australia*	*To North America*
Romania	US$0.04 to $0.08	US$0.06 to $0.13	US$2	US$6	US$4
Moldova	US$0.03	US$0.22	US$1.45 to $2.60	US$5	US$3.55

Maramureş and Southern Bucovina, all calls have to be made via the operator (☎ 191) or through a central switchboard.

Fax, Telegraph & Email
Faxes can be sent or received from any central post office or, in Bucharest, from any Telex-Fax office. It costs US$1.50 within Romania, and US$2-4 per page to send an international fax. The average charge for international telegrams is US$0.20 per word.

An increasing number of hotels, travel agents and associations are getting hooked on to the World Wide Web. Many have email accounts. Cybercafés are also beginning to sprout. So far you can send email and access the Internet in Bucharest, Craiova in Wallachia, Iaşi in Moldavia, Mangalia on the Black Sea coast, Sibiu, Sighişoara and Gheorgheni in Transylvania, Timişoara in the Banat, and Sighetu Marmaţiei in Maramureş. Online access costs around US$3 an hour.

BOOKS
Foreign-language books can be found in Romania's many bookshops. Some of the following books can be found but it's better to try to get the ones you want before you go. Local language phrasebooks and dictionaries are widely available.

Few books written during the WWII period remain in print today. Here we only list those books which were available at the time of writing. Romanian literature is listed in the Literature section of Facts About the Country: most have been published in English by Forest Books (☎ 0181-529 8470; fax 0181-524 7890; email brenda@fores .demon.co.uk) and can be mail-ordered through Grantham Book Services (☎ 01476-541 080; fax 01476-541 061), Isaac Newton Way, Alma Park Industrial Estate, Grantham, Lincs NG31 9SD.

Lonely Planet
If you're travelling elsewhere in eastern Europe, *Eastern Europe on a shoestring* has a useful 858 pages covering 13 countries and including 149 maps. If you're heading further east from Moldova, the 1192 pages of *Russia, Ukraine & Belarus* could be life-saving. Lonely Planet's *Eastern Europe phrasebook* is handy.

Travel
The two classic works are Olivia Manning's *Balkan Trilogy* and Patrick Leigh Fermor's *Between the Woods and the Water*. Manning's colourful portrait of Bucharest at the outbreak of WWII gained a new lease of life since being serialised on British TV as *The Fortunes of War*. Fermor's book, the second in a trilogy, describes Transylvania in the 1930s.

Not surprisingly, a deluge of travelogues emerged after the collapse of communism. Helena Drysdale's *Looking for George – Love & Death in Romania* is a hard-hitting account of the author's search for a Romanian tour guide and defrocked monk she met at Putna monastery in 1979. In 1991 she returns to find him. Psychiatric abuse in post-communist Romania is one of the issues she tackles.

Seventy-three pages of *Exit into History* by Polish-American Eva Hoffman is devoted to Romania during the author's travels across eastern Europe in 1990 and 1991. It is told from an exasperating 'nice, middle-class woman' perspective but does highlight the 'aesthetic torment' a first-time traveller to Romania could suffer. Less lamentive is Robert Kaplan's insightful *Balkan Ghosts* which recounts the journalist's investigative travels across eastern Europe and Romania in the 1990s.

Stalin's Nose by failed British screen-writer Rory Mclean tackles his journey across eastern Europe with his nutty old aunt and her pet pig. Nicholas Crane's *Clear Waters Rising* is the amusing story of a lone hiker tramping from Cape Finisterre (Spain) across the Sierras, Pyrenees, Alps and the Carpathians to Istanbul.

Unbeatable for its fascinating revelations about Roma in Romania is Isabel Fonseca's *Bury Me Standing – the Gypsies and their Journey*. Isabel Fonseca spent several months travelling with Roma in eastern and central Europe between 1991 and 1995. The chapter covering Romania, entitled 'The least obedient people in the world', looks at racial attacks against Roma in Transylvania.

The anguished travels of aid volunteers plummeting from a cushy nine-to-five existence in the west to the torments of Romanian orphanages feature in Sophie Thurnham's *Sophie's Journey – The Story of an Aid Worker in Romania*, and Beverley Peberdy's *Do Robins Cough? – Giving Romania's Children a Chance*.

History & Politics

The Romanians – A History by the head of the Romanian service of Radio Free Europe, Vlad Georgescu, provides a comprehensive account of contemporary history. Also recommended for its clear and succinct account of the events leading up to and the consequences of 1989 is *Romania in Turmoil* by Martyn Rady.

Kiss the Hand You Cannot Bite: the Rise and Fall of the Ceauşescus by Edward Behr provides fascinating background on the revolution. Other titles homing in on the Ceauşescus include *The Rise & Fall of Nicolae and Elena Ceauşescu* by Mark Almond and *The Life and Evil Times of Nicolae Ceauşescu* by John Sweeney. Another pivotal figure of 1989 is the subject of *With God, for the People: the Autobiography of László Tökés*, as told to David Porter.

Ion Pacepa, head of the foreign intelligence service of the Securitate, defected to the US in 1978 and promptly published a behind-the-scenes account of his work in Romania. *Red Horizons* tells the story of one of the highest ranking officials of any communist secret service to defect to the west.

A superb and detailed analysis of the Securitate is presented in Dennis Deletant's *Ceauşescu and the Securitate – Coercion and Dissent in Romania 1965-1989*, written by Britain's leading authority on Romanian history and politics. Information on life inside communist prisons in the 1950s is also included. An even more disturbing, first-hand account of this unfolds in *The Anti-Humans* by political prisoner Dimitru Bacu, published in Romanian in the US in 1963 and later translated into English.

Brilliant for its wit, dead-pan humour and startling insights into the hardships and cruelties encountered by a youth existing on the 'wrong side' of the Securitate is Dan Antal's autobiography *Out of Romania*.

Hannah Paluka's *Marie, Queen of Romania* focuses on the half-English, half-Russian granddaughter of Queen Victoria whose persuasive charm at the 1919 Paris Peace Conference helped Romania obtain Transylvania.

The extraordinary cult following that has sprung up around Bram Stoker's fictitious *Dracula* novel and its association with the historical figure, Prince Vlad Ţepeş is expounded in *In Search of Dracula: History of Dracula and Vampires* by Raymond McNally and Radu Florescu; and in *Dracula – Essays on the Life and Times of Vlad Ţepeş*, edited by Kurt Treptow. Jean Marigny's *Vampires – The World of the Undead* explores the perverse attraction these fictitious and historical bloodthirsty figures offer.

Kurt W Treptow also edited *A History of Romania*, published locally in 1996 by the Romanian Cultural Foundation in Iaşi (see Newspapers & Magazines). This weighty, 726 page book is one of the few to trace the history of Romania from the Stone Age to the 1990s and is worth its weight in lei.

Charles Boner's *Transylvania: It's Products & Its People* is considered the authority on Saxons in Transylvania from the 12th century onwards.

ONLINE SERVICES

The Internet is taking off at lightning speed in Romania. Email account holders can subscribe for free to the Romanian news service *Telegramă* which mails out daily news bulletins. Send a message reading 'subscribe TELEGRAMA English version' to esm@ecst.csuchico.edu. Equally informative are the news bulletins, features and analytical pieces which are mailed out weekly by the *Romanian Press Review* (email rompr@halcyon.com, RoPR1 @aol.com; www.halcyon.com/rompr). A yearly subscription costs US$25.

Hot web sites worth a surf include:

www.huntcol.edu/pmichels/srs.html
  Home page of the *Society of Romanian Studies*; over 400 hot links to every known Romanian-related web site. Definitely the best.
www.bucharest.com
  The *Romanian Internet Directory*; local news, photos of the 1989 revolution, and links galore to Romania-related web sites
www.info.polymtl.ca/romania
  Virtual Romania; news and dozens of Romania links

NEWSPAPERS & MAGAZINES

More than 1000 newspapers appeared after the revolution. Leading daily papers are *Adevârul* and *Tineretul Libera*, both of which favour the opposition PDSR, *România Liberă*, a pro-government voice, and *Evenimentul Zilei*, a popular mainstream paper. *Romániai Magyar Szo* is the main daily in Hungarian. *A Hét* (Hungarian) and *Deutsche Zeitung* (German) are published weekly. Most newspapers are online.

Local foreign-language publications are gradually gaining ground: *România Liberă* publishes a weekly English-language edition on Friday which is distributed for free in major hotels in Bucharest. The other main English-language weekly newspaper is *Nine O'Clock* (☎ 01-222 8280; fax 01-222 3241; email nine@starnets.ro; www.starnets .ro/9clock/), Splaiul Independenţei 202a, Bucharest. It costs US$0.28 but again, is easier to pick up free of charge in Bucharest hotels.

The *Romanian Economic Observer* and *Romanian Business Journal* are business-based, English-language newspapers, published weekly and costing US$1.50. Again, they are usually distributed for free in upmarket hotels in Bucharest. The *Romanian Business Journal* (☎ 01-222 4126; fax 01-222 6407), Piaţa Presei Libere 1, Bucharest, has an overseas subscription system (US$15 per month).

Invaluable for gaining deeper insight into Romanian culture are the informative little journals published by the Romanian Cultural Foundation in its *Romanian Civilization* series. In Romania, the journals, which cover every cultural topic imaginable, cost around US$2 in bookshops. They are US$10 by mail order (☎ 032-219 000; fax 032-219 010; email kurtwt @starnets.ro; The Center of Romanian Studies, Str Poligon 11a, Oficiul Poştală 1, CP 108, RO-6600 Iaşi). The foundation also publishes a biannual *Romanian Gymnastic* journal, which is online at www .romaniangymnastics.ro.

Locally produced city guides are listed in the relevant chapters of this book.

RADIO & TV

All middle and top-end hotels, and some bottom ones too, have a colour TV. Regardless of its decrepit state, if you fiddle with the knobs enough you should be able to pick up various cable channels, including MTV, Euronews and Eurosport in English. Numerous English-language films and American sitcoms (in their original language with Romanian subtitles) are screened on Pro-TV, Romania's main private TV channel which has had a cult following since its launch in the 1970s by Romanian tennis star and business tycoon Ion Ţiriac.

Tune into Radio Hit on 94.9 FM to pick up Voice of America (VOA) or try Radio France International on 93.5 FM. The BBC World Service can only be picked up on shortwave.

Other popular radio stations include Radio Contact on 96.1 FM in Bucharest, 92 FM in Iaşi, 89.8 FM in Cluj-Napoca and on 91.8 FM in Sibiu, Radio Delta on the Danube Delta, and the dancey Radio Vacanţa on the coast on 100.1 FM.

PAL is the main video system used in the region.

PHOTOGRAPHY & VIDEO

Kodak, Agfa and Fuji colour films and basic accessories such as batteries are widely available except in remote villages where there are few shops. Slide and black and white film is so not so widespread so bring your own to prevent running out at the award-winning shot. Stock up on film before leaving Romania for Moldova.

In both countries you are not allowed to photograph military installations, including army barracks, border posts, hydroelectric power plants, dams, and often coal and gold mines. If in doubt, look for a sign featuring a crossed-out camera. This means no photographs allowed in which case you risk having your film confiscated.

TIME

Romanian time is GMT/UTC (Greenwich Mean Time/Universal Time Coordinated) plus two hours, which means there's a one-hour difference between Romania/Moldova and Hungary/Yugoslavia, but no difference between Romania/Moldova and Bulgaria. Romania and Moldova go on summer time at the end of March, when clocks are turned forward an hour. At the end of October, they're turned back an hour. To find out the correct time dial ☎ 958.

The 24 hour clock is used for all transport schedules which are always listed in local time. Dates are listed the American way: the month comes first, followed by the day and year, ie 03/08/97 refers to 8 March 1998 as opposed to 3 August 1998.

ELECTRICITY

Romania runs on 220 V, 50 Hz AC. Most appliances that are set up for 240 V will handle this happily. Sockets require a European plug with two round pins.

WEIGHTS & MEASURES

Romania uses the metric system, often to a ridiculous degree. In most restaurants the Soviet practise of listing on menus the precise gram weight of each ingredient incorporated in the final dish is still alive and well. Prices are often listed per 100g.

Outdated it might seem, but Romanians are not stupid: listing items this way provides the perfect opportunity to rip diners off – see Food section.

LAUNDRY

You can pay a price to get your clothes cleaned in all major hotels. The Vila Helga hostel in Bucharest has a washing machine at guests' disposal. Elsewhere no mechanical washing facilities exist. Hand wash.

TOILETS

The cleanest toilet is behind a bush. Unfortunately bush-squatting is not allowed in towns and cities where you'll be arrested if you pull down your pants in public.

Public toilets in towns and cities come in three grades. Bottom of the pile are those smelly holes in the ground at train and bus stations. These are stinking, vile pits that will leave you gasping for fresh air as you attempt to race in, pee, and race out again without inhaling the stench. Grade two toilets are those touting a cracked seat and a flushing system – marginally less smelly and with a babushka at the entrance doling out squares of coarse toilet paper for a nominal fee. Grade three toilets: McDonald's (in most big cities).

Regardless of grading, all toilets have a plastic bin by their side. This is intended for used toilet paper. Hotel toilets usually comply with western norms. Most homes in rural areas only have an outside toilet. Women's toilets are marked with the letter **F** (femeie) or with a ▲. Men's are marked **B** (bărbaţii) or ▼.

HEALTH

Romania is generally a pretty healthy place to travel around. Provided you make the necessary predeparture preparations, you should hopefully not need to seek medical care while travelling. Potential dangers can seem quite frightening, although in reality few travellers experience anything more than an upset stomach. Be aware that children and pregnant women are more susceptible to disease.

In Bucharest there are private western clinics offering quality care. Elsewhere, however, medical care is *not* up to western standards.

Predeparture planning

Immunisations No immunisations are required for Romania or Moldova but some vaccinations are strongly advisable, particularly if you intend to explore more remote areas or spend any length of time in these countries.

Check that routine vaccinations recommended are up-to-date. These include diphtheria, tetanus, polio and measles.

You should then consider a rabies, typhoid and encephalitis vaccination. Stray dogs are rife in Romanian cities, particularly Bucharest. A rabies vaccination is particularly recommended by those who are cycling, handling animals, caving, travelling to remote areas, or for children (who may not report a bite). Pretravel rabies vaccination involves having three injections over 21 to 28 days. If someone who has been vaccinated is bitten or scratched by an animal they will require two booster injections of vaccine, those not vaccinated require more.

Typhoid is an important vaccination to have if you really intend to rough it in remote areas. A vaccination against encephalitis, a disease transmitted by forest ticks, has to be administered in advance.

Other considerations should be a precaution against Hepatitis A and B. Hepatitis A is a common travel-acquired illness which can put you out of action for weeks. A Havrix 1440 vaccination provides long term immunity (possibly more than 10 years) after an initial injection and a booster at six to 12 months, while Gamma globulin is a ready-made antibody administered close to departure. Depending on the dose, it protects for two to six months. Hepatitis B is spread by blood or by sexual activity. It involves three injections, the quickest course being over three weeks with a booster at 12 months.

All vaccinations should be recorded on an International Health Certificate. Don't leave vaccinations until the last minute; they often have to be spread out over a few weeks.

Health Insurance Make sure that you have adequate health insurance. See Travel Insurance under Documents earlier in this chapter.

Travel Health Guides There are a number of excellent travel health sites on the Internet. From the Lonely Planet home page (www.lonelyplanet.com) there are links at to the World Health Organisation, the US Center for Diseases Control & Prevention and Stanford University Travel Medicine Service.

Other Preparations Make sure you're healthy before you start travelling. If you are going on a long trip make sure your teeth are OK. If you wear glasses take a spare pair and your prescription. You cannot replace lost contact lenses in Romania or Moldova.

If you require a particular medication take an adequate supply, as it may not be available locally. Take part of the packaging showing the generic name, rather than the brand, which will make getting replacements easier. Carry a legible prescription or letter from your doctor to show that you legally use the medication.

Basic Rules

Food & Nutrition Vegetables and fruit should be washed with purified water or peeled where possible. Beware of ice cream which is sold in the street or anywhere it might have melted and been refrozen.

Make sure your diet is well balanced. If you're travelling hard and fast and missing meals, you can start to lose weight and place your health at risk. Cooked eggs and nuts are all safe ways to get protein. Fruit you can peel (bananas, oranges or mandarins for example) is usually safe (melons can harbour bacteria in their flesh and are best avoided) and a good source of vitamins.

Mushroom and berry picking is a national pastime in Romania. Feel free to join in the fun but don't eat anything until it has been positively identified as safe by someone who can be relied on to be correct in their judgement. In 1997, 62 people were hospitalised after eating poisonous mushrooms: nine died.

Milk should be treated with suspicion as it is often unpasteurised, though boiled milk is fine if it is kept hygienically. Tea or coffee should also be OK, since the water should have been boiled.

In summer make sure you drink enough liquid – don't rely on feeling thirsty to indicate when you should drink. Not needing to urinate or small amounts of very dark yellow urine is a danger sign. Always carry a water bottle with you on long trips.

Water You won't die if you drink tap water, but it is advisable to treat it with caution. The locals drink it straight but most travellers and foreigners boil it first. If you don't know for certain that the water is safe assume the worst. Reputable brands of bottled water or soft drinks are generally fine, although in some places bottles may be refilled with tap water. Water fountains on train station platforms and water drawn from wells in villages could give you a stomach upset.

Medical Problems & Treatment

Self-diagnosis and treatment can be risky, so you should always seek medical help.

There are pharmacies in every town and city in Romania, many of which stock basic western items such as aspirin, insect repellent (a definite must for travellers who intend visiting the Danube Delta), and insect bite reliefs. Many pharmacies sell antibiotics over the counter too. These should ideally be administered only under medical supervision.

There are few alternatives to the dismal local medical system, which is short on both facilities and equipment, if you do need serious attention. Medical treatment in state-run hospitals *(spital)* and clinics is free for Romanians and foreigners alike. Some private clinics do offer western-standard medical care in Bucharest but they are expensive. In an emergency seek your hotel's help first (if you're in one) – the bigger hotels may have doctors on call. Emergency care is free in Romania. Secondly, your embassy or consulate may be able to recommend an English-speaking doctor or hospital, but if things are serious be prepared to go straight home. Romanian doctors are paid US$70 a month.

To call an ambulance (in Romanian) dial ☎ 961.

Diarrhoea Simple things like a change of water, food or climate can all cause a mild bout of diarrhoea, but a few rushed toilet trips with no other symptoms is not indicative of a major problem.

Dehydration is the main danger with any diarrhoea, particularly in children or the elderly as dehydration can occur quite quickly. Under all circumstances *fluid replacement* (at least equal to the volume being lost) is the most important thing to remember. Weak black tea with a little sugar, soda water, or soft drinks allowed to go flat and diluted 50% with clean water are all good. With severe diarrhoea a rehydrating solution is preferable to replace lost minerals and salts. Commercially available oral rehydration salts (ORS) are very useful; add them to boiled or bottled water. In an emergency you can make up a solution of six teaspoons of sugar and a half teaspoon of salt to a litre of boiled or bottled water. You need to drink at least the same volume of fluid that you are losing in bowel movements and vomiting. Urine is the best guide to the adequacy of replacement – if you have small amounts of concentrated urine, you need to drink more. Keep drinking small amounts often. Stick to a bland diet as you recover.

Lomotil or Imodium can be used to bring relief from the symptoms, although they do not actually cure the problem. Only use these drugs if you do not have access to toilets. Lomotil and Imodium are not recommended for children under 12. Do not use these drugs if the person has a high fever or is severely dehydrated.

Hepatitis Hepatitis is a general term for inflammation of the liver. It is a common disease worldwide. The symptoms are fever, chills, headache, fatigue, feelings of weakness and aches and pains, followed by loss of appetite, nausea, vomiting, abdominal pain, dark urine, light-coloured faeces, jaundiced (yellow) skin and the whites of the eyes may turn yellow. **Hepatitis A** is transmitted by contaminated food and drinking water. The disease poses a real threat to the western traveller. You should seek medical advice, but there is not much you can do apart from resting, drinking lots of fluids, eating lightly and avoiding fatty foods. People who have had hepatitis should avoid alcohol for some time after the illness, as the liver needs time to recover. **Hepatitis E** is transmitted in the same way, it can be very serious in pregnant women.

There are almost 300 million chronic carriers of **Hepatitis B** in the world. It is spread through contact with infected blood, blood products or body fluids, for example through sexual contact, unsterilised needles and blood transfusions, or contact with blood via small breaks in the skin. Other risk situations include having a shave, tattoo, or having your body pierced with contaminated equipment. The symptoms of type B may be more severe and may lead to long-term problems. **Hepatitis D** is spread in the same way, but the risk is mainly in shared needles. **Hepatitis C** can lead to chronic liver disease. The virus is spread by contact with blood usually via contaminated transfusions or shared needles. Avoiding these is the only means of prevention.

HIV & AIDS HIV, the Human Immunodeficiency Virus, develops into AIDS, Acquired Immune Deficiency Syndrome, which is a fatal disease. Any exposure to blood, blood products or body fluids may put the individual at risk. The disease is often transmitted through sexual contact or dirty needles – vaccinations, acupuncture, tattooing and body piercing can be potentially as dangerous as intravenous drug use. HIV/AIDS can also be spread through infected blood transfusions; some developing countries cannot afford to screen blood.

If you need an injection, ask to see the syringe unwrapped in front of you, or take a needle and syringe pack with you. Fear of HIV infection should never preclude treatment for serious medical conditions.

Romania bears 54% of all Europe's known juvenile AIDS cases. AIDS in Romanian is SIDA. Seek advice, support, or consultation locally from the Romanian AIDS Association (Asociaţia SIDA în România; ARAS) which has offices/support centres in Bucharest (☎ & fax 01-311 068; email aras@kappa.ro), Blvd Gării Obor 23, apartment No 8; in Constanţa (☎ & fax 041-665 350; email arasct@dnt.ro), Str Jupiter 6; in Iaşi (☎ & fax 032-2110 024; email aras@mail. cccis.ro), Str Zmeu 3; in Piatra Neamţ (☎ & fax 033-234 345; email araspn@mail.cccis.ro), Blvd Traian 6, block S5; and in Craiova, Str Petru Rareş 4, room No 123.

Sexually Transmitted Diseases Gonorrhoea, herpes and syphilis are all painfully common in this region. There was a syphilis epidemic in Romania in late 1997, prompting calls yet again for prostitution to be legalised in the country where child prostitution is rife. Many syphilis sufferers are street children.

Sores, blisters or rashes around the genitals, discharges or pain when urinating are common symptoms. In some STDs, such as wart virus or chlamydia, symptoms may be less marked or not observed at all especially in women. Syphilis symptoms eventually disappear completely but the disease continues and can cause severe problems in later years. While abstinence from sexual contact is the only 100% effective prevention, using condoms is also effective. The treatment of gonorrhoea and syphilis is with antibiotics. The different sexually transmitted diseases each require specific antibiotics. There is no cure for herpes or AIDS.

Tick-Borne Encephalitis From May to September there is a risk of tick-borne encephalitis in forested areas. Encephalitis is inflammation of the brain tissue. Symptoms include fever, headache, vomiting, neck stiffness, pain in the eyes when looking at light, alteration in consciousness, seizures and paralysis or muscle weakness. Correct diagnosis and treatment require hospitalisation. Ticks may be found on the edge of forests and in clearing, long grass and hedgerows. A vaccine is available (see the Immunisations details earlier).

Always check your body if you have been walking through a potentially tick-infested area. If found, press down around the tick's head with tweezers, grab the head and gently pull upwards. Avoid pulling the rear of the body as this may squeeze the tick's gut contents through the attached mouth parts into the skin, increasing the risk of infection and disease. Smearing chemicals on the tick will not make it let go and is not recommended.

WOMEN TRAVELLERS

Traditional gender roles are firmly intact. Romania has the lowest percentage (3%) of women in parliament in Europe and few vocal women's groups exist. Male chivalry plays a vital role in daily life. Most Romanian women expect their menfolk to carry their bags and kiss their hands upon meeting, while the vast majority of Romanian men cannot comprehend that a woman is able to step off a bus or train unaided.

The upshot of this for women travellers is that you won't be left to get on with things alone during your entire trip. Romanian women rarely travel unaccompanied. Western women travelling alone are generally accorded respect (because they are 'so brave') and sympathy (because they couldn't find a man to bring along) by both sexes alike.

Romania is a 'safe' place for women travellers, the same rules applying as anywhere else in the world – don't wander about alone late at night, avoid sitting in empty compartments on long-distance and overnight trains; and don't appear unnerved. Some Romanian men have the revolting habit of hissing at women but, beyond that, they'll leave you alone. The only exception is Constanţa and the Black Sea coastal resorts which teem with Romanian *and* western men on the pull. Don't hesitate to be rude if a polite refusal to engage in conversation fails; once they

realise you're not game they'll soon latch onto the next woman till they find someone to play. If things get desperate, shout '*Poliţia!*'

Organisations

The Women's Association of Romania (☎ 01-650 2795; fax 01-659 7931), Calea Victoriei 133-135, RO-71102 Bucharest; and the Women's National Union (☎ 01-212 0967), Calea Dorobanţilor 224, RO-71282 Bucharest, are two information sources.

GAY & LESBIAN TRAVELLERS

Homosexuality in Romania is still illegal and punishable by five years imprisonment. In 1994 the parliament voted against liberalising laws, as demanded by the Council of Europe. In 1996 it then extended Article 200 of its penal code to criminalise homosexual acts in private, gay bars, clubs and newspapers, and all 'attempts to convert'.

The Council of Europe, Amnesty International, and gay and lesbian groups worldwide actively campaign against this anti-gay legislation. In 1996 gay activists armed with banners reading 'Romania! Stop Persecuting Queers!' stormed onto the stage during a performance of *Aida* by the Romanian National Opera in London's Albert Hall. In New York gay and lesbian activists organised a sit-in outside the Romanian consulate, and in Milan campaigners took to the streets masked as Dracula. In 1997 the International Gay & Lesbian Association (ILGA) called for a worldwide boycott on Romanian wine.

Not surprisingly, gay and lesbian Romanians never show affection in public. Those who do are persecuted. The Orthodox Church considers homosexuality a sin, and a surprising number of young Romanians feel that gay and lesbian relationships are 'unnatural'. Hotel managers will turn away openly gay couples, so be discreet if you're travelling with a same-sex partner.

Organisations

Despite being outlawed the Bucharest-based ACCEPT group operates underground. It can be contacted via the human rights group Helsinki Committee (☎ & fax 01-312 4528, 312 4443; email ion@apador.sfos.ro), Calea Victoriei 120, RO-70179 Bucharest.

Romania Action (web@raglb.org.uk; www.raglb.org.uk) is a British-based web site which heads the international campaign for the decriminalisation of homosexuality in Romania. It includes press clippings and full details of Article 200.

DISABLED TRAVELLERS

Disabled travellers will find it difficult, if not downright impossible, to conquer Romania. Street surfaces are woefully uneven, ramps and specially equipped toilets and hotel rooms virtually unheard of. Consider joining a package tour that will cater to your specific needs – some hotels on the Black Sea coast have wheelchair access from the hotel to the beach. Bucharest's Gara de Nord train station has ramps for wheelchairs but offers no solution to the problem of actually getting on the train.

For information contact the National Society for Physically Handicapped Persons (☎ 01-659 3000), Town Hall, Blvd Banu Manta, RO-78171 Bucharest. The Handicapped Persons Sports Club (☎ 01-211 5550, 211 5195), Str Vasile Conta 16, RO-70139 Bucharest, and the Blind Persons' Association of Romania (☎ 01-250 6525, 250 6615), Str Vatra Luminoasă 108, RO-73305 Bucharest, might be of use too.

TRAVEL WITH CHILDREN

If you intend travelling across the region by public transport with young children, take every opportunity to break up the journey. Bus and train journeys between regional cities can be long and arduous with little to make the journey pass quickly. Take sufficient food and drink supplies as none are available on buses and most trains. Children under five travel free on private buses and those under 12 get discounts. TAROM also offers children's discounts on flights.

Many of the larger hotels have family rooms or will put an extra bed in the room.

See Lonely Planet's *Travel with Children* by Maureen Wheeler for some insider tips.

USEFUL ORGANISATIONS

The following Romanian Cultural Centres can supply information on the country:

France
    1 rue de l'exposition, F-75005 Paris (☎ 01-40 62 22 70, 40 62 22 71; fax 01-40 62 22 72)
Hungary
    Iszto út 5, H-1146 Budapest XIV (☎ 1-122 6 293, 142 7388; fax 1-268 0269)
UK
    7th floor, 54-62 Regent St, London WIR 5PJ (☎ 0171-439 4052, 437 0015; fax 0171-437 5908; email radu@radur.demon.co.uk; www.radur.demon.co.uk/RCC.html)
USA
    200 East 38th St, New York NY-10016 (☎ & fax 212-0687 0181)

DANGERS & ANNOYANCES
Street Crime

Crime has soared in the region since the collapse of communism – primarily because daily survival for an increasing number of people is so damn difficult. We're not talking gangland murders, gruesome rapes and protection rackets though. Most crime stems from simple economics – pickpocketing, muggings, theft from hotel rooms etc.

It is unwise to display your wealth. *All* western travellers are considered wealthy in Romania. Be on guard if walking late at night, keep to well lit streets and look purposeful. If you are attacked, don't expect much help from bystanders or the police. Never leave valuables unattended, including in hotel rooms, campsites and in the boot of your car. Motorists with western cars should ensure they lock their vehicle at night, leave not so much as a tourist map on the dashboard and, if possible, park in a guarded parking lot. Upmarket hotels have guarded parking.

Occasionally beggars can be a nuisance. Be especially wary of professional beggars, colourfully dressed women with babies in their arms, or gangs of sweetly-smiling beggar children.

For the police (in Romanian) dial ☎ 955.

Scam Alert!

You may be approached on the street by a man who asks if you want to change money. Within seconds, another man dashes up to you flashing a fake police ID and demands to see your passport and cash as evidence that you did not illegally change money. *Do not* give them either: don't even start to get your passport or cash out. If you do, they will be off with both or alternatively demand even more cash from you in return for your passport. If this happens to you, do not be intimidated by these men. Shout *'poliţia!'* and create a commotion and they usually scarper quickly. If this fails, offer to accompany them to the nearest police station. Wandering off in an unknown city with a thief is not a good idea, however.

This trick is particularly rife in Bucharest, but be careful in every city. *Never* ever part with your passport. ■

Stray Dogs

Bucharest's serious stray dog problem is a bizarre legacy of Ceauşescu's systemisation in the 1980s when scores of city-centre homes were demolished. Replacement tower blocks proved so cramped that many dog-owners faced no alternative but to let their pets loose on the streets. These dogs have since multiplied, a fact immediately evident the moment you set foot in Bucharest. Numerous packs of dogs roam in the city centre, scouring in waste bins and generally making their canine presence known. Most are harmless but bitches with puppies can be snappy. Keep well clear.

In mid-1997 a mass sterilisation programme rumoured to cost in excess of US$1 million was implemented in the capital in a bid to stop Bucharest's 200,000-strong dog population multiplying further.

Attitude

The Romanians' egocentric Latin temperament is apparent when they do things like turn on loud music without consulting those nearby, push in front of others in the queue, monopolise the pavement and insist on being served first. Some bad-mannered Romanians rudely interrupt conversations at ticket and information windows. It's also common for Romanians to squeeze close together in queues and on buses; the notion of 'personal space' has yet to catch on here.

Being late simply is not a concept for most Romanians. Many have no jobs, have nowhere to rush to, hence are happy to spend hours waiting in line at a post office or in shops. Slow service is just not a problem for these people. The upside of this is that most Romanians will go out of their way to help foreign travellers. They are prepared to spend hours talking to you. If you ask someone directions, they will probably insist on accompanying you wherever you want to go.

Drugs

Treat all drugs with caution. There is a fair amount of dope in the region but it is illegal and you can get into serious trouble if you are found dabbling. Since 1989 Romanian police have seized 20 tonnes of drugs smuggled into the country, including heroin and cocaine. The biggest haul was 11 tonnes of cannabis and hashish, found on a boat docked at Constanţa port in 1993.

Other Nuisances

Hay fever sufferers will sneeze their way around the region in May and June when the pollen count is at its highest. Bloodsucking mosquitoes are rife in summer, particularly in the Danube Delta. Water pressure is low and hot water is programmed in many middle and bottom-end hotels; a pathetic dribble of lukewarm water from the shower head is common.

LEGAL MATTERS

If you are arrested you can insist on seeing an embassy or consular officer straight away. Be polite and respectful towards officials.

BUSINESS HOURS

Banking hours are weekdays from around 8 am to noon. Most shops and markets close on Sunday, museums on Monday. Theatrical performances and concerts usually begin at

7 pm, except on Monday and in summer, when most theatres are closed.

PUBLIC HOLIDAYS & SPECIAL EVENTS

The public holidays in Romania are New Year (1 and 2 January), Easter Monday (March/April), May Day (1 May), National Unity Day (1 December) and Christmas (25 and 26 December).

Romania has a juicy calendar of folklore

Total Eclipse of the Sun

On 11 August 1999 night will fall during the day in Romania as the last total eclipse of the century crosses the continent. The next one in Europe cannot be witnessed until 2081.

The shadow of the moon is expected to travel from England's Cornwall, through northern France, southern Germany, Austria and Hungary, into Romania. The path of a totally blackened sky will enter Romania 50km west of Arad and will pass over Timişoara, Piteşti and Bucharest before leaving the country 30km west of Călăraşi.

Romania is the prime spot for amateur astronomers to witness this solar eclipse. It will reach its maximum duration of two minutes and 23 seconds over Bucharest at approximately 2.07 pm (11.07 am GMT). Here the eclipse will have its maximum coverage of the sun and weather forecasters predict the best chances of clear skies in this region.

Don't look at the eclipse with a magnifying glass (unless you want to be left blind or with permanent eye damage).

The International Association Eclipsa '99 (☎ 01-335 6892; fax 01-337 3389; email mstavinschi @roimar.imar.ro), Str Cutitul de Argint 5, RO-75212 Bucharest, is building a 65-seat planetarium in preparation for the event. Alternatively, contact the Timişoara Astronomical Observatory (☎ & fax 056-162 838; email astro@astrotm.sorostm.ro), Piaţa Axente Sever 1, RO-1900 Timişoara), or the Royal Greenwich Observatory (☎ 01223-374 774; fax 01223-374 700; email sab@ast.cam.ac.uk), Madingley Road, Cambridge CB3 0EZ, UK. ■

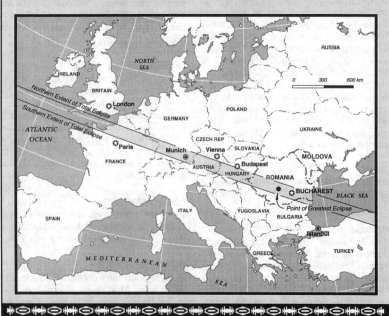

festivals, many of which have become regular events. Numerous smaller festivals remain unpublicised, preserving their authenticity but making them difficult for the traveller to attend. Many festivals are detailed in the relevant regional chapters. Regular annual festivals include:

May
  Feast of Narcisses – spring festival Vlăhiţa-Hărghita district
1-14 May
  Tânjaua de pe Mara Festival – traditional folk festival to celebrate the first ploughing of spring, Hoteni, Maramureş
last weekend in May
  Bucharest Carnival – street carnival, Bucharest
mid-May
  Juni Pageant – traditional folk festival in Scheii district, Braşov
Whit Sunday
  Székely Pilgrimage – the largest traditional Székely folk and religious festival of the year, Miercurea Ciuc
June
  Fundata Fair – traditional folklore fair originally held for people to meet and shepherds to meet their future wives, Fundata near Bran
23/24 June
  Sarbatoare – most evident in Maramureş
Sunday around 20 July
  Girls' Fair (Târgul de fete) – traditional wife-arranging festival, Mount Găina, Avram Iancu
July
  International Chamber Music Festival – concerts in Braşov and Bran
July and August
  National Festival of Light Music – Mamaia
mid-August
  Hora de la Prislop – wild dancing festival on the Prislop Pass
August
  Medieval Days – two-week medieval arts, crafts and music festival in the streets of Sighişoara
August
  International Folk Festival of Danubian Countries – Tulcea
September
  Golden Stag (Cerbul de Aur) – six or seven day pop music festival, Braşov
September
  Sâmbra oilor – a major pastoral festival to mark the 'coming down' (*transhumanţă*) of the sheep from the mountains, Bran and around
mid-September
  Festivalu l Clătitelor – pancake festival in and around Bran

14 September
  Wine Festival – drinking festival to celebrate the start of the grape harvest, Cotnari
December
  De la Colind la Stea – international Christmas festival in Braşov

ACTIVITIES
Romania is rich in things to do all year round, be it skiing, hiking, bear-watching or sheer self-pampering you are after.

Mountain Biking
Given Romania's ideal mountain biking terrain, it is not surprising that the sport has taken off in a big way in recent years, complete with western jargon and trendy, multicoloured gear! The most active biking clubs are in Cluj-Napoca, Sibiu, Oradea and Târgu Mureş.

These clubs can provide information on biking in their area (see individual chapters for contact details). The Sinaia club based at the Bike Shop (☎ 044-311 810), Str Walter Măvăcineanu 2, is the only club to officially rent out mountain bikes and guides. All clubs can do this; contact them well in advance.

The clubs host 12 cross-country and downhill events each year between April and September. The Boua Bikes Club (☎ 069-218 310), Str Avram Iancu 25, 2400-Sibiu, organises the Triatlon Altitude (Altitude Triathlon) in August in the Făgăraş mountains, open to international competitors.

The Bike Sport Club (☎ 059-121 745), Str Nufărului 39, Oradea, publishes the monthly *Mountain Bike Mania* magazine. To subscribe mail Mountain Bike Mania, Oficiul poştal 10, Căsuta poştală 34, RO-3700-Oradea.

If road cycling is more your scene, contact the Romanian Cycling Federation (☎ 01-615 9194; fax 01-312 7042), Str Academiei 2, RO-70417 Bucharest.

Off-Roading
Two-wheelers can contact EnduRoMania (☎ 056-194 11; ☎ & fax 056-194 596; email sergio@adetim.sorostm.ro; www .sorostm .ro/enduro/), Str Lucian Blaga 3, RO-1900

Timişoara. The off-roading motorcycle club arranges events year-round and can also set up tours and expeditions geared to individuals (see Getting Around for more details).

Four-wheelers are steered to Transcarpat Off-Road (☎ 01-613 8315; fax 01-312 1008), PO Box 33-27, RO-70200 Bucharest, an 4 x 4 off-roading club that organises the international Carpat Trophy in Transylvania each year. It is also possible to tour Romania by Land Rover (see Getting Around).

Skiing & Snowboarding

Romania's most famous ski resorts are Sinaia, Predeal and Poiana Braşov, all in the Carpathian mountains between Bucharest and Braşov. They are fully developed, with cable cars, chair lifts and modern resort hotels. Predeal is the smallest resort and attracts few skiers beyond school groups. The ski slopes at Sinaia vary in altitude from 400 to 2800m, with level differences up to 585m, and is considered to offer Romania's most challenging skiing. The downside is that the resort is exposed, meaning cable cars often don't run in windy weather. On top of the Bucegi plateau above the Sinaia resort is an 8km cross-country route, as well as a 13-bend bobsled track where the Ski-Biathlon Club (☎ 044-374 815, 01-211 5550) hosts a biathlon each year.

Poiana Braşov boasts 20km of ski slopes and sled runs at varying degrees of difficulty. This resort, off the main railway line, has few black slopes but offers guaranteed skiing year-round. Advanced skiers can dabble in some off-piste skiing with a local guide. This resort is extremely popular with package tours, and has the best developed ski school. Six days tuition costs US$60 and a six day ski pass is US$40. Poiana Braşov is also popular with snowboarders. Snowboarding lessons are also available. Full details are included in the Poiana Braşov section of the Transylvania chapter.

The ski season runs from December to mid-March. You can hire gear from all the major hotels in the resorts. The cheapest way to ski in Romania is to book a package deal.

Travel agencies specialising in ski holidays are listed in Getting There & Away.

Hiking & Climbing

Romania's Carpathian mountains offer endless opportunities for hikers, the most popular areas being the Bucegi and Făgăraş ranges, south and west of Braşov. Other Carpathian hiking zones include the Retezat National Park, north-west of Târgu Jiu; the Şureanu mountains, between Alba Iulia and Târgu Jiu; the Apuseni mountains, south-west of Cluj-Napoca; and the Ceahlău Massif, between Braşov and Suceava. Buşteni is considered the premier mountaineering centre.

Clearly marked trails traverse most of Romanian mountain ranges and lower lying foothills. Detailed hiking maps are hard to find – check at tourist offices. The best selection of maps is sold at the kiosks outside Bucharest University on Piaţa Universitaţii.

LINK Romania (see Work section later in this chapter) arranges sponsored six-day hikes in the Carpathians.

Mountain Rescue Emergency rescue is provided by the Asociaţia Naţionale a Salvatorilor Montani dîn România (SALVAMONT). This is a voluntary mountain rescue organisation (exclusively male). Its 200 active members are skilled climbers, skiers and medics who serve Romania's hiking resorts in summer then move to its ski resorts in winter. It has 26 stations countrywide, spread between towns and more mountainous regions. Many urban stations have telephones (numbers are listed in the relevant chapters of this book). In an emergency, contact can be made via the local hospital, mayor's office (primăria), or through its headquarters in Braşov (☎ 068-168 719). The crew is on 24-hour alert and contactable by radio. Hikers and climbers intending to spend a few days in the mountains should always alert a SALVAMONT station of their route and schedule.

Bear in mind that this is only a voluntary organisation which relies on limited funding from local authorities. Members receive

US$7 per skiing action and US$4 for a mountaineering action. Equipment is minimal and outdated, and mountain rescue by helicopter is financially impossible.

Clubs Abroad, the British Mountaineering Council (BMC; ☎ 0161-445 4747; fax 0161-445 4500; email office@thebmc.co.uk; www.thebmc.co.uk), 177-179 Burton Road, Manchester M20 2BB, provides up-dated lists of climbing clubs in Romania, including those approved by the Union Internationale des Association d'Alpinisme (UIAA).

In Bucharest contact the Clubul Alpinism și Escaladă (☎ 01-614 8217), Str Câmpineanu 20 and Str Vasile Conta 16; the Clubul Alpin Român (☎ 01-613 8078), Str Gladiolelor 1/14b; or the National Youth Tourist Club (☎ 01-615 4970; fax 01-312 5374), Str Dem Ion Dobrescu 4-6. For a local guide try the National Guides Association (☎ 068-150 448; fax 068-150 504), Complex Favorit, Poiana Brașov.

Regional clubs are listed in the relevant chapters.

Caving

Some 12,000 caves *(peștera)* in Romania have been documented but only four are protected: the Peștera Ghețarul de la Scarișoara, an ice cave in the Apuseni mountains ranked as the world's second largest subterranean glacier; the Peștera Cetățile Ponosului between Cluj-Napoca and Oradea which has 100m-high passages; and the 3566m-long Peștera Muierii, and the Peștera Closani in western Wallachia. All four are gated and only the Scarișoara ice cave is open to tourists.

Serious cavers can however contact local caving clubs and get permission to enter caves not open to the public. The Emil Racovița Institute of Speleology (☎ 064-195 954), Str Clinicilor 5, RO-3400 Cluj-Napoca, can arrange an expedition to Romania's largest cave, the Peștera Humpleu in the Padiș Plateau. This river-cave is 30km-long and large enough to house six full-size football stadiums. The southern Banat, Dobruja and the Apuseni mountains

are considered the most rewarding caving terrain. Much of it is mapped.

The Romanian Speleological Federation can likewise assist cavers and potholers interested in discovering Romania's underworld. It has a list of all 40 of Romania's caving clubs and can usually put you in touch with a local guide. Contact its Cluj-Napoca office (☎ & fax 187 657; email speo @mail.soroscj.ro; www .uib.no/ People/ nglbn/frspeo.htm), Piața 14 Iulie 4, RO-3400 Cluj-Napoca; or at Str Frumoașa 31, RO-78114 Bucharest. Get in touch with both these associations *well* in advance if you hope to organise an expedition through them. Cavers have to provide their own equipment.

Train Spotting

Romania is paradise for train enthusiasts who steam it to Romania to travel aboard one of the country's last remaining nine steam locomotives dating from the 1920s and 1930s. Some pre-war steam locomotives using narrow-gauge lines have been lovingly restored, enabling travellers to train it through some of Romania's most remote regions, while special-gauge steam engines trundle along forestry railway lines in the mountains.

Two specialist companies organise steam train adventures. RomSteam-Aldo (☎ & fax 040-231 431; email romsteam@decebal.ro), Str Plevnei 2, block L2, apartment 58, RO-5600 Piatra Neamț, organises various seven and nine day steam train tours on standard and narrow-gauge lines, including a trip up Europe's only operational inclined plane in the Transylvania. Dracula steam tours are also available. The Ronedo Tourist Agency (☎ 040-231 870; fax 040-231 306), Blvd Decebal 59, apartment 1, RO-5600 Piatra Neamț, offers similar tours. Unfortunately steam costs – expect to pay from US$1079 per person in a group of 15. The *Wälder & Dampf* (Forest & Steam) coffee-table book includes photographs and parallel German and English texts to trace the history of Romania's forestry railways.

Birdwatching

The Danube Delta and the area of Dobruja immediately south of it offer some of the most spectacular birdwatching in Europe, with some 280 bird species having been recorded. Most birdwatchers arrive during the migratory seasons between mid-April and mid-May, and in October. Large bird colonies are protected by the Danube Delta Biosphere Reserve but, to quote a local ornithologist, 'the birds don't know where the protected zones are, do they?' Flocks of white pelicans overhead are a common sight.

Specialist travel agents abroad (see Getting There & Away) organise birdwatching tours. Locally, the Romanian Ornithological Society – sponsored by the British Royal Society for the Protection of Birds (RSPB) – arranges day trips and can provide professional guides. Its headquarters are at Str Gheorghe Dima 49/2, RO-3400 Cluj-Napoca. Cash donations to protect Delta birds are handled by the Berlin Land Association of the Nature Conservation Federation of Germany (NABU; ☎ 030-986 4107), Hauptstr 13, D-13055 Berlin.

Finding Birds in Romania by Dave Gosney, *Important Bird Areas in Europe* by RFA Grimmet & TA Jones, and *Where to Watch Birds in Europe* by John Gooders (the bible) are three books worth bringing along: local guides only know Romanian names for bird species so the pictures in these books come in handy.

Wolf & Bear Watching

ANTREC in Bran (see the Bran section in the Transylvania chapter) can arrange, with notice well in advance, brown bear watching from hideouts close to Zărneşti in the Piatra Craiului region. It can also arrange visits to see the wolf cubs being raised at the Zărneşti field cabin by devoted members of the pioneering Carpathian Large Carnivore Project.

Spas

One-third of all European sources of mineral or thermal waters are concentrated in Romania, which has more than 160 spas. The mud baths on Lake Techirghiol at Eforie Nord go well with the salty lake water and the nearby Black Sea. Other important spas are Băile Felix (near Oradea) and Băile Herculane (known since Roman times).

COURSES

Several Romanian universities offer foreigners two or three-week *cursuri de vară* (summer courses) in Romanian language and civilisation. Tuition includes about 20

Romania's bears thrived under Ceauşescu – only he could shoot them and usually he missed.

hours of instruction a week, accommodation in double rooms at student halls of residence, meals at student cafeterias, cultural events and other activities. Programmes for beginners are offered. Registration (by mail or fax) generally closes around 1 June.

The three week course in July at the Universitatea Alexandru Ioan Cuza (fax 032-146 330), Secretariat Relaţii Internaţionale, Blvd Copou No 11, RO-6600 Iaşi, costs US$400, including a three day excursion to Bucovina. Babes-Bolyai University (fax 40-64-111 905), Secretariatul Cursurilor de Vară, Str Mihail Kogălniceanu 1, RO-3400 Cluj-Napoca, also has a three week course in July (US$550). In late August and early September the University of Timişoara (fax 40-56-116 722), Blvd Vsile Parvan, 1900 Timişoara, offers specialised two week courses in a variety of fields (US$375).

The Romanian Cultural Foundation (☎ 01-212 2854; fax 01-312 7579), Aleea Alexandru 38, RO-71273 Bucharest, runs language courses year-round as do many private language schools in Romania. These are listed in the relevant regional chapters of this book.

WORK

Romania has enough difficulty keeping its own people employed so there is little work for foreigners. What work exists is usually in specialist fields (on a local salary) and requires previous work experience and formal qualifications in that field. Jobs for qualified English-language TEFL teachers, special needs teachers, care assistants, and other positions in Romanian schools, orphanages and medical institutions are occasionally advertised in *Information Romania*, a monthly newsletter published by the Romania Information Centre (see the list later in this section).

The *East European Partnership* (☎ & fax 0181-780 7555), Carlton House, 27a Carlton Drive, London SW5 2BS, is the eastern Europe branch of VSO (Voluntary Services Overseas) and regularly recruits English-language teachers.

Volunteer & Aid Work

There are still plenty of opportunities to be had in the realm of charity work, providing you are prepared to fund the trip yourself.

One of the most exciting opportunities is with the Carpathian Large Carnivore Project. Volunteers can spend two to four weeks working with members of the wolf and brown bear conservation project in the Carpathian mountains. You pay your own air fare and a donation is expected. To apply send your CV and a letter of motivation to Europe Conservation France (☎ 02 54 58 22 22; fax 02 54 58 22 20), BP 44, La Chaussée, F-41260 Saint Victor; or to Travel 'n Care (☎ 040-8891 3955; fax 040-8891 3957), Hohenzollernring 27, D-22763 Hamburg. Few applications are refused.

Many mainstream charities can only place volunteers with work experience or qualifications in a certain field. Charities who fund or carry out aid work in Romania include:

Christian Children's Fund
    4 Bath Place, Rivington St, London EC2A 3DR (☎ 0171-729 8191; fax 0171-729 8339) – sponsor a Romanian child through the CCF
LINK
    20-24 South St, Tarring, Worthing, West Sussex (☎ & fax 01903-529 333; email admin @linkrom.org; www.wordnet.co.uk/linkro.html) – dynamic charity with imaginative projects; sends around 14,000 shoeboxes every Christmas; opportunities to volunteer on group and sometimes individual basis are advertised in newsletter
Powerful Information
    21 Church Lane, Loughton, Milton Keynes MK5 8AS (☎ & fax 01908-666 275) – sets up environmental workshops in Romania
Relief Fund for Romania
    54-62 Regent St, London W1R 5PJ (☎ 0171-439 4052; fax 0171-437 5908) – set up by Romanian expats in the UK; helps Romanian children
Romanian Aid Fund
    2 Torquay Drive, Woodsmore, Stockport, Cheshire SK2 7BB (☎ 0161-612 9013) – Christian-based charity set up in the 1980s
Romania Information Centre
    Southampton University, Southampton SO17 1BJ (☎ 01703-551 328; fax 01703-678 700) – database of over 650 British charity groups working in Romania; can provide contacts and information for registered groups looking for Romanian charities to support

Romania's Unwanted Children

The burden of Romania's communist past weighs most heavily on its children. An estimated 91,000 live in orphanages or children's homes today – 20% more than in 1989. Eight thousand of these orphans or abandoned youngsters are less than three years old.

Tentative steps have been made by Constantinescu's reformist government to overhaul Romania's childcare system and tackle the enormous problem of family poverty – the main factor behind the rising number of children in state institutions. Child benefits were increased from US$1.50 to US$7 a month in early 1997, and paid maternity leave extended from three months to two years. A new child adoption law placing adoption procedures in the hands of an authorised agency has also been enforced in a bid to crack down on illegal adoptions and baby trafficking to the west.

The situation remains dire though. The government's harsh 1997 economic reforms – vital for the country's future economic growth – have provoked further short-term unemployment and poverty. Some 36% of the population is estimated to live below the poverty line and approximately 20,000 of the 300,000 babies born each year are abandoned. In April 1997 a 36-year-old mother abandoned her 14th baby. Three of her children are being raised by her parents, four are in an orphanage, while the remaining seven have died from starvation.

Romania's unwanted children are a legacy of Ceauşescu's ban on contraception and abortion in 1966 coupled with his ruling that women under 45 should have at least five children.

Since communism's collapse the appalling conditions in Romania's orphanages have improved slightly, thanks to the assistance of international aid organisations. The flood of individual 'mercy missions' that swamped Romania in the early 1990s has since receded, aid to Romania today being handled by a focused network of larger organisations which are committed to working alongside local non-government organisations and aid groups as part of a long-term solution to help Romanians help themselves.

Since 1990 foreigners have been able to adopt Romanian orphans. An average 2500 children are adopted by foreigners each year, although the Romanian Adoption Agency says at least 10,000 children have been illegally sold to westerners. In November 1994 a British couple were given a suspended 28 month jail sentence for trying to smuggle a six-month-old baby (which they'd bought for US$6000) out of Romania. In March 1997 four men were charged with illegally selling 48 children to Italian families.

Romania's abortion rate remains among the highest in Europe (2.12 for every live birth), despite contraceptives being available to those who can afford them. New-born babies weigh an average 200g less than those born in western Europe and have a 10% greater chance of dying in the first 12 months of their life. Romania has the second-highest infant mortality rate in Europe. ■

Romanian Information Clearing House
Str Ministerului 1-3, RO-70103 Bucharest (☎ 01-615 000) – database of Romanian and foreign non-government organisations
Romanian Orphanage Trust
21 Garlick Hill, London EC4V 2AU (☎ 0181-675 6114; fax 0181-675 2516; email contextcomms@demon.co.uk) – works with orphanages; its sister organisation *European Children's Trust* supports orphanages in Moldova; sponsor a child in either
Rumänien Info Dienst
Karolinger Strasse 2, D-71322 Waiblingen (☎ 07151-564 307; fax 07151-564 399; email digitas@aol.com) – database of German charities working in Romania

ACCOMMODATION

You have to pay all accommodation charges in lei despite many hotels listing rates in US$. Upmarket hotels accept credit cards. All hotels ask to see your passport when you check in. Many will try to keep it for the duration of your stay; tell staff at reception you need it to change money and they will happily return it to you. Accommodation is widely available in private homes in rural Romania – sharing the breakfast table with a family each morning will bring you closer to the 'real' Romania than any number of nights in a hotel.

Floors are numbered the American way. The ground floor is the first floor.

Reservations

Reservations are only necessary on the Black Sea coast which gets packed in July and August. Consider booking a package deal if you intend to spend more than a few days here.

Camping

Campsites *(popas turistic)* are not like the ones you may know in the west. Most sites comprise little wooden huts *(căsuţe)* which usually sleep two or four people. Bare mattresses are usually provided but you have to provide your own bedding or sleeping bag. Some upmarket căsuţe tout real beds with sheets and even wash basins. Communal wash facilities – showers – in most campsites are basic. Hot water rarely flows while some sites are completely without toilets or showers.

There is usually a space allocated for tents on these sites. Freelance camping is prohibited in cities but not necessarily elsewhere. Camping on the beaches or in fields along the Black Sea coast, unthinkable during the Ceauşescu era, is now fairly common. Wild camping is strictly forbidden in the Danube Delta and you can be fined if you do so: for allocated campsites here you need a camping permit (US$1).

Pitching tents is freely allowed in the mountains but it can get nippy.

The Romanian Ministry of Tourism publishes a *Camping Map* of most of the country's campsites. It's available from tourist offices abroad.

Mountain Huts

In most mountain areas there's a network of cabins or chalets *(cabana)* with restaurants and dormitories. Prices are much lower than those of hotels and no reservations are required, but arrive early if the *cabana* is in a popular location – for example, next to a cable-car terminus. Expect to find good companionship rather than cleanliness or comfort. Many are open year-round and cater for skiers in winter.

You will also come across unattended, empty wooden huts *(refuge)* in the mountains. These are intended as shelter for hikers and anyone can use them.

Homes & Farmstays

Paying to stay in someone's private home is the most down-to-earth type of accommodation anyone wanting to get to the roots of Romanian homelife, tradition and cuisine will ever find! A paying guest you might well be, but that will not deter your host family from welcoming you with open arms. Their spontaneous friendship is free – and not optional! An evening meal costs extra.

Finding a private room in towns and cities is still difficult. Loiter at the train and bus station and someone will proposition you soon enough. By contrast, 'agro-tourism' (B&B in the countryside) has taken off at breakneck speed since the revolution.

The two leading organisations in this field are the National Association of Rural, Ecological and Cultural Tourism (ANTREC) and Opération Villages Roumains (OVR). The Belgian-based OVR was established in 1989 in response to Ceauşescu's systemisation scheme, with 3000 villages in Europe 'adopting' a threatened village in Romania. Today it operates an excellent network of village offices in Romania through which accommodation in rural homes (US$10-12), folklore evenings, local guides, and various cultural activities can be arranged. Details are listed in the relevant chapters of this book.

Abroad, you can book accommodation in advance through:

France
  18 rue A Duparchy, F-91600 Savigny sur Orge (☎ 01 40 15 71 51; fax 01 40 15 72 30)
UK
  The Old Dye House, Spring Gardens, Frome, Somerset BA11 2NZ (☎ 01373-466 555; fax 01373-454 442)

ANTREC bookings can be made through the Eurogîtes country holiday reservation system. Offices abroad include:

France
  56 rue Saint Lazare, F-75009 Paris (☎ 01 49 70 75 75; fax 01 49 70 75 80)
  7 Place des Meuniers, F-67000 Strasbourg (☎ 03 88 75 60 19; fax 03 88 75 37 96)

Germany
    Eschborner Landstrasse 122, D-60489 Frankfurt
    (☎ 069-247 880; fax 069-247 88110)
    Godesberger Allee 142-148, D-53175 Bonn
    (☎ 0228-819 8220; fax 0228-371 870)
Hungary
    Szoboszalai út 2-4, H-1126 Budapest (☎ 1-155
    533 312; fax 1-155 1857)
Ireland
    2 Michael St, Limerick (☎ 0161-400 700; fax
    0161-400 771)
    Irish County Holidays, 84 Merrion Sq, IRL-2
    Dublin (☎ 0167-65 790; fax 0167-65 793)

Hostels

There are three hostels in Romania. The Vila Helga hostel in Bucharest is the only one open year-round. Romania's other two hostels – in Cluj-Napoca and Sighişoara – are housed in student dormitories and hence only open in July and August when the students are on holiday. In Bucharest a bed in a shared room costs US$12, including breakfast, free cigarettes, and free use of the washing machine.

Hotels

Romanian hotels are rated by the government on a star system, one-star being the lowest (and cheapest) and four-star the highest. At the top of the scale (three and four stars) you're guaranteed hot water, a phone, private bathroom and cable TV. Prices at these places range from US$45 to US$90 for a double room. Breakfast *(mic dejun)* is almost always included in the price.

Not much separates one-star from two-star hotels. Hot water *(apă caldă)* at both is common but not guaranteed. Usually it is restricted to a few hours in the morning and evening: the schedule is normally pinned up at reception. Occasionally cold water *(apă reche)* will be programmed too. You can usually choose between a more expensive room with private bath or a cheaper one with shared bath. Both charge US$20 to US$40 for a double. Breakfast is not always included. Ask!

Except for the grottiest hotels, most supply guests with a ration of crisp pink toilet paper neatly rolled up in the bathroom or on your bedside table. Towels and wrapped

tablets of soap are usually included in private bathrooms (even in one and two-star hotels).

All double rooms – even in four-star hotels – do not sport real double beds. A double room effectively translates as a twin with two single beds, occasionally pushed together. Double rooms with a double bed are called 'matrimonial rooms' which are always more expensive than a regular double. Few hotels, even at the top end of the bracket, offer matrimonial rooms.

By law hotels are required to display at reception contact details for its director, the local emergency services, and the county office for consumer protection *(oficiul pentru protecţia consumatorului)*. Theoretically, this is so guests know who to direct their complaints to. The consumer protection head office (☎ 01-642 2553; fax 01-312 1275) is at Blvd Nicholae Bălcescu 21, RO-70114 Bucharest. *Noroc Bun!* (Good luck!)

Ceauşescu's Private Villas

Travellers keen to sleep in Ceauşescu's bed can do so. The former dictator had two or three private residences in all 41 of Romania's counties. He spent lavish amounts of money on them, decking them out with extravagant furnishings and elaborate mechanisms, only to decide he didn't like the final result. Ceauşescu's private villa overlooking Herăstrău park in Bucharest and his lakeside palace in Snagov are said to be priceless.

Since 1989, some of these properties have been turned into upmarket restaurants, hotels or villas. Many remain in state hands, serving as guesthouses for state VIPs (rock star Michael Jackson stayed at Snagov). Others – in Olaneşti, Lacul Roşu, Neptun, Predeal, Sfântu Gheorghe and Sinaia – are open to humble tourists and backpackers. Details are included in the relevant regional chapters of this book. For bookings and information on other properties contact the State Protocol Patrimony Administration (Administraţia Patrimoniului Protocolului de Stat; ☎ 659 4876; fax 312 1091), Str Iancu de Hunedoara 5, Bucharest. Double rooms range from US$29 to US$100 a night.

FOOD

Romanian restaurants are very affordable, and it would be difficult to spend more than US$10 per day on food. On the other hand, restaurants can be hard to find and are often very basic, offering the same things with unnerving consistency: grilled pork, pork liver, grilled chicken, tripe soup and greasy potatoes.

Beware of bring ripped off in city restaurants. A common trick is to price items per 100g on the menu, leading diners to believe this is the final price. When the bill comes, the amount will have doubled or tripled, leaving you wondering how on earth you can prove that the slab of mystery meat happily nestled in your stomach did not in fact weigh 200g.

Gangs of restaurant staff sitting round a table smoking and watching TV is a norm in many older establishments. Despite the horror that crosses their face when customers dare to walk in wanting to eat, they do offer quite nippy service once they get going. In many places hotel restaurants are still the only ones serving proper meals from regular menus. Romanians can seldom afford to dine out.

Over 140 traditional Romanian recipes (including a staggering seven for Romania's infamous *mămăligă!*) are featured in Nicolae Klepper's delectable *Taste of Romania* cookery book (Hippocrene Books, New York, 1997).

Local Food

Mămăligă is Romania's most novel dish. In short, it is a hard or soft cornmeal mush, which is boiled, baked or fried (a Romanian version of Italian polenta) Traditionally it is served with nothing more than a sprinkling of *brânză*, a very salty sheep cheese. Mămăligă is so bland-tasting that it pretty much goes with – and *is* served with – everything! In many Romanian households it is served as a main dish.

Ciorbă (soup) is the other mainstay of the Romanian diet. It is tart and sometimes served with a dollop of *smântână* (sour cream). Favourites include *ciorbă de perişoare* (spicy soup with meatballs and vegetables), *ciorbă de burtă* (a garlicky tripe soup), and *ciorbă de legumă* (vegetable soup cooked with meat stock). The leftovers are transformed into *ghiveciu* (vegetable stew) or *tocană* (onion and meat stew) for the following day's dinner.

Restaurants and beer gardens typically offer *mititei* or *mici* ('meech' – grilled meatballs). Other common dishes are *muşchi de vaca/porc/miel* (cutlet of beef/pork/lamb), *ficat* (liver), *piept de pui* (chicken breast) and *cabanos prajit* (fried sausages). Cooking styles include grilled *(la grătar)*, fried *(prajit)*, boiled *(fiert)* and roasted on a spit *(la îrigare)*. Almost every dish comes with *cartofi* (potatoes) and *pâine* (bread).

Typical desserts include *plăcintă* (turnovers), *clătite* (crşpes) and *cozonac* (a brioche). *Saraille* is a yummy almond cake soaked in syrup.

Folk dishes are hard to find but worth the search, especially *ardei umpluti* (stuffed peppers), *sarmale* (cabbage or vine leaves stuffed with spiced meat and rice) and *creier pane cu sunca* (breaded brains with ham). Another goodie is *tochitură Moldoveneasca*, a Moldavian speciality comprising pan-fried pork in a spicy pepper sauce served with mămăligă and topped with a fried egg. *Crap kebab* (carp kebab) is typical to the Danube Delta as are most fish dishes. Fish is *peşte*, herring is *scrumbie*, pike is *ştuică*, salmon is *somon*, shrimp is *crevete*, sardine is *sardele* and tuna is *ton*.

In the Orthodox calendar, Easter is the most important feast of the year. Traditionally a kosher lamb (a lamb that has not eaten grass) is slaughtered, every part being used in the great culinary celebration that ensues. *Drob de miel* (haggis) is made from its heart, liver, lungs and stomach. A *ciorbă de miel* (lamb soup) is made from its shoulder or leg, while *stufat de miel* (braised lamb), made with the most succulent meat, is served as the main course. The equivalent is done to a pig at Christmas.

Following a death, a *coliva* – a ring-shaped cake with nuts, honey, vanilla and cinnamon – is baked to honour the deceased.

Fast Food

Fast food is storming its way through the region with McDonald's running sit-down restaurants and drive-ins in all the big cities. Pizza Hut and Kentucky Fried Chicken have outlets in Bucharest. Countrywide a variety of locally run outlets offer a cheap feed for less than US$2.

Vegetarian

Romanians who are devoutly Orthodox do not eat meat on Wednesday or Friday, on certain religious holidays, and during Lent. Hence, there are vegetarian dishes to be had, unexciting as they may be. If a plate of mămăligă does not turn you on, try *caşcaval pâine* (cheese covered in breadcrumbs and fried), *salată roşii* (tomato salad), *salată castraveţi* (cucumber salad) and *salată asortat* ('mixed salad' which is tomatoes and cucumbers). Peppers are *ardei* in Romanian, mushrooms are *ciuperci* and eggs are *ou*. Rice is *orez*. Beyond this staggering choice, dishes are meat-based.

Self-Catering

Every town has a central market *(piaţa centrală)* offering a gorgeous array of fresh fruits and vegetables. Fresh fish and dried products are often sold here too. Pastries and cakes are available everywhere for no more than US$0.10 a piece, as is freshly baked bread which, at around US$0.10 a loaf, forms the staple diet of far too many impoverished backpackers! In Bucharest and some other larger cities there are 24 hour shops and western-style supermarkets with push-round trolleys and every imported luxury imaginable. In smaller towns the old, 'don't touch – point at what you want' style of shopping still rules. Here you'll find row upon row of uninspiring pickled peas, cucumbers etc.

DRINKS

This region is noted for its excellent wine, while the local beer is notable mostly for its low price (about US$0.30 for a half-litre). Imported Hungarian and German beers are available but expensive. Among the best

Romanian wines are Cotnari, Murfatlar, Odobesti, Târnave and Valea Călugărească. Red wines are called *negru* and *roşu*, while white wine is *vin alb*. Also look for the words *sec* (dry), *dulce* (sweet) or *spumos* (sparkling) on the labels. *Vin de masă* is table wine. Sweeter wines are automatically mixed with sparkling mineral water: if you want it neat ask for it *sec*. Even at the restaurant of a two-star hotel, a bottle of decent local wine shouldn't be more than US$4. Wine shops and cellars marked *vin* or *vinuri* are found in most towns. This is the cheapest and most fun way to sample locally made wine. You have to provide your own mug or plastic bottle.

In Romania, *Must* is a fresh unfermented wine available during the wine harvest. *Ţuică* (plum brandy) and *palincă* (distilled three times as much as plum brandy) are mind-blowing liqueurs taken at the beginning of a meal. *Crama* refers to a wine cellar, and a *berărie* is a pub or beer hall. A couple of toasts are *poftă bună* (bon appétit) and *noroc!* (cheers!).

In a land where wine rules, non-alcoholic drinks are unvaried. Coke, Fanta etc are sold everywhere, as is *Frutti-Fresh*, a locally produced mixed-fruit drink bottled in Oradea. *Portocală* is orange and *lămâie* or *citron* is lemon. In May and June locals wander in the forests to collect the young green branches from fir trees, from which they make *syrup de brad*. The pines, fermented in sugar to make the syrup which is then drunk with water, are believed to contain healing properties.

Prior to the 1989 revolution coffee was a rare commodity. A coffee substitute known as *nechezoe*, a word derived from the Romanian word for the neigh of a horse, was painfully drunk instead. Today, Romania has *Ness*, which is an awful instant coffee made from vegetable extracts. It's always served super sweet, tepid or downright cold. Some nightclubs serve *Ness-coke* (Ness and Coke mixed). Many cafés serve Ness and *cafea naturală*, a 'real' coffee made the Turkish way with a thick sludge of ground coffee beans at the bottom and a generous spoonful of sugar. Unless you specifically ask, coffee and *ceai* (tea) are always served black and with sugar. If you want it white ask for it *cu lapte* (with milk). *Apă minerală* (mineral water) is cheap and widely available in Romania.

ENTERTAINMENT

Funky bars and clubs are sprouting in Bucharest but outside the capital nightlife remains low-key. For most Romanians a 'night on the town' is a țuică-fuelled sing-song around a campfire which, for travellers from the west,

Topping the Gymnastic Charts

Romanian gymnast Nadia Comăneci wiped the floor at the 1976 Montreal Olympic Games, making her the most well known Romanian after Dracula and Nicolae Ceaușescu. The 14-year-old landed an unprecedented seven perfect 10 out of 10 scores, enabling her to waltz off with three gold medals (for beam, asymmetric bars and the coveted all-round championship), one silver (team) and one bronze (floor).

Comăneci went on to win two gold medals in the 1979 World Cup, two golds and two silvers at the 1980 Moscow Olympics, and became the only woman to win three consecutive European Championship all-round titles. At home she was the youngest Romanian to be awarded Ceaușescu's Hero of Socialist Labour gold medal and attracted the romantic attentions of Ceaușescu's eldest son, Nicu. Abroad she was credited with taking gymnastics to new heights. Tucked double-backs somersaults, 'Comăneci flips', and 'toe-on half-twists tucked-back to dismount' were all new moves pioneered by the fearless Comăneci as she flip-flopped her way to success. In 1984, at the age of 22, she retired.

Comăneci's defection to the West in November 1989 drew international attention to the brutality of the Ceaușescu regime. She was consequently granted political asylum by the US and later married American gymnast Bart Conner from whom she had stolen a first kiss at the American Cup in 1976 where they met. The couple wed in 1995 at Ceaușescu's House of People in Bucharest and exchanged religious vows at Casin Monastery outside the capital. The bride twirled up the aisle in a US$50,000 dress which sported a 6.5m-long train carried by six aspiring young Romanian gymnasts.

Comăneci was inducted in the International Gymnastics Hall of Fame in 1993. The same year she posed in her underwear for a Times Square poster to raise cash for Romania's orphans. She now runs a gymnastics school in Oklahoma, with husband Bart, and is honorary president of the Romanian Gymnastics Federation.

Despite baring all, Comăneci remains a role model for up-and-coming gymnasts throughout the world. The Romanian Gymnastics Federation (☎ 01-210 4616, 211 1087; fax 01-210 4616) is at Str Vasile Conta 16, RO-70139 Bucharest. Romania's top club is Deva, at Cetate Liceul de Educație Fizica și Sport Deva, Str Alexandru Sahia, RO-2700 Deva. ■

can be an enlightening experience and a refreshing change from life in the fast track back home.

One of Romania's unique joys lies in its bulging folk festival calendar. Music plays a vital role in most people's lives and there is an active cultural scene in most towns. Classical music concerts, opera, ballet and cinema feature strongly on the arts agenda, all of them cheap and easily accessible. See the individual sections for details.

SPECTATOR SPORT

Romanians are football (soccer) crazy. Their national team reached the quarter-finals of the 1994 World Cup, and glided through the European qualifiers for the 1998 World Cup, not losing any of its 10 matches. Top club Steaua Bucharest also has a formidable international reputation, first forged when it won the European Champions' Cup in 1986.

At home, the Romanian Football Federation is dogged by allegations that it siphons off 10% of transfer fees paid by foreign clubs. Steaua Bucharest claims the Federation has pocketed US$1 million from its players.

In accordance with a Soviet-style ruling dating from the 1940s, the Steaua sports club is subordinated to the army. Its rugby union squad is Romania's leading rugby side.

Practically every town has a stadium, some better maintained than others. In Bucharest, Steaua plays at the Steaua Stadium (☎ 01-410 0048, 410 3075), Blvd Ghencea 35. Tickets are sold at the stadium gates. Other leading stadiums in the capital include the Dinano Stadium (☎ 01-210 3519), Şoseaua Ştefan cel Mare 18-22, and the Rapid Stadium (☎ 01-220 2855), Calea Giuleşti 18. There is a whopping big stadium in Scorniceşti, built under Ceauşescu as a gift to his home village after bulldozing half the houses there.

Romania's women gymnasts are among the best in the world, but you are unlikely to see them in action within the country.

THINGS TO BUY

Traditional purchases in Romania include plum brandy (ţuică), embroidered blouses, ceramics, wooden sculptures, embroidered tablecloths, handwoven carpets and other handicrafts. The latter are easiest to find at major tourist sights, particularly Bran Castle and Bucovina's monasteries. Romarta stores sell glassware, textiles, women's clothing and ceramics, and Muzică stores sell Romanian records. Pirated rock music cassettes are cheap. If in doubt about a price at stores, offer the vendors a pen and paper and ask them to write it down. Always count your change.

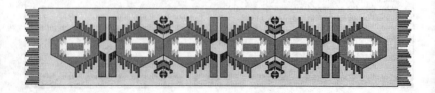

Getting There & Away

Romania, on the main backpackers' route from the west to Turkey via Bulgaria, is easily accessible. Buses, trains and planes galore serve this busy Balkan country making travel to/from here hassle-free.

This chapter includes some information on travel to Moldova, but for additional information see the Moldova chapter.

Remember when travelling that there is a one hour time difference between Romania/Moldova (GMT/UTC plus two) and Hungary/Yugoslavia (GMT/UTC plus one). Arrival/departure times in this chapter are listed in local time.

AIR

There are plenty of scheduled flights to Romania from a dozen or so western countries, and with a single plane change, from a great many more. There are also some charter flights, particularly in summer.

Airports & Airlines

Most flights arrive at Bucharest's Otopeni international airport. There are also flights from the west to Timişoara airport in the Banat and to Mihail Kogălniceanu airport in Constanţa on the Black Sea coast. Some flights from Bucharest to other cities in eastern Europe use Bucharest's Băneasa airport, primarily used by domestic flights.

Aeroflot (Russia), Air France (France), British Airways (UK), Lufthansa (Germany), Malev (Hungary) and THY (Turkey) are among the airlines flying into Romania. Approaching major airlines direct for cheap fares is unlikely to get you any staggering bargains. Dealing directly with Romania's national airline can sometimes prove more lucrative.

National Airline Romania's state-owned carrier TAROM (Transporturile Aeriene Române) has been flying in and out of Bucharest since 1954.

In 1997 TAROM launched its own 'Smart Miles' scheme in conjunction with the international car rental company Avis. Miles credited onto your account for each flight can be cashed in with Avis, and vice versa. The two companies offer 'fly-and-drive' package deals which work out cheaper if you intend hiring a car in Romania. These deals can only be booked through TAROM offices abroad.

TAROM offers youth discounts to people aged under 25. TAROM's offices and sales representatives in other countries include:

France
    38 ave de l'Opéra, F-75002 Paris (☎ 01 47 42 25 42; fax 01 42 56 43 67)
UK
    27 New Cavendish St, London W1M 7RL (☎ 0171-935 3600; fax 0171-487 2913); Terminal 2, Office Block, Heathrow airport (☎ 0181-745 5542; fax 0181-897 4071)
Ukraine
    ulitsa Dimitrievskaja 1, Kiev (☎ 044-274 9961; fax 044-216 2958)
USA
    2724 N. Lehmann Central, Chicago (☎ 312-871 3012; fax 312-404 2888); 342 Madison Ave, suite 213, NY-10173 New York (☎ 212-687 6013/4; fax 212-661 6056)

Other TAROM offices include Vienna, Brussels, Copenhagen, Berlin, Frankfurt/Main, Budapest, Rome, Amsterdam, Warsaw, Moscow, Barcelona, Stockholm and Zürich.

Buying Tickets

TAROM, THY and Malev are among the airlines which offer cheap 'youth' fares to under-26s on some Bucharest flights. Many airlines have 'general sales agents' appointed to sell discounted tickets for certain routes. Also get quotes from student, youth, and general discount ticket agents.

Specialist travel agencies can offer some of the cheapest air tickets to Romania. Also look at the ads in the travel pages of newspapers and 'what's on' magazines.

Romanian embassies, consulates, tourist

offices overseas and émigré organisations may be able to help with information on charter flights or other economical ways of getting to Romania and neighbouring Moldova (look in capital or major-city phone books). Information on travel ticket outlets within Romania and Moldova is given in the relevant sections of this book.

Stand-by & Courier Flights For very cheap flights consider going either stand-by or courier. Airhitch (see Organised Tours) can arrange a one-way, stand-by flight to Europe from the USA but you must be flexible as to time and destination. Costs are US$169 from the East Coast, US$269 from the West Coast, US$209 from the South-East and US$229 from the Midwest. They also have flights from Canada.

Courier flights are another way to fly cheap. Again you have to be flexible. In addition you will only be allowed to bring a limited amount of luggage as you will be transporting a package. For more information call Discount Travel International in New York (☎ 212-362 3636; fax 212-362 3236) for East and West Coast flights. In Canada, contact FB On Board Courier Services (see Travel Agencies).

The magazine *Travel Unlimited* (PO Box 1058, Allston, MA-02134, USA) publishes details of the cheapest air fares and courier possibilities for destinations all over the world to/from the USA, Britain and elsewhere. A single monthly issue costs US$5 and a year's subscription US$25 (US$35 abroad).

Travellers with Special Needs
If you have special needs of any sort – you've broken a leg, you're vegetarian, travelling in a wheelchair, taking the baby, terrified of flying – you should let the airline know as soon as possible so that they can make arrangements. Remind them when you reconfirm your booking (at least 72 hours before departure) and again when you check in at the airport. If you intend flying with TAROM or any of the Moldovan carriers,

check before you book your ticket that they can meet your demands adequately.

Hungary
TAROM has daily flights from Bucharest to Budapest. Flying time is one hour and 20 minutes and a single/return fare (maximum stay one month) is US$255/186. A youth fare (under 25) with no restrictions (valid for one year) is US$108/214.

Malev has twice-daily flights from Bucharest to Budapest. A return (Sunday Rule) is US$150. Malev also offers discounts to under 25s.

Dac Air operates five flights a week between Timişoara and Budapest. A single/return fare is US$95/150. It also has flights to Budapest from Cluj-Napoca for US$125/185.

Turkey
TAROM operates three weekly Bucharest-Istanbul flights which, between 1 May and 14 September, also stop at Constanţa. Departures are on Wednesday, Friday and Sunday and a single/return fare to/from Bucharest/Constanţa is US$190/195.

THY (Turkish Airlines) operates a daily Bucharest-Istanbul flight. A single is US$150 and a return (Weekend Rule) is US$227. Under 25s get marginally discounted fares – US$103/220 for a single/return with the same restrictions.

Ukraine
TAROM and Air Ukraine both have a weekly Bucharest-Kiev flight. Air Ukraine offers the most competitive fares which are US$169/184 for a single/return.

Air Ukraine also has a twice weekly Bucharest-Odessa flight with single/return fares starting at US$60/120. The airline also plans to introduce flights from Bucharest to Cernăuţi (Chernivtsi) in the near future.

Russia & Eastern Europe
TAROM operates four Bucharest-Warsaw flights on Monday, Tuesday, Wednesday and Saturday; twice weekly Bucharest-Sofia flights on Monday and Saturday; twice

weekly Bucharest-Moscow flights on Thursday and Sunday; and three times weekly Bucharest-Prague flights departing on Monday, Thursday and Saturday. It also has a weekly flight from Bucharest to Tashkent.

Dac Air flies from Bucharest to Zagreb on Tuesday and Saturday.

Aeroflot, Air Ukraine, Czech Airlines and LOT (Polish Airlines) all have direct flights from Bucharest to their home countries.

The UK

There are numerous ways of getting to Bucharest from the UK and a continuous price-war rages between the major airlines. They all offer discounted flights. The cheapest options include flying from London's Heathrow or Gatwick to Bucharest with Air France via Paris, Austrian Airlines via Vienna, KLM via Amsterdam, Lufthansa via Frankfurt or Swiss Air via Zürich. A return (Sunday Rule) usually varies between US$260 and US$400. You can also fly from most regional airports in the UK, with just one change of plane, to Bucharest.

British Airways and TAROM both have direct London-Bucharest flights. Single/return fares fluctuate wildly. In mid-1997 a return fare with British Airways was US$379 while TAROM was offering a return fare (maximum stay one month) for US$289. From London you can also fly with Austrian Airlines, via Vienna, to Timişoara in the Banat.

Continental Europe

Bucharest is well linked with all the major European cities. TAROM has regular flights to Amsterdam, Athens, Barcelona, Berlin, Brussels, Copenhagen, Düsseldorf, Frankfurt, Madrid, Milan, Paris, Rome, Stockholm, Thessaloniki, Vienna and Zürich. Return fares including a Saturday night stay start at US$340 or around US$400 for a return ticket with no restrictions.

Malev flies three times weekly from Bucharest, via Budapest, to Münich (US$350 return with Sunday Rule) and Venice (US$280 return with Sunday Rule).

There are also some direct flights from Europe to Timişoara. At the time of writing TAROM had a weekly flight from Timişoara to Rome (single/return US$195/230); one weekly flight to Frankfurt (single/return US$275/350); and a weekly flight to Düsseldorf (single/return US$275/350). Austrian Airlines has a daily flight from Timişoara to Vienna, and Dac Air has three flights to Venice and Munich departing from Timişoara, Cluj-Napoca and Bucharest. A return with Dac Air from Timişoara to Venice/Munich is US$280/350.

In summer there are weekly charter flights with TAROM from Constanţa to Paris. In 1997 a single/return fare including a Saturday night stay in Romania was US$144/289, plus an additional US$8.50/17 supplement in July and August. It also operates flights to Brussels (US$341/330) and Stockholm (US$341/330) out of Constanţa in summer.

The private Italian company Business Jet operates three weekly flights from Arad to Verona (US$240/275) and Rome (US$315/345).

The USA

TAROM has direct flights twice weekly to New York which, at the time of writing, were US$740 for a return. On Friday TAROM operates a Bucharest-Chicago flight via Shannon for US$740 return. A single/return ticket from Shannon costs US$550/630.

Australia & New Zealand

The cheapest flights from Australia to Bucharest are with Qantas to Asia from where you change to a connecting flight with Aeroflot to Moscow, and on to Bucharest. Low/high season fares start at A$1470/1850 return.

More costly flights include via Amsterdam with KLM for A$1650 return in low season or A$2200 in high season; or via Rome with Alitalia for A$1650/2120 return in low/high season.

There are no direct or connecting flights from New Zealand to Bucharest, so you'll need to go via a major European city such as Frankfurt.

Air Travel Glossary

Apex Apex (advance purchase excursion) is a discounted ticket which must be paid for in advance. You must purchase it at least 21 days in advance (sometimes more) and must be away for a minimum period (normally 14 days) and return within a maximum period (90 or 180 days). There are penalties if you wish to change it.

Baggage Allowance This will be written on your ticket: usually one 20kg item to go in the hold, plus one item of hand luggage.

Bucket Shop An unbonded travel agency specialising in discounted airline tickets. Availability varies widely, so you'll not only have to be flexible in your travel plans, you'll also have to be quick off the mark as soon as an advertisement appears in the press.

Bumped Just because you have a confirmed seat doesn't mean you're going to get on the plane – see Overbooking.

Cancellation Penalties If you have to cancel or change an Apex ticket there are often heavy penalties involved; insurance can sometimes be taken out against these penalties. Some airlines impose penalties on regular tickets as well, particularly against 'no show' passengers.

Check In Airlines ask you to check in a certain time ahead of the flight departure (usually 1½ hours on international flights). If you fail to check in on time and the flight is overbooked, the airline can cancel your booking and give your seat to somebody else.

Confirmation Having a ticket written out with the flight and date you want doesn't mean you have a seat until the agent has checked with the airline that your status is 'OK' or confirmed. Meanwhile you could just be 'on request'.

Discounted Tickets There are two types of discounted fares – officially discounted (see Promotional Fares) and unofficially discounted. The lowest prices often impose drawbacks like flying with unpopular airlines, inconvenient schedules, or unpleasant routes and connections. A discounted ticket can save you other things than money – you may be able to pay Apex prices without the associated Apex advance booking and other requirements. Discounted tickets only exist where there is fierce competition.

Economy Class Tickets Economy class tickets are usually not the cheapest way to go, though they do give you maximum flexibility and are valid for 12 months. If you don't use them, most are fully refundable, as are unused sectors of a multiple ticket.

Full Fares Airlines traditionally offer first class (coded F), business class (coded J) and economy class (coded Y) tickets. These days there are so many promotional and discounted fares available from the regular economy class that few passengers pay full economy fare.

Lost Tickets If you lose your airline ticket an airline will usually treat it like a travellers' cheque and, after inquiries, issue you with another one. Legally, however, an airline is entitled to treat it like cash and if you lose it then it's gone forever. Take good care of your tickets.

No Shows No shows are passengers who fail to show up for their flight, sometimes due to unexpected delays or disasters, sometimes due to simply forgetting, sometimes because they made more than one booking and didn't bother to cancel the one they didn't want. Full-fare passengers who fail to turn up are sometimes entitled to travel on a later flight. The rest of us are penalised (see Cancellation Penalties).

On Request An unconfirmed booking for a flight, see Confirmation.

Other Destinations

TAROM has direct flights year-round from Bucharest to Beirut (twice weekly), Cairo (twice weekly), Delhi (twice weekly), Dubai (once weekly), Kuwait (once weekly), Larnaca (three a week), Tel Aviv (once weekly). It also serves a host of other destinations, often just including one stop en route.

LAND

Bus

With an unbeatable train service linking Romania to western Europe and Russia, there is little reason to travel to/from Romania by bus which, in short, is hellish. Romania's public bus system is practically nonexistent while fares offered by the numerous private bus companies operating buses to the west rarely compete with the inexpensive comfort offered by trains.

The exception to this rule is Istanbul. The bus (12 to 14 hours) is substantially cheaper and faster than the train (17¼ hours).

Western Europe Numerous private bus companies operate daily buses between western Europe and Romania. Buses depart

Open-jaws A return ticket where you fly out to one place but return from another. If available this can save you backtracking to your arrival point.

Overbooking Airlines hate to fly empty seats and since every flight has some passengers who fail to show up (see No Shows) airlines often book more passengers than they have seats for. Usually the excess passengers balance those who fail to show up but occasionally somebody gets bumped. And guess who it is most likely to be? The passengers who check in late.

Promotional Fares Officially discounted fares like Apex fares which are available from travel agents or direct from the airline.

Reconfirmation At least 72 hours prior to departure time of an onward or return flight you must contact the airline and 'reconfirm' that you intend to be on the flight. If you don't do this the airline can delete your name from the passenger list and you could lose your seat. You don't have to reconfirm the first flight on your itinerary or if your stopover is less than 72 hours. It doesn't hurt to reconfirm more than once.

Restrictions Discounted tickets often come complete with various restrictions – advance purchase is the most usual one (see Apex). Others include restrictions on the minimum and maximum period you must stay away – such as a minimum of two weeks or a maximum of one year. See Cancellation Penalties.

Stand-by A discounted ticket where you only fly if there is a seat free at the last moment. Stand-by fares are usually only available on domestic routes. To give yourself the best possible chance of getting on the flight you want, get there early and have your name placed on the waiting list. It's first come, first served.

Sunday or Weekend Rule Applies to some return tickets – you must spend one Sunday or weekend in your destination before returning.

Tickets Out An entry requirement for many countries is that you have an onward or return ticket, in other words, a ticket out of the country. If you're not sure what you intend to do next, the easiest solution is to buy the cheapest onward ticket to a neighbouring country or a ticket from a reliable airline which can later be refunded if you do not use it.

Transferred Tickets Airline tickets cannot be transferred from one person to another. Travellers sometimes try to sell the return half of their ticket, but officials can ask you to prove that you are the person named on the ticket. This is unlikely to happen on domestic flights, but on an international flight tickets may be compared with passports.

Travel Agencies Travel agencies vary widely and you should ensure you use one that suits your needs. Some simply handle tours while full-service agencies handle everything from tours and tickets to car rental and hotel bookings. A good one will do all these things and can save you a lot of money, but if all you want is a ticket at the lowest possible price, then you really need an agency specialising in discounted tickets. A discounted ticket agency, however, may not be useful for other things like hotel bookings.

Travel Periods Some officially discounted fares, Apex fares in particular, vary with the time of year. There is often a low (off-peak) season and a high (peak) season. Sometimes there's an intermediate or shoulder season as well. At peak times, when everyone wants to fly, not only will the officially discounted fares be higher but so will unofficially discounted fares or there may simply be no discounted tickets available. Usually the fare depends on your outward flight – if you depart in the high season and return in the low season, you pay the high-season fare. ■

from most cities in Romania. Tickets can be bought from ticketing agencies in Romania's larger cities. Buses go to Germany (usually Frankfurt) from where there are frequent connections to all the European capitals. You can buy a straight-through ticket to your final destination from Romania. If you are under 26 it is worth checking whether the bus company offers reduced youth fares. Many offer 10% discount on tickets from Germany onwards, in which case it is cheaper to buy a ticket from Romania only as far as Germany where you can then pick up a discounted fare.

Inter-Touring Rumänien (☎ 069-252 884, 069-252 822; fax 069-252 983), Baseler Platz 3, D-60329 Frankfurt/Main, is the leading bus company, a branch of Eurolines. In Romania, look for travel agencies with 'Touring' signs in their windows.

Other bus companies operating services between Romania and Europe include Amad Transport International (☎ 069-884 549; fax 069-882 708), Frankfurter Strasse 76-78, D-63067 Offenbach/Main; Betaco (☎ 069-234 611; fax 069-234 697), Baseler Platz 5, D-60329 Frankfurt; Erna Mayer Reisebüro (☎ 0821-486 24 21; fax 0821-486 24 33),

Westheimer Strasse 1, D-86356 Westheim; and König Reisen (☎ 091-031 873; fax 091-005 516), Hindenburg Strasse 80, D-90556 Cadolzburg.

Ticketing agencies in Romania are listed in the relevant chapters in this book. Sample single/return fares include Bucharest-Hamburg US$97/175; Timişoara-Munich US$65/120; Bucharest-Munich US$59/107; Sibiu-Berlin US$114/200; Ploieşti-Cologne US$126/229. Fares increase every three months.

Hungary To/from Hungary the cheapest option is the Hungarian Volanbus. These leave daily from Budapest's Népstadion bus station. For example, Budapest-Oradea is US$8 (246km).

Other cities in Romania which are served by cheaper public buses to Hungary include Arad, Braşov, Cluj-Napoca, Deva, Gheorgheni, Miercurea Ciuc, Satu Mare, Târgu Mureş and Timişoara. A single fare is no more than US$10.

Private bus companies operate buses to Hungary from many other cities. Ticketing agencies and schedules are listed in the relevant chapters in this book. A single Bucharest-Budapest fare (873km, 18 hours) with these companies is around US$18.

Yugoslavia Cheap private buses aimed more at local traders rather than foreign tourists operate daily from Drobeta-Turnu Severin to Negotin and Pojarevat in Yugoslavia. A single fare is US$7. See the Drobeta-Turnu Severin section in this book for details.

Bulgaria Most private bus companies operate buses to Sofia. Various Bucharest travel agencies have single trips to Sofia (512km, 8-14 hours) for around US$11. Compare prices at a couple (or haggle!) and remember to take plenty of food. See individual chapters for details.

Turkey There are daily buses galore between Romania and Istanbul (804km, 14 to 18 hours). Be prepared for a gruelling trip however. Music blasts away and winter heating may be seen as optional. Half the journey is spent waiting at borders or at meal stops.

The leading bus companies – Toros Trans, Ortadoğu Tur, Özlem Tur and Öz Murat – have offices in Bucharest as well as in most of the other Romanian cities. From Bucharest, they all operate between four and eight buses daily to Istanbul. A single/return fare is US$28.50/57. Buses are less frequent from other cities however (see relevant chapters for details). In Istanbul you can buy tickets from the following offices: Toros Trans (☎ 0212-513 5315, 0212-520 1446; fax 0212-547 1739) at Büyük Reşit Paşa Cad. 51/1, Laleli; Ortadoğu Tur (☎ 0212-512 7746, 0212-512 9423; fax 0901-511 7528) at Büyük Reşit Paşa Cad. 50, Laleli; Özlem Tur (☎ 0212-632 6974; fax 0212-658 0522) at Aksaray, Balkan Pazari, Büyük Istanbul Otogari 154.

Moldova & Ukraine There is an overnight bus from Bucharest via Ploieşti to Chişinău (Kishinev), departing from Gara de Nord daily at 6 pm. Journey time (591km) is 15 to 18 hours and a single ticket costs US$10. A weekly bus departs from Bucharest's Gara de Nord to Cernăuţi (Chernivtsi) on Wednesday at 4 pm. A single fare is US$20.

From Moldavia, there are daily Suceava-Cernăuţi and Rădăuţi-Cernăuţi buses. To the republic of Moldova, a daily bus also heads east from Suceava to Chişinău. Four daily buses run between Iaşi and Chişinău.

Train

Travelling by train is one of the most interesting ways of reaching Romania. This applies even more so to Moldova where train travel is the most economical means of getting there. Most travellers fly or train it to Bucharest from where you can take an overnight sleeper to Chişinău in Moldova.

If you plan to do a lot of train travel around Europe, the *Thomas Cook European Time-*

table, updated monthly, gives full intercity timetable listings and indicates where reservations are necessary or supplements payable. It covers as far east as Moscow and is available from Thomas Cook outlets around the world.

Equally handy is *On the Rails around Eastern Europe*, also published by Thomas Cook in 1996. It outlines 30 favoured rail routes intended to show you the best of eastern Europe, and is illustrated with colour city, regional and route maps.

Rail Passes & Youth Tickets There are no rail passes or discounted youth fares available for Moldova.

Romania is included in the Inter-Rail pass scheme, available to anyone under 26 on the first day of travel. The pass provides unlimited 2nd class rail travel for one month. You can also buy zonal inter-rail passes which are only valid in countries within a specified zone. These passes are valid for 15 days or one month and work out cheaper if you intend inter-railing the whole way around Europe. One zonal pass covers Romania, Bulgaria, Hungary, Slovakia, Czech Republic and Yugoslavia. Unfortunately Turkey is included in a separate zone along with Greece, Slovenia and Italy. More expensive two-zone passes are available too. Inter-Rail passes for over-26s are also available; they're more expensive.

Another option if you intend to travel only in Romania is the EuroDomino Freedom pass which entitles you to three, five or 10 days unlimited train travel in a one month period. These passes *must* be bought prior to your departure; they are not available in Romania. In mid-1997 a 1st/2nd class pass for three days travel was US$92/60. For under 26s it costs US$45 (2nd class only). A five day pass costs US$123/76 and for under 26s, US$60. The 10 day pass is US$217/139 and for youths, US$107. Bear in mind however that train travel in Romania is cheap – buying train tickets in-country is more economical than a pass.

Romania is also included in the regional Balkan Flexipass scheme – available to all ages – which offers unlimited travel for five, 10 or 15 days in a one month period around Romania, Bulgaria, Turkey, Greece and Yugoslavia. You can also choose between a 1st or 2nd class pass. These passes can only be bought upon arrival in any of the specified countries. In Bucharest you can purchase a Balkan Flexipass pass at the main train station, Gara de Nord. In mid-1997 a 1st/2nd class five day pass cost US$152/112, a 10 day pass was US$265/197 and a pass valid for 15 days in a one month period was US$296/236.

Romania is included in the Wasteels/BIJ (Billets Internationales de Jeunesse) ticket network too. Student and youth travel offices abroad, and some travel agencies, sell tickets and can give you more information. In Bucharest you can buy train passes and onward discounted tickets at the Wasteels office at Gara de Nord.

Ticket Reservations International train tickets are rarely sold at train stations, but rather at CFR (Romanian State Railways) offices in town – look for the Agenție de Voiaj CFR signs. Tickets have to be bought at least two hours prior to departure. Since the Bucharest offices are crowded, try picking up an open international train ticket to get you out of the country at a provincial CFR office. Many of them are listed in this chapter.

If you're travelling on an Inter-Rail pass, seat reservations (US$2 to $4) are mandatory on all express trains within Romania. Even if you're not travelling with a rail pass, most international trains require seat reservations. When you buy your ticket in Romania, a seat reservation is automatically included in the fare. If you already have a ticket, you may be able to make reservations at the station an hour before departure, though it's preferable to do so at a CFR office at least one day in advance.

Western Europe From Berlin the *Alutus* trundles south-east though Prague and Budapest to Bucharest (1866km, 27¼ hours). It departs daily from Berlin-Lichtenberg at

7.45 pm, arriving in Prague at 12.49 am, in Bratislava at 6.29 am and in Budapest at 9.47 am. It pulls out of Budapest-Keleti at 10.15 am and arrives in Bucharest at 11.58 pm. The return train departs daily from Bucharest at 6 am, arriving in Budapest at 2.02 pm and in Berlin at 9.30 am. In both directions, this train stops at Arad in Banat; at Deva, Alba Iulia, Mediaş, Sighişoara, Braşov, Predeal and Sinaia in Transylvania; at Ploieşti in Wallachia; and at Buzău, Brăila and Galaţi in Moldavia. Sleepers are available on this train.

From Munich there is the daily *Pannonia Expres* train via Budapest to Bucharest, which from Budapest follows the same route as the *Alutus* to the Romanian capital. The overnight *Pannonia Expres* departs from Munich at 11.19 pm and arrives at Budapest-Keleti (714km) at 7.28 am the following morning. It departs from Budapest at 8.15 am and gets to Bucharest at 10.12 pm.

To get to/from Romania to/from elsewhere in western Europe, you have to change trains at Budapest. From Budapest there are numerous trains to western Europe. Major daily services include the *Orient Express* to Paris via Vienna and Munich; the *Prinz Eugen* and *Joseph Haydn* to Hamburg via Bonn, Cologne and Düsseldorf; the *Hungaria* to Berlin and the *Comenius* to Hamburg both via Bratislava and Prague; the *Bela Bartok* to Frankfurt via Vienna; and a daily Budapest-Zürich train via Vienna and Salzburg.

Hungary The Budapest-Bucharest train journey (873km) is around 12 hours. To/from Arad in Romania's Banat, it is a mere 28km to the Hungarian border town of Lököshaza, from where it is a further 225km (4½ hours) to Budapest. It is not cheap to travel between the two countries. In mid-1997 a 1st/2nd class Bucharest-Budapest single fare was US$31/48 on an express international train. A single Arad/Oradea-Budapest fare was US$16-19.

The cheapest way is to cross Romania or Hungary on a local train to the nearest border town, then get another local train over the

border. Two daily local Hungarian trains shuttle between Oradea and Budapest-Nyugati (249km, five hours). Reservations aren't required, but in Romania try to buy an open Oradea-Budapest ticket at a CFR office well ahead. If this is impossible, board the train at Episcopia Bihor, following the instructions given in the Oradea section of the Banat & Crişana chapter.

Local trains also depart from Békéscsaba, Hungary, for Oradea (90km) and Arad (68km) three times daily.

International daily trains between Bucharest and Budapest include the *Dacia Expres*; the *Pannonia Expres* which continues to Munich; the Berlin-bound *Alutus*; and the *Ister* and *Traianus*. In addition, there is the daily *Muntenia* between Galaţi and Budapest.

There are also direct Budapest trains from Baia Mare and Satu Mare in Maramureş; Cluj-Napoca in northern Transylvania; Timişoara and Arad in the Banat; and Constanţa on the Black Sea Coast. The *Bega* that passes through Timişoara and Arad has one through-carriage to Venice, Italy. The daily *Ovidius* from Constanţa stops at Bucharest and then takes a southern route via Craiova, Drobeta-Turnu Severin and Băile Herculane. See the individual chapters for details of train time departures for all these trains.

Yugoslavia The *Bucureşti* and *Banat* express trains run daily between Belgrade-Dunav and Bucharest (693km, 12 to 13 hours) via Timişoara, Băile Herculane, Drobeta-Turnu Severin and Craiova. If you can't get a ticket or reservation for this train, you can get an unreserved early morning train from Timişoara-Nord to Jimbolia (39km), where you change to another local train to Kikinda, Yugoslavia.

The *Banat* departs from Bucharest daily at 10.55 am, arriving in Belgrade at 10.18 pm. On its return journey, it leaves Belgrade at 7 am and gets to Bucharest at 8.10 am. The daily *Bucureşti* leaves Bucharest at 9.05 pm and arrives in Belgrade at 9.23 am. Eastbound, it departs at 8 pm, arriving in

Bucharest the following morning at 9.50 am. In mid-1997 the 1st/2nd class single fare was US$23/16. Sleepers are not available on these trains in either direction.

Bulgaria & Turkey The train service between Romania and Bulgaria is slow and crowded – but cheap. Between Sofia and Bucharest (509km) there are three trains, the *Bulgaria Expres* from Moscow and two nameless trains, all of which stop in Ruse. A Bucharest-Ruse single ticket (2nd class) is US$4.

The *Bulgaria Expres* departs daily from Bucharest at 7.35 pm and arrives in Sofia at 5.55 am. On its return journey the train departs Sofia at 9.25 pm and gets into Bucharest at 7.56 am. It then continues north via Bacău and Suceava to Siret, Romania, where the train crosses the border into Ukraine (see the following Moldova, Ukraine & Beyond section). There are sleepers on both overnight trains – buy your ticket well in advance to guarantee yourself a bunk for the night.

Two more trains depart daily from Bucharest. A speedy train departs at 7.50 am and arrives in Sofia at 4.50 pm, while a slower overnight train leaves Bucharest at 7.35 pm, pulling into Sofia at 7.45 am. Between 1 June and 27 September this second train continues to Greece, arriving in Thessaloniki (335km) at 6.07 pm. This train then connects with a train to Athens departing from Thessaloniki at 6.27 pm and arriving in Athens (510km) at 1.46 am. In mid-1997 a single 1st/2nd Bucharest-Sofia fare cost US$23/33 plus a supplement for a bunk.

The overnight train journey from Bucharest to Istanbul (803km) on the daily *Bucureşti-Istanbul Expres* takes around 17¼ hours. It does not go via Sofia but rather via eastern Bulgaria. A single 2nd class fare is US$38. The train leaves from Bucharest at 12.55 pm and arrives in Istanbul at 6.15 am the following morning. Sleepers are available.

Moldova, Ukraine & Beyond From Bucharest there is one overnight train to Chişinău in the republic of Moldova. This Soviet-made train is the most economical method of getting to Moldova. The *Prietenia* departs daily from Bucharest at 7 pm and arrives in Chişinău (591km) at 8.38 am. There are only 2nd class carriages (some sleepers) on this train, with a single fare costing US$10.

The train stops at the Romanian-Moldovan border at Ungheni at 6.10 am for a two-hour bogie change. Waking up is no problem. The train lurches, vibrates and clanks while the under-carriages are changed to fit the broader gauge tracks of the former Soviet Union. Every carriage is lifted 2m off the ground by a crane so rail workers can change each bogie by hand. Passengers are forbidden to get off the train during this bizarre operation.

On Tuesday and Sunday a second train, the *Romania Expres*, leaves from Bucharest to Chişinău. This train then continues southeast to Tighina (Bendery) and Tiraspol, then veers north to Kiev and Moscow. The *Romania Expres* leaves Bucharest at 11.59 pm, arriving in Chişinău at 1 pm (13 hours), Tighina at 2.57 pm, Tiraspol at 3.31 pm, Kiev at 4.20 am, and Moscow at 8.06 pm. The total journey time from Bucharest to Kiev (1546km) is 28 hours, and to Moscow (2418km) 42 hours. A 1st/2nd class single fare from Bucharest to Kiev is US$72/44; and to Moscow US$121/93. This train returns from Moscow to Bucharest on Tuesday and Friday, passing through Chişinău on Wednesday and Saturday evening at 9.33 pm.

In summer there are also trains to Chişinău from Braşov and Constanţa. The *Basarabia* departs from Braşov on Wednesday, Friday and Sunday at 7.42 pm and arrives in Chişinău (561km) the following morning at 10.56 am. The Chişinău-Braşov train heads west on Tuesday, Thursday and Saturday. From Constanţa the *Basarabia* departs on Tuesday, Thursday and Saturday at 9.10 pm (59km, 13½ hours). The return Chişinău-Constanţa train departs Monday, Wednesday and Friday.

From Romania to Ukraine there is the twice weekly Bucharest-Moscow *Romania Expres* which goes to Kiev. A second train, the Sofia-Moscow *Bulgaria Expres*, which takes a different route through western Ukraine to Cernăuţi (Chernivtsi). It departs from Bucharest at 8.13 am, Cernăuţi at 9.18 pm, then continues to Kiev where it departs at 3.07 pm and arrives in Moscow at 6.22 am. Total Bucharest-Moscow journey time is 46 hours. At Cernăuţi some carriages of this train are unhitched to take an alternative route along the eastern realm of eastern Europe. It goes via Lviv (Lvov), Baranovici and Lida (Belarus), Vilnius (Lithuania) and Daugavpils (Latvia) to St Petersburg. The Bucharest-St Petersburg journey takes 55 hours (2608km).

Poland The aptly-named Bucharest-Warsaw *Carpaţi* crosses the Carpathians twice; first in Romania between Bucharest (8.10 pm) and Arad (5.51 am). The train then continues through eastern Hungary to Kosice, Slovakia (12.32 pm), where it crosses the Carpathians (Tatra mountains) into Kraków (6.16 pm). It arrives in Warsaw (1645km) 26 hours later at 9.11 pm.

Car & Motorcycle

Having your own vehicle has massive advantages in Romania and Moldova, countries where some treasures are impossible to access by public transport. Renting a car is costly and it can be cheaper to take your own vehicle. Car owners who love their vehicles more than their spouse should leave their wheels at home (unless they're of the four-wheel drive variety). Roads here are among the most pot-holed in eastern Europe.

If you do drive your vehicle to Romania, make sure it is in good condition before you leave. Always carry a petrol can, supplies of engine oil and some basic spares. A shovel is handy in snowy weather. A fire extinguisher, first-aid kit and warning triangle are also advisable. Motoring clubs like Britain's AA and RAC are worth checking with for information on regulations, border crossings, and so on – as are the Romanian and Moldovan embassies. For information and tips on driving once you're in Romania and Moldova, see the Getting Around chapter.

Documents Drivers and motorcyclists will need the vehicle's registration papers, liability insurance and a driving licence. Contact your local automobile association for details about all documentation, or alternatively contact the national motoring association in Romania, the Automobil Clubul Român (ACR; ☎ 01-659 3910; fax 01-312 8462), Str Take Ionescu, Bucharest, RO-71054.

In Romania liability insurance for drivers is compulsory, but payouts are low, while in Moldova it is not needed at all. So, either way, you really need comprehensive insurance in case of damage done by another driver.

At the time of writing, the Green Card – a routine extension of domestic motor insurance to cover most European countries – is valid in Romania, but *not* in the republic of Moldova, so you must organise insurance separately. If you have difficulty doing so through your regular insurer, try Black Sea & Baltic General Insurance (☎ 0171-709 9202) of 65 Fenchurch St, London EC3M 4EY. Insurance policies with limited compensation rates can be bought at the Romanian borders.

Border Crossings When crossing the Romanian border by car, expect long queues at checkpoints, especially on weekends. With varying success, some foreigners drive right past the long lines of Romanian vehicles waiting to cross and jump to the head of the queue. Avoid the temptation to bribe the Romanian officials (it no longer works) and beware of unauthorised persons charging dubious 'ecology', 'disinfectant', 'road' or 'bridge' taxes at the border. Ask for a receipt if you are unsure.

Leaving Romania for Bulgaria by car is no longer as time-consuming as it used to be. 'Bad days' with long, slow-moving lines of vehicles at all checkpoints can occasionally still happen however.

The Romanian highway border crossings open to all nationalities are listed here in an anticlockwise direction around Romania. All are open 24 hours a day, except those to/from Ukraine and Moldova, which are open from

8 am to 8 pm. Telephone numbers listed in brackets are for customs authorities on the Romanian side of the border.

Hungary There are border crossings at Petea (☎ 061-730 395) 11km north-west of Satu Mare; at Borş (☎ 059-133 324) 14km north-west of Oradea; at Vărşand (☎ 057-520 669) 66km north of Arad; and at Nădlac, between Szeged and Arad. The borders at Petea, Borş and Nădlac are generally the busiest as they connect with major highways to Budapest.

Yugoslavia You may cross at Jimbolia (☎ 056-250 690) 45km west of Timişoara; at Moraviţa (☎ 056-270 931) between Timişoara and Belgrade; at Naidăş (☎ 055-540 558) 120km east of Belgrade; and at Porţile de Fier (Iron Gate; ☎ 052-211 154, 217 001) 10km west of Drobeta-Turnu Severin.

Bulgaria You can cross at Calafat (☎ 051-231 361) opposite Vidin, Bulgaria; at Giurgiu (☎ 046-222 501) opposite Ruse; at the Ostrov-Silistra crossing (☎ 041-121 397) opposite Călăraşi in Romania; at Negru Vodă (☎ 041-665 227) 37km north-east of Tolbuhin; and at Vama Veche (☎ 041-751 331) 10km south of Mangalia.

Giurgiu is the main border crossing with a 4km-long bridge across the Danube. Queues can be tiresome during peak periods. The toll for the bridge is US$10/3 for a car/motorcycle. A cheaper option is Giurgiu's small ferry, not suitable for lorries and other large vehicles, that ploughs its way across the Danube every half hour or so. The crossing takes 10 minutes and a single ticket is US$6 plus a US$3.50 ecological tax levied by the Bulgarian authorities. There is also a second, larger ferry that crosses the Danube every two hours but this is aimed at heavy-cargo vehicles. A single ticket for a car is US$17 plus the additional ecological tax. It takes 20 minutes to cross.

The border crossing at Calafat also involves a ferry trip. A car-ferry crosses the Danube hourly. The journey takes 30 minutes and it costs US$3.50 to take a car on board. Bicycles cost US$2. Queues on the Romanian side are generally quite bad.

The Ostrov border is on the southern bank of the Danube, practically adjoining the Bulgarian border town of Silistra. To get to Ostrov, you have to cross the Danube by ferry at Călăraşi. A small car-ferry (which would not meet safety regulations in the west) trundles across the water in 10 minutes. A single ticket for a car and four passengers is US$1.20. This border crossing is popular with truckers who say the custom controls are less rigid here.

Moldova From Romania you can cross the border into Moldova at Albiţa (☎ 035-472 859) 65km south-east of Iaşi; at Sculeni (☎ 032-113 112) 24km north of Ungheni and closer in fact to Iaşi; at Sânca Costeşti (☎ 031-512 720) 60km east of Botoşani; or at Oancea (☎ 036-040 826) some 50km north of Galaţi.

All three borders are slow to cross, not so much because of the volume of traffic but simply because of Soviet-style custom officials on the Moldovan side who insist on searching every nook and cranny of each vehicle that passes through. In between searches, they play football regardless of whether cars are waiting in line or not. Most commercial traffic uses the Albiţa crossing. Public buses between Romania and Moldova pass through the Sculeni border. Sânca Costeşti and Oancea are very small borders where foreigners might get hassled by bureaucratic border guards.

For more information, see Getting There & Away in the Moldova chapter.

Ukraine From Romania, there is one border crossing into Ukraine at Siret (☎ 056-250 690) 45km north of Suceava on the main road to Cernăuţi (Chernivtsi). Expect to queue.

From Moldova, there are several border crossings into Ukraine. The Pervomaisc border, 30km south-east of Tiraspol in Transdniestr, is the main Chişinău-Odessa crossing. Volume of traffic coupled with newly established Transdniestr border guards make crossing here a nightmare. Expect to wait at least three or four hours. Odessa is just 183km from Chişinău.

The border 20km north-east of Dubăsari on the main road to Kiev attracts less traffic since the direct M21 route from Chişinău was shut (see the Getting Around section of the Moldova chapter).

The border crossing 11km north of Soroca is closed to foreigners. Cross the border at Otaci, 50km north-west of Soroca. Neither of these borders involve passing through Transdniestr.

Walking

You can walk in or out of Romania at most of its border crossings *except* those with Moldova and Ukraine. Hitch a ride instead. Pedestrians are also not allowed to use the so-called 'Friendship Bridge' to/from Ruse, Bulgaria, but you can go by taxi (US$29). Take the ferry instead.

Bicycle

If you intend cycling around Romania, contact the British Cyclists' Touring Club (☎ 01483-417 217; fax 01483-426 994; email cycling@ctc.org.uk; www .ctc.org.uk), Cotterell House, 69 Meadrow, Godalming, Surrey GU7 3HS. The club offers members guided cycling tours to destinations which change each year. If there's no tour to Romania planned, the club can provide you with detailed travel notes based on previous cycling trips. Annual membership costing US$35 includes free travel insurance.

SEA & RIVER
Turkey

Between May and September a ferry runs twice weekly between Constanţa and Istanbul. Sailing time is 20 hours and the single/return deck fare is US$40/55. This is an amazing bargain if you don't mind skipping Bulgaria. There are no ferries to Turkey in winter.

See the Northern Dobruja chapter for full details.

Bulgaria

There are passenger and car ferries year-round into Bulgaria from Calafat and Giurgiu in Romania. See the Border Crossings section earlier.

To get from Ostrov, Romania, to Silistra in Bulgaria, you have to make a 20 minute ferry crossing from Călăraşi. See the relevant chapter for details.

ORGANISED TOURS

Many travel agencies abroad arrange plane tickets, package deals and specialist tours to Romania.

Australia
> *Eastern Europe Travel Bureau*, 75 King St, Sydney, NSW 2000 (☎ 02-9262 1144; fax 02-9262 4479); 343 Little Collins St, Melbourne 3000 (☎ 03-9600 0299; fax 03-9670 1793) – eastern Europe and Russia specialists; offices in other state capitals too
> *Gateway Travel*, 48 The Boulevarde, Strathfield, NSW 2135 (☎ 02-9745 3333, fax 02-9745 3237; email gatrav@magna.com.au; www.magna .com.au/gatrav) – ex-USSR specialists

France
> *Club Aventure*, 18 rue Séguier, F-75006 Paris (☎ 01 44 32 09 30; fax 01 44 32 09 59; email infos@club-aventure.com; www.club-aven ture.com) – alternative tours of Romania
> *Nouvelles Frontières*, 87 blvd de Grenelle, F-75738 Paris (☎ 01 43 22 98 28; fax 01 43 22 98 28; www.nouvelles-frontieres.com) – large travel agency with offices in London and Bucharest
> *Romania Tours*, 36 ave de l'Opéra, F-75002 Paris (☎ 01 42 47 66 95; fax 01 47 42 50 51) – city breaks and tours to Romania
> *Transtours*, 49 ave de l'Opéra, F-75065 Paris (☎ 01 44 58 26 00) – specialists in the Balkans, Russia and the former Soviet republics
> *Wasteels*, 5 rue de la Banque, F-75002 Paris (☎ 01 42 61 53 21, 01 43 62 30 00; email wasteels @voyages-wasteels.fr; www.voyages-wasteels.fr) – cheap tickets for students and people under 26

UK
> *Exodus*, 9 Weir Rd, London SW12 0LT (☎ 0181-675 5550; fax 0181-673 0779) – discovery and walking holidays, biking adventures and overland expeditions
> *Explore Worldwide*, 1 Frederick St, Aldershot, Hampshire GU11 1LQ (☎ 01252-319 448; fax 01252-343 170) – cultural and adventure holidays in Romania

Footprint Adventures, 5 Malham Drive, Lincoln LN6 0XD (☎ 01522-690 852; fax 01522-501 392; email sales@footventure.co.uk; www.foot venture.co.uk/res.html) – trekking, wildlife and adventure tours for the independent traveller

High Places, Globe Works, Penistone Rd, Sheffield S6 3AE (☎ 0114-275 7500; fax 0114-275 3870; email highpl@globalnet.co.uk) – hiking holidays in Romania

Naturetrek, Chautura, Bighton, Nr Alresford, Hampshire SO24 9RB (☎ 01962-733 051; fax 01962-733 368; email sales@naturetrek.co.uk; www.naturetrek.co.uk) – birdwatching and botanical holidays

Ramblers Holidays, PO Box 43, Welwyn Garden City, Herts AL8 6PQ (☎ 01707-331 133; fax 01707-333 276; email ramhols@dial.pipex.com) – rambling holidays in Transylvania and Moldavia

Romania Travel Centre, Clayfield Mews, Newcomen Rd, Tumbridge Wells, Kent TN4 9PA (☎ 01892-516 901; fax 01892-511 579; email james@romtrav.demon.co.uk; www.londonweb .co.uk/romania/index.html) – UK's major discount centre for flights to Romania; arranges car hire and accommodation in Romania

Sherpa Expeditions, 131a Heston Rd, Hounslow, Middlesex TW5 0RD (☎ 0181-577 2717; fax 0181-572 9788; email sherpa.sales@dial .pipex.com; www.sherpa-walking-holidays .co.uk) – specialists in walking and trekking holidays

Trade Wings, Morley House, 1st floor, suite 31-36, 320 Regent St, London W1R 5AG (☎ 0171-436 515; fax 0171-636 1705) – cheap eastern Europe 'circle' trips taking in a couple of capital cities

Waymark Holidays, 44 Windsor Rd, Slough SL1 2EJ (☎ 01753-516 477; fax 01753-517 016) – walking holidays in Transylvania

USA

Abaco Travel, 14 East 38th St, 10th floor, New York City, NY-10016 (☎ 212-481 1212, 481 1226) – Romania specialists selling plane tickets

Airhitch, 214 Broadway, 3rd floor, New York, NY-10025 (☎ 800-326 2009, 212-864 2000; email airhitch@netcom.com); 110 Sepulveda, Blvd EI Segundo, Los Angeles, CA-90245 (☎ 800-397 1098, 310-726 5000) – specialists in cheap single airfares, often on stand-by to Europe; can also arrange flights from Canada

Council Travel – student/youth/discount travel agency with offices in many cities including NewYork (☎ 212-661 1450) and Los Angeles (☎ 310-208 3551)

Hungarian Travel Agency 18349 Sherman Way, Reseda, CA-91335 (☎ 800-624 9277, 818-996 3510; fax 818-996 5306) – arranges trips and packages from Budapest to Bucharest

STA Travel, 3730 Walnut St, Philadelphia, PA-19104 (☎ 800-777 0112, 215-382 2928; fax 215-382 4716) – student/youth/discount travel agency with offices all over the USA

Quest Tours, 1 World Trade Center, 121 SW Salmon St, Suite 1100, Portland, OR-97204 (☎ 800-621 8687; fax 503-777 0224; email tour@romtour.com; www.teleport.com/tour) – arranges 'Dracula' theme tours, trips to the monasteries and accommodation in spa resorts

LEAVING THE REGION

There is no departure tax when leaving Romania or Moldova. Leaving Romania you have to show your 'exit card' (*talon de iesire*), that wee piece of paper placed in your passport upon entering Romania. If not you risk having to buy a new 30 day visa as a punishment. Also be sure to get an exit stamp in your passport.

WARNING

The information in this chapter is particularly vulnerable to change: prices for international travel are volatile, routes are introduced and cancelled, schedules change, special deals come and go, and rules and visa requirements are amended. Airlines and governments seem to take a perverse pleasure in making price structures and regulations as complicated as possible. In addition, the travel industry is highly competitive and there are many lurks and perks. The details given in this chapter should be regarded as pointers and are not a substitute for your own careful, up-to-date research.

Getting Around

Getting around Romania is painless, Moldova less so (for additional information, see the Moldova chapter).

In both countries, travelling is traditionally viewed as a joyous yet hazardous occupation, be it by horse-drawn cart, ferry or on foot. Romanians frequently bless themselves with a holy Sign of the Cross as a bus or train pulls out of the station. Romanians are also the first to wish foreign travellers a cheery *Drum Bun!* (Good Road!).

AIR

Domestic flights are completely reliable and stable. From Bucharest they all depart from Băneasa airport (there are buses between Băneasa and Otopeni airports). The state-owned carrier TAROM has an extensive network of domestic flights. From Bucharest there are at least four flights weekly to Arad, Bacău, Baia Mare, Cluj-Napoca, Constanţa, Iaşi via Suceava, Oradea, Satu Mare, Sibiu, Timişoara and Târgu Mureş. To many cities there is an early-morning and evening flight. There are no domestic flights on Sunday. Many flights to Constanţa operate only in July and August.

TAROM lists its fares in US dollars but you have to pay in Romanian lei. Unfortunately the airline still touts a two-tier pricing system on all its domestic routes, making flights extremely expensive for foreigners. TAROM does not offer any youth discounts on domestic flights. A single fare is usually around US$50. Return fares offer no saving; they are exactly double the price of a single. Fares are quoted in the relevant sections in this book.

Flights rarely get full and you can usually buy a ticket just hours before departure. TAROM offices at regional airports and in city centres sell tickets. In all cities, TAROM offers a free shuttle service for passengers from its city centre office to the airport. Only 10kg of luggage is carried free but overweight charges are minimal.

BUS

Bus services in Romania are massively underdeveloped compared to the country's rail network. Buses are snail-slow. They are generally used for serving outlying villages and more rural areas. Services are infrequent with just one or two buses a day serving most routes. Buses usually embark on the return journey immediately, making many services useless for day trips.

Heating systems that function or can be moderated and windows that do not leak in rainy weather are rare commodities on long-distance buses. Unless you are a masochist, opt for one of the numerous private buses that have sprung up in recent years to travel between cities.

The handwritten schedules posted in bus stations are often incomplete or out of date, so always ask at the ticket window. Buses in transit are written on the timetable in a different colour (usually red). Many services do not run on Saturday or Sunday so check the timetable carefully. You usually have to purchase your ticket before boarding at a bus station *(autogară)*. Try to reserve a seat by buying a ticket the day before and arriving early at the station.

Travelling by bus is cheap although fares (calculated per kilometre) are upped slightly each month. A list of some destinations, their distance in kilometres, and price can be found in most bus stations. Look for a scrappy piece of A4 paper – handwritten – stuck on the wall. In mid-1997 a 1km to 6km journey cost US$0.20; a 6km to 10km journey cost US$0.28; and an 11km to 15km fare was US$0.42. It cost US$1.70 to travel 100km and US$2.50 to travel 200km.

TRAIN

Rail has long been the most popular way of travelling around Romania. Căilor Ferate

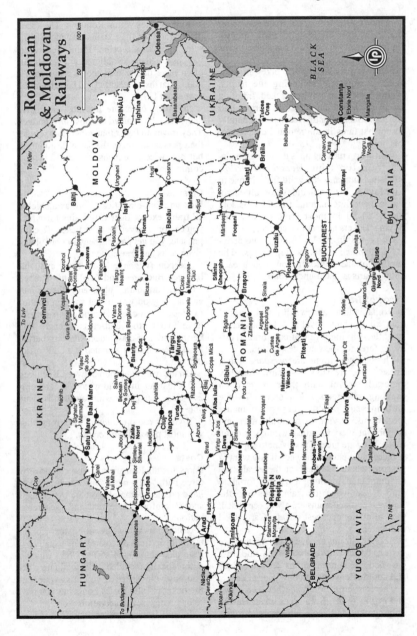

Române (CFR), Romanian State Railways, runs trains over 11,106km of track, providing a frequent service to most cities, towns and larger villages in the country.

Following massive price hikes in mid-1997 less people are using the trains, although they can still get packed. Inflation has been curbed since then but prices still remain variable. For this reason we generally do not list fares in the regional chapters of this book.

Well worth picking up is the comprehensive train timetable *Mersul Trenurilor*, published annually and valid from 1 June to 23 May. It lists schedules for all local, national and international trains and is sold for US$1.50 in most CFR offices (see Buying Tickets later in this chapter).

On posted timetables, *sosire* means arrivals and *plecare* means departures. The number of the platform from which each train departs is listed under *linia*.

Types of Train

In Romania there are five different types of train, all of which travel at different speeds, and offer varying levels of comfort and differing fares for the same destination.

The cheapest trains are *persoane* trains. These trains are slow – so slow that they generally travel with their doors open enabling passengers to leap on or off while the train is still in motion. Persoane trains are local trains, serving more rural routes and stopping at every imaginable train station en route. They are great if you want to enjoy the scenery but a pain in the neck if you want to get somewhere fast. Seats on these trains are not numbered, meaning it is a free-for-all to grab a seat when the train pulls into the station. Persoane trains are always crowded; they offer the cheapest tickets. Carry food and water.

Accelerat trains are one notch up: they are faster, hence more expensive and less crowded. Seat reservations are obligatory and automatic when you buy your ticket.

There is little difference between *rapid* and *expres* trains. Both types travel reasonably quickly and serve international routes

as well as cities within Romania. The speed of, and fares for, these trains are generally the same as those of accelerat trains. Seat reservations are likewise obligatory. These trains often have dining cars too; a meal with a main meat dish, side salad and large beer will cost about US$4.

Inter-City trains are the most expensive and should be avoided by those on a budget. They travel no faster than other trains (other than persoane), serve the same destinations but are twice as expensive – and twice as comfortable.

Classes

First and 2nd-class tickets are available on all trains except Inter-City trains for which you can only buy a 1st class ticket. To compensate, you get complimentary chocolates, clean seats and free coffee.

Sleepers *(vagon de dormit)* are available between Bucharest and Arad, Cluj-Napoca, Oradea, Timişoara, Tulcea and other points, and are a good way to cut accommodation expenses. First-class sleeping compartments have two berths, 2nd-class sleepers four berths and 2nd-class couchettes six berths. Book these well in advance at a CFR office in town.

On the overnight train between Bucharest and Chişinău in Moldova, there are only 2nd-class couchettes with four berths available.

If you're caught riding in the wrong class you must pay a US$6 penalty.

Costs

Fares for all Romanian trains comprise of three parts – the basic fare which is calculated on the kilometres you are travelling, a speed/ comfort supplement, and a seat reservation.

Seat reservations are obligatory for all trains (apart from persoane). You usually pay a supplement of US$0.50 to US$3 which is automatically included in the total fare when you buy your ticket. If you miss your train the ticket is valid for 24 hours but you have to buy a new seat reservation.

In mid-1997 a 1st/2nd class ticket for a

100km journey on a persoane train was US$1.42/0.88. The equivalent on an accelerat was US$2.20/1.12. A 1st/2nd class 100km ticket on a rapid or expres was priced US$2.60/1.87 and an Inter-City 1st class ticket was US$5.60. A 1000km train ride on a persoane cost US$7.90/5 and on an Inter-City US$16. A Bucharest-Chişinău single fare in a 2nd-class couchette costs US$10.

If you board a train without a ticket you'll be hit with a penalty of US$8 to US$11.

Buying Tickets

Tickets can be bought in advance for all trains except local persoane ones. Advance tickets are sold at an Agenţie de Voiaj CFR – a train-ticket office in every city centre. In smaller towns the office is often at the train station. In this book we list CFR offices in city sections under Getting There & Away.

Most CFR offices are only open weekdays. Some are open Saturday. When the ticket office is closed you have to buy your ticket immediately before departure at the station. Whenever possible, buy your ticket in advance. This saves time queuing at the train station and also guarantees you a seat. Tickets for some trains do get sold out.

Theoretically you can buy tickets at CFR offices up to two hours before departure. In reality many do not sell tickets for trains leaving the same day so try to buy your ticket at least the day before you intend to travel.

You can only buy tickets at train stations two hours – and in some cases just one hour – before departure. Get there early as queues can be horrendous. At major stations there are separate ticket lines for 1st and 2nd class; you may decide to opt for 1st class when you see how much shorter that line is. There are often different ticket windows for different trains (a list of destinations should be posted near each ticket window).

Often several trains depart within 30 minutes of each other for the same destination, so note the train number, then check the carriage number (posted on metal signs on every train carriage). Your reservation ticket lists the code number of your train along with your assigned carriage *(vagon)* and seat *(locul)*.

If you have an international ticket right through Romania, you're allowed to make stops along the route but you must purchase a reservation ticket each time you reboard an accelerat or rapid train. If the international ticket was issued in Romania, you must also pay the expres train supplement each time.

CAR & MOTORCYCLE

Most Romanian roads are best suited for four-wheel drive vehicles (in mid-1997 a Frenchman sued the mayor of Craiova after his car was wrecked driving in the city). Do not attempt to drive in Romania unless your car is in good shape and has been recently serviced. Repair shops are common, but unless you're driving a Renault (Romania's Dacia is a descendant of the Renault 12) or a Citroën (the basis of Romania's Oltcit), parts are hard to come by.

Romania has two short stretches of motorway *(autostradă)*: between Bucharest and Ploieşti (114km) and crossing the Balta Ialomiţei from Cernavodă to Fiteşti (15km) into Dobruja. Some major roads *(drum naţională)* are being resurfaced, but generally speaking major roads in both countries are in poor (understatement) condition, with unexpected potholes and irregular signposting. Secondary roads *(drum judeţeana)* can become dirt tracks, while mountain and forestry roads *(drum forestiere)* are often impassable after heavy rain. Concrete roads (such as the Bucharest ring road) were often shoddily constructed and are now quickly deteriorating. Level crossings over railway lines should be approached with caution, as the roads can become very rough at these points. Open manhole covers are a hazard in cities such as Bucharest and Constanţa.

In 1997 the Romanian government dramatically increased the annual tax local motorists have to pay in order to raise the US$183 million a year needed to patch up its roads. Seventy per cent of all roads need repairs!

Even more hazardous than the dire state of the roads, are the obstacles moving about on them. Drivers are aggressive and lack discipline. Horse-drawn carts piled high with hay, cows, pigs, drunkards, playing children and other moving contraptions dart in, out, and along roads without warning, making driving here a downright displeasure. Avoid driving at night. Roads have no markings and are unlit. Many vehicles do not have lights.

It is customary for motorists to wildly blow their horns at anything that moves.

Breakdowns

Members of major foreign automobile clubs (AA, AAA) are automatically covered by Romania's Automobil Clubul Român (ACR). Of course you still must pay: emergency road service costs US$5 to US$10, and towing is US$0.50 per kilometre. In the event of a breakdown, ring ACR's 24 hour free-phone emergency number (☎ 927). The ACR has an office in most cities and these are listed in the relevant sections of this book.

Punctures can be repaired at small workshops labelled *vulcanizare*, abundant in Romania, and found even in the tiniest village in the middle of nowhere.

If you intend hiring a car (see Rental below) consider a Dacia. Romania's national car might well be the source of endless jokes but in the event of a breakdown you'll be grateful you're not driving a Mercedes. Romanians are adept at dismantling/reassembling Dacia engines and take great pride in showing off their engineering skills. If you break down, flag down the first passing car. It will be a Dacia and its driver will be able to make yours go again. Don't worry about not having the necessary tools. Every other Dacia driver will.

Fuel

Petrol is no longer rationed and long lines are a thing of the past. Thank Peco (the state-owned monopoly) and Royal Dutch Shell who have built stations all over Romania. In 1996 Shell announced it would spend US$18 million to build 12 new stations in Bucharest

alone. Stations are less abundant in Moldova.

The types of petrol *(benzină)* available in Romania are normal or regular (88-90 octane), unleaded (95 octane), premium or super (96-98 octane) and diesel. Super is the best. At the time of writing, 1L of regular/premium petrol cost US$0.37/0.41. Unleaded petrol *(fără de plumb)*, costing US$0.40 a litre, is known all over Romania by the German name, *Bleifrei*. Most Peco and Shell stations accept Visa and MasterCard.

There is at least one 24 hour Peco station in every major Romanian city.

Road Rules

The whole region drives on the right. The speed limit for cars is 60km/h in built-up areas or 70km/h on the open road. Motorcycles are limited to 40km/h in built-up areas and 50km/h on the open road. Driving with any alcohol in your blood is illegal.

If you are fined for a traffic violation, insist on a receipt before producing any money. Don't accept a written statement that doesn't specify the exact amount, otherwise the money may go straight into the police officer's pocket.

Useful if you intend driving a lot is the *Romania Ghid Rutier* (Editrura Transport Rutier, 1997) which includes Romania's highway code, road maps, useful contact number listings, and border crossing/customs information. It costs US$4 and is sold in most Bucharest hotels and in ACR offices.

Rental

It's no longer difficult to hire a car in Romania. Avis, Budget, Europcar and Hertz all have offices in most cities. In addition there is Touring ACR.

The new problem is price. On a Ford Fiesta (the cheapest) expect to pay an average US$80 per day for unlimited mileage or US$25 per day plus $0.25 per kilometre. Average weekly rates are US$140 (not including kilometres) or US$420 unlimited mileage. The daily insurance charge is an additional US$17 per day on average. Credit-card insurance is not accepted – everyone must pay the additional fee.

In some cities there are small, private car-rental companies which usually rent out Dacias and massively undercut the larger rental firms. Daily rental including 200km per day starts at around US$45.

A cheaper option if you are flying to Romania on a TAROM flight is to opt for an Avis/TAROM 'fly and drive' deal which you arrange when you book your plane ticket. London-Bucharest return flights for two people plus eight days car rental cost around US$730. Avis also offers 'smart miles' to its clients in conjunction with TAROM. With all the major car-rental agencies you can book car hire in your own country prior to departure, enabling you to pick up a car directly when you land at Otopeni airport in Bucharest. All these companies accept payment by credit card.

Tours

Touring ACR organises caravan and car tours in summer. These tours are for people who bring their own cars to Romania but want the security of travelling in a group and the expertise of an ACR chaperone. The 26 day trek through Transylvania and Maramureş costs US$900, including breakfast, dinner and accommodation (at camping grounds and hotels). You pay for your own petrol. Contact the ACR main office in Bucharest (☎ 01-650 2595; fax 01-312 0434).

EnduRoMania (☎ 056-194 11; ☎ & fax 056-194 596; email sergio@adetim .sorostm.ro; www.sorostm.ro/enduro), Str Lucian Blaga 3, RO-1900 Timişoara, is a member of the International Motorcycle Federation and organises touring, off-road and discovery trips throughout Romania for motorcyclists with their own bikes. It also arranges several competitive off-road motorcycle events each summer.

During tours and events EnduRoMania offers motorcyclists guarded parking for their bikes at night, special access to forest roads otherwise off-bounds to the public, and can arrange accommodation in camping grounds, private homes, monasteries or hotels.

BICYCLE

Providing you are well equipped and prepared for some hard cycling, travelling around Romania on two wheels is one of the most rewarding ways of seeing the country. In many parts of the country you will have the road all to yourself. However, the pot-holed state of Romania's roads makes the going tough for anything less than a robust touring or mountain bike.

Bicycles can be taken on trains. Most trains have a baggage car (vagon de bagaje), marked by a suitcase symbol on train time-tables. Bicycles stored here have to be labelled with your name, destination and the bicycle's weight. But it is easier and safer to simply take your bicycle on the train with you. On local and express trains there is plenty of room at either end of the carriage next to the toilet. You might be charged a minimal 'bulky luggage' fee.

The flashier your bicycle, the more chance there is of it being stolen.

Rental

You can hire mountain bikes in the ski resorts of Poiana Braşov and Sinaia in Transylvania. Rental starts at US$2 an hour or US$15 a day.

There is a well-stocked mountain bike shop in Sibiu which also serves as the base for the Boua Bikes Club (☎ 069-218 310), Str Avram Iancu 25. The club does not arrange bike hire but is more than happy to give advice on, and propose, mountain routes in the Carpathians. It can also provide mountain bike guides. It has a sister club in Cluj-Napoca, the Clubul de Cicloturism (☎ 064 142 953), Str Septimiu Albinii 133, apartment 18 (see Facts for the Visitor – Activities for more details).

HITCHING

Hitching is never entirely safe in any country in the world. Travellers who decide to hitch should understand that they are taking a small but potentially serious risk. People who do choose to hitch will be safer if they travel in pairs and let someone know where they are planning to go.

Hitchhiking in Romania is a common way of getting from A to B and as a westerner you have a greater chance of being picked up. It is common practise in Romania and Moldova to pay the equivalent of the bus fare to the driver. Many local motorists solicit business at bus and train stations as a way of covering their fuel costs.

You may be able to guess where a car in Romania is going by the letters on its licence plate: BV (Braşov), B (Bucharest), CJ (Cluj-Napoca), CT (Constanţa or Mangalia). Moldova plates are marked MD.

Horse, Donkey & Wagon
In many rural parts, the only vehicle that passes will be horse-powered. Horse and cart is the most popular form of transport in Romania and you will see numerous carts, even in cities (although some downtown areas are off-limits to them). Many carts will stop and give you a ride, the driver expecting no more than a cigarette in payment.

BOAT
Boat is the only way of getting around much of the Danube Delta. NAVROM passenger ferries sail along the three main channels from Tulcea to Sulina and Sfântu Gheorghe on the Black Sea and to Periprava just south of Romania's border with Ukraine. You can easily hire private motorboats, rowing boats and kayaks in Tulcea and all the Delta villages to explore the smaller waterways. Local fishermen and boatmen double as guides. From Tulcea passenger ferries also sail to Galaţi in Moldavia.

Combined car and passenger ferries depart from Constanţa to Istanbul between 1 May and 1 September. See the Nothern Dobruja chapter for details.

To get to Ostrov, the Romanian border town with Silistra in Bulgaria, you have to cross the Danube on a shoddy ferry that does not meet international safety standards. It is 'suitable' for cars and foot passengers.

Ferries also cross the Danube river at Calafat and Giurgiu. See the Wallachia chapter for details on all three crossings.

LOCAL TRANSPORT
Bus, Tram & Trolleybus
Buses, trams and trolleybuses (buses run by electricity with wires overhead) provide transport within most towns and cities in Romania and Moldova. An increasing number of quite good-quality city guides include public transport routes and numbers.

All three forms of public transport are generally crowded. Getting on a bus can be a feat in itself. Expect to engage in battle at least two or three times before succeeding on clambering aboard one of the infrequent sardine cans that pass by. Shoving, pushing, elbowing and stamping on toes are allowed.

Buses, trams and trolleybuses usually run from about 5 am to 11 pm daily, with a reduced service on Saturday and Sunday. Services can get thin on the ground after 7 pm in more remote areas. You must purchase tickets at kiosks marked *bilet* or *casă de bilet*, and then validate them once aboard. In most cities only double-journey tickets are sold, each end of the paper-scrap being valid for one ride. You're supposed to validate both ends of a ticket when carrying bulky luggage. Tickets cost less than US$0.20.

Ticket kiosks close around 5 pm. They also close without warning for sporadic intervals during the day so buy a handful of tickets when you first arrive in town. Tickets cannot usually be bought from the driver.

If you travel without a validated ticket or with no ticket at all you risk a hefty US$5 fine or more. Spot checks are carried out on all modes of public transport by plain-clothed ticket inspectors who have no qualms about making a spectacle of the 'stupid foreigner' before physically removing you from it. The best option in these cases is to just shut up and pay.

Taxi
Government taxis are distinguishable by a chequered design on the side and have meters (you pay what the meter displays).

Unmetered private taxis with the letters 'P' or 'PO' on the roof are more expensive but often easier to find. If there's no meter, bargain for a price beforehand. Outside Bucharest, many taxis still tout old pre-revolution meters which clock up fares in tens of lei rather than thousands. In these cases the driver will multiply the digits on the meter by 100. These meters are not reliable and are tantamount to a rip-off.

In cities the official rate is US$0.20 per kilometre but as a foreigner you usually end up paying a lot more. In smaller towns you will be charged US$0.14 per kilometre. You are charged 'waiting time' almost everywhere.

It is always cheaper to telephone for a taxi than to hail one in the street. Numbers for local taxi firms are listed in the regional chapters of this book.

ORGANISED TOURS

Most travel agencies offer a stunning array of guided tours around Romania, enabling you to see the prime sites in a minimum amount of time. Few agencies have yet to acknowledge the existence of independent travellers and it can be impossible to sign up for a guided tour unless you are part of a group of 20 or more.

The Transylvanian Society of Dracula (☎ 01-222 5195; fax 01-312 3056; ☎ & fax 01-679 5742) in Bucharest organises eight day historical tours of Vlad Ţepeş' old haunting grounds – Târgovişte, Sighişoara, Braşov and Bran Castle from US$675 including meals. The shorter Vlad Ţepeş

'escape' tour includes a hike across the mountains in the footsteps of Ţepeş while the Queen Marie tour takes in the former royal residences in Bran and Sinaia. The society also organises more gimmicky Dracula tours which are graded according to spookiness, with clients being awarded a certificate at the end to prove they survived. These tours start at US$60 per person a day, including meals, for groups of 10 or more. The society also arranges more costly day trips which are individually tailored for independent travellers.

Alternative tours to parts of Romania inaccessible to most people are offered by Roving Romania (☎ 034-311 625; fax 034-311 082), 201 Harga, Oituz, RO-5461 Oneşti, Bacău. Roving Romania organises off-roading and mountain tours for two to six people in a Land Rover. Tours are individually tailored and can incorporate a range of activities from birdwatching and trekking to mountaineering. A typical seven day 'mountain pass' tour costs US$560 per person for a group of five, including accommodation in mountain cabanas or private homes, and three meals a day. Roving Romania also organises camping tours, and caving tours led by a professional speleologist. Advance bookings can be made in the UK through Trailmasters (☎ 01474-873 277; fax 01474-873 517), PO Box 299, Seven Oaks, Kent TN15 7U2.

Travelling by steam train is another fun way of discovering a different side of Romania (see Facts for the Visitor – Activities for details).

Bucharest

• *area code ☎ 01, pop 2,037,278*

Tree-lined boulevards, park-girdled lakes, pompous public monuments and its very own Arc de Triomphe give Bucharest (Bucureşti) a smooth Parisian flavour. The city is at its best in spring and summer, when relaxed crowds fill the beer gardens and parks. As well as having the usual complement of museums, Bucharest has a gentle Latin air that goes well with the mysticism of its Orthodox churches.

On the other hand, few travellers fall in love with Romania's capital, largely thanks to its petulant street hustlers and expensive restaurants which spur far too many travellers to leave as quickly as possible. Bucharest can be fascinating if you approach it with patience and humble expectations. Back streets bustle with hawkers and artists; 18th century monasteries and churches hide behind pretty walled gardens (or monumental apartment blocks!); while the decaying elegance of the city's historic quarter is riddled with a charm of its very own.

During the 1980s southern Bucharest was transformed by Nicolae Ceauşescu's attempt to recast Bucharest as a grandiloquent socialist capital, with the behemoth House of the People as its centrepiece. The 1989 revolution put an end to the city's Stalinist makeover, yet reminders of the Ceauşescu era remain – the turn of every corner unveils a bullet-pocked building, a candle quietly burning by a memorial statue, or a marble-covered apartment that once housed Communist Party elite.

History

Bucharest derives its name from a legendary shepherd named Bucur (*bucurie*; literally 'joy') who allegedly founded the city and built a church on the right bank of the river Dâmboviţa.

The city, which lies on the Wallachian plains between the Carpathian foothills and

HIGHLIGHTS

Bucharest

• Tour the city cemeteries to see the Ceauşescus' graves
• Stroll around Bucharest's historic heart
• Visit the House of the People, the world's second largest building
• Take in a movie on the 4th floor of the National Theatre
• Trace the steps of the 1989 revolutionaries
• Mingle with the elite on Şoseaua Kiseleff
• Take a day trip to Cotroceni Palace and Lenin's graveyard

the Danube river, was settled by Geto-Dacians as early as 70 BC. By 1459, a princely residence and military citadel had been established under the chancellery of Prince Vlad Ţepeş. By the end of the 17th century, the city had become the capital of Wallachia and was among the wealthiest in south-eastern Europe. Bucharest became the national capital in 1862.

The early 20th century witnessed Bucharest's golden age. The city's narrow, winding streets were replaced with wide, tree-lined boulevards as Romania looked to France for its cultural and architectural inspiration. Much of Bucharest was redeveloped with the assistance of French architects: large neo-classical buildings sprang up, fashionable parks were laid out and landscaped on Parisian models and, by the end of the 1930s, Bucharest was known throughout

Europe as 'Little Paris' or the 'Paris of the Balkans'.

Bombing by the allies during WWII coupled with a 1940 earthquake measuring 7.4 degrees on the Richter scale destroyed much of Bucharest's pre-war beauty. In March 1977 a second major earthquake claimed 1391 lives and flattened countless buildings. Ceauşescu's criminal redevelopment of the city marked the final death knell of Romania as the 'Paris' of eastern Europe.

Orientation

Bucharest's main train station, Gara de Nord, is a few kilometres north-west of central Bucharest. Luggage can be left at the special 24 hour foreigners-only cloakroom *(bagaje de mână)*, which is on the right side of the central hall if your back is to the train platforms. The other luggage rooms are not open to foreigners.

The Metro conveniently connects Gara de Nord with the centre. Otherwise it's a 20 minute walk – next to the station is Calea Griviţei, which you follow east to Calea Victoriei, then south to Piaţa Revoluţiei and the Ateneul Român (Romanian Athenaeum). The latter is a good orientation point in central Bucharest. Across the square is the Palace of the Republic, and two blocks east of Piaţa Revoluţiei is the ONT tourist office.

Another central focal point is Piaţa Universităţii, a busy student hangout close to the Municipal Museum, National Theatre and Hotel Inter-Continental (Bucharest's tallest building). The city's northern focal point is Piaţa Victoriei, from which Şoseaua Kiseleff leads north past Herăstrău Park to the airports at Băneasa (8km) and Otopeni (17km). Just south of the centre is Piaţa Unirii, the pick-up and drop-off point for express buses to the airports.

Most embassies are clustered along Blvd Dacia, east of Piaţa Romană, and around Str Jean Louis Calderon, south of Blvd Dacia.

Maps Vendors in front of the university building on Blvd Republicii sell city maps of Bucharest published by the Ministry of Tourism, and the best selection of regional and country maps in town. The Ministry of Tourism's *Bucureşti – Romania*, is distributed for free in tourist offices abroad.

If you arrive at Otopeni airport, head straight for the newspaper kiosk in the arrival hall to buy a copy of the *Bucharest 1:18, 000* map with a city map insert (1:9000), published by Cartographia, Budapest (1995). Some street names are out of date but it is still the most detailed, accurate map of Bucharest available.

A pretty dodgy city-centre map depicting only major streets is included as a pull-out inside *What, Where, When Bucureşti* (see Media later). Small maps are included in *The Guide Bucureşti* (see Media later); some are difficult to read.

Information

Information provided by Romanian tourist offices abroad is markedly more useful than anything in-country.

Tourist Offices Bucharest has no national tourist office. ONT Carpaţi (☎ 614 0759, 614 1138, 614 4058; fax 312 0915) at Blvd General Magheru 7 claims to be the city's main tourist office, priding itself on the 'international tourist services' it offers. Visiting this office however is the most momentous blast-to-the-past you are likely to encounter in Bucharest. Staff are frighteningly stern-faced and surprisingly reluctant to part with information. Each of the unmarked desks deals with different types of information; ask at each until you get what you want.

The office can arrange hotel accommodation as well as rooms in private homes, starting at US$15/20 with/without breakfast. Make sure you know exactly where the suggested room is before you pay. Some landlords will collect you from the ONT office. It also arranges a variety of city and regional tours, rents out cars, changes money, cashes travellers cheques and gives cash advance on Visa/MasterCard and Diners Club (see Money). The office is open weekdays from 8 am to 7 pm, Saturday from 8 am to 2 pm.

Moldova has a national tourist office in Bucharest. Moldova Tur (☎ 312 7070, extension 2310), is behind Hotel Bucureşti at Str Luterană 2-4, apartment 10. The office provides general information on the former Soviet republic and issues invitations for visas (see Moldova – Facts for the Visitor, Visa & Documents); it is open weekdays from 9 am to 3 pm.

Agenţie de Turism Patriot (☎ 337 44 75), well signposted from the ONT office, is run by students from the university. It arranges car rental, hotel accommodation in Bucharest and trips to the Black Sea.

Touring ACR (☎ 211 0410; fax 211 4366), part of the Automobil Clubul Român (ACR) network, is near Piaţa Romană at Str Stanislav Cihoschi 2 (open weekdays from 8 am to 8 pm, Saturday from 8 am to 3 pm, Sunday from 8 am to 2 pm). The helpful, English-speaking staff assist visiting motorists, act as the official agent for Eurodollar rental cars, give out free city maps, make hotel reservations, and arrange private accommodation.

The main ACR office (☎ 650 2595; fax 312 0434) at Str Take Ionescu 27, books package trips and group caravan tours throughout Romania. It's not really equipped to help individual tourists (unlike its branch offices).

Embassies Foreign representatives in Bucharest include the following:

Australia
    Honorary Consulate: Blvd General Magheru 29, apartment 45 (☎ 312 9097)
Bulgaria
    Embassy: Str Rabat 5 (☎ 230 2150; fax 312 7654)
    Consulate: Str Vasile Lascăr 32 (☎ 211 1106)
Canada
    Embassy: Str Nicolae Iorga 36 (☎ 222 9845; fax 312 0366)
France
    Embassy: Str Biserica Amzei 13-15 (☎ 312 0217; fax 312 0200)
    Consulate: Intrarea Cristian Tell 6 (☎ 312 0217)
Germany
    Embassy: Str Rabat 21 (☎ 230 2580, 230 2680; fax 312 9846)
    Consulate: Str Rabat 19 (☎ 230 0332; fax 230 2155)

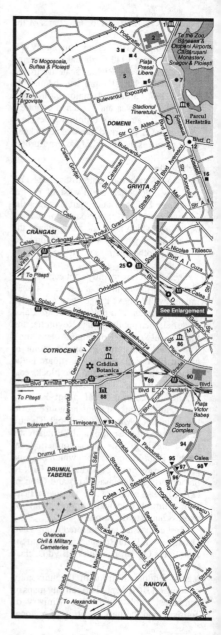

Bucharest

0   0.5   1 km

PLACES TO STAY
3 Hotel Parc
4 Hotel Turist
6 Hotel Sofitel;
   Manhattan Café;
   World Trade Centre
13 Hotel Helvetia
16 Hotel Triumf
26 Economy Academy
    Student Dorms
43 Hotel Minerva
48 Hotel Dunărea
50 Hotel Marna
51 Hotel Grivița
52 Hotel Nord
54 Hotel Bucegi
55 Hotel Cerna;
    Cofetăria Ema
56 Hotel Astoria
68 Hotel Dorobanți
82 Villa Helga Hostel
91 Hotel Veneția

PLACES TO EAT
14 TGI Friday
18 Brutărie
    Deutschland; Café
    Einstein

19 Il Buogutaio
    Ristorante
20 Doina
37 Springtime Fast
    Food
42 Victoria Conti Club
44 Nan Jing
46 Grădină
    Vernescu
47 Casino Palace
49 Restaurant QM Grill
59 Hong Kong
61 Moby Dick
64 Ristorante Italia
    Pizzeria
65 Cofetăria Diplomat
70 Il Gattopardo
75 McDonald's
78 Aquarium
79 Capriccio Italiano
81 Beijing
83 Nicorești
85 Transilvania Club
89 Brădet
93 Golden Blitz
95 Grota Vampirilor
96 Sahib
97 Pizzeria Magia

98 La Florărie
99 Le Petit Paris
100 Grădină Tariștea
103 Dorem Steakhouse
104 Dunkin' Donuts
107 McDonald's
108 Horoscop Pizzeria
111 Tandoori

OTHER
1 Minovici Museum of
   Ancient Western
   Arts
2 Press House
5 Romanian EXPO
7 Expo-Market
8 Village Museum
9 Primăvera Palace
10 Former Residence
    of Gheorghe
    Gheorghiu-Dej
11 Transylvanian
    Society of Dracula
12 Triumphal Arch
15 Romanian
    Television
    Headquarters
17 White Horse Pub

Hungary
  Embassy: Str Jean Louis Calderon 63 (☎ 614 6621, 614 6622; fax 312 0467)
  Consulate: Str Henri Coandă 5 (☎ 312 0468; fax 312 7470)
Ireland
  Consulate: Str Vasile Lascăr 31 (☎ 211 3967; fax 211 3970)
Moldova
  Embassy: Aleea Alexandru 40 (☎ 230 0474; fax 312 9790)
  Consulate: Str Câmpina 47 (☎ 666 5720, 312 8631; fax 312 8631)
Russia
  Embassy: Șoseaua Kiseleff 6 (☎ 222 3170, 617 1318)
  Consulate: Str Tuberozelor 4 (☎ 617 1309, 617 1655)
Turkey
  Embassy: Calea Dorobanților 72 (☎ 230 0279)
UK
  Embassy: Str Jules Michelet 24 (☎ 312 0303, 312 0304; fax 312 0209)
Ukraine
  Embassy: Calea Dorobanților 16 (☎ 222 3162, 211 6986; fax 211 6949)
  Consulate: Str Tuberozelor 5 (☎ & fax 223 2702)
USA
  Embassy: Str Tudor Arghezi 7-9 (☎ 210 4042,

210 0149; fax 210 0395)
  Consulate: Str Nicolae Filipescu 26 (☎ 211 3360)
Yugoslavia
  Consulate: Calea Dorobanților 34 (☎ 210 0359, 211 9871)

Money Currency exchanges are dotted all over the city, and all of them accept US dollars, British pounds, Deutschmarks, French francs and most of the other major currencies. The currency exchange inside ONT Carpați (see Tourist Offices earlier) offers good rates but charges a scandalous 8% commission for changing travellers cheques and 12% for cash advance on credit cards.

Outlets of the OK Exchange House are dotted the length and breadth of Blvd General Magheru and Blvd Nicolae Bălcescu. They give cash advance on Visa/ MasterCard (9% commission) and cash travellers/Eurocheques (7% commission). There is a 24 hour outlet just around the corner next door to Librărie Noi at Str Batiștei 16. The Electrotechnica currency exchange opposite

KFC at Blvd General Magheru 33 also cashes travellers cheques and gives cash advance on Visa/MasterCard, as does the Casă Romană Exchange House close by at Str Pictor Verona.

Unless you have to, however, it is better not to cash travellers cheques or get cash advance on credit card at currency exchanges. All banks charge lower commission rates – and have the advantage of keeping you well away from the eyes of potential pickpockets. Bancă Comercială Română, opposite the university at Blvd Republicii 14, charges 3% commission for cashing travellers' cheques into US dollars/Romanian lei or giving cash advance (in lei only) on credit card. It also has an ATM accepting Visa/MasterCard – as does its branch at the northern end of Calea Victoriei close to Piaţa Victoriei. Both branches are open weekdays from 8 am to 2.30 pm.

BANCOREX, BCIT and Bancă Agricola all give cash advance in dollars or lei on credit card; all three banks only open for a few hours in the morning. BANCOREX has branches at the northern end of Calea Victoriei overlooking Piaţa Victoriei at No 155 (open weekdays from 8.30 am to 2 pm); and at Blvd Nicolae Bălcescu 11. There is an ATM outside the branch at Calea Victoriei 155. BCIT has a branch west of Piaţa Victoriei in Şoseaua Nicolae Titulescu 1, and at Str Doamnei 12 (both open weekdays from 9 am to 2.30 pm). Bancă Agricola has branches at Str Lipscani 27, and at Str Smârdan 3.

Marshal Tourism (☎ 659 6812, 650 2347; fax 223 1203; email office@marshal .eunet.ro) at Blvd General Magheru 43 is a representative for American Express and can issue travellers' cheques to AmEx card holders. It can also replace lost American Express travellers' cheques. It is open weekdays from 9 am to 6 pm.

TAROM operates a currency exchange at Băneasa airport. At Otopeni airport you can get cash advance on Visa/MasterCard at the exchange next to the information desk in the arrival hall; opposite, there is also an ATM accepting Visa/MasterCard.

Post The central post office (Poştă Română Oficiul Bucureşti 1) is close to the Hotel Continental, just off Calea Victoriei at Str Matei Millo 10. Poste Restante letters (see Facts for the Visitor – Post & Communications at the front of this book) can be collected here; letters are kept for one month. It is open weekdays from 7.30 am to 8 pm, Saturday from 7.30 am to 2 pm. Smaller post offices are dotted all over town: handy ones include the 'Poştă Română' next to the telex-fax office on Str Take Ionescu (open weekdays from 7 am to 8 pm, Saturday from 7 am to 2 pm); the office at Str Ion Câmpineanu 21 (open weekdays from 7.30 am to 8 pm); and the one close to the train station at Str Gării de Nord 6-8 (open weekdays from 7.30 am to 8 pm, Saturday from 7.30 am to 2 pm).

To mail a parcel you must take it unsealed to Post Office No 67, Str Virgiliu 45, between Gara de Nord and Eroilor, on weekdays from 8 am to 2.30 pm. All packages are carefully inspected. The state-run Express Mail Service (EMS) is available weekdays from 8.30 am to 5 pm.

Private, express mail services include DHL (☎ 312 2661; fax 312 8489; email chutina@buh-co.ro.dhl.com), at the side of Hotel Bucureşti inside the Condor Travel & Trade travel agency on Str George Enescu; International Rom-Express Service (☎ 211 1580; fax 211 6719) at Str Polonă 22; TNT Express Worldwide (☎ 210 5050, 312 8117; fax 210 5900), Blvd General Magheru 16-18, 4th floor, apartment 35; and UPS (☎ 336 1732; fax 337 3230), Calea Rahovei 195. They are all closed on Sunday.

Telephone There are numerous public phones – both coin-operated national (blue) and card-operated international (orange) ones – all over the city. Finding a phone is not a problem.

All calls can be made from the central telephone office close to Hotel Continental on the corner of Calea Victoriei and Str Matei Millo. International calls can be booked via one of the operators, or made from any of the orange public card phones. The 24 hour office is always jam-packed with impatient people.

The telephone office (officiul telefonic de Cabina; fax 311 419, 311 429) a few doors down on Str Matei Millo, marked by a large blue telephone sign outside, is smaller, calmer and markedly more pleasurable to call from. The blue public phones – for local and national calls only – accept coins. Rom Telecards for the orange international cardphones are sold at the counter marked *punct de distribuire a cartelelor telephone*, on the left as you enter the building. Cards cost US$3 (20,000 lei) or US$6 (40,000 lei). The automatic phonecard dispenser inside the doorway accepts 10,000 lei notes – preferably not creased.

From this office you can also make freephone calls to order a taxi (☎ 953), get SNCFR train information (☎ 952), and make calls to the Automobil Clubul Român (ACR; ☎ 927). Each booth is marked with the relevant organisation and telephone number above the door. This telephone office is open daily from 7 am to 9 pm.

You can rent a mobile telephone from the Telemobil Rental Agency (☎ 614 8251), Blvd General Magheru 7. It also has an office at Otopeni airport (☎ 860 025).

Fax & Telex Faxes can be sent and received for reasonable rates at the telephone office on Str Matei Millo. It costs US$1 per A4 page within Bucharest; US$1.50 per page elsewhere in Romania; and US$2 per page for international faxes. Faxes and telexes can also be sent from the modern 'Telex-Fax' offices dotted around the city centre. Noteworthy outlets include the office (☎ 650 4896; fax 210 788, 210 1155, 210 1085; telex 11948 CTBXR) around the corner from Teatrul Nottara on Str Pictor Verona (open weekdays from 7.30 am to 8 pm, Saturday from 7.30 am to 2 pm); and the office (fax 312 4591, 312 5349; telex 10260 CBTXR) just off Blvd General Magheru on Str Take Ionescu (open weekdays from 7.30 am to 8 pm, Saturday from 7.30 am to 8 pm).

The business centres inside some of the major hotels offer a more costly fax service.

Online Services Logging-in is not a problem in Bucharest (unlike the rest of the country where cybercafés have yet to make their mark).

The French Institute (Institut Français; ☎ 210 0224, 211 3836; fax 210 0225; email adm@instfrbuc.ro; www.instfrbuc.ro) operates a thriving cybercafé, Le Bistro, in the main institute building at Blvd Dacia 77. Thirty minutes online access costs US$1.50. A monthly 10 hour package deal is US$21 and the café also offers a one hour Internet orientation course for US$5. Le Bistro is open weekdays from 10 am to 11 pm.

Similarly priced is the popular 24-hour Internet Café (email icafe@icafe.kapp.ro), just off Piaţa Rosetti at Blvd Carol I, 25. To send emails, it costs US$1/1.75 for 15/30 minutes computer use. To access the Internet it is US$4 an hour. You can also set up your own mailbox at the café for US$2 a month, plus US$3 an hour to access it.

Slightly more expensive and not so well located is the trendy *Web Club* (☎ 650 6417; email web@web.club.ro; http://web .club.ro) at Blvd 1 Mai, 12. An hour online costs US$7. The club has five computers and is open 24 hours.

Cinor (☎ 312 0579; fax 312 0580; email cinor@starnets.ro; http://cinor.starnets.ro) behind Hotel Bucureşti at Str Luterană 11 is an Internet provider.

Travel Agencies With the painful absence of a national tourist office, private travel agencies offering a moderate range of services have mushroomed in the city. Some are better than others.

Dacia Tours
(☎ 210 4568, 210 4547; fax 210 4515), Blvd General Magheru 1-3 – acts as an agent for most airlines including TAROM, Dac Air and Air Moldova

Marshal Turism
(☎ 659 6812, 650 2347; fax 223 1203; email office@marshal.eunet.ro; www.romania .eu.net/clients/marshal), Blvd General Magheru 43 – member of the American Society of Travel Agents and Romania's only representative for American Express (see Money). Its head office (☎ 410 5304; fax 312 4657) is at Blvd Unirii 20

Continental Tours
(☎ 312 4342; fax 312 0134), Calea Victoriei 56 – rents Avis cars

Atlantic Tours
(☎ 312 7689, 650 2848; fax 312 6860; email atlantic@kappa.ro; www.kappa.ro/clients/atlantic), Calea Victoriei 202 – arranges tours, including a half day tour of Ceauşescu's House of the People for around US$25

Paralelea 45 Turism
(☎ 613 4450, 613 4542; fax 312 2774), Blvd Mihail Kogălniceanu 7-9 – arranges hotel accommodation, city and regional tours, sells Eurolines tickets, and has a discreet currency exchange offering good rates

Nouvelles Frontières/Simpa Turism
(☎ 615 9615, 312 7496; fax 312 7465) on the corner of Str Jean Louis Calderon and Blvd Republicii – arranges a number of day trips, folk evenings (US$21), trips to the Danube Delta (US$31). It has a sister office in Braşov.

Bookshops An excellent selection of dictionaries, reference books and city, country and regional maps are sold at the line of kiosks outside the university, which are just west off Piaţa Universităţii on Blvd Republicii.

The Humanitas bookshop almost opposite Hotel Bucureşti at Calea Victoriei 120 has a small selection of books in English; it is open weekdays from 10 am to 7 pm, Saturday from 10 am to 2 pm. Past the Hotel Inter-Continental, the more expensive Librărie Noi at Blvd Nicolae Bălcescu 18, stocks English and French-language, art and history books and Penguin classics as well as an excellent range of secondhand and antique books. It is open weekdays from 10 am to 6.30 pm, Saturday from 10 am to 4 pm. Librărie Mihai Eminescu, on the corner of Blvd Republicii and Str Academiei, is another good bet.

For secondhand novels try the Universitate Populară Ioan I Dalles bookshop, bang next door under the arches. If you're lucky you should also find some old copies of the *Muntri Nostri* hiking map and guide book series published in the 1980s (see Activities – Hiking at the front of this book for more details).

An excellent bet for city maps, glossy picture books and guides about Romania, phrasebooks and dictionaries, and books published by the British-based Blackwells, is the English-language bookshop, Fundaţia Carţii Librărie (☎ & fax 650 3473) close to Piaţa Romană at Blvd Lascăr Catargui 3 (formerly Blvd Ana Ipătescu). It is open weekdays from 10 am to 6 pm.

The bookshop inside the French Institute at Blvd Dacia 77 sells a vast range of French-language novels, reference books, newspapers and magazines; it is open weekdays from 10.30 am to 6.30 pm. For German-language books go to Euromedia at Str General Berthelot 41.

Media English-language tourist guides, newspapers and magazines are plentiful in Bucharest; they are just amazingly difficult to find if you don't know where to look. Head straight for any of the major hotels where the most useful of the locally produced publications are distributed for free. These include the multilingual listings guide *What, Where, When Bucureşti*; the pocket-size monthly *Bucharest Info Top*; the English-language weekly newspaper *Nine O'Clock* published Thursday and usually available in hotels on Friday; the business-orientated *Romanian Economic Observer*; and the comparable *Romanian Business Journal*. One guide you definitely have to pay for is the useful but pricey, 208-page *The Guide Bucureşti*. It costs US$7 and is sold in some upmarket restaurants (see Facts for the Visitor – Newspapers & Magazines at the front of this book for details on these publications).

Libraries The British Council Library (Biblioteca Consiliuliu Britanic; ☎ 210 0314, 211 6635; fax 210 0310; email bc.library@bc-bucharest.sprint.com; www.britcoun.org/romania) at Calea Dorobanţilor 14 is open weekdays from 10 am to 6 pm, Saturday from 10 am to 1 pm, and is closed in August. Many cultural centres in Bucharest also have well stocked libraries or reading rooms where you can digest the latest newspapers and magazines from home.

Cultural Centres Cultural centres can be valuable sources of information.

French Institute
(Institut Français de Bucharest; ☎ 210 0224, 211 3836; fax 210 0225; email adm@instfrbuc.ro; www.instfrbuc.ro), Blvd Dacia 77 – arranges film retrospectives, music and theatre festivals, art exhibitions, conferences and a host of other cultural events each month

Soros Foundation for an Open Society
(Fundaţia Soros pentru o Societate Deschisă; ☎ 650 6325, 659 0720; fax 312 0284, 312 7053; email programs@buc.soros.ro; www.sfos.ro/), Calea Victoriei 155 – supports a host of cultural and social insitutions including the useful Student Advisory & Placement Center (☎ 637 4497; fax 220 7750; email apc@buc.soros.ro, at Str Vergiliu 61, apartment 5 – arranges a variety of cultural and social events; well stocked library and reading room

American Cultural Centre
(☎ 210 1602, 210 16 03, 210 1604), Str Jean Louis Calderon 7-9 – open Tuesday to Friday from 1 to 4 pm

Hungarian Cultural Centre
(Magyar Koztarsasag Kulturalis Kozpontja; ☎ 210 4884; fax 210 4811), Str Batiştei 39 – arranges various cultural events, aimed mainly at Bucharest's Magyar community

German Democratic Forum
(Demokratisches Forum der Deutschen; ☎ & fax 211 2224), Str Batiştei 15 – has offices in most Transylvanian cities too

These are closed, or only offer a minimal service, from 15 July to 15 September.

Photography & Video Fuji, opposite Marshal Turism on the corner of Blvd General Magheru and Piaţa Romană, develops films for US$1 plus an additional US$0.14 for each print. It also runs a more expensive 30 minute photo developing service and makes passport photos for US$3.25. There is a second Fuji outlet almost opposite the ONT Carpaţi tourist office on Blvd General Magheru. Both are open weekdays from 8 am to 9 pm, Saturday from 8 am to 6 pm.

The most central Kodak Express outlet offering a one hour film development service is just off Calea Victoriei on Str Edgar Quinet. Film development is US$1 plus

US$0.21 per print; it is open weekdays from 9 am to 7 pm, Saturday from 9 am to 1 pm.

Laundry Self-service laundrettes have yet to hit Bucharest: wash your clothes by hand, take them to one of the upmarket hotels and pay a small fortune to get them smelling good again, or stay at the Villa Helga hostel (see Places to Stay – Hostels) where you can machine-wash your clothes for free!

The Spălătorie Ecologica, north of the centre at the eastern end of Şoseaua Ştefan cel Mare (Metro: Obor), is a modern dry-cleaners offering a 24 hour and 'urgent' six hour dry-cleaning service (open weekdays from 7.30 am to 9 pm, Saturday from 8.30 am to 4 pm).

Medical Services Foreigners with non-emergency medical problems are referred to the Policlinic Batiştei (☎ 613 3480), Str Tudor Arghezi 28, opposite the American Embassy. Many physicians here speak English and consultations begin at US$30. It's open weekdays from 7 am to 9 pm.

Highly efficient and recommended by the British Embassy is the Centrul Medical Unirea (☎ 336 1696; fax 336 8792) in the same block as Dunkin' Donuts on Piaţa Unirii. The official address is Blvd Unirea 27, block 15, 5th floor. It is open weekdays from 8 am to 8 pm, Saturday from 9 am to 2 pm. Doctors speak English and German; in an emergency call ☎ 092-286 770 or leave a message on the medical centre's pager (☎ 250 9090, No 20563).

The Biochemie Austria pharmacy on the corner of Blvd General Magheru and Str Pictor Verona is open daily from 8 am to 8 pm. On the door is an up-to-date list of other pharmacies open until late; there are 24 hour pharmacies at Str Iuliu Maniu 30, Blvd General Magheru 18, Blvd Nicolae Grigorescu 20, and at Otopeni airport.

Farmacie Victoriei, close to Piaţa Victoriei at Şoseaua Nicolae Titulescu 3, block A1, is open weekdays from 7.30 am to 7.30 pm, on Saturday from 8 am to 2 pm, and Sunday from 9 am to 1 pm. If you're staying at Hotel Bucureşti, head for the Farmacie opposite

the Lutheran church on Str Ştirbei Vodă; it is open weekdays from 7 am to 8 pm, Saturday from 8 am to 4 pm. If you're at the Continental, go to the Farmacie Academia at Blvd Academia 35-37 (open daily from 8 am to 9 pm), or Farmacie No 1 on Str Edgar Quinet (open weekdays from 7 am to 8 pm, Saturday from 8 am to 1 pm).

Around Gara de Nord, the Nordfarm opposite Hotel Astoria on Blvd Dinicu Golescu is open weekdays from 7.30 am to 6.30 pm, Saturday from 8 am to 1 pm. There is another, very large pharmacy (open the same hours) close to Hotel Dunărea at Blvd Gheorghe Duca 10.

There is a German-run dental clinic, Dentexflex (☎ 650 6526) at Piaţa Romană 9. It has another outlet (☎ 614 2668, 312 2758) at Str Ştirbei Vodă 4. Dent-a-America (☎ 230 2608, 230 2826) at Str Varşovia 4 and Novident (☎ 410 1222) at Str Apolodor 13-15, apartment 52, are private dental clinics with English-speaking staff.

The Romanian-American optical company, Optinova, is based inside Magazinul Unirii at Blvd Unirii 3.

Emergency Emergency first aid is free at hospitals, but anything more and you have to pay. For general emergencies go to the 24 hour Spitalul de Urgenta (☎ 679 6490, 230 0106, 21 1943) at Calea Floreasca 8. There is a children's hospital (☎ 650 4046, 650 4194) at Str Grigore Alexandrescu 27; and at Splaiul Independenţei 200 (☎ 638 5725). Colentina hospital (☎ 210 5485), close to Parcul Circului at Şoseaua Ştefan cel Mare, specialises in rabies treatments.

To call (Romanian only) an ambulance dial ☎ 961; police ☎ 955; fire brigade ☎ 981.

Dangers & Annoyances Despite all the horror stories about Bucharest related to backpackers in Budapest, Sofia and other neighbouring capitals, Romania's capital is not especially dangerous. For details on stray dogs, scams and other annoyances you might encounter, see Dangers & Annoyances in the Facts for the Visitor chapter.

Other annoyances include: banks closing

for the day at lunchtime; noisy trams rattling beneath your hotel window late at night/early in the morning; aggressive drivers who have a complete disregard for pedestrian rights; holes in the road and uncovered manholes in the pavements; and bloodsucking mosquitoes.

The Historic Heart & West of Calea Victoriei

The historic heart of Bucharest – flanked by Splaiul Independenței to the south, Blvd Republicii to the north, Blvd IC Brătianu to the east and Calea Victoriei – sprang up around the **Old Princely Court**, or **Old Court** (Curtea Veche), in the 15th century. Artisans and traders – whose occupations are still reflected in street names like Str Covaci (trough-makers street) and Str Șelari (saddle-makers street) – settled here in the 14th century, but it was not until the reigning prince of Wallachia, the notorious Vlad Țepeș, fortified the settlement and built a **Prince's Palace** (Palatul Voievodal) that it started to flourish as a commercial centre. The palace served as the official residence of the Wallachian princes until the end of the 18th century, when, heavily damaged by earthquakes and fires over the years, it was auctioned off to local merchants. Ruins are all that remain today. To enter the court at Str Iuliu Maniu 31 from the north-eastern side of Piața Unirii, cut along Str Șelari then immediately veer right along Str Iuliu Maniu.

The **Old Court Church** (Biserica Curtea Veche), built between 1546 and 1559 during the reign of Mircea Ciobanul (Mircea the Shepherd), is Bucharest's oldest church. Much of the interior has blackened with time, but the original 16th century frescoes next to the altar, and the unusual horizontal strips of alternating plaster mouldings and brick which adorn the spire, remain beautifully preserved. The carved stone portal was added in 1715. Left of the church stands the **Manuc's Inn** (Hanul lui Manuc), Bucharest's only remaining 19th century inn, built as shelter for travelling merchants. Restored in 1968, it now houses a hotel,

restaurant and attractive courtyard. The city's **oldest café** dating from 1801 is close by at Str Covaci 14. Romanian poet Mihai Eminescu stayed in the house next door when he was in Bucharest in 1880.

Continue west on Str Iuliu Maniu a few blocks, and when you see a large white church turn right on to Str Poștei and then make your way to **Stavropoleos Church**, a UNESCO-protected building on the corner of Str Stavropoleos (literally 'town of the cross'). It was built by the Greek monk Ioanichie Stratonikeas in 1724 in a typical Brâncoveanu style, characterised by a harmonious blend of Renaissance and baroque elements with traditional Romanian architectural forms. The richly ornate wood and stone carvings, coloured with paintings and frescoes, inside the blackened interior are badly smoke damaged and are currently being restored. Those in the church porch remain well preserved. The votive inscription carved in stone above the entrance is written in Greek and Romanian (in the Cyrillic alphabet). Tombstones engraved in Romanian, Greek and Serbian lie behind the church alongside the tomb of Metropolitan Grigorie I of Wallachia (1627-37). A lively, song-filled service is held on Sunday at 10.30 am with additional services on Wednesday at 5 pm, Friday and Saturday at 6 pm. At other times it is open daily, except Tuesday, from 8.30 am to 6 pm.

Constantin Brâncoveanu, the great Wallachian prince (1688-1714) known as 'Altân-bey' (Golden Prince) by the Turks and renowned within Romania for his innovative architectural achievements, is buried in **New St George's Church** (Biserica Sfântu Gheorghe-Nou; 1699). Brâncoveanu introduced fiscal reforms in Wallachia in 1701. In April 1714 he was captured by the Turks following his refusal to take part in the Russo-Turkish War (1711). He and his four sons were taken to Istanbul where they were tortured then decapitated. His wife, Maria, smuggled Brâncoveanu's mutilated body back to Romania and buried it in the church on Str Lipscani. A couple of blocks north, also on Blvd IC Brătianu, is the 17th century

Colţea Church & Hospital (Biserica Colţea), built between 1699 and 1704 by Mihail Cantacuzino. Its church tower, demolished in 1888, used to be a fire tower.

From Colţea Church walk back south past New St George's church, then walk back west along **Str Lipscani**, a bustling, pedestrianised street filled with hawkers flogging pumpkin and sunflower seeds, and Roma selling copper pots and wooden spoons. Market stalls line the recently repaved, stone street which is slowly being transformed back into the fashionable, Parisian-style mall it was in the 1930s.

At its western end, Str Lipscani crosses **Calea Victoriei**, another of Bucharest's most historic streets built under the orders of Brâncoveanu in 1692 to link his summer palace in Mogoşoaia, 14km north-west of Bucharest, with the heart of his capital city. The road became known as **Mogoşoaia Bridge** (Podul Mogoşoaia), because of the wooden oak planks laid over the potholes to ensure a smooth carriage ride for the prince. In 1878, at the end of the Romanian War of Independence, the street was renamed Calea Victoriei.

Bucharest's financial houses moved to the historic heart in the 19th century after the princely residence was moved to the north of the city (see Piaţa Revoluţiei to Piaţa Victoriei section). On the corner of Str Lipscani and Calea Victoria stands a modern mirrored building, which will eventually house the **Bucharest Financial Plaza** when building work is completed in early 1998. Next door is the **Economic Consortium Palace** (CEC, Casă de Economi şa Conseminatuni), designed and built by French architect Paul Gottereau between 1894 and 1900.

Opposite the Economic Consortium Palace at Calea Victoriei 12 is Bucharest's most important museum, the **National History Museum** (☎ 615 7056). The museum is housed in the former Post Office Palace, built in a neo-classical style between 1894 and 1900. The 600,000 exhibits tell the story of the country from prehistoric times to WWI. The highlight of the museum is the fabulous treasury in the basement, full of gold objects and precious stones. There's also a complete plaster cast of Traian's Column that depicts the conquest of Dacia by Rome. Information in English and French is posted in most rooms. The museum is open daily from 10 am to 5 pm.

Heading north along Calea Victoriei, you pass **Casă Capşa**, a historic café renowned as the meeting place of the most eminent artists, literary figures and politicians of the 1930s.

Piaţa Revoluţiei to Piaţa Victoriei

Proceed north on Calea Victoriei. After four or five long blocks, just south of Piaţa Revoluţiei, stands **Creţulescu Church** (1722) on the left, a red-brick structure that was badly damaged in the 1989 revolution. To the side of it stands a **memorial bust** of Corneliu Coposu, who was secretary to National Peasant Democratic Party (PNTCD) leader Iuliu Maniu and later president himself. He spent 17 years in prison for his anti-communist activities and, prior to his death in 1995, was awarded the Légion d'honneur by the French government.

At the rear of the church is a haunting statue of a headless human form, kneeling, with six arms desperately outstretched; it is a **memorial** to those who died during the 1989 revolution.

Piaţa Revoluţiei was at the very heart of the 1989 revolution. Ceauşescu made his last fateful speech from the balcony of the former **Central Committee of the Communist Party** building (1950), the long, white stone edifice across the square from Creţulescu Church. Following the revolution, the building became home to the Senate. Outside the main entrance there is a memorial plaque dedicated to the 'young and courageous people' who 'drove out the dictator', thus 'giving the Romanian people back their freedom and dignity'. In front of the building is a large triangular, white marble memorial. Prior to 1989, most of the buildings next to the Central Committee were occupied by Securitate. Many are still pockmarked with bullet holes made by fire from army troops.

BUCHAREST

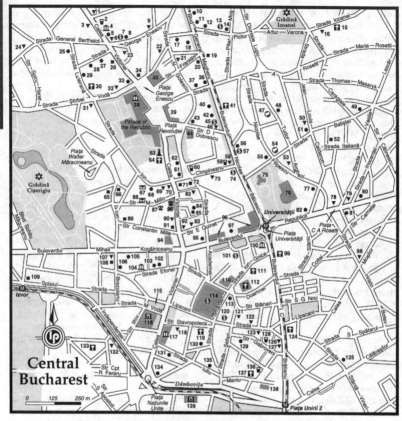

90 Simplan Fast Food
92 Casă Capşa
93 Brăutria Deutschland
98 Golden Falcon Casă Chebab
107 McDonald's
118 Caru cu Bere
121 Casă Rapsodia
122 Cofetăria Excellent
123 Café de Joie
126 London Lucky Burgers
127 Sheriff's Fast Food
132 Springtime Fast Food

OTHER
2 Green Hours Jazz Club; Humanitas Bookshop
4 Da Vinci Galeriile de Art
5 Andrew's Antiques
7 Excellent Currency Exchange
8 Malev Airlines
10 Nottara Theatre
11 Biochemie Austria
12 Lufthansa & Swiss Airlines
13 Casă Română Exchange
14 Telex-Fax Office
15 Church of the Icon
17 Agenţie de Turism Patriot
18 ONT Carpaţi
25 Cinor Internet
27 Entrance to Hotel Bucureşti Swimming Pool
28 DHL; Condor Travel & Trade Travel Agency
29 Moldova Tur
30 German Lutheran Church
33 ANTREC; Lar Tours
35 Romanian Athenaeum

36 Dacia Tours
37 Casino Lido
38 National Art Museum
39 Central University Library
40 Turkish Airlines Office
41 Italian Church
42 Unic Supermarket
43 Shell of Building
44 Former Central Committee of the Communist Party
45 OK Currency Exchange
47 American Embassy
48 Policlinic Batiştei
49 Hungarian Cultural Centre
51 Galeriile Jean-Louis Calderon
54 US Consulate
55 Air Moldova Airline Office
56 Librărie Noi
57 24-Hour OK Exchange House
59 London Bar
60 Atlantic Club
61 Farmacie Academia
62 Excelsior Theatre
63 Memorial Bust of Corneliu Copusu
64 Creţulescu Church
67 Post Office
68 Cinemateca Română
74 BANCOREX
76 National Theatre
77 American Cultural Centre
80 Internet Café
82 Nouvelles Frontiéres/ Simpa Turism
84 Odeon Theatre
86 Central Telephone Office
87 Telephone Office
88 Central Post Office
94 Militar Cercul

95 Librărie Mihai Eminescu
96 University
97 Map Vendors
99 Colţea Church & Hospital
100 Municipal History & Art Museum
101 Bancă Comercială Română & ATM
102 Café Indigo; Cinema
103 African Art Shop
104 Eforie Art Gallery
105 Paralelea 45 Turism
106 TAROM; Agenţie de Voiaj CFR
110 Romanian National Library
111 Student Church
112 Russian Church
113 Bancă Comercială Ion Ţiriac
114 National Bank of Romania
115 Bucharest Financial Plaza
116 Economic Consortium Palace
117 National History Museum
119 Stavropoleos Church
120 Bancă Agricola
124 New St George's Church
125 Choral Temple
128 Hard 'n Heavy
129 Hat Shop
130 Comedy Theatre
131 24-hour Pharmacy
133 Prince Mihai Monastery
134 Double T Travel Agency
135 Priest Vestments Shop
136 Cofetăria Veche
137 Old Princely Court Church
139 Palace of Justice

In the centre of the square is a **wooden cross** in memory of anti-communist heroes who died between 1945 and 1989.

The **Central University Library** (1895) – named the Carol I University Foundation until the end of WWI – between the Central Committee and the Ateneul Român, was rebuilt after being gutted by fire during the 1989 revolution.

One block north of the library is the neo-classical **Romanian Athenaeum** (Ateneul Român), a circular, temple-style building with a 41m-high dome. Scenes from Romanian history are featured on the interior fresco inside the Big Hall on the first floor. The peristyle is adorned with mosaics of five Romanian rulers, including Moldavian prince Vasile Lupu (1512-21), Wallachian Matei Basarab (1632-54), as well as King Carol I (1866-1914). The Athenaeum was built in 1888 as a culture house for the Athenaeum academic and literary circle. Set up in 1865, the group met in the palace of Prince Constantin Ghica until 1873 when it started selling lottery tickets for one leu in order to raise the cash needed to build their own meeting house. George Enescu made his debut in the Athenaeum in 1898, followed five years later by the first performance of his masterpiece *Romanian Rhapsody*. Today, it is home to the **George Enescu Philharmonic Orchestra** and its concert hall. At the time of writing, the Athenaeum was under restoration but concerts are still held inside. A bronze **statue** of Romantic poet Mihai Eminescu stands in the small park in front of the building.

Adjacent to the Athenaeum on the north side of Piaţa Revoluţiei is the prestigious **Athenee Palace**, Bucharest's fanciest hotel in the 1930s. It was designed and built in 1914 by French architect Téophile Bradeau who ensured it was the first building in Bucharest to use reinforced concrete. It suffered heavy bombing during WWII and had to be extensively rebuilt in 1945. A new wing was added in 1966. The hotel was notorious for being a den of iniquity and cradle of high-class prostitution at the turn of the century. In October 1997, following a US$50 million facelift, it repoened as Bucharest's classiest and most expensive hotel.

Dominating the square to the east at Calea Victoriei 49-53 is the massive **Palace of the Republic** (1937), formerly the royal palace and the seat of the State Council until 1989. Built between 1812-15 by Prince Dinicu Golescu, the palace did not become the official royal residence until 1834 under the rule of Prince Alexandru Ghica (1834-42). The current façcade dates to the 1930s.

The palace was the scene of heavy fighting during the revolution, and the extensive collection of Romanian and European art in its four storey **National Art Museum** (Muzeul Naţional de Artă al României; ☎ 614 9774) was badly damaged. The palace has since been repaired and the museum displays a collection of over 100,000 pieces of European art. It's open daily, except Monday and Tuesday, from 10 am to 6 pm. Every May, a handful of monarchists keen to see the monarchy re-established in Romania, gather outside the former royal palace to celebrate Romania's former national day (10 May).

West of Piaţa Revoluţiei is the **German Lutheran Church** (Evangelisch-lutherische Kirche), behind Hotel Bucureşti on Str Luterană. Services are held in German on Sunday at 10 am. Services are held in Italian at the Roman-Catholic red-brick **Italian Church** at Blvd Nicolae Bălcescu 28.

North again at Calea Victoriei 107 is the **Ceramics Museum** inside the Ştirbei Palace, which dates from 1856. A smaller branch of the **National Art Museum** (Muzeul Naţional de Artă al României; ☎ 613 3030) is housed further north at Calea Victoriei 111. Adjoining the museum is the excellent **Art Collection Museum** (Muzeul Colecţiilor de Artă; ☎ 650 6132), formed from several private art collections. Note the many fine works by the 19th century Romanian painter Nicolae Grigorescu. Both museums are open daily, except Monday and Tuesday, from 10 am to 6 pm. Don't miss the much-acclaimed contemporary art gallery, **Galerie Catacomba**, hidden in the catacombs of the art museum building (see Art Galleries later in this chapter).

National composer George Enescu (1881-1955) lived for a short time in the former Cantacuzino Palace at Calea Victoriei 141. Built in the early 1900s in a French baroque style, the building features a fantastic clam-shaped *porte-cochère* above the main entrance. The **George Enescu Museum** (Muzeul George Enescu; ☎ 659 7596), now occupying the building, exhibits the musician's manuscripts and personal belongings. A collection of Bach belonging to Queen Elizabeth of Romania is on display; the museum is open daily, except Monday, from 10 am to 5 pm.

Piaţa Victoriei, at the northern end of Calea Victoriei, is dominated by the massive, heavily guarded **government building** (1938), on the north-eastern side of the square. On the north-western side of Piaţa Victoriei is the worthwhile **Grigore Antipa Natural History Museum** (Muzeul de Iistorie Naturală Grigore Antipa; ☎ 650 4710). The museum's showpiece is a 4.5m reconstruction of a fossil mammoth skeleton (Deinotherium Gigantissimum), found in the Bârlad valley in Moldavia and the only surviving skeleton of its type in the world. The museum is open daily, except Monday and Tuesday, from 10 am to 6 pm.

A short walk south-east of Piaţa Victoriei is **Piaţa Romană**, at the northern end of which is a statue of **Lupoaica Romei** (the wolf of Rome) and the two abandoned children, **Romulus & Remus** which the wolf fed and cared for, enabling them to found the city of Rome. East of Piaţa Romană at Blvd Dacia 12 is the **Museum of Roman Litera-**

ture (Muzeului Literaturii Române). Temporary art exhibitions are held on the 1st floor. It is open daily from 10 am to 4 pm; admission is free. Close by on Str Icoanei is the **Church of the Icon** (Biserica Icoanei), built by the monk and former privy secretary Mihail Babreanu between 1745-50. Around the corner at Str Schitu Darvări 3 is the **Mănăstirea Sfântă Slujbe**, a pretty monastery, recently renovated and surrounded by a lush walled garden.

North-west of Piaţa Romană at Blvd Lascăr Catargui 21 is an **Astronomic Observatory** (☎ 650 3475) run by the Astronomical Institute of the Romanian Academy. It houses an astronomic history museum; you have to book a visit in advance. On 11 August 1999, hundreds of stargazers will congregate here to witness the last total solar eclipse of this century.

Piaţa Universităţii & Around

From Piaţa Romană, the centre's other main artery – Blvd General Magheru leading into Blvd Nicolae Bălcescu – runs parallel to Calea Victoriei. It leads south to Piaţa

Romolus & Remus wolf down a couple of pints in Bucharest.

Universității, the hub of Bucharest's intellectual and political life.

Immediately north of the university square is the **Ion Mincu Institute of Architecture** (Institutul de Arhitectură Ion Mincu), housed in several sombre 20th century buildings dating from 1912 to 1917.

A red and white **pillar** bearing the inscription 'Centrul Libertăț Democratiei 0km' (Centre of Liberty and Democracy 0km), in front of the **National Theatre** opposite the fountain, marks the anti-communist zone set up by students in 1990.

On the north-western corner of Piața Universității, adjoining Blvd Republicii, is the main **university** building, built 1856-68 and inaugurated in 1869.

The faded green domes of the **Student Church** (Biserica Studenților), dedicated to St Nicolae (Sfântu Nicolae), peep at the university from the south-eastern side of the square on Blvd Republicii. To get to the church cut down the street next to the Romanian Commercial bank onto Str Ion Ghica. One block south, in a small yard off Str Doamnei, is Bucharest's small **Russian Church** (Biserica Rusească).

On the south-western corner of Piața Universității is the **Municipal History & Art Museum** (Muzeu al Municipiului București; ☎ 613 2154), housed in the former Șuțu Palace at Blvd IC Brătianu 2. Designed by two Austrian architects, the neo-Gothic building was built between 1832 and 1834 for the Șuțu family, notorious for the high-society parties they threw. The museum has displays on turn-of-the century Bucharest. The document, issued by Vlad Țepeș in 1459, in which the city of Bucharest was chronicled for the first time, is also here. The museum is open daily, except Monday, from 9 am to 5 pm.

Heading east from Piața Universității along Blvd Republicii, you pass a 19th century **fire tower**. The tower was restored in the early 1960s and made into a fire museum; the museum appears to be closed today. Further east at Blvd Carol I 43, is the **Museum of the Armenian Community** (Muzeul Comunitii Armene; ☎ 613 9070), housed inside the Armenian Orthodox church; the museum is open daily, except Monday, from 10 am to 4 pm.

The Civic Centre

In the last years of Ceaușescu's reign, the southern section of central Bucharest around **Piața Unirii** was 'systemised' to create a new civic centre (referred to behind closed doors as 'Ceaușima' by Bucharest's unhappy residents). Some 26 churches, two synagogues, and a monastery in the city's most historic quarter were bulldozed, and about 70,000 people forced from their homes to make way for the megalomaniac leader's grandiose building plans.

From Piața Unirii Metro station walk over to the large ornamental **fountain** in the middle of the square to get your bearings. On the north-eastern side of the square is the **Unirea Department Store** (good photos of the fountain can be taken from the top floor); the main **city market** is a long block behind it – shop here for fresh fruit and vegetables. The **Dâmbovița river** snakes up to the north-eastern corner of Piața Unirii before disappearing underground, beneath the square, on its journey to the south-west of the city. The natural twists and turns of the river were canalised between 1880 and 1883 and further enhanced with concrete during the mid-1980s.

The fortified **Văcărești Monastery**, built by Prince Ioan and Nicolae Mavrocordat on the south bank of the river between 1718 and 1722, was completely destroyed in 1985. Its neighbouring 16th century **Prince Mihai Monastery**, built under the orders of Mihai Viteazul (1593-1601), was moved 279m east to a patch of wasteland in between apartment blocks at Str Sapienței. The Mihai Vodă church – one of the last remaining architectural treasures from pre-Ceaușescu Romania – is currently being renovated. To reach the church, cut down the alleyway by the side of Springtime fast food at Splaiul Independenței 7.

The tiny **St Apostles' Church** (Biserica Sfântii Apostoli), built in the 17th century at Str Apostoli 33a, survived systemisation to a degree. It was not moved but the parkland and many of the trees surrounding it were ripped up and blocks of flats planted there instead. Cut through the alleyway close to the Dorem Steakhouse at the western end of Blvd Unirii. On the opposite side of the street, south of Blvd Unirii at Str Antim, you'll find the surviving **Antim Monastery** (Mănăstirea Antim), a walled complex built in 1715 by the metropolitan bishop Antim Ivireanu.

South-east of Piaţa Unirii, aloft Patriarchy Hill, is the majestic **Patriarchal Cathedral & Palace**, south-west of Piaţa Unirii on Blvd George Coşbuc. During the 15th century a small wooden church surrounded by copious vineyards stood on the hill. The cathedral, consecrated the Metropolitan centre of Wallachia in 1868, and was built between 1656 and 1658 by Wallachian prince Şerban Basarab. None of the original interior paintings or icons remain bar a single icon (1665) depicting Constantin and Helen, the cathedral's patron saints. The present-day frescoes were painted by Dimitrie Belizarie in 1923. The icons embedded in the gold iconostasis were wrought in iron in the Romanian Patriarchy's workshops in 1965. To the west of the cathedral is a small **chapel**, linked by a balcony to the **Patriarchal Palace**, the south-wings of which date to 1932. Three beautifully carved, 16th and 17th century **stone crosses** flank the northern wall of the cathedral. Alongside is a belfry (1698) and the **Chamber of Deputies**, housed in the former parliament building dating from 1907.

Other surviving churches include the 16th century **Mănăstirea Radu Vodă**, south-west of Piaţa Unirii on Str Radu Vodă; and the nearby **Church of Bucur** (Biserica Bucurie) at Str Mircea Ciobanul, a small church believed to have been built by Bucur in the 18th century.

East from the fountain on Piaţa Unirii runs **Blvd Unirii**, a wide boulevard intended to replicate the Champs Élysées. Exactly 3.2km in length, the 'boulevard of the Victory of Socialism' as it was originally named, is flanked by towering concrete blocks and leads to a large square at its western end, large enough to hold 300,000 people.

Towering over the square to the west is Ceauşescu's infamous **House of the People** (Casă Poporului), the second largest building in the world after the Pentagon. The incredible Stalinist structure was almost finished when Ceauşescu was overthrown in 1989 and was subsequently renamed the Palace of the Parliament (Palatul Parlamentului), an official title that has not yet caught on with the locals!

Since 1989, intense debate has surrounded the House of the People – many in Bucharest would like to see it torn down, but the government has instead ordered a reluctant parliament to move in. The House of the People is open to visitors; informative guided tours in English, Spanish, Italian and Romanian are available on the hour daily, except Monday, between 10 am and 4 pm. Admission costs US$2/1 for adults/students and a US$2/1.50 fee is charged if you want to take in a camera/video camera. The International Conference Centre (☎ 311 3611) inside the building has an information desk. For tours, take the second entrance on the right, heading west along Calea 12 Septembrie.

Various government ministries as well as the state prosecution office and the Romanian Intelligence Service (the successor of the Securitate) are today housed in the vast civic centre buildings bordering the square to the north-east and south-east. The converging streets are lined with towering apartment buildings once intended to house privileged bureaucrats employed in nearby ministries.

On the southern side of the House of the People is the huge **National Institute for Science & Technology** of which Elena Ceauşescu was president. West is the new **Ministry of Defence**. Ceauşescu planned to have the remodelling of Bucharest complete by the end of 1990 and literally hundreds of gigantic, almost finished buildings can be seen around the city, especially in this southern part.

House of the People – Vital Statistics

- Built in 1984 as the centrepiece of 'Ceauşima' (alias Ceauşescu's Civic Centre) in central Bucharest
- It was built to house the Central Committee, the president's office, and all the state ministries
- Twelve churches, three monasteries, two synagogues, and 7000 homes were bulldozed to accommodate the monstrous building which is 84m tall and has a surface area of 265,000sq metres
- Ceauşescu intended it to be the largest building in the world. It is, in fact, the second after the Pentagon in the US
- It has three registers, 12 storeys, and over 1000 rooms. Two of its 60-plus galleries are 150m long and 18m wide. One of its 64 reception halls is large enough to land a helicopter in
- Beneath the edifice is a vast nuclear bunker
- In the 1980s, when lit, it consumed a day's electricity supply for the whole of Bucharest in a mere four hours
- When Ceauşescu was toppled, building work was still not completed. He had not yet quite decided on the final roof design
- It was renamed Parliament Palace (Palatul Parlamentului) after Romania's first post-communist parliament moved in, but is still known locally as 'it', the 'thing', or as the House of the People (Casă Poporului)
- Locals have a love-hate relationship with the house – it's among the world's worst eyesores yet its interior is a fantastic showpiece of Romanian craftsmanship
- Over 400 architects and 200,000 workers laboured on it. Up to 25,000 were on site at any one time
- Estimated building costs range from US$760 million to US$3.3 billion
- The Alexandru Ioan Cuza Hall is 2000sq metres and is topped by an 18m-high gold-gilded ceiling.
- The carpets coating the floor of Unity Hall weigh 14 tonnes ■

Western Bucharest

In order to make Bucharest a great capital like Paris or Moscow, Ceauşescu decided that his new city needed a river. So the Dâmboviţa was rechannelled through southern Bucharest in a tremendous engineering project.

To ensure a regular supply of water for the Dâmboviţa, he had a massive dam built across the river on the western side of Bucharest, thereby creating **Dâmboviţa Lake**. The Crângaşi (Crîngaşi) Metro station is only about 500m from the dam, which is visible from the station.

From the Dâmboviţa Dam or Crângaşi Metro stations board a southbound tram No 41 to the end of the line. From here it's two stops east on tram No 8 or 48 to **Ghencea Civil & Military Cemeteries** on Blvd Ghencea. Alternatively, walking from the southern side of the House of the People it's a straight 2.5km trek along Calea 13 Septembrie.

The **burial place** of Nicolae and Elena Ceauşescu was supposed to have remained secret but it is now common knowledge that they are buried at Ghencea Civil Cemetery (Cimitrul Civil Ghencea). Their graves are on opposite sides of the main avenue that leads to the church in the cemetery's centre; Nicolae to the left and Elena to the right. Following their secret burial here on 30 December 1989, the couple's graves were humbly marked with simple wooden crosses bearing the pseudonyms of two reserve colonels – 'Colonel Popa Dan 1920-1989' and 'Colonel Enescu Vasile 1921-1989 – in an attempt to prevent their graves becoming a place of pilgrimage.

In May 1990, the wooden crosses were replaced with small, elaborate tombstones. Nicolae's grave today in fact consists of three crosses – a heavy cross made from stone bearing no name; a black steel cross inscribed with Nicolae's name and date of birth and death (26 January 1918 – 24 December 1989); and a more ornate, marble cross put up in May 1996 by the Romanian Workers' Party. Fresh flowers adorn his grave and candles burn around the clock thanks to the handful of disgruntled pensioners who tend his grave and pay homage to the man who granted them an adequate monthly pension, rent-free apartments and free medical treatment – none of which they receive today. Fewer flowers adorn Elena's more modest grave, marked by a plain wooden cross mounted on a heap of stones. Her name is scrawled on the cross with a black magic marker.

The **grave** of their son Nicu (1951-96) lies to the left side of the white church. Reputed to be a notorious playboy, womaniser and drunkard, Nicu died in Vienna of liver cirrhosis in September 1996. The Ceauşescu family would like the remains of all three to be moved to Nicolae's ancestral village, Scorniceşti, some 70km south-west of Bucharest.

The Ghencea Military Cemetery (Cimitrul Militar Ghencea) is next to the civil cemetery. Most tombstones bear a photograph of the deceased. Propeller blades stand upright amid the sea of graves. A silver-domed, white church stands in the centre of the cemetery.

From the cemetery take eastbound tram No 48 as far as the stop called 'Razoare', where the tram turns for the second time. Walk for two long blocks on Blvd Geniului (the road made from stone bricks), then turn right at the T-junction onto Şoseaua Cotroceni.

For the last half of this walk you'll be following the high wall of the 19th century **Cotroceni Palace**, one of many buildings restored by Ceauşescu as a personal residence but never occupied by him. The palace, which housed the royal court from 1893-47, was built between 1891-3 as a gift from King Ferdinand to his wife, Marie. Today the palace houses the **National Cotroceni Museum** (Muzeul Naţională Cotroceni; ☎ 638 7975, 613 3763) and the **Presidency of Romania** in its wings. Visits to the museum have to be booked in advance; no visits are allowed on Monday.

The entrance to Bucharest's **Botanical Garden** is on the northern side of Şoseaua Cotroceni, a little further east. Originally part of the Cotroceni palace park (1860-66), the gardens were replanted in the university grounds in the 1870s and finally relocated to the present site in 1884. The gardens – spread over 17 hectares and home to some 20,000 plant species from all over Romania – are open daily, but the **Botanical Museum & greenhouse** is only open Tuesday, Thursday and Sunday between 9 am and 1 pm; admission to the gardens is US$0.15.

Heading back east towards the centre along Şoseaua Cotroceni/Str Mircea Vulcănescu, you pass the **National Military Museum** (Muzeul Militar Naţional; ☎ 637 3830, 638 7630) at Str Mircea Vulcănescu 125-127. As with most museums in the country, the history of the Romanian army comes to an abrupt halt at WWII. The museum is open weekdays from 9 am to 5 pm; admission is US$0.50. From here, if you bear south along Calea Plevnei, you eventually come to the **Opera House** (Opera Română; ☎ 613 1857, 615 7939). A **statue** of George Enescu, whose opera *Oedipus* was premiered here, stands in front of the building.

Close by, opposite the university hospital, is a giant half-built edifice which Ceauşescu ordered to be built in 1984 to house his tomb and the National History museum. Since building work stopped in 1989, local authorities have scratched their heads over what to do with it; if enough cash is ever raised (an unlikely option) the plan is to move the national radio station into it.

Northern Bucharest

The pleasant, tree-lined **Şoseaua Kiseleff**, with its elegant mansions and beautifully tended lawns and flower beds, stretches north from Piaţa Victoriei to Herăstrău park in the north of the city. At its most southern end is the **Museum of the Romanian Peasant** (Muzeul Tăranului Român; ☎ 650 5360) at Şoseaua Kiseleff 3. Built on the site of Bucharest's former Mint and Mavrogheni Palace, a small textile museum opened here in 1875. In 1953, following immense success as host of major international folk art exhibitions, the museum was shut down by the post-war communist government who turned the building into a **Museum of the Communist Party History & Revolutionary Democratic Movement**. It was not until 1990, following the closure of the Communist Party museum, that the Romanian Peasant museum returned to its original premises. The museum today houses Romania's largest collection of peasant treasures, including an 18,000-piece pottery collection. An 18th century wooden church stands in the grounds of the museum which is open daily, except Monday, from 10 am to 6 pm. Opposite the peasants' museum on Şoseaua Kiseleff is a **Museum of Geology** (Muzeul Geologie), open daily, except Monday, from 10 am to 6 pm.

During the communist era Şoseaua Kiseleff was the most prestigious residential area in the city, parts of it reserved strictly for Communist Party officials (*nomenklatura*). Nicolae and Elena Ceauşescu, had their private residence, **Primăvera Palace**, at Blvd Primăverii 50. To get here from Piaţa Charles de Gaulle (Metro: Piaţa Aviatorilor), walk north-east along Blvd Primăverii to the corner of Blvd Mircea Eliade. The Ceauşescu mansion is on the south-western, right-hand corner. The palace today is reserved for state guests and dignitaries and there is always a guard at the gate.

Just across Blvd Mircea Eliade from the entrance to Ceauşescu's mansion is the **former residence** of Gheorghe Gheorghiu-Dej, Romania's communist ruler until Ceauşescu took over in 1965.

Piaţa Charles de Gaulle, formerly Piaţa Aviatorilor, was renamed in early 1997 to mark the visit of French president Jacques Chirac to Bucharest. Some 500m west of the square is the **Triumphal Arch** (Arcul de Triumf). Its resemblance to the Arc de Triomphe in Paris was intentional and gives some evidence of the strength of French-Romanian cultural ties prior to WWI. The 11m-tall arch, constructed from reinforced concrete and granite mined in Deva was built between 1935 and 1936 to commemorate the reunification of Romania in 1918.

The sites of the battles in which the Roma-

nian front fought in WWI are inscribed inside the arch and King Ferdinand and Queen Marie feature on its southern façade. A makeshift triumphal monument allegedly made from cardboard and wood had been erected on the site in 1878 to mark the achievement of Romanian independence the previous year. In 1922 a new wooden structure was hastily thrown up in time for King Ferdinand's triumphant entry into the city as the first king of a united Greater Romania. The arch was so equally ludicrous that composer George Enescu was motivated to write to the city mayor, demanding to know when, in fact, a 'real' triumphal arch would be erected.

On Calea Dorobanţilor, near Piaţa Charles de Gaulle, is the headquarters of **Romanian Television**. In the late 1980s, the TV was reduced to a mere two hours air-time, one devoted to presidential activities. In December 1989 revolutionaries broke into the television building and announced the collapse of the government on air. Bullet holes from the fighting still pockmark the building. In front of it is a small **memorial** to those killed here.

A short walk north from the arch along Şoseaua Kiseleff is one of Bucharest's best sights, the **Village Museum** (Muzeul Satului; ☎ 617 1732, 617 5929, 222 9110), which contains full-scale displays of nearly 300 churches, wooden houses, windmills, roadside crosses and farm buildings. Established in 1936, it is one of the largest and oldest outdoor museums in Europe, and should *not* be missed if you don't plan to travel to Romania's more rural regions. It is open daily between May and October, except Monday, from 9 am to 8 pm, and from November to April, daily, except Monday, from 9 am to 5 pm. Admission is US$1.50. The main entrance to the museum is at Şoseaua Kiseleff 28-30; the northern entrance opens into Herăstrău park (see Parks & Lakes later in this chapter).

North-west of the village museum at Blvd Expoziţiei is the **Exhibition Pavilion & Conference Centre**, home to the Romanian EXPO. The modern **World Trade Centre**, housing a fashionable shopping mall and five-star hotel, stands on the same site.

At its northern end, Şoseaua Kiseleff splays out into Piaţa Presei Libere, on the northern side of which stands Bucharest's giant **Press House** (Casă Presei Libere), a Stalinist, wedding-cake structure dating to 1956. Until 1990 the house was officially called the 'House of the Sparks' (Casă Scânteii); behind closed doors it was known as the 'House of Lies'. The red marble pedestal on which a **statue of Lenin** stood is still in front of the building; Lenin was immediately levelled following the 1989 revolution and dumped in the grounds of Mogoşoaia estate (see Around Bucharest later in this chapter). North-east of the square at Str Dr Nicolae Minovici 3 is the **Minovici Museum of Ancient Western Arts** (Muzeul de Artă Veche; ☎ 657 1505), housed in an English-style castle; open daily from 9 am to 5 pm.

Jewish Bucharest

Little remains of the old **Jewish quarter** of Vacareşti, north-east of Piaţa Unirii in Bucharest's historic heart. During the Iron Guard's fascist pogrom, entire streets of houses were burnt to the ground, synagogues looted and Jewish-run business razed. What remained of the quarter's narrow cobbled streets, small wooden houses, synagogues and schools was levelled in the mid-1980s to make way for Ceauşescu's civic centre.

Jewish merchants and traders first settled in Bucharest in the 16th century. By 1861 more than 6000 Jews – mainly from Russia, Turkey and Balkan regions south of the Danube – lived in the capital. There were around 30 synagogues at this time. Mounting anti-Semitism in the latter part of the 19th century, coupled with increasing internal conflicts within the Jewish community, prompted many Jews to leave Bucharest. As early as 1801, an estimated 100 Jews died during anti-Semitic riots. Nevertheless, on the eve of WWII, there were an estimated 95,000 Jews in Bucharest and 80 working synagogues.

The **Jewish History Museum** (Muzeul de Istorie al Comunitaţilor Evreişti dîn Română), is housed in the former tailors' synagogue at Str Mămulari 3. It dates to 1850 and is one of just three of Bucharest's pre-WWII synagogues to survive. Its centrepiece is a moving sculpture of a mourning woman, in memory of the estimated 100 to 150,000 Jews who were deported to hard-labour camps in Transdniestr (see Moldova chapter), and the 200,000 from Transylvania who died in Auschwitz. Six candles burn in tribute to the six million Jews killed during the Holocaust. The museum is open on Wednesday and Sunday from 9.30 am to 1 pm. Admission is US$0.50.

Close by at Str Vineri 9 is the **Choral Temple**, built in 1857 and still serving Bucharest's remaining Jewish community of 8000. Its magnificent Moorish turrets, choir loft and organ remain intact. The **Federation of Jewish Communities** (☎ 613 2538) in Romania is also based here. A **memorial** to the victims of the Holocaust, put up in 1991, stands in front of the temple. A third, smaller synagogue close to Piaţa Amzei on Str Take Ionescu, is no longer in use.

The main **Sephardic Jewish Cemetery** (Cimitrul Evreisc de rit Sefard) lies opposite Belu cemetery (see following section) on Calea Şerban Vodă, in the south of the city (Metro: Eroii Revoluţiei). Two rows of graves date to 21-23 January, 1941, marking the Iron Guard's pogrom against the Jewish community in Bucharest, during which at least 170 Jews were murdered. Monuments representing various villages and towns in Romania stand in memory of 185,000 Jews from northern Bucovina and Bessarabia killed in death camps in Transdniestr.

Belu Cemetery

The main city cemetery, Belu Cemetery (Cimitrul Belu), borders the south-western edge of the Youth park. Amid the vast sea of graves lie those of some of Romania's most notable writers and poets, including the 20th century comic playwright and humorist, Ion Luca Caragiale (1852-1912); novelist Ion Liviu Rebreanu (1885-1944); Moldavian-born writer and historian Mihail Sadoveanu

(1880-1961); and national poet Mihai Eminescu (1850-89). Eminescu's grave is on the northern side of plot No 9 – sadly, his dying wish to be buried under a lime tree did not come to pass. A plan of the cemetery and a list of some of the people buried in it is posted on a board at the main entrance in Calea Şerban Vodă.

The heroes of the 1989 revolution are buried in the **Heroes' Cemetery** (Cimitrul Eroii Revoluţiei) at the northern end of Belu cemetery. Since 1993 the Orthodox church in Romania has been struggling to find the cash to finish building the new **Martyrs' Church** (Biserica Eroilor Martiri) which stands, half-complete, in the Heroes' cemetery; it should open by 1998.

The post-war communist leader Gheorghe Gheorghiu-Dej who died of cancer in 1965 after ruling Romania for two decades, is buried in the modest **military section** of Belu cemetery.

Parks & Lakes

The lush, well-kept parks and not-so-clear-blue lakes in Bucharest's suburbs provide a welcome escape from the hustle and bustle of the city. To the north lies Herăstrău lake, surrounded by Bucharest's largest park; to the south is the Youth park and Carol I park; and just west of the centre close to Piaţa Universităţii are Cişmigiu gardens (Grădină Cişmigiu), dubbed the 'lovers' park'.

You can rent boats and swim in **Herăstrău lake** which stretches almost the entire width of the city from east to west, north of Piaţa Charles de Gaulle (Metro: Piaţa Aviatorilor). The surrounding 200-hectare pleasure park opened in 1936. Indoor bowling enthusiasts and billiard fans should hit Club Champion (☎ 222 9321), in the small **amusement complex** bordering the south-western edge of the park at Şoseaua Kiseleff 32. Bowling/billiards cost US$4/1.50 an hour and the complex is open 24 hours. From Club Champion steps lead to the western shores of Herăstrău lake. From the small landings here, you can cross or circle the lake in a cruising boat. Two boats sail daily between May and October. To take the 10 minute,

return crossing (US$0.50), go to the landing marked 'traversari vaporase'. The circular, 30 minute cruise (US$1.40) leaves from the central landing ('debarcaderu centrul').

Ten kilometres north of Bucharest lies **Băneasa Park**, surrounded by deep forest. The **zoo** (☎ 233 0502), at the southern edge of the park, is open daily from 8 am to 8 pm. Admission is US$0.20; hide your camera at the entrance to avoid paying the US$2.50 photography fee. Fast-food kiosks and huts cooking traditional Romanian spicy sausages *(mititei)* are plentiful. To reach the park from the centre, take bus No 301 from Piaţa Romană.

The park and circus is a 10 minute walk from the Obor metro stop. Alternatively take tram No 34 one stop westbound along Şoseaua Ştefan cel Mare. Scattered throughout this quiet park is a unique collection of **sculpted wooden caricatures**, entitled 'Wooden Spirits' (Spirite în Lemn). The totem pole style sculptures, the work of local sculptor Titi Teodorescu, are carved from the trunks of trees that have died in the park. A peasant *(ţăran)*, a mother and child *(mama şi copii)*, lovers *(îndrăgosti)*, a monkey *(maimuţă)* and an elephant *(elefant)*, along with Pinocchio, Superman and opera tenor Luciano Pavarotti, are just some of the 'spirits' to haunt the park.

Equally central are the historic **Cişmigiu Gardens**, Bucharest's oldest park, dating from the early 19th century. The pretty gardens were landscaped in classical English style by a gardener from Berlin. You can rent rowing boats.

The **Youth park** (Parcul Tineretului; Metro: Tineretului), at the southern limits of the city centre, is a popular haunt for city dwellers in summer. You can rent rowing boats from the small boathouse on the north-eastern shores of the lake in the centre of the park, which, despite its murky waters, people still swim in. Cycling paths circle the lake. Sporting events, fashion shows, conferences and open-air concerts take place in the **Sports & Culture Palace** (Palatul Sporturilorşi Culturii; ☎ 330 2820; fax 615 3985) in the centre of the park. The **Carol I**

park, a five minute walk north-east of the youth park on Calea Şerban Vodă, was inaugurated in 1906. An eternal flame burns in memory of the unknown soldier and bands play regularly in the bandstand. The centrepiece of the park is a 20m-tall **mausoleum**, built in 1958 from Black Norwegian granite and topped with five arches of red Swedish granite. It was put up in memory of 'the Heroes of the Struggle for the People's and the Homeland's Liberty, for Socialism'. Until 1991 Gheorghe Gheorghiu-Dej was buried beneath the arches along with other early Romanian communists. In 1991 the mausoleum was disinterned.

Since then indecision has surrounded the future of the communist monstrosity which remains guarded by police today. The Romanian Orthodox Church announced in 1997 that it intended to build the country's largest Orthodox cathedral in the park, the bell of which will hang from the arches. From the mausoleum, stairs lead north through the park to a square where you get to tree-lined Str 11 Iunie; this brings you into Blvd George Coşbuc and Piaţa Unirii.

Pantelimon Park (Parcul Pantelimon; Metro: Piaţa Iancului) has been earmarked for even grander plans. According to recent press reports, a giant, 9.2 hectare amusement park is to be built around the lake by the year 2000. The complex, which is estimated to cost around US$20 million, will include hotels, restaurants, shops and amusements which its ambitious Canadian-American investors say will compete with EuroDisney in Paris.

Art Galleries

Contemporary art exhibitions are held in the Galeriile de Artă at Str Academiei 15; the Casă Memorială Cornel Mederea at Str General Budişteanu 16; Căminul Artei at Str Biserica Enei 16; Klaus & Andrew's Galerie de Artă inside the national history museum at Calea Victoriei 118; Galerie de Artă Eforie at Str Eforie 4-6; the Galerie Dominus Practică and Galerie Naţională de Artă Apollo, both inside the National Theatre at

Blvd Nicolae Bălcescu 2; and Dominvszart inside the adjacent opera theatre.

Galerie Catacomba, tucked in the catacombs of the art collection museum at Calea Victoriei 111, is one of Bucharest's finest galleries; it is open daily, except Monday and Tuesday, from 10 am to 7 pm.

Activities

You can swim, have a sauna, or work-out at Ceauşescu's former private club, Clubul Ilie Năstase (☎ 679 6385; fax 312 9970), named after the Romanian tennis champion, at Blvd Mircea Eliade 1 overlooking Herăstrău lake. It is open daily, except Monday, from 12.30 to 4.30 pm and from 8 pm to midnight. The Hotel Bucureşti and Hotel Parc (see Places to Stay) have outdoor swimming pools which are open to non-guests.

The karting club Automobilism şi Karting (☎ 222 4123; fax 222 4124) has its headquarters at Blvd Banul Manta 21. Cycling enthusiasts should contact the Cycling Society (☎ 615 9194; fax 312 7042) at Str Academiei 2. The Canotaj rowing club (☎ & fax 211 5566) and the Kayak canoeing club (☎ & fax 211 5576) both have an office inside the Ministry of Sports at Str Vasile Conta 16.

Many national clubs and organisations which organise various activities in other regions in the country – caving, climbing, mountaineering, orienteering, off-roading, fishing – have an office in Bucharest.

Language Courses

The private language school, Fiatest Centru Educational (☎ 312 2104, 613 1880; fax 312 2106), Str General Berthelot 24, offers private and group tuition in Romanian, German, French, Italian and English. Romanian classes for up to five people cost US$10 an hour. The school also has branches in Braşov, Sibiu, Baia Mare and Cluj.

The French Institute (see Information – Cultural Centres) offers French and Romanian courses from 1 September to 1 July; courses consist of 10 hours of group tuition a week.

The PROSPER-ASE Language (☎ & fax

211 7800; email muresan@eurisc.iiruc.ro) is sponsored by the British Council and upon special request can arrange Romanian courses. It's at Calea Griviţei 2-2a.

Organised Tours

Practically every travel agency in town organises city tours and day trips around Bucharest (see Information – Travel Agencies). The Transylvanian Society of Dracula (☎ 222 5195; fax 312 3056; ☎ & fax 679 5742), opposite Ceauşescu's villa at Blvd Primăverii 47, arranges Dracula tours, some more spooky than others. The 'Classic Dracula Tour' and the 'Twilight Zone Dracula Tour' start in Bucharest (see Getting Around – Organised Tours at the front of the book). Bookings can also be made in Bucharest through Romantic Travel (☎ & fax 312 3056, 638 9144), Str Mămulari 4.

Special Events

Bucharest plays host to numerous theatre and music festivals. Annual events worth attending include:

last weekend in May
: *Bucharest Carnival* – a week-long carnival with street-dancers, street-theatres, folk-dancers dressed in 1900 period costume and live bands performing in Bucharest's historic heart

mid-June
: *Dreher Beer Festival* – four day beer festival with live bands, drinking contests and the like in Herăstrău park

21 June
: *Feşte de la Musique* – annual French music festival organised by the French Institute

1 August
: *Hora Festival* – three day dance festival attracting traditional folk dance troops from all over the country; held in the village museum

15 August
: *Craftsman's Fair* – local craft fair hosted by the village museum with guest crafters from all over Romania

September
: *International George Enescu Music Festival* – held every two years, last held in 1997, attracting musicians from all over the world

October
: *National Theatre Festival* – a week-long theatre festival held every year in the national theatre

last week of October
: *St Dimitrie Day* – a two day carnival celebrating Bucharest's patron saint

Places to Stay – bottom end

Gone are the dark days when you needed a pre-paid hotel coupon to guarantee a room for the night. Staying in Bucharest is exactly the same as staying anywhere else in the world. Budget accommodation can get fully booked, especially in summer. Most staff at hotel receptions will ask to see your passport when you check in; some may want to keep your passport for the duration of your stay. If you tell them you need it to change money, they will happily return it to you. Do this even if you do not want to change money!

Private Rooms ANTREC (☎ 615 3276, 615 3206), inside the Lar Tours travel agency at Str Ştirbei Vodă 2-4, arranges private rooms in villages surrounding Bucharest for around US$10 per person a night. Hopefully it will extend its service in the future to cover the city too.

The ONT tourist office arranges private rooms at US$25 per person. This does not usually include breakfast. Room quality varies considerably; if you're not satisfied with what you get, go back and ask for something else. Ask to be shown exactly where it is on the map before you agree; most rooms are in the southern suburbs.

Occasionally people at the station or on the street outside offer private rooms. Evaluate these people carefully; ask them to point out the location of their rooms on a map and do not hand over any cash – or your passport – until you have seen the room and are satisfied.

Campuses Theoretically it is possible to book a room in advance in one of the university student dormitories. In reality however, the procedure is so bureaucratic that most travellers will run out of patience before receiving a response from the relevant authority. The best student dorms are just off Calea Victoriei at Str Mihai Moxa 11. Bookings must be made in writing, in advance, and in Romanian only, to the academy director (☎ 659 2463), Strada Mihai Moxa 11, Bucureşti RO-76021. A bed for the night is US$1 per person.

Hostels Backpackers should head straight for the *Villa Helga* hostel (☎ 610 2214), brilliantly located five minutes from Piaţa Romană at Str Salcâmilor 2. Housed in a spacious villa with a wonderful, vine-covered terrace, it is one of the most homey places to stay in Romania. The hostel is run by a young, dynamic team who go out of their way to make travellers feel at home. It has hot water round-the-clock, cable TV, tons of tourist guides/reference books, and offers laundry and locally produced Carpaţi cigarettes for free. A bed in a two, eight or 10-bed room costs US$12 a night. Take bus Nos 79, 86 or 133 from Gara de Nord to Piaţa Galaţi; or bus No 783 from Otopeni airport to Bâneasa airport and then tram No 5.

Hotels Euro Service Amerom has an office at Otopeni airport (☎ & fax 322 5829) and at Str Radu Cristian 6 in central Bucharest (☎ 230 0022, extension 1567; 322 7420) and arranges accommodation in a variety of bottom-end hotels at slightly lower rates than the hotels offer.

Around Gara de Nord is a cluster of cheap hotels. As you exit the station, walk 30m to the right for the noisy but surprisingly clean *Hotel Bucegi* (☎ 637 5225), at Str Witing 2. Single rooms have shared bath and cost US$6. Doubles with/without bath are good value at US$10/11. All triple and four-bed rooms have private bath and cost US$13/14. Breakfast is not included.

Across the street, the recently renovated *Hotel Cerna* (☎ 637 4087; fax 311 0721), Blvd Dinicu Golescu 29, charges US$7/12 for a single/double with shared bath, and US$17/23 for a single/double with private bath. It also has apartments for US$35 a night. Again, breakfast is not included in the price but the adjoining and modern Cofetârie Ema serves good cakes and pastries daily from 8 am to 8 pm.

To the left of the station is *Hotel Dunârea*

(☎ 222 9820; fax 222 9822) at Calea Griviţei 140. The 'Danube' is a bit dingy but rooms are good value at US$11/17/24 for singles/doubles/triples with private bath. The noisy trams rattling along the street outside late at night can be a nuisance. Further down the same street is the even dingier, 59-room *Hotel Griviţa* (☎ 650 2327) at Calea Griviţei 130. Singles/doubles with shared bath are US$6/10 a night. The bar is smoky and off-putting, and women travelling solo should head elsewhere.

Two blocks down, and around the corner to the left, is *Hotel Marna* (☎ 650 6820) at Str Buzeşti 3. It's overpriced at US$25/37 with bath.

Places to Stay – middle
There are lots of worn-out 2nd-class hotels in Bucharest and it's usually no problem finding a room, even in midsummer. Avoid accepting a room that faces a busy road, and check whether breakfast is included in the price. There are two clusters of middle-range hotels: one around the train station and another in the city centre.

Around Gara de Nord The one-star *Hotel Astoria* (☎ 637 7640; fax 638 2690), close to the train station at Blvd Dinicu Golescu 27, deserves far more stars than the paltry one it has. The hotel has been renovated in recent years and is quite luxurious, attracting business travellers as well as backpackers. Singles/doubles with private bath are not bad value at US$35/57, including breakfast.

At the time of writing the *Hotel Nord* next to the bus station on Calea Griviţei was under renovation.

In the Centre At Piaţa Mihail Kogâlniceanu 2, facing a busy roundabout, is *Hotel Veneţia* (☎ 615 9149). You'll pay US$25/43 for a single/double with bath. The entrance to quiet *Hotel Dâmboviţa* (☎ 615 6244), Blvd Schitu Mâgureanu 6, is actually off Str Gutenberg. It costs US$21/34 without bath, US$25/42 with bath.

Some rooms at *Hotel Opera* (☎ 323 6065), Str Brezoianu 37, have sweeping views over the park, so ask for one. The price is US$28/38 with bath. A short walk away is *Hotel Carpaţi* (☎ 615 7690), at Str Matei Millo 16. It's the nicest in the area, is fully equipped with TV and phone, and costs US$25/40 with bath. Much less exciting is nearby *Hotel Palas* (☎ 615 3710), Str Constantin Mille 18, at US$21/28 without bath, US$35/60 with bath. *Hotel Muntenia* (☎ 614 6010, 614 1783; fax 714 1782) at Str Academiei 19-21 is noisy but has a great location near the university. It costs US$25 for a single room with shared bath. Double rooms with private bathroom are US$50. Breakfast is not included although the hotel has a deal with the nearby Pasajul Victoriei restaurant.

Quite good value is the aptly named *Hotel Central* (☎ 312 1549; ☎ & fax 615 5637), well located at Str Brezoianu 13. Despite the decrepit sign hanging outside, the rooms inside are more than adequate. The doubles on the less expensive 5th floor have been redecorated less recently than those on the lower floors and cost around US$35. Doubles on the other floors cost US$50. Solo travellers simply get a double room with a 20% discount.

Doubles with/without private shower cost US$75/40 a night at the small, 21-room *Hotel Banat* (☎ 613 1056; fax 312 6547), close to Piaţa Universitǎţii at Piaţa Rosetti 5. Doubles with bath start at US$100. Don't be put off by the Lady Puf Showgirls snack bar immediately next door; it's not part of the hotel. Nearby at Str Dr Emanuel Bacaloglu 2 is the small *Hotel Batişte* (☎ 614 0880, 614 9022; fax 614 0887). Singles/doubles with shared bath are US$35/42. The hotel, in a quiet location, is usually fully booked.

Among the most idyllic places to stay in town (despite its adjoining rip-off restaurant) is the 52-bed, two-star *Hanul lui Manuc* (☎ 613 1415; fax 312 2811), housed in a 19th century merchants' inn bang in Bucharest's historic centre at Blvd Iuliu Maniu 62-64. Single/double rooms with private bath start at US$45/53 a night. Staff can be a bit surly.

North of the Centre Heading north towards the Triumphal Arc at Şoseaua Kiseleff 12 is

the elegant, two-star *Hotel Triumf* (☎ 222 3172; fax 223 2411) with singles/doubles for US$38/56 a night. The hotel grounds are superb.

East of the Press House on Blvd Poligrafiei are two towering concrete blocks, housing the two-star *Hotel Parc* (☎ 222 8480; fax 222 5938) at No 3, and the one-star *Hotel Turist* (☎ 222 8450; fax 222 8315) at No 5. The Parc charges US$31/47, including breakfast. Its outdoor swimming pool can be used by non-guests too (admission US$1.50). Ask for a room on one of the upper floors to escape the disco beat. Rooms at the Turist are cheaper – and quieter – at US$14/23. Triples cost US$30. The price includes breakfast.

Places to Stay – top end
All of Bucharest's upmarket hotels accept Visa/MasterCard, have multilingual staff, include breakfast in their nightly rates, and have a restaurant specialising in European cuisine.

In the Centre The attractive, 83-room *Hotel Minerva* (☎ 650 6010, 311 1550; fax 312 2734), Str Gheorghe Manu 2-4 near Piaţa Romanǎ has telephones and cable TV in every room. The cost is US$118/147 with bath. It is bright, clean and modern.

The four-star *Hotel Lido* (☎ 614 4930; fax 312 6544) at Str CA Rosetti 1 is a fine 1930s building with all mod cons inside. Singles/doubles cost US$220/240. A luxury apartment is US$345 a night. Room rates drop by 10% at weekends. A 22-storey, 130m-tall glass building housing the five-star hotel, the *Hotel Star Lido & Conference Centre*, is currently being built behind the Hotel Lido on Blvd General Magheru; it will open in 1999.

Similarly priced is the *Hotel Ambasador* (☎ 615 9080; fax 312 3595) on the opposite side of the street at Blvd General Magheru 8-10. The hotel caters largely to Bucharest's visiting business community. Close by at Blvd Nicolae Bǎlcescu 4 is the top of the range – in luxury and height – *Hotel Inter-*

Continental (☎ 210 7330; fax 312 0486). It has 423 rooms, 27 suites, 24 hour room service, a health club, nightclub, casino and gourmet restaurants to satisfy the most insatiable appetite! Not-so-simple singles/doubles cost US$230/274; the luxury equivalents are US$256/274. A two-room suite with two bathrooms costs US$390; breakfast is an American-style buffet.

Along Calea Victoriei are hotels offering slightly more competitive rates. Doubles start at US$200 at the *Hotel Bucureşti* (☎ 312 7070, 633 525; fax 312 0927, 312 1047), Calea Victoriei 63-81; the hotel has a fitness club and one of the few outdoor swimming pools in town (admission US$3.50). The *Hotel Continental* (☎ 312 0132, 638 5022; fax 312 0134) at Calea Victoriei 56 has singles/doubles for US$150/190 and luxury suites for US$250. The *Hotel Majestic* (☎ 210 2746; fax 311 3363) close by at Str Academiei 11, has singles/doubles for US$195/240, suites for US$290 and apartments for US$310. All prices include breakfast. Cheaper still is the three-star *Hotel Capitol* (☎ 615 8030; fax 312 4169), one of the few top hotels to list their prices in lei (most list them in US dollars). Simple singles/doubles/triples cost around US$75/85/150. Luxury singles/doubles cost in the region of US$85/110, including breakfast.

East of Piaţa Romană at Calea Dorobanţilor 1-7 is *Hotel Dorobanţi* (☎ 211 5450; fax 210 0150) which has single/double rooms for US$103/129. The hotel stocks one of the most comprehensive ranges of English-language newspapers and magazines in Bucharest.

Steeped in history is the five-star *Athenee Palace Hilton* (☎ 315 1212; fax 315 2121), housed in the restored 1914 Athenee Palace hotel at Str Episcopiei 1-3. Heavily damaged during the 1989 revolution, the building has been completely restored by the Hilton hotel group over the past three years. The exquisite glass-dome ceiling in the banquet hall in particularly impressive. Single/double rooms cost US$310/350. Luxury suites on the even plusher executives' floor start at

US$620. The hotel has a restaurant, coffee shop and English bar.

Standing next to the ministry of defence behind the House of the People on Str Izvor is an ugly, half-built monstrosity which will eventually become the five-star *Hotel Grand*.

North of the Centre *Hotel Helvetia* (☎ 223 0566, 222 8180; fax 223 0567), close to Parcul Herăstrău at Piaţa Charles de Gaulle 13, is a bright, modern building with singles/doubles costing US$188/235.

US president Bill Clinton stayed at the *Hotel Sofitel* (☎ 223 4000, 212 2998; fax 222 4650), adjoining the World Trade Centre at Blvd Expoziţiei 2, when he was in town in mid-1997. Some of Bucharest's most expensive, elegant and luxurious hotel rooms are US$200/305 for a single/double. The in-house Darclée restaurant specialises in French and Romanian cuisine.

Places to Eat

Restaurants Dining out in Bucharest is not cheap. There has been a rapid influx of flashy, upmarket restaurants offering a dazzling array of international cuisine with prices to match. However, it is still easy to track down traditional Romanian cooking – generally at a less painful price. Even places which purport to be Turkish, Spanish or Greek will generally have at least one local dish on the menu.

Reservations are not needed in most restaurants. Practically all the upmarket places accept Visa/MasterCard.

Near Piaţa Revoluţiei One of Bucharest's best spots is *Bistro Ateneu* (☎ 613 4900), Str Episcopiei opposite the Ateneul Român. The high-quality food and friendly, 'Frenchy' atmosphere draw large crowds; a violin and keyboard duo plays most evenings. Make a reservation or be prepared to squeeze in at the bar. Food is served until 1 am; particularly good value is the self-service, fill-your-bowl-as-high-as-you-can salad bar costing a mere US$1.40.

The *Ristorante Italiano Business Club* (☎ 312 0143), close to the Hotel București in a dusty back alley at Str Nicolae Crețulescu 14, serves a wide range of salads, pasta and other Italian-inspired delights in a pretty uninspired setting at the bottom of a flashy, mirrored staircase. A simple mixed salad – naked lettuce, cucumber and tomato to be exact – costs US$2. It is open daily from 1 pm to 1 am.

Close by is the best pizza restaurant in town – *Casă Veche* (☎ 615 7897) at Str George Enescu 15-17 – which serves a mind-boggling array of authentic Italian pizzas. Some members of the staff here can apparently down an entire pizza measuring 112cm in diameter and five regular-sized pizzas in 53 seconds! Luckily they don't expect their clientele to eat quite so fast! The restaurant is open daily from 11 am until the last customer leaves.

Restaurant Menuet, behind the Ateneul Român at Str Nicolae Golescu 14, is a simple cellar restaurant serving average food at average prices. The *Minion Restaurant* on the corner of Calea Victoriei and Str Piața Amzei is a small green restaurant which sports a cabaret show from 10 pm until 4 am; food is served any time between 10 am and 11 pm.

West of Piața Revoluției at Str Ştirbei Vodă 2-4 is *Velvet* (☎ 615 9241), an expensive but classy restaurant, great for a corporate bank account. It is open daily from noon to 4 pm, and from 7 pm to midnight. Close by at Str General Berthelot 24 is the far more reasonable *Hanul Maramureş*. Set in a modern wooden house typical of the Maramureş region, the inn serves traditional Romanian dishes and local beers in a rustic setting. You can eat here for around US$3 – be sure to sink at least one fiery *palincă* (plum brandy) while you're at it.

Tucked inside the atmospheric Pasajul Victoriei, south of Piața Revoluției off Calea Victoriei, is the *Pasajul Victoriei* restaurant. The vibrance of this tiny alley makes eating here an enjoyable experience although unsavoury types sometimes lurk late at night.

Around Piața Universității *Le Premier* (☎ 312 4397), which is behind the Hotel Inter-Continental and National Theatre at Str Tudor Arghezi 16, is considered to be Bucharest's finest restaurant – at least by the city's expat community. A drink on its covered terrace is a must, even if you cannot afford to eat here. It is open daily from 10 to 2 am. For a panoramic view of the square, catch the lift to *Balada* on the 21st floor of the Hotel Inter-Continental. Be warned; this hotel restaurant is expensive and you might well feel a bit of a misfit in jeans. It is open daily from 7 pm onwards.

Founded in 1852, *Casă Capşa* (☎ 613 4482), a short walk west of Piața Universității at Calea Victoriei 36, has long been Bucharest's most prestigious bohemian hang-out, attracting a glittering crowd of the city's elite literati since 1852. It is open daily from 12.30 pm to midnight.

Hanul lui Manuc (literally 'Manuc's Inn'; ☎ 613 1415), an 1812 inn in the old city at Str Iuliu Maniu 62, is a rip-off. The old-world atmosphere is great, the terrace overlooking a courtyard the best in Bucharest, and there is no doubt that tourists love it. But be warned! The waiters are surly, bolshy, and bring you whatever dish they fancy then shrug their shoulders stupidly when you complain that it is not what you ordered. To add insult to injury, items on the menu are priced per 100g, meaning your final bill is at least five times more (around US$10 a head without alcohol). Have a drink here but nothing more. Apparently, the original 19th century owner was poisoned by a fortune-teller who had to murder him to make his prophecy – that the inn-keeper would die – come true. Hanul lui Manuc is open daily from 7 am to midnight. The restaurant closes at 8 pm and does not accept credit cards on Sunday.

Don't be overawed by the lavish decor at the Gothic-style *Caru cu Bere* (☎ 613 7560), Bucharest's oldest and most ornate beer hall, dating from 1875 at Str Stavropoleos 3. The traditional Romanian dishes are among the cheapest in town – stuffed vine leaves *(sarmele)* are US$0.80 and meat dishes start at US$1. Roma bands play from noon onwards; it is open daily from 10 to 1 am.

The stylish *Café de Paris* (☎ 312 7013), part of a worldwide American-run chain, at Str Jean Louis Calderon 33, serves tantalising French-inspired dishes including steak with lobster for US$25 and tiger prawns with Pernod sauce for US$14. Lunchtime salads, grilled sandwiches and pastas start at US$5. It is open Monday to Saturday from 11.30 to 3 am, Sunday from 10.30 am.

Equally refined is *Da Vinci* (☎ 312 2494), a cool, calm and collected Italian restaurant-cum-café serving a small selection of cakes and light savoury snacks inside a small shopping mall at Str Ion Câmpineanu 11. It is open daily from noon to midnight.

South-east of Piaţa Universităţii at Str Histro Botev 18-20 is Bucharest's only Turkish restaurant. The *Golden Falcon Casă Chebab* (☎ 614 2825, 613 2833) serves delicious Turkish food. The pita bread is so large it won't fit on your plate. A full meal costs around US$5. The restaurant is open daily from noon to midnight. Reservations are recommended at weekends. Further east along Blvd Republicii, at Blvd Carol I 76, is the elegant *Transilvania Club* (☎ 615 1933), open daily from noon to 3 am. The *Dragon Palace* (☎ 018-600 583) at Blvd Carol I 96, is as Chinese as you can find with the menu and signs outside, all written in Chinese.

The *China House* (☎ 613 0650) at Blvd Nicolae Bălcescu 25, is an atmospheric place for above-average Chinese food. Main courses cost about US$5. Visa is accepted; it is open daily from noon to 1 am. The *Salt & Pepper* bar bistro (☎ 312 3717), which is at Str Ion Câmpineanu 2 opposite the Hotel Inter-Continental, serves breakfast from 7.30 am. It also serves wholesome homemade meals such as potato musaka for US$2.40, boiled beef for US$3 and chicken curry for US$3.50. A good choice of salads starts at US$1 and the coffee is excellent. *Dunărea* (literally 'Danube'), a couple of doors down, is a restaurant-cum-cabaret bar open 24 hours.

Heading north from Piaţa Universităţii up Blvd Nicolae Bălcescu towards Piaţa Romană, you come to the Greek-inspired *Élysée* (☎ 659 7522) at Blvd Nicolae Bălcescu 29. Live bands often play in this popular basement restaurant-cum-bar, open daily from 10 am to midnight.

Piaţa Romană & Around Backpackers seeking wholesome cheap food should head straight for *Nicoreşti*, close to the Villa Helga hostel on the corner of Str Maria Rosetti and Str Toamnei. It only serves Romanian dishes, costing no more than US$1 each. It's open daily from 10 am to 10 pm.

One of the most enticing terrace restaurants in this area is the *Casă Oamenilor de Ştiinţă Grădină de Vară* (COS; ☎ 210 1284), housed in the lush gardens of the late 19th century Scientists' House, close to Hotel Dorobanţi at Piaţa Alexandru Lahovari 9. It is open daily from noon to midnight.

Equally favoured for its unique atmosphere is the upmarket Italian restaurant, *Il Gattopardo* (☎ 659 7428), named after the famous Fellini film inside the Writers' Union house (Uniunea Scriitorilor) close to Hotel Bucureşti at Calea Victoriei 115. Authentic Italian dishes by Italian chefs start at around US$5 for a main dish. It is open daily from noon to midnight.

Heading east along Blvd Dacia, close to Piaţa Galaţi, is the well recommended *Aquarium* (☎ 211 2820), inside an old villa at Str Alecu Russo 4 (entrance on Blvd Dacia) which specialises in fish and Italian-inspired cuisine; it is open daily from noon until midnight. At the eastern end of the boulevard at Str Mihai Eminescu 185, is the authentic enough *Beijing* Chinese restaurant (☎ 210 2466). Fast service is the name of the game here; it is open daily from 1 to 10 pm.

The *Moldova Grădină de Vară* (☎ 211 3781) at Str Icoanei 2 specialises in typical Moldavian food. It also offers a pricier three course business lunch for US$10. The restaurant is open daily from 10 to 2 am. Close by, on the corner of Str Schitu Darvări and Str Aurel Vlaicu at Str Icoanei 18-20, is the good value *Capriccio Italiano* (☎ 211 5308) which serves good pizza and pasta; it is open daily from noon to midnight.

Special lunch menus are also offered at the upmarket *Grădină Vernescu* which adjoins the *Casă Vernescu* (☎ 659 3442), west of Piaţa Romană at Calea Victoriei 129-133. Particularly appetising is the 'Romanian Corner' (Polţul Românesc) menu for US$10. The restaurant and canopied summer garden is open daily from noon until 12.30 am.

Bucharest's first Chinese restaurant, the *Nan Jing* (☎ 650 6010), north of Piaţa Romană next to the Hotel Minerva at Str Gheorghe Manu 2, serves expensive but exquisite Chinese food. It is also one of the few places in town to have a separate dining room for nonsmokers. West of the square, heading towards the train station at Calea Griviţei is the small and poky – but less expensive – *Hong Kong* (☎ 659 5025). It's open daily from noon to midnight.

North of Piaţa Victoriei *Moby Dick* (☎ 222 4190), a short stroll north-west of Piaţa Victoriei at Blvd Banul Manta 27, is about the only restaurant in town to specialise solely in fish dishes. It has a pretty terrace garden and an indoor restaurant. Its tripe soup *(ciorba de burtă)* is superb. The restaurant is open daily from 9 to 12.30 am.

Il Buogutaio Ristorante (☎ 230 2623) is an upmarket Italian restaurant, inside a luxury shopping mall at Calea Dorobanţilor 172. The restaurant is open daily from noon to 3 am.

At the time of writing, the global chain *TGI Friday* was set to open a restaurant on the corner of Calea Dorobanţilor and Str I Emil Pangratti. *La Belle Blu*, opposite the entrance to Parcul Circului on Şoseaua Ştefan cel Mare, serves a variety of pizzas in a very blue setting; it's open daily from noon to midnight.

Heading north along Şoseaua Kiseleff at No 8 is the elegant *Doina* (☎ 222 3179). Extremely expensive but delicious Romanian dishes are served in its beautiful terrace garden. Service is full-on, but incredibly slow. A full meal without alcohol is about US$15. Further north out of town but well worth the trip is *Doi Cocosi* (☎ 667 1998) at Şoseaua Bucureşti-Târgovişte 6. One of the

first private restaurants to open, its specialities include garlic fried chicken, schnitzel stuffed with mushrooms and a delicious array of homemade cheese. Traditional folk bands play in the summer garden in the evening; it is open daily from noon to 4 am.

Elite (☎ 312 9973), close to Băneasa airport at Str Ficusului 2, is a large but intimate restaurant housed in one of Ceauşescu's former food factories. The nosh is good though, as is the service; it is open daily from 12.30 to 5 pm and from 7.30 pm to midnight.

Piaţa Unirii & Around The *Dorem Steakhouse* on a terrace at Blvd Unirii 13, has karaoke some evenings and offers a wonderful view of the 'big house' at the end of the boulevard; it is open daily from noon to midnight.

Le Petit Paris (☎ 330 3888, 335 4079), behind the Civic Centre at Str George Georgescu 46-48, is a light and airy place, well worth dining in if you fancy a splurge. Typical Romanian dishes – beautifully translated into French! – are listed on the menu as well as mouth-watering French dishes. The restaurant is open daily from noon until the last customer leaves. Opposite, on the corner of Str George Georgescu and Str Gladiolelor, is the cheaper *Grădină Tariştea*.

For dinner by candlelight dine at *Café de Joie*, a small and intimate restaurant tucked down the narrow Str Zarafi, off Str Lipscani. It is difficult to find; the sign outside reads 'bistro'. Close by at the northern end of Str Şelari is the equally romantic *Casă Rapsodia*; walk through the heavily furnished restaurant to get to the pretty summer garden.

South of Piaţa Unirii at Str Budai Deleanu 4 is the spicy *Tandoori* (☎ 335 4247), specialising in Indian cuisine. Business travellers tend to hang out here. It is open daily, except Tuesday, from 9 am to 11 pm.

East of the square at Str Poenaru Bordea 2 is one of Bucharest's most historic restaurants: *Bucur* (☎ 336 1592) was a major hotspot in the 1970s; today it attracts a dwindling crowd, most of whom come for its casino rather than the Romanian food. It is open daily from noon until the early hours.

West of the Centre German beers, fondues and pancakes served with rose-petal jam are just some of the house specialities served at *Bistrot Pierrot* (☎ 223 0258) at Blvd Alexandru Ioan Cuza 73. Run by a Bavarian entrepreneur, this small bistro is always packed; it's open daily from 11 to 1 am.

Close to Cotroceni Palace and the military museum is Bucharest's *Golden Blitz* (☎ 410 5100) on the corner of Str Razorae and Blvd Geniului. Its traditional Italian bruschetta is particularly yummy; the restaurant is open daily from noon to 2 am.

One place which definitely merits a special trip from the centre is *Brădet* (☎ 638 6014) at Str Carol Davila 60. From the Eroilor Metro station walk three blocks south-west down Blvd Eroilor. It serves authentic Lebanese cuisine, cooked by Lebanese chefs. Swill it down with Lebanese wine. Well worth the US$6-8 splurge; it is open daily from noon to 2 am.

Sahib (☎ 410 2223), Calea 13 Septembrie 127-131, is another high-priced spot with Bucharest's best Indian dishes; the chef is of Indian origin. From the House of the People's southern side follow Calea 13 Septembrie to the intersection of Şoseaua Panduri.

Grota Vampirilor (☎ 410 4336; fax 411 1252) at Calea 13 Septembrie 108-122 might well be a glamorous cabaret club with a topless show, but its decor alone is well worth a peek before dark. Sheepskin-lined walls and chairs are strung with spiders, garish masks and other ghosts and ghouls. It is open daily from noon to 2 am.

Pizzeria Magia close by on the corner of Calea 13 Septembrie and Str Sabinelor has a nice terrace – handy if you want a quick bite. It is open daily from 10 am to midnight.

Cafés Some of the best pastries in town can be eaten standing up at the *Patisserie* adjoining the Casă Veche restaurant at Str George Enescu 15-17; it is open Monday to Saturday

from 7 am to 8 pm, and Sunday from 7 am to 1 pm.

The *Caffé Piano* (☎ 312 1068), behind the National Art museum on the corner of Str Ion Câmpineanu and Str Ştirbei Vodă, is a calm and tranquil café. At night it serves an exotic array of cocktails. It is open daily from 10 am until the last customer leaves.

Lacto Vegetarian, close to Hotel Continental at Str Ion Câmpineanu 25, is a small, cheap basement café (mind your head!), which, in spite of its name, caters for the carnivorous-minded too. It's open daily from 10 am until the last customer leaves. Opposite the Hotel Continental on Calea Victoriei is the popular, 24 hour *Terasa Anda*, a sun-filled terrace serving light cheap buns, hot dogs and beer. You'll find some incredibly rich cakes that will please the sweetest tooth at *Cofetăria Victoria*, Calea Victoriei 18. *Cofetăria Ambasador*, next to Hotel Ambasador, Blvd General Magheru 10, serves some of the best coffee and cakes Bucharest has to offer.

The *Cofetăria Diplomat* at Calea Dorobanţilor 20-28 is a clean and bright, indoor café serving freshly-made cakes and pastries and other temptations for the sweet-toothed. It is open Monday to Saturday from 8 am to 8 pm, Sunday from 10 am.

Heading north of Piaţa Victoriei, the highly recommended, French-run *Manhattan Café* (☎ 666 2295) is inside the shopping plaza in the World Trade Centre at Blvd Expoziţiei 22. In the summer it offers an eat-as-much-as-you-can cold lunch buffet for US$3 a head. Its cold tomato soup for US$1 is absolutely delicious and as good as you will get anywhere in the world. The café-cum-bar is open daily from noon to 2 am.

The *Brutărie Deutschland & Café Einstein*, on the northern side of Piaţa Dorobanţilor, is a German-style café specialising in lush ice-cream sundaes and fruity cakes. Drinks are pricey however; it's open daily from 10 am to 10 pm. Takeaway chickens are roasted on a spit in the entrance hall.

Close to Piaţa Unirii, *La Florărie*, down a

tree-lined avenue at Calea Septembrie 3, overlooks the House of the People. For a more charming view, try *Cofetăria Excellent*, close by at the eastern end of Str Lipscani. It has a fat range of cakes, pastries and chocolates, and is open weekdays from 10 am to 6 pm, and on Saturday from 10 am to 2 pm.

Fast Food Bucharest is plastered with small fast-food outlets and 24 hour kiosks selling hot dogs, burgers, popcorn and other delights. Ketchup is generally generously doused on everything, be it a burger, toasted sandwich or pizza. 'Nu vreau ketchup' means 'I do not want ketchup'.

Simplan Fast Food, opposite Hotel Majestic on Calea Victoriei, serves a healthy variety of salads and filled sandwiches as well as burgers and hot dogs. It is open daily from 7 to 1 am. South of Piaţa Revoluţiei off Calea Victoriei is the charming Pasajul Victoriei, a narrow alleyway crammed with fast-food kiosks.

McMoni's, two minutes walk from Piaţa Universităţii at Piaţa Rosetti 3, is always packed. It's open weekdays from 7 am to 10 pm, weekends from 11 am.

East of Piaţa Romană, the *Ristorante Italia Pizzeria* at Calea Dorobanţilor 56, slaps out pizza 24 hours a day.

Zodiac Fast Food at Calea Victoriei 116 is open daily from 10 am to 10 pm. *Springtime* at Piaţa Victoriei A6 is part of a fast-food chain. It doles out burgers, fries, cakes and ice cream daily from 9 to 1 am. Outlets at Calea Floreasca 131 and Str Ştefan cel Mare 42 are open 24 hours.

Burger Ranch is considered one of the best fast-food joints in town. It has a giant outlet at Piaţa Dorobanţilor 2 and another at Şoseaua Colentina; both are open 24 hours.

McDonald's has seven outlets in town. Prime locations include Blvd General Magheru 24 (open daily from 7 am to 1 am); the eastern side of Piaţa Unirii at Splaiul Unirii 1 (open Sunday to Thursday from 6 am to midnight, Friday and Saturday from 6 to 1 am); and on the corner of Blvd Kogălniceanu and Str Brezoianu opposite

the main entrance to Cişmigiu Park (open daily from 7 am to midnight).

KFC is next to McDonald's on Blvd General Magheru. *Dunkin' Donuts* faces McDonald's on the western side of Piaţa Unirii at Blvd Unirii 27 (open 24 hours).

Just north of Piaţa Unirii heading towards Piaţa Universităţii along Blvd IC Brătianu is *London Lucky Burgers*, a large burger bar decked out with pool tables and packed from noon to midnight. Next door is *Sheriff's Fast Food*, a vast burger 'n shake outlet; its clean toilets rival McDonald's. It is open daily from 10 am to 8 pm.

Turkish döner kebabs and German schnitzels are dished out at *Pegas*, next to the Comedy theatre on Str Mândineşti.

Pizza Hut (☎ 210 8413) has a giant-sized restaurant and more modest terrace, close to Hotel Dorobanţi at Calea Dorobanţilor 3-5. It is open daily from 11 am to 11 pm.

Self Catering *Piaţa Amzei* (Amzei Market), just off Calea Victoriei on Piaţa Amzei, is open daily from sunrise to sunset and has the juiciest selection of fresh fruit and veg in Bucharest. Another open-air market, *Piaţa Gemini*, is within spitting distance of the Villa Helga hostel at Piaţa Galaţi.

Most peanut butter and chocolate spread freaks in town swear by *La Fourmi* (The Ant), close to McDonald's on the eastern side of Piaţa Unirii. It is the most advanced supermarket in Bucharest, complete with real trolleys and every imaginable imported food product money can buy. It is open Monday from 10 am to 6 pm, Tuesday to Friday from 7 am to 8 pm, and Saturday from 8 am to 2 pm. *Supermarket Orient* on the corner of Calea Dorobanţilor and Str Pitarul Hristache also has vast amounts of luxury foods. It's open daily, except Sunday, from 9 am to 9 pm.

The upmarket *Vox Maris* supermarket chain has outlets strategically located close to McDonald's off Blvd General Magheru on Str George Enescu; and on Piaţa Victoriei. Both are open 24 hours; the one on Piaţa Victoriei also sports a 24 hour restaurant, café and disco.

Patisserie Parisienne, is a small chain of French-style bakeries selling delicious croissants, pastries and cakes – there's a branch close to Hotel Bucureşti at the northern end of Calea Victoriei, and another on the corner of Piaţa Romană and Blvd Dacia. Both are open Monday to Saturday from 7 am to 10 pm, Sunday from 9 am to 9 pm.

For Schwarzbrot, Nussbrot and other nutty German breads, look no further than *Brutărie Deutschland*, close to Hotel Continental at Str Edgar Quinet 5. It is open weekdays from 7.30 am to 8 pm, Saturday from 7.30 am to 5 pm. Fresh coffee beans of varying origins are sold at the *Café de Oro*, close to the Hanul Manuc at Str Şepcari 22.

Entertainment

Cinema Most films are shown in their original language with Romanian subtitles and cost less than a dollar. There's a cluster of cinemas on Blvd Nicolae Bălcescu between Hotel Inter-Continental and Piaţa Romană, and another on Blvd Kogălniceanu, between Calea Victoriei and Cişmigiu Park.

Up-to-date listings of what's on where are available on the Net at www.pcnet.ro. The most popular downtown cinemas include *Cinemateca Română* (☎ 613 4904) at Str Ion Câmpineanu 21 and at Str Eforie 2; *Cinema Dacia* (☎ 650 3594) at Calea Griviţei 137; *Cinema Scala* (☎ 211 0372) at Blvd General Magheru 2-4; *Cinema Patria* (☎ 211 8620) at Blvd General Magheru 12-14; the *Luceafărul* (☎ 615 8767) at Str IC Brătianu 6; and the *Martin* (☎ 230 3243) at Str Iancu de Hunedoara 61.

In summer alternative films are screened at the hip *Prima Club*, on the 4th floor of the national theatre at Blvd Nicolae Bălcescu 2 (see Bars, Pubs & Nightclubs later). The French Institute screens French films every Wednesday (see Cultural Centres earlier).

Theatre Bucharest has countless theatres, offering a lively mix of comedy, farce, satire and straight contemporary plays in a variety of languages. Tickets to most productions cost less than US$3. All theatres are closed in July and August.

The most sought-after tickets are those for performances at the *Ion Luca Caragiale National Theatre* (Teatrul Naţional Ion Luca Caragiale; ☎ 614 7171, 615 4746), opposite Hotel Inter-Continental at Blvd Nicolae Bălcescu 2 (Metro: Universităţii). The theatre, named after the 20th century playwright who started off his career as a prompter, was built in the 1970s. The original theatre dating from 1852 was destroyed during WWII. The national theatre box office is on the southern side of the building facing Blvd Republicii.

The *Ion Dacian Opera Theatre* (Teatrul de Operetă Ion Dacian; ☎ 614 1187, 617 7174) adjoins the national theatre at Blvd Nicolae Bălcescu 2. The box office, inside the theatre, is open daily from 11 am to 6 pm.

The *Ţăndărică Puppet Theatre* (Teatrul de Marionete şi Păpuşi Ţăndărică; ☎ 211 0829), just off Piaţa Lahovari near the Hotel Dorobanţi at Str Eremia Grigorescu 26 (Metro: Piaţa Romană), presents innovative, amusing puppet shows.

A variety of films and contemporary plays are performed at the *Odeon Theatre* (Teatrul Odeon; ☎ 614 7234, 615 5053), founded in 1946 next to Hotel Majestic at Calea Victoriei 40-42. The box office (open daily from 11 am to 7 pm) is in a separate building at the side of the main theatre. A similar program is hosted at the *Nottara Theatre* (Teatrul Nottara; ☎ 659 3103), Blvd General Magheru 20. Its box office is open daily from 10 am to 2.15 pm and from 2.45 pm to 7 pm.

For more of a laugh, try a play at the *Comedy Theatre* (Teatrul Comedy; ☎ 616 4000, 613 1791), close to Piaţa Unirii at Str Măndineşti 2. Sparkling musicals and cabarets are hosted at the *Victoriei Theatre* (Teatrul Victoriei; ☎ 312 9516) at Calea Victoriei 174.

International theatre troupes often perform at the *Lucia Sturza Bulandra Theatre* (Teatrul Lucia Sturza Bulandra). The theatre has two stages – one is in the Schitu Măgureanu hall (Sală Schitu Măgureanu; ☎ 614 7547, 613 9750) at Blvd Schitu Măgureanu 1; and another is in the Toma Caragiu hall (Sală Toma Caragiu;

☎ 211 3441, 614 9696) at Str Jean Louis Calderon 76a.

Plays in Hebrew and Yiddish are held at the *Jewish State Theatre* (Teatrul Evreiesc de Stat; ☎ 323 4530) at Str Iuliu Barash 15.

Folk Theatre *Rapsodia Romană* (Teatrul Pan), Str Lipscani 53 in the old town, is a folk theatre that combines music, poetry and dancing – well worth visiting.

Opera & Ballet Not to be confused with the Opera theatre, is the *Opera House* (Opera Română; ☎ 614 6980, 615 7939) at Blvd Regina Elisabeta 70, west of Cişmigiu park.

Classical Music If at all possible, attend a performance at the *Ateneul Român* (☎ 615 0026) (see Things to See), home to the George Enescu philharmonic orchestra and the main concert hall in Bucharest at Str Benjamin Franklin 1. Tickets are sold in the office on the left as you enter; the office is open daily from 10 am to 4 pm as well as one hour before performances start.

Pubs, Bars & Nightclubs For the cheapest, strongest and most authentic drink in town, head for the *Vin Superior* shop, close to the train station at Calea Griviţei 115. Locally brewed plum brandy *(ţuică)* is a mere US$0.78 a litre; palincă (brandy distilled more than three times and even stronger) is US$2.20 a litre; and Romanian Cabernet and Muscat wines start at US$0.50 a litre. Bring your own bottle and get it filled! Vin Superior is open weekdays from 7 am to 8 pm, on Saturday from 7 am to 2 pm, Sunday from 8 am to noon.

If you speak English and plan to spend more than a few weeks in Bucharest, you might just find that the private members-only pub and club run by the British Embassy in its grounds every Wednesday for pining-for-home Brits comes in useful. Contact the embassy (see Facts for the

Visitor – Embassies) for membership details and fees.

Imported beers, wines and spirits are available in most bars and music clubs in town, including the following:

Berăria Europa
    Str Jean Louis Calderon 76 (☎ 210 0152) – Hungarian-inspired beer bar serving mug fulls of Dreher beer and Romanian and Hungarian dishes; open daily from 11 to 1 am
Burlane
    Str Grigorescu – busy bar run by Romanian rock singer of *Holograf*, one of the country's biggest pre-1989 bands
Café Indigo
    Str Eforie 2 (☎ 312 6336) – hip jazz club inside Cinemateca Română with live bands most night; open 24 hours
Caffé Piano
    Str Ion Câmpineanu 33 – Black Russians, Good Mothers, Dirty Mothers and Sex on the Beach starting at US$3.50 are served here by night; live piano music in an upmarket setting behind the national art museum
Carioca Jazz Club
    Blvd Dacia 97 (☎ 210 6086) – popular jazz club close to the embassies; open daily from noon to 2 am. Pricey
Club Art Papillon
    Str Matei Vodă 66a – a bohemian art café filled with students from the film academy across the street; enter through the green wooden gates
Cofetăria Veche
    Str Covaci 14 – 24 hour disco, bar and restaurant housed in Bucharest's oldest café dating to 1801
Dubliner Irish Pub
    Blvd Titulescu 18 (☎ 222 3737, 222 9473) – ask the taxi driver for 'Bar Irlandez'. A handful of chairs and a couple of tables on the street outside. Open daily from noon to 2 am. Guinness costs a staggering US$3
Green Hours Jazz Club
    Calea Victoriei 120 – hip cellar bar with occasional live jazz in the evenings; by day mellow out in the cool outside café to the sound of Beethoven, Brahms and Enescu. Open Monday to Saturday from 10 to 2 am, Sunday from 4 pm to 1 am
Hard 'n Heavy
    Str Gabroveni 14 – the hippest place in town, mixing hard live rock with prerecorded rock. Pay US$1.20 at the door and cash it in at the bar. Open weekdays and Sunday from 8 pm to 3 am, Saturday 8 pm to 5 am
Kontakt Deutscher Pub
    Str Berzei 60 – German everything; open daily from noon until late

COLIN D SHAW

MATTHIAS LÜFKENS

NICOLA WILLIAMS

Bucharest
Top: Recycled German tram near Piaţa Victoriei
Bottom left: St Apostles' Church
Bottom right: Calea Victoriei

NICOLA WILLIAMS

NICOLA WILLIAMS

NICOLA WILLIAMS

MATTHIAS LÜFKENS

MATTHIAS LÜFKENS

Bucharest
Top left: Arc de Triumf
Middle left: House of the People
Bottom left: Dumped Lenin statue

Top right: Cişmigiu Gardens
Bottom right: Nicolae Ceaşescu's grave

Prima Club

Blvd Nicolae Bălcescu 2 – trendy, roof top bar (also known as Leptărie) on the 4th floor of the National Theatre; live jazz most weekends and occasional outside film screenings at 9.30 pm; look for the poster inside the unmarked entrance at the side of the theatre opposite the Dominvszart gallery

Sardele

northern end of Str Vasile Lascăr – live Roma music most nights

Sydney Bar & Grill

Calea Victoriei 224 – Australian-run terrace bar. Provided you don't mind breathing in the car fumes as Bucharest's crazy motorists roar by, a good place to hang out; open 24 hours. Serves food too

White Horse

(☎ 679 7796), Str George Călinescu 4 – British pub and restaurant serving steak or egg and mayonnaise sandwiches; you can call a black London cab (US$0.50/km) from the red phonebox outside to take you home; open daily from noon to 3 am

Salsa, You & Me

Str 11 Iunie 51 (☎ 311 2322) – bongos, steel drums and lots of body-beat dancing; open nightly from 10 pm to 4 am

Vox Maris

Calea Victoriei 155 (☎ 311 1994) – supposedly the 'biggest-and-the-best' club in Bucharest with lots of slot machines and one-armed bandits; open nightly from 10 pm to 4 am

Why Not?

Str Turturelelor 11 (☎ 323 1450) – also meant to be the biggest and best; open from 10 pm until the wee hours

Things to Buy

The main departmental store, Cocor, is 100m south of Piaţa Universităţii on Blvd IC Brătianu. There are two indoor Expo Markets selling everything from pots and pans to clothes and books: one is north of the centre in the amusement complex off Şoseaua Kiseleff, open daily, except Sunday, from 10 am to 6 pm; the other is close to Gara Basarab and Gara de Nord on Şoseaua Orhideelor, open Monday to Saturday from 9 am to 7 pm, Sunday from 9 am to 2 pm. A free shuttle bus runs between Gara de Nord and the market.

Bucharest's quality art galleries and antique shops are clustered in 'embassy land' around Str Jean Louis Calderon in the eastern part of the city. Another bunch of art and antique shops worth a browse is at the northern end of Calea Victoriei. At No 214, close to the George Enescu museum, is the Galeria Anemone; at No 118 near Hotel Bucureşti is Andrew's Antiques. The Da Vinci Galeriile de Artă is in the same block.

For beautifully made woven rugs, table runners, national Romanian costumes, ceramics and other local crafts, look no further than the excellent folk art shop inside the Romanian Peasant Museum at Şoseaua Kiseleff 3. It is open daily, except Monday, from 10 am to 6 pm. There is another folk art

Off-Court Tennis Stars

Nasty by name. Nasty by nature. That's what sport critics said about Ilie Nastăse, Romania's first tennis player to score stardom in the west. The former on-court wildcat stood as a Social Democrat candidate for the mayorship of Bucharest in 1996 but was defeated at the polls by Victor Ciorbea, Romania's current prime minister.

At the peak of his career in 1971-75 Nastăse was ranked No 1 in the world. During his 26 year career he won 57 singles titles including the 1972 US Open and the 1973 French Open. In 1972 he wed a Franco-Belgian model. In 1982 the couple split, and in 1984 he married Alexandra King, a US model and soap-opera actor, with whom he set up home in Manhattan.

Nastăse's doubles partner was Romanian Ion Ţiriac. Together they took Romania to the 1972 Davis Cup final in Bucharest, but the home country lost to the US. Ţiriac subsequently settled in Germany where he managed German tennis champion Boris Becker. Since 1990 Ţiriac has promoted foreign investment in Romania: he owns the Ion Ţiriac Commercial Bank (Bancă Comercială Ion Ţiriac; BCIT); is a major shareholder in Pro TV, the country's first private TV channel; established Mercedes-Benz in Romania; and opened Romania's first cash-and-carry, Metro, in Bucharest. In his home town of Braşov Ţiriac 'adopted' 100 children and set up the Waldorf school for orphans. Ion Ţiriac is a national hero in Romania today. ∎

shop inside the Village Museum at Şoseaua Kiseleff 28-30.

The narrow alleys and passages winding off Str Lipscani in the old part of the city are a delight to explore. Tucked in a courtyard at Str Iuliu Maniu 13 there is a tiny tailor's shop, Croitorie, which sells exquisite, hand-made vestments for Orthodox priests *(de veşminte preoţeşti)*. They cost US$120 upwards. Close by, at the western end of Str Gabroveni, is a good hat shop. Wrought iron gates lead from the eastern end of Str Lipscani to Str Hanul Cu Tei, a narrow passage filled with art and antique shops, Roma selling sunflower seeds and local crafters selling their wares.

Guess what African Art at Str Eforie 2 sells!

Getting There & Away

This section concentrates on transport between Bucharest and other places in Romania and the republic of Moldova. See Getting There & Away for details on air, bus and train links with other countries.

Air Most international flights use Otopeni airport (☎ 230 1602, 230 0042, 230 0022), 17km north of Bucharest on the road to Ploieşti. TAROM flights to Chişinău, Kiev and Sofia and all domestic flights use Băneasa airport (☎ 232 0020), 8km north of the centre at Şoseaua Bucureşti-Ploieşti 42. The information number is ☎ 633 0030.

The Otopeni airport information desk (☎ 230 0042, 230 0022, 230 0038) is on the right as you enter the main arrivals hall; there is another in the departures hall. Both are open 24 hours and the staff speak excellent English. There is a left-luggage room inside the Lufthansa office next to the baggage claim area in the arrivals hall.

Romania's national airline, TAROM, has two main offices in Bucharest. The domestic branch (☎ 659 4185) is off Piaţa Victoriei at Str Buzeşti 59 (open weekdays from 7.30 am to 7.30 pm, Saturday from 7.30 am to 1.30 pm). The international office is on the 1st floor of the CFR office at Str Domniţa Anas-tasia 10-14 (open weekdays from 8 am to 7.30 pm, Saturday from 8 am to noon).

From Băneasa airport there are flights every day except Sunday to Arad, Cluj-Napoca, Constanţa (summer only), Oradea, Timişoara; two flights weekly to Bacău; four flights weekly to Baia Mare, Satu Mare and Târgu Mureş; and twice-daily flights on Monday, Wednesday and Thursday to Iaşi and Suceava. To Sibiu there is a morning and an evening flight from Bucharest on Monday, Wednesday and Friday. Fares are quoted in relevant chapters in this book but don't expect any bargains. Foreigners pay at least double the price that Romanians pay.

Bus Bucharest is served by a poor domestic bus system, so much so if you ask someone where the bus station (Autogară) is, they will look at you in astonishment. Many will tell you that Bucharest does not have a bus station.

The central bus station – a bus stop rather than a fully-fledged station – is outside Hotel Nord on Calea Griviţei. Services change regularly and it is wise to check the timetables stuck on the lamp posts at the bus stop first. At the time of writing there was a daily bus to Curtea de Argeş (140km); five buses a day to Piteşti (108km); three daily to Câmpulung Muscel (249km); and one bus to Galaţi (212km), Piteşti (113km), Ploieşti (59km), Râmnicu Vâlcea (171km) and Tulcea (263km). More usefully, there are also 13 daily buses to Târgovişte (78km). Buy your ticket from the driver.

Moldova Tickets for a daily bus to Chişinău (15 to 18 hours; US$10 single) in Moldova, departing from Gara de Nord at 6 pm, are sold at the Autotrains kiosk, next to the Ortadoğu Tur office on Piaţa Gara de Nord.

Turkey Daily buses to Istanbul depart from the Filaret bus station (☎ 641 0692), Piaţa Gării Filaret 1; or from the Militari bus station (☎ 769 7042) at Blvd Păcii 141. Bus companies operating these buses run a shuttle service, 30 minutes before departure, from Gara de Nord to the appropriate bus station. Major bus companies include Toros Trans (☎ 638 2424, 223 1898), Str Gării de Nord (four daily buses departing at 7, 11 am, and 2 and 4 pm); Ortadoğu Tur (☎ 31 2423, 637 6778), Piaţa Gara de Nord 1 (four buses daily at 10 am, noon, 3 and 4 pm); and Öz Murat (☎ 618 4095, 638 3992), Str Dinicu Golescu 31 (six daily at 6.30, 7, 8 and 9 am, and 3 and 4 pm).

Western Europe Daily buses to western Europe depart from the bus stop at the northern end of Calea Dorobanţilor, close to the German embassy. Leading bus companies operating buses to Germany and western Europe include Atlas Reisen (☎ 230 7980), Str Ankara 4; Double T (☎ 613 3642; fax 615 8166), Calea Victoriei 2; and Touring (☎ 633 1661; fax 312 8543), Str Sofia 26. They all have offices abroad too (see Getting There & Away).

Train Bucharest is served by a comprehensive train network linking the capital to most other towns, cities and villages in Romania. The main train station – from which all international and most national trains arrive and depart – is Gara de Nord (☎ 223 0880, 223 0455) at Blvd Gării de Nord 2. Some local trains to/from Cernica and Constanţa use Gara Obor (☎ 635 0702; 223 0880, extension 152, 238), east of the city centre. Local trains to/from Snagov and a couple of seasonal *accelerat* trains to/from Mangalia on the Black Sea coast and Cluj-Napoca sometimes use Gara Băneasa (☎ 223 0880, extension 3537), on the northern edge of town on Şoseaua Bucureşti-Ploieşti. A very few unreserved local trains to/from Braşov, Craiova, Piteşti, Sibiu, Suceava, Timişoara, and so on, arrive at and depart from Gara Basarab (☎ 637 5705), which is a long block north-west of Gara de Nord. All local trains to/from Giurgiu arrive at Gara Progresul (☎ 685 6385l; 223 0660, extension 153, 135), on the far southern side of Bucharest (take tram No 12).

Most tourists have no reason to set foot in Gara Basarab, a small, stinky station filled with children running wild and people sleeping rough. Should you have the misfortune to have to use this station, there is a 24 hour left-luggage office (US$0.40/50 per small/large bag) at the information desk in the main ticket hall.

Tickets for all trains can be bought in advance from the Agenţie de Voiaj CFR office in Bucharest. You have to pay a nominal reservation fee (no more than US$1) but this is well worth it, if only to avoid queuing for hours at the train station. A seat reservation is mandatory if you are travelling with an Inter-Rail pass. All international tickets have to be bought in advance.

The main CFR office (☎ 613 2644, 613 2642, 614 5528) is a block past Hotel Central at Str Domniţa Anastasia 10-14. The domestic ticket office (Bucureşti 1) is on the ground floor and the international ticket office (Bucureşti 3) on the 1st floor. Train timetables costing US$0.75 are sold at the ticket desks in the domestic ticket hall. Some staff speak English. Both halls are open weekdays from 7.30 am to 7.30 pm, Saturday from 8 am to noon.

Tickets for local and national trains can be bought from two hours before departure at the train station. At Gara de Nord, different windows sell tickets for different trains, as noted on small signs displayed in the window. There are separate ticket halls for 1st and 2nd class. The ticket hall for international destinations, 1st-class tickets and sleeping compartments – marked *Casele de bilete Cl. 1* – is on the right as you enter the station at its main entrance. Window No 1 (*Casă internaţionale*) is for international tickets; window No 2 is for inter-city tickets, windows Nos 6 & 7 are for 1st-class tickets; and windows Nos 8 and 9 are for sleepers and couchettes on national trains.

To get to the 2nd-class ticket hall – which is marked *Casă II* – walk past the 1st-class ticket hall and turn right when you reach the tracks.

Timetables are in the main aisle of the station building opposite the first-class ticket hall. On the left side of the aisle is a currency exchange, mother & baby room (*mama şi*

BUCHAREST

copilul) and left-luggage office (open 24 hours). It costs US$0.25/0.50 to leave a small/big bag for 24 hours. Up-to-date notice boards listing ticket prices are displayed in the second-class ticket office. Prices change every month. Train timetables are sold at the information desk, at the end of the main aisle opposite the tracks.

Wasteels (☎ 222 7844) which sells discounted tickets to western Europe for the under 26s (see Getting There & Away) is on the right as you enter the main station building. It is open weekdays from 10 am to 6 pm.

Car & Motorcycle There are plenty of 24 hour gas stations around the city which sell a great array of imported junk food as well as petrol, oils, accessories etc. Well located stations include the Inter-Continental at Str Tudor Arghezi 7; the Dorobanţi at Calea Dorobanţilor 180; and the Cotroceni station west of the centre on Splaiul Independenţei. Heading north to the airports, there is the Băneasa Service at Şoseaua Bucureşti-Ploieşti 2; Shell Otopeni 13km north from the centre along the same road; and AGIP at Otopeni airport.

Car Rental Many of Bucharest's travel agents and major hotels are agents for the major car rental firms too. Shop around for the best deal. Check whether the price offered includes the required 18% VAT. At the time of writing Budget offered the most competitive rates. All the major car rental agencies have desks directly opposite the customs area as you enter the main arrival hall at Otopeni airport. Through Avis, Budget, Europcar and Hertz, you can book a car in advance through any office overseas and arrange to collect it upon arrival at Otopeni.

Avis
  Otopeni airport (☎ 212 0011)
  Vacanţa Agenţie de Turism, Blvd Nicolae Bălcescu 35 (☎ 210 7388)
  Str Polona 35 (☎ 210 4344, 210 4345; fax 210 6912)
Budget
  Otopeni airport (☎ 230 0022, 230 0038, 230

0042; extension 1667)
  Hotel Dorobanţi, Calea Dorobanţilor 1-7 (☎ 210 2867; fax 210 2995)
Eurodollar
  Touring ACR: Otopeni airport (☎ 230 4040)
  Str Cihoschi 2 near Piaţa Romana (☎ 211 0410; fax 211 4366)
  Str Take Ionescu 27 (☎ 650 2595; fax 312 0434)
Europcar
  Otopeni airport (☎ & fax 312 7078)
  ONT Carpaţi, Blvd General Magheru 7 (☎ 613 1540; fax 312 0915)
Euro Service Amerom
  Otopeni airport (☎ & fax 322 5829)
  Str Radu Cristian 6 (☎ 230 0022 extension 1567, 322 7420)
Hertz
  Otopeni airport (☎ 230 3257)
  Hotel Dorobanţi, Calea Dorobanţilor 1-7 (☎ 210 6555; fax 210 6521)

Getting Around
To/From the Airports To get to/from Otopeni or Băneasa airport take bus No 783 from Bucharest city centre, which departs every 15 minutes between 6.30 am and 9 pm from Piaţa Unirii and various bus stops on the eastern side of Blvd Brătianu, Blvd Nicolae Bălcescu and Blvd General Magheru. An easy stop to find is the one outside KFC on Blvd General Magheru (Metro: Piaţa Romana). Double-journey tickets costing US$0.90 are sold at silver ticket booths marked *bilete şi cartele magnetice* next to bus stops. Punch tickets inside the bus. TAROM also runs a shuttle bus to the airport. It leaves from outside its office on Str Domniţa Anastasia and also stops outside KFC. It is free for TAROM flyers and US$0.70 for everyone else.

Băneasa is 20 minutes from the centre. Get off at the *aeroportul Băneasa* bus stop. Bus No 313 also runs between Băneasa and Piaţa Romana. Bus No 205 goes from Băneasa to Gara de Nord.

Otopeni is a good 35 minutes from the city centre. The bus stops outside the departures hall and then continues to the arrival hall. To get to the centre from Otopeni, catch bus No 783 from the stop immediately on the right as you exit the main terminal. A silver booth here sells tickets. Single-journey tickets are not available.

Don't believe taxi drivers if they say the airport buses have stopped running or don't exist. In fact, avoid taxi drivers at both airports at all costs – unless you are quite happy to fork out between US$25 and US$40 for the 20 to 35 minutes ride.

Sky Services (☎ 232 9691; fax 232 9891), which has a desk at the far right end of Otopeni arrival hall, can arrange transfers between the international airport and most of the major hotels in the city. It charges US$5/10 single/return by 'Eldorado' shuttle bus or an absolutely ridiculous US$30/55 by limousine. Tickets can be bought from the airport desk or booked in advance by telephone.

Some tour operators supply transfer from the airport to the centre or vice versa at competitive rates.

Bus, Tram & Trolleybus For buses, trams and trolleybuses buy tickets (US$0.12) at any RATB (Régie autonome de Transport de Bucureşti) street kiosk, painted yellow or silver and marked *Casă de bilet* or simply *bilet*. Tickets have to be punched once on board. Tickets are spot-checked by inspectors who have no qualms about fining you

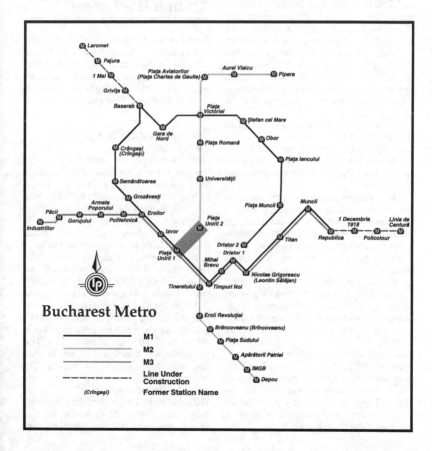

Bucharest Metro

——————— M1
——————— M2
——————— M3
– – – – – – Line Under
            Construction
(Crîngaşi) Former Station Name

US$7.50 if you don't have a validated ticket. Single and two-journey tickets are available as well as a handy US$0.75 one-day pass which entitles you to unlimited travel on buses, trams and trolleybuses. A two-week/one-month pass costs US$4.20/8.40. Students get a 50% discount on day and monthly passes.

All public transport runs daily from 5 am to midnight, with a reduced service on Sunday.

Metro Bucharest's metro opened in 1985 and has three lines which are helpful for getting around the city centre. Trains run every five to seven minutes during peak periods and a lot less frequently – about every 20 minutes – during off-peak times. During off-peak times don't be fooled by the 0:00 reading on the digital stopwatch on the platform which theoretically means a train is about to arrive: These stopwatches were designed to clock up only 9:59.

To use the metro buy a magnetic-striped ticket (US$0.20) at the subterranean kiosks inside the main entrance to the metro station. All tickets are valid for two journeys. For routes see the Bucharest metro map included in this book.

Metro stations are poorly signposted so sit near the front of the train to give yourself a better chance of seeing the station names. At platform level, the name of the station where you are is the one with a box around it. The others indicate the direction the train is going.

Metro station names are prone to change: Leontin Sălăjan is now Nicolae Grigorescu (after the Romanian painter), while Piaţa Aviatorilor has been Piaţa Charles de Gaulle since the French president visited. Just to confuse things these new names do not yet appear on all metro maps or at the metro station itself! Moreover the busy Piaţa Romană metro stop is not marked on any of the route markers or maps in the metro stations. There are two new lines under construction will which probably never be completed due to lack of cash.

Taxi Don't flag a taxi down in the street unless you want to be ripped off. The most unscrupulous taxi drivers hang out at the airports and at Gara de Nord where you'll be asked as much as US$10 for the 3km ride to the centre. Avoid!

The cheapest type of taxis are those you book by telephone (☎ 941, 944, 945, 946, 948, 956, 965). The fixed metered rate usually works out at US$0.25 per kilometre. Most drivers charge US$1.50 an hour for waiting.

Around Bucharest

Dracula's tomb, Lenin's graveyard, Ceauşescu's luxury summer pad and the former Communist Party hotel – all of them surrounded by unspoilt forests and lakes – are among the varied sights within an easy day's reach of Bucharest. Who said Bucharest was dull?

MOGOŞOAIA PALACE & LENIN'S GRAVEYARD
One of Romania's most remarkable palaces lies just 14km north-west of Bucharest in Mogoşoaia (literally Mogoş' wife). Mogoşoaia Palace was built by Wallachian prince, Constantin Brâncoveanu, between 1698 and 1702 as a summer residence for his family and an inheritance for his son Ştefan. It is considered to be among the country's finest examples of Brâncoveanu architecture. Built within a large court and surrounded by a lake and oak forests, the palace's main feature is a traditional balcony that winds around the front façade.

Following the gruesome death of Ştefan, his three brothers and his princely father at the hands of the Turks in Istanbul in 1714, the palace was turned into an inn. In 1821 fire destroyed much of the edifice. The palace was plundered and made into a warehouse by the occupying Russian forces in 1853. In the late 19th century the Mogoşoaia estate was handed down to the Bibescu family, descendants of the Brâncoveanus through the female line. A large guesthouse was built and, in 1912, Prince George Valentin Bibescu (1880-1941) relinquished the entire estate to his wife, Martha (1886-1973). It was under her guidance that Italian architect Domenico Rupolo was hired to help restore the entire estate. A black and white chequered marble floor was laid in the main palace and the ornate gilded arched doorways were restored, both of which remain today. The guesthouse was rebuilt, taking the fish market in Venice as its model, and the gardens were laid out English-style.

In 1945 Martha Bibescu left for Paris leaving her daughter Valentino to manage the estate. In 1956 she joined her mother in Paris and the estate was given to the state. It stood as a museum until the 1970s when Ceauşescu ordered the building to be closed and all the furniture removed, presumably for his own personal use. There are tours in English and French around the furnitureless palace. An **art gallery** is housed in the palace kitchens, the unusual building of archways on the right as you pass under the guards tower into the estate enclosure.

Prince George Valentin Bibescu is buried in the small, white, 1688 church on the estate. A path from the main entrance to the palace leads to the **Bibescu family tomb** where Elizabeth Asquith (1898-1945), the daughter of former British prime minister Henry Herbert Asquith lies. She married Prince Antoine Bibescu in London in 1919.

Lenin's grave is also ironically at Mogoşoaia. Following his downfall in 1989 when all communist statues in Bucharest were rapidly levelled, Lenin, who stood outside the press house in Bucharest, was removed from his pedestal and dumped on wasteground behind the palace kitchen on the Mogoşoaia estate. The head of his 5m-tall bronze body lies peacefully against that of **Petru Groza**, the communist prime minister at the head of the 1945 government which forced King Michael to abdicate in 1947. Entering the main enclosure, turn right after the kitchen into the field, the turn right again.

The Brâncoveanu complex is open daily, except Monday, from 10 am to 6 pm. Admission to the estate is US$1.20. Guided tours are free. The estate at Str Valea Parcului also houses the **Mogoşoaia National Cultural Centre** (☎ 01-223 4689, 668 4990), a centre funded by the European Council aimed at promoting culture and arts in the region. Various theatre workshops, art exhibitions and classical music concerts are held here.

Places to Stay & Eat

There is a small motel on the right as you enter Mogoşoaia village from Bucharest. the *Popas La Prepeleac* (☎ 01-668 5832) at Şoseaua Bucureşti-Târgovişte 32 has a handful of double rooms with shared bath for US$15 a night. It has a small adjoining restaurant.

Restaurant Mogoşoaia inside the Mogoşoaia National Cultural Centre at Str Valea Parcului 1 has a delightful wooden terrace on which authentic Romanian dishes are served. It is open daily, except Monday, from 10 am to 11 pm. Traditional folklore evenings are occasionally held here.

Getting There & Away

A daily Bucharest-Snagov train departs at 7.25 am from Gara de Nord, arriving at Mogoşoaia at 7.51 am. The return train leaves Mogoşoaia at 9.13 pm, arriving at Gara de Nord at 9.38 pm. Some Bucharest-Galaţi trains, departing from Gara de Nord, stop at Mogoşoaia (five daily; 25 minutes).

CĂLDĂRUŞANI MONASTERY

Tennis champion Björn Borg married Romanian player, Mariana Simionescu at the picturesque Căldăruşani Monastery, some 27km further north along the same train line. The monastery, built in 1638 under the guidance of Wallachian prince Matei Basarab (1632-54), gained recognition during the 18th century as home to one of Romania's most distinguished icon painting schools. The 17-year-old Nicolae Grigorescu spent some months at the monastery in 1855, painting several icons for the church.

Getting There & Away

Some Bucharest-Galaţi trains, departing from Gara de Nord, stop at Greci (five daily; 50 minutes) where you alight for Căldăruşani. The monastery is a 2km hike north from the train station.

BUFTEA

Up until 1989, the 19th century **Ştirbei Palace**, 18km north of Bucharest, was an official Communist Party hotel. The palace was built by the Wallachian prince, Barbu Ştirbei between 1855-64, and it was here, on 5 March 1918, that the Romanian government signed a preliminary peace treaty with Germany to WWI. Following WWII, the palace – or Buftea Castle – as it was also known, was handed over to the state and transformed into a luxury guesthouse for people deemed 'very important' by the government. Today the pretty castle enclosed in lush park land at Str Ştirbei Vodă 36, is open as a hotel (☎ 613 1500; fax 311 2417) and restaurant.

Getting There & Away

From Bucharest's Gara de Nord, there are 17 local trains to Ploieşti daily between 5.05 am and 10.52 pm which stop at Buftea (34 minutes).

SNAGOV

Snagov, 38km north of Bucharest, is a favourite picnic spot for city dwellers, with a famous 16th century **church and monastery** tucked away on an island in Snagov Lake, inhabited by no one bar an elderly abbot and nun who take care of Snagov monastery. Deep forest surrounds the lake, estimated to be 576 hectares large and an impressive 18km long.

A simple wooden church was built on the island in the 11th century by Mircea cel Bătrân. A monastery was added in the late 14th century during the reign of King Dan I (1383-6) and, in 1453, the wooden church was replaced by a stone edifice which later sank in the lake.

In 1456 Vlad Ţepeş the Impaler built fortifications around the monastery. He also built a bridge from the lake to the mainland, a bell tower, a new church, an escape tunnel, and a prison and torture chamber. Nicolae Bălcescu, leader of the 1848 revolution in Wallachia, and other 1848 revolutionaries were imprisoned in Snagov prison for a short time. A mass grave for those who died in the prison was dug in the grounds. The remains of the prison behind the present-day church can still be seen today.

The present stone church, listed as a UNESCO heritage building and currently under renovation, dates from 1521. The paintings were done in 1563 by painter Dobromir cel Tânăr. The body of Vlad Ţepeş was reputedly buried below the dome, just in front of the church's wooden iconostasis, but when the grave was opened in 1931 it was found to be empty. The humble grave inside the church, marked by a simple portrait of Vlad Ţepeş, is simply known as 'Dracula's tomb' today. Daily services are held in the new wooden church which stands next to the stone church. Admission to the monastery complex is US$0.70.

The early 20th century **Snagov Palace**, just across the lake from the island, was built by Prince Nicolae, brother of King Carol II, in the Italian Renaissance style. During the Ceauşescu era it was used for meetings of high-level government officials and today it houses the Snagov Complex (☎ 311 3782; fax 311 3781) restaurant, conference centre and hotel reserved exclusively for state guests. Ceauşescu had a summer home on Snagov Lake, **Villa No 10**, which is now rented out to rich and famous tourists. When Michael Jackson played in Bucharest in 1992 and again in 1995, this is where he stayed. In response to his question 'Have I got enough money to buy this villa?', the mega-millionaire pop star was politely told that the property was, in fact, priceless. Ceauşescu's two large yachts, both named *Snagov*, are moored majestically on the lake shores; they too are reserved exclusively for very important people.

You can hire a boat to the island from outside the Dolce Vita restaurant. The return journey in a motorboat for up to six people costs US$7. The restaurant also organises **water-skiing** around the lake; it rents out skis, wet suits etc. One ski run is US$7. At the time of writing it was planning to buy a couple of **snowmobiles** to hire out in winter. In December and January, it is often possible to walk or ice skate across the frozen lake to the monastery.

Places to Stay & Eat

There are two *campsites* in the lakeside oak forest plus a few *beer gardens* and *food stands*. The lakeside *Dolce Vita* (☎ 018-604 075), run by an American, serves traditional Romanian dishes on its floating restaurant on the lake. It is pricey, like everywhere in Snagov. Expect to pay around US$4 for a simple pork chop *(cotlet de porc)*. The bar and restaurant is open 24 hours.

If you think you are sufficiently rich and famous to stay in *Snagov Palace*, contact the State Protocol Patrimony National Corporation (☎ 659 4876; fax 312 1091), inside the government building in Bucharest at Str Iancu de Hunedoara 5.

Getting There & Away

From June to September two trains a day run from Bucharest's Gara de Nord to Snagov Plajă at 7.25 and 8.30 am, returning at 6.10 and 8.25 pm (one hour). In winter these trains only run at weekends. Note however that Snagov Plajă is still a good hike to the monastery complex. Private mini-buses departing from Gara de Nord also go to Snagov.

The Villa Helga hostel in Bucharest (see Places to Stay – Hostels) arranges informal, guided tours to Snagov; the trip works out fairly cheap as the hostel has a friend – the burly Ana – at the lake who takes tourists over to the island in her rowing boat; she has been doing this for the past 20 years!

CERNICA

The 19th century monastic complex of Cernica (Sfânta Mănăstirea Cernica), nestled on a small island in the middle of Cernica lake 14km east of Bucharest, is one of Romania's most idyllic – yet least visited – monasteries. Two churches, some chapels, a cemetery, seminary and a **religious art & typography museum** are contained within the fortified complex, founded on the site of a former 17th century church in 1781. A smaller, **St Nicolae's Church** (Biserica Sfântu Nicolae din Ostrov) was built in 1815, but it was not until the mid-1800s, under the guidance of St Calinic of Cernica, that the monastery really flourished. Between 1831 and 1838 **St Georghe's Church** (Biserica Sfântu Gheorghe) was built, a library and seminary was opened, and a school for religious painting set up. Following WWII, the monastery was shut down; it was not until 1995 that the seminary reopened. Some 80 monks live on the island complex – joined by a causeway to the mainland. The graves of Romanian painter Ion Ţuculescu, and writer and priest, Gala Galaction, lie in the cemetery on the lake shores, in front of St Georghe's Church.

Getting There & Away

Two trains daily depart from Bucharest's Gara Obor to Cernica. One leaves at 7.30 am, arriving in Cernica at 8.26 am. The return train departs from Cernica at 5.54 pm.

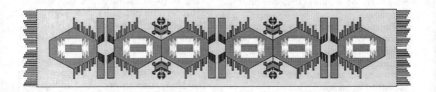

Transylvania

To most people, the name Transylvania conjures up images of haunted castles, werewolves and vampires. Certainly, the 14th century castles at Râşnov and Bran could be straight out of a Count Dracula movie.

Yet the charms of Transylvania are far more diverse – mountain scenery, some of Romania's best hiking and skiing, glimpses of ancient Roman and Dacian settlements, plus scores of rural villages that haven't changed much since the 18th century.

For lovers of medieval art and history, it's an unparalleled chance to have an overlooked corner of the old Austro-Hungarian empire all to themselves. Most travellers head straight up the Prahova valley to the old Saxon merchant town of Braşov and the citadel of Sighişoara and don't move on. Move on! It's well worth it.

Transylvania consumes the entire central region of Romania, bordered to the east, south and west by the Carpathian mountains. The south-eastern region, most accessible by public transport from Bucharest, is dominated by the Prahova valley with Romania's leading ski resorts. The Făgăraş mountains and a string of medieval cities founded by the Saxons in the 12th century are within easy reach.

Romania's Hungarian enclave embraces south-east Transylvania, stretching to Târgu Mureş in central Transylvania, which is the cradle of Magyar culture. This eastern region is known as Székely land.

Transylvania's ethnic diversity is most prevalent in the great cultural centre of Cluj-Napoca in northern Transylvania, a potpourri of Romanians, Saxons and Hungarians.

The south-western region of Transylvania is home to a string of awe-inspiring Dacian and Roman citadels, including the fantastic remains of the Roman capital of Sarmizegetusa which are slowly being unearthed by archaeologists.

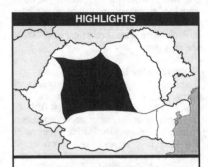

HIGHLIGHTS

- Watch wild wolves in the Carpathians near Piatra Craiului
- Eat home-made cheese and bread in a family home around Bran
- Stroll through the medieval streets of Braşov, Sighişoara & Sibiu
- See Roman remains at Sarmizegetusa
- See how the royals lived at Peleş Castle in Sinaia
- Sleep in Ceauşescu's bed in a Sfântu Gheorghe castle
- Take a trip back in time up a forest railway at Covasna

History

For a thousand years, right up to WWI, Transylvania was associated with Hungary. In the 10th century a Magyar tribe, the Székelys, settled in what it called Erdély ('beyond the forest'). In the 12th century, Saxon merchants arrived to help defend the eastern frontiers of Hungary. The seven towns they founded – Bistriţa (Bistritz), Braşov (Kronstadt), Cluj-Napoca (Klausenburg), Mediaş (Mediasch), Sebeş (Mühlbach), Sibiu (Hermannstadt) and Sighişoara (Schässburg) – gave Transylvania its German name, Siebenbürgen ('seven boroughs').

Medieval Transylvania was an autonomous unit ruled by a prince responsible to the Hungarian crown. The indigenous

Romanians were mere serfs, their presence only noted in chronicles in relation to peasant revolts. After the 1526 Turkish defeat of Hungary the region became semi-independent, though it still recognised and paid tribute to Turkish suzerainty

In 1683 Turkish power was broken at the gates of Vienna, and Transylvania came under Habsburg rule in 1687. The Catholic Habsburg governors sought to control the territory by favouring first the Protestant Hungarians and Saxons and then the Orthodox Romanians. In 1848, when the Hungarians revolted against the Habsburgs, the local Romanian population sided with the Austrians.

After 1867, Transylvania was fully absorbed into Hungary. In 1918, Romanians gathered at Alba Iulia to demand Transylvania's union with Romania. Following the Trianon peace treaty signed with Hungary on 4 June 1920, Transylvania, along with Maramureş (actually part of Transylvania), Bessarabia, Bucovina and Banat, was united with its Romanian motherland.

This has never been fully accepted by Hungary and from 1940 to 1944 much of the region was re-annexed by Hungary's pro-Nazi fascists. After the war, the Romanian communists put a tight lid on Hungarian nationalist sentiments. Since 1989 right-wing politicians in Hungary have beaten the Greater Hungary drum. Nationalist politicians in Romania have responded with equal vehemence. The 'Transylvania Question' continues to cast a small but looming cloud over relations between the two countries.

Saxon Land & the Prahova Valley

The area colonised by the Saxons from the 12th century onwards lies north of Bucharest. Frequent attacks on these early cities by Tartars and Turks prompted the Saxons to fortify their churches and towns with sturdy walls.

The Prahova valley snakes its way north along the course of the Prahova river from Sinaia, the 'Pearl of Carpathians', to Predeal, just south of Braşov. Romania's kings, queens and dictators had summer residences along this 48km stretch today renowned for skiing and hiking. The Bucegi mountains lie immediately to the west, straddled closely by the Făgăraş chain which dominates the southern region between Braşov and Sibiu.

BRAŞOV
• *area code* ☎ *068 , pop 319,908*

Braşov is a pleasant medieval town flanked by verdant hills. Established on an ancient Dacian site at the beginning of the 13th century, today it is one of Romania's most visited cities. Piaţa Sfatului, the central square, is the finest in the country, lined with baroque façades and pleasant outdoor cafés. Within easy reach by bus and train are the ski resorts of Sinaia and Poiana Braşov, the castles of Bran and Râşnov, and trails that lead into the dramatic Bucegi mountains.

Braşov started as a German mercantile colony named Kronstadt (Brassó in Hungarian), and its strategic location at the meeting point of three principalities helped it to become a major medieval trading centre. The Saxons who lived there built ornate churches and townhouses, all protected by a massive wall that still remains. The Romanians lived at Schei, just outside the walls to the southwest. During the Stalinist era, Braşov (and the entire Braşov district) was renamed 'Staline', with the communist leader's name carved in bold letters on the side of Tâmpa mountain.

It was here that one of the first public oppositions to the Ceauşescu government flared in 1987. Thousands of disgruntled workers, angered by wage cuts, long hours and rationing, took to the street demanding basic foodstuffs. Ceauşescu called in the troops and three people were killed.

More recently, in 1997, 6000 workers at Braşov's state-run Roman SA truck manufacturing company blocked city streets to protest at the government's market forms. These threatened the future of the factory

TRANSYLVANIA

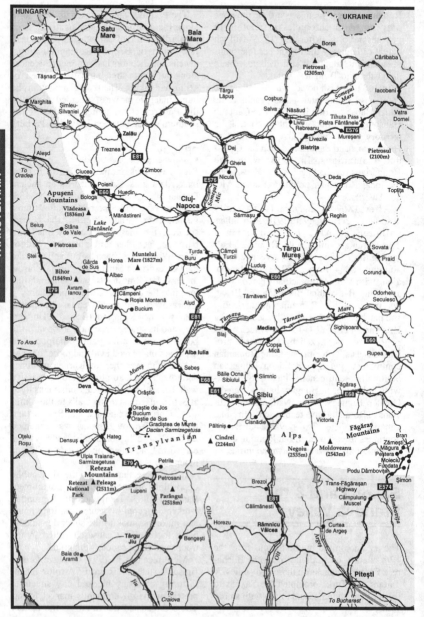

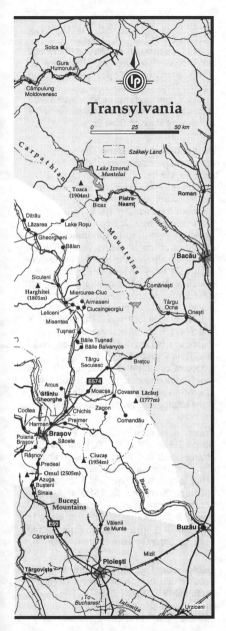

whose output had steadily declined since its heyday under communism.

Orientation

The train station is to the north-east, far from the centre of town. Take bus No 4 (buy your ticket at a kiosk) to Parcul Central. Str Republicii, Braşov's pedestrian-only promenade, is crowded with shops and cafés. At the train station, the left-luggage office (open 24 hours) is on the left in the underpass that leads from the main ticket hall to the tracks.

Braşov has three bus stations: bus station No 1 (Autogară 1) is next to the train station on Blvd Gării. Buses to Târgu Mureş, Târgovişte and international buses arrive/depart from here. Buses to/from Curtea de Argeş, Făgăraş and Câmpulung depart from bus station No 2 (Autogară 2), west of the train station at Str Avram Iancu 114. Few buses use bus station No 3 (Autogară 3) in the east of the town.

Mount Tâmpa (formerly spelt Mount Tîmpa) towers over the town to the south.

Maps & Guides The fold-up *Braşov Ghid Turistic şi Commercial* contains a detailed map of the city. It is published annually and sells for US$1.20 in most bookshops. Most museums publish English-language guides.

For an online map and tourist guide to Braşov go to www.deuroconsult.ro/brasov.

Information

Tourist Offices There's a tourist desk in the lobby of the Hotel Aro Palace at Blvd Eroilor 25; it is not much use except to buy a map, or book an overpriced excursion (a city tour of Braşov costs US$5). It also arranges day trips to Sibiu (US$38), the Bicaz gorges (US$28), Sighişoara (US$26), Bran (US$7.50) and Sinaia (US$14).

The Touring ACR desk (☎ 118 920) in Hotel Capitol provides assistance for motorists. The main Automobil Clubul Român office (ACR; ☎ 135 476) is further from the centre, at Str Bucureşti 68.

Money The IDM currency exchange on Str Apollonia Hirscher offers good rates; it is

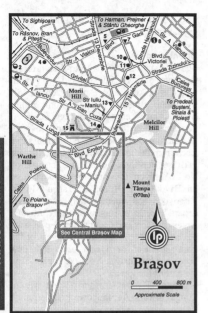

Braşov

0   400   800 m
Approximate Scale

1   Bus Station No 2
2   Stadium Tineretului Bus Stop
3   Braşov FC Stadium
4   Fabrica de Bere
5   Restaurant Faget
6   Train Station; Bus Station No 1
7   Sarmis Pizza
8   Tourist Information Resource Centre
9   International Trade Centre
10 Bradul 24-hour Shop
11 Farmacie Thea
12 Deuronet
13 Restaurant Timiş
14 Dimm Travel Agency;
    Heroes' Cemetery
15 Citadel

open weekdays from 10 am to 6 pm, Saturday from 10 am to 2 pm. It also has an office on Piaţa Sfatului which cashes Eurocheques; this office is open weekdays from 8 am to 7.30 pm, Saturday from 9 am to noon.

BANCOREX, Str Republicii 20a, changes travellers cheques and gives cash-

advance on Visa/MasterCard. It's open weekdays from 8.30 am to 2 pm.

BCIT, on the corner of Str Republicii and Str Weiss, also gives cash advance on Visa/MasterCard; it is open weekdays from 9 am to 2 pm.

Out of hours, get cash on Visa/MasterCard from the ATM outside the restaurant of the Hotel Aro Palace on Blvd Eroilor.

Post & Communications The central post office is opposite the Heroes' Cemetery, next door to the municipal council on Blvd Eroilor; it's open weekdays from 7 am to 8 pm, Saturday from 8 am to noon.

Braşov has a number of telephone centres. The small centre at Str Republicii 12 is open weekdays from 10 am to 6 pm; the old central telephone office on a side street off Blvd Eroilor next to the ethnographic museum is open daily from 6.30 am to 10 pm; and the sparkling centre one street further east off Blvd Eroilor is open weekdays from 7 to 1 pm and from 2 to 7 pm.

DHL Worldwide Express (☎ 151 232; fax 144 844) has an office inside the Hotel Aro Palace at Blvd Eroilor 27; it is open weekdays from 9 am to 5 pm.

DeuroConsult (☎ 319 222; fax 318 637; email deuro@deuroconsult.ro; www .deuroconsult.ro) at Blvd Kogălniceanu 19, is the leading Internet provider in town.

Travel Agencies Nouvelles Frontières/ Simpa Turism (☎ 151 173), Piaţa Sfatului, changes cash at a good rate and has cheap deals on international plane tickets; the office is open weekdays from 9 am to 5 pm.

Dimm Travel (☎ & fax 151 084), Str Iuliu Maniu 13, can arrange accommodation in private rooms in Braşov and other towns in Romania; it is open weekdays from 9 am to 6.30 pm, Saturday from 10 am to 2 pm.

Bookshops The Librărie Unirea on Str Politechnicii, the Librărie George Coşbuc at Str Republicii 29, the Librărie Universitas on the northern side of Piaţa Sfatului, and the Librărie Sfântu Iosif at Str Mureşenilor 14 all sell a small selection of English-language novels.

The best bookshop for city maps, postcards, guidebooks and maps of Transylvania is the Librărie Aldus at Str Apollonia Hirscher 4; it is open daily, except Sunday, from 9 am to 5 pm.

Cultural Centres The new International Trade Centre (☎ 322 025; fax 322 006; email itc@deltanet.roknet.ro), close to the train station at Str Alexandru Vlahuţă 10, should be open by 1998. It will house a business centre, conference halls and auditorium.

The German Democratic Forum (Demokratisches Forum der Deutschen) has an office in the Schei district on the corner of Str Dr Gheorghe Baiulescu and Str Prundului. The Alliance Francçaise (☎ & fax 411 626) is at Str Furcii 1.

Medical Services The pharmacy opposite the market at the northern end of Str Nicolae Bălcescu is open weekdays from 7 am to 8 pm, Saturday from 8 am to 2 pm.

The branch west of Piaţa Sfatului on Str Gheorghe Bariţul is open weekdays from 8 am to 8 pm, Saturday from 8 am to 2 pm. Farmacie Thea on Blvd Victoriei is a three minute walk from the train station; it is open weekdays from 7.30 am to 7.30 pm, Saturday from 8 am to 1 pm.

Farmacie Hyron, Str Republicii 18, is open weekdays from 7 am to 9 pm, weekends from 8 am to 9 pm.

Emergency The voluntary mountain rescue organisation, SALVAMONT (Asociaţia Naţionale a Salvatorilor Montani dîn România), has its Braşov office (☎ 416 550, 168 728) inside the municipal council building at Blvd Eroilor 8; its regional headquarters are inside the district council office (☎ 152 367) across the park at the northern end of Str Postăvarului.

The Walled City
Piaţa Sfatului is the heart of medieval Braşov. During Saxon rule it was here, in the centre of the fortified city, that markets, fairs and the general bustle of city life would unroll. In the square's centre stands the **council house** (Casă Sfatului; 1420) in which the town councillors, known as centurions, would meet. The 'keeper of the fairs' lived in the 58m **Trumpeter's Tower** on top of the council house. The council house today houses the **Braşov Historical Museum** (Muzeul de Istorie; ☎ 143 685) in which the history of the Saxon guilds is recounted. It is open daily, except Monday, from 10 am to 6 pm.

Opposite is the Renaissance **Hirscher House**, also known as the 'Merchants House'. It was built between 1539 and 1545 by Apollonia Hirscher, the widow of the Braşov mayor Lucas Hirscher following the death of her daughter. Adorned in the family's finest jewels. the daughter was buried there. Some hours later she returned to life after a grave digger broke into the coffin in an attempt to steal the jewels. So overjoyed was the widow by the resurrection that she built the Hirscher House and donated it to the city. Today it shelters the Cerbul Carpaţin restaurant.

Braşov's famed **Black Church** (Biserica Neagră), said to be the largest Gothic church between Vienna and Istanbul and still used by German Lutherans today, looms just south of the square. The church's name comes from its blackened appearance after a fire in 1689. Construction started on the church in 1383 and it was finally completed in 1477. The original statues on the exterior of the apse are now inside at the back of the church, and Turkish rugs hang from every balcony. Worshippers drop coins through the wooden grates in the floor.

The church's organ, built by Buchholz of Berlin in 1839, has 56 keys, 76 stops and 4000 pipes and is believed to be the only Buchholz preserved in its original form. Since 1891, organ recitals have been held in the church during July and August. Recitals are on Monday, Tuesday and Saturday at 6 pm; admission costs US$0.20. Equally impressive is the church's bell. It weighs seven tonnes and is said to be the largest in Romania.

TRANSYLVANIA

TRANSYLVANIA

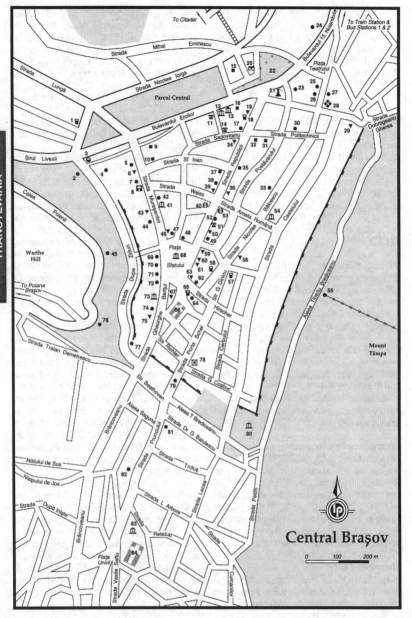

Central Braşov

0   100   200 m

PLACES TO STAY
9 Hotel Aro Palace
10 Hotel Aro Sport
16 Hotel Capitol
31 Hotel Postăvarul;
    Pizza Postăvarul
32 Hotel Coroana

PLACES TO EAT
6 Mamma Mia
19 McDonald's
29 Le Bastion Café
34 Crama Postăvarul
36 Pâine (Bread Shop)
39 Lacto-Snack
43 Rita Impex Bufet
    Expres
46 Ristorante Italiano
50 Ciao
56 Pizza Iulia
59 Restaurantul
    Chinezesc Marele
    Zid
60 Casata Cafea
    Arabică
61 Sirena Gustari
63 Cerbul Carpaţin
67 Transilvania
75 Cofetăria
    Vatra-Ardalului

OTHER
1 No 1 Disco
2 County Library
3 Bus Stop for buses to
   Poiana Braşov
4 Student Culture
   House
5 Artă Populare
7 GEEN 24-Hour Shop

8 Roman Catholic
   Church
11 Telephone Centre
12 Ethnographic Museum
13 Art Museum
14 Telephone Centre
15 Municipal Council
17 Agenţie de Voiaj
    CFR; TAROM
18 Britannia Arms Pub
20 Post Office
21 Memorial to Victims
    of 1989 Revolution
22 Heroes' Cemetery
23 District Council
24 Sică Alexandrescu
    Drama Theatre
25 Pharmacy
26 Bârsa Super
    Magazin; Casă de
    Comenzi Patiseri
27 Fruit & Vegetable
    Market
28 Star Department Store
30 Librărie Unirea
33 Reparaţii Biciclete
    Shop
35 Fuji Film Centre
37 Librărie George
    Coşbuc
38 Pro-Activ Sports Shop
40 Bancă Comercială
    Ion Ţiriac (BCIT)
41 Sală Artă
42 Librărie Sfântu Iosif
44 Royal Cinema &
    Bingo
45 White Tower
47 Nouvelles Frontiéres/
    Simpa Turism

48 Librărie Universitas
49 Agenţie Teatrală de
    Bilete
51 Telephone Centre
52 Farmacie Hyron
53 BANCOREX
54 Asociaţia Artiştitilor
    Plastici Gallery
55 Tâmpa Cable Car
    (Telecabina)
57 Grenadier Pub
58 Scotch Club
62 BAM Currency
    Exchange
64 Childrens' Theatre
65 President Disco
66 Black Church
68 Trumpeter's Tower;
    Braşov Historical
    Museum
69 IDM Currency
    Exchange
70 Pharmacy
71 Bentaco Travel
    Agency
72 Astro Sports Shop
73 Galerie de Artă
74 Kron-Tur
76 Black Tower
77 Blacksmiths' Bastion
78 Synagogue
79 Schei Gate
80 Weavers' Bastion
81 German Democratic
    Forum
82 First Romanian Lycee
83 First Romanian
    School Museum
84 Saint Nicholas'
    Cathedral

TRANSYLVANIA

The Black Church is open to visitors daily from 10 am to 5 pm. Admission is US$0.20. Services are held on Sunday.

Head north-east into the new town along Str Republicii, the main pedestrianised street. At its northern end, in front of the Braşov District council offices is a **wooden cross** to commemorate victims of the December 1989 revolution. In the **Heroes' Cemetery** opposite, on the northern side of Blvd Eroilor, a memorial slab lists 62 people – aged six to 67 – who died in Braşov on 23 December 1989.

Head west along Blvd Eroilor to the **Art Museum** (Muzeul de Artă; ☎ 144 384) and the **Ethnographic Museum** (Muzeul de

Etnografie; ☎ 143 990) which adjoin each other at Blvd Eroilor 21. The former has a permanent pottery and decorative arts exhibition in its basement and a national art gallery of Romanian paintings from the 18th century to contemporary times on the 1st floor. Temporary exhibitions are housed in the two halls on the ground floor. Admission to all three floors is US$0.50.

Silver crafted by members of Braşov's 16th century silver manufacturers guild, and fur and sheepskin coats woven by members of the 270-member-strong furrier guild are among the exhibits displayed in the excellent ethnographic museum. Costumes worn by the various inhabitants of Braşov are also exhibited: rich Saxon guild members wore thick cloth costumes decorated with lace and ribbon imported from abroad, silk blouses and girdles, and solid silver accessories. Romanians from the Schei district wore girdles with flashy metal buckles and a chain of golden coins. Saxon embroidery, noted for its black and red symmetrical motifs on a white background, is also displayed. Admission to the ethnographic museum is US$0.20.

Both museums are open daily, except Monday, from 10 am to 6 pm.

The art museum has a small gallery, **Sală Artă**, at Str Mureşenilor 12; it hosts temporary exhibitions of contemporary art and photography and is open daily, except Monday, from 11 am to 6 pm.

Continue west to the end of Blvd Eroilor then turn right along Aleea Dupa Ziduri, following the western **defensive wall**, built by Braşov's inhabitants in the 15th century to protect themselves against the Turks. The wall was 12m high and 3000m long. Seven bastions were also raised around the city at the most exposed points of the defensive wall. Each bastion – approximately 110m apart – was defended by a guild whose members, pending danger, would toll their bastion bell to beckon other guilds to take up their posts. The **Blacksmiths' Bastion** (Bastionul Fierarilor) is at the southern end of Aleea Dupa Ziduri. West of the Blacksmiths' Bastion lie the **Black Tower** (Turnul Neagră) and **White Tower** (Turnul Alba). Parts of the remains of the Black Tower collapsed in 1991 but have since been restored.

From here, continue to follow the city wall south-west, past **Catherine's Gate** (Poarta Ecaterinei, 1559) to the 16th century **Weavers' Bastion** (Bastionul Ţesătorilor) on Str Castelui. Visit the **Weavers' Bastion Museum** (Muzeul Bastionul Ţesătorilor; ☎ 144 590) with a fascinating scale model of Braşov as it was in the 17th century. The model itself was created in 1896. The museum is open daily, except Monday, from 10 am to 4 pm.

Above the bastion is a pleasant promenade through the forest overlooking Braşov. Halfway along you'll come to the **Tâmpa cable car** (Telecabina Tâmpa), which operates daily, except Monday, from 10 am to 8 pm and costs US$0.80 return. It offers a stunning view of the entire area.

Braşov's original defensive fortress was built on this mount but, by the time Vlad Ţepeş attacked Braşov (1458-1460), the citadel had been dismantled, which perhaps accounts for the ghastly death of 40 merchants who Ţepeş impaled on top of Mount Tâmpa during one of his attacks on the city. You can hike to the top following a series of zigzag trails marked by red triangles from the telecabina station (one hour) or yellow triangles from Aleea Brediceanu opposite the Le Bastion café. It is worth the effort.

In 1580 a new citadel was built in Braşov, this time on top of Citadel hill (Deal Cetăţii). Today it houses two good beer patios, a so-so disco and an expensive restaurant. Steps lead up to it from Str Nicolae Iorga.

Schei District

In Saxon Braşov, Romanians were not allowed to enter the walled city. They were banished to the Schei quarter which lay in the south-west outside the 12m-tall city walls. The entrance to this quarter from the walled city was marked by the **Schei Gate** (Poarta Schei).

As soon as you pass through the Schei Gate at the southern end of Str Poarta Schei the urban landscape changes from the sober rows of Teutonic houses in the walled old town to the smaller, simpler houses of the former Romanian settlement. Almost immediately on the left after you have passed under the gate, you come to **Str Storii**, the narrowest street in Braşov. Further south along Str Prundului, you come to the first **Romanian lycee** which opened in Braşov in 1850. It was here that the first Romanian opera *Crai Nou (New Prince)*, written by Ciprian Porumbescu (1853-83), was performed in 1882. The lycee today houses the Andrei Saguna National College (Colegul Naţional Andrei Saguna).

Continue south to Piaţa Unirii. Here you

will find the black-spired Orthodox Church of **St Nicolae din Scheii**, first built in wood in 1392 and replaced by the stone church in 1495 by the Wallachian prince Neagoe Basarab (1512-21) who, along with other princes in Wallachia, lent great support to the Romanian community in Saxon-dominated Transylvania. In 1739 the church was enlarged and its interior heavily embellished. Beside the church at Piaţa Unirii 2 is the **First Romanian School Museum** (Muzeul Prima scoli Romaneşti) on the site of a Romanian school built in 1495. Wallachian Orthodox priests came in 1556 and opened a printing press. The church is open daily from 6 am to 9 pm, and the museum is open daily, except Monday, from 10 am to 6 pm. Admission is US$0.20.

The School Museum has a small **ethnographic section** in which the history of the century-old Schei **Juni Pageant** (Sărbătoarea junilor) colourfully unfolds. This traditional folk festival takes place on the first Sunday in May. Single men – Juni – don the traditional Schei armour based on military uniforms worn by different regiments of the medieval Transylvanian army. Sword in hand they then ride on horseback from Piaţa Unirii, through the Schei Gate, to Piaţa Sfatului. They are followed by the married men – the Old Juni. During Saxon domination, this was the one day of the year when Romanians were allowed to enter the walled city.

Activities
Hire a helicopter for an aerial twirl of Braşov. Call Brex Trans (☎ 143 666; fax 151 248). The downside? It's US$320 an hour.

Braşov is the main centre for Transylvania's numerous climbing and mountaineering clubs. If you intend heading south to the Bucegi mountains or west to the Făgăraş range, consider contacting a local club beforehand. Leading clubs include:

Nature Protection Society
  (Asociaţia Pentru Protecţia Naturii), Str Mr Cranţă 41 (☎ 119 210)

Liliecii Mountain Tourism Club
  (Clubul de turism Montaru Liliecii), Str Octavian Goga 38, block 209, apartment 10
Carol Lemaru Mountain Club
  (Montaru Club Carol Lemaru), Str Republicii 14
Dinama Braşov
  Str Nicopole 34 (☎ 419 751)

Language Courses
Polish up your Romanian at the Fiatest Centru Educational (☎ & fax 410 152), Str Gheorghe Dima 2. Romanian-language classes for up to five people cost US$10 an hour. The school has branches in Bucharest, Sibiu, Baia Mare and Cluj too.

The British Council runs the PROSPER-Transilvania Language Centre (☎ & fax 153 668) at Blvd Eroilor 25.

Organised Tours
Happy Travel (☎ 153 980), Str Sadoveanu 1, opposite Hotel Coroana, arranges cheap ski packages to Poiana Braşov (US$120-150 per week for accommodation and lift tickets). Kron-Tur (☎ 471 473, 410 515; ☎ & fax 410 715) on Str Gheorghe Bariţul offers similar deals and is an agent for most private German bus companies.

Micomis Agenţie de Turism (☎ 152 086, 153 184; fax 410 321) inside the Agenţie de Voiaj CFR at Str Republicii 53, is an agent for TAROM It arranges cheap skiing packages and a variety of regional tours including an eight day 'Dracula Classical Tour'. It also arranges car rental (see Getting Around).

Special Events
Beyond the fantastic Juni Pageant (see Schei District earlier) in mid-May, Braşov hosts other annual festivals which are well worth attending

June/July sees the return of Romania's largest international pop festival, the Golden Stag (Cerbul de Aur) which attracts thousands of spectators and some top bands every year. James Brown, Boy George, Culture Beat and the Temptations have all played here. The festival runs for six or seven days and an outside stage is erected in Piaţa Sfatului. A day pass to the festival costs around US$10. Classical music lovers might prefer a ticket to the International Chamber Music Festival, usually held the first week in July in various venues around town (look for posters outside the Philharmonic), with a final concert at Bran Castle.

In August an International Photographic Art Exhibition is hosted at the art museum and in September/October, Piaţa Sfatului hosts to a one week International Beer Festival – another goodie.

December welcomes the beautiful De la Colind la Stea (From the Carol to the Star) music festival. Choirs and theatre groups from more than 28 countries perform their own traditional Christmas carols and nativities. The four day festival is usually held in the Sică Alexandrescu Drama Theatre.

Places to Stay

Camping The closest campsite is a good 3km south-east of the centre, on the road to Bucharest – *Camping Darste* (☎ 259 080; ☎ & fax 315 863) at Calea Bucureşti 285 has wooden huts for around US$5 a night as well as plenty of space for tents.

The only other convenient campsite near Braşov is at Râşnov (see Râşnov later).

Private Rooms It's hard to miss Maria and Grig Bolea (☎ 311 962) at the train station, as they meet almost every train from 8 am until 8 pm. Maria speaks perfect English and will happily show you written testimonials from satisfied customers (and photocopied extracts from Lonely Planet's *Eastern Europe on a shoestring*). Some travellers have said they found the couple too pushy (they *are* on the pushy side) and Grig can be a bit alarmist about the dangers of Braşov, (ignore his advice: the same rules apply as in any other city in the world). However, they arrange private rooms for US$10-12 per person in the city centre or in an apartment 15 minutes from the old town. The latter is the closest Romania gets to a hostel – four rooms just for travellers, with a kitchen and two bathrooms.

Hotels The only medium-priced option is the one-star *Hotel Postăvarul* (☎ 144 330;

fax 141 505) at Str Politechnicii 2 in the old town. Rooms with shared bath cost US$14/20 a night, including breakfast. Doubles with private bath are US$22. Next door and sharing the same telephone number/address is the affiliated, more upmarket, two-star *Hotel Coroana*. Doubles with/without private bath at the 'Crown' which opened its doors as a hotel in 1910, cost US$63/54, including breakfast. City maps are sold at reception.

Alternatively try the rather miserable *Hotel Aro Sport* (☎ 142 840), behind the Aro Palace Hotel at Str Sfântu Ioan 3. It has 34 rooms which often get booked out; singles/doubles are US$11/16 a night. No rooms have private bath.

The high-rise, three-star *Hotel Capitol* (☎ 118 920; fax 115 834) at Blvd Eroilor 19, is a bland relic of the 1960s with singles/doubles for US$61/79, including breakfast. Visa and AmEx are accepted. It has 180 rooms.

The four-star *Aro Palace* (☎ 142 840; fax 150 427), on Blvd Eroilor facing Parcul Central, has an Art Deco façade and amenities aimed at business travellers, including plush rooms with cable TV, telephone and fridge. Nice if you can afford US$80/113. The ridiculously large hotel reception area is the biggest in Romania. Visa/MasterCard and AmEx are accepted. The in-house Pergola restaurant specialises in Italian cuisine.

Places to Eat

Restaurants *Pizza Iulia*, a pizza and pasta spot on Str Nicolae Bălcescu has good food, low prices and friendly staff. The kitchen is open until 10.30 pm.

Despite its superb location at Piaţa Sfatului 14, *Sirena Gustari* doesn't overcharge for high-quality food. This is a good place to try Romanian specialities like sarmale (stuffed vine leaves) and mămăligă (corn porridge). The service can be a bit slow. It's open daily from 10 am to 10 pm; the menu is in English.

Braşov's most famous restaurant is the adjacent *Cerbul Carpaţin* in the Hirscher

House. The wine cellar opens in summer from 7 pm to midnight and a humungous restaurant upstairs serves meals until 10 pm year-round. Some nights folk bands play; to reserve a seat in advance call ☎ 143 981, 142 840, 144 622. The terrace bar is open daily from noon to midnight.

Ristorante Italiano, on the north-eastern side of Piaţa Sfatului, serves small but fairly authentic portions of spaghetti and lasagna as well as 15 different types of pizza. Again, service is on the slow side but at least the food is worth waiting for; the restaurant is open daily from noon to midnight. The downstairs pizzeria opens at 11 am.

Restaurantul Chinezesc Marele Zid (☎ 144 089) at Piaţa Sfatului 10, serves wonderfully delicious Chinese food at staggering prices – US$14 for a six-course set meal. Beef with peppers and special fried rice will only set you back US$5. Sadly, Braşov's ultimate splurge does not accept credit cards; it is open daily from 11 am to 11 pm.

Crama Postăvarul, on Str Republicii, opposite Hotel Coroana, is a wine cellar that serves typical Romanian dishes. It's a bit of a dive but the food and drinks are cheap, and there's often live music. The *Restaurant Faget*, close to the train station on Str Aurel Vlaicu, is OK to while away a couple of hours until your train leaves; it has an outside terrace overlooking the busy street. Alternatively, walk up Blvd Victoriei to *Sarmis Pizza*.

For a bird's eye view of Braşov, hike up to the superb *Cetate Braşov* terrace restaurant, housed within the walls of the old fortress. Chamber music recitals and folk dances are regularly held in the medieval saloon restaurant; it is open daily from 11 am to 11 pm.

Cafés *Le Bastion*, at the southern end of Aleea Tiberiu Brediceanu, serves light snacks and delicious cappuccinos on its pleasant outside terrace. The conservatory-style, inside café is warm and cosy on rainy days; it is open daily from 10.30 am to 7.30 pm.

Top notch for ice-cream floats, cakes and coffee is *Casata Cafea Arabică*, Piaţa Sfatului 12. The outside terrace is always full so get there early; it is open daily from 10 am to 10 pm.

Offering an even more mouth-watering array of gooey cakes, biscuits and gateaux is the delectable *Cofetăria Vatra-Ardalului* at Str Gheorghe Bariţul 14. The inside café is a little gloomy but you can also buy takeaway cakes; it is open daily from 9 am to 6 pm.

Mamma Mia at Str Mureşenilor 25 and *Ciao* at Str Republicii 4 sell a decadent array of banana splits and ice cream for around US$1.

Fast Food The large *Transilvania* complex off the southern end of Piaţa Sfatului on Str Gheorghe Bariţul slaps out fast food to the tinkle of one-armed bandits; it is open daily from 10 am to 10 pm.

For a healthier option, try *Lacto-Snack*, opposite the BCIT bank on the corner of Str Republicii and Str Weiss. Despite its name, it serves a meaty variety of filled bread rolls, hot dogs and kebabs for no more than US$1. It is open weekdays from 8 am to 9 pm, weekends from 9 am to 9.30 pm. The *Rita Impex Bufet Expres* at Str Mureşenilor 7 sells a good choice of sandwiches and filled rolls.

McDonald's, at the northern end of Str Republicii, is open Sunday to Thursday from 7 am to midnight, Friday and Saturday from 7 to 1 am.

Self Catering Braşov's *fruit & vegetable market* is at the northern end of Str Nicolae Bălcescu, next to *Star*, the central department store. Star is open weekdays from 9 am to 8.30 pm, Saturday from 9 am to 3 pm. The *Bârsa Super Magazin* and adjoining *Casă de Comenzi Patiseri*, directly opposite Star on Str Nicolae Bălcescu, is handy for tinned and dried products and freshly baked breads; it is open daily from 8 am to 8 pm.

Pâine, at Str Republicii 22, is a small but good bakery. *GEEN*, at Str Mureşenilor 23, is a top quality, 24-hour shop. There is another, the *Magazin Alimentar Bradul*, close to the train station on Blvd Victoriei.

Things to Buy

The Braşov Asociaţia Artiştitilor Plastici has a gallery at Str Nicolae Bălcescu 18, filled with paintings. It is open daily, except Sunday, from 9 am to 6 pm. Unusual ceramics can be picked up at the Galerie de Artă at Str Gheorghe Bariţul 4. Artă Populare at Str Mureşenilor 27 sells traditional folk costumes.

For water bottles, whistles, boots and anything else you might need for hiking (except maps) go to the superb Astro Sports shop on the eastern side of Piaţa Sfatului; it accepts credit cards. The smaller Pro-Activ sports shop at Str Republicii 17 has a good selection of sportswear and shoes.

Entertainment

Cinema Braşov has six cinemas, all of which show films in their original language with subtitles in Romanian. The most central are the *Royal* (☎ 419 965) at Str Mureşenilor 7, and the *Astra* (☎ 419 621) at Str Lunga 1.

Bars & Discos The top pub in town, with traditional smoke-filled atmosphere, is the *Britannia Arms Pub*. Despite its name, it has absolutely no connection with anything British. The pub is tucked down an alleyway next to McDonald's on Str Republicii. Those who crave a touch of the British Isles should go to the *Scotch Club* at Str Nicolae Bălcescu, open daily from 10 pm to 5 am.

Second in line for a quick pint is the *Grenadier*, opposite Pizza Iulia on the corner of Str Nicolae Bălcescu and Str Grigoraş Dinicu. Beer is more expensive here and attracts a more elite crowd; it is open Monday to Saturday from 2 pm to midnight, Sunday from noon to midnight.

Taste various Romanian wines at the *Cetate Braşov* wine cellar; it is open daily from 8 pm. Fill up your water bottle with locally brewed *Kronstadt* beer (US$2 a bottle) at the Kronstadt beer factory close to the train station at Blvd Griviţei 14.

Two of Braşov's best discos are in the Sică Alexandrescu Drama Theatre: *Disco Thalia* and *Disco Cristolety*. Both charge US$1 to US$2 admission, and US$0.75 for a beer. *No*

1 (☎ 134 444, 310 410), at the southern end of Str Lunga, is another hot spot; it is open daily from 10 pm to 6 am. In summer there is a disco outside in the *Grădină de Vară*, up the hill in the citadel, on Saturday and Sunday from 7 pm to 2 am; admission is US$1.20. The *No 1 Disco* is on Str N Iorga and the even less modest *President Disco* is next to the Children's Theatre.

The *Student Culture House* (Casă de Cultură Studenteasca), next to the Transylvania University at Blvd Eroilor 29, hosts everything from discos to drama. Performances by the Student English Theatre Club (Clubul de Teatrul în Engleza) are held here occasionally.

Theatre & Classical Music The *Sică Alexandrescu Drama Theatre* (Teatrul Dramatic Sică Alexandrescu; ☎ 151 486) on Piaţa Teatrului, has plays, recitals, and opera year-round. The *Gheorghe Dima State Philharmonic* is at Str Mureşenilor. Ask for details about both at the Agenţie de Teatrală at Str Republicii 4, just off Piaţa Sfatului. There is a *Children's Theatre* (Teatrul Pentru Copii; ☎ 142 289) at Str Apollonia Hirscher 10, and a *Puppet Theatre* (Teatrul de Păpuşi Arlechino; ☎ 142 873) on Str Ciucaş.

Getting There & Away

Bus From Autogăra 1, buses marked 'Moieciu-Bran' depart for Râşnov, Bran and Moieciu every half hour or sooner if the bus is full; pay the driver on board. Other major daily bus services from this station include one to Iaşi (326km), Miercurea Ciuc (101km), Piatra Neamţ (238km), Târgu Neamţ (280km), Târgu Mureş (172km) and Sfântu Gheorghe (32km); two to Gheorgheni (150km) and Târgovişte (90km); and four to Bacău (179km).

Major daily bus services to/from Autogăra 2 include one daily to Făgăraş (65km) and Câmpulung (84km); two to Curtea de Argeş (184km) and Piteşti (143km); and seven to Zarneşti (19km).

Hungary & Turkey International buses depart from Autogăra 1. A public bus to

Budapest departs from Braşov on Thursday at 7 am (17 hours, US$14). The return bus leaves Budapest on Saturday at 3 pm.

A private bus to Istanbul departs from Braşov on Thursday at 8 am (16 hours, US$33). The return bus leaves Istanbul on Sunday at 8 am. Tickets are sold at the Ortadoğuu Tur office (☎ 150 670) at Autogăra 1.

Germany Daily early morning and evening private buses depart from Braşov to Germany. Ticketing agencies include Double T (☎ 410 466), Str Republicii 9; Kron-Tur (☎ 151 070, 471 473), Str Baritiu 12; and Touring (☎ 150 402), Piaţa Sfatului 25.

Train Advance train tickets are sold at the Agenţie de Voiaj CFR office (☎ 142 912), Str Republicii 53, on weekdays from 7 am to 7.30 pm, Saturday from 9 am to 1 pm. International tickets are not sold at the train station.

From Braşov there is one overnight train to Chişinău (15 hours) in Moldova, departing at 7.42 pm.

The *Dacia* and *Pannonia Expres* from Bucharest to Budapest both stop at Braşov (8½ hours). The morning *Dacia* departs from Braşov at 11.11 am, arriving in Budapest at 20.47 pm. The *Pannonia* night train leaves Braşov at 7.11 pm and gets to Budapest at 6 am the following morning. In addition Budapest-bound trains, *Ister*, *Muntenia*, *Traianus* and *Alutus*, all stop at Braşov. From Budapest the *Alutus* continues to Bratislava, Prague and Berlin.

There is a daily train to Warsaw, departing from Braşov at 23.04 pm and arriving in Warsaw (22¼ hours) at 21.18 pm the next evening.

Braş is on the main Bucharest-Cluj-Napoca line.

Getting Around

Bus Bus No 4 runs from the train station and Autogăra 1 into town, stopping at Piaţa Unirii in the centre. From Autogăra 2, take bus Nos 12 or 22 from the 'Stadion Tineretului' stop on Str Stadionului into the centre. Turn right out of the bus station, walk to the end of Str Avram Iancu, then turn right onto Str Stadionului. The bus stop is in front of the stadium.

The main bus stop in town is the 'Livada Postei' at the western end of Blvd Eroilor in front of the County Library (Biblioteca Judeţeana). From here, take bus No 20 to Poiana Braşov (12km); it departs every half hour between 7 am and 9 pm. Buy your ticket from the kiosk opposite the Student Culture House before boarding. Bus No 25 leaves every half hour between the same hours for Cristian (5km).

Bicycle Try the Reparaţii Biciclete shop at Str Nicolae Bălcescu 55, or the Biciclete shop close to the train station at Blvd Gării 30. Both shops repair bikes and sell spare parts. Both are open weekdays from 8 am to noon, and 12.30 to 4.30 pm.

Car Rental The Micomis Agenţie de Turism (see Information – Travel Agencies earlier) arranges car rental for US$194 day, unlimited mileage.

Avis (☎ 142 840; fax 150 427) has an office inside Hotel Aro Palace, open weekdays from 9 am to 1 pm, and 5 to 7 pm.

Hertz (☎ 153 974) has an out-of-town office at Str Feldioaret 4-8.

Taxi Rip-off taxi drivers hover at every street corner. Calling a taxi is cheaper (☎ 319 999, ☎ 953).

AROUND BRAŞOV

There are plenty of things to see and do around Braşov. As well as the Saxon fortresses of Prejmer, Hărman and Râşnov, you can easily visit the mountain resort of Poiana Braşov or the acclaimed Bran Castle (you'll be disappointed) in a day.

Four kilometres east of Braşov in **Săcele** is a small ethnographic museum in which the traditional occupations of the villagers of Săcele are vividly illustrated. The most important day in this village is 20 July when the Sântilia shepherd festival takes place.

Prejmer & Hărman

Prejmer (Taertlauer) is an unspoiled Saxon town, first settled in 1240, with a picturesque 15th century **citadel** surrounding the 13th century **Gothic Evangelical church** in its centre. The fortress was the most powerful peasant fortress in Transylvania. Its 275 small cells on four levels lining the inner citadel wall were intended to house the local population during sieges. Villagers also stored valuables here. Its outer defensive wall – 4.5m thick and 14m tall in parts – were the thickest of all the remaining Saxon churches. The original moat surrounding the fortress was filled in 1850.

Hărman (Honigburg – literally 'honey castle') is a small Saxon village, also with a 16th century peasant citadel at its centre. Inside the thick walls is a weathered **clock tower** and a 15th century **church**. The colourful houses facing the main square are typical of the Saxon era, with large rounded doors and few windows. Like Prejmer, rural Hărman hasn't changed much since the 19th century.

Getting There & Away

From Braşov, trains leave for Ilieni (the station closest to Prejmer Citadel) at 0.12, 4.02, 5.58 and 8.20 am, and 12.08, 1.09, 4.19 and 8.13 pm (20 minutes). As you arrive at Ilieni look for the tall tower of the citadel church, to the right (south) of the railway line. Walk south on Str Nouă for about 500m, then left on Str Alexandru Ioan Cuza, which you follow to the end. Turn left to reach Str Şcolii on the right. The citadel is straight ahead.

From Ilieni trains leave for Hărman and Braşov at 1.51, 5.27, 7.27 and 9.27 am, 1.43 pm, 4.08 pm, 5.31 pm and 9.23 pm. If you decide to visit Hărman – seven minutes by train from Ilieni – walk 200m north-east from its station, turn left, cross the highway and continue straight for 2km to the centre of town.

Râşnov

Râşnov (formerly spelt Rîşnov) offers both a convenient campsite and the ruins of the late 13th century Râşnov Castle. Everyone who makes the trip agrees Râşnov's hilltop fortress is more dramatic and less touristy than the castle at Bran. As with Hărman and Prejmer, the fortress was built by the local population as protection against Tartar, and later Turkish, invasions. Indeed, almost immediately after its completion, the fortress suffered its first Tartar attack in 1335. The fortress remained functional until 1850 when it was abandoned and fell into ruin. The church, chapel, weapons' tower and jail which remain today at Râşnov were closed for restoration at the time of writing. They are expected to open again by mid-1998. Visitors who do make their way here can wander around the grounds and peer down the 154m-deep well.

Places to Stay & Eat Râşnov's campsite, *Camping Valea Cetaţii* (☎ 068-186 346), is directly below the castle on the road to Poiana Braşov, less than a kilometre from Piaţa Unirii or about 2km from the bus route to/from Braşov. There are 30 cabins at US$5 per person and camping is US$2.50 per tent. It's reliably open from June to August only.

Getting There & Away Buses marked 'Bran-Moieciu' leave hourly from Braşov's County Library (Biblioteca Judeţeana) for both Râşnov (40 minutes) and Bran (one hour). It's best to visit Bran first (see Bran later) and then stop at Râşnov on the way back.

From the bus stop in Râşnov, walk 100m east towards the mountains, turn right at Piaţa Unirii and watch for the hillside stairs in the courtyard of the unmarked Casă de Cultură (on your left). The castle is a 15 minute walk uphill.

POIANA BRAŞOV
• *area code ☎ 068*

Poiana Braşov (1030m) is Romania's premier ski resort – hordes of merry-making British tour groups head for the purpose-built resort on the slopes of Postăvarul Massif in the southern Carpathians for a cheap week of skiing and booze. Unlike its sister resort of Sinaia, 'Braşov's Clearing' –

renamed 'Stalin's Clearing' during the Stalinist era – offers few challenges for advanced skiers. But the beauty of this intermediate resort, lies in its sheltered, forested location which guarantees good skiing between early December and mid-March. Some years, you can ski here as late as May. In summer, take the cable car to the top of Mount Postăvarul (1802m) for a panoramic view of Braşov and the surrounding Carpathians.

Orientation & Information

Streets aren't named but a large map of the resort in the car park (next to the central bus stop) indicates exactly where the hotels and cable cars are.

The cheapest hotels are centred around the Complex Favorit at the eastern end of the resort. The information centre, post office and pharmacy are also here.

There is a 24 hour shop and currency exchange (open daily from 10 am to 8 pm) at the foot of the Hotel Alpin. The currency exchange also cashes travellers cheques. To make international telephone calls, go to the cable car (telecabina) station next to the Hotel Bradul, where there is an international cardphone.

Tourist Office The tourist office (☎ 262 310, 262 325, 262 271; fax 150 504) is inside the Complex Favorit. From the main bus stop turn left along the main road and then immediately right; the tourist office is 50m along this road on the left.

The tourist centre acts as the coordinating body for all the hotels in the resort except for the Sport, Bradul and Poiana. It has information on all types of accommodation in the resort and can tell you which hotels, villas and cabanas have vacancies; if you do not have pre-arranged accommodation come here and the staff can book you into a hotel or cabana to suit your budget.

The central ski school for the resort is also based in the tourist centre; you can arrange ski school and ski hire here or through one of the centre's reps in each of the hotels.

Emergency The resort clinic *(dispensar medical)* is next to the Complex Favorit; it is open daily from 8 am to 1 pm and operates a 24 hour emergency service (☎ 262 121).

The mountain-rescue team, SALVAMONT (Asociaţia Naţionale a Salvatorilor Montani dîn România; ☎ 186 176), has a permanent base at the Cabana Cristianul Mare (1690m) at the end of the gondola line on Mount Postăvarul. In case of extreme emergencies it has radio contact with its headquarters in Braşov (☎ 152 367).

Activities

Skiing From the resort there are two cable cars and a gondola to take you up to the mountain. The gondola, which is stationed near Hotel Teleferic, takes you to Cristianul Mare at 1802m. The two cable cars – one departing next to the gondola station and the other departing from near Hotel Bradul – drop you off near Cabana Cristianul Mare (1690m). Six drag lifts *(teleski)* are spread around the slopes to ease the long lug back up. Poiana Braşov has 10 slopes in all, ranging from 485m-long nursery to 2860m black slopes.

The cable cars and gondola run every half hour between 9 am and 4 pm. The trip up takes six minutes and costs US$1.20 return. Skiers can get day lift passes for unlimited rides on all cable cars, drag lifts and the gondola for US$11. A four/five/six day pass costs US$40/50/60. Children get 50% discount.

Sign up for ski school at any of the hotels or through the tourist centre (see Information – Tourist Offices earlier). A six day ski school, consisting of four hours' group tuition (eight to 10 people) a day, costs US$60/45 for adults/children. A five day course is US$40/30; and a day course US$10/8. Private lessons are US$15 an hour. Ski instructors speak English, German and French.

Skis, poles and boots can be hired through the ski school inside the tourist centre or through its hotel reps. Skis with poles/boots are US$8/12 a day and its costs US$10 a day to hire cross-country skis.

TRANSYLVANIA

When your legs can't stand any more, hire a toboggan from the central ski school and give your backside a pummelling instead.

Snowboarding & Heli-Skiing The ski school inside the tourist centre rents snowboards for US$10 a day; it also offers a six day snowboarding course comprising of two hours tuition a day for US$55. Private snowboarding lessons cost US$15 a day.

Advanced skiers can try their hand at heli-skiing in Poiana Braşov's sister resort of Sinaia. The central ski school in Poiana Braşov can arrange for skiers to go to Sinaia for the day, accompanied by an experienced heli-skier. An hour's heli-skiing costs around US$35 per person.

Ice Skating There is an outdoor ice-skating rink close to the Hotel Stadion; rent skates from the hotel reception.

Horse Riding & Sleigh Rides In winter the private horse-riding centre (☎ 262 161; Centrul de Echitaţie), 300m down the road to Braşov, arranges sleigh rides around Poiana Braşov for US$5 an hour. In summer it offers horse-riding lessons and trekking in the foothills. The centre is open daily from 10 am to 5 pm.

Hiking Various hiking trails are marked around the resort. The tourist centre can also provide you with a hiking map. You can easily hike to Braşov, Predeal, Râşnov and Timişu de Jos and Sus.

A trail marked by red crosses leads to the top of Cristianul Mare (three hours). From the top, the trail marked by red triangles leads down to the road which links Timişu de Jos (on the rail line from Sinaia to Braşov) with Timişu de Sus (2½ hours). Turn left for Jos, right for Sus.

From Cabana Cristianul Mare you can also hike down to Timişu de Jos in three to four hours. The trail is marked from the cabana with blue stripes, then blue crosses. Instead of following the blue cross trail where the path diverges, you can continue to follow the blue striped trail which eventually

takes you over the top of Tâmpa mountain into Braşov. This trail – 1½ hours – actually follows the old Braşov road.

No direct trail leads from Poiana Braşov to Cabana Cristianul Mare. Follow the marked trail (red crosses, two hours) from the resort to Cabana Postăvarul from where it is an easy one hour climb to Cristianul Mare.

From Poiana Braşov it is an easy downhill walk to Râşnov. The 9km trail, marked by blue stripes (two to three hours), follows a road for much of its descent.

From Poiana Braşov you can also hike to the neighbouring resort of Predeal (yellow stripe, five to seven hours). For those who want to break the journey, you pass the *Cabana Poiana Secuilor* and the *Cabana Trei Brazi* (☎ 018-608 917) (see Predeal – Places to Stay). From the Cabana Trei Brazi a road leads to Predeal.

A more interesting route is the hike from Poiana to the top of Cristianul Mare (1802m) from where you can follow a 3½ hour trail, marked by red triangles to the Râsnoavei gorges (Cheile Râsnoavei). From here, head south-east to Predeal (blue triangles, three hours).

Mountain Biking The Hotel Caraiman (☎ & fax 262 061) has eight mountain bikes which it rents out for US$2 an hour or US$8 a day. The Hotel Sport charges identical rates for its five bikes.

Other Activities You can hire rowing (*barcă*) and paddle boats (*hidrobicicletă*) from the Cristal Fitness Centre, open daily from 9 am to 8 pm. Boats cost US$1.20/1 an hour. A mini-golf course and tennis courts are on the road leading to Hotel Bradul. Both are open daily from 9 am to 7 pm. Mini-golf/tennis, including racquet and ball hire, costs US$1.20 an hour.

Organised Tours
The tourist office inside the Complex Favorit offers various day trips from Poiana Braşov. Excursions include Bran castle followed by

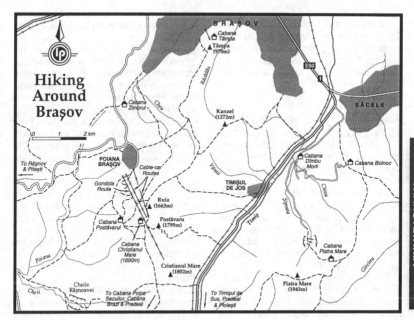

Hiking Around Braşov

BRAŞOV

Cabana Tâmpa
Tâmpa (970m)

Cabana Zimbrul

Kanzel (1272m)

SĂCELE

To Râşnov & Piteşti

POIANA BRAŞOV

Cable-car Routes

Gondola Route

Ruia (1663m)

Postăvaru (1799m)

Cabana Postăvarul

Cabana Christianul Mare (1690m)

Cristianul Mare (1802m)

Cabana Dîmbu Morii

Cabana Bolnoc

TIMIŞUL DE JOS

Cabana Piatra Mare

Cheile Râşnoavei

To Cabana Poipa Secuilor, Cabana Brazi & Predeal

To Timişul de Sus, Predeal & Ploieşti

Piatra Mare (1843m)

TRANSYLVANIA

a traditional Romanian lunch in Moieciu (US$14), the spa resort of Covasna (US$12), Sinaia (US$9), Bucharest (US$28), the Bicaz gorges (US$23), Sighişoara (US$16), Sibiu (US$19), Sâmbăta de Sus monastery (US$15), and a drive across the Trans-Făgăraşan highway (US$18). The centre also arranges various traditional folklore evenings in the resort. It's open daily from 8 am to 8 pm. Tours can also be booked through one of the centre's reps in each of the hotels.

Places to Stay

Most travel agencies in Braşov take bookings for hotels in Poiana Braşov. Except for a couple of weeks over Christmas and New Year, you can always find a room at the resort. Nightly rates in all the hotels include breakfast.

Cabanas The *Cabana Cristianul Mare* (☎ 186 545), at 1690m, offers 56 beds in two to eight-bed rooms at US$3 per person. This large wooden chalet and the attached restaurant, both overlooking the slopes, are open throughout the year, except for a few weeks in November.

Fifteen minutes downhill from Cristianul Mare is the calmer *Cabana Postăvarul* (☎ 186 356), at 1585m. It also charges US$3 a night for a bed in a shared room. It has a better atmosphere than Cristianul Mare, with fewer cable-car tourists, but it's sometimes closed.

The *Cabana Poiana Secuilor* is at 1070m and, further along, there is the *Cabana Trei Brazi* (☎ 018-608 917) at 1130m. A bed in a shared room costs US$11 to US$17 in both.

Villas Luxury, private villas offering private rooms are sprouting up all over Poiana Braşov. The tourist centre can arrange accommodation in villas for around US$20 a night. Rooms are cheapest in the *tourist village*, opposite Complex Favorit.

Among the nicest places to stay in Poiana Braşov is the *Casă Viorel* (☎ 262 042), run by the same enterprising couple who run the thriving Outlaws' Hut (see Places to Eat). It has 10 rooms, costing US$30 a night for a double.

Hotels The cheapest hotel in Poiana Braşov is the slightly shabby *Poiana Ursului* (☎ 252 216, 262 308), next to the tourist village in the 'cheap end' of the resort. Double/triple rooms with shared bathroom are US$14/19 a night.

The *Hotel Ruia* (☎ 262 202) and the *Villa Alunis* (☎ 262 320; fax 150 472), adjoining each other just south of the Poiana Ursului, are overpriced for the grotty rooms and sour service they offer. Singles/doubles in the Alunis are US$30/35; the Ruia has 20 doubles for US$30.

The 66-room *Hotel Caraiman* (☎ & fax 262 061), behind the Cristal Fitness Centre, has single/double rooms with private bathroom for US$14/20. Luxury apartments cost US$30. It also rents out mountain bikes (see Activities).

Next door is the two-star *Hotel Piatra Mare* (☎ 262 226) which has singles/doubles for US$32/55. The hotel has an efficient tourist office and a currency exchange which gives cash advance on Visa.

Close by on the same street is the two-star *Hotel Şoimul* (☎ 262 111; fax 262 154). It has 107 doubles, costing US$23. Directly opposite is the more inviting *Hotel Ciucaş* (☎ & fax 262 181), also two-star, but offering a more friendly – and expensive – service in a modern setting. Singles/doubles cost US$43/55. The Pontica art gallery in the hotel lobby sells the best selection of paintings and souvenirs.

The Sport, Bradul and Poiana hotels at the southern end of the resort are owned by the separate Hotel Ana group – the *Poiana* (☎ 262 313, 150 480; fax 262 130) has singles/doubles for US$38/50. The *Bradul* (☎ 150 480, 262 313; fax 262 130), hidden among trees, charges US$33/44 for singles/doubles, and is one of the few hotels

in the resort to have triple rooms, costing US$58.

The *Hotel Sport*, wedged between the Poiana and Bradul, is the most exclusive in the resort, charging US$43/56 for singles/doubles. It also rents out mountain bikes. Poiana Braşov's other top hotel is the three-star *Hotel Alpin* (☎ 262 343; fax 252 211) which you pass as you enter the resort from Braşov. It has 129 rooms, most with a balcony and all with a mini bar and cable TV. Singles/doubles are US$62/80. Luxury doubles cost US$117 and apartments are a staggering U$179.

En route to Poiana Braşov from Braşov you pass the *Hotel Restaurant Valea Cetăţii* (☎ 230 266), a pretty chalet, beautifully furnished (for the price), with bargain rooms at around US$7. It's not in the resort centre but it's cheap.

Places to Eat

All the hotel restaurants make an effort to serve typical Romanian dishes. Nothing can beat Poiana Braşov's famed *Coliba Haiducilor* (☎ 262 137) or 'Outlaws' Hut' as it is generally known. It is beautifully decorated in a traditional rustic style with dried corn cobs strung from the ceiling and sheepskins lining the walls. A fire burns in the hearth in winter and live folk bands play. In autumn, jars of pickles adorn the small 'museum' outbuilding in which traditional weaving looms are displayed. The restaurant, at the southern end of the resort, is open year-round from noon to around 1 am.

Animal lovers may want to avoid the *Sura Dacilor* (Dacians' Grange; ☎ 262 327), next to the Cristal Fitness centre, which has even more sheepskins on the walls than the Outlaws' Hut, plus a couple of wild boar skins. Enough to put you off eating. The food is excellent however (yes, they do serve bear steaks!) and the waiters are dressed in traditional costume. Very charming. It is open daily from 11 am to midnight.

A bit of a trek north, but worth it, is the *Stână* (Sheep Farm) restaurant, housed on a genuine, working sheep farm. Home-made cheese and other delectable products of the house are served here; it is also open daily from 11 am to midnight.

Entertainment

The Caraiman, Şoimul and Bradul hotels all have popular discos, open from around 10 pm until the early hours of the morning. There is a *Disco Ski Club* inside the Cristal Fitness Centre, open 10 pm to 4 am; and the *Disco Violeta* is on the right as you enter the resort from Braşov.

Complex Favorit touts a cinema, cabaret hall, nightclub, restaurant, bowling alley and other fickle amusements.

Getting There & Away

From Braşov, bus No 20 runs from the Livada Postei bus stop opposite the County Library (Biblioteca Judeţeana) at the western end of Blvd Eroilor to Poiana Braşov every 20 minutes between 6.30 and 8.30 am, and every 30 minutes from 8.30 am until 7.30 pm. The journey takes 30 minutes. Upon arrival in Poiana Braşov, the bus waits 15 minutes before embarking on the return journey.

BRAN
• *area code* ☎ *068*

For many travellers Bran, 30km south of Braşov, is their first (or only) glimpse of rural Romania. And indeed, for most, the experience lives up to expectation. This was the first part of Romania to be developed as a tourist hub in the 1960s. Many properties were never nationalised and cash was poured into the little village to make it the gold mine it is today.

Travellers who set foot further afield in other rural parts of the country will quickly realise that Bran, with its luxury villas and private cottages kitted out with hot water and indoor bathrooms, is not representative of Romania.

The town is nestled in a mountain pass between the Bucegi and Piatra Craiului ranges and during the 15th and 16th centuries was an important frontier town on the main road leading from Transylvania into Wallachia.

Orientation & Information

The centre of Bran lies either side of the main Braşov-Piteşti road (Str Principală) which cuts through the village from north to south. The entrance to the castle, signposted 'Muzeul Bran', is on the left as you enter the town from Braşov. The main cluster of shops and cafés and the currency exchange are centred around this junction.

The bus stop is further south on Str Principală, next to the park. From the bus stop, turn right along Str Principală and then right onto Str Aurel Stoian to get to the Bran Imex tourist office. The central post and telephone office is south of Bran centre, past the Vama Bran museum on the road to Moieciu.

Bran Castle

Despite popular myth, Bran castle, commonly known as 'Dracula's castle', was *not* built by Vlad Ţepeş, the Wallachian prince upon whom the 19th century novelist Bram Stoker is (incorrectly) supposed to have based his bloodthirsty vampire count. The 14th century castle, perched atop a 60m peak in the centre of Bran village, was in fact built by the people of Braşov in 1382 to defend the Bran mountain pass against Turks. In 1413, the Wallachian ruler allowed the people to set up custom posts on the Braşov road and Bran pass. The customs house just south of the castle levied a 3% tax on all commercial goods carried along the Bran pass.

From 1920 the castle was inhabited by Queen Marie. Bran Caste remained a summer royal residence until the forced abdication of King Michael in 1947.

Bran Castle, with its fairytale turrets and Mediterranean whitewashed walls, is far from menacing. Much of the original furniture imported from Europe by Queen Marie is still inside the castle's thick stone walls. A fountain in the courtyard conceals a labyrinth of secret underground passages. Tour guides will tell you that Vlad Ţepeş, upon whom Bram Stoker allegedly based his vampire Count Dracula, might have sought refuge for a few days in Bran on his flight

A castle fit for a vampire ... but Vlad Țepeș probably never stayed here.

from the Turks in 1462 following their attack on Poienari fortress in the Argeş valley (see Poienari & Arefu in the Wallachia chapter).

Free guided tours of Bran Castle are available in English, French, Romanian and Italian. Admission to the castle's 57 recently restored rooms costs US$2 (US$1.50 with a student card). This also includes entrance to the open-air **ethnographic museum** at the foot of the castle. The complex is open daily, except Monday, from 9 am to 5 pm.

Around Bran Castle
From the castle, walk south along Str Principală past the centre of the village to the **Vama Bran Museum** (Muzeul Vama Bran), housed in the former customs house. Various archaeological treasures as well as rather too many photographs of the castle from varying angles are displayed; admission costs US$2/1.20 for adults/students.

Opposite the former customs house, next to the campers' field, are some remains of the old **defensive wall** which divided Transylvania from Wallachia (best viewed from the soldiers' **watchtower** in the castle). On the southern side of the wall is a small stone **chapel**, built in 1940 in memory of Queen

Marie. The church, now abandoned and boarded up following attacks by vandals, is a copy of a church in the queen's palace grounds in Balcic, Bulgaria (formerly southern Dobruja). A **memorial tomb** to the queen has been carved in the mountain, on the north side of the wall at the western end of the campers' field.

Special Events
In mid-September, Bran hosts the Festivalul Clătitelor (Pancake Festival) and vast amounts of pancakes topped with decadent delights are washed down with locally produced plum brandy (ţuică).

September is also the month of the Sâmbra oilor, a major pastoral festival celebrated with great gusto in Bran and its surrounding villages.

On 31 October the US Peace Corps host a Halloween party in Bran Castle and the town is also considered the top venue in Romania to celebrate the new millennium.

Places to Stay
Camping You can camp for free in the field across the stream from the Vama Bran Museum, just below Bran Castle. Otherwise, *Cabana Bran Castel* (☎ 236 404), a rustic chalet on the hillside 600m from the castle, provides accommodation for US$3 per person in a double/triple room with shared bath. Meals are served and it is open year-round, but fills up quickly in summer. From the bus stop, turn right along Str Principală then right along Str Aurel Stoian (or cut across the park instead); continue for 50m and then turn left onto a narrow path by the side of the hospital (a yellow-painted building). Cross the bridge over the stream and bear left up to the cabana.

Private Rooms Bran-Imex (☎ 236 642; fax 152 598), the agent for ANTREC in Bran at Str Aurel Stoian 395, is one of the most organised – and successful – tourist agencies in Romania. It arranges accommodation in some 250 different private homes in Bran and nine surrounding villages (see Around

The Warrior Queen

'There is only one man in Romania and that is the Queen.' At least, that is how the French minister in Bucharest described Queen Marie of Romania who, upon his advice, went on an SOS mission to the Paris Peace Conference in 1919 to bolster Romania's flagging image abroad. Her subsequent diplomatic coup contributed to her legendary status.

Queen Marie (1875-1938) was the granddaughter of Britain's Queen Victoria and the oldest daughter of the Duke and Duchess of Edinburgh. She married Ferdinand I (1865-1927), heir to the Romanian throne, in 1892. Despite widespread horror in Britain at the young princess being ill-matched to a prince of a 'semi-barbaric' country, Marie subsequently developed a strong kinship with Romania, prompting her final declaration 'My love for my country [Romania] is my religion'.

Seventeen-year-old Marie spent the first two years of married life pining for the glittering courts of western Europe and producing heirs. Following an alleged love affair with the American aristocrat, Waldolf Astor, she knuckled down to twisting her tongue around the Romanian language, acquainting herself with Romanian politics, and meeting as many of her future subjects as possible.

In 1913 during the second Balkan war the princess ran a cholera hospital for Romanian soldiers on the Bulgarian side of the Danube. The following year, after the death of Carol I, Ferdinand I was crowned king and Marie became queen.

Despite proving herself to be a 'viable political force', handsomely equipped with all the 'necessary tools of statemanship', Queen Marie remained the 'people's princess' throughout her reign. At the outbreak of WWI she wrote her first book, *My Country*, to raise funds for the British Red Cross in Romania.

Prior to her evacuation of Iaşi in 1916, she worked in hospitals in Bucharest, distributing food and cigarettes to wounded soldiers during daily rounds of the wards. In Iaşi she set about reorganising the appallingly makeshift hospitals, demanding fuel and sanitation equipment be brought in. Dressed in white, she kept a ready supply of crosses and icons in her apron pocket to give to dying soldiers and became famed for her courageous refusal to wear rubber gloves in the typhus wards.

After she represented Romania at the peace conference in Paris, the French press dubbed her the 'business queen'. A mother of six, she wrote over 100 diaries from 1914 until her death in 1938. During her lifetime 15 of her books – fairytales, romances and travelogues – were published. Her autobiography, *The Story of my Life*, appeared in two volumes in 1934-5.

Queen Marie is buried in Curtea de Argeş. Her heart, originally encased in a gold casket and buried in Balcic, southern Dobruja, is safeguarded in the treasury of Bucharest's national history museum. ∎

Bran – Places to Stay). The office is open in summer daily from 8 am to 9 pm, and in winter from 10 am to 6 pm. If you call in advance, staff will meet you out of office hours too. The agency can also arrange long and short-term rentals for an entire property.

For a whirlwind of luxury and decadence – even by western standards – go for the *Vila Alba*, an incredibly large mansion with a master bedroom and en suite bathroom that would have made even Ceauşescu's hair curl. The villa is owned by a rich Romanian émigré; the house is run, however, by a down-to-earth, friendly couple who do everything to make you feel at home. A night's stay, including full board, is US$55. Bookings can be made through ANTREC.

Hotels The one-star *Han Bran* (☎ 236 556),

two blocks from the castle on the right as you enter Bran from the north along Str Principală, charges US$10 per person for a bed in one of its 22 double rooms with private shower and toilet. Hot water flows from 8 pm to midnight. The front terrace is a good place for a meal.

Opposite the main bus stop on Str Principală in the centre of the village is the *Casă de Creatic* (☎ 236 738). The hotel has 25 beds in double/triple rooms with shared bathroom. A bed costs US$3 a night, including breakfast. The hotel has no sign outside; it is the large, wooden chalet-style building at the foot of the castle. Its restaurant is open daily from 10 am to 10 pm; there is a pool table in the adjoining bar.

The *Bran Benzin* petrol station (☎ 151 675) at the northern end of Bran has six rooms above the station. Doubles with private/shared bath are US$10/9 a night and a more spacious apartment is US$11.

Places to Eat

Both hotels have restaurants. However, nothing can beat the home-made cheese, jam, ţuică and other culinary delights you will be treated to if you stay in a private home. The *Bella Italia Pizzeria*, opposite the Vama Bran museum on the road south out of the village, serves good pizza for around US$1.20. It is open daily from 11 am to 10 pm. Campers can stock up on provisions at the *Dracula Market*, on the corner of Str Principală and the turn-off to the castle; or at the *alimentar* close by on Str Principală.

Entertainment

At weekends, Bran youths flock to the Cabana Bran Castel to boogie the night away in its terrace disco; it is open Friday and Saturday from 9 pm to 5 am, Sunday from 6 pm to midnight.

Getting There & Away

Buses marked 'Bran-Moeciu' leave hourly from Braşov's Central bus station. The journey takes one hour. From the bus stop in Bran the castle is easy to spot. Return buses to Braşov depart from Bran every hour between 5.40 am and 7.40 pm; at weekends buses run between 6.40 am and 5.40 pm. All buses to Braşov stop at Râşnov and Cristian.

From Bran there are also buses daily, except Sunday, to Zarneşti (40 minutes) departing at 6, 9 and 11 am, and 2, 5 and 6 pm; and to Moieciu hourly between 7.30 am and 9.30 pm (15 minutes).

AROUND BRAN

The villages around Bran are spectacular, both in riches and rural attractions. Modern luxury villas abound but the wild landscape remains untouched. Traditional occupations such as sheep farming, wool weaving and cheese making are vital to villagers' daily survival. Agro-tourism is well developed

and finding a bed for the night in a rural home is no problem.

Some 3km south-east along a dirt road from Bran is the village of **Şimon**. Its 19th century water-powered saw mills were moved to Bran's ethnographic museum long ago; today people come to see the big brown bears, which roam in the forests nearby. Bran-Imex (see Places to Stay) arranges bear-watching tours here. Hiking trails lead into the Bucegi mountains (see the Bucegi Mountains section).

Until 1992, **Moieciu**, 4km south of Bran on the road to Câmpulung, was famed throughout Romania for the pine-aroma cheese it produced in its village factory. This was forced to close in 1992 when machinery became outdated and it could not afford to modernise. Most families in the village, however, make their own *casă caşcaval* (homemade cheese). The village **trout farm** remains afloat.

From Moieciu, a dirt track leads northwest to **Peştera** (literally 'Cave'). The 160m-long cave from which the village gains its name is home to a colony of bats. Bran-Imex (see Places to Stay) arranges rural accommodation here as well as visits to a shepherds' *stână* where you can taste the local cheese and milk. From here it is an easy 6km ride north through **Măgura** to Zărneşti (see the Piatra Craiului section).

A few kilometres south-east of Moieciu is **Cheia**, home to one of the region's few remaining 19th century painted churches which have not been shifted to Bran's ethnographic museum. Wool has been manufactured in this village since the Middle Ages. Continuing south along the upper course of the Moieciu river, you come to the village of **Moieciu de Sus** with another pretty church. Various hiking trails into the Bucegi mountains are marked from here (see the Bucegi Mountains section).

Fundata, 25km south of Bran on the road to Câmpulung, is a popular cross-country skiing spot and host to the annual Nedeea Munţilor folklore festival on 25 August. Continuing south along the Câmpulung road, you come to **Podu Dâmboviţei**, home

MARK DAFFEY

COLIN D SHAW

NICOLA WILLIAMS

Transylvania
Top: 'Dracula's Castle', Bran
Bottom left: Peleş Castle, Sinaia
Bottom right: Prefecture, Târgu Mureş

Transylvania
Top: Forest track, Harghita mountains, near Odorheiu Secuiesc
Bottom: Lake Colibiţa, near Bistriţa

to the Peştera Dâmbovicioarei. The cave, 870m deep, is not particularly noteworthy but the drive to it is. Sheer rockfaces line either side of the road. It is a popular picnic stop.

Piatra Craiului

Local climbers rave about the twin-peaked 'Stone of the Prince' mountain in the Bâsei depression in the south-west Carpathians. They might not be the highest – Piatra Mică peaks at 1816m and Piatra Mare at 2238m – but these mountains offer climbers one of Romania's greatest challenges.

The range, 25km in length, stretches from Zărneşti in the north to Podu Dâmboviţei in the south. Piatra Mică's summit is marked by a large stone cross, visible from Cabana Plaiu Foii, the main access point to Piatra Craiului at the foot of the range. Since 1939 the entire area has been protected. Its trea-

sures include mountain cocks, black goats, wolves, stags and unusual hazel-coloured bears.

The *floare de colt* ('flower of stone', better known as the edelweiss) is also common to Piatra Craiului, as is the pink, vanilla-perfumed *sângele voinicului* ('blood of a brave man') which flowers in May and June. Traditionally, villagers ate this flower in the belief that it was a source of superhuman strength.

Piatra Craiului is a limestone ridge characterised, particularly in the north-west, by its numerous *padine* – valleys totally without water. Above 1200m the range does not retain water, while the eastern ridge is a rich karst area boasting numerous caves.

Hiking A great deal of Piatra Craiului is inaccessible to tourists due its deep rocky gullies and sheer rock faces. The best access

TRANSYLVANIA

Cry Wolf!

The Carpathian Large Carnivore Project (CLCP) is the biggest of its type in Europe. Through its extensive pioneering research and field studies coupled with its innovative ecotourism program, it works towards the future survival of Romania's large wolf and brown bear populations.

Based in the Bucegi-Piatra Craiului Biosphere Reserve in the southern Carpathians, the project has its headquarters in Prejmer, near Braşov. Its field cabin in Zarneşti is home to two wolves called Crai and Poiana. These wolves were rescued as cubs by project workers from a fur farm in central Romania. Crai and Poiana were subsequently hand-raised at the field cabin, today happily mingling with tour groups and serving as a vital educational tool for the Large Carnivore Project.

Tracking radio-tagged wolves and brown bears by four-wheel drive vehicles, snowmobiles, ultralight deltaplane, on skis and on foot, is an equally integral part of the wardens' work. Since 1994 10 wolves have been briefly ensnared by steel leg-hole traps, tranquillised, fitted with a collar bearing a radio tag, then set free to roam wild once more in their natural habitat. Project wardens can then follow the feeding and behaviour patterns of the pack at large.

Timiş, a female wolf tagged since 1995, spends most of her time prowling around the village of Timişul de Jos near Bran. In summer her 'downtown' pack ventures by night into Dârste, a Braşov suburb, to raid waste bins for food. Given the large number of stray dogs prevalent in most Romanian cities, few Braşov dwellers realise that Timiş is in fact a wolf!

Sheep provide another rich food supply for the pack in summer. Between May and July 1997 the downtown pack killed 30 sheep from one flock. Wild red deer and garbage bins provide the mainstay of Timiş's diet during the winter months.

The radio tags also enable wardens to discern the extent of human persecution of wolves. Of the 10 wolves tagged, two have been shot by hunters, one shot by a shepherd, and another poached.

Research of Romania's impressive brown bear population is still in its early stages. This will soon change however thanks to the radio tags worn by a sow and her two cubs who were successfully trapped and collared in April 1997. The three bears were ensnared while feeding by night from a garbage bin in Racadav, a Braşov suburb.

The CLCP is a joint venture between the Munich Wildlife Society (☎ 8822-921 20; fax 8822-921 12; email wgm.ev@t-online.de), Linderhof 2, D-82488 Ettal; and the Wildlife Research Department, Şoseaua Ştefaneşti 128 sect 2, Bucharest RO-72904. ∎

is from Zărneşti, some 15km north-west of Bran along a forest road, or from Dimbovicioara, 25km south of Bran. Hiking trails are marked from villages.

If you plan to hike from Bran, the quickest route is along the dirt road to Predulut, through the village of Tohaniţa to Zărneşti. From Zărneşti, follow the road signposted *spre Cabana Plaiu Foii 12km*. Some 2km along this road, a trail marked by blue stripes takes you to Colţul Chiliei (two hours).

From Peştera, you can hike along the dirt track to Măgura and again head north to Zărneşti. From Cabana Plaiu Foii, a 6km trail marked by yellow triangles leads to Fantăna lui Botorog and eventually to Cabana Curmătura (three hours).

A trail marked by red circles takes climbers along the most challenging route from Cabana Plaiu Foii, through the Cheile Zăruestiului to the Regugiul Grind and, ultimately, up to Vârful Omu (three to four hours). This route is not possible in winter and is only recommended for experienced climbers; ropes are needed in places.

In May/June and September Piatra Craiului gets heavy rainfall. Summer storms are frequent and in winter much of the mountain cannot be accessed. Avalanches are common.

A map with all the trails marked is inside the SALVAMONT office at the foot of the mountain close to Cabana Plaiu Foii. If you intend venturing up the mountain for any length of time, you should inform the voluntary mountain rescue team of your plans, including an outline of the route you intend to follow. The emergency hut is staffed from 1 May to 1 October. Between 20 December and 20 April the team is based at Cabana Postăvarul (see Poiana Braşov) for the skiing season.

In the central square in Zărneşti village, there is a small noticeboard with contact telephone numbers for leading SALVAMONT members. You can also contact the Primăria Oraş Zărneşti for information (☎ 068-220 455).

Six kilometres from Zărneşti, en route to Cabana Plaiu Foii, you pass Cabana Lupului,

the base camp for the Carpathian Wolf project. The project – the largest of its type in Europe – was set up in 1993 as a joint Romanian-German-French project. Wolf cubs are being raised at the camp and the project includes studies into the movements of Romania's wolf and bear populations which total 40% and 60% respectively of the world's total wolf and bear populations. Visitors must book well in advance through an authorised agent abroad (see Facts for the Visitor – Activities and the boxed aside on the project for more details).

Places to Stay

Bran-Imex (☎ 068-236 642; fax 068-152 598), Bran's ANTREC agent at Str Aurel Stoian 395, Bran, arranges accommodation in private homes in Şimon, Fundata, Moieciu and Moieciu de Sus, Cheia and Peştera. It also provides English or French-speaking guides to show you around the Bran area; and arranges hiking, fishing, bear watching, and cheese tasting tours in the area.

In Moieciu de Sus, the *Crăiasa Muntilor* (☎ 068-153 900), in the centre of the village at No 17, has 11 comfortable double rooms with original pottery stoves and wooden furnishings for US$11 a night. Bathrooms are shared. Breakfast costs US$2 extra.

The *Cabana Plaiu Foii*, at the foot of Piatra Craiului, is a large complex attracting many frivolous climbers who spend most of their stay just looking at the mountain while drinking around their camp fire. The cabana has beds in double/triple/four-bed rooms for US$3 per person a night. In a five or six-bed room a place is US$2. You can also pitch your tent in the field. It is signposted from the centre of Zărneşti.

Some 200m north, there is a private *Cabana*, which was being renovated at the time of writing. It should be open by early 1998. It has 20 upmarket rooms in a main building and lots of tent space. Serious climbers come here.

PREDEAL
• *area code* ☎ *068*

It might well be Romania's highest (1033m)

but it's definitely not Romania's hottest skiing spot. Unlike its sister resorts, Predeal has just a couple of slopes, which generally attracts hordes of local kids on school camps. Few tour groups come here.

Orientation
The shops and main facilities in the resort are centred around the train station at the western end of town. Shops selling hiking gear and the resort's only currency exchange are inside the Complex Commercial; turn right out of the train station and walk 50m along Blvd Mihai Săulescu.

Information
Tourist Offices The Agenţie de Turism Ingrid (☎ 456 972; fax 456 376), inside the train station building, sells a good selection of hiking maps of the Bucegi and Făgăraş mountains as well as tourist guides for Sinaia and Predeal. It arranges accommodation in hotels, villas and cabanas in the resort *(dispecerat cazare)*, although it is not always up to date on the cheapest places to stay. The office is open daily, except Sunday, from 9 am to 6 pm. The staff do not speak English.

Staff at the Biroul de Turism (☎ 455 042), behind the post office at Str Ponduri 6, are better informed about nightly rates in hotels and cabanas and are willing to phone around to see where there are vacancies. It is open daily from 10 am to 6 pm. There is a third tourist office, Predeal SA, (☎ 256 545) at Blvd Mihai Săulescu 74.

Money You can change money in the Bachide Exchange (☎ 456 870) inside the Complex Commercial on Blvd Mihai Săulescu; the office is open weekdays from 7 am to 9 pm and at weekends from 10 am to 6 pm. None of the hotels has currency exchanges.

Post & Communications The central post office, opposite the Complex Commercial on Blvd Mihai Săulescu is open weekdays from 7 am to 8 pm. The telephone office, in the same building, is open daily from 7 am to 9 pm.

Emergency The emergency clinic (dispensar policlinic; ☎ 456 313) is opposite the Hotel Bulevard on Blvd Mihai Săulescu.

Activities
Skiing Predeal has just two slopes served by two chair lifts *(telescaun)* and two drag lifts *(teleski)*, all run by the Clăbucet Zona de Agrement (☎ 456 451) at the eastern end of Str Telefericului. The chair lifts operate daily year-round, between 9 am and 5 pm. The drag lifts only run in winter, from around mid-December to mid-March. It costs US$0.70 for the chairlift and US$0.35 for the drag lift.

Ski passes are sold on a point *(puncte)* system; in the 1996-7 ski season, a five/10/20 point card cost US$1.30/2.40/4.20. A ride on a chair lift/drag lift costs two/one points. The ticket office is open daily, except Monday, from 9 am to 5 pm.

Predeal has one central ski school, the Fulg de Nea (literally 'Snow Flake'; ☎ 456 089) close to the ski lifts at Str Telefericului 1. A six-day ski school comprising two/four hours per day group tuition costs US$17/35 (not including a ski pass). Private lessons are US$3 an hour and a day's rental of skis, poles and boots is US$2. Most of the hotels also arrange ski school and hire; however, they simply go through the ski school and add their own commission. Staff at the ski school speak English – go directly to them.

The centre also has an ice skating rink in winter; it costs US$0.80 for three hours plus another US$0.70 for skate hire. A horse-drawn sledge ride is a hefty US$1.20 per person per kilometre. At the time of writing, the ski centre was still partly under construction; a ski club with fitness centre and sauna on the 1st floor will open by 1998.

Tennis The Hotel Orizont has two outdoor tennis courts. Private tennis lessons cost US$5 an hour, court hire is also US$5 an hour and the hire of two racquets and balls is US$1.50 an hour. Courts should be booked in advance.

The Fulg de Nea has three courts, costing

US$2.20 an hour for the court, US$0.60 for a racquet and US$0.15 for a ball.

Places to Stay

Some of Predeal's larger hotels and cabanas get booked out during the skiing season. Many of the hotels which include breakfast in their nightly rate issue breakfast vouchers which can, in fact, be spent anywhere in the hotel.

Private Rooms Providing you arrive in Predeal at a reasonable time of day, you will be surrounded by a swarm of babushkas the minute you step off the train offering you a room *(cazare)* for the night. Buy a map of the resort from the tourist office inside the train station building (see Information – Tourist Offices above) and clarify exactly where the room you are being offered is before you agree to even see it. Bargain too! The going rate in mid-1997 was around US$10 a night.

Cabanas The *Cabana Clăbucet-sosire* (☎ 456 541) at the foot of the ski lift (telescaun) has 70 places in double and triple rooms costing US$6 a night. Its sister cabana, the *Cabana Clăbucet-plecare* (☎ 456 312), at the top of the ski lift run (1714m) has 80 places in shared rooms with private bath, also for US$6 a night. Both cabanas get full in winter. You can pitch your tent on the wasteland below the ski lift along Str Teleferic.

Five kilometres from Predeal in Trei Brazi is the *Cabana Trei Brazi* (☎ 018-608 917). Double/triple/four-bed rooms with private bath are US$11/17/17 a night, including breakfast. Doubles with shared bath and no breakfast at the *Chalet Vânătorul* (☎ 455 285), some 3km west of the resort on the road to Trei Brazi, cost US$8. Hiking trails lead from the Trei Brazi to Poiana Braşov (see Poiana Braşov – Hiking).

Hotels The cheapest hotel beds in the resort are at the one-star *Hotel Rozmarin* (☎ 256 422; fax 256 894), tucked away at the north-eastern end of the resort at Str Mihai Săulescu 159. Clean singles/doubles with shared shower cost US$6/12 a night, including breakfast. Close by is the cheap, but not so cheerful, *Hotel Cirus* (☎ 456 035), in front of the Orizont hotel on Str Avram Iancu. It has 35 doubles with private bath for US$16 a night, excluding breakfast. The entrance to the hotel is off Str Trei Brazi.

The *Hotel Carmen* (☎ 456 656, 456 517), at Str Mihai Săulescu 121, is a bright and cheerful hotel, close to the train station, with singles/doubles with private bath reasonably priced at US$12/21.

East of the railway tracks, heading towards the ski lifts, is the *Hotel Carpaţi* (☎ 456 273; fax 455 411) at Str Nicolae Bălcescu 1. It has 77 doubles with private bath for US$15. Budget-conscious backpackers should ask for a room in the hotel's *Villa Bălcescu*, on the same street. Double/four-bed rooms with private bath cost a bargain US$8/10.

Close by, at the western end of Str Muncii at No 6, is the one-star *Hotel Robinson* (☎ & fax 456 753) which has 19 doubles costing US$15. Rooms are pretty shabby. Slightly more inviting is the ageing *Hotel Predeal* (☎ 456 705) opposite. Singles with private bath are US$12 and doubles with/without balcony are US$24/20. The price includes breakfast. The Predeal also takes bookings for the dilapidated *Hotel Tourist* which looks more like a prison than a hotel. Singles/doubles/triples are appropriately cheap at US$6/5/5 a night.

At the north-eastern end of the resort up a steep hill on Str Libertăţii you'll find the two-star *Hotel Cioplea* (☎ 456 870, 456 871). Doubles/triples with private bath cost US$20/42.

Predeal's top hotel is the three-star *Hotel Orizont* (☎ 455 150), a large, modern, chalet-style building at Str Trei Brazi 6. It has all the mod cons including a health club, swimming pool, sauna, and massage parlour. It has a Romanian and Chinese restaurant as well as the flash Bahamas cocktail bar overlooking the swimming pool and the Cristal nightclub. Singles/doubles with cable TV and private bath cost US$23/28. The hotel accepts credit cards.

Villas Predeal boasts villas galore, many very luxurious and privately owned. A handful of these upmarket properties – including one which belonged to Ceauşescu (see Places to Eat) – are owned by the government and managed by the Predeal Protocol Service (☎ 455 222; fax 455 435), Str Nicolae Bălcescu 39. Some villas are for rent; most have two or three double rooms, a dining room, kitchen and lounge with colour TV, and cost between US$58 and US$154 a night for the entire villa. Bookings can made through the Hotel Robinson (☎ & fax 456 753).

The Fulg de Nea ski school (see Activities) operates a 20-bed villa behind the ski centre. A bed in a double room with private bath is US$13. Book in advance as it is often filled with groups of school children. The centre also plans to open a hotel on the 2nd and 3rd floors of the ski centre on Str Telefericului; it should be open by 1999.

Places to Eat

Most hotels have a restaurant of sorts. The *Restaurant Vultural*, below the dashing town council building at the western end of Str Panduri, serves wholesome meals at a reasonable price. Junk food addicts will find a clean, modern *fast food* outlet opposite the Hotel Carmen, close to the train station, on Blvd Mihai Săulescu.

The pizzeria and restaurant inside the *Fulg de Nea* ski centre serves hearty portions in a warm and cosy atmosphere; it sometimes has live folk bands and a bonfire outside in summer. It is open daily from 8 am to around 10 pm.

A definite must is the resort's prime restaurant, *Casă Ţărănească*, housed inside what was Ceauşescu's private holiday villa at Str Libertăţii 63. The luxury villa with its large, lamp-lit terrace surrounded by a sky-high fence of fir trees, is now a folklore restaurant. It serves traditional Romanian dishes to the jolly sound of violinists who strut around serenading diners. A meal costs around US$6 without alcohol. It is open daily from 11 am to midnight.

Getting There & Away

The Agenţie de Voiaj CFR (☎ 456 203) is inside the train station building at Str Intrarea Gării 1.

The *Dacia* and *Pannonia Expres* trains to Budapest both call at Predeal exactly five minutes before/after calling at Braşov. The *Muntenia, Ister, Traianus* and *Alutus* – all of which go to Budapest –also stop in Predeal (see Braşov – Getting There & Away). In addition, the Constanţa-Kraków train stops at Predeal, departing daily at 5.47 am and arriving in Kraków (23 hours) at 4.51 am the following morning. This train only runs from 2 June to 29 September.

Travellers heading east to Moldova can hop on the overnight Chişinău train from Braşov that passes through Predeal at 8.24 pm, arriving in Chişinău (14 hours) the next morning at 10.56 am.

Predeal is on the main Cluj-Napoca-Braşov-Bucharest line with most local and express trains which serve this route stopping at Predeal. Between Predeal and Braşov (35 minutes to 45 minutes) there are some 35 trains daily. Most trains that arrive/depart from Braşov call at Predeal too.

BUŞTENI
• *area code* ☎ 044

Ten kilometres south of Predeal, along the main road running through the Prahova valley between Braşov and Sinaia, is Buşteni (885m), a pleasant market town tucked below the mighty Caraiman (2284m) and Coştila (2490m) peaks to the west and Mount Zamora (1519m) dotted with villas to the east. Between the Caraiman and Coştila peaks lie the highest conglomerate cliffs in Europe. Buşteni, coupled with Sinaia, is the main starting point for hikes into the Bucegi mountains (see The Bucegi Mountains section). Rock climbers consider it Romania's premier climbing centre.

Orientation

The train station backs onto the main street, Blvd Libertăţii, and is easily identifiable by the large WWI memorial in front of it. The cable car, Hotel Caraiman, post office and

TRANSYLVANIA

commercial complex are at the southern end of town. Turn left out of the train station and walk straight down Blvd Libertăţii. The *primărie*, post office and Hotel Caraiman are clustered together 20m from the station on the left. To get to the cable car, continue along Blvd Libertăţii for 200m then turn right along Str Telecabinei.

The tourist office is 50m north of the train station; from the station turn right along Blvd Libertăţii.

Maps There is a large-scale map of Buşteni on Blvd Libertăţii in front of the post office on which all the hotels, cable car station and walking trails are marked. Unfortunately, pocket-maps of the town do not exist.

First-class hiking maps of the Bucegi mountains, *Munţii Bucegi Hartă Turistică*, published by the National Youth Tourist Club in Bucharest in 1997, are sold for US$1.20 at the foot of the cable car station next to the Hotel Silva.

Information
Tourist Offices The Carpatours tourist office (☎ 320 027; fax 320 120), Blvd Libertăţii 202; is open weekdays from 8 am to 8 pm, and weekends from 8 am to noon.

Money Change money at the Exchange House, 20m past the Hotel Caraiman on the right at Blvd Libertăţii 142; it is open daily from 10 am to 5 pm.

Post & Communications Call home from the post and telephone office 20m south of the train station; it is open weekdays from 7 am to 8 pm.

Emergency Mountain rescue volunteers SALVAMONT (☎ 320 048, 320 835, 320 750) have a contact point inside the primărie next to the post office at Blvd Libertăţii 91. They have a permanent base at the Cabana Caraiman (☎ 320 817), halfway up Caraiman mountain at 2025m.

Cezar Petrescu Memorial Museum
Between the wars, Buşteni was home to Romanian novelist, Cezar Petrescu (1892-1961), whose realist works attempted to reflect a 'psychology of failure' in modern Romanian life. His house at the northern end of the town on Str Tudor Vladimirescu is now a memorial museum, open daily, except Monday, from 9 am to 3 pm. Turn right out of the train station along Blvd Libertăţii; Str Tudor Vladimirescu is the fourth street on the left.

Activities
Hiking Hiking up to the giant cross – a WWI memorial – on the top of Caraiman or to the red and white TV transmitter (which looks like a rocket about to take off) atop Coştila peak are the two main activities in Buşteni. From these two easily identifiable landmarks a variety of clearly marked trails lead hikers further afield into the Bucegi mountains (see the Bucegi Mountains section).

Buşteni's lone cable car station is behind the Hotel Silva at the western end of Str Telecabinei. The cable car (US$0.70/1.20), which runs every half hour daily, except Monday, from 8 am to 5 pm, whisks you up to Cabana Babele (Babele literally means 'Old Ladies') at 2206m from where a trail marked by red crosses leads to the WWI memorial cross *(crucea eroilor)* at 2284m (a bout a half-hour hike). From here, an unmarked footpath heads north to the Coştila peak.

For those who do not want to take the cable car, a three to four hour trail, marked by blue crosses, leads from the cable car station to the Cabana Caraiman (2025m) where you can pick up a red circled trail (one hour) to the WWI cross.

Hiking trails (see The Bucegi Mountains section) are also marked from the train station, Căminul Alpin on the north-western edge of town, and from the Chalet Gura Diham, 3km further north at 987m (see Places to Stay below).

Mountain Biking You can hire a set of sturdy wheels from the Hotel Silva next to the cable car station for US$2/9 an hour/day.

Places to Stay
Camping The *Chalet Gura Diham* (☎ 321 108), 3km north of Buşteni along a dirt road, has a campsite where you can pitch a tent. It also has 20 doubles for US$5 per person and 16 five-bed rooms for US$3 per person. Bathrooms are shared. Minibuses depart from outside the train station every hour for Guru Diham (see Getting There & Away). To hike, turn right out of the train station along Blvd Libertăţii and take the third left along Str Horea; the chalet is at the northern end.

Further north is the *Căminul Alpin* (☎ 320 167). A bed in a four-bed room is US$5 a night. Wild camping is permitted. Turn right out of the train station along Blvd Libertăţii and take the second left along Str Viitorului until the road forks. Bear left at the fork and continue along Str Clabucet; the Alpin is at the end of the street on the right. Its street address is Str Morarului 2.

Cabanas The *Cabana Babele* (☎ 320 817, 311 750) at 2206m, has provided refuge to hikers since 1937. Today it offers 84 places in beds in double rooms and mattresses on dormitory floors, costing between US$3 and US$9 depending on the season and level of comfort you want. The Babele is open year-round.

The *Cabana Caraiman* (☎ 320 817) at 2025m, also home to the SALVAMONT team who are great for grilling about hikes in the hilltops, has 40 places in shared rooms. Prices start at US$3. The Caraiman is only open in summer.

For details of other cabanas in the Bucegi mountains see Places to Stay & Eat in the Bucegi Mountains section later.

Private Rooms Carpatours (see Information – Travel Agencies) arranges accommodation in hotels, villas and cabanas in Buşteni, charging a 5% commission on top of every booking it takes. It is worth visiting though; it says it can find rooms for US$3 a night.

Hotels The most central hotel is the dreary *Hotel Caraiman* (☎ 320 156) at Blvd Libertăţii 89, which still sports a two-tier

pricing system. Foreigners pay US$20 for a double room with private shower. Breakfast is not included. The hotel has a restaurant, café and disco.

A cheaper and more cheerful option is the *Hotel BTT* (☎ 320 138; fax 320 056) at the other end of Blvd Libertăţii at No 153. Double rooms start at US$9 per person, including breakfast. Other facilities include a basketball court and disco, open daily from 8 pm to 4 am.

The *Hanul Cu Flori* (☎ 320 505), at Str Telecabinei 46, is a family-run pension. It has eight places in three rooms with a shared bathroom for US$9 per person. Continuing west along Str Telecabinei, you come to the large *Hotel Silva* (☎ 312 412; fax 320 950), nestled beneath the cable car station. Double rooms with TV, telephone and private bath cost US$22, including breakfast. The in-house *Disco You & Me* is open daily from 9 pm to 4 am.

Places to Eat
You can stock up on supplies in the commercial complex at the southern end of Blvd Libertăţii or at the cluster of shops at the foot of the cable car station. The *Vinuri la litru*, housed in a small caravan on the right on Blvd Libertăţii, en route to the cable car, sells home-made wine for US$0.50 a litre or more potent Rachiu Tescovină (39.4% proof) for US$1 a litre. The caravan is open daily from 9 am to 1 pm. Take your own bottle. Excellent, freshly baked, jam-filled buns and breads are sold at the *Pâine* shop close by at Blvd Libertăţii 35.

Getting There & Away
Bus From Buşteni, buses depart every 45 minutes from the main bus stop on Blvd Libertăţii between 6 am and 10 pm, to Azuga and Sinaia.

Minibuses marked *Guru Diham* depart on the hour, every hour, between 7 am and 10 pm from outside the train station. Return buses leave Guru Diham hourly between 7.30 am and 10.30 pm.

Train Buşteni has no Agenţie de Voiaj CFR.

Buy tickets at the train station on Blvd Libertăţii. As with Predeal, Buşteni is on the main Bucharest-Cluj-Napoca line with all local trains between Braşov and Bucharest stopping at Buşteni.

From Buşteni, you can also hike 8km south to Sinaia or 10km north to Predeal (see The Bucegi Mountains section).

SINAIA
• *area code* ☎ 044

This well known winter ski resort snuggles at an altitude of 800m to 930m in the narrow Prahova Valley, at the foot of the fir-clad Bucegi mountains. Cable cars whisk skiers and hikers up to 1400m at the foot of Mount Furnica (2103m) and further up still to 2000m. Sinaia is a convenient day-trip from Braşov.

The resort is alleged to have gained its name from Romanian nobleman Mihai Cantacuzino who, following a pilgrimage he made to the biblical Mount Sinai in Israel in 1695, founded the Sinaia monastery.

Sinaia later developed into a major resort dubbed the 'Pearl of the Carpathians' after King Carol I selected Sinaia for his summer residence in 1870. His palace, open to visitors today, is considered the most beautiful in Romania. Until 1920, the Hungarian-Romanian border ran along Predeal Pass, just north of Sinaia.

For reader convenience, this area has been included in Transylvania in this book, even though, strictly speaking, it is part of Wallachia.

Orientation
The train station is directly below the centre of town. From the station go up the stairway across the street to busy Blvd Carol I. The left-luggage office on platform No 1 at the train station is open 24 hours. It charges US$0.25/0.50 per day for a small/large bag.

Maps
The *Sinaia Ghid Turistic*, published in 1997 by Bel Alpin Tour, includes a good town map as well as a small hiking map of the southern Bucegi mountains. Ironically, it is practically impossible to find in Sinaia.

Purchase a copy for US$1.20 in Buşteni or Predeal where they are sold in tourist offices and kiosks.

Information
Tourist Offices The Palace Agenţie de Turism (☎ 312 051; ☎ & fax 310 426), opposite Villa Parc at Str Octavian Goga 11, is an agent for Hertz car rental (for rental prices see Getting Around at the front of this book). It is open weekdays from 8 am to 8 pm, Saturday from 9 am to 2 pm, Sunday from 9 am to noon.

The Luxor Agenţie de Turism (☎ 314 124; fax 314 051) at Blvd Carol I, 22 arranges day trips to Bran (US$3) and Poiana Braşov (US$5).

Money There are currency exchanges inside the Hotel International and Hotel Sinaia. The currency exchange inside the Luxor Agenţie de Turism also offers good rates; it is open weekdays from 9 am to 5 pm.

Cash travellers cheques is at the Bancă Comercială Română on Blvd Carol I next to the primărie, just past the Hotel Montana. You can get cash advance on Visa/MasterCard here too. It is open weekdays from 8 am to 11 am and has an ATM outside. BANCOREX, a five minute walk from the Hotel International at the southern end of Calea Bucureşti at No 33, gives cash advance on Visa/MasterCard; it is open weekdays from 8.30 am to 2 pm.

Post & Communications The central post and telephone office is between the Hotel Sinaia and Hotel Montana on the opposite side of Blvd Carol I. The telephone office is open daily from 7 am to 8 pm; the post office is only open weekdays. There is a phone-card dispensing machine and an international cardphone outside.

Emergency SALVAMONT (☎ 313 131) is based inside the primărie, opposite Hotel Montana on Blvd Carol I. The 10-man team is on 24-hour alert. It also has a small base next to the cable car station at Cota 1400.

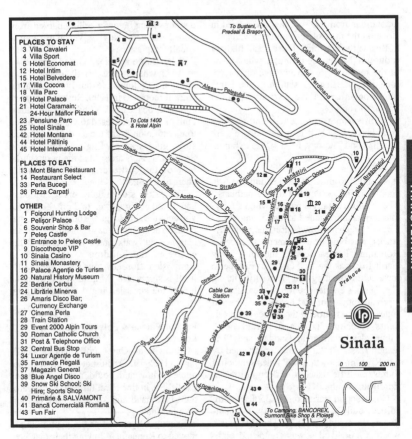

PLACES TO STAY
3 Villa Cavaleri
4 Villa Sport
5 Hotel Economat
12 Hotel Intim
15 Hotel Belvedere
17 Villa Cocora
18 Villa Parc
19 Hotel Palace
21 Hotel Caramain;
   24-Hour Maflor Pizzeria
23 Pensiune Parc
25 Hotel Sinaia
42 Hotel Montana
44 Hotel Păltiniş
45 Hotel International

PLACES TO EAT
13 Mont Blanc Restaurant
14 Restaurant Select
33 Perla Bucegi
36 Pizza Carpaţi

OTHER
1 Foişorul Hunting Lodge
2 Pelişor Palace
6 Souvenir Shop & Bar
7 Peleş Castle
8 Entrance to Peleş Castle
9 Discotheque VIP
10 Sinaia Casino
11 Sinaia Monastery
16 Palace Agenţie de Turism
20 Natural History Museum
22 Berărie Cerbul
24 Librărie Minerva
26 Amaris Disco Bar;
   Currency Exchange
27 Cinema Perla
28 Train Station
29 Event 2000 Alpin Tours
30 Roman Catholic Church
31 Post & Telephone Office
32 Central Bus Stop
34 Luxor Agenţie de Turism
35 Farmacie Regală
37 Magazin General
38 Blue Angel Disco
39 Snow Ski School; Ski
   Hire; Sports Shop
40 Primărie & SALVAMONT
41 Bancă Comercială Română
43 Fun Fair

TRANSYLVANIA

Sinaia

0   100   200 m

Sinaia Monastery

From the train station, walk up the stairway to town, turn left and then make a quick right onto Str Octavian Goga, which passes Vila Parc before curving left at the Mont Blanc Restaurant. There's a stairway here, at the top of which is Sinaia Monastery (Mănăstirea Sinaia). Some 20 monks live here today. The large Orthodox church (Biserica Mare) dates from 1846, and the smaller, older church (Biserica Veche) from 1695. Monks retreated into the Bucegi mountains from the 14th century but it was not until the late 17th century that they built

a monastery. The original church is currently under restoration. Many of the original frescoes are still evident.

Take Ionescu (1859-1918), a leading liberal statesman who led the Romanian delegation at the Paris Peace Conference (1918-20) and briefly headed one of the first postwar governments in Romania (December 1921 to January 1922) is buried here. Born in Ploieşti, Ionescu contracted cholera as a child and was sent to Sinaia monastery to convalesce. Following his death, his second wife Adina Olmazu built a vast mausoleum at the monastery in his memory.

Quotations from his speeches are carved in stone on the mausoleum's interior walls.

Beside the new church is a small **history museum** (Muzeul de Istorie) in which some of the monastery's treasures are displayed, including the first translation of the Bible into Romanian (in the Cyrillic alphabet) dating to 1668.

Admission to the entire monastery complex is US$1; it is open daily, except Monday and Tuesday, from 10 am to 6 pm.

Peleş Castle

It is apt that Romania's most exquisite castle should lie in the 'Pearl of the Carpathians'. The magnificent royal palace, with its fairytale turrets and pointed towers rising above acres of green meadows sprinkled with haystacks, was built as a summer residence by Romania's longest serving monarch, King Carol I. It was the first castle in Europe to have central heating and electricity. During Ceauşescu's era, its 160 rooms were used as a private retreat for leading communists and statesmen from around the globe. US presidents Richard Nixon and Gerald Ford, Libyan leader Moamar Gaddafi and PLO leader Yasser Arafat were all entertained by the Romanian dictator in Peleş's fanciful rooms, each furnished to reflect a different European country.

Construction started on the 3500sq metre edifice, built in a predominantly German-Renaissance style, in 1875. The first part – where Carol lived – was completed eight years later. More than 400 craftsmen laboured on the palace which was finally completed 39 years later, just months before the king died in 1914.

Tour guides whirl visitors through a succession of grandiose rooms. Rembrandt reproductions line the walls of the king's office while a row of books in the library conceals a secret escape passage leading to the 2nd floor of the castle. There is a gallery of mirrors and the dining room has a leather-clad ceiling. Scenes from age-old Romanian fairytales adorn the stained glass windows in the poetry room.

In the Florence hall, Michelangelo reproductions hang below a ceiling carved from gilded linden wood. The Venetian room is equally impressive.

Peleş Castle remained closed from 1947 to 1975 when it was briefly opened as a museum. Following extensive renovation work it reopened in 1990. Restoration work continues on the castle's 2nd floor and attics, both of which are closed to visitors. Guided tours (45 minutes) of the castle are compulsory; guides speak English, French and Spanish. Tickets are sold at the booth at the foot of the castle drive. Foreigners are charged US$4.50.

The castle is open daily, except Monday and Tuesday, from 9 am to 3 pm. To ensure you get a tour in a language other than Romanian, do not enter the castle through the main entrance but walk under the arches in the centre of the building to the entrance signposted 'foreign tourists'. The castle itself is signposted 'Muzeul Peleş' from the top of the steps leading down to the train station.

Pelişor Palace & Foişorul Hunting Lodge

Marie, wife of King Carol's nephew Ferdinand (1865-1927), did not get on with her uncle-in-law and could not stand Peleş Castle. So, in fine royal fashion, King Carol built Ferdinand and Marie a castle of their own in Sinaia.

Exactly 10 years after the young couple moved to Romania following their marriage in 1892, Pelişor Palace, just a few hundred metres uphill from Peleş, was completed. Built in a mock German-medieval style, the interior was furnished according to Marie's own designs – pretty pastel decorations in a simple Art-Nouveau style. Most of the furniture was imported from Vienna. Marie had four apartments while Ferdinand had just one.

The bed in which Romania's second king died at the age of 62 from cancer can still be seen today. Marie died nine years later in the golden room, the walls of which are entirely covered in heavy gold leaves.

Pelişor Palace is open daily, except

The Four Kings

Romania had four kings. **Carol I** (1839-1914), Prussian cousin of Kaiser Wilhem I, was the first. He entered Romania incognito in 1866, and proposed to his future queen, Elizabeth of Wied, on their second meeting (said to be the peak of their relationship, after which it degenerated rapidly). He was crowned king of Romania in 1881. His last act before dying in 1914 was to refuse to enter WWI on the side of his German cousin.

His widowed queen (1836-1916) was a cranky poet who wrote under the pen-name Carmen Sylva and decreed that everyone in the royal court should wear folk costume. As a child she had been regularly taken to lunatic asylums to observe the inmates. Elizabeth's failure to produce an heir – the couple's only daughter died at the age of four – ensured she died diabolical.

Carol I's nephew, **Ferdinand I** (1865-1927) was Romania's second monarch. Beckoned from Germany to the Balkans to prepare for his regal role, he promptly fell in love with his Aunt Elizabeth's favourite lady-in-waiting, Helene Vacaresco. King Carol, horrified at this, banished his wife and her lady-in-waiting to Germany, then packed Ferdinand off to Europe, armed with a list of eligible young princesses. The best move Ferdinand – renounced for his weak character and protruding ears – ever made was to wed Marie, Queen Victoria's granddaughter, under whose shrewd guidance he successfully ruled the country from 1916 until his death from cancer in 1927.

Ferdinand and Marie's son, **Carol II** (1893-1953), was Romania's third king. The notorious playboy was said to be great in bed and the only man in town able to satisfy the 'crow', an infamous Bucharest prostitute of the 1930s. In 1918 the 24-year-old Carol deserted his military unit to elope with a commoner called Jeanne Lambrino or Zizi. The lovestruck pair crossed the Romanian border incognito and wed in Odessa. The marriage was later annulled although the couple remained together in exile for some time in France. In 1919, following his parent's refusal to allow him to remarry the pregnant Zizi, Carol renounced his right to the throne. Soon after however he returned to Romania and, in 1921, married Princess Helene of Greece, only to elope two years later with the promiscuous Jewish divorcee Elena Lupescu.

In 1930 Carol II returned to Romania to resume his role as king. His 10 year rule was abruptly terminated in 1940 when he fled the country with Lupescu, taking nine railway carriages of stolen state treasures as bounty. The couple wandered aimlessly through Europe until the end of WWII when they finally wed and settled in Brazil, then Portugal. After Carol's death in 1953 Lupescu, who lived another 25 years, moved in with one of Carol's former prime ministers.

Carol and Princess Helene's son, **Michael** (1921-), became king for the first time following Ferdinand's death in 1927. The knickerbockered King Michael (Mihai) was five years old at the time. Following his father's shock return to Romania in 1930 the nine-year-old was forced to abdicate. Following King Michael's second forced abdication in 1947, the entire royal family was exiled from their homeland.

Michael married Princess Ana de Bourbon Parma in 1948 and subsequently settled in Versoix, Switzerland, where he still lives today. The eldest of his two daughters, Marguerite, who is married to the actor Radu Duda, is alleged to have had a five year affair with Britain's Chancellor of the Exchequer, Gordon Brown.

The exiled king, a former test pilot and technical consultant, returned to Romania for the first time in 1990, only to be deported 12 hours later. In 1992 he returned again for Orthodox Easter, being greeted by a crowd of 500,000. It was not until 1997 however that he was given back his Romanian passport and officially welcomed 'home' by the Romanian government. He made it clear during his state visit that he was committed to helping Romania in its NATO and EU bid, and that he hoped to settle permanently in Romania in the near future. He did not rule out the possibility of a return to a constitutional monarchy. ■

Monday and Tuesday, from 9.30 am to 4.30 pm. Admission is US$3 for foreigners and 20 minute tours of 20 of the castle's 70 rooms (in English or French) are compulsory.

At the western end of the Peleş estate is the Swiss chalet-style Foişorul Hunting Lodge, built as a temporary residence by King Carol I before Peleş Castle was completed. Here, Marie and Ferdinand spent their first summer together in Romania. Here also their son, later to become King Carol II, briefly lived with his mistress Elena Lupéscu. During the communist era, Ceauşescu used it as his private hunting lodge. The building remains in state hands today and is closed to visitors.

Bucegi Nature Reserve Museum

Behind the Hotel Palace in the central park is a small Natural History Museum (Muzeul Rezervatiei Bucegi; ☎ 311 750) featuring some of the natural wonders of the Bucegi Nature Reserve which protects the entire 300sq km mountain range. Two rooms in the cellar exhibit various stuffed animals, flowers and birds, including the edelweiss, which is abundant on the Bucegi mountains. Temporary art exhibitions are displayed on the ground floor. In summer, the museum is open on Monday from 8 am to 4 pm, Tuesday to Friday from 7 am to 7 pm, and weekends from 10.30 am to 7 pm. In winter, it is open daily from 9 am to 5 pm. Admission is US$0.50.

Activities

Skiing Sinaia has no artificial slopes, but offers wild skiing around Mount Furnica. Unlike Poiana Braşov and Predeal, however, which are both shielded by forest, Sinaia's exposed position often sees its cable cars grinding to a halt as the wind blows up. Skiing is, on average, guaranteed four days out of seven.

Sinaia has two cable car routes. From the rear of Hotel Montana a cable car whisks you up to Cota 1400 (a station near Hotel Alpin) where you can either continue on the cable car or take the ski lift up to Cota 2000 (near Cabana Mioriţa). A map showing the various skiing routes and ski lifts is inside the Montana station. Both stations are open Tuesday to Friday from 8 am to 4 pm, weekends from 8 am to 5 pm. Both are closed on Monday. At the time of writing the Cota 1400 car departed every half hour between 8.30 am and 3.30 pm, while the car to Cota 2000 left every half hour between 8.45 am and 3.34 pm.

Most hotels arrange ski school and ski hire. It is cheaper to go direct to the central ski school however, the *Snow* (☎ & fax 311 198), behind the Hotel Montana at Str Cuza Vodă 2a. Private lessons cost US$7 an hour; group tuition for two to four people is US$6 per person an hour; and it costs US$4.50 per person an hour for groups of five to 10 skiers.

The centre also hires boots, poles and skis for US$5 a day.

There is a storage room and second ski hire outlet at the Cota 1400 cable car stations. Various drag lifts are spread between the two cable car stations.

Ski passes for the cable car, chair lift and drag lifts do not exist. If you book into the ski school, the centre can negotiate a day or weekly fee for a pass entitling you to unlimited use of all the teleferic services. Individual skiers simply have to pay for each trip up the mountain (US$0.35).

Hiking Sinaia is the queen of hiking in the Bucegi mountains and even chain-smokers should take the cable car up to Cota 1400 and further to Cota 2000 (see Skiing above).

Incredibly, there are no official climbing clubs in Sinaia. All members of SALVAMONT are experienced climbers, however, who are quite happy to take tourists hiking in the mountains for a small fee.

The Palace Hotel also organises hikes led by experienced guides for less confident hikers. Most hikes start in Buşteni, taking climbers to the top of Caraiman mountain, to the bats' cave in Peştera (see Around Bran), and to Piatra Craiului. Each hike costs US$3.50 per person and is well worth doing if you are not sure of which route to take.

Numerous hiking trails are marked from Sinaia leading you through the 300sq km mountain range. See the Bucegi Mountains section later in this chapter.

Mountain Biking The Snow ski centre (see Skiing above) rents out mountain bikes for US$2 an hour or US$9 a day. It can also arrange a guide. The Surmont Bike Shop (☎ 311 810) out of town at Str Walter Măvăcineanu 2, is run by a group of mountain bike enthusiasts; it is open daily from 6 to 9 pm. At the time of writing, Surmont was also planning to set up a bike hire and guide service. Follow Calea Bucureşti for 1km past the factories; the shop is signposted on the right.

Places to Stay

Camping There's a *campsite* at Izvorul Rece, 4km south of central Sinaia, but only three buses a day go there from a stop on Blvd Carol I, just past Hotel Montana.

Cabanas The *Hotel Alpin* (☎ 312 351; ☎ & fax 117 650) is at Cota 1400 – at 1400m no less – next to the cable car station, making it a prime spot for beer-thirsty skiers.

Just below the station at 1300m is the *Cabana Brădet* (☎ 311 551) which offers beds in shared rooms for around US$3 a night. It is generally packed year-round. Prices are similar at the *Cabana Valea cu Brazi* (☎ 314 751) which has 43 beds in shared rooms. It is just above the cable car station at 1500m; a path leads to it from Hotel Alpin.

For details of other cabanas within hiking reach of Sinaia see the Bucegi Mountain section.

Private Rooms Hang around the train station for a few minutes and you'll probably be offered a private room. The going rate is US$6 to 9 per person.

Hotels Among the cheapest places to stay is the small *Pensiune Parc* (☎ 313 856, 312 391), next to the Berărie Cerbul at the northern end of Blvd Carol I; you pass it coming from the train station to the centre of town. Double rooms with shared bath are US$10. Breakfast is not included and there is only hot water from 6.30 to 10.30 am, and from 7 to 11 pm.

The main two hotels in the centre of the resort are the high-rise *Hotel Sinaia* (☎ 311 551; fax 314 098) at Blvd Carol I 8 and *Hotel Montana* (☎ 312 751; fax 314 051) at Blvd Carol I 24. The Sinaia is geared more to tour groups and generally reluctant to let out rooms for one or two nights. Singles/doubles with private bath, telephone and cable TV are good value at the Montana at US$16/27 a night, including breakfast.

The attractive, two-star *Hotel Păltiniș* (☎ 314 651; fax 111 033) at Blvd Carol I 65-67, in the southern end of the resort, is a dark hotel with wooden panelling and heavy furnishings. Singles/doubles with private bath cost US$11/23 a night, including breakfast.

Opposite is the luxurious *Hotel International* (☎ 313 851, 314 515; fax 313 855) at Str Avram Iancu 1. This three-star hotel, aimed very much at wealthy foreign travellers, has 159 rooms; singles/doubles/triples are US$33/54/70 a night, including breakfast. It also has a handful of doubles with matrimonial beds. Other facilities include an unfriendly tourist agency, hairdressers, shop and telephone and fax centre.

Heading north up Str Octavian Goga, you come to Sinaia's most elegant hotels. The *Hotel Palace* (☎ 312 051/2/3; fax 374 633) stands majestically next to the central park at Str Octavian Goga 4. Dating to 1911, it has all facilities including a mini-casino, night bar, restaurant and nightclub. Singles/doubles are US$32/46 a night; admission to the nightclub (10 pm to 4 am) is US$1.20. Opposite, at No 5, is the smaller, more intimate *Villa Cocora* which has 10 luxury apartments costing US$63; bookings can be made through the Palace. Behind the Palace is the *Hotel Caramain* (☎ 311 151; fax 310 625), overlooking the park with its entrance on Blvd Carol I. Singles/doubles are US$28/37 a night. The hotel has a pizzeria, open 24 hours.

If your budget cannot stretch this far, go to the tiny *Villa Parc* (☎ 313 856) at Str Octavian Goga 2. Doubles with/without private bath are US$14/10.

West of Str Octavian Goga heading towards Sinaia monastery at Str Mănăstirii 7 is the small *Hotel Belvedere* (☎ 313 754, 313 198). It has four doubles costing US$14 a night. Needless to say, it is often fully booked. Its outside restaurant is cheap and popular. Close by at Str Funicar 1 is the one-star *Hotel Intim* (☎ 311 754, 311 127). Double rooms with private bath cost US$17. There is hot water between 7 and 9 am and 7 and 9 pm.

Rivalling Hotel Palace in location and luxury is the *Hotel Economat* (☎ 311 151; fax 311 150), housed in a wonderful 19th

TRANSYLVANIA

century manor house inside the Peleş Castle complex at Aleea Peleşului 2. The hotel has 36 rooms, singles/doubles with all the mod cons, costing US$21/43 a night. The hotel also takes bookings for the luxury, four-star *Villa Cavaleri*, directly opposite Pelişor Palace, and the eight-room *Villa Şipot* close by. Both villas are often inhabited by state guests but it is possible to stay here if you book in advance. It costs around US$535 a night for an entire villa.

Places to Eat

The *Perla Bucegi*, at Blvd Carol I 18, serves Romanian food including tripe soup (ciorbă de burtă) for US$1.50 and excellent beef steaks topped with a fried egg (biftec cu ou) for US$3; it is open daily from 10 am to 10 pm.

Restaurant Select, close to the Palace hotel on Str Octavian Goga, is a large establishment with slow service and below-average food. The terrace is a popular hangout though, as is the disco bar, open daily from midnight to 2 am. Food is served in the restaurant from noon to midnight.

For a touch of France, try the *Mont Blanc* French restaurant (☎ 310 105), further north along Str Octavian Goga opposite the Palace hotel. Dishes, starting at around US$6, include 'filet de boeuf au poivre' (peppered beef steak), 'salade de foie de volailles' (chicken liver salad) and a typical 'salade Lyonaise' (salad with croutons and a fried egg). It is open daily from 11 am to 11 pm.

Pizza fans can dine at *Pizza Carpaţi* next to the magazin general on Blvd Carol I or the more popular *pizzeria* inside the Perla Bucegi complex opposite at Blvd Carol I 18; it is open daily from 10 am to 10 pm. The *Maflor Pizzeria*, inside the Caraiman hotel on Blvd Carol I, is open 24 hours.

Entertainment

Films are often shown in English with Romanian subtitles at the *Cinema Perla*, opposite the Sinaia hotel on Blvd Carol I. During the summer season, there is a small fun fair and dodgem cars for kids outside the

Hotel Păltiniş at the southern end of Blvd Carol I.

Bars & Discos The *Berărie Cerbul* at the junction of Blvd Carol I and Str Octavian Goga is a traditional bar serving Romanian beer and barbecued şaşlik, hot dogs and grilled meats in its summer garden. It is generally packed.

There are discos practically everywhere you turn in Sinaia. The *Discotheque VIP* inside the Complex Ceremică close to Peleş Castle on Aleea Peleşului rocks from 9 pm to 4 am; it attracts a mobile-phone crowd. The *Blue Angel Disco* next to the magazin general opposite the Hotel Montana is open the same hours. Alternatively, try the crowded *Black Horse Disco* inside Hotel Sinaia, open from 10 pm to 3 am.

Getting There & Away

Bus Buses run every 45 minutes between 6.20 am and 10.45 pm from the central bus stop on Blvd Carol I to Azuga and Buşteni.

Train Sinaia is on the Bucharest-Braşov rail line – 126km from the former and 45km from the latter. All express trains stop here, and local trains to Buşteni (8km), Predeal (19km) and Braşov are quite frequent. Approaching Sinaia from the south, don't get off at the 'Halta Sinaia Sud' – a small stop 2km south of Sinaia centre.

In summer there are two trains daily to Constanţa (four hours). This service is reduced to one daily in winter.

THE BUCEGI MOUNTAINS

The Bucegi Mountains – 300sq km – are Romania's best kept secret, rivalling Slovakia's Tatra mountains and even the Alps when it comes to trekking. The horse-shaped massif, forming part of the southern Carpathians, boasts the highest cabana in the whole of the Carpathians. It sits atop Mount Omu (2505m), the highest peak in the Bucegi chain. The Ialomiţa river carves a deep valley through the limestone mountains while the glacier valleys in the north are cut through with rocky ridges known as *custuri*.

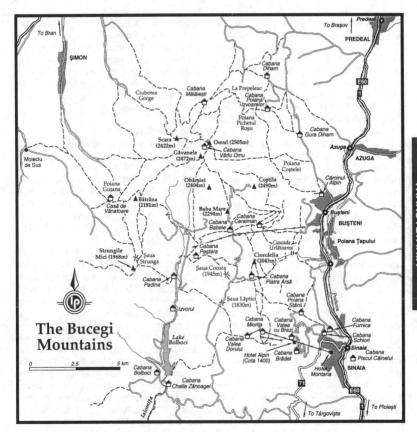

The Bucegi
Mountains

0   2.5   5 km

Getting lost in the Bucegi mountains is difficult, thanks to a network of marked trails, while most of the mountain huts are open year-round to shelter and feed hikers and cross-country skiers. The only danger is the weather: winter is severe, waist-deep snow lingers as late as May and summertime thunderstorms are common. Day hikes from Sinaia and Buşteni require no special equipment, but freelance campers should bring food, water and warm clothes to combat the elements. If you sleep in cabanas, it's still a good idea to bring extra food.

Regardless of the route you intend to take,

you should get a hiking map before even setting foot in the mountains. The best one is the excellent, up-to-date *Munţii Bucegi Hartă Turistică*, published by the National Youth Tourist Club in 1997. To purchase a copy before leaving home contact the club (☎ 01-615 4970; fax 01-12 5374) at Str Dem I Dobrescu 4-6, Sector 1, Bucharest.

Day Hikes

Catch a morning train from Braşov or Sinaia to Buşteni, then take the Buşteni cable car up to Cabana Babele (2206m). From Babele hike south following a blue triangle trail to

Cabana Piatra Arsă (1950m), where you pick up a blue striped trail that descends to Sinaia via Poiana Stânii (a five hour walk in total). The beginning of the blue trail is poorly marked at Piatra Arsă, so study the large map on the wall in the cabana carefully and look around. Once you're actually on the trail, it's no problem. This trip across alpine pastures and through forest is varied and downhill all the way.

A variation on the above involves taking the Sinaia cable car all the way up to Cabana Mioriţa (1957m), near the crest. You then walk north to Cabana Piatra Arsă (1½ hours) and on to Cabana Babele (another hour), where you can catch the Buşteni cable car down the mountain. The problem with this hike is it's uphill (350m gain) and you must take two cable cars.

Longer Hikes

A more ambitious expedition involves taking one of the two cable cars mentioned above and hiking north-west across the mountains all the way to Bran Castle, from where there are buses to Braşov. You can do this in one strenuous day if you get an early start from Babele, but it's preferable to take two days and camp freelance or spend a night at Cabana Vârfu Omul.

As you look north from Babele, you'll see the red and white TV transmitter on top of Coştila peak. To the left is a yellow-marked trail that leads to Cabana Vârfu Omul (two hours) on the summit (2505m). North of Babele the scenery becomes dramatic, with dizzying drops into valleys on either side.

To go from Omul to Bran Castle takes another six hours and involves a tough 2000m drop (don't even think of climbing up from Bran to Omul). The yellow-triangle trail is easy to follow, and chances are that you will have this glorious landscape all to yourself. From Omul, you begin by crossing Mount Scara (2422m), before dropping into Ciubotea Gorge (the grassy valley at the bottom of the gorge is ideal for freelance camping). Once you clear the treeline the trail descends through thick forest. This is the only point where the markers are hard to

follow – don't get lost by the abandoned horse corral; the marker is uphill by the picnic table. Eventually you come out on a logging road beside a river, which you follow for 2½ hours right to Bran Castle.

You could extend this hike for a day or two by including Cabana Padina and any of a dozen well marked trails.

Places to Stay & Eat

Cabanas invariably close for renovations at some time or other and it is always a good idea to check with the local tourist office or the SALVAMONT team before heading off.

For details on *Cabana Babele* and *Cabana Caraiman* see Buşteni – Places to Stay. *Cabana Brădet*, *Cabana Valea cu Brazi* and the *Hotel Alpin* are listed under Sinaia – Places to Stay.

The *Cabana Piatra Arsă* (☎ 044-311 751) is a large, modern chalet offering good accommodation. It charges between US$3 and US$9 for its 112 beds. It also serves inexpensive meals and drinks, and is open from May to September.

Only open in summer too is the *Cabana Mioriţa*, further south, which has 50 places in shared rooms. It also has a small snack bar.

Cabana Vârfu Omul (☎ 320 677) is small and basic, with 35 mattresses in dormitories for US$2 per person. Meals (soup, bread and omelette) are served only occasionally; bring your own food. Although blankets are provided, a sleeping bag would be useful. Omul is dependably open from May to September.

The *Cabana Peştera* and *Cabana Virful cu Dor* were closed for renovations at the time of writing but should be open by the time this guide sees the light. The *Cabana Mălăieşti*, at 1720m, has 40 places in shared rooms, starting at US$3 a night.

THE FĂGĂRAŞ MOUNTAINS

In summer, a small but steady stream of backpackers descends on the Făgăraş mountains (Munţii Făgăraşului), a section of the Carpathian mountains in the centre of Romania. It is the most spectacular hiking area in the country.

The Făgăraş mountains stretch for some

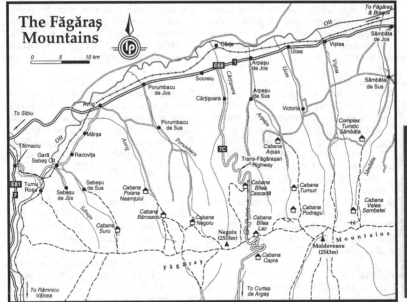

The Făgăraş Mountains

75km south of the main Braşov-Sibiu road and are dotted with more than 40 glacial lakes, the highest of which is Lake Mioarele (2282m). The famed Trans-Făgăraşan highway cuts through the Bâlea valley across the mountains from north to south, linking the Făgăraş depression with the southern Argeş valley. This mountain pass, open for just two or three months of the year, is said to be the highest road in Europe. The Bâlea tunnel cutting between Mount Negoiu (2535m) and Mount Moldoveanu (2543m) – Romania's highest mountains – at 2060m, is 845m long.

The main drawback to the Făgăraş mountains is the difficulty in getting there. From train stations along the Braşov-Sibiu line, most trailheads are 8km to 15km south, poorly serviced by bus and difficult to hitch (few cars can accommodate hitchhikers and their packs). The main access points are the villages of Victoria and Complex Turistic Sâmbăta (see following sections).

To hike the Făgăraş you must be in good physical shape and have warm clothing and sturdy boots. The trails are well marked, but keep the altitude in mind and be prepared for cold and rain at any time. There is a SALVAMONT refuge at the northern end of the Trans-Făgăraşan highway next to the Cabana Bîlea Lac (2040m).

From November to early May these mountains are snow covered; August and September are the best months to visit. Basic food is available at the cabanas but carry a supply of biscuits and keep your water bottle full. It is easiest to buy quality hiking maps in Bucharest, although some shops in Sibiu do sell maps. The best available are the *Munţii Făgăraşului Pliant Turistic* (EMCO, US$1.20) and the *Munţi Făgăraş Hartă Turistică* (Ministry of Tourism, 1982).

Făgăraş

Despite being named after Romania's most famous mountain range, Făgăraş town (with a 47,000 population) is not the prime access point to this stately massif. Most hikers pass straight through the town en route to neighbouring Victoria. Its only attraction is its 13th century fortress, surrounded by a moat and housing the **Făgăraş County Museum** (Muzeul Ţării Făgăraş), open Tuesday to Friday from 8 am to 6 pm, weekends from 9 am to 3 pm. Organ recitals are regularly held in the **evangelical church** (Biserica Evangelică), Piaţa Republicii 16.

Opération Villages Roumains (☎ 068-215 170), Str Gheorghe Doja 53, arranges rural accommodation in Făgăraş and its surrounding villages for US$10 a night.

Făgăraş bus and trains stations are next to each other on Str Negoiu. There are daily bus services to Braşov (65km), Târgu Mureş (150km), Sibiu (92km) and Victoria (36km). Trains from Făgăraş to Braşov and Sibiu stop at Ucea (see Victoria).

Victoria

Victoria is a nondescript town, of no interest except as a starting point to hike south into the mountains. Marked hiking trails leading

from the town into the mountains are shown on a faded map outside the town's lone hotel, the *Hotel Victoria* (☎ 068-241 916, 242 091) on the main square, Piaţa Libertăţii. Double rooms with/without private bath are US$5/4 a night.

Victoria is serviced by buses from Făgăraş. Most hikers access the town by train, however. The nearest train halt is 7km north of Victoria at **Ucea**. All local trains from Braşov, Făgăraş and Sibiu stop here. Buses then depart from outside Ucea station to Victoria, departing daily at 1, 7, 8.45 am, and later at 1, 2, 2.30, 4.25, 5.25, 7.30 and 9.15 pm.

Buses in both directions are supposedly timed to connect with trains to/from Ucea – a debatable point given the steady stream of backpackers seen hiking the 7km road (in summer) from Ucea to Victoria.

The bus station in Victoria is on Str Tineretului; buses stop outside the Hotel Victoria on Piaţa Libertăţii too. Buses depart from Victoria to Ucea at 4.30, 6.30, 7.45 and 8.40 am, noon, and 1, 1.30, 3.10, 3.40, 4.40, 7.05, 8.20 and 11.30 pm.

The Forest Brothers

An aggressive Stalinist policy of collectivisation was ruthlessly pursued following the communists' creation of the People's Republic in 1947. Despite widespread opposition to this absorption of privately owned land, the collectivisation process was completed by 1962. Just 6% of agricultural land remained in the hands of private owners.

Peasants who refused to give up their land were persecuted. Following the arrest of some 80,000 peasants, thousands more fled into the mountains from where they engaged in guerrilla warfare against the communist authorities.

Romania's 'forest brothers', who survived in the mountains on wild berries and food parcels smuggled to them by sympathetic villagers, succeeded in outwitting the authorities until as late as 1960 in some regions.

Partisan Gheorghe Arsenescu put up armed resistance from his camp in the southern Făgăraş mountains until 1952 when he went into hiding. In 1960 he was caught and imprisoned in Câmpulung Muscel prison where he promptly committed suicide. In the northern Făgăraş mountains the partisan fight was led by engineer Gavrila whose mountain stronghold remained unconquered until 1956. His forest brother, Dumitru Moldoveanu, was shot in the intestines during battle and captured. Despite being tortured, he refused to betray his brothers in the mountains. Another camp surrendered only after its families and friends living in the low-lying villages were captured and tortured by the communist army.

In the Vrancea mountains the armed resistance was split between the 'juniors' and the 'seniors' (over 40 years old). The two divisions were betrayed in 1949 by a communist spy who infiltrated one of the groups. Just two mountain fighters escaped: one was recaptured and shot, the other imprisoned and executed. ■

Sâmbăta

Ten kilometres south of Victoria lies the Sâmbăta complex, home to one of Romania's greatest and wealthiest monasteries and a key access point to the Făgăraş mountains. Nicolae Ceauşescu rightly deemed the place sufficiently idyllic to build a private luxury villa for himself and Elena in the grounds of the red-roofed monastery.

The **Brâncoveanu Monastery** (Mănăstirea Brâncoveanu), dating from 1696, derives its name from its original founder, Wallachian prince Constantin Brâncoveanu (1688-1714), who built the Orthodox monastery on the family estate which spread for some 10km as far north as Sâmbăta de Sus. The Brâncoveanu monastery, seen by the Hapsburg authorities as the last bastion of Orthodoxy in the Făgăraş region, was practically destroyed.

In 1926, restoration work started on Sâmbăta's scanty ruins, the new monastery being modelled on its original Brâcoveanu style and completed in 1946. Despite not being an original, the monastery remains a fitting testament to the great art renaissance inspired by the 17th century Wallachian prince. Its fame today is derived from its workshops of glass icons, run by the 35 monks who have been resident at Brâncoveanu Monastery since the early 1990s. There is a **glass icon museum** (☎ 068-241 239, 241 237) on the complex and visitors can tour the workshops. The monastery is open daily, except Monday, from 10 am to 6 pm.

Places to Stay & Eat The *Complex Turistic Sâmbăta*, in the monastery grounds close to the main entrance, has 12 wooden huts for US$4 a night. Bathrooms are shared and there is a small bar and restaurant.

Campers should head straight to the *Cabana Sâmbăta Popas* (810m), signposted 1km north from the monastery complex. A bed in a wooden hut is US$4 a night and you can pitch your tent for free. Staff here are experienced climbers and good for providing local advice on the area/routes etc.

From the cabana, a three hour trail marked by red triangles leads to the *Cabana Valea Sambetei* (1401m). From here, further trails go to the Moldoveanu and Negoiu peaks.

Hiking

The easiest access is from Sibiu, and local trains on the Făgăraş line to Braşov pass many starting points.

One of the best places to get off is Gară Sebeş Olt (24km from Sibiu), from where you can hike to *Cabana Suru* (1450m, 60 beds) in about five hours via Sebeşul de Sus (450m). The first leg is boring, but the scenery is stunning once you start the ascent. The next morning head for *Cabana Negoiu* (1546m, 170 beds), seven hours east of Cabana Suru across peaks up to 2306m high.

If you've had enough, hike seven hours to the railway line at Porumbacu de Jos (41km from Sibiu). Otherwise, eight gruelling hours east of Cabana Negoiu is *Cabana Bîlea Lac* (2034m, 170 beds), where there's a cable car down to *Cabana Bîlea Cascadă* (1234m, 63 beds) and to a road leading out of the mountains. On this section you will pass Mount Negoiu. If you decide to end your trip here by hitching or hiking north from Bîlea Cascadă to the railway at Cârţa (formerly spelt Cîrţa) 51km from Sibiu, check out the ruins of a fortified 13th century Cistercian monastery about a kilometre north of Cârţa station.

A seven-hour hike east of Cabana Bîlea Lac is *Cabana Podragu* (2136m, 100 beds), which you can use as a base to climb Mount Moldoveanu. From Cabana Podragu you can easily walk down to the railway at Arpaşu de Jos (420m) or Ucea (59km from Sibiu) in a day.

SIBIU
• *area code* ☎ *069 , pop 91,000*

Sibiu is just far enough off the beaten track to be spared the tourist tide that occasionally engulfs Braşov. Founded in the 12th century on the site of the former Roman village of Cibinium, Sibiu (Hermannstadt to the Saxons, Nagyszében to Hungarians) has always been one of the leading cities of Transylvania. During the peak of Saxon

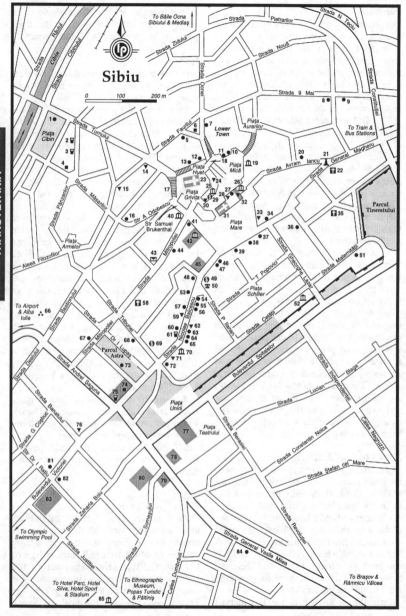

influence, Sibiu had some 19 guilds, each representing a different craft, within the sturdy city walls protected by 39 towers and four bastions.

Under the Habsburgs from 1703 to 1791 and again from 1849 to 1867, Sibiu served as the seat of the Austrian governors of Transylvania. Much remains from this colourful history, especially in the old town, one of the largest and best preserved in all Romania.

Sibiu's few remaining Saxons continue to follow in their ancestors' footsteps playing a leading role in the town's cultural life. Sibiu's remaining German-speaking Saxon

community celebrates the traditional Maifest on 1 May when they flock to Dumbrava forest. The town also hosts an International Astra Film Festival in May and an International Theatre Festival in June.

Orientation

The adjacent bus and train stations are not far from the centre of town. Exit the station and walk straight up Str General Magheru four blocks to Piaţa Mare, the historic centre. The left-luggage office at the train station is clearly marked at the western end of the main platform (open 24 hours) next to track No 1.

TRANSYLVANIA

Maps The Hotel Bulevard sells a rather cumbersome, poster-size, city map (1997) for US$0.40.

The Agenţie de Turism inside the Hotel Continental gives away a free handier city map, published in the mid-1990s with all the tourist sights clearly marked and accompanied by short historical explanations in English.

Topnotch is the multilingual *Sibiu... de la A la Z*, published in 1996 with text in English, German and Romanian. It includes maps, hotel and restaurant listings, historic sights etc and is sold for US$3 in most bookshops.

Information

Tourist Offices Sibiu lacks an efficient tourist office. The official Agenţie de Turism (☎ 218 100; fax 210 125) inside the Hotel Continental is useless (except for its free map). The staff and do not appear to be interested in trying to assist tourists.

The Hotel Bulevard and Hotel Împăratul Romanilor do not have official tourist offices but staff at reception smile, speak every European language between them, and are willing to help.

The Automobil Clubul Român (ACR; ☎ 447 359) at Str General Vasile Milea 13, is two blocks east of the Hotel Continental.

If you plan to head out to Păltiniş, contact the Agenţie de Turism Păltiniş (☎ 218 319) opposite BANCOREX on Str Tribunei. The office is open daily, except Sunday, from 10 am to 5 pm.

Foreign Consulates There is a German consulate (☎ 211 133, 433 127; fax 214 180) at Str Lucian Blaga 15-17.

Money There are currency exchanges inside the Hotel Bulevard and Hotel Împăratul Romanilor. There are IDM exchanges giving cash advance on Visa/MasterCard at Piaţa Mic 9, Str Papiu Ilarian 12, and Parcul Tineretului 20. All three are open weekdays from 8 am to 8 pm, Saturday from 9 am to 2 pm.

BANCOREX, close to the Hotel Bulevard at Str Tribunei 6, changes travellers cheques and arranges Visa/MasterCard cash advances. It is open weekdays from 8.30 am to 2 pm. The Bancă Comercială Română at Str Nicolae Bălcescu 11, also changes travellers cheques and gives cash advance on Visa/MasterCard. It is open weekdays from 8.30 am to noon and has an ATM accepting Visa/MasterCard outside.

BCIT, behind the Hotel Continental on Str Someşului, offers the same services (no ATM). It is open weekdays from 8.30 am to 6 pm, Saturday from 8.30 to 11 am.

Post & Communications The central post office is on Str Mitropoliei, open weekdays from 7 am to 8 pm. Sibiu's telephone centre, at Str Nicolae Bălcescu 13, is open daily from 7 am to 7 pm. DHL Worldwide Express (☎ 211 567; fax 217 786) has an office next door to TAROM at Str Nicolae Bălcescu 10; it is open weekdays from 9 am to 6 pm.

You can send emails and access the Internet at PVD Net-Group (☎ & fax 216 771; email pvd@pvd.logicnet.ro; www.pvdnet .logicnet.ro) at Str Nicolae Bălcescu 5; the entrance is in a courtyard off the main street. Online access for 30 minutes/one hour is US$1/1.20 and it costs US$3.50 a month to set up your private mailbox. PVD also offers monthly packages starting at US$8 for six hours online access a month. The office is open weekdays from 9 am to 6 pm.

Bookshops Sibiu has a number of quality bookshops which sell English and German-language books as well as city guides, dictionaries and postcards; the Librărie Dacia Traian at Piaţa Mare 6 has the best stock of guides and books. It also sells a hiking map for the Retezat mountains, as does the Librărie Mihai Eminescu at Str Nicolae Bălcescu 31. Neither sells maps of the Făgăraş range.

The English-language bookshop, Librărie Thausib at Piaţa Mică 3, has the largest selection of English-language novels. The Librărie Humanitas Academic bookshop opposite Kodak Express on Str Nicolae Bălcescu sells textbooks and reference books mainly, including the excellent 724-page *History of Romania* published by the Romanian Cultural Foundation, Iaşi, in 1996. It costs US$11.

Libraries & Cultural Centres The British Council Centre & Library (☎ & fax 211 056) is housed in the main building of the Lucian Blaga University at Blvd Victoriei 10. It is open Monday and Thursday from 1 to 7 pm, Tuesday and Friday from 9 am to 3 pm. An annual subscription to the library is US$1.20. The American Library of Romania is next door to the British library in the same building.

The American Centre & Library (☎ 216 062, extension 121) and the German Cultural Centre & Library (☎ 216 062, extension 123) are also housed in the university; just to confuse things however, they are inside the block on the opposite side of the street. Both buildings have the same street address – Blvd Victoriei 10. The Americans open Monday to Thursday from 8.30 am to 4 pm, Friday from 8 am to 3 pm; the Germans are open weekdays from 8 am to 4 pm.

The French Cultural Centre (☎ 218 287) is inside the Student Culture House (Casă de Cultură Studenteasca) at Str Mitropoliei 3. It is open Monday, Wednesday and Thursday from 8 am to 4 pm; Tuesday from 1 to 6 pm; and Friday from 8 am to 2 pm.

The Democratic Alliance of Hungarians in Romania (RMDS; Romániai Magyar Demokrata Szövetség; ☎ 436 751), at Str General Magheru 1-3, arranges a variety of cultural events.

Medical Services The best-stocked pharmacy, selling everything from tampons to herbal medicines, is the Farmacie Nippur-Pharm, opposite the Hotel Împăratul Romanilor at Str Nicolae Bălcescu 5; it is open weekdays from 8 am to 8 pm, Saturday from 9 am to 2 pm. The Farmasib pharmacy, which is close to the Hotel Bulevard at Str Nicolae Bălcescu 53, is open daily from 8 am to 6 pm.

There is a small pharmacy outside the train station, open weekdays from 7 am to 7.30 pm, Saturday from 8 am to 2 pm.

Things to See & Do
Central Sibiu is a perfectly preserved medieval monument, and there's no better place to begin your visit than at the top of the former **council tower** (turnul statului) which links Piaţa Mare with its smaller sister square Piaţa Mică. It was built in 1588 as a defensive tower. Its clock would toll the beginning and end of the guard's night watch. Later, the tower was used as a cereal storehouse and, more recently, as a small **History Museum** (Muzeul de Istorie). At the time of writing it was closed for restoration but it should be open by early 1998. The view of Sibiu's red roofs with the Făgăraş mountains beckoning to the south is superb.

Walk along Piaţa Mare to the baroque **Roman Catholic Cathedral** (Biserica Romano Catolică), built between 1726 and 1733 by a Jesuit order. The monument inside the church marks the resting place of general commander Otto Ferdinand, Count of Abensberg (1677-1747) who served as military commander of Transylvania between 1744 and 1747. In front of the cathedral on the square you will find a large **memorial statue** to the people who fought in the 1848 peasant uprisings.

Close by at Piaţa Mare 4-5 is the **Brukenthal Museum** (Muzeul Brukenthal; ☎ 217 671), the oldest and finest art gallery in Romania. Founded in 1817, the museum is in the baroque palace (1785) of Baron Samuel Brukenthal (1721-1803), former Austrian governor. Apart from the paintings, there are excellent archaeological, folk art and butterfly collections. Brukenthal's library is still intact, containing some 280,000 books. The museum is open daily, except Monday, from 9 am to 5 pm; admission costs US$1.

At Piaţa Mare 10 is the 15th century Gothic **Haller's House** (Casă Haller), which belonged to the family of Mayor Petrus Haller for 350 years. Next door is the house in which linguist **Andreo Cseh** (1895-1978)

TRANSYLVANIA

Unwanted People

Roma (Gypsies) are the second largest minority in Romania, comprising 1.8% of the population. The Mongols and Tartars brought the first enslaved Roma to Romania in 1242. Nomadic Roma *(corturari)* from India settled in Romania from the 15th century onwards.

Around 50% of the world's Roma population was wiped out by the Holocaust: 40,000 were deported from Romania to Auschwitz. In the communist era, Roma were again persecuted, the authorities robbing these traditionally nomadic people of their nonconformist lifestyle. Despite two-thirds of Romania's Roma population being assimilated with the broader Romanian culture *(vătraşi,* literally 'settled'), they remain an unwanted people.

Today Romania has around 2000 nomadic Roma. They are split between 40 different clans comprising 21 castes, each of which has its own traditional costume, superstitions and taboos. Unlike other ethnic minorities, they do not seek their own nation state. Rather, they aspire to the rival leadership of Roma King Florin Cioba and Roma Emperor Iulian Radulescu – two self-proclaimed chieftains who battle for Roma rights in Romania between battling against each other. Their flamboyant lifestyles represent the glittering uppercrust of Romania's largely impoverished Roma community.

Forty-one-year-old Florin Cioba was crowned king of 'all Roma everywhere' in Sibiu in February 1997. The Pentecostal minister inherited the 24-carat gold coin crown from his late father, Ioan Cioba.

Ioan Cioba crowned himself Roma king in 1992. He was a survivor of a WWII Transdniestran concentration camp and served as president of the Nomadic Metal-Working Gypsy trade union during the Ceauşescu era. As king he fought for Roma children to be accepted into state schools and, being illiterate himself, established the first adult education centres for fellow Roma. His more grandiose plan of building a replica of the Taj Mahal in Romania as a pilgrimage spot for Roma to celebrate their Indian heritage never came to fruition.

Self-styled emperor Iulian Radulescu – a cousin of the late Cioba – holds court at his palace on the same upmarket street in Sibiu as his rival king. Radulescu's 20-room villa is painted pink, blue, grey and green, and is guarded by a wizened old fortune teller and two stone elephants.

He crowned himself emperor of all Roma in 1993, marking the occasion by marrying his common-law wife with whom he had lived for 35 years. The couple – the first of the coppersmith clan *(căldărari)* to wed in church – were paired off by their parents during childhood. Traditionally Roma are forbidden from marrying *gaujes* (non-Roma). The emperor's crown, comprising 40 gold coins studded with diamonds and rubies, was valued at US$87 million. His bride wore a blue dress symbolising the nomadic clan's traditional roof – the sky – and bore a chain made up of nine 14g gold coins minted in Austria in 1915. Throughout the ceremony she refrained from touching her groom. Under Roma law, a wife is subordinate to her husband and is therefore expected to demonstrate her subservience in public.

In 1994 Emperor Radulescu was briefly imprisoned for allegedly selling stolen copper to Turkey. The previous year he embarked on a four week tour of India, sponsored by the Romanian Roma community, in a bid to retrace his clan's ancestral roots. In anticipation of his death he plans to build a US$30 million marble mausoleum for himself near Sibiu as a 'symbol of Roma pride'.

Note: Roma unanimously voted in favour of the term 'Roma' as opposed to 'Gypsy', *'tsigane'* or *'gitano'* at the first World Romany Congress held in London in 1971. Romania participated in the congress for the first time in 1918. ■

first expounded his modernist theories on the teaching of Esperanto in 1920.

Just west along Str Samuel Brukenthal, at Str Mitropoliei 2 is the **Primăria Municipiului** (1470), now the **City History Museum** (Muzeul de istorie; ☎ 218 143) which contains further exhibits from Brukenthal's palace.

Nearby, on Piaţa Huet, is the Gothic **evangelical church** (Biserica Evangelică; 1300-1520), its great five-pointed tower

being visible from afar. Note the four magnificent baroque funerary monuments on the upper nave, and the organ with 6002 pipes (1772). The tomb of Mihnea Vodă cel Rău (Prince Mihnea the Bad), son of Vlad Ţepeş, is in the closed-off section behind the organ. This prince, who ruled Wallachia from 1507-10, was murdered on the square in front of the church after attending a service in March 1510. Don't miss the fresco of the Crucifixion (1445) up in the sanctuary. The church is open weekdays from 9 am to 1 pm, and organ concerts are held every Wednesday at 6 pm – check the schedule outside for dates. Opposite is the **Brukenthal School** (Liceul Brukenthal).

To reach the lower town from here, walk down the 13th century **staircase passage**, on the opposite side of the church from where you enter or down the stairs beneath the 18th century **Staircase Tower** (Turnul Scarilor). Otherwise, cross the photogenic **Iron Bridge** (1859) on nearby Piaţa Mică. The bridge's nickname is 'Liar's Bridge' after the tricky merchants who met here to trade and the young lovers who declared their undying love. It is meant to collapse if anyone tells a lie while standing on it. It didn't when Ceauşescu crossed it.

Piaţa Mică is small and quaint with buildings a muted rainbow of pretty pastel colours. The wonky stairway leading to Piaţa Aurarilor at its eastern end is particularly idyllic and leads down to a maze of narrow cobbled-stone streets. At Piaţa Mică 26 is the **Pharmaceutical Museum** (Muzeul de istorie Farmaciei; ☎ 218 191), with a small collection of antique drug jars and medical tools. It is open daily, except Monday, from 10 am to 6 pm. Admission is US$0.80.

A couple of doors down on the same side of the square is the **Artists' House** (Casă Artelor), an exhibition hall which hosts various temporary exhibitions. Its contemporary photographic exhibitions are particularly noteworthy; it is open daily, except Monday, from 9 am to 5 pm.

The **Franz Binder Museum of World Ethnology** (Muzeul de etnografie universală Franz Binder; ☎ 218 195) at Piaţa Mică 11, has some fun permanent displays including traditional Japanese toys, folk costumes from China and an Egyptian mummy. It is open daily, except Monday, from 10 am to 6 pm; admission is US$1.20.

Heading north-east from Piaţa Mică along Str Avram Iancu, you come to the **Ursuline Church**. Founded by Dominican monks in the 15th century, it was later transformed into a school, then turned over to the Ursulines in 1728.

Go back to Piaţa Mică, then walk southwest along Str Mitropoliei to the **Orthodox cathedral**, a monumental red and white brick building dating from 1906 and said to be a miniature copy of the Hagia Sofia in Istanbul. The church bells call worshippers to prayer daily at 6 and 8 am.

Str Mitropoliei is lined with memorial plaques on almost every house wall. Avram Iancu, Romanian leader of the 1848 revolution, stayed for a few days at Str Mitropoliei 7 in 1848 on his way to the Apuseni mountains. Poet Mihai Eminescu rested at Str Mitropoliei 22 between 18 and 30 June 1868.

The influential **Transylvanian Association for Romanian Literature & Culture**, known as ASTRA, was founded in 1861 at Str Mitropoliei 20. It was created in protest at the intense Magyarisation of Transylvania in the mid-19th century. ASTRA's nationalist calls for Romanians to stand up for their liberty and identity were voiced in *Tribuna*, Transylvania's first Romanian newspaper, written and printed in Sibiu from 1884.

The house at Str Mitropoliei 19 bears a **memorial plaque** to Transylvania's Memorandumists of 1892, the leaders of the Romanian National Party who addressed a memorandum to the emperor Franz Joseph in Vienna in 1892 in which they called for an end to discrimination against Romanians in Romania. The emperor forwarded it to the Hungarian government who sent it back without opening it, and 29 members of the National Party were convicted of agitating against the state and imprisoned.

At the southern end of Str Mitropoliei, turn left onto Str Tribunei, then right along Str Cetăţii, the start of a pleasant walk northeast along a section of the old **city walls**, constructed during the 16th century. As in Braşov, different guilds protected each of the 39 towers – such as the Linenmakers' Tower, the Potters' Tower and the Barbers' Tower. Walk north up Str Cetăţii, past the **Thick Tower**, also built in the 16th century and later used to house Sibiu's first theatre. Close by at Str Cetăţii 1 is the **Natural History Museum** (Muzeul de istorie Naturală; ☎ 436 868), dating from 1849.

TRANSYLVANIA

The **Haller Bastion** stands at the northernmost end of Str Cetăţii. The bastion is named after the 16th century city mayor, Petrus Haller, who had the red-brick tower built with double walls in 1551. When Sibiu was hit by the plague, holes were drilled through the walls to enable corpses to be evacuated more quickly from the city. The bastion was consequently dubbed the 'gate of the corpses'.

South of the centre, close to the **university**, is a **Museum of Hunting Arms & Trophies** (Muzeul de arme şi trofee de Vânătoare; ☎ 217 873) at Str Scoala de Înot 4. At the south of this street is the city **stadium**, backing into the 21-hectare **Sub Arini Park** (Parcul Sub Arini) filled with tree-lined avenues and beautifully laid-out flower beds. The **Complex Nataţie Olimpia** is also here, complete with swimming pool, canoeing and rowing facilities, and tennis courts.

If you have an extra afternoon, it's worth taking in the **Museum of Popular Techniques** (Muzeul civilzaţiei Populare tradiţionale Astra Dumbrava Sibiului; ☎ 420 215) further south in Dumbrava Park (take trolleybus No T1 from the train station). It's open from May to October, from Tuesday to Sunday between 10 am and 5 pm. A great many authentic rural buildings and houses have been reassembled in the park to create an open-air **ethnographic museum**. Ask about guided tours of the site in English. At the adjacent **zoo** you can hire a boat and row yourself around the lake. The **city cemetery** is also here.

Activities

The Boua Bikes Club (☎ 218 310), based at the SurMont sports shop at Str Avram Iancu 25 welcomes all fellow mountain-bikers to join its clan. The club arranges mountain biking expeditions in the Făgăraş mountains and if you contact them in advance they can probably supply you with a bike too. Every year in mid-August the club also hosts the gruelling *Triathlon Altitude – Surmont*, in the Făgăraş mountains (see Facts for the Visitor – Activities, Mountain Biking).

Language Courses

The Fiatest Centru Educational (☎ & fax 213 446) at Blvd Vasile Milea, Pavilion 5, offers Romanian language courses, costing US$10 an hour for a group of up to five people.

Places to Stay

Camping The closest campsite is *Popas Turistic* (☎ 422 831, 214 022), beside the Hanul Dumbrava Restaurant 4km southwest of town (take trolleybus No T1 from the train station direct to the site). There are 204 rooms in worn-out cabins at US$11 for either single or double. Pitch your own tent on the shady lawn for US$4.50. There's plenty of space and it's open from June to September.

There is also a *campsite* 14km north of Sibiu in Ocna Sibiului (see Around Sibiu later).

Private Rooms If you hang out at the bus or train station long enough, you're bound to get an offer. Alternatively, try ANTREC (☎ 220 179; fax 215 481), Calea Dumbrăvii 120. It arranges rooms in private houses in Sibiu and surrounds for around US$10 a night, including breakfast.

Hotels – in the centre On the first side street below the Iron Bridge is *Hotel La Podul Minciunilor* (☎ 217 259), a small, three-room pension at Str Azilului 1. Singles/doubles cost US$13/18 if you are lucky enough to turn up when it has vacancies. In the same vein is the more friendly, four-room *Hotel Halemadero* (☎ 212 509) at Str Măsarilor 10. It overlooks a pleasant garden and patio and costs US$15 for a double with private bath and TV. Breakfast is not included in either pension. The adjacent bar is a friendly hangout.

Sibiu's most colourful hotel is the central three-star *Hotel Împăratul Romanilor* (Roman Emperor; ☎ 216 500; fax 213 278) at Str Nicolae Bălcescu 4. It was founded in 1555 as a restaurant called 'La Sultanul Turcilor' (The Turks' Sultan). The hotel has 102 rooms, split into three categories: 'A' rooms, with a street view, are the most expensive at US$29/44 for a single/double;

'B' rooms face the backyard and cost US$27/40 a night; 'C' rooms, for US$25/38, are 'very small'. All rooms have a private bath and TV; rooms with a shower are US$1 cheaper. Breakfast is included.

Another appealing old place is the *Hotel Bulevard* (☎ 216 060), Piaţa Unirii 2-4. Dating from 1876, it was here, in what was then the 'Haberman Café', that 19th century poet George Coşbuc came to brainstorm. The hotel today is a worthwhile splurge at US$18/28 for a spacious single/double with remote-controlled TV and modernised, private bathrooms.

The nearby, 15-storey *Hotel Continental* (☎ 218 100; fax 210 125) at Calea Dumbrăvii 2-4, was recently renovated with business travellers in mind. Every room now has a colour TV and porters to carry in your bags. It's US$43/69 for singles/doubles, including breakfast. An apartment costs US$90.

Hotels – south of the centre There is a cluster of hotels next to the stadium, a few blocks south of Hotel Continental (a taxi from the train station costs US$1.50). The largest is the grim, eight-storey *Hotel Parc* (☎ 424 455) at Str Scoala de Înot 3, way overpriced at US$11/17 for singles/doubles with private bath, TV and telephone. Prices include a breakfast of stale bread and instant coffee.

A better choice is the chalet-style *Hotel Silva* (☎ 442 141; fax 217 945) overlooking the tennis courts in the tranquil, tree-filled Sub Arini park at Aleea Eminescu 1, 30m to the right of Hotel Parc. Rooms cost US$17/23 night and an apartment is US$33. All rooms have private bath and TV. Breakfast is included.

Much better value than either of these – although not as comfortable – is the ageing two-storey *Hotel Sport* (☎ 422 472), at Str Octavian Goga 2, on the eastern side of Hotel Parc. Rooms here are US$4 per person, although it is often fully booked by sporting groups. Bathrooms are communal and the hot water supply is somewhat erratic.

Places to Eat
Restaurants & Cafés Sibiu has a shortage of restaurants, which means you may eat more than one meal in a hotel restaurant. The one in the Împăratul Romanilor is rather stuffy, but several readers have commented that they found the food superb; it is generally full of rich tourists speaking loudly and gaping in amazement at the elaborate, sliding glass ceiling. The *Restaurant Bumita*, further south along Str Nicolae Bălcescu, is cheaper, more local, and has nice wooden tables with red tablecloths on the street; it is open daily from 8 am to midnight.

Lacto Bar Liliacul, Str Nicolae Bălcescu 18, is a good place for breakfast on week-days, if you don't mind consuming your mămăligă and yoghurt standing up. *Restaurant Mara*, at Str Nicolae Bălcescu 21, is a small, quiet bistro with an English-language menu. Everything here is good except the spaghetti, truly a crime against Italians.

La Turn, next to the old council tower on Piaţa Mare, has a large terrace overlooking the square and serves traditional Romanian cuisine; its downside is its proximity to the permanent jam of impatient, horn-honking motorists queuing to drive beneath the council tower onto Str Avram Iancu. The restaurant is open daily from 10 am to 10 pm.

Dori's, close by at Piaţa Mică 14, is the top place in Sibiu for a cheap – and delicious – fill. The tiny patisserie only serves freshly baked, sesame-seed bread (the best in the whole of Romania) and yoghurt (!), but it is permanently packed, nevertheless, with people waiting for the next batch of bread to come out of the oven – literally. It is open weekdays from 8 am to 8 pm, Saturday from 10 am to 8 pm. There are a couple of tables, always full, outside on the square. The ageing *Restaurant Union*, opposite at Piaţa Mică 7, fails to attract the same sort of crowds.

On the opposite side of the square is the upmarket, very trendy *Domar Cafetărie & Patisserie*. It has a great selection of naughty-but-nice cakes and pastries and serves excellent fresh coffee. Again, it's always packed.

Another fun café is the more bohemian *Art Café*, inside the state philharmonic building on Str Filharmonicii. The café is through a red and gold-painted door which leads to the cellar; its walls are covered with graffiti and adorned with musical instruments. It is open weekdays from 8 am to midnight, weekends from 10 am.

Restaurant Select, west of the centre at Str Târgu Peştelui 2, is a small, upmarket restaurant serving traditional Romanian food at slightly above-average prices; it is good for a splurge though.

If you want to eat dirt-cheap food with the locals, go to *Restaurant Timiş*, not far from the market on the corner of Str Tumului. It is open daily from 7.30 am to 8 pm.

Fast Food On the eastern side of Piaţa Mare is the *Pupa* alimentar and fast food outlet; hot dogs, hot sandwiches and vegetarian pizza slices for less than US$1 are served through a small window facing the street. Sit on the chairs outside and watch the world go by.

Self Catering Stock up on vegetables and fruits at the *market* on Piaţa Cibin, north-east of Str Măsarilor near Hotel Halemadero. *Capa*, opposite the history museum at Str Mitropoliei 1, is a small but clean food shop selling a good variety of products; it is open daily, except Sunday, from 8 am to 6 pm. The *Magazin centrală* at Str Nicolae Bălcescu 15 is your typical 'Soviet-style' shop touting rows upon rows of the same product; it is open weekdays from 6 am to 8 pm, Saturday from 8 am to 1 pm.

For foreign imports go to *Prima* at Str Nicolae Bălcescu 2; it is open weekdays from 7 am to 9 pm, Saturday from 7.30 am to 5 pm, Sunday from 9 am to 1 pm.

Entertainment

Cinema Sibiu has three cinemas: *Cinema Pacea* at Str Nicolae Bălcescu 29 is your conventional cinema, with screenings daily at 10 am and 12.30, 3, 5.15 and 7.30 pm. The *Cinema Tineretului* (☎ 211 420), adjoining the hip Bar Meridan on Str Alexandru

Odobescu, is quite a treat. The auditorium-cum-bar is filled with sofas and coffee tables, inviting you to sit back in comfort and relax over a beer while watching your favourite Hollywood hero in action. Films are screened daily at 11 am and 1, 3 and 5 pm.

The Studionul Astra (☎ 218 195, extension 26) at Piaţa Mică 11, screens alternative art films; it also hosts the annual International Astra Film Festival in May.

Clubs & Bars The *Disco-Bar Meridan* (☎ 212 166) inside the Cinema Tineretului complex is an alternative cellar club with tribal art-style paintings on the wall, dim lighting and fascinating relics. Its mellow blues and funky jazz attracts a fun, bohemian crowd. The bar is open 24 hours; the disco runs from 10 pm to around 5 am. The *Disco Bar Mega Vox*, downstairs in the Culture House (Casă de Cultură) in front of Hotel Continental (entry from the rear of the building), is popular on summer weekends (but not as cool).

The *Cocktail Club*, around the corner from the Hotel Halemadero at Str Croitorilor, is open daily from noon to midnight. Heading north, the *Caliba Billiard Bar* at Str Croitorilor 7 has one billiard table, two tables and about five chairs. It is open pretty much non-stop.

On Str Nicolae Bălcescu, opposite the Prima food shop, is the bikers-style *Scorpion Bar* with blacked out windows and a dark and smoky atmosphere; it is open daily from noon to midnight.

Theatre & Classical Music Performances at the *Philharmonic*, on the corner of Str General Magheru and Str Filharmonicii, and the *Radu Stancu State Theatre* (Teatrul de Stat Radu Stancu; ☎ 413 114) just off Piaţa Unirii at Blvd Spitelor 2-4, are well worth attending. Plays at the theatre are usually in Romanian, but there is a German-language section within the theatre. Tickets for both venues are sold at the Agenţie de Teatrală (☎ 211 990), Str Nicolae Bălcescu 17, open weekdays from 10 am to 1 pm and from 5 pm to 6.15 pm. The Radu Stancu State

Theatre hosts the International Theatre Festival in June.

The *Puppet Theatre* (Teatrul de Păpuşi; ☎ 211 420), in the same building as the Cinema Tineretului on Str Alexandru Odobescu, is only open between October and July. Ask at the cinema for details of shows.

Things to Buy

SurMont Sports, Str Avram Iancu 25, has tents, climbing ropes and water bottles, plus a good selection of hiking maps (some for sale, some for reference only). It's open weekdays from 9 am to 5 pm.

Craving a CFR train conductor's cap? How about a fez? The Aleman Nicolae Ceaprazărie (☎ 431 764) hat shop at Str 9 Mai 50 is open weekdays from 9 am to 1 pm. If you want a hat made to fit go to the no-name hat shop, a couple of doors down at Str 9 Mai 46.

Art Antic, behind the evangelical church on Piaţa Huet, sells contemporary and antique arts and crafts; it's open weekdays from 10 am to 6 pm, Saturday from 9 am to 1 pm. Another goodie for antiques and old ceramic pieces glued together is La Fresca Antichitati at Piaţa Mică 22; it is open weekdays from 10 am to 6 pm.

The Galerile de Artă, at Str Nicolae Bălcescu 37, sells some tasteful objects and is probably the least 'touristy' of Sibiu's many art and craft shops.

Getting There & Away

Air TAROM operates a morning and evening flight to Bucharest on Monday, Wednesday and Friday. Single/return tickets (US$25/50) are sold at TAROM (☎ 211 157), Str Nicolae Bălcescu 10, open weekdays from 8 am to 7 pm, Saturday from 8 am to noon.

Bus The bus station is opposite the train station at the eastern end of Str Nicolae Teclu Major, on Piaţa 1 Decembrie. Daily bus services include one to Cluj-Napoca (230km), Sibiu (175km), (Târgu Mureş (125km) and Piteşti (260km); and two daily to Sighişoara (92km).

Western Europe Mihu Reisen (☎ 211 744, 214 979), Str 9 Mai 52, operates buses to Germany. Its office is weekdays from 8 am to 8 pm. A bus departs from outside its office on Tuesday and Saturday at 2.30 am. It stops at various cities in Hungary, Slovakia and the Czech Republic en route to Germany. The return bus leaves Aschaffenburg in Germany on Wednesday and Friday. Atlassib (☎ 229 224), at Str Tractorului 14, offers identical services.

Trans-Europa (☎ 211 296; ☎ & fax 210 364), Str Nicolae Bălcescu 41, sells tickets for buses to western Europe too. The Touring Eurolines office (☎ 218 100) is inside the Hotel Continental. Reisebüro Kessler (☎ 228 118), Str Beiltz 22, has a daily bus departing from Sibiu to Germany at 6 am.

Train The Agenţie de Voiaj CFR office (☎ 216 441) next to the Împăratul Romanilor Hotel at Str Nicolae Bălcescu 6, is open weekdays from 7 am to 7.30 pm.

The train station is at the eastern end of Str General Magheru, on Piaţa 1 Decembrie. For Sighişoara (95km) you may have to change at Copşa Mică or Mediaş. For Alba Iulia (92km) you may have to change at Vinţu de Jos.

Getting Around

To/From the Airport Sibiu airport (☎ 229 296, 229 269) is 5km west of the centre; TAROM runs a shuttle bus to/from the airport. It departs from its city centre office one hour before flights depart.

Bus & Trolleybus Tickets for public transport cost US$0.22 for a double-journey ticket and are sold from kiosks next to most bus stops. Trolleybus Nos 1 and 2 depart from the train station to the centre.

From Sibiu, buses for Păltiniş depart from the bus stop at the eastern end of Str 9 Mai at 7 and 11 am and at 3.30 pm (32km, 1½ hours). Tickets costing US$0.75 can be bought directly from the driver. Return buses depart from the central bus stop in Păltiniş at 9 am, and 1 and 5.30 pm.

Taxi There are taxi ranks outside the Hotel Bulevard and Hotel Continental. To call a taxi dial ☎ 444 444, 222 222 or 212 121.

AROUND SIBIU
Băile Ocna Sibiului
The bubbling spa resort of Băile Ocna Sibiului, 18km north of Sibiu on the railway line to Copşa Mică, is packed during summer weekends. Known as Salzburg to the Saxons, the many natural pools and geological curiosities around Ocna Sibiului make it a popular bathing resort. Some of the bubbling lakes are formed in abandoned salt mines. There is a large *campsite* in the forest next to the train halt: Get off at Băile Ocna Sibiului, *not* Ocna Sibiului, 2km north.

From Sibiu there are 11 local trains daily to Băile Ocna Sibiului (12km, 15 minutes).

Cisnădie & Răşinari
Eight kilometres south of Sibiu, on the road to Păltiniş, is the Saxon fortified church of Cisnădie (Heltau in German, Nagydisznód in Hungarian). Work started on defensive walls around the church in 1430 but they were destroyed by a Turkish attack on the town in 1493. In 1601, the Habsburg general George Basta murdered three villagers on the church porch.

Ask in the village for the key to the bell tower which offers fantastic views of this red-roofed town. Three main streets run through Cisnădie; the church is south of the middle street.

The shepherd village of **Răşinari**, famed for its local carpentry and sheep farming, is 4km south of Cisnădie. Ethnographic exhibits – including the long wooden ladels *(tâlv)* used for sampling the plum brandy *(ţuică)* stored in large wooden kegs – are displayed in the **Răşinari village museum**. The village is also the birthplace of Romanian poet and politician Octavian Goga (1881-1939) who served as prime minister for 44 days in 1937.

You can hike to Răşinari from Păltiniş (see Păltiniş – Activities).

Places to Stay *Opération Villages Rou-mains* operates a thriving agro-tourism scheme from its small office in **Sebeşu de Sus**, 15km east of Cisnădie. It arranges rooms in private homes in Sebeşu de Sus and the surrounding villages for US$10 to US$12 per person a night, including breakfast. It also has French and English-speaking tour guides who charge a daily fee of US$10. Advance bookings can be made through its central office in Cluj-Napoca.

In Răşinari there is the *Cabana Curmătura Stezii* (☎ 069-557 310).

Getting There & Away Local buses run from Sibiu bus station to Cisnădie (8km, 30 minutes) every half hour between 5.15 am and 11 pm.

To get to Răşinari, take trolleybus No T1 from Sibiu train station.

Păltiniş
Păltiniş, out on a limb 32km south-west of Sibiu, nestles at an altitude of 1442m at the foot of the Cindrel Mountains (also known as the Cibin Mountains). Its peaks – Mount Cindrel (2244m) and Mount Frumoasa (2170m) – shelter two large glacier lakes from which the Cibin river flows to make its way downstream to the fantastic **Cibin gorges** (Cheile Cibinului).

Păltiniş is generally snow-covered from December to March. In summer, hikers follow in the footsteps of the Saxon members of the *Siebenbürgische Karpatenverein* (Transylvanian Carpathian Association) who established the resort in the late 19th century and managed it until 1944. Păltiniş in the 1920s was a fashionable resort, the last remnants of its golden past being wiped out in 1992 when its wooden, nine-pin bowling *(popice)* alley was moved from Păltiniş to the open-air museum in Sibiu.

From Păltiniş it is an easy day's hike to most of the villages in Mărginimea Sibiului.

Activities Skis and sledges can be rented from the Club Sportiv behind the Gaudeamus villa at the south-eastern end of the resort. Alternatively, try the Cabana Păltiniş a few hundred metres south of Club Sportiv.

The cabana is next to the teleferic station where you can get a chair lift up the mountain; it costs US$1.20 for a return trip.

Hiking trails are well marked. From Club Sportiv it is a 4km walk along a road to Şanta where there is a small refuge for campers to spend the night. The most popular route, however, is a 3½km trail marked by red circles which descends downhill to the Cibin Gorges (Cheile Cibinului). From here the trail continues north-east, past Lake Cibin to the Cabana Fântânele (Fîntînele). The next day you can continue in the same direction to Sibiel village (see Mărginimea Sibiului below); this trail (3-3½ hours) is marked by blue crosses. Alternatively, follow a blue cross trail to the neighbouring village of Fântânele (Fîntînele).

Heading back south from Cabana Fântânele, a 7½ to eight hour trail (red crosses and blue circles) cuts down the valley to Şaua Şerbănei where you pick up a blue circle trail leading to the Cînaia refuge. The mountain rescue team SALVAMONT has a base here.

More adventurous alpinists who want to climb to the summit of Mount Cindrel (Vârful Cindrel, 2244m) should follow the red striped trail from Cabana Păltiniş south, past the Cînaia refuge (5½ to 6½ hours). Heading northwards, red stripes also indicate the way to Răşinari village (six to seven hours).

Places to Stay Bookings for Păltiniş's *Villa Sinaia* can be made in advance through the Păltiniş tourist agency (☎ 215 223; fax 218 319), Str Tribunei 3, Sibiu. Comfortable double rooms with private bath cost US$14 a night, including breakfast.

The family-run *Vila Andreea* (☎ operator 991; ask for ☎ 135) has four rooms costing US$3.50 per person a night. The Păltiniş tourist agency also takes bookings. The somewhat ghastly 39-room *Hotel Cindrelul* (☎ 213 237), the mainstay hotel in the resort, has doubles/triples starting at US$13.

Getting There & Away From Sibiu, buses for Păltiniş depart from the bus stop at the eastern end of Str 9 Mai at 7 and 11 am and at 3.30 pm (1½ hours). Tickets can be bought directly from the driver. Return buses depart from the central bus stop in Păltiniş at 9 am, and 1 and 5.30 pm.

Mărginimea Sibiului

Mărginimea Sibiului (literally 'borders of Sibiu') embraces the predominantly pastoral region west of Sibiu which runs along the county border towards Sebeş. Traditional occupations such as shepherding, weaving and carpentry are still very much alive in its pretty little villages where painting icons on glass and colouring eggs outweighs any 20th century invention.

Lying 15 km west of Sibiu is the delightful **Cristian** (Grossau in German, Kereszténysziget in Hungarian). The village, settled by Saxons since the 14th century, is a picture postcard of red-roofed houses and vibrant washed walls, overshadowed by a grandiose fortified church in the centre of the village. Visitors can climb the tower of the church for an aerial view. Ask for the key to the tower *(turnul)* and church at the green-painted house, down the road behind the eastern fortress wall. The history of the church is told in the small village museum *(muzeul sătesc)*, next to the local prefecture in the centre of the village. It is theoretically open daily, except Monday, from noon to 5 pm; if it is closed during opening hours ask for the museum key at the prefecture (comuna Cristian consulul locale).

From Cristian, it is worth making a short detour through **Orlat**, home to one of the largest village orphanages in Romania, to **Sibiel**. Sibiel has one of Romania's best **glass icon museums** (muzeul de coane pe sticlă), well worth visiting. The museum, in a blue-painted building next to the village church (1765), houses a collection of more than 600 icons richly painted on glass. An icon of the Virgin Mary meanwhile would traditionally be included in a young girl's dowry, representing both the virginity and fertility of the bride-to-be.

From Sibiel, head back north to **Sălişte**, another quaint village rich in local folklore.

In **Galeş**, 2km west of Sălişte, is a small ethnographic and art museum (muzeul de etnografie şi artă populară). It is at the southern end of the village, across the bridge opposite a salami factory. If you get lost ask in the village for the salami factory (fabrica de salamuri). A dirt track leads from Galeş to **Poiana Sibiului**, famed for its fantastic col-.oured eggs decorated with brightly coloured geometric motifs.

Places to Stay & Eat In Cristian, you can stay at the *Hotel Spark* (☎ 069-559 262). Staying here is comparable to a cosy night at home. The small, family-run pensione has 14 beds in doubles/triples costing US$13 per person, including breakfast. The hotel does not provide evening meals so bring your own supplies.

In Sibiel you can have the real McCoy. Some 25 families open their homes to tourists, feeding you with fresh eggs and milk for breakfast and laying on a small feast of home-grown produce at dinnertime. The successful agro-tourism scheme is run by Dorina Petra (☎ 554 198) who can generally be found at the museum (☎ 553 818). A night's accommodation costs US$9 per person; meals are around US$3.

Getting There & Away Local trains from Sibiu to Sebeş stop at Cristian (15km, 15 minutes), Sibiel (23km, 25 minutes), Sălişte (30km, 35 minutes), and Miercurea Sibiu (58km, 1¼ hours). There are seven trains daily between Sibiu and Sebeş.

MEDIAŞ & COPŞA MICĂ
• *area code ☎ 069, pop 75,500,*

Mediaş is a small but thriving industrial town, 55km from Sibiu, on the banks of the river Târnava Mare. It was in Mediaş (Mediasch in German, Medgyes in Hungarian) that Saxon church leaders met in 1544 to mark the first Lutheran synod in Transylvania. Today a predominantly Romanian town, the Saxon influence lives on in the painted houses which glow in the sunlight.

Not quite so radiant is the black pit of Copşa Mică, 11km south of Mediaş and a major junction for connecting trains between Sibiu and Sighişoara.

During the communist era, the town was home to the Carbosin carbon-black processing plant which belched out thousands of tons of soot annually, leaving *everything* black and killing off all vegetation within a 6km radius. Finally, in 1993, international pressure forced the soot-spouting monster to shut up for good.

But its legacy lives on. Lung and heart diseases are higher than average in Copşa Mică (population 30,000). Should you have the misfortune to change trains in Copşa Mică, you can view the abandoned plant from the train platform. It stands derelict on wasteland alongside the entire length of the station, its blackened buildings testimony to the living nightmare it must once have been. The permanent cloud of grey smoke that lingers above it comes from the chemical plant, yet to be shut down, at its southern end.

Orientation
Mediaş train station is at Str Unirii 3. Left luggage (open daily from 7 to 9 pm) is in the main ticket hall. The bus station (☎ 814 326) is a couple of blocks further north on Str Unirii. The Hotel Central is a three minute walk from the train station: turn right along Str Unirii and then right onto Str Stephan Ludwig Roth. Cross the roundabout and cut through a small alleyway on the other side of the street towards the red and white building with the satellite dish on top. To get to the centre, turn right at the roundabout and continue along Str Stephan Ludwig Roth until you reach Piaţa Regele Ferdinand I. Walk up Str George Enescu, at the northern end of the square, to reach the church.

Information
The tourist office (☎ 811 885), inside the Hotel Central, sells tickets for buses to Germany and maps of the Sibiu district; it is open weekdays from 8 am to 3.30 pm, Saturday from 8 am to 1 pm.

Change money and get cash advance on Visa/MasterCard at the Bancă Agricola, next to the Hotel Central on Str Mihai Eminescu. It is open weekdays from 8 am to 1 pm.

The telephone office is a couple of blocks further north, towards the fresh fruit and veg market (piaţa agrolimentară) on Str Mihai Eminescu. The post office is next to the train station on Str Unirii.

Things to See

The fortified **evangelical church of St Margaret** dominates the old town. A church was built on the site in the 13th century but it was not until 1447 that the present edifice was constructed. A 74m-tall tower (later struck by lightning four times) was added in 1482 while the church's altar, dating from 1485, is considered one of Transylvania's most precious pieces of medieval Saxon art.

Close to the church is the Mediaş' **school** (Liceul Teoretic) in which a small exhibition on the life and works of Stephen Ludwig Roth (1706-1849) is housed. Born into a middle-class Saxon family in Transylvania, Ludwig Roth studied in Germany and Switzerland but returned to Mediaş where he worked as a professor at the school. He actively opposed Habsburg efforts to introduce Hungarian as the official teaching language. In 1848, Habsburg forces arrested him and on 11 May 1849 he was executed in Cluj-Napoca. A statue of the teacher, writer and activist stands in the small park in front of the school.

There is a small local **history museum** (☎ 811 299), next to the Hungarian Reformed church on Str Viitorului; it is open daily, except Monday, from 10 am to 5 pm.

Places to Stay & Eat

Despite being the only hotel in town, 128-room *Hotel Central* (☎ 811 787) at Str Mihai Eminescu 4-7, does not charge astronomical prices. Nightly rates depend on the floor you stay on and whether you have cable TV. A basic single/double with private bathroom starts at US$8/13 a night, including a good breakfast. All the staff speak excellent English.

There is a good *fast food* outlet, next to the telephone office on Str Mihai Eminescu. It

doles out egg and cheeseburgers for less than US$1 and has an excellent patisserie counter too. The *Ana Café*, opposite the theatre school on Str George Enescu, is a pleasant local hangout with a terrace overlooking the fortified church.

Getting There & Away

Bus There are eight daily buses to Târgu Mureş (71km) but few others. Tickets for private buses to western Europe are sold at the travel agency inside the Hotel Central on Str Mihai Eminescu; buses depart from outside the hotel. A bus departs from Mediaş to Germany on Tuesday at 4.30 am.

Train The Agenţie de Voiaj CFR (☎ 811 351) is on the central square at Piaţa Regele Ferdinand I, 5. Mediaş is on the main Cluj-Napoca-Bucharest line. To get to Sighişoara from Sibiu you have to change trains at Copşa Mică or Mediaş.

All international trains between Bucharest and Budapest stop at Mediaş (see Sighişoara – Getting There & Away).

SIGHIŞOARA

* *area code* ☎ *065 , pop 38,000*

Sighişoara (Schässburg in German, Segesvár in Hungarian) is a perfectly preserved medieval town in beautiful hilly countryside. Nine towers remain along Sighişoara's intact city walls, which encircle sloping cobbled streets lined with 16th century burgher houses and untouched churches.

Settled by the Romans, the town was first documented as Castrumex in 1280. Saxon colonists, under whom traditional medieval trades such as tailoring, shoemaking, rope-making and goldsmithery flourished, settled here from the 12th century onwards. These Saxons were nicknamed 'sasi' by the local population. Today the town continues to burst with life, particularly on Wednesday and Saturday when Roma and villagers from outlying regions come into town on their horse-drawn wagons to sell their wares at the

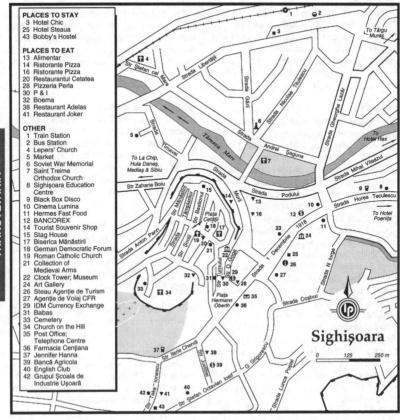

PLACES TO STAY
3 Hotel Chic
25 Hotel Steaua
43 Bobby's Hostel

PLACES TO EAT
13 Alimentar
14 Ristorante Pizza
16 Ristorante Pizza
20 Restaurantul Cetatea
28 Pizzeria Perla
30 P & I
32 Boema
38 Restaurant Adelas
41 Restaurant Joker

OTHER
1 Train Station
2 Bus Station
4 Lepers' Church
5 Market
6 Soviet War Memorial
7 Saint Treime
   Orthodox Church
8 Sighişoara Education
   Centre
9 Black Box Disco
10 Cinema Lumina
11 Hermes Fast Food
12 BANCOREX
14 Tourist Souvenir Shop
15 Stag House
17 Biserica Mănăstirii
18 German Democratic Forum
19 Roman Catholic Church
21 Collection of
    Medieval Arms
22 Clock Tower; Museum
24 Art Gallery
26 Steau Agenţie de Turism
27 Agenţie de Voiaj CFR
29 IDM Currency Exchange
31 Babas
33 Cemetery
34 Church on the Hill
35 Post Office;
    Telephone Centre
36 Farmacia Centiana
37 Jennifer Hanna
39 Bancă Agricola
40 English Club
42 Grupul Şcoala de
    Industrie Uşoară

Sighişoara

0   125   250 m

twice-weekly market. In summer, Sighişoara is packed every day with tourists.

Sighişoara was also the birthplace of Vlad Ţepeş and therefore attracts hordes of Dracula tourists.

Prior to 1989 there were some 3000 Saxons living in Sighişoara. Since 1990 however, the Saxon community has plummeted to less than 500. The city band still plays but its dulcet tones are ringed with nostalgia for its top tenor, who has departed for Germany, along with the better part of the choir.

All trains between Bucharest and Buda-pest (via Oradea) pass through here, so look out for it from the window if you're foolish enough not to get off.

Orientation

Follow Str Gării south from the train station to the Soviet war memorial, where you turn left to the large Orthodox church. Cross the Tîrnava Mare River on the footbridge here and take Str Morii to the left, then keep going all the way up to Piaţa Hermann Oberth and the old town. Many of the facilities you'll want are found along a short stretch of Str 1 Decembrie 1918.

A legend is born ... 'Dracula' Vlad Ţepeş entered the world in Sighişoara.

The left-luggage office is on the main platform at the train station (open 24 hours).

Maps The most up-to-date and detailed map of the city, and the fortified old town, is the *Sighişoara Touristic Map* (US$0.50), published by FRH Impex in 1997 with brief historical explanations in English, German and Romanian.

The A5-sized *Sighişoara Tourist Guide* (US$0.70) includes a detailed history of the old town in English, French, German and Romanian, and a centrefold city map.

The *Medieval Sighişoara Tourist Guide* is pretty much a repeat of the information presented in the other two.

All three are sold at the reception of the Hotel Steau and at the Librărie Hyperion bookshop opposite the Hotel Steau at Str 1 Decembrie 1918 11.

Information
Tourist Offices The Steau Agenţie de Turism (☎ 771 072; fax 771 932), next to the Hotel Steau at Str 1 Decembrie 1918 12, sells city guides, maps and tickets for weekly buses to Hungary and Germany. It also arranges accommodation in private rooms for around US$3 a night. It is open weekdays from 9 am to 5 pm, Saturday from 9 am to 2 pm.

Money The currency exchange inside the Steau Agenţie de Turism, is open weekdays from 9 am to 5 pm, Saturday from 9 am to 1 pm. The IDM Exchange, next door to the Pizzeria Perla on Piaţa Hermann Oberth, gives cash advance on Visa/MasterCard and is open weekdays from 9 am to 6 pm.

Change travellers cheques and get cash advances on Visa/MasterCard at Bancă Agricola at Str Justitiei 7, open weekdays from 8 am to noon; or from BANCOREX at Str 1 Decembrie 1918 39. It's open weekdays from 8 am to 2 pm.

Post & Communications The post and telephone centre is close to the Hotel Steau on Str Herman Oberth; it is open daily from 7 am to 9 pm.

You can send emails and access the Internet at the Sighişoara Education Centre, also funded by Eastern Nazarene College, next to the Black Box disco at Str Horia Teculescu 37; it is open weekdays from 9 am to 8 pm; in July and August it closes at 5 pm.

Cultural Centres English speakers meet for coffee and a chat at the Coffee Club, held every Tuesday and Thursday at 7 pm at the English Club. The charitable organisation is funded by the Eastern Nazarene College in the US which, among other things, runs a very successful programme aimed at helping Sighişoara's street children. The club house is at Str Ştefan Octavian Iosif 10.

Things to See
All Sighişoara's sights are in the old town – the medieval citadel – perched on a hillock and fortified with a 14th century wall, 930m long. A century later the 14 towers and five artillery bastions were added. Today, the citadel, which is on the UNESCO World Heritage list, retaining just nine of its original towers and two of its bastions. Today,

there are 164 houses and 13 public buildings within the citadel.

Entering the citadel, you pass under the massive **clock tower** (turnul cu ceas). Formerly the main entrance to the fortified city, the tower is 64m tall with sturdy base walls measuring an impenetrable 2.35m. Inside the 1648 clock, 2.40m in diameter, is a pageant of figurines, each representing a character from the Saxon pantheon: Peace bears an olive branch, Justice has a set of scales and Law wields a sword. The executioner is also present and the drum-player strikes the hour. Above stand seven figures, each representing a day of the week.

The figurines can be inspected through glass from the **History Museum** (Muzeul de Istorie), in the 14th century tower. The museum has a good collection of WWI-era photographs, a bust of the museum's founder Dr Joseph Bacon (1857-1941), a scale model of the town and a superb view of Sighişoara from the walkway on top of the 7th floor. It is open Tuesday to Friday from 9 am to 5 pm, weekends from 9 am to 3 pm. Admission is US$0.50.

Immediately inside the citadel, on the western side of the clock tower is the 15th century **Biserica Mănăstirii** (Church of the Dominican Monastery). The Gothic church became the Saxons' main Lutheran church in 1556. The church is open daily from 10 am to 6 pm and a Sunday service is held at 10 am. Classical, folk and baroque concerts are often held here.

Opposite the church on the western side of the clock tower is a small house containing a **collection of medieval firearms** (colecţia de arme medievale). It is open daily, except Monday, from 10 am to 3.30 pm. Admission is US$0.20.

Continuing west towards Piaţa Cetăţii, you come to the house in which Vlad Ţepeş was born in 1431 and reputedly lived until the age of four. The Dracul house, complete with its original river-stone floor, is now a beer bar and restaurant (see Places to Eat).

Piaţa Cetăţii, complete with benches and fine old houses, is the heart of old Sighişoara. It was here that markets, craft fairs, public executions and witch trials were held. In 1603 a nobleman was tried in the square in front of 12 judges for high treason. He was found guilty and had his right hand chopped off before being impaled. The 17th century, panelled **Stag House**, overlooking the square on the corner of Str Şcolli Bastionul, is considered the most representative example of the citadel's architecture. It is currently under restoration (until 2001).

From the square, turn left up Str Şcolii to the 172 steps of the **covered stairway** (scara acoperită) which has tunnelled its way up the hill since 1642 to the Gothic **Church on the Hill** (Biserica din Deal). This Gothic Bergkirche – also Lutheran – dating from 1345 is currently undergoing a DM5 million restoration, paid for by the city of Munich. A path leads from in front of the church to the adjacent **German cemetery**. The gates are open between May and October from 8 am to 8 pm and from November to April from 9 am to 4 pm.

Behind the church are the remains of the **Goldsmiths Tower**. The goldsmiths, tailors, carpenters and tinsmiths, the only craftsmen to have their guilds and workshops inside the citadel, built eight fountains (34m deep) within the city walls to ensure a continuous water supply during times of siege. Guilds existed until 1875.

From the church, head back down the hill, cross Piaţa Cetăţii, then head down Str Bastionul. At its northern end is a **Roman Catholic Church**, built in 1894. From here turn east (right), then south along Str Mănăstirii. At No 4 is a fantastic green-painted house with a wooden roof, ornate overhanging eaves and wonderfully crooked wooden shutters covering the windows. This is the oldest surviving house in the citadel, dating to the 13th or 14th centuries.

Apart from their two churches in the citadel, Sighişoara's Saxon community had a third Lutheran church, deliberately sited well outside the city walls. The church, just west of the train station off Str Libertăţii, was used in the 17th century as an isolation compound for victims of the plague and later of leprosy. Many, however, were taken to the

leprosarium (Siechhof) adjoining the small Lutheran church. Church records show that as many as 38 people died every day.

To get to the church, turn right out of the train station along Str Libertăţii, then right along Str Ştefan cel Mare. The tin-spired church is on the right.

Out of Town Heading west out of town towards Mediaş, you pass a large roofed turret on the hilltop, known as **La Chip**. Legend has it that the turret was built in memory of a Turkish warrior who, as he approached the citadel by elephant with his army, was hit by an arrow shot by a goldsmith. The Turkish troops buried their leader and his elephant on the spot.

Just 4km north-east of Sighişoara is **Albeşti** (Fehéregyháza in Hungarian). The village is home to the **Petőfi Sándor Museum** (Muzeul Petőfi Sándor; ☎ 771 108). The Hungarian poet Petőfi Sándor (1823-49) died here in battle. Petőfi, who is credited with making Hungarian poetry more accessible, led the 1848 revolution with Lajos Kossuth against the Habsburgs. He was killed by Tsarist troops.

The only downside of the museum is that the entire exhibition is explained in Hungarian. It is open daily, except Monday, from 9 am to 3.30 pm. Admission is US$0.50. In its grounds – the site of the battle – stands an obelisk topped with a vulture in memory of those revolutionaries who died alongside Sándor on 31 July, 1849.

To get to Albeşti, take any of the northbound buses which leave every 10 minutes from the main bus stop at the southern end of Str Podului. In Albeşti, get off at the bus stop in the centre of the village and turn right along Str Muzeului, a gravel road. At the fork, bear left and continue along the road, past the *magazin* mixt and village cemetery until you reach a church; the museum is opposite.

Special Events

During the first two weeks in August, Sighişoara hosts its Medieval Days (Festivalul de Artă Medievală Sighişoara)

during which people dress in traditional costume, and stage music and theatrical performances. The two week festival did not take place in 1997 but is expected to happen in 1998. For information, contact the Fundaţia Festivalul de Artă Medievală Sighişoara (☎ & fax 774 566, 775 844), Str Plopilor 32.

A music festival takes places every year in mid-July.

Places to Stay

Camping You can camp on a hill above the town, but it's a stiff, half-hour hike up from the train station. Walk east along the train tracks to a bridge, then cross the tracks and turn left to a road which leads up.

At the end of this road is the *Dealul Gării Restaurant* (☎ 771 046), where you can camp for US$3 or rent a bungalow for US$10 a double.

There's a better campsite at Hula Daneş (☎ 771 052), but it's 4km out of town on the road to Mediaş, with 11 buses a day marked 'Cris' from the bus station, beside the train station. Bungalows here cost US$9 a double.

Hostels One of Romania's three lone hostels is in Sighişoara: *Bobby's Hostel* (☎ 772 232) at Str Take Ionescu 18, is a clean, cheap hostel run by a local management student – called Bobby – who leases out the dormitories of the adjacent technical school each year between 15 June and 1 September. Double rooms cost US$6 and a bed in a dormitory is US$5. The communal bathrooms have hot water between 9 and 10 am and 8 and 9 pm. The hostel has a small common room with cable TV and the reception has useful city, regional and country maps, train timetables, and lists of the latest 'in' places. Bobby will meet backpackers at the train station. The hostel is a 25 minute walk from the train station; the reception is in the building behind the Grupul Şcoala de Industrie Uşoară. Note it is closed from 1 September to 14 June.

Private Rooms The Steau Agenţie de Turism (see Information – Tourist Offices) arranges rooms in private homes in the centre of Sighişoara starting at US$3 a night. Contact them in advance as few travellers take advantage of this service, hence they cannot always organise a room on the spot.

Hotels An OK deal if you don't mind staying directly opposite the noisy train and bus stations is the *Hotel Chic* (☎ 775 901; fax 164 149) at Str Libertăţii 44. It has seven rooms with private bathroom costing US$10 per person. The impossible-not-to-see sign above the hotel reads 'Non-Stop Hotel Restaurant'.

The *Hotel Steaua* (☎ 771 594; fax 771 932), Str 1 Decembrie 1918 12, is a comfortable, two-star place that attracts individual tourists and American tour groups in their droves in summer. Rooms are clean and comfortable though, with private bathroom. Singles/doubles are US$10/20 a night, including breakfast.

More upmarket is the luxurious *Hotel Poeniţa* (☎ 772 739), a 20 minute walk from the centre, amid rolling hills, squawking children and chickens at Str Dimitrie Cantemir 24. A double in this seven-room mansion costs US$20, including breakfast and free use of the miniature swimming pool in the front garden. At the time of writing, the hotel was building a second little mansion with six more rooms.

Hotel Rex (☎ 166 615), 1km north-east of the centre at Str Dumbravei 18, is the most modern hotel in town with 16 tastefully furnished double rooms for US$20 a night, including breakfast. The hotel restaurant is the finest in town. If you don't fancy the 15 minute walk along a busy road, take any bus to Albeşti for one stop from the bus stop at the southern end of Str Podului.

Places to Eat
Restaurants & Cafés Dracula freaks can indulge their ghoulish hunger by dining at *Restaurantul Cetatea*, in Vlad Dracul's former house in the citadel. There is a restaurant upstairs and a *berărie* (beer bar) downstairs. The food here is above average and reasonably priced.

Beyond that, the popular place to hang out – for tourists at least – is the brilliantly located *P & I*, a large, terrace café and patisserie above the park at Piaţa Herman Oberth 7. It only serves sweet snacks but is a pleasant place to lounge in the sun. For a plate of spaghetti, go to the small *Babas* opposite P & I, at the southern end of Str Turnului; it is open daily from 10 to 2 am.

Pizzeria Perla on Piaţa Herman Oberth has a good selection of pizzas and pastas, as well as traditional soups and cutlets etc. Try the Dracul pizza for a spicy treat or, if you're desperate to take a break from your daily diet of pork and fries, go for the pelmeni topped with cheese and ham. It's good. The restaurant is open daily until 11 pm (until 9 pm in winter).

The Italian-inspired *Ristorante Pizzeria 4 Amici* has two outlets, one at Str Morii 7 and the other across the park at Str Octavian Goga 12. Both have tables outside and compete with the P & I to be the busiest hang-out in town; they are open daily from noon to midnight.

Good, traditional Romanian dishes are served at the small, seldom-frequented *Restaurant Adelas*, just off the main street on Str Cooperatorilor; the day's menu is listed on a blackboard outside. It is open daily from 8 am to 10 pm.

More expensive is the modern *Restaurant Joker*, opposite the entrance to Bobby's Hostel on Str Take Ionescu. It is open Monday to Saturday from noon to 11 pm, Sunday from 2 to 11 pm.

The unexciting *Boema*, in a courtyard off Str Şcolii at Str Muzeului 6, has a monopoly on outdoor dining in the citadel. The menu is an ode to pizza and pastries; it's open 24 hours.

Fast Food & Self Catering *Hermes Fast Food*, opposite the cinema at Str 1 Decembrie 1918 54, doles out burgers daily between 8 am and 10 pm.

The daily *market* off Str Târnavei has a good selection of fruits, vegetables and cheese. There is a large, modern *Alimentar* next to the Dacia car sales room on the corner of Str Podului and Str Morii.

Entertainment
Cinema *Cinema Lumina*, on the corner of Str 1 Decembrie 1918 and Str Mihai Viteazul, screens films in their original language (usually English); there are daily showings at 10 am and 5 and 7 pm. Tickets cost A$0.30.

Bars & Discos One of the most colourful bars in town – seldom frequented by tourists, which is part of its delight – is the small and cosy *Jennifer Hanna*, not far from Bobby's Hostel on Str Ilarie Chendi. Run by a Roma, it attracts a completely local crowd and serves Bere Ciuc brewed in Miercurea Ciuc as its house beer.

Dance under the moonlight at *Grădină de Vară* disco, close to the Hotel Steava. Walk down the alleyway through the large iron gates under the archway at Str 1 Decembrie 1918 8; it is open daily from 10 to 2 am. The more upmarket *Black Box* disco at Str Horea Teculescu 35 charges a hefty US$3 fee to enter its small, black box-room filled with members of the mobile-phone brigade.

Classical, Baroque & Folk Music Look out for posters on the billboards in the small park on Piaa Herman Oberth, or under the arches of the Casă de Cultură at the entrance to the citadel. Organ concerts and performances by local folk and baroque groups in the Monastery Church in the citadel are advertised in both places.

Getting There & Away
Bus The bus station (☎ 771 260) is next to the train station on Str Libertăţii. Many surrounding villages are served by bus. Daily bus services include two to Sibiu (92km); one to Bistriţa (146km) and Făgăraş (92km); nine to Târgu Mureş (54km); and four to Criş (17km) and Apold (15km).

A private bus to Germany departs on Tuesday from outside the Hotel Steaua at 3.30 am. Another departs daily at 6 am and there are numerous others. Tickets and schedules are available at Pahomar-Prodtur (☎ 771 072, 772 630), Str 1 Decembrie 1918 10 and from most travel agencies.

Train The Agenţie de Voiaj CFR (☎ 771 820) at Str 1 Decembrie 1918 2, is open weekdays from 7.30 am to 7.30 pm. International tickets can only be bought here.

All trains between Bucharest and Budapest stop at Sighişoara. The daily *Dacia* and *Pannonia Expres* pass through at 12.55 pm and 8.54 pm, arriving in Budapest 8½ hours later. The daily *Muntenia*, *Alutus* and *Traianus* trains to Budapest also stop in Sighişoara; from Budapest the *Alutus* continues to Prague and Berlin.

For trains to Sibiu you have to change at Copşa Mică or Mediaş. All trains between Bucharest (via Braşov) and Cluj-Napoca stop at Sighişoara.

Getting Around
Taxis Taxis are not allowed in the citadel which is restricted to residents only. There is a taxi stand outside the train station and in town outside the Hermes Fast Food outlet. To call a taxi dial ☎ 771 484 (24 hours).

SAXON FORTIFIED CHURCHES
The Târnave plateau, which stretches for some 120km between Braşov and Sighişoara, is traditionally known as Burzen Land (Ţara Bârsei in Romanian, Birsenland in German). It was to this region, inside the Carpathian arch, that Saxons – mainly from the Franken region in western Germany – were invited by the Hungarian King Geza II in 1123. In the 15th and 16th centuries, following the increased threat of Turkish attacks on their towns, the settlements were strengthened with bulky city walls and fortified churches. Defensive towers in the churches served as observation posts and entrances were guarded with a portcullis that could be quickly lowered as the enemy advanced.

Since 1989, following the mass exodus of Saxons to Germany, Saxon communities and culture have faced extinction. German president Roman Herzog warned Romania's

TRANSYLVANIA

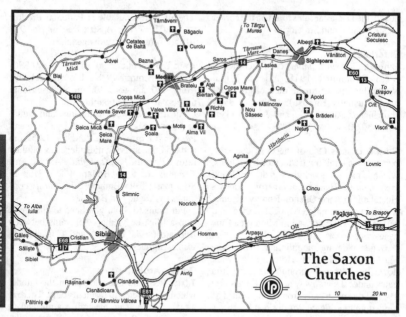

The Saxon Churches

Saxons during a state visit: 'You can't pack your homeland in a bag and take it with you to Germany.'

Saxons in Romania today are elderly and fear for the future of their sturdy village churches. Most village priests have already left.

Particularly fine examples of the Saxon churches are the numerous fortified churches which dominate settlements immediately west of Sighişoara and around. These pin-prick villages are poorly served by public transport but within easy hiking distance of one another.

Around Mediaş

Bazna (Baassen) a small village first settled in 1302, is 15km north-west of Mediaş. Its late Gothic St Nicholas' church was built at the start of the 16th century on ruins of a 14th century original. Its highlight is the three pre-Reformation bells (1404) in the church tower. The 6m-tall wall that surrounded the

church was partly dismantled in 1870 because the villagers needed bricks to build a wall around the village school.

From 1842 onwards the village developed as a small sap resort following the discovery of natural springs which released natural gases. Wooden huts were built over the springs to contain these sulphurous gases. Villagers suffering from rheumatic pains would then take a 'smelly bath' in these huts. To get to Bazna from Mediaş head north towards Târnaveni (formerly spelt Tîrnaveni) for 10km then turn left to Bazna.

Băgaciu (Bogeschdorf) is 12km north of Mediaş. Follow the main northbound road, then turn right along a minor road signposted 'Delenii'. The pre-Reformation, late-Gothic altar, restored in Vienna in 1896, is considered to be the best preserved Saxon church altar.

Heading 4km south along the dirt track you come to **Curciu** (Kirtsch). The decorative stone frieze above the western door, featuring apes and other animals, are unique to this 14th century village church. In 1366 the Saxons of Curciu and Băgaciu joined forces and broke into the house of local noble Thomas von Kend. They killed the noble in revenge for a toll he introduced on the bridge across a small river close to both villages.

Towards Sibiu

There are a number of fine churches south-west of Mediaş along the road to Sibiu via Copşa Mică. In Copşa Mică, make a small detour by heading south along a dirt track to **Valea Viilor** (Wurmloch). The village dates to 1263 and has a quaint church, dedicated to St Peter. This fortified church was raised at the end of the 15th century and surrounded by 1.5m-thick walls.

Further south along this dirt track you come to Motiş. From Motiş, return to Copşa Mică and continue south-west along the main Sibiu road. After just a couple of kilometres, you pass through the village of **Axente Sever** (Frauendorf) with a Saxon church dating from 1322-1323.

Şeica Mică (Kleinschelken), first settled in 1316, is 5km further south. The village was engulfed by fire several times during the 16th century but remarkably, its local church, dedicated to St Catherine and built in 1414, survived. Its beautiful baptismal font is late-Gothic (1447) and cast from iron. In the church courtyard stands an old well, surrounded by 15m-tall walls.

There are also small fortified Saxon churches in **Şoala**, 4km east along a dirt track from Şeica Mică, and in **Şeica Mare**, 13km south of its sister village.

From Mediaş you can also head south towards Agnita. Ten kilometres south along this minor road is **Moşna** (Meschen). Its village church, dating from the 14th century, was completely rebuilt in 1485 in a late-Gothic style. Its centrepiece, however, is the tall bell tower, eight storeys high.

Alma Vii (Alemen) is just a few kilometres south of Moşna. The four-towered church was built at the start of the 14th century and fortified in the early 16th century.

Towards Sighişoara

The eastward journey from Mediaş to Sighişoara is probably the most delightful. Some 5km east on the main road is the village of Brateiu. From Brateiu, continue east along the main road for a further 5km then turn right at the turn-off for **Aţel** (Hetzeldorf). The church, dating from the 14th century, was heavily fortified in 1471. In 1959, the northern tower was levelled to uncover a secret tunnel leading to a neighbouring farmstead.

Heading back along the main road, you come to a turn-off on the right for what is considered to be among the most fantastic of the Saxon heritage. The fortified church of **Biertan** (Birthälm), 9km south of the main road, is listed as a UNESCO World Heritage site, and rightly so. The present church was built by the Saxons in the late 15th century. Its altar (1483-1550), modelled on a Viennese altar, has 28 panels. The magnificent 15th century walls which fortify the church stand 12m tall. Biertan's Saxon priest, who cared for six other parishes after their priests left for Germany, abandoned his 400-strong congregation in 1995. He too moved to Germany.

Six kilometres south of Biertan is the small village of **Richiş**, likewise dominated by a fantastic stone church.

From Biertan you can also head east for 2km along a dirt track to **Copşa Mare** (Grosskopisch). The church dates from the early 14th century and was fortified to fend off Turkish and Tartar invasions in the 16th century but failed to fend off Székely troops, who attacked the village in 1605 and destroyed the church.

Continuing east along the main Mediaş-Sighişoara road, you arrive at **Laslea**, less than 1km off the road just before **Daneş** village. Nine kilometres south of Daneş is **Criş**. From Laslea, energetic hikers can trek for some 10km south to **Nou Săsesc**; bear right where the road forks or, alternatively, bear left to get to **Mălincrav**.

From Sighişoara there are a number of churches you can easily hike to. Fifteen kilometres south is **Apold** and 6km further south is **Brădeni**. Four kilometres further south-west is **Netuş**. The Saxon church trail is endless!

Viscri is some 45km south-east of Sighişoara. Follow the road towards Braşov and turn right in Buneşti. From here, a dirt track leads to the remote village. First mentioned in 1400, the village was heavily destroyed by fire in 1638. Its one-room church, dedicated to St Nicholas, was built in the 12th century by Székelys and taken over by Saxon colonists in 1185. The baptism font inside the church was built from a pillar taken from a Roman church.

Today, no more than 40 Saxons live in Viscri today – more than 90% of the village's population is Romanian. Just eight German-speaking children attend the local village school.

Székely Land

The eastern realms of the Carpathians are home to the Székelys, an ethnic group closely related to the Magyars whose people have their own national anthem, their own language (actually a dialect of Hungarian) and their own distinctive folk culture.

The Székelys' origins are disputed. Debates rage as to whether they are descendants of the barbaric Attila the Hun, who arrived with his troops in Transylvania in the 5th century; or of his predecessors, the Magyars, who migrated from southern Russia to Transylvania in the early Middle Ages. The simplest explanation is that the Székelys are direct descendants of Hungarians who settled in Transylvania from the 9th century onwards, defending Hungary's borders in the 12th century in return for their liberty and other privileges. Three 'nations' were recognised in medieval Transylvania: the Székelys, the Saxons and the nobles.

During the 18th century the Székelys, famed for their warrior virtues, suffered at the hands of the Habsburgs, who attempted to convert this devout Protestant ethnic group to Catholicism. Thousands of young Székely men were conscripted into the Austrian army. Local resistance throughout Székely Land (Ţara Secuilor in Romanian, Székelyföld in Hungarian) led to the massacre of Madéfalva in 1764. Martial law was subsequently imposed while thousands of Székelys fled across the border into Romanian Moldavia. These refugees were dubbed the Csángó people.

Following the union of Transylvania with Romania in 1918, some 200,000 Hungarians – a quarter of which were Székelys – fled to Hungary. It was during this period that the Székelys, who regard Transylvania as their homeland, composed their own national anthem.

Maps

The *Ţara Secuilor, Székelyföld, Székely Land* map, published by Budapest-based Ábel Térképészeti in 1997, includes a detailed map (1: 250,000) of the region complete with lengthy historical explanations in Hungarian. It is sold for US$4 in bookshops and travel agencies.

TÂRGU MUREŞ
• *area code ☎ 065 , pop 165,000*

Târgu Mureş (formerly spelt Tîrgu Mureş) is traditionally a Hungarian stronghold. First documented under the name 'Novum Forum Sicolorum' in 1322, the town overlooking the Mureş river in central Transylvania developed as a leading garrison town and later as an important cultural and academic centre. In 1658 it was attacked by Turks who captured 3000 inhabitants and transported them back to Istanbul as slave labour. In Hungarian, Târgu Mureş is called Marosvásárhely, in German Neumarkt.

During the Ceauşescu regime, Târgu Mureş was a 'closed city' with all ethnic groups other than Romanians forbidden to settle here. Large numbers of ethnic Romanians from other parts of Romania, notably Moldavia, were also moved into Târgu Mureş to further dilute the Hungarian community. Not surprisingly, the town's Hungarian population gradually dwindled.

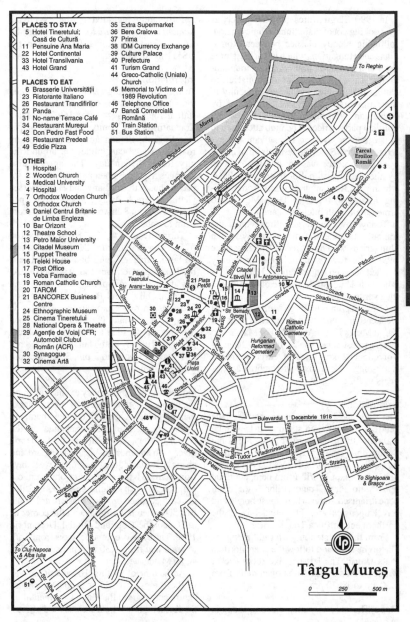

PLACES TO STAY
5 Hotel Tineretului;
  Casă de Cultură
11 Pensune Ana Maria
22 Hotel Continental
33 Hotel Transilvania
43 Hotel Grand

PLACES TO EAT
6 Brasserie Universităţii
23 Ristorante Italiano
26 Restaurant Trandifirilor
27 Panda
31 No-name Terrace Café
34 Restaurant Mureşul
42 Don Pedro Fast Food
48 Restaurant Predeal
49 Eddie Pizza

OTHER
1 Hospital
2 Wooden Church
3 Medical University
4 Hospital
7 Orthodox Wooden Church
8 Orthodox Church
9 Daniel Centrul Britanic
  de Limba Engleza
10 Bar Orizont
12 Theatre School
13 Petro Maior University
14 Citadel Museum
15 Puppet Theatre
16 Teleki House
17 Post Office
18 Veba Farmacie
19 Roman Catholic Church
20 TAROM
21 BANCOREX Business
  Centre
24 Ethnographic Museum
25 Cinema Tineretului
28 National Opera & Theatre
29 Agenţie de Voiaj CFR;
  Automobil Clubul
  Român (ACR)
30 Synagogue
32 Cinema Artă

35 Extra Supermarket
36 Bere Craiova
37 Prima
38 IDM Currency Exchange
39 Culture Palace
40 Prefecture
41 Turism Grand
44 Greco-Catholic (Uniate)
  Church
45 Memorial to Victims of
  1989 Revolution
46 Telephone Office
47 Bancă Comercială
  Română
50 Train Station
51 Bus Station

Târgu Mureş

0   250   500 m

TRANSYLVANIA

In 1990, Târgu Mureş gained notoriety as the cooking pot of major inter-ethnic tension, following bloody clashes between Romanians and Hungarians which left at least three dead and hundreds injured. Hungarian students staged a peaceful demonstration calling for a Hungarian language faculty in their university. They were attacked by Romanians who raided the local Hungarian political party offices. The mob attempted to gouge out the eyes of Transylvanian playwright András Sütőwho remains blind in one eye. The violence was apparently stirred up by the nationalist political group VATRA which paid Romanian peasants from outlying villages to travel to Târgu Mureş, and armed them with pitchforks and axes.

Today, however, Târgu Mureş is quiet and tranquil. Despite the many Transylvanian Hungarians who have fled to Hungary since 1990, the town's population is evenly divided between Romanians and Hungarians who both demonstrate a sense of shame over the events of 1990.

Carnival comes to Târgu Mureş on the last weekend in June when the city hosts its Târgu Mureş Days. At the end of May, a two day Art-Fest takes place. In the village of Voivodeni, 25km north of Târgu Mureş, a week-long folk festival is celebrated most years in June or July.

Orientation

The train and bus stations are south of the centre. From the train station – a 15 minute walk into town – turn right along Str Mihai Sadoveanu, bearing right where the road forks. Continue north, across the river, until you reach Piaţa Unirii. From here, continue north onto Piaţa Trandafirilor – the main pedestrianised street where most hotels and travel agencies are. The citadel is at the northern end of Piaţa Trandafirilor.

From the bus station, turn right along Str Gheorghe Doja and follow the street north to Piaţa Unirii. The left-luggage room (ticket windows Nos 9 and 10) is open daily from 5.30 am to 10.30 pm.

Maps The only city map existing today is unfortunately included in the expensive *Romania Atlas Turistic Rutier*, published by Editura Fast Print in 1994 and sold for US$11 in bookshops.

Information

Tourist Offices Târgu Mureş has no official tourist agency but the enthusiastic smiles of staff at Total Tours (☎ & fax 169 343), Piaţa Trandafirilor 6-8, compensate. The competent English, French and German 'young road managers' can guide you around the city for US$16 a day. The agency also arranges trips to Sovata and sells tickets for private buses to Germany and Hungary (see Getting There & Away). The office is open weekdays from 8 am to 4 pm, Saturday from 9 am to noon.

Turism Grand (☎ 160 287; ☎ & fax 160 675), Piaţa Trandifirilor 21, is not as clued up but it arranges hotel bookings and sells bus tickets for Germany too. It is open weekdays from 9 am to 6 pm.

Automobil Clubul Român (ACR; ☎ 161 515) has an office next to the Agenţie de Voiaj CFR at Piaţa Teatrului 1. It is open Monday, Wednesday and Friday from 8 am to 3 pm, Tuesday and Thursday from 8 am to 3 pm and from 5 to 7 pm, Saturday from 8 am to 1 pm.

Money There are currency exchanges in all the hotels as well as plenty of pushy, black-market money changers outside them all. Ignore them! The IDM Exchange on the corner of Piaţa Trandafirilor and Str Horia gives cash advance on Visa/MasterCard and changes Eurocheques. It is open weekdays from 8 am to 8 pm, Saturday from 9 am to 1 pm. You can cash travellers cheques and also get cash advance on Visa/MasterCard at the Bancă Comercială Română on the corner of Str Gheorghe Doja and Blvd 1 Decembrie 1918. The bank is open weekdays from 8 am to noon and from 1.30 to 6 pm and there is an ATM outside.

At the time of writing, BANCOREX was in the throes of building a giant business centre across from the Hotel Continental on Str Kossuth. It will house a bank and offices.

Post & Communications The central post office is at the northern end of Piaţa Trandafirilor at Str Revoluţiei 2. The telephone centre is close to the Hotel Grand on the corner of Piaţa Victoriei and Blvd 1 Decembrie 1918. Both are open daily, except Sunday, from 7 am to 8 pm.

Bookshops The Librărie Mihai Eminescu and the Librărie Hyperion, on the east and western side of Piaţa Teatrului respectively, stock a good selection of Penguin Classics in English as and French as well as Romanian-English and Romanian-Hungarian dictionaries. The Hyperion also sells the *Romania Atlas Turistic Rutier* (see Orientation – Maps). You'll find both shops are open weekdays from 9 am to 8 pm, Saturday from 9 am to 2 pm.

Cultural Centres The Democratic Alliance of Hungarians in Romania (Romániai Magyar Demokrata Szövetség; ☎ 161 928, 162 907; fax 214 077) has its office at Piaţa Trandafirilor 5.

Piaţa Trandafirilor

Târgu Mureş's main sights are focused around Piaţa Trandafirilor. At the northern end of the square cross Piaţa Petőfi and head east onto Piaţa Bernády György. Towering above this small square is the **Citadel Church & fortress**, founded on the site of the stronghold around which Târgu Mureş developed during the 13th and 14th centuries. The citadel, perched on a hillock, remains the focal point today. The Hungarian Reformed church it shelters serves a congregation of 5000 – the largest by far of the 10 Reformed churches in the town.

The church, dating from 1316, was built by the Dominicans on the site of a former Franciscan monastery. Daily services are held at 6 pm and on Sunday at 10 am.

The fortress, comprising six towers, was built around the church between the 15th and 17th centuries. Its **gate tower**, heavily restored in the 1960s and 1970s, today shelters a small branch of the **county museum**.

Admission to the museum, open daily except Monday, from 10 am to 4 pm, is US$0.20.

Nestled beneath the citadel walls on Piaţa Bernády György is the yellow-painted, baroque **Teleki House**, built between 1797 and 1803. Joseph Teleki served as governor of Transylvania between 1842 and 1848. The house was built as a motel bearing the name 'Kis Pipa' (Small Pipe). Following the 1848 revolution, in which Hungarians rebelled against Habsburg rule, Hungarian forces took over the fortress, using part of Teleki House as its administration headquarters. Revolutionary poet Petőfi Sándor is said to have sought shelter in Teleki House on the night of 29 July 1849 while en route to Albeşti, near Sibiu. He was killed in battle two days later. In 1935 the Teleki family donated the building to the Hungarian Reformed Church which today uses it as its administrative headquarters.

Walk back to Piaţa Trandafirilor, the northern end of which is dominated by the magnificent **Orthodox Cathedral** (Catedrăla Ortodoxă). The interior is one of the most breathtaking of Romania's modern churches. Built between 1933 and 1938, the cathedral partially replaced the tiny wooden church *(biserica de lemn)* that had served the local Orthodox community since 1773. and which is still used for services today. It is worth a visit. The church is north of the citadel at Str Doiceşti.

On the western side of Piaţa Trandifirilor, completely overshadowed by the Orthodox Cathedral, is the baroque-style **Roman Catholic Church** (Biserica Sfântul Jonos). Dating from 1728, it is under renovation.

Continue south down Piaţa Trandifirilor. At No 11 is Târgu Mureş's **Ethnographic Museum** (Muzeul Etnografic), open Tuesday to Friday from 9 am to 4 pm, on Saturday from 9 am to 4 pm, Sunday from 9 am to 1 pm.

West of Piaţa Trandifirilor, at Str Aurel Filmon 21, is Târgu Mureş's leading **synagogue**, currently under restoration. Dating from 1900, it was designed to seat a congregation of over 500. Prior to WWII, some 5500 Jews lived in Târgu Mures, making up almost a third of the town's population. Some 300 Jews live in the town today. A memorial outside the synagogue pays homage to the holocaust victims. East of the square, at Str Bolyai 17, is the **Bolyai-Teleki Library** (Biblioteca Bolyai-Teleki). The library, built between 1799 and 1805 in an imposing Empire style, houses the private book collection of Samule Teleki, which he donated to the city in 1802.

The southern end of the square is dominated by the fantastic **Culture Palace** (Palatul Cultural; ☎ 137 625), built in secessionist style between 1911 and 1913. Its glittering steepled roofs, tiled in colourful geometric patterns, shelter a history museum, art museum and a stained glass window museum, better known as the **Hall of Mirrors** (Salǎ de Oglinzi). Scenes from traditional Székely fairytales, ballads and legends are featured in the 12 stained-glass windows which fill the entire length of one wall of the long hall. Two giant mirrors cover the walls either end of the hall. The ground floor of the palace houses a contemporary **Art Gallery** (Galeria de Artǎ) featuring some unusual ceramics, paintings and sculptures. Many are for sale. The Culture Palace is open Tuesday to Friday from 10 am to 4 pm, weekends from 9 am to 1 pm.

The **Prefecture**, with a tiled roof and bright green spires that sparkle in the sun, is next door to the Culture Palace. A plaque on its facing façade pays tribute to those from Târgu Mureş who died during WWI. In the small park in front is a statue of **Lupoaica Romei** (the wolf of Rome), identical to that in Bucharest. The statue of Romulus and Remus suckling the wolf was given to Târgu Mureş by the city of Rome in 1924. Close by, at the most southern end of the pedestrianised street, on Piaţa Uniri, is the town's **Greco-Catholic Cathedral**, a Romanian Orthodox church until its congregation opted to accept the authority of the Vatican.

Behind the church is a **memorial** to the victims of the 1989 revolution. Following the news of the bloody clashes between the army and civilians in Timişoara on 17 December 1989, protesters took to the streets in Târgu Mureş. On 20 December the army was called in to Târgu Mureş to squash the demonstration, during which six people were shot. The memorial comprises six interwoven wooden crosses, each carved with the name and age of the victims. A hand carved in wood, making the sign of victory, stands on top of the crosses.

University & Around

Târgu Mureş enjoys a strong academic tradition and its medical and drama schools are considered the most distinguished in the country. Eminent scholars include mathematicians Farkas Bólyai (1775-1856) and his son János Bólyai (1802-1860) who revolutionised Euclidean geometry.

The university area lies north-east of the citadel. From Piaţa Bernády György walk east along Str Bernády György onto Str Mihai Viteazul. Immediately behind the citadel walls is the private **Petru Maior University** (Universitatea Petru Maior). It is named after a leading 19th century intellectual and staunch defender of the rights of Romanians living in Transylvania, who published *The History of the Origin of the Romanians in Dacia* in 1812.

Immediately opposite is Târgu Mureş's **Theatre School**. Founded primarily as a Hungarian school before the war, it quickly became renowned as the top drama school in Transylvania. However, during the ethnic purges on all non-Romanians during Ceauşescu's regime, the school's flawless reputation suffered serious damage; Romanian students were given preferential treatment over Hungarian students and by the end of 1989 ethnic Hungarians filled less than one-third of the school register.

Continue north-east along Str Mihai Viteazul, then turn onto Str Nicolae Grigorescu. Immediately after the students' Culture House, turn left along Str Dr Gheorghe Marinescu. The **Medical University** (Universitatea de Medicinǎ şi Farmacie) is a magnificent 1950s building beyond the hospital. Hungarian students from this university took to the streets of Târgu Mureş on 16 March 1990 with banners and placards calling for a Hungarian-language faculty. Some classes are now held in Hungarian.

Directly opposite the university is the **Romanian Heroes' Park** (Parcul Eroilor Români). dominated by a large memorial to those who died during WWII.

Language Courses

Dan Antal, author of the riveting *Out of Romania* (see Facts for the Visitor – Books at the front of this book), is no longer out of Romania. For private or group Romanian language lessons, go straight to his school, the Daniel Centrul Britanic de Limba Engleza (☎ & fax 216 950) at Str Cosminului 10. Lessons start at US$3 an hour.

Places to Stay

The cheapest bet is the *Hotel Sport* (☎ 131 913), a five minute walk from the train station at Str Griviţa Roşie 33. It is popular with locals passing through town for the night. Singles/doubles/triples cost US$4.50/8/9.50 a night. Two rooms share one bathroom. A two-room apartment with private bath is US$13.

In the centre, the cheapest is the unexciting *Hotel Grand* (☎ 160 711, 160 844; fax 130 289) at Piaţa Victoriei 28-30. It has 124 clean, old-fashioned rooms, most of which are usually guestless. Singles/doubles with private shower are US$14/22 a night, including a coffeeless breakfast (coffee is an extra US$0.20).

Drab from the outside but bright inside is the *Hotel Continental* (☎ & fax 160 999) overlooking Piaţa Teatrului at No 6. Plush singles/doubles/triples with private bath have been recently refurbished and cost US$42/54/69, including breakfast.

Hotel Transilvania (☎ 165 616; fax 166 028), in a prime spot at Piaţa Trandafirilor 46, has singles/doubles/triples for US$14/31/37 a night, including breakfast. Staff are a tad grumpy.

The *Hotel Tineretului* (☎ 217 441, 216 774) inside the university students' Culture House (Casă de Cultură) at Str Nicolae Grigorescu 17-19 has 44 double rooms with shared bath for US$21.50 a night.

East of the centre near the theatre school is the upmarket, *Pensiune Ana Maria* (☎ 164 401) at Str A L Papui Ilarian 17. It is a small, privately run hotel with eight beautifully furnished rooms complete with 'real' double beds and crisp white linen sheets. Singles/doubles are US$28.50/36, including the best breakfast in town.

Places to Eat

Restaurants & Cafés Beyond the countless, plastic chair-type snack bars, and the hotel restaurants, eating choices are limited. One of the most modern – and pricey – places in town is the *Ristorante Italiano* behind the Hotel Continental on Piaţa Teatrului. It serves good espresso, cappuccino, fresh strawberries and chocolate-filled crepes on its terrace; for a full meal you are obliged to eat inside. It is open daily from noon to 10 pm. The terrace of the cheaper *Roti Bar*, beneath the Librărie Mihai Eminescu bookshop on the same square, is a popular lunch spot although it only serves light snacks.

Older establishments – generally lacking a menu (or only serving a couple of items featured if they do have one) – include the *Restaurant Trandifirilor* next to the cinema at Piaţa Trandifirilor 14. Your average pork cutlet is no more than US$0.50. The restaurant is open daily from 7 am to 10 pm.

The *Restaurant Mureşul* was traditionally the top restaurant in town. It has a pleasant terrace overlooking the street and the beef steak served on a wooden platter and topped with a fried egg (US$1.20) is quite a treat. It is open daily from 10 am to 10 pm.

There is a handful of cafés and small terrace restaurants around the student Culture House at Str Nicolae Grigorescu 17-19. The *Brasserie Universităţii* on Str Mihai Viteazu is a small shopping and café complex which serves the student fraternity.

Fast Food *Don Pedro Fast Food* outside the Hotel Grand is a crowded, stand-up affair. Light snacks and hot dogs are served from a kiosk. The small, modern *Panda* at Piaţa Trandifirilor 15 serves microwaved pizza and an excellent choice of 'pick and mix' salads priced by weight and served in plastic tubs costing US$0.20 or US$0.75. It is open daily from 10 am to 10 pm.

Prima, on the eastern side of the square close to the *Extra supermarket*, serves microwaved meatballs, cutlets and sniţel for around US$0.70.

Eddie Pizza, south of the centre on the way to the bus station at Str Gheorghe Doja, serves pizzas for US$2, ham and sniţel burgers for US$0.50 and a small range of omelettes. It is open daily from 10 am to 10 pm.

Self Catering Stock up on groceries at the *Extra* supermarket at Piaţa Trandifirilor 36-41. It's open weekdays from 6.30 am to 9 pm, Saturday from 6.30 am to 6 pm. For cut meats and other delicatessen products, go to *Prima*, a couple of doors down on the same side of the square. It is open Monday to Thursday from 8 am to 4 pm, Friday from 8 am to 6 pm, Saturday from 8.30 am to 1 pm.

Entertainment

Cinema All the cinemas in Târgu Mureş screen films in English. The *Cinema Tineretului* at Piaţa Trandifirilor 14 has showings daily at 10 am, 2.30, 4.40 and 6.30 pm. The *Cinema Artă* on the opposite side of the square runs films at 9 and 11 am, and 1, 3, 5 and 7 pm; and the *Cinema Unirea*, Piaţa Unirii, at 3 and 5.30 pm. Admission for all three is US$0.60/0.28 for adults/students.

Discos Students from the university hold regular Friday and Saturday night discos inside their *Culture House* (Casă de Cultură; ☎ 2216 066) at Str Nicolae Grigorescu 17-19. The disco rocks from 9 pm to 2 am on Friday and from 9 pm to 4 am on Saturday. Before you hit the dance floor, go for a drink at *Bere Craiova* in a courtyard off Piaţa Trandafirilor.

Opera & Theatre The main focus of Piaţa Teatrului is the *National Opera & Theatre* (☎ 127 030) which hosts a colourful array of plays and operettas in Romanian. Tickets for performances can be bought in advance from

the ticket office (☎ 125 060) inside the main theatre building. It is open Tuesday to Friday from 10 am to 1 pm and 5 to 7 pm, and at weekends from 10 am to 1 pm. The theatre breaks for summer in July and August.

Târgu Mureş also has a small puppet theatre just north of Piaţa Petőfi on Blvd Timişoarei.

Getting There & Away

Air TAROM operates four weekly flights between Bucharest and Târgu Mureş. A single/return fare is US$45/90. The TAROM office (☎ 135 200) at Piaţa Trandafirilor 6-8 is open weekdays from 8 am to 6 pm, Saturday from 8 am to noon.

Bus The bus station (☎ 121 458, 137 774) is a five minute walk south of the train station on Str Gheorghe Doja. Daily bus services include one to Dej (162km) via Gherla, Braşov (172km) and Sibiu (125km); two to Bistriţa (92km), Cluj-Napoca (108km), Corneşti (20km), Făgăraş (146km), Miercurea Ciuc (140km) and Ordorheiu Secuiesc (115km); three to Găleşti (25km); six to Sovata (67km); eight to Mediaş (71km); and nine to Sighişoara (54km).

Hungary A public bus departs from Târgu Mureş for Budapest on Friday at 8 am, arriving at Budapest Nep Stadion at 6.45 pm. The return bus leaves Budapest on Sunday at 2 pm, arriving in Târgu Mureş at 1.45 am the following morning. Single/return tickets costing US$7/11.50 are sold in advance at the bus station in Târgu Mureş.

More expensive private buses also depart daily from Târgu Mureş for Budapest. Impex EuroTours (☎ 165 341), Blvd 1 Decembrie 1918 163, operates a daily bus to Budapest, departing at 3.30 pm from outside its office and arriving at Budapest Nep Stadion at 4 am the following morning. The return bus leaves Budapest at 4 pm, arriving in Târgu Mureş at 5 am. Single/return tickets costing US$12/17 are sold at the Impex Euro Tours office at the more central Total Tours travel agency (see Information earlier).

Western Europe A Trans-Europa bus from Targu Mureş to Germany departs from outside the Hotel Grand on Tuesday, Thursday and Saturday at 3 am. Tickets can only be bought in advance from Total Tours.

The German bus companies Hartig Reisen and Mihu Reisen also operate buses to/from Târgu Mureş. Buses leave from outside the Hotel Grand on Monday, Friday and Saturday at 8.10 am. Tickets have to be bought in advance from the Turism Grand travel agency (see Information – Travel Agencies above).

Train The Agenţie de Voiaj CFR (☎ 166 203) at Piaţa Teatrului 1 is open weekdays from 7.30 am to 7.30 pm. Its staff speak English and are of the rare species who smile.

From Târgu Mureş there is one train daily to Budapest: the *Claudiopolis* departs at 1.28 pm, arriving in Budapest (783km, 8¾ hours) at 10.18 pm. The return train leaves Budapest at 12.10 pm and arrives in Târgu Mureş at 10.55 pm.

Târgu Mureş is at the end of a branch line off the main Cluj-Napoca-Bucharest line. To get to Alba Iulia from Târgu Mureş, you often have to change trains at Războieni or Teiuş.

Getting Around
To/From the Airport Târgu Mureş airport (☎ 132 738) is 10km south of the city in the Ungheni district. TAROM operates a shuttle bus for its clients; it meets incoming flights and leaves 1½ hours before outgoing flights.

Bus Târgu Mureş is small enough to cover by foot. Bus Nos 2, 4, 16 and 17 go to the bus station. Bus Nos 11, 18, 20 and 23 run from the centre along Str Mihai Eminescu to the hospitals and university area.

Taxi To call a taxi dial ☎ 132 222.

Bicycle Bicycle is a popular form of local transport in Târgu Mureş although at the time of writing it was still not possible to hire one. Maybe if enough people pester the young and trendy staff at Hike & Bike – a well stocked shop at Str Horia 16 which sells all the gear for biking and hiking (not maps) – they will realise there is a market to be filled. Most staff at the shop are members of the Robike mountain biking club (see Facts for the Visitor – Activities for more details).

AROUND TÂRGU MUREŞ
Sovata spa resort, Praid salt mines, and Corund, famed for its traditional black pottery, can all be visited in a day from Târgu Mureş.

Sovata Bai & Praid
Sovata Bai (Szováta in Hungarian) is 67km east of Târgu Mureş. The salt mines and lakes of Praid are an easy 7km south from Sovata.

The spa developed as a fashionable resort in the early 19th century and retains much of its former elegance. Five lakes dominate the resort, bearing such colourful names as Red Lake (Lacul Roşu), Hazelnut Lake (Lacul Aluniş) and Black Lake (Lacul Negru). Each is renowned for its curative waters although it was the largest lake – aptly named Bear Lake (Lacul Ursu) – which most bathers flocked to during the 19th century. It allegedly cured sterility. The Hazelnut and Black lakes were popular for their sapropelic mud. Sovata's salted lakes continue to draw crowds today, maintaining an average temperature of 19 to 20°C on the surface and 30 to 40°C below.

In Praid (Parajd in Hungarian), 7km south, asthma sufferers and folk with bronchial disorders are treated in the underground sanatorium sheltered in part of the giant salt mines, still operational today. Guided tours are available.

Trans-Tur (☎ 066-240 272; ☎ & fax 066-570 484), Str Principală 21, is an agent for ANTREC and arranges rooms in rural homes in Praid and its surrounding towns and villages. Some 31 families are involved in the flourishing agro-tourism scheme in this region. A bed for the night starts at US$15 and meals cost an additional US$2.

Getting There & Away Sovata Bai is 3km

TRANSYLVANIA

east of Sovata village. From Târgu Mureş there are six buses daily to Sovata Bai (1½ hours), which depart at 6.15 and 9 am, and 1.45, 2.30, 3.30 and 6 pm. There are no buses from Târgu Mureş to Praid. From Miercurea Ciuc there are two buses daily to Sovata Bai via Praid, both of which depart at 6.45 am and 2.30 pm.

. All the hotels arrange excursions to Praid. From the train halt (a scheduled stop) in Sovata village, there are three local trains daily to Praid (7km, 15 minutes). Trains depart from Sovata at 10.17 am, 6.40 and 9.19 pm. From Praid, trains leave for Sovata at 3.21 and 11.38 am, and 7.30 pm.

Corund

Continuing for 12km south from Praid towards Odorheiu Secuiesc you pass through the small village of Corund (Korond) where the age-old craft of pottery remains the mainstay of the village today with coachloads of tourists descending on the place in summer en route to/from Sovata and Praid.

Local potters sell their wares – which today embrace everything from handwoven rugs to sheepskin jerkins and knitted sweaters – from open-air stalls set up in the centre of the village. Many simply lay out their colourful crafts on the grass.

The history of this potters' village is briefly outlined in the small **History Museum** (Muzeul de Istorie), housed in a small white cottage down a mud road, just off the main road, in the centre of the village. If it is locked, continue along the mud road to house No 461 and ask for the key. Entering the village from the north, the mud road is on the left immediately before the main cluster of craft stalls.

Trans-Tur in Praid (see Sovata & Praid previously) can arrange accommodation in private houses in Corund for US$15 a night.

GHEORGHENI & AROUND
Gheorgheni

Approximately 90% of the population (23,000) of Gheorgheni ('gore-gen'; Gyergyószentmiklós in Hungarian) is

Hungarian. Sunk in the Gurghiu depression between the volcanic Gurghiu mountains and the eastern Carpathians, the town suffers longer, harsher winters and shorter summers than the rest of Romania. Gheorgheni is frequently dubbed the 'cold pole'.

There is little to see in Gheorgheni itself but it makes a good base for exploring the surrounding region

The **Tarisznyás Márton County Museum** (Városi Múzeum Tarisznyás Márton), named after its Szkéley founder in an 18th century building on Piaţa Petőfi Sándor, is worth a visit. Gheorgheni's main church, the **Hungarian Reformed Church**, is in pride of place on the central square, Piaţa Libertăţii.

Places to Stay There is a campsite at the *Motel 4* (☎ 161 585), 4km east of the centre on Blvd Lacul Roşu. Camping costs US$2 per person. In Gheorgheni, the *Szilágyi Hotel* (Szilágyi Szálló; ☎ 162 591) on Piaţa Libertăţii, has rooms with private bath for US$5 per person.

The *Hotel Mureş* (Maros Szálló; ☎ 161 904) at the western end of Blvd Frăţiei, opposite the culture house, has doubles with private bath for US$13. Doubles with shared bath cost US$6 at *Hotel Sport* (Sport Szálló; ☎ 161 270), Str Stadionului 11.

Getting There & Away The bus and train stations are 1.5km west of the centre on Str Gării. Buses to Budapest (635km) depart on Wednesday at 7 pm and on Thursday at 8.30 am. Tickets cost US$10 one-way. Tour Inform (☎ & fax 066-161 568), Piaţa Libertăţii 17, sells tickets for private buses to Hungary.

There are daily buses to Cluj-Napoca (168km), Braşov (150km), Lăzarea (6km), Odorheiu Secuiesc (102km), Miercurea Ciuc (57km) and Remetea (14km). Buses to Piatra Neamţ (82km) and Târgu Neamţ (160km) stop at Lacul Roşu and Bicaz. The Agenţie de Voiaj CFR (☎ 161 805) is at Blvd Frăţiei 9.

Lăzarea & Ditrău

Just 6km north of Gheorgheni on the road to Topliţa is the tiny village of 3060 people, Lăzarea (Gyergyószárhegy). Dating from 1235, it is dominated by its 16th century castle. It was to Lăzarea Castle that Gábor Bethlen, later to become prince of Transylvania (1613-29) came to seek solace following the death of his son in 1590. The castle is open to visitors daily, except Monday, from 9 am to 5 pm. Each summer artists from throughout Romania descend upon the castle for a summer camp when they help restore the castle's frescoes and fantastic Renaissance hall. Contemporary sculptures are scattered amid the haystacks in the castle grounds.

Below the castle rests a 17th century Franciscan monastery. Signposts from the centre of the village also direct tourists to the village water mill and water-powered saw mill. Lăzarea is predominantly Hungarian. At the time of writing there were just four Romanian families living here.

Ditrău (Ditró), 8km north of Lăzarea, was the site of a bloody battle on 6 August 1658 between Turkish-Tartar forces and a local army of some 300 villagers from Ditrău. The Székely army, which included many women, forced the Turks to retreat but many lost their lives in the process. An obelisk in memory of those who died stands on the hilltop, known as 'Tartar Hill'. Each year, on 6 August, locals climb the hill to pay homage to their heroic ancestors.

Places to Stay Lăzarea has a thriving agrotourism scheme, thanks to the Belgian charity Opération Villages Roumains. A bed for the night followed by a hearty home-cooked breakfast the next morning is US$10 per person. Full board costs US$15. It is also possible to hire a local guide to show you around for US$10 a day. The agro-tourism office (☎ & fax 161 464), signposted 'Birou OVR' is in the centre of the village next to the post office at Str Principală 1082. If it is closed, ask for the house of Emma Pap. She lives at house No 1285.

Lacul Roşu

From Gheorgheni the road heads east 26km across the Bucin mountain pass to dramatically reveal Lacul Roşu (Red Lake in English, Gyilkos tó in Hungarian). The lake is strangely filled with dead tree stumps which jut out of its murky waters at 45° angles and is considered one of Romania's weirdest natural wonders. Legend has it that the 'red lake' or 'killer lake' was formed from the flowing blood of a group of picnickers who had the misfortune to be sitting beneath the mountain side when it collapsed, crushing them to death. In fact, a landslide did occur in 1838, eventually flooding the valley and damming the Bicaz river. The wild tree stumps remain preserved thanks to the lake's unnaturally high content of calcium carbonate and iron oxide.

The thriving alpine resort, which sprang up around Lacul Roşu in the 1970s, is today, unfortunately, as dead as the tree stumps in the lake. You can hire rowing boats to tour the lake from the small boat station, open daily from 10 am to 6 pm. A 3.6km hiking trail (red cross, one hour) circles the lake.

From Lacul Roşu, the road continues east to the magnificent Bicaz Gorge in Moldavia. This road is among the most dramatic in the country and should not be missed (see Bicaz & Bicaz Gorge section in Moldavia).

Places to Stay Accommodation overlooking the lake is not a problem. Wild camping is permitted, every other house displays a *cazare* (room) sign and there are plenty of empty hotels and villas to choose from.

Topnotch is the *Vila Borş*, a little white palace overlooking the southern end of the lake. Once Ceauşescu's hunting lodge, it is palace is open to all and visitors can even sleep in the dictator's former bedroom for an undisclosed sum. Regular double with private bath costs US$14. The villa – amid pine trees in a fenced compound – is signposted on the left almost immediately after you enter Lacul Roşu from the south.

Less startling options include the 18-room *Hotel Făget* which has double/triple/four-bed rooms with shared bath for US$10/15/11 a night. The hotel overlooks the lake in the centre of the resort. Less sterile is the red and black wooden *Vila 14*, opposite the lake, which has beds on offer for US$3 a night. Hot water and breakfast is not included. Despite its ferocious name, the *Vila Vultural* (Eagle Villa), is among the most friendly. It has eight doubles, one four-bed room and two singles, all for US$3 per person a night. The hotel also has a small terrace restaurant overlooking the lake.

Getting There & Away There are two buses daily from Gheorgheni to Lacul Roşu, departing from Gheorgheni bus station at 12.30 and 3.05 pm (26km). The first bus continues along the eastern side of Bicaz lake to Târgu Neamţ (134km). The second bus heads east to Piatra Neamţ (56km).

From Miercurea Ciuc there is one bus daily to Piatra Neamţ via Lacul Roşu. It departs from Ciuc daily at 10.20 am.

Siculeni

In Siculeni (Madéfalva), 49km south of Gheorgheni on the road to Miercurea Ciuc, is a large roadside memorial to the victims of the Massacre of Madéfalva. Some 200 Székelys in this village were killed by Habsburgs troops after they revolted against orders issued by the Habsburg queen Marie Therese (1740-80) to round up all men in the village to serve in the Habsburg army. The victims were later buried in a mass grave, today known as the 'Hill of Death' (Vészhalom). Hundreds more villagers were captured and taken to the castle in Miercurea Ciuc where they were tortured. Following the bloody attack, many of the remaining villagers fled across the Carpathians into Romanian-ruled Moldavia.

MIERCUREA CIUC

• *area code* ☎ 066, *pop 46,029*

Miercurea Ciuc (Csíkszereda in Hungarian), 10km south of Siculeni and 85km east of Sighişoara, is the capital of Székely land. It is also renowned for the *Ciuc* beer (pronounced 'chook' as in 'hook') that it is brewed here.

The city was founded during the reign of Hungarian king Ladislaus I (1077-95) around a castle the king built for himself. Craft fairs were held every Wednesday around the citadel walls and Miercurea Ciuc quickly developed into a prosperous commercial centre and the hub of Székely cultural activities. Today, 83% of the population is ethnic Hungarian.

Miercurea Ciuc is the stronghold of Székely culture. Most signs in the town are written in Hungarian. Given its location in the Ciuc depression, Miercurea Ciuc is one of the coldest towns in Romania. Its annual average temperature is 5.9°C.

Orientation

The train and bus stations are a 10 minute walk west of the centre on Str Braşovului. Exit the train station and bear right along Str Mihail Sadoveanu towards Piaţa Majláth Gusztáv Károly. At the crossroads, turn left along Blvd Timişoara to get to Piaţa Libertăţii – the other main square. The bus station is 50m north of the train station.

Maps Buy a copy of the quality *Miercurea Ciuc Map* when you arrive. It is published by Topo Service in English, Romanian and Hungarian, and costs US$1.20 in bookshops. Go directly to the Topo Service office (☎ & fax 123 028) at Str Iancu de Hunedoara 33.

Information

Tourist Offices The Hotel Bradul has a tourist office at Blvd Timişoara 10 although staff at the hotel reception are helpful and speak English.

The SRL Român Travel Agency (☎ 211 319) at Str Kőrösi Csoma Sándor 51 sells tickets for private buses to Hungary and arranges excursions to Praid, Lacul Roşu and other places of interest in the region.

Money Change money and get cash advance on Visa/MasterCard at the Bancă Comercială Română (Kereskedelmi Bank), Str Florilor 19. The bank is open weekdays from 8 to 11 am and it has an ATM outside.

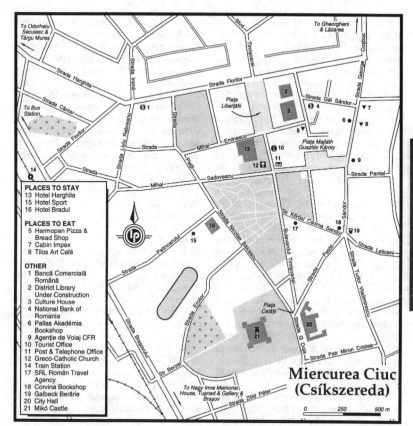

Miercurea Ciuc (Csíkszereda)

PLACES TO STAY
13 Hotel Harghita
15 Hotel Sport
16 Hotel Bradul

PLACES TO EAT
5 Harmopan Pizza & Bread Shop
7 Cabin Impex
8 Tilos Art Café

OTHER
1 Bancă Comercială Română
2 District Library Under Construction
3 Culture House
4 National Bank of Romania
6 Pallas Akadémia Bookshop
9 Agenţie de Voiaj CFR
10 Tourist Office
11 Post & Telephone Office
12 Greco-Catholic Church
14 Train Station
17 SRL Român Travel Agency
18 Corvina Bookshop
19 Galbeck Berărie
20 City Hall
21 Mikó Castle

Post & Communications The central post and telephone office is at the western end of Piaţa Majláth Gusztáv Károly on the corner of Blvd Timişoara. It is open weekdays from 7 am to 9 pm, Saturday from 9 am to 1 pm.

Cultural Centres The Democratic Alliance of Hungarians in Romania (Romániai Magyar Demokrata Szövetség; ☎ 113 221; fax 171 211) is based at Str Mihai Eminescu 2.

City Centre
Miercurea Ciuc's centrepiece is its **Mikó**

Castle which today houses the impressive **Székely Museum of Csík** (csíki Székely Múzeum; ☎ 111 727). The castle, which was constructed between 1611 and 1621 in a rectangular shape with four bastions, was built as a residence for the Hungarian commander-in-chief of the Székely districts, Ference Mikó. Dubbed the 'Golden Bastion' for its sheer luxury and Renaissance finery, the castle was burnt to the ground by Tartars in 1661.

The history of the town is told in the museum, and a library of some 8000 books survives from Miercurea Ciuc's 17th century

Franciscan monastery. There are also many archaeological exhibits and an ethnographic section featuring the traditional, brightly coloured woven fabrics known as *festékes* (literally 'painted'). The museum is open daily, except Monday from 9 am to 5 pm. Admission is US$0.50. Statues of the 1848 revolutionary Nicolae Bălcescu (1819-1961) and Hungarian poet Petőfi Sándor (1823-1849) stand in front of the entrance.

Miercurea Ciuc's **Palace of Justice** (1904) and **city hall** (1884-1898), both built in an eclectic style face Nicolae and Petőfi on the opposite side of Piaţa Cetăţii.

From Piaţa Cetăţii walk back north up Blvd Timişoara into the modern centre. At the northern end of Piaţa Libertăţii turn right onto Str Florilor, then take the first right. This leads you to the heart of the city's **Civic Centre**, created in the late 1980s as part of Ceauşescu's systemisation plans. While most of the older buildings in this area were bulldozed to make way for the concrete blocks you see today, a canary yellow, regal building, dating from 1903, which housed the **National Bank of Romania** managed to survive – just. On 30 July 1984, the entire building was uprooted from its foundations and moved 128m east on rollers to make way for the **district library** which is still under construction today.

Miercurea Ciuc was also the birthplace of the revered Székely painter Nagy Imre (1893-1976). The **Imre-Nagy Art Gallery** (Nagy-Imre Galéria; ☎ 113 963), south of the centre at Str Nagy Imre 175, displays various works by the artist whose body rests in the walls of the whitewashed church. The gallery is open daily, except Monday, from 9 am to 5 pm. Admission is US$0.30.

The Székely Pilgrimage

Two kilometres south of the centre in the Şumuleu district, (Csíksomlyó in Hungarian) is a fine **Franciscan Monastery**, built in 1442 by Iancu de Hunedoara (János Hunyadi), governor of Hungary (1446-52) to commemorate his great victory against the Turks at Marosszentimre.

The monastery today is a major pilgrim-age site for Székelys who flock here on Whit Sunday to celebrate their brotherhood. Traditional costumes are worn, songs sung and religious services held in celebration of their Protestant faith. The pilgrimage dates from 1567 when, in an attempt to convert the Székely peoples to Catholicism, Hungarian troops attacked the monastery. On Whit Sunday a bloody battle was fought on a field close to the monastery from which the Székelys emerged triumphant. Since then pilgrims have travelled to the monastery every year.

An early 19th century sculpture of the Virgin Mary, carved from wood and 2.27m tall, is considered one of the church's greatest treasures.

Places to Stay

Miercurea Ciuc's bargain-basement hotel is surprisingly user-friendly; the *Hotel Sport* (Sport Szálló; ☎ 116 161) close to the stadium at Str Patinoarului has double rooms with shared bath for US$7 a night. It also has four rooms with private bath for US$12. The hotel reception is in room No 19 on the 2nd floor.

Around the corner is the *Hotel Bradul* (Fenyö Szálló; ☎ 111 493; fax 172 181) next to the town's hockey club at Str Nicolae Bălcescu 11. It is a 198-room tower block with singles/doubles with private bath for US$10/19. The price does not include breakfast.

The *Hotel Harghita* (Hargita Szálló; ☎ 116 119; fax 113 181) overlooking the central Piaţa Libertăţii on the corner of Str Mihai Eminescu and Blvd Timişoara, considers itself the classy joint in town. Single/double rooms with private bath are US$16/26 a night. Again, breakfast is not included.

Places to Eat

Miercurea Ciuc has some funky places to eat and have some fun. The extremely stylish *Tilos Art-Café* (Cafeneaus Tilos; ☎ 116 814) is decked out like an old-fashioned bookshop inside and has tables on the street outside in summer. The town's young bohemians hang out here. It is open daily from 8 am to 10 pm and always packed.

The *Harmopan Pizza* slaps out microwaved pizza doused with ketchup for less than US$1 a slice. It also has a *bakery* inside which sells great fresh breads and cakes. From the southern end of Piaţa Libertăţii turn left onto Str Mihai Eminescu.

Cabin Impex at the end of Str Gál Sándor, is a traditional restaurant serving more substantial meals. It is open daily from 10 am to 11 pm.

Entertainment

Off-beat art films are screened once a week at the *Kriterion Art-Video Film Klub*, inside Kriterion House (Ház Kriterion) above the Pallas Akadémia Bookshop on Str George Coşbuc. Showings start at 7 pm; look for posters inside the Tilos Art-Café.

Folk dances are held in the *Culture House* (Városi Művelődési; ☎ 112 453) every Tuesday between 7 and 9 pm. Admission is US$0.20.

For a good old pint of British bitter look no further than the *Galbeck Berărie* (Galbeck Söröző) on the corner of Str Petőfi Sándor and Str Leliceni. Look out for the great NATO mural painted on the wall outside.

Getting There & Away

Bus The bus station (☎ 113 333) is 50m north of the train station on Str Braşovului. Miercurea Ciuc is quite well served by buses to other destinations in Romania. Daily services include one to Târgu Mureş (140km), and Târgu Neamţ (217km) and Piatra Neamţ (139km) via Gheorgheni (57km); two to Sovata Bai via Praid (92km), and Braşov (101km) via Sfântu Gheorghe (78km); five daily to Odorheiu Secuiesc (48km); and four to Băile Tuşnad (29km).

There are numerous buses to Budapest from Miercurea Ciuc. Tickets for buses to Budapest and western Europe are sold by the Itas agency (☎ 111 555) at the eastern end of Str Mihai Eminescu. Single/return tickets, which have to be bought in advance, cost

US$12/18. The Itas agency is open weekdays from 9.30 am to 4.30 pm.

The SRL Român Travel Agency also sells bus tickets for Budapest. A single/return ticket costs US$13/20. Tickets, again, have to be bought in advance.

Train The Agenţie de Voiaj CFR (☎ 111 924) at the eastern end of Piaţa Majláth Gusztáv Károly at Str Petőfi Sándor 23 is open weekdays from 7.30 am to 7 pm.

AROUND MIERCUREA CIUC

Székely villages lie within easy reach of Miercurea Ciuc, enabling travellers to get a glimpse of traditional rural life in the area.

Just 4km south-east of the town lies **Leliceni** (Csíkszentélek) where houses are arranged in four distinct clusters, known as *tizes* (tens). The village has been laid out this way ever since the early 17th century when, following a Tartar attack on the town in 1614, the entire village was destroyed bar those houses standing where the 'tens' are today. Traditionally, village meetings would take place under the 100-year-old linden tree next to the 15th century Gothic village church.

Two kilometres south is **Misentea** (Csíkmindszent), one of the most historic villages in the region, dating from the 12th century. An inscribed stone unearthed in the village shows that Székelys settled here from 1188 onwards. The church, dating from the 13th century, still has its original Gothic apse.

From Misentea, continue south for a couple of kilometres then bear left (north) along a dirt track to **Ciucsingeorgiu** (Csíkszentgyörgy). The village was settled from the early 14th century and the fortified village church dates from this period. Close to the church is a sacred piece of land – rich in clay – which villagers believe was coloured red by the blood of a local priest who was killed here. The red earth, which villagers use to colour their houses, is said to have protective powers.

Much of the original 13th century church also remains in the village of **Armaseni**

(Csíkménaság), 2km further north along the dirt track. The church's 17th century wooden altar is today displayed in the National Museum in Budapest. Frescoes inside the church feature pagan images of the sun and moon.

ODORHEIU SECUIESC
• *area code* ☎ *066, pop 40,000*

Odorheiu Secuiesc (Székelyudvarhely in Hungarian) lies 48km east of Miercurea Ciuc on the road to Sighişoara. Settled on an ancient Roman military camp, Odorheiu Secuiesc developed as a small craft town during the reigns of the Hungarian Árpád kings between the 11th and 13th centuries. In 1485, King Matthias Corvinus (1458-90), son of Iancu de Hunedoara, granted Odorheiu Secuiesc 'free royal town' status enabling its many different craft guilds to host commercial fairs. Trade boomed until the 1600s when, following a series of damaging attacks by the Turks, the town fell into decline. Today, it is a quiet, humble place, with that inexplicable sense of tranquillity that seems to pervade most of Romania's Hungarian towns.

Orientation
The train station at Str Bethlen Gábor 63 is a 10 minute walk from the centre. Exit the station and turn left (south) down Str Bethlen Gábor until you come to Piaţa Harghitei. From here bear right to get to Piaţa Libertăţii.

The bus station is 100m south of the train station at Str Târgului 10. Exit the bus station and turn right on to Str Bethlen Gábor then head south into town.

Many of the sights are centred around Piaţa Libertăţii. To get to the citadel, walk north-east from the square along Str Cetăţii. Str Kossuth Lajos runs south off Piaţa Libertăţii.

Maps Buy a copy of the excellent city map *Odorheiu Secuiesc Map of the Town* (Top-Gráf; 1996) for US$1 from the Corvina bookshop at Piaţa Libertăţii 23. It is open weekdays from 9 am to 6 pm, Saturday from 9 am to 1 pm.

Information
The Agenţie de Turism, adjoining the Hotel Târnava, is open weekdays from 7 am to 3 pm.

The post and telephone office at Str Kossuth Lajos 33 is open weekdays from 7 am to 7 pm. The Automobil Clubul Român (☎ 212 046, 211 804) has an office in the same building; the entrance is around the back down an alley off the main street. Get cash advance on Visa/MasterCard and cash travellers cheques at the BANCOREX at Str Morii 5. It is open weekdays from 8.30 to 11 am.

Things to See
Odorheiu Secuiesc's medieval **citadel** (vár), built between 1492 and 1516, is almost fully intact today, and houses an agricultural college. Visitors can freely stroll in the grounds around its inner walls.

Odorheiu Secuiesc has no less than two Greco-Catholic, two Orthodox, three Hungarian Reformed, and four Roman-Catholic churches. From the citadel, walk south down Str Cetăţii towards the main square, Piaţa Libertăţii. At the western end of the square stands a **Franciscan Monastery & Church** (Szent Ferencrendi Templom és Kolostor) constructed 1712-79. Walk east past the impressive eclectic **city hall** (1895-6) to the 18th century baroque **Hungarian Reformed Church** (Református Templom). Bearing right onto Piaţa Márton you come to one of the town's **Roman Catholic Churches** (Római Katolikus Plébánia-templom), the first to be built, between 1787 and 1791.

Unfortunately, the town's best church lies 2km south of the centre on Str Bethlen Gábor. The **Chapel of Jesus** (Jézus kápolna) is among the oldest architectural monuments in Transylvania, built during the early 13th century. The little chapel gained its name from the war cries of Székely warriors who, during a Tartar invasion on their town in 1241, cried to Jesus for help while in battle. They won and built a chapel on the battlefield to commemorate their victory.

Odorheiu Secuiesc's colourful history is

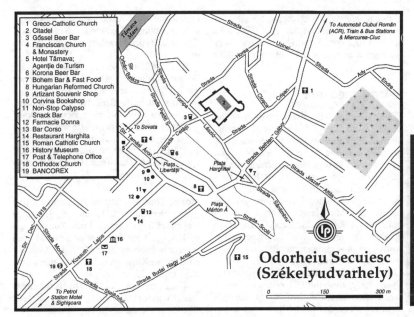

1 Greco-Catholic Church
2 Citadel
3 Gössel Beer Bar
4 Franciscan Church
   & Monastery
5 Hotel Târnava;
   Agenţie de Turism
6 Korona Beer Bar
7 Bohem Bar & Fast Food
8 Hungarian Reformed Church
9 Artizant Souvenir Shop
10 Corvina Bookshop
11 Non-Stop Calypso
   Snack Bar
12 Farmacie Donna
13 Bar Corso
14 Restaurant Harghita
15 Roman Catholic Church
16 History Museum
17 Post & Telephone Office
18 Orthodox Church
19 BANCOREX

Odorheiu Secuiesc
(Székelyudvarhely)

0   150   300 m

TRANSYLVANIA

explained – in Hungarian – in the **Haáz Rezsó Museum** (Haáz Rezsó Múzeum) at Str Kossuth Lajos 29. The museum was founded from a collection of folk objects belonging to local art teacher Haáz Rezsó from 1900 onwards. It is open daily, except Monday, from 9 am to 4 pm.

Places to Stay & Eat

Mediocre single/double rooms cost US$15/22 a night, including breakfast at the two-star *Hotel Târnava* (Târnava Szálló; ☎ 213 963; fax 213 970) in the centre of town at Piaţa Libertăţii 16. The only other alternative is a room in the motel above the petrol station, on your left as you enter Odorheiu Secuiesc on the main road from the south.

The *Restaurant Harghita* at Str Kossuth Lajos 19 is your typical large, empty, age-old restaurant. For fast food, look no further than the *Bohem* bar and fast food joint on Piaţa Harghitei; the place is open daily from 10 am to 10 pm.

The *Korona Bar* overlooking Piaţa Libertăţii and the *Gössel* beer bar opposite the citadel ruins on the corner of Str Cetăţii and Str Tompa Lázló are two pleasant drinking holes.

Getting There & Away

Bus The bus station (☎ 212 034) is north-east of the centre at Str Târgului 10. From Odorheiu Secuiesc there are two buses daily to Gheorgheni (102km) and Târgu Mureş (115km); and five buses a day to Miercurea Ciuc (48km).

Train The Agenţie de Voiaj CFR (☎ 212 916), for advance train tickets, is at the train station (☎ 213 653) at Str Bethlen Gábor 63. Odorheiu Secuiesc is on a branch line off the main Braşov-Cluj-Napoca railroad. From Odorheiu Secuiesc there are local trains to Sighişoara from where you can take a train to Cluj-Napoca, Copşa Mică, Braşov, Mediaş Oradea, Predeal, and Târgu Mureş.

Local trains from Odorheiu Secuiesc to Sighişoara (1¼ hours) depart at 6.20, 2.33 am, and 10.25 pm. Return trains depart from Sighişoara at 4.20 and 11.49 am, and 8.20 pm.

SFÂNTU GHEORGHE
* *area code* ☎ *067, pop 76,000*

Sfântu Gheorghe (Sepsiszentgyörgy), on the banks of the Olt river is a truly Hungarian stronghold with more than two-thirds of its population laying claim to Székely origin. The town has its own Hungarian daily newspaper, *Háromszék*, and one of Romania's two Hungarian State Theatres, while most street signs and shop boards bear just one language – Magyar. Only one of its 10 schools is Romanian, and Hungarian remains the predominant language of the town's small Roma community.

First documented in 1332, Sfântu Gheorghe developed as a cultural centre for the Székelys from the 15th century onwards when it became a free town, bearing the right to host commercial fairs. The town was left devastated by Turkish attacks between 1658 and 1671, its population dwindling further after the plague swept through the city in 1717.

Orientation
The bus station and train stations are on Str Avanţului, 10 minutes walk from the centre. Top-Gráf produces the superb *Sfântu Gheorhge Map of the Town*, published in 1997, with a city map, larger scale city centre map, Romanian-Hungarian street register, and a short historical explanation of the town in English, German, Romanian and Hungarian. It is sold for US$1 in most bookshops and travel agencies.

Information
Tourist Offices International Trade & Tourism (☎ 316 375; fax 151 194, 150 551) at Str Grigore Bălan 1 is the top travel agency-cum-tourist office in town. Its friendly English-speaking staff arrange car and mini-bus rental, guided tours in the region, plus accommodation at Ceauşescu's former hunting lodge 3km south of the town. The office is open weekdays from 9 am to 5 pm.

BTT (☎ 324 869; fax 324 939) at Str General Grigore Bălan 18 also arranges guided tours to Sovata, Praid and other tourist spots in the Székely region. It operates a small rent-a-car service, has local guides and translators for hire and is also an agent for the national rural tourism body ANTREC (see Places to Stay & Eat). Its staff speak English. The office is open weekdays from 9 am to 4 pm.

Money There is a currency exchange inside Tref Turism on Str 1 Decembrie 1918, open weekdays from 9 am to 4 pm. You can get cash advance on Visa/MasterCard and cash travellers cheques at BANCOREX at the south of Str Klossuth Lajos. It is open weekdays from 8.30 am to 2 pm.

There is an ATM which accepts Visa/MasterCard outside the Bancă Comercială Română west of the centre on Str Nicolae Iorga. The bank is open weekdays from 7.30 to 11 am.

Post & Communications The central post and telephone office at the junction of Str Oltului and Str 1 Decembrie 1918 is open weekdays from 7 am to 8 pm.

Cultural Centres The Democratic Alliance of Hungarians in Romania (Romániai Magyar Demokrata Szövetség; ☎ 316 152; fax 314 839) has its office at Str Gábor Áron 14. It has a small library with material in English as well as Hungarian and publishes the monthly *Magyar Közélet* newsletter.

Things to See
It was inside the building at Str Gábor Áron 14 (today housing the Democratic Alliance of Hungarians in Romania) that revolutionary Áron Gábor announced to his comrades on 23 November 1848 that the town should 'Bring in the cannons!' in their fight against Habsburg rule. The cannons he was referring

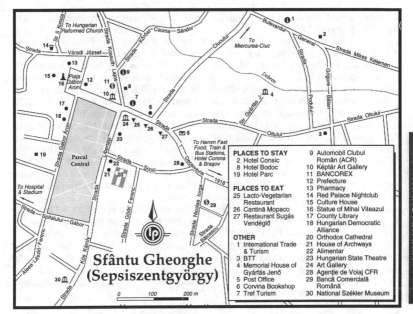

PLACES TO STAY
2 Hotel Consic
8 Hotel Bodoc
19 Hotel Parc

PLACES TO EAT
25 Lacto-Vegetarian
   Restaurant
26 Cantină Mopaco
27 Restaurant Sugás
   Vendéglő

OTHER
1 International Trade
  & Turism
3 BTT
4 Memorial House of
  Gyárfás Jenő
5 Post Office
6 Corvina Bookshop
7 Tref Turism
9 Automobil Clubul
  Român (ACR)
10 Képtár Art Gallery
11 BANCOREX
12 Prefecture
13 Pharmacy
14 Red Palace Nightclub
15 Culture House
16 Statue of Mihai Viteazul
17 County Library
18 Hungarian Democratic
   Alliance
20 Orthodox Cathedral
21 House of Archways
22 Alimentar
23 Hungarian State Theatre
24 Art Gallery
28 Agenţie de Voiaj CFR
29 Bancă Comercială
   Română
30 National Székler Museum

Sfântu Gheorghe
(Sepsiszentgyörgy)

0   100   200 m

TRANSYLVANIA

to were cast in his small village workshop just outside of Sfântu Gheorghe (see Around Sfântu Gheorghe section).

From Str Gábor Áron walk south to the end of the park then turn left along Str Spitatului Gábor. At the junction turn right along Str Kós Károly until you reach the **Székely National Museum** (Székely Nemzeti Múzeum; ☎ 312 442). The building itself is a masterpiece, designed by leading Hungarian architect Kós Károly (1883-1977) between 1911 and 1913. The museum, founded in 1879, provides the most comprehensive visual display of Székely culture today, while the helpful English-speaking tour guides possess a wealth of fascinating facts they're keen to share.

The museum has a large open-air section exhibiting Székely porches, gates and wooden houses. In the main building there is a large exhibit on the 1848 revolution.

The museum is open weekdays from 9 am to 4 pm, Saturday from 9 am to 1 pm. It is closed Sunday. Admission is US$0.50 and guided tours in English or French are free.

From the museum, walk north up Str Kós Károly, past the modern **Greco-Catholic Church** (Unitárius Templom) built in 1991 on the right, until you come to the **Orthodox Cathedral** (Román Ortodox Katedrális), set slightly back off the road. Dating from the 16th century, the church was only designated a cathedral in the early 1990s following the establishment of a bishopric for Covasna and Harghita counties.

Continue north along Piaţa Libertăţii, past the Hungarian State Theatre and adjoining **art & crafts shop**, then head west towards Piaţa Gábor Áron. At the northern end of the park you pass the **Képtár Art Gallery** which hosts a fine range of contemporary international art exhibitions.

Places to Stay
Private Rooms International Trade & Tourism (see Information – Tourist Offices)

arranges rooms in private houses throughout the Székely region for US$8 to US$10 a night. It can also arrange rooms in the centre of Sfântu Gheorghe providing you give staff some notice. The agency works with rural tourism experts ANTREC.

BTT (see Information – Tourist Offices) is also an agent for ANTREC and arranges rooms in private houses in rural villages around Sfântu Gheorghe, including Băile Tuşnad, Băile Bálványos, Covasna and most other villages. A bed for the night starts at US$15.

Hotels The cheapest is the *Hotel Consic* (☎ 326 984) at Str Grigore Bălan 31. Double rooms without/with private bath are US$5/6 per person, not including breakfast.

The busiest is the *Hotel Corona* (☎ 35 479, 351 151) opposite the train station on Str Gării. Singles/doubles with shared bath are US$9/12, including breakfast. Its bar is open 24 hours.

The friendliest is the *Hotel Parc* (☎ 311 058; fax 311 307) in wooded grounds at Str Gábron Áron 14. Doubles with private bath and cable TV are US$11, including breakfast.

The dreariest is the *Hotel Bodoc* (☎ 31 292; fax 153 787) at Str 1 Decembrie 1918, your old-style state hotel which has 40 singles/doubles on offer for US$23/29, including breakfast.

Castle The Arcus Castle, built in 1870 in a large park by the Baron Szentkereszti, was extensively renovated under the orders of Ceauşescu. He poured huge amounts of cash into and he stayed there only twice. Travellers, however, can stay in the castle for just US$29 for a luxury apartment. Meals can also be provided for an additional US$10 per person. Bookings can be made through the International Trade & Tourism agency, which can also provide transport to the castle. Some local buses go to Arcus.

Places to Eat
Sfântu Gheorghe offers few eating options. The hot spot in town is the cheap and cheer-

ful *Lacto-Vegetarian Restaurant* at the north-eastern end of Piaţa Libertăţii. Despite its name, it serves tons of meat dishes too on an outside terrace overlooking the main street. It is open daily from 7 am to 9 pm.

The cheapest joint in town is the *Cantină Mopaco* 100m further east along Piaţa Libertăţii. Pizza costs a bargain US$0.20, quality not guaranteed. It is open daily, except Sunday, from 8 am to 10 pm. Marginally more upmarket is the large and dreary *Restaurant Sugás Vendéglő* which has all the characteristics of an old Soviet-type ghetto. It is open daily from 10 am to midnight and is just a couple of doors east from the riveting *cantină*.

At the southern end of Str 1 Decembrie 1918 there is a *Hamm* fast food outlet which churns out the junk food 24 hours.

Stock up on supplies at the *Alimentar* opposite the central park on the corner of Str Şcolli and Piaţa Libertăţii. *Eves* is a 24 hour shop opposite the train station on Str Gării.

Entertainment
Plays are performed in Hungarian at the *Tamási Áron Hungarian State Theatre* (Állami Magyar Színház; ☎ 313 886; fax 312 104) at Piaţa Libertăţii 1.

Guaranteed fun can be had at the *Red Palace Nightclub* on the corner of Str Váradi József. An alleyway leads from the pharmacy on Piaţa Gábor Áron to the club. It is open daily, except Sunday, from 8 pm to 5 am.

Discos are held in the culture house on Piaţa Gábor Áron on Friday and Saturday night. Admission is US$0.20.

Getting There & Away
Bus The bus station is 50m north of the train station on Str Avanţului. Daily bus services include eight to Arcus (3km); three to Covasna (28km) and Târgu Secuiesc (37km); one bus a day to Băile Tuşnad (32km) and Miercurea Ciuc (78km); two daily to Bodoc (11km); and one bus daily to Târgu Neamţ (315km), Piatra Neamţ (214km), and Braşov (32km).

Train The Agenţie de Voiaj CFR (☎ 311 680) at Str Şcolli 3 is open weekdays from 7 am to 7 pm.

AROUND SFÂNTU GHEORGHE

The Fairy Queen Valley, the only inclined plane railway still in use in Europe, and the birthplace of the composer of the first English-Tibetan dictionary are all here.

Covasna

The spa town of Covasna (Kovászna in Hungarian), 28km east of Sfântu Gheorghe in the 'Fairy Queen Valley' (Valea Zânelor) has long been dubbed the 'valley of a thousand springs' for its popular curative mineral water. The black mud that bubbles from the resort's 'Devil's Pond' (Baia Dracului) is more menacing.

The main appeal of this typical Romanian spa resort (560m) is its unique **inclined plane**, the starting point of Romania's oldest narrow-gauge forestry railway which snakes 10km up the western flanks of Mount Vrancrei (1777m) to **Comandău** village.

The forestry railway, completed in 1890, was the first of its kind in the country to use iron rails and steam locomotives. Its purpose was to transport wood down the valley from Comandău, a primitive logging settlement. The line remains the only functional one of its type in Europe. Also unusual is the fact that the sawmill and administrative buildings of this logging community lie, not in the valley of Covasna, but at the top of the line in Comandău (1012m). Today, about 100 people live in this male-dominated village where the rules are firmly set: men cut wood, women stay at home, huts are made of wood, the station has a bell, the men smoke too much and no one has any money. The scene is straight out of a cowboy movie.

Every weekday two steam trains transporting trimmed wood lumber 10km down the valley to **Siclău** (1236m). Here the wood is loaded on to open wagons to make the final part of its journey down the inclined plane to Covasna. Horses are used to manoeuvre the loaded wagons into position then, with the careful use of brakes, the wood is slowly lowered down the mountain. Its weight is counterbalanced against empty wagons at the bottom of the line.

You can view the inclined plane and unloading of the wood from the bottom of the line in Covasna. A dirt road leads southwest from the centre of Covasna. Ask for *fabric de lemn* or *mocăniţa*. At the time of writing, the logging operation was halted due to fire.

Places to Stay Check with International Trade & Tourism in Sfântu Gheorghe to see if the inclined plane is operational. ITT can arrange accommodation in private homes in Covasna and trips to the inclined plane (see Information – Sfântu Gheorghe section).

Covasna resort is centred around Valea Zânelor (formerly spelt Valea Zînelor) at the south-eastern end of Covasna village proper. The *Hotel Covasna* (☎ 067-340 401; fax 067-151 945) on Str 1 Decembrie 1918 has singles/doubles for US$40 a day in high season. This includes three meals a day plus three health treatments of your choice. The concrete blocks of the more upmarket *Hotel Căprioara* (☎ 067-340 825; fax 067-151 945) and the low-budget *Hotel Turist* (☎ 067-340 573; fax -67-340 622) are next door.

Getting There & Away RomSteam-Aldo and Ronedo in Piatra Neamţ (see the Moldavia chapter) both organise 'adventures with steam' in Romania and can arrange for groups to visit Comandău or explore the forestry railways in this region. It can be costly unless you are part of a large group (see Activities – Facts for the Visitor at the front of this book).

Travel agencies all over the country arrange package tours and cheap weekend deals to Covasna spa. From Sfântu Gheorghe there are three buses daily to Covasna (28km).

Covasna is on a small branch railway line between Sfântu Gheorghe and Breţcu. Daily train services from Covasna include six trains daily to Sfântu Gheorghe (40 minutes); five trains daily to Târgu Secuiesc

(30 minutes); and four trains daily to Brețcu (two hours).

Chiuruş & Zagon

Along a dirt track 2km south-west of Covasna is the village of Chiuruş (Csomakörös in Hungarian). This is the birthplace of an outstanding Székely linguist Şándor Körösi Csoma (1784-1842) who walked to Tibet, wrote the first English-Tibetan dictionary and, upon his death, was buried in Darjeeling in India. Chiuruş is also home to one of the oldest Hungarian Reformed churches in Székely Land.

Following this track 9km further south you come to Zagon (Zágon in Hungarian), the home of Kelemen Mikes, the devoted secretary of Hungarian Transylvanian Prince Francis Rákóczi II who led the 1703-11 revolution in Transylvania against Habsburg rule. Mikes voluntarily went to live in Rhodes where he outlived Rákóczi and the rest of his exiled generals. During the solitary time he spent on the island, he wrote letters to a fictitious aunt in Székely Land in which he lamented the loss of his homeland. Two oak trees, said to have been planted by Mikes, stand in Zagon today. The house in which he was born is now a memorial house.

Târgu Secuiesc & Around

Continuing 16km north, you come to Târgu Secuiesc (Kézdivásárhely), a quiet market town famed for the role a local ironsmith from here played in the 1848 uprising led against Habsburg rule of Hungary.

The 1848 revolution in Székely Land was primarily led by Hungarian Liberation Front leader Lajos Kossuth and poet Petőfi Sándor. From October 1848 until June 1849 the revolutionaries were supplied with canons cast by Székely ironsmith Áron Gábor who ran a small foundry in Târgu Secuiesc. Gábor cast the cannons from melted-down church bells, donated by surrounding Székely villages happy to lose their church bell for the 'cause'. The canons consequently became known as 'canons of brass' while Áron Gábor was immortalised in a folk song written about him in praise of his warfare creations. One of the canons and tools used by the enterprising ironsmith are displayed in Târgu Secuiesc's **Áron Gábor Museum**. A statue of Áron Gábor stands in the central square.

Gábor was born 16km east of Târgu Secuiesc (literally 'market town'), in the village of **Brețcu** (Bereck). On 2 July 1849, following the intervention of Russian troops on behalf of the Habsburgs, he was shot in battle at **Chichis** (Kökös), 10km south of Sfântu Gheorghe. Revolutionaries attempted to carry their wounded leader to his home village for burial but in **Moacşa** (Maksa), 20km short of Târgu Secuiesc, he died. Fearing the approach of Russian troops, they buried Gábor in Moacşa. A large memorial tombstone rests above his grave in the centre of the village today.

In **Ghelinta** (Gelence), 9km south-west of Târgu Secuiesc, there is a fine Gothic church, built in the 13th century and later fortified by the local Székely community.

Getting There & Away There are three buses daily from Sfântu Gheorghe to Târgu Secuiesc (44km, one hour), departing at 6.30 and 11.30 am, and 1.30 pm.

Local trains from Sfântu Gheorghe to Târgu Secuiesc via Covasna, depart daily from Sfântu Gheorghe at 5.30 and 9.10 am, 1.30, 5.55 and 9.25 pm. Return trains from Târgu Secuiesc depart at 7.20 am, noon, and 3.25, 7.25, 11.15 pm.

Băile Bálványos & Băile Tuşnad

From Târgu Secuiesc, it is a straight 26km drive north to the unusual spa resorts of Băile Bálványos and Băile Tuşnad, which nestle in the eastern and western shores of Lake St Anne (Lacul Sfântu Ana; Szt Anna tó). Approaching from Sfântu Gheorghe, you cross the spectacular Tuşnad Pass.

Lake St Anne, inside a volcanic crater on Mount Ciumatu (950m), is steeped in legend. It is also the site of a Székely pilgrimage each year on 26 July. Since the 12th century pilgrims have flocked here to pay homage to St Anne, the traditional protector of young women. Székely women unable to conceive would also come here to pray for a child. A wooden chapel was built during the 12th century, which, by the 17th century had been replaced by a larger, stone building to serve the 30 to 40,000 pilgrims who visited the lake each year. It remains a popular pilgrim site today. Large expanses of peat bogs surround the lake, many of which are protected under a nature reserve.

Băile Bálványos is a small spa overlooking the lake to the east. It is the hot springs in Băile Tuşnad (Tusnádfürdó), on its western shores however, that attract most travellers.

Places to Stay In Băile Bálványos, you can stay at the *Hotel Carpaţi* (☎ 068-1154 059, 067-361 449). It has 65 doubles and 13 singles starting at US$15/25 a night. The hotel offers numerous hot bath and therapy treatments.

In Băile Tuşnad, you can camp at *Camping Univers* (☎ 066-116 319; fax 153 447), Str Voinţa 18. There are also plenty of small villas and private houses displaying *cazare* (rooms) signs outside.

The leading hotel for beds and pampering is the *Hotel Tuşnad* (☎ 068-151 258; fax 066-115 074), Str Olt 45. It offers a mind-boggling choice of health treatments including mud wraps, medical gymnastics and cures for nervous-system disorders. In summer a night in one of its 108 doubles is US$25, including three meals a day. The hotel is popular with group tours.

Getting There & Away There are daily buses to Băile Tuşnad from Miercurea Ciuc (29km) and Sfântu Gheorghe (32km). One bus daily departs from Sfântu Gheorghe at 3.30 pm. From Miercurea Ciuc there are four buses daily.

Băile Tuşnad is also served by local trains from Braşov (1½ hours), Sfântu Gheorghe (3/4 hours), Miercurea Ciuc (3/4 hours) and Gheorgheni (two hours). Nine trains daily follow this route. Don't alight at Tuşnad station, 6km north of Băile Tuşnad, by mistake.

Northern Transylvania

During WWII, northern Transylvania fell under pro-Nazi Hungarian rule. Under the Diktat of Vienna of 30 August 1940, the Axis powers, Germany and Italy, forced Romania to cede 43,493sq km and a population of 2.6 million to Hungary. During the four years of occupation, thousands of Romanians were imprisoned and tortured while entire villages were massacred. Northern Transylvania was not recovered until 25 October 1944 when, following the liberation of Satu Mare, the territory fell back into Romanian hands.

CLUJ-NAPOCA
● *area code ☎ 064, pop 328,000*

Cut in two by the Someşul Mic River, Cluj-Napoca is as Hungarian as it is Romanian. Its position near the middle of Transylvania has long made it a crossroads, which explains its present role as an educational and industrial centre. Known as Klausenburg to the Germans and Kolozsvár to the Hungarians, the old Roman name of Napoca has been added to the city's official title to emphasise its Daco-Roman origin.

The history of Cluj-Napoca goes back to Dacian times. In 124 AD, during the reign of Emperor Hadrian, Napoca attained municipal status and Emperor Marcus Aurelius elevated it to a colony between 161 and 180 AD. Documented references to the medieval town, known as 'Castrum Clus', date back to 1183. German merchants arrived in the 12th century and, after the Tartar invasion of 1241, the medieval earthen walls of *castrenses de Clus* were rebuilt in stone. From 1791-1848 and after the union with Hungary in 1867, Cluj-Napoca served as the capital of Transylvania.

Though less picturesque than either Sighişoara or Braşov, it has several good museums and a relaxed, inviting atmosphere. You could see all the sights in a busy afternoon, but cheap accommodation makes it easy to spend a few days. Nearby Turda Gorge (Cheile Turzii) is also worth a look.

TRANSYLVANIA

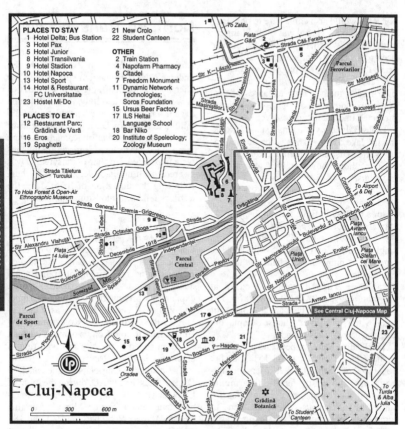

PLACES TO STAY
1   Hotel Delta; Bus Station
3   Hotel Pax
5   Hotel Junior
8   Hotel Transilvania
9   Hotel Stadion
10 Hotel Napoca
13 Hotel Sport
14 Hotel & Restaurant
    FC Universitatae
23 Hostel Mi-Do

PLACES TO EAT
12 Restaurant Parc;
    Grădină de Vară
16 Eros
19 Spaghetti

21 New Crolo
22 Student Canteen

OTHER
2   Train Station
4   Napofarm Pharmacy
6   Citadel
7   Freedom Monument
11 Dynamic Network
    Technologies;
    Soros Foundation
15 Ursus Beer Factory
17 ILS Heltai
    Language School
18 Bar Niko
20 Institute of Speleology;
    Zoology Museum

Cluj-Napoca

TRANSYLVANIA

Orientation

The train station is 1.5km north of the centre, so walk left out of the station, buy a ticket at the red Coca-Cola kiosk across the street and catch tram No 101 or a trolleybus south down Str Horea. Get off the trolleybus immediately after crossing the river; on tram No 101 you go two stops and then continue walking south until you cross the river. The left-luggage office inside the train station is near the restaurant (open 24 hours).

Cluj-Napoca has two bus stations. Bus Station No 2 (Autogară No 2) is over the bridge from the train station, north of town.

Bus Station No 1 (Autogară No 1) is on Str Aurel Vlaicu on the far eastern side of town (no left luggage). Trolleybus No 4 connects Autogară No 1 to the centre of town and the train station.

Maps The quality *Cluj-Napoca, Kolozsvár, Klausenburg* map, published in 1997, includes a city map, detailed city centre map and lists the major sights in Romanian and Hungarian. It is US$3 in most bookshops. If you cannot find it go direct to the map distributor, Apex SRL (☎ 196 213, 195 981; fax 190 316), Str Innocenţiu Micu Klein 17.

Information

Tourist Offices Turism Feleacul (☎ 184 935; fax 197 306), the official tourist office at Calea Moţilor 1, is useless beyond arranging package deals to the coast. For practical help and information approach one of the private agencies (see Travel Agencies later in the chapter). Turism Feleacul is open weekdays from 8 am to 8 pm, Saturday from 7 am to 1 pm.

The Automobil Clubul Român (ACR; ☎ 116 503) has an office close by at Str Memorandumului 27.

The Transylvanian Ecological Club (☎ 197 399; fax 190 404), run mainly by university students at Blvd Eroilor 2, is open weekdays from 9 am to 6 pm. It arranges tours and activities in rural areas in northwestern Transylvania, publicises local environmental issues, and publishes the yearly magazine *EcoForum* which lists other ecological societies in Transylvania.

Foreign Consulates The US embassy in Bucharest operates an information bureau (☎ 193 815, 193 868) at Str Universităţii 79. It is open Monday and Thursday from 10.30 am to 1 pm, 2.30 to 6 pm, Tuesday from 2.30 to 4 pm, Wednesday and Friday from 10.30 am to noon.

The Hungarian Consulate is on Piaţa Unirii.

Money Black-market moneychangers (all very fat) lurk in front of the Agenţie de Turism KM0 on Piaţa Unirii, outside the Hotel Continental and around the taxi rank in front of St Michael's Church. Most change forints for lei and vice versa, but be extremely careful (scams are common).

Change money officially at the Platinum Currency Exchange on Str Gheorghe Doja. You can change travellers cheques and get Visa/MasterCard cash-advances at BANCOREX next door at Str Gheorghe Doja 8 or at its branch at Piaţa Unirii 10. Both are open weekdays from 11 am to 5.30 pm, Saturday from 10.30 am to 1 pm.

If the queues are too long at BANCOREX, try the Bancă Comercială Română on the opposite side of the square at Piaţa Unirii 7. It gives cash advance on Visa/MasterCard, cashes travellers cheques, and is open weekdays from 8.30 am to 12.30 pm.

The Bancă Agricola, on the corner of Str Ştefan Ludwig Roth and Str Emil Racoviţă, only gives cash advance on Visa. It is open weekdays from 8.30 am to 1.30 pm and from 3.30 to 6 pm. A second branch is under construction on Str George Bariţiu, close to the telephone office.

The IBM Exchange, Str Samuil Micu 3, accepts Eurocheques.

Post & Communications There is a small telephone office at Piaţa Unirii 5, open weekdays from 7 am to 9 pm. The main telephone office is behind the central post office at Str Gheorghe Doja 33; both open weekdays 7 am to 8 pm, Saturday 7 am to 1 pm. Queues are shorter at the post office opposite the student culture house on the corner of Piaţa Lucian Blaga and Str Petru Maior. It's open weekdays from 8 am to 3.30 pm.

DHL World-wide Express (☎ 190 692, 191 824; fax 190 481) at Blvd Eroilor 10 is open weekdays from 8.30 am to 3 pm.

Dynamic Network Technologies (☎ 420 006; fax 420 478; email sales@dnttcj.ro; www.dntcj.ro) inside the Soros Foundation building at Str Tebei 21 provides full email and Internet access starting at US$9.90 a month for 10 hours online access monthly.

Travel Agencies The Continental Agenţie de Turism (☎ 195 405, 195 406; fax 193 977) inside the Hotel Continental at Str Napoca 1 arranges tours, makes hotel bookings, and offers the cheapest car rental service in town. It is open weekdays from 9 am to 5 pm, Saturday from 9 am to 2 pm.

Consus Travel (☎ 192 928; ☎ & fax 193 044; email consus@cjx.logicnet.ro; www.consustr.logictl.com) at Str Gheorghe Şincai 15 can book you into most hotels at a slightly better rate than if you approach the hotel direct. It also arranges weekend trips to the Apuseni mountains, Maramureş, and Poiana Braşov for around US$220. It is open weekdays from 9 am to 5 pm.

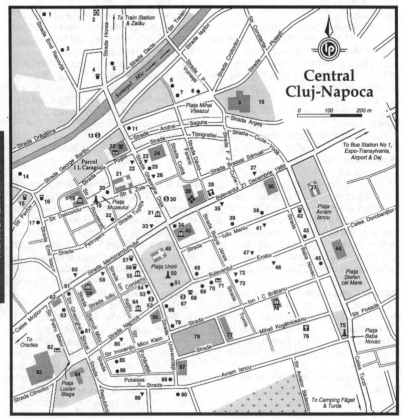

Central Cluj-Napoca

Staff at the Agenție de Turism KM0 (☎ 191 114; fax 196 557), Piața Unirii 10, cannot take bookings for Avis car rental despite advertising otherwise. The staff arrange trips to other parts of Romania and take bookings for Cluj-Napoca hotels. It is open weekdays from 8 am to 6 pm, Saturday 10 am to 2 pm.

Bookshops & Newsstands The University Bookshop (Librărie Universității), Piața Unirii 9, stocks English-language novels. It is open weekdays from 9 am to 5 pm.

Newsstands on Piața Unirii sell current copies of *Newsweek*, *Time* and *The Economist* at a lower price than in the west.

Libraries & Cultural Centres The Students' Union (Federația Organizațiilor Studențești Cluj; ☎ & fax 196 263; email fosc@mail.soroscj.ro) inside the Culture House in room No 4, is happy to fill you in on the latest hip things to hit town. Its office is open Monday from 2 pm to 6 pm, Tuesday from 6 pm to 8 pm, Wednesday from 2 to 8 pm, Friday and Saturday from noon to 2 pm.

The Soros Foundation for an Open Society (Fundația Soros pentru o Societate

Deschisă România; ☎ 420 480; fax 420 470; email office@soroscj.ro; www.soroscj.ro) at Str Tebei 21 runs a small English-language library which stocks the latest issues of *Time*, *Newsweek*, *The Economist* as well as some British dailies. It is open between October and mid-July on Monday from noon to 7.30 pm, Tuesday to Thursday from 11 am to 7.30 pm, Saturday from 10 am to 2 pm.

The German Cultural Centre (Deutsches Kulturzentrum; ☎ 194 492), Str Universităţii 7-9, hosts cultural events, film evenings etc.

Its library is open Monday, Wednesday and Friday from 10 am to 2 pm, Tuesday and Thursday from noon to 4 pm. The German Democratic Forum (Demokratisches Forum der Deutschen; ☎ & fax 196 389) is represented at Str Memorandumului 8.

The American Studies Center & Library (☎ 194 315, extension 134), Str Universităţii 7-9, is open Monday to Thursday from 12.30 to 4.30 pm, Friday from 10.30 am to 1 pm.

There is a British Council library (☎ & fax 194 408) at Str Avram Iancu 11. It has an excellent stock of books, magazines and videos and is open Monday and Wednesday from 2 to 5 pm, Tuesday, Thursday and Friday from 9 am to 2 pm. You have to be a member (US$1.20 a year) to borrow books.

The French Cultural Centre (Centre Culturel Francčais; ☎ 198 551, 197 595; fax 193 536; email ccfc@mail.soroscj.ro), inside a branch of the art museum at Str Ion Brătianu 22, arranges contemporary art exhibitions, modern music festivals, jazz nights, and other cultural events. Its library is open weekdays from 9 am to 5 pm.

Medical Services The Napofarm pharmacy on the corner of Piaţa Unirii and Blvd Eroilor is open weekdays from 8 am to 8 pm, and at weekends from 8 am to 2 pm. It has another branch close to the train station at Str Horea 87, open weekdays only from 8 am to 8 pm.

The Spernat Napoca pharmacy on the corner of Piaţa Ştefan cel Mare and Str Iuliu Maniu is open weekdays from 8 am to 8 pm, Saturday from 8 am to 2 pm. On Sunday go to the central pharmacy at Piaţa Unirii 11 which is open daily from 8 am to 8 pm.

Piaţa Unirii

The vast 14th century **St Michael's Church** dominates Piaţa Unirii. The neo-Gothic tower (1859) topping the Gothic hall church creates a great landmark. The church is considered to be one of the finest examples of Gothic architecture in Romania and was built in four stages. The three naves and vestry were the last to be completed at the end of the 16th century. The choir vaults, built in the 14th century, were rebuilt in the 18th century following a fire. Daily services are held in Hungarian and Romanian and organ concerts often take place in the evening. Look for posters in the church porch.

Flanking the church to the south is a huge **equestrian statue** (1902) of the famous Hungarian king Matthias Corvinus (Mátyás Corvinus), the son of Iancu de Hunedoara (János Hunyadi) and ruler of Hungary between 1458-90.

Since 1993, this statue has been at the centre of controversy, largely due to the efforts of the notoriously anti-Hungarian mayor of Cluj-Napoca, Gheorghe Funar. Having erased the *Hungariae* of the original *Hungariae Matthias Rex* inscription on the statue, Funar later gave the go ahead for an archaeological dig to take place in front of the statue. In May 1997 the newly appointed National History Museum director called a halt to the excavation works and made it clear that the statue would not be removed or destroyed. Digging, 'for archaeological, not political reasons', will recommence in 1998. Given the fact that the central forum of the old Roman city is known to lie north of St Michael's Church and that the area currently being excavated is south of the church, the dig is expected to be somewhat futile. Archaeologists have yet to prove that the remains of a Roman temple of the wine god does, in fact, lie in the ugly pit scarring Piaţa Unirii.

On the eastern side of the square is the excellent **National Art Museum** (Muzeul de Artă; ☎ 196 952) housed inside the 18th century baroque Banffy Palace, built in 1791. Its 22 rooms are filled with priceless paintings and artefacts, including a 16th century church altar. It is open daily, except Monday, from 10 am to 4 pm. Admission is US$0.40. The art museum runs a smaller gallery close to the university at Str Ion Brătianu 22.

A **pharmaceutical museum** (Muzeul Farmaciei) is diagonally across the street at Str Gheorghe Doja 1, on the site of Cluj-Napoca's first apothecary (1573). It is open weekdays from 10 am to 4 pm.

If you want to see locally-produced contemporary arts and crafts – which are also for sale – cross the square to the stylish **art gallery** (Galeria de Artă) on the western side of Piaţa Unirii. It is open weekdays from 9 am to 5 pm, Saturday from 10 am to 2 pm.

On the south-western corner of the square, at the eastern end of Blvd Eroilor stands an obelisk monument, topped with a bronze bell, in honour of Transylvania's Memorandumists of 1892.

The Memorandumist monument was

Hungarians

In 1996 Romania and Hungary met to negotiate a groundbreaking 'Basic Treaty' covering trade, border regulations, and the rights of Transylvania's 1.8 million Hungarians. It was followed later in the year by a more concrete accord in which Hungary officially agreed to relinquish all territorial claims on Transylvania. The government in Budapest consequently admitted the move was a 'sell-out' but added that it was a 'necessary' step towards the two countries' admission to the European Union and NATO.

In Cluj-Napoca Hungarian nationalists proclaimed a day of mourning and conducted a death march in the town. A horse-drawn funeral procession snaked through the streets and a death bell tolled.

Despite Cluj-Napoca's citizens re-electing their nationalist major, Gheorghe Funar, the community remains split in 1996 over his blatant anti-Hungarian stance. Amid much controversy the city's Hungarian consulate, which was closed by Ceauşescu in 1988, reopened in July 1997. While hundreds of Romanians and Hungarians gathered in the central square to cheer its opening, Funar said ' I would like to declare the consul *persona non grata* but unfortunately I do not have such power'. In an open letter to the government, the mayor asked that the Hungarian flag and emblem be removed from the consulate building, arguing that the diplomatic mission would encourage movements towards Hungarian autonomy.

As it was, three municipal employees subsequently stole the flag, a second attack on the reinstated flag being thwarted by police just one week later. Funar denied giving his employees the orders but praised their act and gave them each one million lei as a reward for their heroism.

In September 1997 Funar called for the citizens of Târgu Mureş to oust their Magyar mayor, Fodor Imre. He was the first city mayor to implement a governmental decree allowing bilingual signs in cities where an ethnic minority comprises more than 20% of the population. Târgu Mureş became notorious in 1990 as a hotbed of ethnic violence after six people were killed in inter-ethnic clashes. Imre's bilingual signs were vandalised several times by Romanian nationalists who painted over the Hungarian city name with the Romanian tricolour. The signs at the entrance to the city are now protected by six policemen.

Given the vigorous opposition towards granting more language rights to Transylvania's Hungarian minority, the government's promise to reopen the Hungarian section of Cluj-Napoca's Babes-Bolyai university was shelved in late 1997. Despite all this, for most Romanians and Hungarians today, ethnic rivalry is a luxury they can't afford amid the greater financial battle of trying to keep their heads above water. ■

erected in 1994 following an archaeological dig which unearthed remains of what is believed to have been the largest brooch factory in the Roman empire. A treasure trove of 40 different brooches and 8000 moulds was found, some of which are now displayed in Cluj-Napoca's history museum.

An **ethnographic museum** (Muzeul Etnografic al Transilvaniei) with Transylvanian folk costumes, household items and farm implements is just west off the square at Str Memorandumului 21. It is open daily, except Monday, from 9 am to 5 pm. Admission is free but a donation is expected. This is only the indoor section however and true ethnographic fiends should head to the **open-air section** (secţia în aer liber) north-west of the centre in the Hoia forest. Traditional saw mills, wells, wine and oil presses, roadside crosses, fruit dryers,

potters' workshops, sheepfolds and much more are all here in this marvellous outdoor display of folk architecture. Note, however, that many of the exhibits have been 'imported' from the Maramureş region.

Back in town, Str Matei Corvin leads from the north-western corner of the square to the **birthplace** of Matthias Corvinus. The house – No 6 – is closed to the public. A block ahead is a beautifully decorated **Franciscan Church** (Biserica Franciscanilor).

Piaţa Muzeului & Around

At the northern end of Str Matei Corvin, Str Roosevelţ leads into Piaţa Muzeului. At the western end of the square, inside the archaeology and art history institute at Str Constantin Daicoviciu 1, you'll find the **National History Museum of Transylvania** (Muzeul Naţional de Istorie a Transilvaniei;

☎ 191 718, 195 677), open since 1859. All the captions are in Romanian but the museum can usually provide you with an English or French-speaking guide. This museum presents one of the most comprehensive accounts of Transylvanian history. It is open daily, except Monday, from 10 am to 4 pm. Admission is US$0.20.

On the southern side of the square, behind the **statue** of Constantin Daicoviciu (1898-1973), are the remains of an archaeological dig. The remains of two original Roman walls uncovered on the north-eastern corner of the square, opposite the music school housed in a former monastery on Str Victor Deleu, will be preserved as an **archaeological park** (parc arheologic). Excavations started in 1991 after construction workers uncovered parts of walls while laying the foundations for a block of flats. A wooden trunk filled with bronze statuettes and 1268 silver coins dating to the 1st and 3rd centuries were later found. Local archaeologists are also keen to excavate the remains of the northern wall and gate of the Roman city, believed to lie further north of Piaţa Muzeului beneath the small **Caragiale Park** opposite the central telephone office.

Another **Franciscan Church** (Biserica Franciscanilor) stands at the western end of the square. A five minute walk from the square heading towards the river at Str Emil Isac 23 is the **Emil Isac Memorial House**, open daily, except Monday and Tuesday, from 1 to 5 pm. Emil Isac (1886-1954) was a Memorandumist, who lived much of his free life in this house. Continuing north towards the river you pass the **Hungarian State Theatre**, one of two in Romania today.

From here, turn right along Str Gheorghe Bariţiu, then left along Str Independenţei to **Central Park** (Parcul Central) where you can hire boats to row on the small lake. East of the park is the Ursus Beer Factory where Ursus beer has been brewed since 1878. Alternatively, continue walking east along Str Gheorghe Bariţiu then cross the bridge over the river. Bear west towards the towering Hotel Transilvania on top of **Citadel Hill**. On top of the hill is an obelisk monument in

memory of those who died during WWI. Some ruins of the 15th century citadel, enlarged in 1715, still remain. Above the entrance to the crumbling edifice opposite the hotel is a plaque to commemorate the 1848 revolutionary Stephen Ludwig Roth (1706-1849) who was executed here by Habsburg troops on 11 May 1849.

Head back down the hill then bear north along Str Horea. At No 23 is the **Synagogue of the Deportees**. The grand Moorish-style building is just one of three remaining synagogues in Cluj-Napoca. This was built in 1887 in memory of the 16,700 Jews deported to Auschwitz from Cluj-Napoca in 1944. Some 18,000 Jews once lived in the ghetto. In the early 1990s an institute for Jewish and Hebrew studies was established at Cluj-Napoca's Babeş-Bolyai University.

University & Around

The Babeş-Bolyai University of Cluj (☎ 194 315; fax 191 906; email staff@staff .ubbcluj.ro), home to some 17,500 students, is the largest university in Romania after Bucharest. It was founded in 1872 and Hungarian remained the predominant language at the university until 1918 when Transylvania became part of Romania.

The main university building is south of Piaţa Unirii at Str Mihai Kogălniceanu 1. It is named after 19th century mathematician Farkas Bólyai (1775-1856) and scientist Victor Babeş who founded Romania's first school of microbiology and morphology in the early 1900s.

Internationally, Cluj-Napoca's Babeş-Bolyai University is famed for being home to the world's only university institute of speleology. From the main university building walk west to Piaţa Lucian Blaga, then continue along Str Clinicilor. Bear right where the road forks and walk up the small hill. At the top, on the left, is a small **Museum of Zoology**, housed in the university's geology and biology faculty at Str Clinicilor 5. The museum is open weekdays, except Monday, from 9 am to 3 pm, and at weekends from 10 am to 2 pm. Admission is US$0.20.

The **Emil Racoviţă Institute of Speleology** (Institutul de Speologie Emil Racoviţă; ☎ & fax 195 954) is housed on the 2nd floor in the same building. The institute was set up in 1920 by Romanian biologist Emil Racoviţă (1868-1947) and a small **museum** inside the institute has a fascinating collection of his work. It includes extraordinarily detailed drawings of whales, plus original transparencies invented by Racoviţă in 1905. The museum is open weekdays from 9 am to 5 pm. English-speaking professors are happy to show genuinely interested visitors around the museum.

Str Avram Iancu runs west from the university. At No 20 is a memorial plaque to those Romanians who died in the 1848 revolution. Revolutionary leaders Nicolae Bălcescu and George Bariţu both stayed in this house. On Str Mihail Kogălniceanu, running eastwards, parallel to Str Avram Iancu, is a **Hungarian Reformed Church**, built by the king of Hungary Matthias Corvinus in 1486. The statue of St George slaying the dragon in front of the church is a replica of the 14th century original, carved by the Hungarian Kolozsvári brothers, which is now displayed in Prague. Organ concerts are regularly held in the church.

Further east is Piaţa Ştefan cel Mare, at the southern end of which is Piaţa Baba Novac on which **Tailors' Bastion** stands. The bastion, dating from the 1550s, is the only one that remains from the medieval fortified city. The square on which it stands is named after one of Mihai Viteazul's generals who was executed by Hungarian nobles here in the 17th century.

Cluj-Napoca's fragrant **Botanic Gardens** (1930) lie just south of the university at Str Republicii 42. Covering 15 hectares, the green lawns embrace greenhouses, a Japanese garden and a rose garden with some 600 different varieties. In summer, allow several hours to explore it. The gardens are open daily from 9 am to 8 pm.

Trade fairs and exhibitions take place at **Expo-Transylvania** (☎ & fax 419 075), east

---

Brave New World

Emil Racoviţă (1865-1947) was Romania's most heroic scientist. He created a new branch of science through which the great mysteries of the underground world came to be unravelled.

The son of an Iaşi nobleman and a Sorbonne graduate, Emil Racoviţă's first pioneering move was in 1897 aboard the *Belgica* for a polar expedition led by Norwegian explorer Roald Amundsen (the first man to reach the South Pole in 1911).

In March 1898 the *Belgica*, a wooden whaler, became trapped in Antarctic ice. It remained grounded until March 1899 when the intrepid explorers succeeded in cutting a 75m-long channel through the 6m-thick icepack. Ice drifts shifted the ship 3500km during the 12 months it was stuck. Not surprisingly, the 19-strong crew was given up for dead. The expedition provided the first meteorological data recorded hourly over a one year period, as well as a collection of 1600 botanical and zoological specimens.

Emil Racoviţă's adventures whirled him around the globe. In 1904 he discovered a new species of cave crustacean in Majorca. In 1905 he pioneered the use of photographic slides. And in 1907 he published a paper on the problems of biospeleology *(Essai sur les problèmes biospéléologiques)* marking the birth of biospeleology as an independent science. During his lifetime he explored some 1200 caves in Europe (many of which were in Romania) and Africa.

In 1919 Emil Racoviţă was offered the post of zoology professor at Cluj-Napoca university. He refused, explaining he could only come to Cluj-Napoca if a speleology institute were established. On 26 April 1920 the world's first institute of speleology headed by Romania's greatest biologist opened.

Emil Racoviţă remained in Cluj-Napoca until 1940 when, following the Hungarian occupation of northern Transylvania, his institute sought refuge in Timişoara. He returned to Cluj-Napoca in 1944, only to be struck down by pneumonia. Even on his deathbed, Emil Racoviţă remained loyal to his homeland: while famine raged through the country, the heroic professor gracefully declined a dish of chicken and sour cream offered to him, explaining he would eat the same as his famine-struck countrymen – dry *mămăligă*. ■

of the centre on Str Aurel Vlaicu. Also east of the centre, is the **university stadium**, home to FC Universitatea who have matches here regularly. The stadium is close to the Olympic-sized swimming pool (☎ 188 919) at the southern end of **Dr Iuliu Haţieganu University Sports Park** (Parcul Sportiv Universitar Dr Iuliu Haţieganu). Here you will find outside tennis courts, a fitness club, running tracks, an athletes pavilion and the FC Universitatea's club house. Enquire here about footie games. The park is open daily from 9 am to 9 pm. Admission to the park is US$0,20.

Activities

Mountain Biking Mountain bike enthusiasts should contact the Cluj-Napoca Moutain Bike Club (Clubul de Cicloturism; %y142 953) at Str Septimiu Albinii 133, apartment 18, for local advice on good pedalling terrain in the Cluj area. Staff at the Hobby Bike shop at Piaţa Muzeului 4 – all members of the club – are equally well informed and happy to help with queries (see Facts for the Visitor – Activities, for general information on mountain biking in Romania).

Caving Some 12,000 caves have been documented in Romania with about 10 new caves being discovered each year. Many caves are gated and you have to contact the caving club responsible for that cave for permission to enter.

Staff at the Emil Racoviţă Institute of Speleology (☎ & fax 195 954), Str Clinicilor 5 are happy to advise experienced cavers on accessibility etc and can occasionally help arrange expeditions. Staff here speak some French or English

Students from the institute run their own caving club (☎ 195 315, extension 149; email ubbmail@utcluj.ro) which has an office on the ground floor of the main institute building. Meetings are held every Monday and Thursday between 6 and 8 pm. The club arranges expeditions and trips to caves in the region.

See Activities – Caving in the Facts for the

Visitor chapter for more information about caving.

Language Courses

The Hungarian-run ILS Heltai International Language School (☎ 190 811) at Str Clinicilor 18 runs Romanian, Hungarian, English and German language courses. A one month course (24 hours group tuition) costs US$10 per person. The school also offers a one day, six hour course for US$3. The office is open weekdays from 1 to 5 pm.

The ACCESS Language Centre (☎ & fax 420 476; email ovidiu@access.soroscj.ro, ovidiu@lmae.ubb.soroscj.ro), inside the Soros Foundation building at Str Tebei 21, does not run regular Romanian-language courses but can arrange them if there is sufficient demand.

The Fiatest Centru Educational (☎ 135 561), which you'll find at Str Horia 3, provides one hour Romanian-language lessons, costing US$10 for up to five people.

Places to Stay

Camping Up in the hills, 7km south of Cluj-Napoca is *Camping Făget* (☎ 196 234). It opens from mid-May to mid-October and the site's 143 bungalows go for US$5/7 a double/triple. It's US$2/3/5 (single/double/triple) to camp with a tent. The summer-only restaurant here closes at 8 pm. To reach the camping site take bus No 35 from Piaţa Mihai Viteazul south down Calea Turzii to the end of the line. From here it is a marked 2km hike to the site.

Private Rooms Rural tourism experts ANTREC (☎ 215 585, 195 675; fax 191 414) at Piaţa Avram Iancu 15, can arrange rooms in private houses around Cluj-Napoca from US$15 a night. Meals cost extra. The office is open weekdays from 9 am to 5 pm.

The Clubul Ecologic Transilvania (☎ 197 399; fax 190 404), Blvd Eroilor 2, publishes a glossy, 24-page brochure featuring black and white photographs of all the private homes you can stay at in the Apuseni mountains and north-western Transylvania. Houses are graded according to comfort, with a bed for the night costing between US$10 and US$20, including breakfast. Accommodation can be booked at their office or in advance. The club's mailing address for advance copies of its brochure is CP 518, OP 9, RO-3400 Cluj-Napoca.

Opération Villages Roumains (☎ & fax 420 516) arranges rural accommodation in villages throughout the Cluj district and Transylvania. Reservations can be made through its central Cluj-Napoca office, Str Grozavescu 13, RO-3400 Cluj-Napoca. It charges US$10 to US$12 a night, including breakfast. It also has guides to show you around for US$3 an hour or US$10 a day.

Hostels Between 1 July and 1 September the *Hostel Mi-Do* (☎ & fax 186 616) at Str Braşov 2-4 is open. A bed in a four-bed dormitory costs US$7/6 a night, including breakfast. The hostel has lockers. From the train station take trolleybus No 3 three stops to Piaţa Cipariu. From the square walk south along Str Andrei Mureşanu, then take the first left along Str Zrínyi Miklós. At the end of the street turn left onto Str Braşov. The hostel is 50m on the right.

At the time of writing the university's Student Union (Federaţia Organizaţiilor Studenţeşti Cluj; ☎ & fax 196 263; email fosc@mail.soroscj.ro) was making massive efforts to reopen the hostel it formerly ran at its campus on Str Observatorului, 2km south of the centre. Its other major student campus is closer to the centre, straddling Str Bogdan P Haşdeu and Str Professor Ion Marinescu. Contact the Students' Union in room No 4 of the student culture house at Piaţa Lucian Blaga 1-3 for an update.

Hotels – bottom and middle The five-storey *Hotel Delta* (☎ 132 507), at Bus Station No 2 across the bridge from the train station, is convenient and cheap. It costs US$3 for a bed in a shared room with communal bath.

Opposite the train station is the basic *Hotel Pax* (☎ 136 101), Piaţa Gării 1-3. It is noisy but clean and in summer you'll have to battle with hordes of other backpackers for a room.

Singles/doubles/triples with shared bath are US$18/33/39 a night.

Some 150m further east along Str Căii Ferate – a three minute walk from the train station – is the relatively unknown *Hotel Junior* (☎ 432 028), with simple but modern doubles/triples with private bath for US$14 per person.

The best value of the centrally located hotels is the *Hotel Melody* (☎ 197 465), Piaţa Unirii 29. It only has one single for US$10 with shared bath (always busy) and plenty of clean doubles with shared bath for US$17. The downside is you have to queue for a shower in the morning. Close by at Str Gheorghe Doja 20 is the less packed *Hotel Vlădeasa* (☎ 194 429). Single/double/triple/four-bed rooms with private bathroom are US$21/36/43/54. The reception is through an archway adjacent to the Restaurant Vlădeasa.

Overlooking Piaţa Unirii at Str Napoca 1 is the jaded *Hotel Continental* (☎ 195 405, 191 441). Its rooms have seen better days and the tacky restaurant music blasts away until 5 am at weekends. Singles/doubles with shared bath cost US$17/22. Rooms with private bath are US$34/51. You can sometimes get cheaper rates if you book through the first-floor tourism agency inside the hotel.

Further afield, the *Hotel Stadion* (☎ 182 826; fax 182 315), behind the Hotel Napoca at Str General Eremia Grigorescu 5-7, has doubles/triples with private shower for US$22/28. It has no singles.

Football fans can try their luck at the staggeringly plush *Hotel FC Universitatea* (☎ 186 777) west of the centre in the Parcul Sportiv Dr Iuliu Haţeganu. The entrance from the road is on Str Plopilor. Singles/doubles are US$30/45.

The quietest of the cheaper hotels, due to its location on a small, tree-lined avenue, is the three-room *Hotel Piccola Italia* (☎ 136 110), next door to the four-star Vila Casă Albă at Str Emil Racoviţă 20. Doubles with TV and private bath cost US$22. The hotel is run by an elderly couple and has no bar or restaurant.

Hotels – top end A good splurge is the nine-room, four-star *Vila Casă Albă* (☎ & fax 432 277) at Str Emil Racoviţă 22. It's surrounded by gardens on a quiet side street near the base of Citadel Hill and costs US$88 for a double with bath, including breakfast. The hotel has one of the best restaurants and terrace cafés in town.

. Well located in the centre is the elegant, four-star *Vila Continental* (☎ 195 582; fax 1933 977) at Str Gheorghe Şincai 6. Wonderfully luxurious singles/doubles cost US$81/117. Even more decadent apartments are US$140.

Expensive for the ageing rooms it offers is the towering *Hotel Napoca* (☎ 180 715; fax 185 627), close to the central park at Str Octavian Goga 1-3. Singles/doubles with private shower cost US$35/49, including breakfast. A double with private bath is US$49 and luxury apartments start at US$60. The hotel accepts credit cards.

Similarly priced is the *Hotel Sport* (☎ 195 859; fax 193 921), opposite the stadium at Str George Coşbuc 15. Uninspiring singles/doubles/triples are US$39/63/83, including breakfast. Rooms have a telephone and remote-controlled TV.

Attractive from a distance but ugly close up is the three-star *Hotel Transilvania* (☎ 432 071; fax 432 076), overlooking the city on Citadel Hill. It remains an old favourite with business travellers. Luxury singles/doubles/triples with satellite TV and telephone are US$68/88/116, including breakfast.

A fair bet is the modern *Hotel Victoria* (☎ 197 963; fax 197 573) at Blvd 21 Decembrie 1989, 52-54. Its 18 rooms have cable TV and cost US$45/43/67. The hotel has a pleasant terrace café.

Out of Town *Hotel Liliacul* (☎ 488 129; fax 438 130), 2km south of Cluj-Napoca on the Cluj-Turda highway at Str Calea Truzi 252, is a modern motel with a fine restaurant and luxurious singles/doubles/triples with private bathroom and colour TV for US$25/28/36. It also has a handful of US$10 wooden cabins.

Further afield is *Motel KM17 17* (☎ 231 425), 17km north of Cluj-Napoca in Jucu village. Singles/doubles cost US$6/12. Breakfast is an extra US$3.50.

Places to Eat

Restaurants Among the top places to eat in town is the trendy *Napoca 15* (☎ 190 655) street-terrace café and restaurant at Str Napoca 15. Its oozing hot breaded cheese, for US$1.20, just melts in your mouth. Have a Napoca house salad with it and you'll be coming back here time and time again. It is open daily from 9 am to midnight.

The *P&P Ristorante* (☎ 192 666) at Blvd Eroilor 12b serves good pizza, as well as breakfast omelettes and sunny-side-up eggs. Beyond that, the menu is uninspiring although a couple of meat dishes do crop up occasionally. It is open daily from 10 am to 11 pm. *Primăvara Pizza* at Blvd Eroilor 26 has a terrace garden, open weekdays from 8 am to 9 pm, Saturday from 10 am to 9 pm, Sunday from noon to 8 pm. Opposite is the local *Restaurant Crişul*.

For hearty portions of meat, potatoes and more traditional soups, spicy meatballs and hot breaded cheese, the *Restaurant Specializat*, close to Hotel Vlădeasu on Str Gheorghe Doja, is the place to go. This small restaurant tends to attract a lot of older people thanks to the US$1.20 'pensioners special' it offers but is worthy of a visit nonetheless. It is open daily from 9 am to 11 pm.

Also serving local cuisine in a somewhat greyer setting is the ageing *Restaurant Fetitele Vienezel* at Str Memorandumului 11. The restaurant has clearly been around for years; a pork cutlet is US$0.70, grilled mushrooms are US$1 and pizzas served in its adjoining *Saloon Pizza* start at US$0.30. It is open weekdays from 9 am to 10 pm, weekends from 10 am to 8 pm.

If you want game (quail on good nights), head for *Hubertus* at Blvd 21 Decembrie 1989 22. It has a small courtyard decorated in hunting motifs. Cognac is the traditional start to a meal here. It is closed on Sunday.

Popular for its lakeside location rather

than the cuisine is the *Restaurant Parc* and adjoining *La Grădină* terrace café on the south-western edge of Central Park. It is open Monday to Thursday from 10 am to 10 pm, Friday, Saturday and Sunday from 8 pm to 3 am. It has live bands playing most weekends.

Diners who are into football, look no further than the upmarket *FC Universitatea* restaurant in Parcul Sportiv Dr Iuliu Haţeganu. The entrance from the road is on Str Plopilor.

Any student will be the first to tell you that the food slapped out in the *student canteen* on the Str Professor Ion Marinescu campus is pretty disgusting. The canteen cuisine on the Str Observatorului campus is considered no better. However, if you want a full meal for less than US$1, these are the places to go, Both are open daily during term (September to July) from 9 am to 6 pm.

The *Ceasar Restaurant* close to the main university building at Str Avram Iancu 16 is small and simple but smells really good!

Cafés The *Boema Grădină de Vară* at Str Iuliu Maniu 34 is a pleasant terrace café in a courtyard off the main street. It has live music some evenings and is open daily from 10 am to 11 pm.

If you want to mingle with a younger crowd try the *Student Club*, run by university students in a garden directly behind the student culture house. You can enter from the street of Piaţa Lucian Blaga 1-3 or from the official entrance inside the house. *Bar Niko* and *Spaghetti*, behind the student campus on Str Piezişă, are two other, busy, students' haunts worth a drink or two. Close by at Str Molilor 2 is the low-budget *Eros* café. On the wall outside there is a memorial plaque to eight people who died here on 21 December 1989.

Students also hang out at *New Crolo*, a popular pizzeria up the hill on Str Victor Babes near the botanical gardens. It is open daily from 8 am to 5 pm and 6 pm to 1 am.

The *Coroana* beer garden, shaded beneath trees in the small park opposite the Hungarian opera and theatre, on the corner of Str Emil Isac and Str Pavlov serves lots of Coroana beer and is always packed. It is open daily from 10 am until sunset. Opposite, on the corner of Str Emil Isac and Str Gheorghe Baritiu is its direct competitor, the *Decanat* beer garden, which only serves Ursus brew for US$0.30 a glass.

The *Continental Café*, adjoining the Hotel Continental at Str Napoca 1, serves calorie-laden chocolate cakes and other sweet delights.

Fast Food Ask any student and you'll get the same reply: the *Fast Food* joint next to the central department store on Str Gheorghe Doja is the only genuine fast food outlet in town. Pizzas start at US$0.75 and a plate of vegetables, spaghetti, meat stew, cutlet and fries etc – served from a canteen-style counter – is around US$1. It is open weekdays from 9 am to 9 pm, Saturday from 9 am to 7 pm.

Almost directly opposite on the same street is the Italian-inspired *Pizza Pazza* which, with its bizarre concoction of toppings, certainly lives up to its 'nutty' name. It is open daily from 9 am to 9 pm.

Dorna, at Piaţa Unirii 14, sells a great selection of cakes and pastries and also filled rolls and sandwiches to take away. It is open daily, except Sunday, from 10 am to 7 pm.

Fast Food Max, at Str Memorandumului 24, is a clean, modern outlet with an open front onto the street. It is open daily from 10 am to 10 pm.

McDonald's, in front of the central market on Piaţa Mihai Viteazul, is open weekdays from 7 am to midnight and at weekends until 1 am.

Self-Catering For fresh produce, stroll through the packed *central market*, behind McDonald's on Piaţa Mihai Viteazul. For tinned and dry products try the central department store *Centrală* on Str Gheorghe Doja, open weekdays from 8 am to 9 pm, Saturday from 9 am to 3 pm.

The small *supermarket & shopping mall* on the corner of Str Memorandumului and Str Dávid Ferenc is open 24 hours. The

Paniro Patisserie at Blvd 21 Decembrie 1989, 37 is the place to go for fresh cakes and pastries.

Entertainment

Posters advertising what's on where are displayed on bill boards outside the student culture house on Piaţa Lucian Blaga.

Cinema All cinemas in Cluj-Napoca show films in their original language with subtitles in Romanian. The *Cinema de Artă* on the corner of Str Universităţii and Str Ion Brătianu; the *Cinema Republicii* on Piaţa Mihai Viteazul; *Cinema Victoriei* on Blvd Eroilor; and the *Cinema Favorit* at Str Horea 6, all have daily showings at 11 am, 1, 3, 5 and 7 pm. Tickets cost US$0.75/0.50 for adults/students.

Bars & Clubs A favourite haunt among students, expats and diplomats alike is the alternative and very funky *Music Pub* (☎ 432 517), not far from the train station at Str Horea 5. The beer flows from 9 to 3 am inside this trendy cellar bar which hosts live folk, jazz and rock bands most weekends. Ursus Premium Pils is US$0.50 a pint.

Popular with Cluj-Napoca's bright young things is the more expensive *Diesel Club* (☎ 198 441) at Piaţa Unirii 17. During the day it is a simple café; at night it's transformed into a vibrating music club. Live concerts are regularly held in the vast cellars. It is open daily from 9 to 1 am.

The *Art Club*, next door to the Agenţie de Teatrală at Piaţa Ştefan cel Mare 14, is the last of Cluj-Napoca's elitist trio. Posters advertising rock concerts, jazz festivals and plays plaster the walls of the hip café, so laidback you're compelled to sit, smoke and chat for hours on end. It has one pool table and is open weekdays from 9 am to midnight, weekends from noon to midnight.

The *Harley Davidson Club*, a couple of doors down from the Diesel Club at Piaţa Unirii 15, was clearly not 'in' at the time of writing given its distinct lack of clientele. It does have billiard tables, however.

Theatre & Classical Music The neo-baroque *National Theatre & Opera House* (1906) on Piaţa Ştefan cel Mare was designed by the famous Viennese architects Fellner and Hellmer and a performance here is well attended. Tickets can be bought in advance from the Agenţie de Teatrală (☎ 195 363) at Piaţa Ştefan cel Mare 14. The ticket office is open Tuesday to Friday from 11 am to 5 pm. Tickets for classical concerts hosted by the *State Philharmonic* (filharmonia de stat; ☎ 430 060) at Str Mihail Kogălniceanu are also sold here. Look out for performances at the *Puck puppet theatre* (Teatrul de Păpuşi Puck) in a courtyard at Blvd Eroilor 8.

Plays and operas in Hungarian are performed at the *Hungarian State Theatre & Opera* at the northern end of Str Emil Isac, close to the river. Tickets are sold in advance at the box office (☎ 193 4468) inside the theatre.

Organ recitals are held two or three times a week in St Michael's Church (see Piaţa Unirii earlier). The Salā de Expoziţii inside the Lucian Blaga university library (Bibliotecii Lucian Blaga) on Piaţa Lucian Blaga occasionally hosts classical music and organ concerts. Ask for information at the library office, open weekdays from 8 am to 1.45 pm and from 2.30 to 9 pm.

Things to Buy

Stylish crafts, paintings and out-of-the-norm souvenirs are sold at the small Artistilor Plastik art gallery close to the Hotel Continental on Str Napoca; it is open weekdays from 9 am to 5 pm, Saturday from 10 am to 2 pm.

Getting There & Away

Air TAROM has daily flights, except Sunday, to/from Bucharest via Oradea. A single/return Cluj-Napoca-Bucharest fare is US$45/90. Tickets can be bought at the airport one hour before departure or from the TAROM city office (☎ 432 524) at Piaţa Mihai Viteazul 11. It is open weekdays from 7 am to 7 pm, and Saturday from 9 am to 1 pm. Air Transilvania (☎ & fax 194 963) inside the Hotel Victoria, and Air Tracia

(☎ 197 806; ☎ & fax 192 097), Blvd Eroilor 6-8, are both agents for TAROM.

Bus Buses to southern and central Transylvania depart from Autogară 2. Daily bus services include one daily to Abrud (127km), Alba Iulia (99km), Brad (165km) and Sibiu (230km); and four daily to Câmpeni (116km); and five to Zalău (86km).

From Autogară No 1 buses also run to Turda (27km) every half hour between 5.30 and 10 pm.

A daily bus from Cluj-Napoca to Budapest departs from Autogară No 1 at 7 am (399km). Single tickets costing US$6 are sold at the bus station.

There are also many more expensive, private buses that trundle their way west to Hungary and further on to western Europe. The Agenţie de Turism KM0 sells tickets for these.

Train The Agenţie de Voiaj CFR (☎ 432 001) at Piaţa Mihai Viteazul 20, is open weekdays from 7 am to 8 pm. Tickets for international trains have to be bought in advance from this office.

From Cluj-Napoca, there is one daily train to Kraków, departing from Cluj-Napoca at 10.50 am and arriving in Kraków (20 hours) at 4.50 am.

The speedy *Ady Endre* train to Budapest leaves Cluj-Napoca daily at 7.50 am (4¼ hours). Slower daily Braşov-Budapest trains which stop at Cluj-Napoca include the *Corona* and the *Claudiopolis*. Journey time is 6½ hours.

Cluj-Napoca is well served by national trains. For Sibiu you sometimes have to change trains at Copşa Mică. For Alba Iulia, you often have to change at Teiuş.

Getting Around

To/From the Airport Cluj-Napoca airport (☎ 192 238, 145 077) is 8km east of the town centre in Someeni district. Bus No 8 runs from Piaţa Mihai Viteazul to the airport.

Car The cheapest rental deal in town is offered by Jet Tour (☎ & fax 194 498), Str Doja 7, which rents out sturdy white Dacias for US$44 a day, including 500 free kilometres a day. Bookings can also be made through the Continental Agenţie de Turism (see Information – Travel Agencies).

The Automobil Clubul Român (see Information – Travel Agencies) charges US$71/60/51 a day unlimited distance for a one-to-three/four-to-six/seven day deal on a Dacia 1410. The daily rate for a Ford Fiesta starts at US$83.

The more expensive Consus Rent a Car (☎ 192 928; ☎ & fax 193 044; email consus @cjx.logicnet.ro; www.consustr.logictl .com) at Str Gheorghe Şincai 15 rents Ford Escorts/Audi 80s for US$65/95 a day or US$150/220 for a weekend. A chauffeur-driven car costs US$130 a day.

Avis (☎ 432 071; fax 432 076) is based inside the Hotel Transylvania. It charges US$97 a day unlimited distance for a Ford Fiesta.

Tram, Trolleybus & Bus Tram No 101 runs from the train station into town. Trolleybus No 4 connects Bus Station No 1 to the centre. Bus No 27 takes you within a 10 minute walk of the open-air ethnographic museum north west of the centre in Horea forest.

Taxi To call a cab dial ☎ 166 666, 166 866.

Bicycle Ask about rental at the Cluj-Napoca Mountain Bike Club (Clubul de Cicloturism) (☎ 142 953) (see Mountain Biking earlier in this section). The Hobby Bike shop on Piaţa Muzeului 4 sells spare parts and fixes broken bicycles; it is open weekdays from 10 am to 6 pm.

TURDA
* *area code* ☎ *064, pop 58,000*

Turda, 27km south-east of Cluj-Napoca, was the seat of the Transylvanian diet in the mid-16th century and hence once one of the richest towns in the region. Today, this small market town preserves a number of stately baroque and Magyar façades. Your reason for coming here will, however, be strictly practical – to hike or catch a bus to Turda

Gorge (Cheile Turzii), 9km west. In the 13th century this was an important salt mining town.

Turda hit the national headlines in 1997 when hundreds of crows attacked the town, Hitchcock-style.

Orientation & Information

Turda's handful of shops is centred around the main street, Str Republicii. The central post and telephone office is at Str Republicii 31. It is open daily from 6 am to 8 pm. The Agenţie de Voiaj CFR (☎ 11 672), Str Republicii 35, is open weekdays from 8 am to 7 pm.

You can change money at the Bancă Comercială Română at Str Republicii 29, open weekdays from 8.30 am to 2 pm. The Cambio Currency Exchange is next door to the CFR office at Str Republicii 34. It is open weekdays from 8.30 am to 4.30 pm, Saturday from 9 am to 1 pm.

Salt Mines

Salt was first mined at the Turda salt mines (☎ 311 690) at Str Salinelor 54 in 1271. Following their closure in 1932, the abandoned 45sq km mines were used as a cheese deposit for the region. Today, part of the site serves as a day centre for people suffering from lung and bronchial diseases, as the centre remains at a constant 10°C.

Most of the deeper mines, including Ghezala (80m), which is partially filled with a lake, are no longer safe. Visitors can, however, have a one hour guided tour around the Rudolph mine and along a 400m stretch of the 900m-long main tunnel. It is open daily from 9 am to 3 pm. Admission is US$1.20.

To get to the mine, turn left at the first fork in the village (approaching from the north) onto Str Besarabiei. Go straight across the crossroads to the end of Str Tunel, then turn left onto Str Salinelor.

Turda Gorge

Turda Gorge (Cheile Turzii) is a short, but stunning, break in the granite mountains south-west of Turda. You can hike the gorge's length in under an hour, so plan on camping for a night or two in order to explore the surrounding network of marked trails – the map outside the Cabana Cheile Turzii, at the southern foot of the gorge, details a half dozen different routes. Staff at the cabana also distribute free photocopies of the *Cheile Turzii şi Împrejurimi Trasee Turistice* map indicating all the major hiking trails and cabanas in the region. There is some form of accommodation at the end of most trails (see Places to Stay & Eat later in this section).

From Turda village a trail marked by blue crosses (three to four hours) leads hikers the 13km from the village, through Mihai Viteazul village to the Cabana Cheile Turzii at the southern foot of the gorge. An alternative cross-country route (two hours) from Turda to the gorge is also clearly marked (red crosses).

A good two hour trek is the circular red cross trail through the gorge, followed by the steep red circle trail up and over the peak before returning to the Cabana Cheile Turzii (450m). It's also possible to go from Turda Gorge to Cluj-Napoca, along the vertical red stripe trail via Deleni and Camping Făget (on the outskirts of Cluj-Napoca). Signs claim you can do this 29km hike in 10 hours, but 12 hours is more realistic.

From the Cabana Cheile Turzii, another trail marked by red triangles heads west to the Cabana Buru (12.5km, four to five hours). To get to Corneşti, follow the yellow triangle trail from the Cabana Cheile Turzii. It is 9.2km and should take about four hours.

Most people access the gorge from the Cabana Cheile Turzii, 7km north-west of Mihai Veatuzul village. The turn-off marked Cheile Turzii is signposted 2km west of Mihai Veatuzul on the main Turda-Abrud road.

It is also possible to approach the gorge at its more dramatic northern end, from the village of Petreşti de Jos. Upon entering the village, bear left at the first fork; from here, a trail is marked with red crosses.

Băile Turda

Only 2km east of Turda lies the small spa

resort of Băile Turda, allegedly built on the site of an old Roman saltmine. The resort's outdoor swimming pool gets packed in summer. There are a couple of tennis courts and a small **zoo** (parcul zoologic), open daily except Monday and Friday from 10 am to 6 pm.

Câmpii Turzii

Lying 5km east of Băile Turda is the small village of Câmpii Turzii. This is the place where the Wallachian prince Mihai Viteazul was assassinated, but the Wallachian prince is still hailed as the crusader of Romanian nationalism.

Viteazul's head, severed upon his capture, was buried in Dealu Monastery just outside Târgovişte. It was at this monastery that Mihai Viteazul had sworn his allegiance to the Hungarian emperor Rudolph II in 1598.

Places to Stay & Eat

Turda's lone hotel is the *Potaissa* (☎ 311 691) on the corner of Piaţa Republicii and Str George Coşbuc. It is a basic place priced at US$16 a night for a bed in a single/double with shared bath, including breakfast.

In Băile Turda the *Hotel Bradul* (☎ 315 029), Str Ceanului 1, has singles/doubles in what is no more than a private house for US$7 per person a night. The bathroom is shared and hot water is not guaranteed. Close by, on Str Ceanului next to the bus stop, is the busier *Hotel Ariesul* (☎ 316 844; fax 311 124) which offers medicinal baths, saunas and massages as well as double rooms for US$11 a night, including breakfast.

The best bet is the *Cabana Cheile Turzii* at the southern foot of the Turda Gorge. A bed in a single/double/triple in the main building costs US$4/3.50/3 a night including a 'cheese, ham and herbal tea' breakfast. A night's sleep in a wooden hut is US$2. Simple sausage meals are cooked up in the small, family restaurant. Alternatively pitch your tent for free in the grassy valley close to the river.

Heading west from the Turda gorge there are a couple of options within easy hiking reach: 3km west of Mihai Viteazul in the village of Corneşti is the modern and flashy *Motel Ciprian* (☎ 315 923). A bed in a double room with shared bathroom is US$10. The adjoining restaurant is open 24 hours.

Six kilometres further west, in the village of Buru, is the *Cabana Buru*, a two-star restaurant and hotel with wooden bungalows in the forest which can be rented for US$3 per person a night. Single/double/triple rooms in the main building are US$11/7/6 a night.

Getting There & Away

From Cluj-Napoca's Autogară 1 buses depart every half hour between 5.30 and 10 pm for Turda village (27km). The last bus back from Turda to Cluj-Napoca is at about 5.30 pm.

From Turda there are buses to Corneşti and less frequent ones to Câmpeni. Both depart from Piaţa Republicii in the centre of the town. Both stop 2km west of Mihai Viteazul village, next to the signposted turn-off for Cheile Turzii.

From here it is a 5km hike along a gravel road to the Cabana Cheile Turzii. If you are driving, do not attempt this steep road after heavy rains.

From Turda there are two local trains daily to Abrud (five hours). Stops en route include Cabana Buru (40 minutes), Câmpeni (83km) and Roşia Montană (4¾ hours).

From the centre of Turda, bus No 2 runs hourly from Str Republicii to Băile Turda.

ZALĂU

● *area code* ☎ *060 , pop 51,000*

Zalău, 86km north-west of Cluj-Napoca, is an uninspiring provincial town in the foothills of the Meşes mountains. The first town to be chronicled in Transylvania, it was here that the Roman-Dacians built what is believed today to have been the most important military and cultural stronghold in the Roman-Dacian empire.

Orientation & Information

The bus station is 1km north of the centre at Str Mihai Viteazul 54. Bus No 1 runs from the centre to the train station which is 6km north of the centre in the village of Crişeni.

You can change money, cash travellers cheques and get cash advance on Visa/MasterCard at the Bancă Comercială Română at Piaţa Iuliu Maniu 2. It is open weekdays from 8.15 to 11.45 am and 2 to 8 pm, Saturday from 10 am to 6 pm.

Roman Porolissum

The Roman settlement of Porolissum stood on the ultimate northern boundary of Roman Dacia. The Romans built a camp here in 106 AD. The small settlement was rapidly fortified with earth and stone walls, ditches and small fortlets following which it developed as a leading administrative, economic and civilian centre. By the end of the 2nd century, it had been granted the status of a municipality.

The 'Municipium Septimium Porolissensis', which some historians believe could even have briefly served as the capital of Dacia, was built within the walls of a giant castle. The 20,000 inhabitants who lived behind the walls – which measured 230m by 300m – were defended by some 7000 soldiers.

Many of the walls have today been rebuilt on the original site of the Porolissum – a windy and wild heath above Zalău town. The main entrance to the castle, the stadium and the amphitheatre, have all been partially reconstructed enabling visitors to appreciate the enormity of an original Roman stronghold. A lone shepherd, who tends the site, guides visitors around for US$0.20 per person. If he is not at the main entrance to the complex, try the house marked *casă* on the small dirt track leading up to the castle. To get to the Porolissum, take bus No 8 from the central bus stop on Str Mihai Viteazul to the village of Moigrad. From here it is a good 20 minute hike uphill to the fortress.

The history of the Roman fortress is explained in the **Zalău History Museum** (Muzeul de Istorie; ☎ 612 223) in Zalău town centre at Str Unirii 9. Various Roman-Dacian statues unearthed in the Porolissum are displayed here. The museum is open

daily, except Monday, from 10 am to 6 pm. It also has a small **art museum** (Muzeul de Artă; ☎ 633 137) close by at Str Gheorghe Doja 6.

Places to Stay

Zalău has two hotels next door to each other. Ranking bottom is the hideous *Hotel Porolissum* (☎ 615 220) which has outdated singles/doubles/triples for US$9/16/22. Bathrooms are shared.

Next door is the marginally more modern *Hotel Mereş* (☎ 661 050, 616 431) at Str Unirii 5. Singles/doubles/triples with private bathroom and hot water all day are US$16/24/18, including a breakfast of fresh bread, jam, eggs and decent coffee. It accepts Visa/MasterCard.

Some 10km south of town on the main Zalău-Cluj-Napoca road is the *Popasul Romanilor* (☎ 060-661 094). It is a large upmarket place with a small campsite and comfortable double rooms with private bathroom for US$20.

Getting There & Away

Bus The bus station is 1km north of the centre at Str Mihai Viteazul 54. Daily bus services from Zalău include two to Baia Mare (100km), Dej (102km) and Huedin (58km); one to Târgu Lapuş (76km) and Ciucea (31km); three to Bucium (15km); and five to Cluj-Napoca (86km) and Oradea (176km).

Train The Agenţie de Voiaj CFR (☎ 612 885) is at Str Tudor Vladimirescu 2. Zalău is a small branch line between Carel and Jibou. To get to Dej, Braşov, Székely Land, Baia Mare and Bucharest, change trains at Jibou. From Zalău there is one direct train daily to Satu Mare (two hours), 12 trains daily to Jibou (seven hours).

TREZNEA & IP

Following the annexation of 43,493sq km of northern Transylvania to pro-Nazi Hungary in August 1940, police plundered the village of Treznea, massacring 86 villagers. They then continued north-west to Ip, 16km west of Şimleu Silvaniei, where they murdered a further 158 villagers. Both villages have been known ever since as 'villages of the Romanian Martyrs' (Locaclităţi Martir ale Neamului Românesc).

In the old cemetery in Treznea is a **memorial grave** to the victims. The oldest killed was 86, the youngest three years old.

To get to Treznea, follow the Zalău-Cluj-Napoca road for 10km, then turn left at the signpost for the *Locaclităţi Martir ale Neamului Românesc*. One bus daily departs at 4.15 pm for Treznea from Zalău bus station.

Ip is only accessible by private transport. Head 4km north from Zalău then turn left to Şimleu Silvaniei. Ip is 42km west along this road.

CLUJ-NAPOCA TO BISTRIŢA

There are four places worth stopping at on the main road north-east from Cluj-Napoca to Bistriţa. Three are pleasant, the fourth appalling.

Gherla

A predominantly Armenian settlement called Armenopolis in the 17th century, the small market town of Gherla, 45km north of Cluj-Napoca, has a pretty Renaissance-style castle and a baroque Armenian church (1784-1804).

The town is best known, however, for its prison. **Gherla prison**, still functioning today, gained notoriety in the 1950s for its so-called 'student re-education programme'. Under this scheme, hundreds of dissident students were psychiatrically manipulated so that they became torturers of fellow inmates. In 1951 the re-education programme was halted but conditions inside the prison remained harsh. In 1970 during floods, 600 prisoners drowned in their cells after the prison director ordered the inmates to be locked in before fleeing the building himself.

In the cemetery close to the prison is a **memorial** to those who died at Gherla, erected in 1993.

The prison, Str Andrei Mureşan 2, is the large white building on the left as you enter

Gherla at its southern end. As you face the prison from the main road, the cemetery is to the right on Str Dejelui. An overgrown Hungarian cemetery is next to the Romanian one.

Gherla has a small **History Museum** (Muzeul de Istorie) just off the main square at Str Mihai Viteazul 6. The exhibition conveniently fails to mention the existence of any prison in Gherla. It is open weekdays from 8 am to 3 pm.

Places to Stay There is a cheapo, one-star *hotel* on the main square, Piaţa Libertăţii. Just 1km south of the town is the *Băile Băiţe* (✆ 060-241 576), a large complex with an outside swimming pool, tennis courts, terrace restaurant and bar. It has 24 double rooms costing US$20 a night.

Nicula

Nine kilometres east of Gherla is the small village of Nicula, famed for its 16th century monastery and exquisite icons painted on glass.

The age-old folk art of painting on glass was practised in Nicula as early as the 11th and 12th centuries. Icons of the saints were painted and put in peasants' houses to keep evil spirits at bay. Nicula only became famed for its glass icons in the 18th century when, according to legend, an icon of the Virgin Mary in the wooden church of the village monastery miraculously started shedding tears. Henceforth, icons painted on glass in Nicula became a much sought after item as it is believed that an icon of the Virgin Mary contains healing powers. Peasants wash the icon with water from the epiphany then give this water to people consumed by an evil spirit.

Năsăud & Around

Năsăud is actually 24km north of Bistriţa. At Beclean, 26km east from Dej on the Cluj-Napoca-Bistriţa road, you can continue south-west to Bistriţa or bear left to make a detour via **Năsăud**.

This region is best known for its strong folk traditions and for the many writers who have sought inspiration in these parts. In **Salva**, 2km west of Năsăud men still don their traditional straw or felt hats topped with peacock feather while women adorn their hair with dozens of tiny braids.

Nine kilometres north of Năsăud is **Coşbuc,** a small village overlooking the river Szalva and named after the poet George Coşbuc (1866-1918) who was born and spent his childhood years in the village. The life and works of the man known as the 'poet of peasantry' are recounted in the small memorial museum – a white cottage in the centre of the village.

The novelist Liviu Rebreanu (1885-1944) was born in the village of the same name, 3km south of Năsăud on the road to Bistriţa. Rebreanu left his village at the age of 23 (1908) to serve a year in the Habsburg army before moving to Bucharest to establish himself as a writer. The **Liviu Rebreanu Memorial House** (Casă Memorial Liviu Rebreanu) is immediately on the right as you enter the village from the north.

Both museums are open daily, except Monday, from 9 am to 5 pm. Admission is US$0.20.

Places to Stay Năsăud's lone hotel, the two-star *Sălăuta* (☎ 063-372 601) at Str Ioan Prodan is an age-old establishment with grim, but dirt-cheap singles/doubles for US$2.50/5 night. A supposedly 'luxury' apartment is US$10. Rooms have private bathrooms but there is no hot running water. Breakfast is not included.

BISTRIŢA
• *area code* ☎ *063 , pop 79,500*
Bistriţa lies at the south-western end of the Bârgău valley and Tihuta mountain pass which leads from Transylvania into Moldavia. This small market town is at the heart of 'Dracula land'. It was here that Bram Stoker made his leading character, Jonathan Harker, stay the night on the eve of St George's day before continuing his journey east to Dracula's castle.

First chronicled in 1264, Bistriţa (Bistritz in German) was one of the seven towns

founded by the Saxons whose presence still lives on in the old town's quaint 15th and 16th century merchants houses. Witch trials were common in Bistriţa during medieval times.

Orientation
The bus and train stations are next to each other at the western end of town on Str Rodnei. Exit the station and walk to the eastern end of Str Rodnei then turn right along Str Gării. At the crossroads, turn left along Str Gheorghe Şincai to get to the central square, Piaţa Centrală.

The hotels are clustered north-east of the central square around Piaţa Petru Rareş. The Bistriţa river cuts across the south of the town.

Maps The accurate *Hartă Stradală a Municipiului Bistriţa*, published by Mediaprint, is sold for US$0.20 in bookshops and newsagents.

Information
Tourist Offices The tourist office (☎ 211 872, 216 465; fax 216 260) inside the Coroana de Aur on Piaţa Petru Rareş sells tickets for private buses to Germany, arranges day trips to Dracula's castle on the Tihuta pass, and is an agent for TAROM and rural tourism specialists ANTREC. The office is open weekdays from 9 am to 7 pm, Saturday from 9 am to noon.

The Transylvanian Society of Dracula (☎ 231 803, 232 260) has an office inside the Agenţie de Turism (☎ 212 056; fax 232 260) at Piaţa Petru Rareş 7a. Staff can arrange expensive, tacky Dracula tours. The office is open weekdays from 10 am to 4 pm.

The Automobil Clubul Român (ACR) has an office at Str Dornei 45.

Money You can change money, cash travellers cheques and get cash advance on Visa/MasterCard at the Bancă Comercială Română next to the Hotel Bistriţa on Piaţa Petru Rareş. The bank is open weekdays from 8 am to 3.15 pm, Saturday from 8 am to noon. It has an ATM outside.

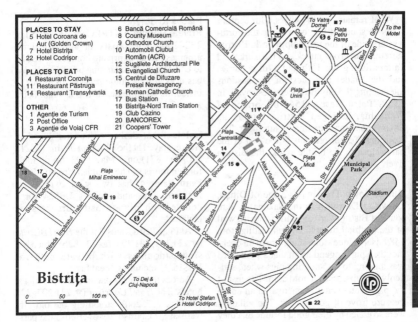

PLACES TO STAY
5 Hotel Coroana de
  Aur (Golden Crown)
7 Hotel Bistrița
22 Hotel Codrișor

PLACES TO EAT
4 Restaurant Coronița
11 Restaurant Păstruga
14 Restaurant Transylvania

OTHER
1 Agenție de Turism
2 Post Office
3 Agenție de Voiaj CFR

6 Bancă Comercială Română
8 County Museum
9 Orthodox Church
10 Automobil Clubul
   Român (ACR)
12 Sugălete Architectural Pile
13 Evangelical Church
15 Centrul de Difuzare
   Presei Newsagency
16 Roman Catholic Church
17 Bus Station
18 Bistrița-Nord Train Station
19 Club Cazino
20 BANCOREX
21 Coopers' Tower

Bistrița

To Vatra Dornei
To the Motel
To Dej &
Cluj-Napoca
To Hotel Ștefan
& Hotel Codrișor

TRANSYLVANIA

BANCOREX has a branch on the corner of Str Lupeni and Str Gării. It is open weekdays from 8 to 11 am.

Post & Communications The post office is sandwiched between the CFR office and the Agenție de Turism on Piața Petru Rareș.

Bookshops Some books and city maps are sold in the Centrul de Difuzare Presei opposite the church on Piața Centrală. It is open weekdays from 9 am to 3 pm, Saturday from 9 am to noon.

Media Listen to the latest scandals with Radio Bistrița on 71 FM.

Things to See
The large **evangelical church** (Biserica Evangelica) dominates the central Piața Centrală. Built by the Saxons in the 14th century, the Gothic-style church with its magnificent 76.5m-tall steeple still serves

the small Saxon community that remains in Bistrița today. At the time of writing the church was being renovated.

Facing the church on the north side of the square is the **Sugălete** pile, the domain of Bistrița's Saxon merchants. Built between 1480 and 1550, the 13 houses were bound together with stone arches. In the 16th century, a portico was added to the length of the terraced buildings, providing shelter in bad weather for those frequenting the merchants' workshops on the ground floor.

Walk east along Blvd Liviu Rebreanu to Piața Unirii. Here an **Orthodox Church** (Biserica Ortodoxă), built between 1270 and 1280, is the centrepiece. A **statue** of Romanian novelist Liviu Rebreanu stands on the square. The **Bistrița County Museum** (Muzeul Bistrița) is just off Piați Unirii at the western end of Blvd General Grigore Bălan. More inspiring museums exist elsewhere. This one is open daily, except Monday, from 10 am to 6 pm. Admission is US$0.20.

What remains of the city's 13th century walls lie south of the town along the north-western side of the **municipal park**. Bistriţa suffered numerous attacks by the Turks and Tartars during the 16th and 17th centuries and the citadel and most of the bastions intersecting the city wall were destroyed. In 1530, Petru Rareş (1541-6), prince of Wallachia, besieged Bistriţa forcing its Saxon inhabitants to finally surrender. The **Coopers' Tower** remains at the east of the park, close to the bridge across the Bistriţa river.

Out of Town The small village of **Dipşa**, known as Dürrbach to the Saxons, is 7km south of Bistriţa. On top of the southern wall of the Gothic Lutheran church, dating from 1489, is a unique stone sculpture of an open-mouthed pig. Legend has it that a swineherd was tending to his snouting pigs when, suddenly, one disclosed a gold coin. The rest of the pigs then excitedly uncovered an entire treasure trove of gold pieces. The villagers were so elated by their good fortune that they built a church in thanks to the pigs.

Activities

The Transylvanian Society of Dracula (see Information – Tourist Offices) arranges Dracula tours which take in the kitsch castle on the Tihuta pass. It also arranges mock 18th century **witch trials** in Bistriţa. Women suspected of witchcraft had their feet and hands bound before being immersed in the river. If they sank, it meant they were innocent. Survival was the ultimate proof of a pact with the devil, and the woman was then taken to the central square and burnt at the stake.

The Dracula Society re-enacts these gruesome events, down to a 'witch', judge and jury and a thronging crowd. Fortunately for the society, tradition says that if a man from the onlooking crowd asks the judge for the woman's hand in marriage, she is saved. To book a trial you have to contact the society well in advance. The show is only put on for groups.

Places to Stay

Private Rooms ANTREC (☎ 231 803; fax 232 260), specialists in agro-tourism, arranges rooms in private homes for US$12 to US$15 a night, including breakfast. It also has a local tour guide service. Its office is inside the Agenţie de Turism at Piaţa Petru Rareş 7a.

Hotels Bram Stoker's character Jonathan Harker stayed at the *Coroana de Aur* (☎ 211 870, 211 871) on 3 May 1893. So do most foreign tourists. The 'Golden Crown', Piaţa Petru Rareş 4, has two stars, exploits its fictitious links and charges US$24 for a double with private bath. Breakfast is included.

At Piaţa Petru Rareş 2 is the *Hotel Bistriţa* (☎ 231 154, 231 205; fax 231 826) which has singles/doubles with private bath for US$15/23 including breakfast.

Across the river is one of Bistriţa's nicest hotels. The *Hotel Codrişor* (☎ 231 207, 222 919; fax 232 260), straddling the old city walls at Str Codrişor 29 overlooks the park, has an outside swimming pool (packed in summer) and a pleasant terrace restaurant. Luxury double rooms with cable TV cost US$20 and larger apartments are US$30. The pool fee for non-guests is US$0.20.

The *Hotel Ştefan* (☎ 221 255), south of the centre off Blvd Independenţei 11, is a small, family-run hotel with nine doubles with private bath costing US$35 a night, including a good breakfast.

The *Motel* (☎ 063-260 165, 260 129), 2km east of the centre towards the Tihuta pass, has five doubles with shared bathroom for US$11. The downstairs restaurant is open 24 hours and attract lots of truckers.

Places to Eat

Breaded brains and Golden Mediaş wine, officially endorsed by the Transylvanian Dracula Society, is served in the *Restaurant Coroniţa* adjoining the Coroana de Aur hotel. The expensive, ghoulish restaurant is open daily from 10 am to 11 pm.

For something a bit more fishy try the

Restaurant Păstruga next to the ACR office at Str Dornei 23. This small fish restaurant, run by the Bistriţa-Năsăud Fishing Association, is open daily from 11 am to 10 pm.

Getting There & Away

Bus From Bistriţa bus station there are two daily buses to Târgu Mureş (92km) and Vatra Dornei (83km); and one to Sighişoara (146km).

Train The Agenţie de Voiaj CFR is next door to the Transylvanian Dracula Society on Piaţa Petru Rareş. It is open weekdays from 8 am to 7 pm.

Bistriţa is at the end of a branch line from Ludus. You have to change trains at Sărăţel to get to Braşov, Baia Mare and Satu Mare, and the Székely Land. There are 15 local trains daily from Bistriţa to Sărăţel (15 minutes).

BÂRGĂU VALLEY

From Bistriţa the road runs east up the Bârgău valley and across the Tihuta mountain pass, to Vatra Dornei in Moldavia. From here, the painted monasteries of southern Bucovina can be easily accessed.

June is a fine time to travel this stretch. Tiny, wild strawberries the size of redcurrants are abundant. Villages along this road are dotted with peasants and children selling the sweet berries. Expect to pay about US$4 for a 2L bottle.

Eight kilometres east of Bistriţa is the village of **Livezile**, home to a small folk museum. And 2km south, in **Bistriţa Bârgăului**, is a *Popasul Montana* where you can camp. From **Mureşeni** the road starts to climb steeply on its approach to the **Tihuta Pass** which peaks at 1200m. A trail marked by red circles leads from here to the **Piatra Fântânele** at the top of the Tihuta pass.

The main reason why most people break their journey at Piatra Fântânele is not so much for the fine hiking that it offers but rather for the grand **Hotel Castel Dracula**, a complete commercial con that somehow manages to persuade guests otherwise, despite its blatant tackiness. The castle-hotel, which towers 1116m on the spot where Stoker sited his fictitious Dracula's castle, claims to be the only hotel in the world named after Stoker's blood-sucking monster. During its construction in the 1980s, members of the Dracula Society in London wrote a stiff letter of complaint about such a kitsch castle being built so close to southern Bucovina's great medieval painted monasteries.

Places to Stay

The *Cabana Valea Strajii* in Mureşeni has a handful of wooden bungalows which it rents out in summer. The restaurant is a local drinking hole for the woodcutters on their way back down from the valley. On the opposite side of the main road is the *Popasul Turistic* restaurant; it's open daily from 8 to 1 am.

The *Hotel Castel Dracula* (☎ 063-266 841; fax 366 119), better known as Dracula's castle, is a feat of modern marketing but remains the star attraction for tourists following the Dracula trail. The architect who designed the jagged-edged, angular building clearly watched the *Dracula* movie. Rooms are kitted out thematically, the highlight being 'Dracula's vault' where visitors are given a short, candlelit tour of the life and loves of Dracula. A coffin said to contain Dracula's bones rests in one corner.

Singles/doubles/triples with private bath cost US$35/43/52, including breakfast. Luxury apartments are US$57. The hotel accepts credit cards and has a sauna, restaurant and bar. Non-guests can visit Dracula's vault for US$0.20.

Heading further east towards Vatra Dornei, *La Vil dîn Carpaţi* (☎ 030-374 312), 6km south of Poiana Stampei and 26km east of Vatra Dornei, has five modern double rooms with a shared bath between two rooms for US$12 per person. It also has wooden cabanas to rent. Tantalising smells of homemade cooking waft from the motel kitchen.

South & West Transylvania

Traces of ancient civilisation are more evident in this region south of Cluj-Napoca than anywhere else in Romania. The cradle of the early Dacian kingdom was in the south-western realms of these parts. The kingdom managed to withstand attacks by its powerful Roman neighbour until 106 AD when the Dacian stronghold was finally conquered. The Roman emperor Trajan created a new capital north of the Retezat mountains. Remains of the great gold, copper and salt mines are still evident.

The union of Transylvania with Romania in 1600 and again on 1 December 1918 was proclaimed in Alba Iulia, the largest city in this region. Every 1 December hundreds of people descend upon the city to celebrate Romania's national day. During the 18th and 19th centuries this region served as a stronghold of resistance against Habsburg domination, giving birth to the first great uprising by Romanian peasants in 1784 and remaining the only region not be conquered by Habsburg forces during the 1848-9 revolution.

The northern tip of west Transylvania is dominated by the Apuseni mountains, a heavily karstic area offering hikers numerous trails to the fantastic caves and grottos that lie west on the Banat-Transylvania border.

THE APUSENI MOUNTAINS

South-west of Cluj-Napoca, the western Carpathians harbour the Apuseni mountains. At their southern foot lies the Arieş valley which follows the course of the Arieş river west from Turda. The mountains cover an area of 20,000sq km, 55% of which is forest-covered. The central part is dominated by the peaks of Bihor (1849m) and Vlădeasa (1836m). Most travellers head straight for the Padiş plateau, a heavily karstic zone in the central region of the Apuseni mountains

where numerous caves and hollows nestle beneath the earth's surface.

Mining and logging are the traditional occupations in this region. For information on the western part of the Apuseni mountain region, including the Bears' Cave and the Scarişoara Ice Cave, see the Banat & Crişana chapter.

Abrud

Abrud is a dull and dusty town, appealing only as a base to explore the mines of Roşia Montană and Roşia Poiena.

Ten kilometres east of Abrud are the staggering basaltic twin peaks of the **Detunătele** (1169m). The main access point for these magnificent peaks – known as Detunăta Goală (Hollow) and Detunăta Flocoasă (Flocky) – is in **Bucium** village. From Abrud, continue along the main Abrud-Alba Iulia road for 1km. Turn right at the turning signposted for Mogos and continue for 9km until you reach Bucium. The trail leading to the top of the Detunătele, marked by red stripes, begins at the bottom of a narrow dirt track to the side of the white church in the village centre. From the Detunătele a 2½ hour trail marked by blue circles and red triangles leads to Roşia Montană.

Places to Stay The *Hotel Abrud* (☎ 058-780 466) at the southern end of the town at Str Republicii 12 has 40 doubles with private bathroom for US$20.

Getting There & Away From Abrud bus station there are regular daily buses to Roşia Montană. Other daily services include six daily to Câmpeni (10km); one daily to Avram Iancu (30km), Brad (32km), Deva (68km) and Sibiu (175km); one daily to Cluj-Napoca (127km); and four daily to Alba Iulia (150km).

Train-wise, there are two daily local trains from Abrud to Turda, stopping at Roşia Montană and Turda.

Roşia Montană

Roşia Montană is 7km north-east of Abrud. From Câmpeni, follow the road south to

Abrud then turn left 4km north of Abrud at the signpost for the Roşia Montană (literally 'red mountain').

Gold has been mined in this village (population 4500) since Dacian times. The Romans exploited this gold mine which enjoyed its most lucrative period during their rule. Enough gold was allegedly mined to build a road of gold from Roşia Montană to Rome, the miners frequently uncovering hefty 24-carat chunks. Between WWI and WWII Romania was ranked second in Europe in gold extraction, mainly due to Roşia Montană's lucrative gold mine.

From 1854, open-casting mines were used to extract the gold ore. The primary gold reserves exploited by the Romans have long dried up and only secondary reserves remain today. A detonator blasts its way into the rock each Tuesday at 2.30 pm causing an unearthly roar through the entire village. Just one or two grams of gold are extracted from every tonne of blasted ore.

In mid-1997 an Australian company invested US$20 million in Roşia Montană to conduct a two year feasibility study into the mine's future profitability. The mine is currently working with outdated equipment, meaning only 50% of the potential gold is extracted from the ore. If the Australians agree to invest further it will mean new technology for the mine as well as the reprocessing of the mine's surrounding mountains of mined ore in order to extract the remaining 50% of gold!

A 400m-long stretch of the **old Roman galleries** is open to visitors. More than 150 dark, wet steps lead down to the galleries, believed to be over 2000 years old and snaking 2km underground. A larger chamber, where the miners would camp for weeks at a time, is still intact, as are the tracks along which small children or ponies would lug up the carts of ore to the surface. The miners underground always kept good stocks of cheese, believing that, in imminent disaster, mice would scamper away from the cheese, thus warning the miners to flee too.

Outside the mine entrance is a **museum** with reproductions of water-powered wooden stamps used to crush the ore in the 18th century. The crushed ore would subsequently be sorted by hand on a sheepskin rug, the gold filings falling deep into the fur and the lighter stones remaining on its surface. The rug would then be washed to extract the gold. During the 19th century there were 700 such stamps positioned on the shores of Roşia Montană's surrounding lakes. Each winter, when the lakes froze, work at the mine would grind to a halt.

October 6 remains an important feast day for the village of Roşia Montană. The holiday celebrates Varvara, the patron saint of the mine.

The gold mine (☎ 058-780 088, 780 979) is opposite the police station at the western end of the main street of Str Principală. The museum is open daily from 7 am to 3 pm. There is also a **gold museum** in Brad, 32km south-west of Abrud.

Getting There & Away Roşia Montană is served by regular buses from Abrud (3km), the first one departing from Abrud bus station at 6.10 am to take the miners to work.

There are also two local trains daily from Abrud (3km, 10 minutes) to Roşia Montană, departing from Abrud at 6.13 am and 4.54 pm. This train continues east to Turda. Return trains to Abrud depart from Roşia Montană at 11.19 am and 8.23 pm.

From Roşia Montană you can hike to Bucium (see Abrud section earlier). From Cluj-Napoca there is one bus daily to Brad (165km).

Roşia Poieni
The copper mine at Roşia Poieni, 12km east of Abrud, is far less tourist-friendly than its golden neighbour. Tours of the vast mine have to be arranged prior to arrival and involve the Soviet method of seeking written authorisation from a surly mine director who is never in his office.

Equally unfriendly are the methods used by the mine to extract copper from the ore. These have been slammed in the local press as 'pollutive' and 'unconventional'. Unfortunately, more than one million tons of copper reserves are yet to be exploited at the mine. Between 0.2g and 0.4g of copper are extracted from every tonne of mined ore. Some 2000 miners work at the copper mine and live in nearby concrete tower blocks. For a tour, contact Roşia Poiena's headquarters (☎ & fax 054-213 641) in Deva.

The mine is signposted immediately on the left after you leave Abrud, on the main Abrud-Alba Iulia road.

Avram Iancu & Mount Găina

From Câmpeni, head west for 6km then turn left along the dirt track, through the village of Vidra, to Avram Iancu. This logging village was known as Vidra de Sus until it was renamed after the revolutionary leader Avram Iancu (1824-1872) who was born in the village. A memorial and small museum honour the village's greatest hero. Unlike other revolutionaries, Avram Iancu did not die in battle. Legend has it that he went insane, spending the last years of his life wandering in the mountains playing a flute.

About 9km from Avram Iancu, on the hilltop of Mt Găina (1486m), a Girls' Market (Târgul de fete) is held every year on a Sunday around 20 July. The 'market' is the biggest event of the year for the surrounding villages whose people flock to the mountain top every year to sing, dance and light bonfires. The fair originated as a crude matchmaking venue. Today, it is just another excuse for a big party.

Horea

Continue 20km west along the main road from Câmpeni to Albac. Turn right here and follow the dirt track to Horea village, named after the peasant revolutionary. Horea (1730-85) who was born here as Vasile Nicola-Ursu, led the great peasant rebellion of 1784 following which the Habsburg emperor Joseph II abolished serfdom.

Horea, Cloşca and Crişan were arrested by Habsburg forces, and put to a ghastly death in Alba Iulia. On 22 August 1785 Emperor Joseph II abolished serfdom among Romanian peasants in Transylvania.

Gârda du Sus, the entryway to the awe-inspiring **Scarişoara ice cave**, is 10km west of Albac. See the Peştera Ghețarul de la Scarişoara section in the Crişana & Banat chapter.

Places to Stay At the time of writing, rooms in the *Cabana Umbra Văii* in the centre of Horea were under construction. The *Homul Giorgioma* (☎ 771 149), in Albac 7km north of Horea, has comfortable double/four-bed rooms to let with private bathroom and hot water for US$4 per person a night. The family serve excellent pork cutlets in their small restaurant and are happy to cook for guests whatever the time of day.

Opération Villages Roumains (☎ & fax 771 812) arranges rural accommodation in the region. Its office is in Albac inside the primăria in the centre of the village. It charges US$10 to US$12 a night, including breakfast and also offers half/full-board starting at US$13/15. Out of hours, ask in the village for local representative Lucian Morar who lives at house No 16.

Getting There & Away There are three buses daily from Câmpeni to Horea (28km).

THE PADIŞ PLATEAU

The Padiş plateau (Platel Padiş) lies north of the Arieş valley on the Transylvania-Banat border, covering just a small area in the central Apuseni mountains. Its highest peaks, Mount Măgura Vinăta (1642m) and Mount Cârligatele (1694m) mark the plateau's eastern and northern boundaries respectively. The Galbenei river, which snakes along the Galbenei valley, straddles the plateau to the south-west.

Padiş is a heavily karstic region, harbouring a treasure trove of undiscovered caves, hollows and underground waterpools. Its limestone foundations do not retain water. The plateau, characterised by a cold, damp and foggy climate, is protected as an ecological area.

Hikers should beware of drinking what appears to be natural spring water. The plateau is shot with small springs bursting from the mountain sides, many of which originate from polluted rivers. Environmentalists are particularly concerned about the polluted Ponorului river which flows downstream from the Cabana Padiş in the south-east of the plateau. During the Soviet administration immediately following WWII, vast areas of pine forest in the Padiş plateau were cut, yet to be regenerated. As a result, the region suffers from frequent flooding. Wild boars, deer, stags and bears continue to inhabit the pine forests, but their future survival is jeopardised by uncontrolled hunting in these parts.

Access Routes

The Clubul Ecologic Transilvania in Cluj (see Cluj – Information) publishes the handy *Padiş* guide. It is all in Romanian but lists all the hiking trails marked in the plateau. Buy a copy from their Cluj office for US$1.20. The club also publishes a map of the Padiş zone which has all the trails marked on it. This is available from the Romanta travel agency in Bologa (see Places to Stay).

You can access Padiş by road from the east in **Poiana Horea** or from the west in **Pietroasa**. Both roads – dirt tracks – are difficult to navigate in bad weather but eventually lead to the Cabana Padiş (1280m) from where numerous hiking trails are marked.

The area is practically impossible to reach by public transport. From Bieuş (see the Crişana & Banat chapter) there is one bus daily to Pietroasa (20km). You can then hike from here, or alternatively access the plateau from **Gârda de Sus** which is 10km west of Albac. From here a blue striped trail is marked to the Cabana Padiş (five to six hours). Few hikers access Padiş from **Stâna de Vale** in the north-west although it is possible (red stripes, 5½ to six hours).

In the Plateau

From the Cabana Padiş the most popular trail is a six hour circular one (blue circles) which leads south-west along the polluted Ponorului river to the fantastic **Ponor Citadela** (Cetăţile Ponorului). The citadel is one of the plateau's greatest natural wonders, leading underground to a wet and damp chamber in which the Ponor river sinks its way through the chamber's numerous holes. Some are as deep as 150m.

Another trail, marked first by red stripes then red circles, leads from the cabana north along a dirt track to **Poiana Vărăşoaia**. From here, red circles bear east to the **Rădesei Citadel** (Cetăţile Rădesei), another underground chamber with impressive rock formations. The route then circles **Someşul Cald**, one of the plateau's three natural storage lakes, before heading back south to the cabana. If you continue to follow the red stripes north, you eventually arrive in the dying ski resort of **Stâna de Vale**. This route does take you over the Cârligatele peak (1694m) however, offering breathtaking views of this unique region.

No marked trails follow the course of the Valea Rea river (literally 'bad valley' river). Crossing the north-eastern part of the plateau, this river is notoriously wild, running through 1800m of underground galleries before shooting out wildly from the mountain side. The river cascades down numerous waterfalls, eventually becoming tamer around Pietroasa where it joins the Valea Bulzului river.

Places to Stay

The *Cabana Padiş* has 45 beds in 14 rooms. Bookings can be made through the Romanta travel agency (☎ & fax 064-251 585) in Bologa (see Huedin & Around). The agency can also arrange rooms in rural homes in surrounding villages and guided tours in the Padiş zone.

HUEDIN & AROUND

Huedin, 52km west of Cluj, lies at the heart of a predominantly Hungarian enclave known as Kalotaszeg by the ethnic Hungarians who populate the 44 villages in this region. Kalotaszeg is seen as the stronghold of Magyar culture in Transylvania today although this only becomes evident if you take the time to explore the pinprick villages where folk culture remains an integral part of rural life.

Huedin (Bánffyhunyad in Hungarian) itself is a small, unexciting place, serving merely as a stepping stone from Transylvania to the Banat or to the surrounding villages. Its village church, famed for its painted, wooden-panel ceiling – a gem of local wood craftsmanship – is worth a brief stop. Huedin has one hotel, and that's the dreary *Hotel Vladeasa* (☎ 064-251 590) on Str Republicii.

Poieni, Bologa & Săcuieu

Twelve kilometres west of Huedin is the small village of Poieni, 2.8km from Bologa. The ruins of a 13th century **medieval fortress** dating from the 13th century towers above it. Some 81m of the original wall remains, as do remnants of the citadel's bastions, complete with stone spiral staircase inside. You can hike up the hill to the ruins from the centre of the village.

Equally interesting is the old **watermill** (apă moara), still functioning and in use today. Clothes continue to be washed in the whirlpool close to the mill. The entrance to the mill is marked by large iron gates in the centre of the village. The citadel can clearly be seen opposite.

In Săcuieu, 10km south of Bologa, 950m high on top of Dealul Domnului (literally 'God's Hill') there is one of Romania's few Sequoia trees, which the predominantly Hungarian residents are extremely proud of.

Mănăstireni

Mănăstireni (Magyargyerömonostor in Hungarian) is 16km south-east of Huedin. A minor road from the main Cluj-Napoca-Huedin roads leads south, through Bedeciu to the village, noted for its 13th century church. It was built by the Gyeröffy family with a Gothic apse added in the 15th century. Many original wood carvings are visible inside the church which also boasts a fine wooden-panelled ceiling. During the 1848 revolution, 200 Hungarians died at the battle of Mănăstireni; they were buried in a mass grave which today rests beneath lake waters in the village.

Heading back to Huedin you pass Izvorul Crisului, known as Körösfő to Hungarians. Towering on a hilltop above the village is a small church, dating from 1764 and considered to be among the most representative of the Protestant churches in this region.

Places to Stay The *Pension Romanta* (☎ & fax 064-251 585), next to the Bologa turn-off on the main Huedin-Poieni road, has three doubles for US$11 a night.

Housed in the same building is the efficient Romanta tourism agency (☎ & fax 064-251 585) which arranges rural accommodation in Bologa, Huedin, Poieni, Săcuieu, Ciucea and Mănăstireni. A bed for the night, including breakfast, starts at US$6. The agency also arranges hiking trips in the Padiş area, folk evenings, cycling and fishing trips. In winter it offers tours around the surrounding villages on a horse-drawn sleigh. The office is open daily from 8 am to 4 pm. Accommodation and trips should be booked in advance; they can be made through the Eurogîtes reservation system (see Facts for the Visitor at the front of this book). The agency publishes a colour brochure of all its properties.

Ciucea

Ciucea village is a place of pilgrimage for Romanians and Hungarians alike, having been home to Romanian poet and politician Octavian Goga (1881-1939) and to Hungary's most controversial poet of the 20th century, Endre Ady (1877-1919).

The house in which Octavian Goga lived, at the eastern end of the village next to the whitewashed, silver-spired church, is today a memorial **museum** (Muzeul Octavian Goga). Goga was born in a small village close to Sibiu but lived in a mansion in Ciucea between 1915-17 prior to his move into politics which led to his disastrous reign as prime minister in 1937 for just 44 days. In the beautifully landscaped park surrounding the house-museum is a monumental shrine to the statesman.

Goga, who campaigned fervently for the rights of Romanians in the face of Hungarian domination, bought this country mansion from the controversial Hungarian poet Endre Ady. The poet, who slammed Hungary as a cultural backwater, spent several years living in Ciucea towards the end of his life.

Also on the complex is a **wooden church**, dating from 1575 and transported to Ciucea from the Cluj region at the end of the 16th century. It is today cared for by a group of nuns. The park and museum are open daily, except Monday, from 9 am to 5 pm. Taking photographs of any of the buildings is forbidden.

Places to Stay The Romanta travel agency arranges accommodation in private homes in Ciucea (see Poieni, Bologa & Săcuieu above).

ALBA IULIA
• *area code ☎ 058 , pop 72,300*

The imposing fortifications of Alba Iulia (known as Karlsburg and Weissenburg to Germans, Gyula Fehérvár to Hungarians), near the Mureş River between Cluj-Napoca and Deva, dominate the south-western flank of Transylvania.

Alba Iulia was known by the Dacians as Apulum, serving both as the capital of Upper Dacia and later, during Roman times, as the largest centre in the Dacian province of the Roman empire. During the 9th and 10th centuries, Apulum was known as Bălgrad-Cetatea Albă.

From 1542 to 1690 Alba Iulia served as the capital of the principality of Transylvania and it was here in 1600 and again on 1 December 1918 that the union of Transylvania with Romania was proclaimed. Romania's national day on 1 December continues to be a time of major celebrations in Alba Iulia today.

Modern Alba Iulia is the seat of Alba County and the source of some of Romania's best champagne (three million bottles a year are produced here). Alba Iulia's 18th century citadel is justly famous, but there's not much else to see or do – you'll find that four hours here is plenty.

Orientation
The city is divided into three parts. The citadel – the pedestrianised 'upper town' – houses all the historic sights, museums and university buildings. The new town is west of the citadel, while the lower town area resembles a building site – most of the town's older buildings were bulldozed under Ceauşescu to make way for a civic centre that never happened.

The adjacent bus and train stations are 2km south of the citadel Take any bus marked *centru* (US$0.20, pay on board) to the second stop, on Blvd 1 Decembrie 1918 close to the culture house *(casă de cultură)*. The left-luggage office inside the train station is open daily 24 hours.

The central department store, Magazin Universal Unirea, on the corner of Str Tudor Vladimirescu and Calea Moţilor in the lower town, is open weekdays from 8 am to 5 pm, Saturday from 8 am to noon.

Information
Tourist Offices The OJT tourist office adjoining the Hotel Transilvania at Str Iuliu Maniu 22 sells comprehensible city maps for US$0.10 and maps of the Alba district for US$0.80. The hotel also sells them. The tourist office is open weekdays from 9 am to 5 pm. The Cetate Apuseni tourist office (☎ 815 152; fax 831 501) inside the Complex Hotelier Cetate, Str Unirii 3, offers similar services. It is open weekdays from 8 am to 4 pm.

The Clubul de Ecologie şi Turism (☎ 822 775) at Str Vănătorilor 26, block VI 2, apartment 10, and EcoTur (☎ 820 511) at Str Vulturului 7a, block 15b, apartment 34, are environmental groups worth contacting if you are interested in hiking in the area. Both can arrange hikes and expeditions in the Alba district (Judeţul Alba).

The Automobil Clubul Român (ACR; ☎ 812 485) has an office and service centre close to the bus and train stations at Str Republicii 64.

Money Change money at the Cambio Exchange inside the Alimentar close to the

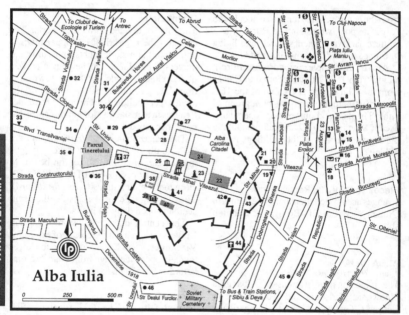

Alba Iulia

0   250   500 m

Hotel Transilvania on Piaţa Iuliu Maniu. It is open weekdays from 9 am to 5 pm, Saturday from 8 am to 2 pm. The Romania Exchange, close to the Magazin Universal Unirea at Str Moţilor 3, is open weekdays from 9 am to 6 pm, Saturday from 9 am to 4 pm. There are also currency exchanges inside the Hotel Parc and Hotel Cetate.

You can change travellers cheques and get cash advance on Visa/MasterCard at BANCOREX near the Magazin Universal Unirea on the corner of Piaţa Iuliu Maniu and Str Avram Iancu. It is open weekdays from 8.30 to 11 am.

The Bancă Comercială Română, Str Tudor Vladimirescu 35, cashes travellers cheques and gives cash advance on Visa/MasterCard. It has an ATM too which is stupidly inside the bank, hence only accessible during banking hours – weekdays from 8.30 am to 7 pm, Saturday from 8 to 11 am.

Post & Communications The central telephone centre and post office are next to each other on Piaţa Eroilor in the lower town. The telephone office is open daily from 7 am to 7 pm; the post office is open the same hours but only on weekdays.

There is another post office in the new town at Blvd Transilvaniei 12, open weekdays from 7 am to 7 pm.

Travel Agencies BTT (☎ 812 140; fax 810 385) at Str Parcului 2 is pretty useless on the map and practical information side. It can however arrange private rooms in the villages around Alba Iulia for US$10 to US$12 a night. The office is open weekdays from 9 am to 5 pm, Saturday from 9 am to 1 pm.

Medical Services The pharmacy on Piaţa Iuliu Maniu is open weekdays from 7 am to 8 pm, Saturday from 8 am to 2 pm. There is an optician next door. The pharmacy on Blvd Horea in the new town is open weekdays from 8 am to 1 pm and 4 to 7 pm. Its branch

PLACES TO STAY		6	BANCOREX	32	Eco Tur
8	Hotel Transilvania	7	Cambio Exchange;	34	Humanitas Bookshop
16	Hotel Parc		Alimentar	35	Pharmacy
20	Mini-Hotel	9	Pharmacy	36	Casă de Cultură
29	Hotel Cetate	10	Agenţie de Voiaj CFR	37	Orthodox
		11	Romania Exchange		Cathedral
PLACES TO EAT		12	Central Market	38	Catholic Cathedral
2	Ristorante Roberta	13	Students' Culture	39	Catholic Episcopal
15	Prometeu		House; Disco-Bar		Palace
19	P & H Terrace Café	14	BTT	40	Former Princely
21	Română Grădină de	17	Post Office		Court (Military
	Vară	18	Telephone Centre		Base)
31	Club Casă Alba	22	Military Base	41	Equestrian Statue of
33	Eis Kaffe Paradis	23	Costozza Monument		Mihai Viteazul
		24	University	42	Entrance to Horea's
OTHER		25	Unification Hall		Cell
1	Bancă Comercială	26	Unification Museum	43	1784 Uprising
	Română	27	Batthyaneum Library		Memorial
3	Small Market	28	Former Military	44	Wooden Church
4	Magazin Universal		Hospital	45	Automobil Clubul
	Unirea	30	Ursus Grădină de		Român (ACR)
5	Grădină de Vară		Vară	46	Fork's Hill

at Blvd Transilvaniei 9 is open on Sunday from 8 am to 2 pm.

Alba Carolina Citadel

The imposing Alba Carolina Citadel, with its seven bastions and six gates, richly carved with sculptures and reliefs in a Baroque style, dominates the city of Alba Iulia. It was originally constructed in a Vauban style in the 13th century, although the fortress you see today was built between 1714-38 according to the design of Italian architect Giovanni Morandi Visconti.

Str Mihai Viteazul runs up from the lower town to the triumphal arc-shaped **first gate** of the fortress, heavily adorned with Baroque sculptures inspired by Greek mythology. From here, a stone road leads to the **third gate** of the fortress, dominated by an equestrian statue of Carol VI of Austria. Above the gate is **Horea's death cell** (celula lui Horia), now housing a small museum to commemorate the leader of the great 1784 peasant uprising.

Opposite the gate stands an **obelisk**, erected in 1937 in tribute to the peasant uprising.

A footpath leads from the gate to a small wooden **Orthodox church**, (Biserica Memorială Sfânta Treime), outside the south-eastern corner of the inner fortress walls. The wooden church, brought to Alba Iulia in 1990 from Maramureş, stands on the site of a former Metropolitan cathedral built by Mihai Viteazul in 1597 and destroyed by the Habsburgs in 1713. The remains of the destroyed cathedral were later used to build a new church in the south of the city, close to the train and bus station. Weekly services are held in the wooden church on Saturday at 6 pm, Sunday at 8.30 and 10 am.

There is a small army base in the building immediately on your right as you enter the citadel. Some remains of the wall of the old medieval town still stand along the southern side of Str Mihai Viteazul.

Thoday the Romanian army also occupies the **Princely Court**, former residence of the princes of Transylvania which was built in several stages from the 16th century onwards. In front of it, on Str Mihai Viteazul, stands a large **equestrian statue** of Mihai Viteazul (Michael the Brave), ruler of Romania from 1593 to 1601. On 1 November 1599 he visited Alba Iulia to celebrate the unification of Wallachia, Moldavia and Transylvania – a union that crumbled after his assassination a year later.

The statue faces **Unification Hall** (Sală de Unirii), built between 1898 and 1900 as a military casino. It was in this hall, renovated in 1922 and again in 1968, where the act of unification between Romania and Transylvania was signed during the Great Assembly of 1 December 1918. Admission costs US$0.10; tickets are sold at the Unification Museum.

In the park, on the eastern side of Unification Hall, is a **Costozza monument**, to commemorate the soldiers and officers of the 50th infantry regiment of Alba Iulia who were killed while fighting in the Habsburg army against Italy in the battle of Custozza in 1866.

On the western side of Unification Hall inside the former Babylon building (1851) is the impressive **Unification Museum** (Muzeul Unirii) which opened in 1887. The museum vividly recounts the history of Romania from the Paleolithic and Neolithic periods through to 1944 and is considered one of the top museums in the country on the history of Transylvania. Of particular interest is the Apulum exhibit which includes statuettes and ceramic pots discovered during excavations around the citadel on the site of the old Roman town.

Another corner is devoted to the peasant revolutionaries Cloşca, Crişan and Horea. The highlight is a replica of the wheel used to crush Cloşca and Horea to death in 1785 (Crişan sensibly killed himself in prison before he could be tortured to death). A plaque on the wall recounts the orders issued by the judge who determined their ghastly death:

... they are to be taken to the torture place and there killed by being tied to a wheel and squashed – first Cloşca, then Horea. After being killed their bodies are to be cut into four parts and the head and body impaled on the edge of different roads for everyone to see them. The internal organs – their hearts and intestines – will be buried in the place of torture ...

The museum is open daily, except Monday, from 10 am to 5 pm. All information is presented in Romanian. Admission is US$0.20.

Just beyond the statue is the 18th century **Catholic cathedral**, built on the site of a Romanesque church destroyed during the Tartar invasion of 1241. Many famous Transylvanian princes are buried here.

The nearby **Orthodox cathedral** – or 'Church of the Coronation' as it was originally known – was built on the old site of the citadel guardhouse between 1921 and 1992 for the coronation of King Ferdinand I and Queen Marie on 15 October 1922. Their frescoed portraits remain intact on the rear wall of the church. Designed in the shape of a Greek circumscribed cross by architect Gheorghe Stefănescu, the cathedral is surrounded by a wall of decorative colonnades which form a rectangular enclosure. A 58m-tall bell tower marks the main entrance to the complex. Marble inscriptions within the church pay homage to the most important events in Alba Iulia's history, including the printing for the first time in 1648 of the New Testament in Romanian by Metropolitan Simeon Ştefan. During the communist era, many of the cathedral's original frescoes were plastered over. Many have since been repainted.

The **Batthyaneum Library**, founded at the end of the 18th century in a former church; the former **military hospital**; and the late-Renaissance **Abor Palace** are situated in the north-eastern area of the citadel.

Fork's Hill

Fork's Hill (Dealul Furcilor), the spot where peasant revolutionaries Horea, Cloşca and Crişan died, is marked with a small **obelisk monument**. A year after their grizzly deaths, on 22 August 1785, Emperor Joseph II abolished serfdom among Romanian peasants in Transylvania.

Places to Stay

Camping The *Hanul Dintre Sălcii* campsite, on Highway DN1 3km south of town, was closed at the time of writing.

Private Rooms Rural-tourism specialists ANTREC (☎ 811 774; fax 830 782), Str

Rozelor 3, arranges rooms in private houses in Alba Iulia and its surrounding villages for around US$10 to US$15 a night. The office is open weekdays from 9 am to 5 pm.

Hotels The cheapest is the excellent value *Mini Hotel* (☎ 813 778), next to the western entrance to the citadel at Str Mihai Viteazul 6. It has two double rooms for US$7, one triple for US$11 and a five-bed room for US$18. All rooms have private bathroom.

Next in line for the budget-conscious is the two star, 12-storey *Hotel Cetate* (☎ 811 780; fax 815 812) in the new town at Str Unirii 3, overlooking the citadel at its western end. Singles/doubles with private bath cost US$18/34 a night, including breakfast. Triples are US$36 and you have to pay US$1 per person extra if you want a room with a black and white TV. It accepts credit cards.

The slightly more expensive, 1960s *Hotel Transilvania* (☎ 812 547) at Str Iuliu Maniu 22 only has double rooms with private bath and cable black and white TV for US$26; the single price for a double room is US$21, including breakfast on the terrace.

Across the park at Str Primăverii 4 is the *Hotel Parc* (☎ 811 723; fax 812 130) which has expensive singles/doubles for US$29/36, including breakfast. It accepts credit cards.

Out of Town In Vinţu de Jos, 10km south of Alba Iulia there is the *Motel Lutsch 2000 Plus* (☎ & fax 743 851). It has 16 reasonably priced double rooms.

Places to Eat
Restaurants Alba Iulia has few private restaurants serving, making it difficult to avoid the hotel restaurants.

The sparkling *Ristorante Roberta* at the northern end of Str Tudor Vladimirescu in the lower town was under construction at the time of writing but is set to become the top, western-style restaurant in town. The same management also runs a hi-tech *pizza parlour* in the new town close to the Cinema Dacia.

In the new town is the flash *Club Casă Alba* close to the Hotel Cetate on Blvd Horea. It has an upmarket restaurant, billiard hall and terrace café – all of which are great as long as you can stand the deafening music. Equally loud is the *Ursus Grădină de Vară* directly opposite. Both are open daily from 11 am to late.

The *Restaurant Română* on Blvd Transilvaniei is a typical, age-old establishment offering few thrills or frills; it is open daily from 10 am to 10 pm.

Cafés If you are only seeking a light snack, there are plenty of terrace cafés to choose from.

Prometeu, in the lower town at Str Parcului 4, is a modern, clean café touting a fast food-type menu and open daily from 10 am to 10 pm. The *Grădină de Vară*, close by at Str Tudor Vladimirescu, sells *Ursus* beer for US$0.20 a bottle or US$0.17 on tap; it is open daily from noon to 10 pm.

Light night-time snacks are served in the *Club Eduard*, inside the Magazin Universal Unirea on the corner of Str Tudor Vladimirescu and Calea Moţilor; it is open weekdays from 1 pm to midnight and at weekends from 7 pm to 3 am. Occasional discos are held in the students' culture house (casă de cultură studenteasca) in the small park on Str Parcului.

There are no cafés or kiosks in the citadel. The *P & H* terrace café under the trees next to the western-end entrance at Str Mihai Viteazul 7, or the bright and breezy *Română Grădină de Vară* nestled beneath the fortress walls on the other side of the street, is the closest you'll get. Both are open daily from around 10 am to 11 pm.

Beyond that, most cafés are centred in the new town. The best is the *Eis Kaffe Paradis* at Blvd Transilvaniei 14. It serves the most scrumptious ice-cream sundaes you're likely to encounter in the whole of Romania. Expect to pay around US$0.50 for a bowl of chocolate, vanilla, peach melba and fruit ice cream topped with fresh fruit, chocolate sauce and lots of cream. It is open daily from 10 am to 7 pm.

Self-Catering There are two small *markets* selling fresh fruit and vegetables as well as dried and tinned products; one is behind the Agenţie de Voiaj CFR office off Calea Moţilor on Str Nicolae Bălcescu; the other is close by at the northern end of Str Doinei. Both can be reached from Calea Moţilor.

There is a 24 hour *Alimentar* in the new town at Blvd Transilvaniei 2. The *Dacia* supermarket on the corner of Str Vasile Goldiş and Blvd 1 Decembrie 1918 is also open 24 hours.

Getting There & Away

Bus Direct services from Alba Iulia's bus station include one daily to Cluj-Napoca (99km), Sibiu (71km) and Oradea (251km); four daily to Abrud (150km) and Aiud (16km); and six daily to Câmpeni (75km).

Train The Agenţie de Voiaj CFR (☎ 813 689) at Str Moţilor 1 is open weekdays from 7 am to 7 pm. International train tickets for the four daily Budapest trains that stop at Alba Iulia (6¼ hours) can only be bought in advance from this office.

To get to Alba Iulia from Sibiu, you have to change trains at Vinţu de Jos. From Târgu Mureş you often have to change at Războieni or Teiuş.

AIUD & AROUND

Heading 16km north from Alba Iulia towards Turda and Cluj-Napoca, you pass through Aiud where wine has been produced since 1293. One of urban Transylvania's oldest fortresses, dating from the 14th century, stands in the town, while the former 17th century Bethlen college now houses a local **history museum**. More ominously, Aiud is known as the former home of a **communist prison** in the 1950s where some 3500 political prisoners were interned.

Blaj, 26km north-east of Alba Iulia, is best known as being the hotbed of Romanian nationalism. Three mass rallies took place on the 'field of liberty' (*câmpul libertăţii*) here between April and September 1848 sparking off a countrywide revolution. Blaj is on the main Braşov-Bucharest-Cluj-Napoca line

and plenty of daily express and local trains stop here.

DEVA

● *area code* ☎ *054 , pop 77,737*

Deva is a small mining town with a fantastic history museum that anyone intending to head further south to explore Transylvania's Dacian citadel and cities should take time out to visit. Deva has its own citadel, blown to smithereens in 1849 after its gun powder deposits exploded, but is still a popular haunt with visitors nonetheless.

Orientation

The train and bus stations are a five minutes walk from the centre at Str Mihai Viteazul 32. Exit the train station and walk straight up Str Libertăţii until it meets Str 1 Decembrie. From the crossroads, Str 1 Decembrie leads into Piaţa Victoriei and Str 22 Decembrie to the east. The main hotels, post office, Cinema Patria and the Ulpia central department store are centred around Piaţa Victoriei and Str 1 Decembrie. Citadel hill is at the western end of Str 1 Decembrie.

Information

The no-name hiking shop at Piaţa Libertăţii 4 is run by an enthusiastic bunch of young climbers and mountaineers who can give local advice about hiking in the Retezat mountains. The shop sells water bottles, rucksacks, tents and clothing (but not maps) and is open weekdays from 10 am to 6 pm.

Tourist Offices The official Agenţie de Turism (☎ & fax 213 173) is inside the Hotel Sarmis at Piaţa Victoriei 3. It is open weekdays from 9 am to 4 pm.

Mondo Turism (☎ 212 162), opposite the Hotel Decebal at Str 1 Decembrie 11, is open weekdays from 9 am to 5 pm; it sells city maps for US$0.30.

The Automobil Clubul Român (ACR; ☎ 612 822; fax 619 419) has an office behind the Hotel Sarmis at Str G Coşbuc 22. It's open weekdays from 8 am to 6 pm.

Money There are currency exchange offices

NICOLA WILLIAMS

MARK DAFFEY

NICOLA WILLIAMS

Transylvania
Top left: Culture Palace, Târgu Mureş
Top right: Window boxes, Sighişoara
Bottom: Piaţa Mare, Sibiu

MARK DAFFEY

NICOLA WILLIAMS

COLIN D SHAW

COLIN D SHAW

Top left: Vlad Tepeş' birthplace, Sighişoara, Transylvania
Top right: Piaţa Mare, Sibiu, Transylvania
Middle right: Fishponds near Odorheiu Secuiesc, Transylvania
Bottom: Curtea de Argeş monastery, Wallachia

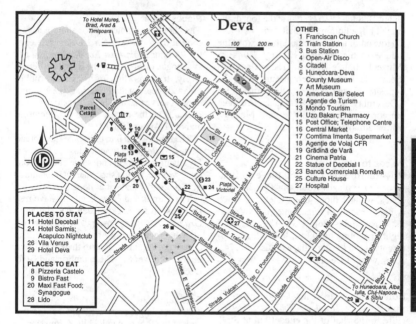

Deva

0   100   200 m

OTHER
1 Franciscan Church
2 Train Station
3 Bus Station
4 Open-Air Disco
5 Citadel
6 Hunedoara-Deva
  County Museum
7 Art Museum
10 American Bar Select
12 Agenţie de Turism
13 Mondo Tourism
14 Uzo Bakan; Pharmacy
15 Post Office; Telephone Centre
16 Central Market
17 Comtina Imenta Supermarket
18 Agenţie de Voiaj CFR
19 Grădina de Vară
21 Cinema Patria
22 Statue of Decebal I
23 Bancă Comercială Română
25 Culture House
27 Hospital

PLACES TO STAY
11 Hotel Decebal
24 Hotel Sarmis;
   Acapulco Nightclub
26 Vila Venus
29 Hotel Deva

PLACES TO EAT
8 Pizzeria Castelo
9 Bistro Fast
20 Maxi Fast Food;
   Synagogue
28 Lido

TRANSYLVANIA

inside the Hotel Sarmis and Hotel Deva. Change travellers cheques and get cash on Visa/MasterCard at the Bancă Comercială Română behind the Hotel Sarmis on Str G Coşbuc. It has an ATM outside. The bank is open weekdays from 8.30 am to 12.30 pm, and 1.30 to 6 pm.

Post & Communications The central post and telephone centre is on the corner of Str Libertăţii and Str 1 Decembrie. It is open weekdays from 7 am to 7 pm. There is also a post office adjoining the main train station building.

Citadel
Standing on top of a volcanic hill, the 14th century Cetatea (300m) magnificently crowns the small mining town below. Building work started on the stone fortress in 1385 under the Habsburg Ardeal kings. Legend says that the wife of the mason was buried alive in the fortress walls to ensure its safekeeping.

In the 16th century, religious activist Dávid Ferenc (1510-79), advocator of the Greco-Catholic faith, was imprisoned in Deva citadel where he died. In 1784, during the peasant uprising led by Horea, Crişan and Cloşca, the fortress served as a refuge for terrified nobles fearful of being killed by the militant peasants. In 1849 Hungarian nationalists attacked Austrian generals sheltering in the fortress. They besieged it for four weeks. The siege ended with the mighty explosion of the castle's gun powder deposits which left the castle in ruins.

A brief history of Deva and its sister citadels as well as extensive archaeological findings from the various sights amid the Orăştie mountains are exhibited in the small, but excellent **Hunedoara-Deva County Museum** (Muzeul Judeţan Hunedoara-Deva), housed in the former Magna Curia palace. This palace was built by Prince

Gábor Bethlen in 1621. It is at the foot of the citadel hill adjoining a small park.

Housed in a separate building next to the palace is the **Natural History Museum** (Muzeul Stintale Naturii). The **art section** (Secţia de Artă) of the museum is on the opposite side of the park on the corner of Str 1 Decembrie and Str Avram Iancu. All three museums are open daily, except Monday, from 9 am to 5 pm.

Places to Stay

Private Rooms Contact the excellent Opération Villages Roumains (☎ 623 160), Aleea Armatei, block 4, apartment 50, which arranges rooms in rural homes in Deva and its surroundings from US$10 per person a night, including breakfast. It also has a representative in Lesnic village (house No 174), 10km west of Deva.

Hotels The cheapest hotel in town (still a rip-off) is the *Hotel Decebal* (☎ 211 976) close to the foot of the citadel hill at Str 1 Decembrie, 14. The hotel still blatantly touts a two-tier pricing system with foreigners paying US$23/34/46 for a double/triple/four-bed room. Bathrooms are shared and there is no running hot water.

The *Hotel Sarmis* (☎ 214 730, 214 731; fax 215 873) at Piaţa Victoriei 3 and the *Hotel Deva* (☎ 211 290; fax 615 873) further east at Str 22 Decembrie 110 are run by the same company. Both are two-star, concrete blocks with large restaurants and tourist agencies inside; the Nightclub Acapulco adjoins the Sarmis (open daily from 9 pm to 5 am). Singles/doubles with private bath are US$28/49. The Deva has a few triples for US$58.

Enjoyable if you can afford it is the luxurious, four-star *Vila Venus* (☎ 217 106, 619 507; ☎ & fax 612 243), behind the culture house at Str Mihai Eminescu 16. Double rooms start at US$57, including breakfast.

Out of town, in Ilia village, 20km west of Deva on the road to the Banat, is the one-star *Motel Mureş*, Str Principală 1.

Places to Eat

The choice is simple: a poor attempt at fast food at *Bistro Fast* on Str 1 Decembrie or at the 24 hour *Maxi Fast Food*, adjoining the synagogue on Str Gheorghe Bariţiu. Alternatively, try a portion of rock-solid-rubber breaded cheese at the *Pizzeria Castelo* which doesn't serve pizza. It is opposite the county museum on the corner of Str 1 Decembrie and Str 1 Avram Iancu.

The third option is to buy some fresh bread from *Uzo Bakan* patisserie close to Maxi on Str Gheorghe Bariţiu and some cheese from the *Comtima Imenta* supermarket opposite at Str Libertăţii 1 and eat at home.

The Sarmis and Deva hotels do have restaurants. Beer seekers can try the vast *Grădină de Vară* opposite the synagogue on Str Gheorghe Bariţiu or the excellent *Lido* terrace café and bar close to the Hotel Deva on the corner of Str 22 Decembrie and Blvd Decebal.

Entertainment

There is a large, *open-air disco* behind the park at the foot of citadel hill. Admission is US$0.75 and it is open weekends from 10 am to midnight.

Getting There & Away

Bus The bus station is next to the train station at Str Mihai Viteazul 32. Local buses leave here for Hunedoara every half hour between 6 am and 10 pm (22km).

Other daily bus services include one bus daily to Câmpeni (83km); one bus to Abrud (68km) and Târgu Jiu (150km) via Petroşani (93km); and two buses to Oradea (190km), Reşita (156km) and Timişoara (159km).

A bus also departs from Deva to Budapest (403km) every Thursday at 7 pm.

Train The Agenţie de Voiaj CFR (☎ 218 887) at Str 1 Decembrie, block A, is open weekdays from 8 am to 8 pm. Buy tickets in advance here for the four daily trains from Deva to Budapest (403km, 4½ hours).

There are no direct trains to Hunedoara but plenty of buses.

HUNEDOARA

Hunedoara is famous for two things – grim steel mills and an intact 14th century Gothic castle considered to be one of Transylvania's greatest architectural gems. The factories abutting the site could easily have been built elsewhere. But Ceauşescu wished to tarnish this symbol of Hungarian rule (both János Hunyadi and his son Matthias Corvinus, two famous Hungarian kings, made notable improvements to Hunedoara Castle).

Still, the 14th century **castle** itself, believed to be built on old Roman fortifications, is evocative, with three huge pointed towers, a drawbridge and high battlements. Five marble columns with delicate ribbed vaults support two halls (1453), the Diet Hall above and Knight's Hall below. The castle wall was hewn out of 30m of solid rock by Turkish prisoners.

The fortress was extensively restored by Iancu de Hunedoara (János Hunyadi in Hungarian) from 1452 onwards. The castle was restored in 1952; a handful of its 50 rooms today houses a **feudal art museum**.

Hunedoara castle is mostly of interest to environmentalists and Greenpeace activists. To get to the castle from the adjacent bus and train stations, head south along Blvd Republicii, then turn right onto Blvd Libertăţii. The castle is signposted from the bridge. It is open daily, except Monday, from 10 am to 5 pm. Admission is US$0.20.

Places to Stay

You can camp at the *Cinciş Lake* campsite, 7km south of Hunedoara on the shores of Lake Cinciş. Hunedoara has one hotel, the *Hotel Rusca* (☎ 712 001; fax 717 575), a five minute walk from the train station at Blvd Dacia 25.

Getting There & Away

The bus and train stations are at Blvd Republicii 3. There are buses every half hour from Deva to Hunedoara (22km).

From Bucharest, Braşov, Sibiu and Arad take a train to Simeria then change onto a local train to Hunedoara. Alternatively, take a train as far as Deva then get a bus. From Alba Iulia there are three daily trains to Hunedoara (2½ hours).

Local train services from Hunedoara include three trains daily to Orăştie (1¼ hours), Vinţu de Jos (1¾ hours) and Teiuş (2½ hours); and 14 trains to Simeria (30 minutes).

THE DACIAN & ROMAN CITADELS

The area immediately south of Hunedoara is an archaeologist's delight, being home to the capital of Dacia (Sarmizegetusa), a church built from a Roman soldiers' mausoleum (Densus), as well as the capital of Roman-conquered Dacia (Ulpia Traiana Sarmizegetusa).

Archaeologists at the National History Museum of Transylvania (☎ 064-191 718, 195 677) in Cluj-Napoca arrange frequent digs and summer camps and don't mind serious archaeologists digging in. Contact the museum in advance to arrange some volunteer work on site.

Sarmizegetusa

Dacians settled in what is today Romania from the 3rd century BC onwards. In 101 BC the Romans moved in to conquer these lands but not before the Dacians had built up a magnificent kingdom, centred in Sarmizegetusa and surrounded by a defensive circle of fortifications in the Orăştie mountains.

The Dacian capital of Sarmizegetusa remained unconquered by the Romans until 106 AD when, following a great battle, the Roman forces led by Trajan forced the Dacians to retreat north. The Dacian city was divided into three parts – two civilian areas and the middle sacred zone which contains the places of worship. Visitors are allowed to walk around the ruins.

Dacian Sarmizegetusa is a good 30km south of Orăştie along a dirt road, past the villages of Oraştioara de Jos, Bucium and Oraştioara de Sus. The ruins are actually 8km from the village of Gradiştea de Munte, at the end of the dirt track.

Costeşti

Sarmizegetusa was defended in the north-west by a fortress at Costeşti on the banks of the Oraşului river, the ruins of which remain. From Sarmizegetusa follow the road back north towards Orăştie and bear right at the turn-off for Costeşti.

The fortress at Costeşti, conquered by the Romans in 102 AD, was 45m by 45m square and was defended by several surrounding walls. The entire northern stretch from here along the banks of the Orăşului to Orăştie was protected by lookout towers and bastions. Remains of a Roman camp once fortified with ramparts and ditches still remain between the villages of Bucium and Oraştioara de Jos.

Densus

The church in Densus is on Romania's top 10 list of fabulous historic treasures. The stone church, built between the 11th and 12th centuries, stands on the ancient site of an edifice dating from the 4th century which archaeologists believe to have been the mausoleum of a Roman soldier. The church was constructed from stones taken from the Roman city of Ulpia Traian-Sarmizegetusa, many of the ancient Latin inscriptions remaining clearly evident on portions of its sturdy stone walls. Some bear funerary inscriptions.

Archaeologists conclude that the church, believed to have been built as a court chapel, was built by a Romanian *boyar* (noble) family, only falling under Hungarian rule from the 14th century onwards. There are fragments of a 15th century fresco inside the church.

Densus is east of Sarmizegetusa. From Orăştie bear 18km west to Simeria then continue south for 33km to Haţeg. From here, follow the Caransebeş road 7km south-west to Toteştii. In Toteştii, turn left. Densus is at the end of this dirt track.

Ulpia Traiana-Sarmizegetusa

Following the Romans defeat of Decebal's forces in 106 AD, they built up a spectacular array of towns for themselves, setting their capital of conquered Dacia in Ulpia Triana, some 15km south of Densus on the main Caransebeş road. Just to confuse things, the name of the former Dacian capital was added to the Roman city's name. It was now known as Ulpia Traiana-Sarmizegetusa.

Archaeologists have unearthed just 5% of the great city which was believed to have covered an area of 60 hectares. During the early 14th century, the stones of the Sarmizegetusa ruins were used by local villagers to build churches and it was not until the 1800s that the dismantled ruins fell under the protection of the Deva Archaeological Society and later of the National Museum of Transylvania. Remains of the Roman Forum, complete with 10m-tall marble columns, have already been uncovered, as have numerous temples devoted to the Roman deities, the amphitheatre, the palace of Augustales, a mausoleum and two suburban villas on the northern side of the town. Many tools, ceramics, ivory combs and other Roman treasures yielded from Sarmizegetusa are exhibited in the Deva history museum.

Every summer, between 21 July and the end of August, archaeologists from Cluj-Napoca descend upon Sarmizegetusa to continue their long task. There is a permanent archaeological base close to the site (*baza arheologico*; ☎ 054-762 170) which welcomes visitors year-round.

Places to Stay

The top people to contact for information and a bed for the night in a private house followed by a great home-cooked breakfast are those at *Opération Villages Roumains*, Str Principală 63a in Beriu, 8km south of Orăştie on the road to Dacian Sarmizegetusa. They arrange accommodation in rural homes throughout the region for US$10 to US$12 a night, including breakfast. They can also supply tourists with an English or French-speaking guide for US$3 an hour or US$6/10 for a half/full day. Bookings can be made in advance through the Opération Villages Roumains office in Cluj-Napoca.

There is a *Popasul Turistic* in the village

of Ulpia Traiana-Sarmizegetusa. Staff at the archaeological base can also help with accommodation and can often point you in the direction of rooms in private homes.

The Agenţie de Turism Mareş-Tur (☎ 054-641 446) in Orăştie at Str Unirii 5 can arrange rooms in private homes in Orăştie and surrounding villages. Be sure to book any accommodation through them in advance.

In Hateg, the two-star *Motel Pascom* (☎ & fax 054-777 480) at Str Viilor 42 has 10 doubles starting at US$15 a night. Three kilometres south-east of Hateg at Sântămaria Orlea is the cheap and cheerful *Hanul Sântămaria Orlea* (☎ 054-770 435). Its one-star doubles and triples cost around US$10/15.

THE RETEZAT MOUNTAINS

The Retezat mountains lie immediately south of Ulpia Traiana-Sarmizegetusa, 20 hectares of which form the Retezat National Park. The mountains, comprising two peaks, gain their name, meaning 'cut off', from the flat-topped pyramid shape of these peaks. The mountains shelter 82 glacial lakes. Year-round, black mountain goats, bears, foxes and stags roam the wilds here while, come migration season, the monk eagle is known to pass by.

East of the mountains lies the Jiu Valley, Romania's largest mining region, centred around Petroşani, Petrila and Câmpii lui Neag in the northern end of the valley and Târgu Jiu in the south. Traditionally, the miners have served as the militant voice of Romania's manual workforce and were used by Illiescu's post-revolution government in 1990 and 1991 to quash anti-communist protests in Bucharest. The miners' militant days however are now over. In a bid to close some of Romania's most unprofitable coal mines, the government in 1997 struck a deal with the miners, offering lucrative packages to those who agreed to take voluntary redundancy.

Maps

The pre-revolution *Trasee Turstice În*

Masivul Retezat, published in 1983 by Publiturism, is still quite widely available and much easier to use than the more recent *Hartă turistică montană Munţii Retezat* published by Cartografica in 1997. Both maps list 31 almost identical trails but the 1983 map is at a larger scale. Both cost around US$1 and are sold in some bookshops and travel agencies. At the time of writing they were widely available in Sibiu and Predeal.

Hiking from the North

One of the main access points to these mountains is north-west from Roman **Ulpia Traiana-Sarmizegetusa** from where a 6½ hour trail (19.5km) marked by red crosses leads to the privately run **Cabana Gura Zlata**. This trail actually follows a dirt track which, in dry weather, is suitable for vehicles too. Continuing 12km south past the Cabana Gura Zluta, you come to the **Lacul Gura Apei**, the 'mouth of the water'.

From the north you can also access the mountains from **Nucşoara**. Hikers can catch a local train from Simeria (36km), Petroşani (44km) or Târgu Jiu (94km) to the Ohaba de Sub Patria halt from where a six to seven hour trail marked by blue stripes leads south, through Nucşoara, to the **Cabana Peitrele**. This and the Gura Zluta are the two most popular cabanas in the Retezat mountains with numerous hiking trails marked from each.

The **Cabana Baleia** in the north-east of the range is also popular with hikers although at the time of writing it was closed for a re-fit. Check with the tourist office in Deva before heading out here. From Ohaba de Sub Patria (9km), Simeria (45km), Petroşani (35km) or Târgu Jiu (85km), take a local train to **Pui** train station from where you can hike 3km south along a paved road to Hobiţa. From Hobiţa a 4½ hour trail marked by blue triangles leads to the Cabana Baleia.

Hiking from the East

The main starting point from the east is the mining town of **Petroşani**, at the northern end of the Jiu valley (see Târgu Jiu section

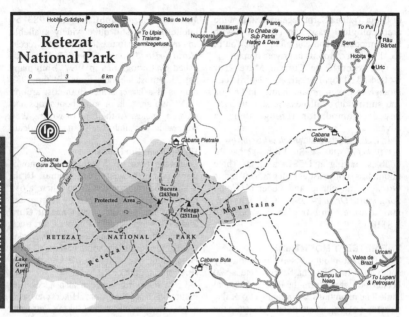

in the Wallachia chapter). Petroşani offers plenty of accommodation choices.

From here there are also regular daily buses to the mining village of **Câmpu lui Neag**, 28km west of Petroşani and the main point of attack for trails to the **Cabana Buta** in the south-eastern part of the Retezat mountains. There are also numerous local trains from Petroşani to **Lupeni**, 14km east of Câmpu lui Neag and easily hikeable. There is a cabana in Câmpu lui Neag where you can take a breather before submerging yourself in alpine glory (see Places to Stay).

From Câmpu lui Neag, a 3½ to 4-hour trail continues west to the Cabana Buta from where you can pick from a number of mountain trails.

From Petroşani you can also head 57km south down the Jiu valley to Târgu Jiu (see the Wallachia chapter). The southbound road running parallel to this road to the east is said to be the highest road in Romania, peaking at 2142m. It is only possible to cross the

mountains along this road by four-wheel drive.

Places to Stay

The *Cabana Gura Zlata* (☎ operator 991; ask for Gura Zlata) is a private chalet, meaning it is not possible to make advance bookings unless you are brave enough to do combat with a Romanian-speaking telephone operator.

The *Cabana Pietrale* (☎ 991; ask for village Poi, Casă Vonica) has double rooms in the main building for US$3 per person a night. Bathrooms are shared and hot water is a hit and miss affair. You can pitch tents here.

There is a small *campsite* in Pui. *Cabana Câmpu lui Neag* is open year-round and charges similar prices to the Pietrale. Another option is the *Motel Valea de Peşti* (☎ & fax 147 572), 2km east of Câmpu lui Neag towards Petroşani.

Petroşani has a cluster of downmarket, one-star hotels. The *Hotel Pârang* (☎ 543

582) at Str 1 Decembrie 1918 88, has two singles, 12 doubles and 14 triples starting at US$7 per person a night. This hotel was formerly called the 'Central'. Close by, at Str 1 Decembrie 1918, 120, is the Cameleonul International (☎ 542 122; fax 350 961). The *Hotel Intim* at Str Constantin Brâncuşi 10 and the *Mini-Hotel* at Str Nicolae Bălescu 10 are both quite reasonably priced too. Five kilometres south of Petroşani, on the road to Târgu Jiu, you pass the cheap *Motel Gambrinus* (☎ & fax 054-543 400).

Getting There & Away

Daily bus services to/from Petroşani include one to Târgu Jiu (57km) and eight daily to Deva (93km).

From Târgu Jiu (see Wallachia chapter) there are eight trains daily to Petroşani (1¼ to 1¾ hours).

To get to Petroşani from Hunedoara and Deva, take a local train to Simeria from where there are 12 trains daily to Petroşani (1½ to 2½ hours). There are also a couple of direct trains a day from Bucharest, Braşov, Sibiu and Arad to Petroşani. Alternatively, take a train to Simeria and change trains for Petroşani there.

In summer there is a daily train to Constanţa (eight hours) from Petroşani.

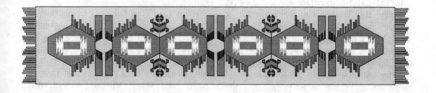

Wallachia

Wallachia is a flat, tranquil region of farms and small-scale industrial complexes stretching across the Danube plain north to the crest of the Carpathian mountains. Although the mighty Danube river flows right along the southern edge of Wallachia, the river is best seen between Moldova Veche and Drobeta-Turnu Severin in the west, where it breaks through the Carpathians at the legendary Iron Gate, a gorge of the Danube river on the border of Romania and Yugoslavia.

Towns such as Calafat, Giurgiu and Călăraşi are industrial river ports with little to offer – most travellers quickly pass through on the way to/from Bulgaria by ferry, car, or on foot. Other towns, including Târgu Jiu in the Jiu valley and Curtea de Argeş, are jumping-off points for the southern Carpathians.

Târgu Jiu is the second home town of the famous Romanian sculptor Constantin Brâncuşi, who between 1937 and 1938 created a striking WWI memorial column in the town's central park. Curtea de Argeş contains two splendid churches, a 14th century princely church and a monastery with dazzling pseudo-Islamic decorations outside and the tombs of the early 20th century Romanian royal family inside. From here the spectacular Trans-Făgăraşan highway – said to be one of the highest roads in Europe – cuts dramatically across the Făgăraş mountains, passing en route what is considered to be Romania's most authentic 'Dracula's Castle'.

History

Prior to the formation of Romania in the 19th century, the Romanians were known as Vlachs, hence Wallachia. These days the name Wallachia is seldom used in Romania since both it and the term *Vlach* are considered derogatory – they originated in the 3rd century with the Goth word for 'foreigner' (Wales and Welsh come from the same

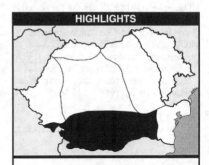

HIGHLIGHTS

- Stretch your neck at Târgu Jiu – Brancuşi's *Endless Column* is 29.35m high
- Learn what sytemisation meant in Scorniceşti, Ceauşescu's home village
- Hike up 1480 steps to the 'real' Dracula's castle at Poienari
- Take a train trip along the Danube from Drobeta-Turnu Severin to Băile Herculane
- Peek into Bulgaria from Ostrov then head east to the Dervent Monastery

source). Romanians call Wallachia *Ţara Românească* (land of the Romanians).

Founded by Radu Negru in 1290, this principality was subject to Hungarian rule until 1330 when Basarab I (1310-52) defeated the Hungarian king Charles I at the Battle of Posada and declared Wallachia independent, the first of the Romanian lands to achieve independence. The Wallachian princes (*voievode*) built their first capital cities – Câmpulung Muscel, Curtea de Argeş and Târgovişte – close to the protective mountains, but in the 15th century Bucharest gained ascendancy.

After the fall of Bulgaria to the Turks in 1396 Wallachia faced a new threat and in 1415 Mircea cel Bătrân – Mircea the Old (1386-1418) – was forced to acknowledge Turkish suzerainty. Other Wallachian princes such as Vlad Ţepeş (1448, 1456-62, 1476) and Mihai Viteazul (1593-1601) became national heroes by defying the Turks and refusing to pay tribute.

In 1859 Wallachia was united with Moldavia, paving the way for the modern Romanian state.

PLOIEŞTI
• *area code ☎ 044, pop 253,623*

Ploieşti ('ploy-esht'), the main city in Prahova county, lures few tourists except those passing through on the way from Bucharest to the Carpathian mountain resorts.

Oil has been refined in Ploieşti since 1857, accounting for Romania's ranking as first in Europe and sixth in the world in oil production between WWI and WWII. In 1936, Romania produced 8.7 million tons of oil. Sadly, since the mid-1970s Ploieşti's oilfields have rapidly declined. Today the town is heavily industrial with frighteningly bad pollution.

Orientation
Ploieşti has four train stations although most travellers will only use the southern (Gara Sud) and western train stations (Gara Vest). If you are arriving from Moldavia you'll alight at Gara Sud, a 15 minute walk from the town centre. Exit the station and head north up Blvd Independenţei until you reach Piaţa Victoriei. All the hotels, museums and restaurants are centred on this square.

If you arrive in town from Transylvania you will probably arrive at Gara Vest. From here, take bus No 1 or 2 to Piaţa Victoriei in the centre.

If you are coming from Bucharest or Târgovişte you could arrive at either station; get off at the southern station, as it's closer to the centre.

Information
Tourist Offices The best of the bunch is the Romania Passion tourism agency (☎ 114 507; fax 115 118) at Str Mihail Kogălniceanu 1. BTT (☎ 146 172; fax 122 775) has an office at Str Poştei 4-6.

The Automobil Clubul Român (ACR;

☎ 113 629), close to the Passion agency on Str Mihail Kogălniceanu, sells road maps and arranges car rental from Bucharest. The office is open Monday to Thursday from 8.30 am to 5 pm, Friday from 8.30 am to 4 pm, and Saturday from 8 am to noon.

Ploieşti does not have an airport but TAROM has an office (☎ 145 165) next to the Agenţie de Voiaj CFR at Blvd Republicii 17 (entrance from the pedestrianised street next to the Omnia department store). The office is open weekdays from 9.30 am to 4 pm.

Money The currency exchange at Ploieşti's Gara Sud is open daily from 9 am to 5 pm. The exchange office inside the Hotel Prahova is open daily from 8 am to 8 pm and offers the best rates in town.

You can cash travellers cheques and get cash advances on Visa/MasterCard at the Bancă Agricola, on the corner of Str Cercelus and Blvd Independenţei (open weekdays from 8.30 to 11.30 am and from 2.30 to 6 pm). The Bancă Comercială Ion Ţiriac (BCIT) next to the port office on Blvd Independenţei (open weekdays from 8.30 am to 2.30 pm) and Bancă Română de Comerţ Exterior (BANCOREX) on the corner of Piaţa Victoriei and Str Take Ionescu (open weekdays from 8.30 am to 3 pm) both offer the same services.

Post & Communications The central post and telephone office is south of Piaţa Victoriei on Blvd Republicii. It's open weekdays from 7 am to 8 pm, Saturday from 9 am to 1 pm. DHL Worldwide Express has an office (☎ 113 400; fax 111 370) inside the Hotel Central (open weekdays from 8.30 am to 5.30 pm).

Cultural Centres There is a French Cultural centre (Alliance Française de Roumanie; ☎ & fax 110 792) at Str Cooperaţiei 2.

Things to See
Ploieşti is most noted for its **Clock Museum** (Muzeul Ceasului), housed in a 19th century

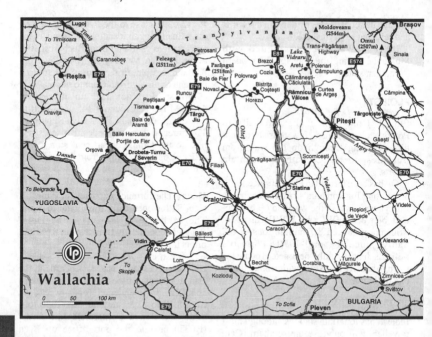

building at Str Nicolae Simachei. Cuckoo clocks, baroque clocks, musical clocks, Austrian clocks, German clocks, clocks in paintings and ancient clocks are all displayed in this museum, founded by Ploieşti history teacher, Nicolae Simachei, in 1963. Included in the collection is an 18th century, rococo Austrian clock which belonged to the Wallachian prince, Alexandru Ioan Cuza, responsible for bringing about the Union of the Principalities in 1859. The museum is open daily, except Monday, from 9 am to 5 pm. Admission is US$0.50. Ring the bell to enter.

Close by on Str Dr Bagdasar 8 is Europe's only **Museum of Oil** (Muzeul Naţionale al Petrolului; ☎ 123 564; fax 119 542). All the captions are in Romanian but it has some nice scale models of Ploieşti's oilfields and refineries. It is open daily, except Monday, from 9 am to 5 pm. Admission is US$0.50. Again, ring the bell to enter.

The **History & Archaeology Museum**

(Muzeul de Istorie şi Arheologie), housed in a former girls' school dating to 1865 at Str Toma Caragui 10, is by no means your conventional history museum. In the 'medal room', various war medals and honours are displayed, including a silver replica of a gold medal awarded to Mihai Viteazul in 1600. The original is displayed in a Vienna museum. Countless 'denaris', dating to the 2nd century BC, as well as coins from the reign of Carol I, are displayed in the 'coin room'. There is also a one million lei banknote which was used prior to the communists getting a grip on inflation in the 1950s. The museum also has a memorial room to the Romanian novelist, Ion Bassarabescu (1870-1952), famed for his novel *Priza* published in 1927. The house in which he lived from 1940 until his death still stands on Str Ştefan cel Mare. The history museum is open daily, except Monday, from 9 am to 5 pm. Admission is US$0.50.

In the central park on Piaţa Victoriei, there

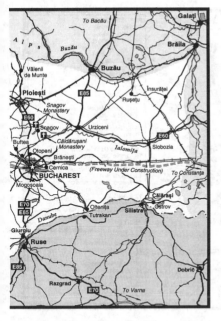

is a **memorial** to the victims of the 1989 revolution who died in the Ploieşti square during fighting on 22 December. The **Culture Palace** (Palatul Culturii), at the northern end of the square, houses a rather dull **Biology Museum** (Muzeul de Biologie Umană), aimed more at local schoolchildren than foreign tourists, and an **Art Museum** (Muzeul de Artă Populare). Both are open daily, except Monday, from 10 am to 6 pm. The main **Art Museum** (Muzeul de Artă) is housed in a large white building at Blvd Independenţei 1 (open Tuesday to Saturday from 9 am to 5 pm, Sunday from 9 am to 1 pm).

Opposite the **Culture House** (Casă de Cultură), continuing further north up Blvd Republicii, lies the impressive **St John's Cathedral**, dating from 1810 but extensively rebuilt in 1840. If the main door at the front is locked, try the side door. To its east lies the central market, partly housed in two large domed buildings.

Places to Stay

Private Rooms The rural tourism agency ANTREC (☎ 122 082; fax 192 977), at Blvd Bucureşti, block 10a, apartment 28, arranges rooms in private homes around Ploieşti and in the Prahova valley. A bed for the night costs from US$10, including breakfast.

Hotels Ploieşti has three hotels: the cheapest and friendliest is the two star *Hotel Prahova* (☎ 126 850) at Str Dobrogeanu Gherea 11. Single/double rooms with private bathroom cost US$20/30 a night, including breakfast. If you want a room with TV, it costs an extra US$0.30 per person a night.

Next in line is the battered-looking *Hotel Central* (☎ 126 641), overlooking Piaţa Victoriei at Blvd Republicii 9. Basic singles/doubles – also with private bathroom, breakfast and a TV for an extra charge – are US$14/26 a night. This two-star hotel has a few triple rooms too for US$34 and apartments for US$50. Other facilities include a restaurant, café, currency exchange and travel agency.

The empty, three-star *Hotel Turist* (☎ & fax 190 441) is inside a modern building with balconies overlooking the street at Str Take Ionescu 6. Guests are hard to spot. A room costs US$41 a night, regardless of whether there is one or two of you. Breakfast is included.

Places to Eat

Eating options are as limited as hotel beds. The *Braserie* above the Cinema Patria on Piaţa Victoriei offers prime views of the city and serves a variety of uninspiring buns and light snacks. It's open daily from 9 am to 11 pm. Equally unappealing in the cuisine field but favoured for its prime views of the cathedral is the *Restaurant Ciocirlia*, next to the Europa Bingo at Blvd Republicii 65. A bland beef steak and naked tomato salad costs US$2, but the fountain in front of the terrace is nice. The *Boulevard* near the Clock Museum has the best summer garden in town.

Vast amounts of vegetables, dry products, alcohol and fresh fish are housed in the two

WALLACHIA

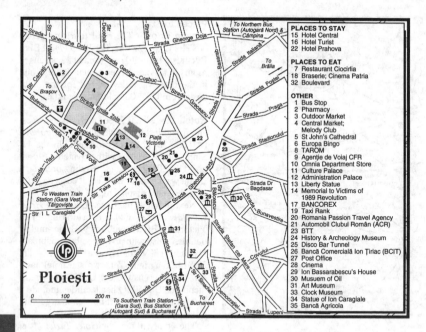

PLACES TO STAY
15 Hotel Central
16 Hotel Turist
22 Hotel Prahova

PLACES TO EAT
7 Restaurant Ciocirlia
18 Braserie; Cinema Patria
32 Boulevard

OTHER
1 Bus Stop
2 Pharmacy
3 Outdoor Market
4 Central Market;
  Melody Club
5 St John's Cathedral
6 Europa Bingo
8 TAROM
9 Agenţie de Voiaj CFR
10 Omnia Department Store
11 Culture Palace
12 Administration Palace
13 Liberty Statue
14 Memorial to Victims of
  1989 Revolution
17 BANCOREX
19 Taxi Rank
20 Romania Passion Travel Agency
21 Automobil Clubul Român (ACR)
23 BTT
24 History & Archeology Museum
25 Disco Bar Tunnel
26 Bancă Comercială Ion Ţiriac (BCIT)
27 Post Office
28 Cinema
29 Ion Bassarabescu's House
30 Musuem of Oil
31 Art Museum
33 Clock Museum
34 Statue of Ion Caragiale
35 Bancă Agricola

monster-sized halls which make up the *Central Market* (Halele Centrale), close to the cathedral on Blvd Unirii. The complex is open daily, except Sunday, with varying hours between 6.30 am and 7 pm.

Getting There & Away

Bus There are two stations: long-distance buses arrive at/depart from the northern bus station (Autogară Nord) at Str Griviţei 25. Buses to nearby villages use the southern bus station (Autogară Sud), a two minute walk from the southern train station on Str Depoului. Few people use buses as the service is so dire.

Daily services to/from the southern bus station include one to Bucharest (59km), six to Câmpina (32km) and two to Târgovişte (52km).

Train Trains to/from Bucharest, Târgovişte and Moldavia use the Gara Sud station at Piaţa 1 Decembrie 1918. This is closest to

the town centre. Trains to/from Transylvania use Gara Vest.

Advance train tickets are sold at the Agenţie de Voiaj CFR (☎ 142 080) at Blvd Republicii 17. The entrance to the office, open weekdays from 7.30 am to 3.30 pm, is on a pedestrianised street to the side of the Omnia department store.

From Gara Sud there is one train to Chişinău in Moldova, departing daily at 7.46 pm (13¾ hours). The *Bulgaria Expres* stops at Gara Sud at 6.22 pm, arriving in Sofia at 5.55 am. Northbound, the train departs from Ploieşti at 9.08 am, arriving in Cernăuţi (Chernivtsi) at 8.40 pm.

Five trains to Budapest from Bucharest stop at Ploieşti-Vest, departing daily at 2.20, 6.42 and 9.14 am, and 5.13 and 8.30 pm (12 hours). The daily Warsaw train departs from Ploieşti-Vest at 8.53 pm (13½ hours).

Getting Around

Bus, tram and trolleybus tickets are sold at

the public transport office (☎ 143 761) marked 'Coreco' on your left when you exit from Gara Sud. Bus Nos 1 and 2 go from Gara Sud to Piaţa Victoriei in the centre and then on to Gara Vest. From Gara Vest, bus No 2 continues to the university.

AROUND PLOIEŞTI

Heading north into the Prahova valley you come to **Câmpina** (formerly spelt Cîmpina). Approaching this small town, 32km north of Ploieşti, you pass a memorial to pioneering, dare-devil pilot, Aurel Vlaicu, who met an untimely death after his plane crashed as he attempted to cross the Carpathians.

Câmpina's main attraction is its **Nicolae Grigorescu Museum** (Muzeul Nicolae Grigorescu), Blvd Carol I 166, dedicated to the life and works of one of Romania's most exciting painters (1838-1907). The artist started his career painting icons, at the age of 10, to support his peasant family. He went on to study in Paris, spending a short stint at the studio of Sebastion Cornu where he studied with Jean Renoir. His works attracted the attention of the Barbizon group and of Napoleon III who bought two of his paintings at an exhibition in Fontainbleau in 1867. During the Romanian War for Independence (1877-78), Grigorescu worked as a frontline correspondent as an artist.

Further north along Câmpina's main Blvd Carol I at No 145 is **Haşdeu Castle**, dating from 1888 and considered one of the most bizarre castles in Romania. It was built by history professor Bogdan Petriceicu Haşdeu in memory of his academically brilliant daughter, Iulia, who died of tuberculosis at the age of 19. Iulia is actually buried in the Belu cemetery in Bucharest but it was in this spiritual temple that her father held seances to communicate with his daughter after her premature death. A bust of Iulia, who would have been the first woman, had she not died in 1888, to be awarded a degree from the Sorbonne in Paris, stands in the main castle hall.

The two-star *Hotel Muntenia* (☎ 044-333 090; fax 044-333 092) at the northern end of Câmpina's main thoroughfare, Blvd Carol I

61, has reasonably priced single/double rooms for US$15/25 a night.

Getting There & Away

From Ploieşti's southern bus station there are six buses daily to Câmpina (32km).

TÂRGOVIŞTE
• *area code ☎ 045, pop 99,173*

All eyes were on Târgovişte, 49km north-west of Bucharest, following the dramatic arrest here of communist president Nicolae Ceauşescu and his wife Elena on 22 December 1989. Four days later, the first bloody images of the hastily arranged court session and execution inside Târgovişte's military garrison flashed across the world's TV screens to prove that the two were really dead.

The Ceauşescus, who had fled Bucharest by helicopter just hours before their arrest, hijacked a car in Titu, 44km north-west of Târgovişte, where they were spotted by two soldiers who finally caught up with them in Târgovişte. The Ceauşescus were promptly taken to the military garrison in the town where they were tried in secret on Christmas Day and shot by a firing squad three hours later.

Târgovişte (formerly spelt Tîrgovişte) is a charming market town dating from 1396. It served as capital of Wallachia from 1418 until 1659 when the capital was moved to Bucharest. During the 15th century, Vlad Ţepeş, the notorious impaler with whom the fictitious Dracula has come to be associated, held princely court here.

Orientation

The train station is a good 20 minutes walk west from the centre. Exit the station and head east, past the military barracks (see Things to See later) up Blvd Castanilor, then turn right into Str Victoriei. All eastbound buses along this street stop in the centre. The bus station and central market are 3km north-west of town; turn right as you leave the station, then cross the large roundabout and take any eastbound bus down Calea Câmpulung.

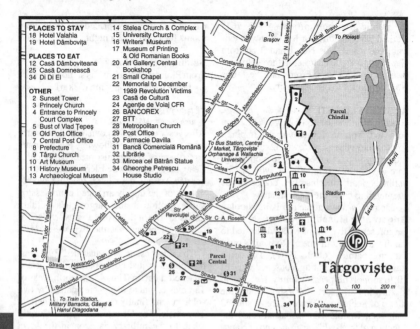

PLACES TO STAY
18 Hotel Valahia
19 Hotel Dâmboviţa

PLACES TO EAT
12 Casă Dâmboviteana
25 Casă Domnească
34 Di Di El

OTHER
2 Sunset Tower
3 Princely Church
4 Entrance to Princely
   Court Complex
5 Bust of Vlad Ţepeş
6 Old Post Office
7 Central Post Office
8 Prefecture
9 Târgu Church
10 Art Museum
11 History Museum
13 Archaeological Museum

14 Stelea Church & Complex
15 University Church
16 Writers' Museum
17 Museum of Printing
   & Old Romanian Books
20 Art Gallery; Central
   Bookshop
21 Small Chapel
22 Memorial to December
   1989 Revolution Victims
23 Casă de Cultură
24 Agenţie de Voiaj CFR
26 BANCOREX
27 BTT
28 Metropolitan Church
29 Post Office
30 Farmacie Davilla
31 Bancă Comercială Română
32 Librărie
33 Mircea cel Bătrân Statue
34 Gheorghe Petrescu
   House Studio

Târgovişte

0   100   200 m

Târgovişte centre is divided into two parts, both within close proximity of each other. The main shops, banks and hotels are in the modern centre clustered around Central Park, which is straddled by Blvd Libertăţii to the north and Str Victoriei to the south. The princely court and key museums are in the older part of town, along Str Nicolae Bălcescu (known locally as Calea Domnească) which cuts across the town from north to south.

Information

Tourist Offices Staff at the tourist office (☎ 634 491) adjoining Hotel Valahia speak some English but are not helpful. Your best bet is to head straight for the Princely Court where you can buy tourist brochures in English or French covering all the main sights.

Money There is a currency exchange inside the Hotel Valahia. Travellers cheques can be cashed and money withdrawn on Visa/MasterCard at the Bancă Comercială Română which backs onto the central park on Str Victoriei. The bank is open weekdays from 8 to 11 am and there is an ATM outside.

The former Hotel Turist, a little further down the street at Str Victoriei 1, has been rebuilt to house the flashy BANCOREX. It is also only open mornings.

Post & Communications There is a small post office next to the pharmacy on Str Victoriei, open weekdays from 8 am to 3.30 pm. You can collect post restante here. The central post and telephone office is a couple of blocks north on Str Ion Rădulescu. The telephone section (on the left as you enter) is open daily from 7 am to 8.30 pm. Telephone cards are sold from the desk in the post office section (on the right as you enter), only open weekdays.

The old post office, dating from 1906 and no longer functional, at the eastern end of

Calea Câmpulung, is preserved as an architectural monument.

Things to See

The **military barracks**, where Nicolae and Elena Ceauşescu were tried and executed on 25 December 1989, are immediately on the right as you leave the train station. At the hasty trial, which lasted just three hours, the Ceauşescus faced joint charges of being accomplice to the murder of some 60,000 people, of genocide, and of attempting to flee Romania with state money, totalling US$1 billion, stashed away in foreign bank accounts. None of the charges were proved.

It is forbidden to enter the garrison at the western end of Blvd Castanilor although guards at the entrance – some of whom claim to have witnessed the bloody execution – are extremely friendly. It is also forbidden to take photographs.

The bloodthirsty prince Vlad Ţepeş resided at the **Princely Court** (Curtea Domnească). The court was built in the 14th century for Mircea cel Bătrân (Mircea the Old) and remained a residence for Wallachia's princes until the reign of Constantin Brâncoveanu (1688-1714). Mircea cel Bătrân fortified his court with defensive towers. The **Sunset Tower** (Turnul Chândiei), 27m tall, served as a military observation post and later as a prison. Its walls are 9m thick. It was so named because it was from here that guards would announce the closing of the city gates as the sun went down. The tower was rebuilt in a neo-Gothic style in the mid-19th century. Today it houses a small exhibition recounting the life and horrors of Vlad Ţepeş's life. All the captions are in Romanian.

Immediately south of the entrance to the court is a small **Art Museum** (Muzeul de Artă). The court and museum are open daily, except Monday, from 10 am to 5 pm. Admission is US$0.35.

Heading south from the court you come to the local **History Museum** (Muzeul de Istorie Dâmboviţa) on the corner of Str Nicolae Bălcescu (Calea Domnească) and Str Justiţei; it's open Tuesday to Friday from 9 am to 5 pm, and at weekends from 10 am to 6 pm.

A fascinating **Museum of Printing & Old Romanian Books** (Muzeul Tiparului şi al Cărţii Româneşti Vechi; ☎ 612 877) is housed in a 17th century palace built by Constantin Brâncoveanu for his daughter Safta at Str Justiţei 3-5. Its prize exhibit is a manuscript dating from 1521, believed to be among the earliest texts written in Romanian (in the Cyrillic alphabet) to be preserved. Until the 17th century, texts were written in the official Slavonic language. The final hall is dedicated to the 19th century, marking the switch from Cyrillic to the Latin alphabet. A small **Writers' Museum** (Muzeul Scriitorilor Dâmboviţeni) adjoins the book museum. Opposite is the **University Church** (Biserica Universităţii), dating from the 19th century. In front of it are busts of local academics Ienăchiţa Văcărescu (1740-97) and Radu de la Afumaţi (1522-1529). Both museums are open daily, except Monday, from 9 am to 5 pm. Admission to each is US$0.15.

Heading south-west along Str Stelea towards the modern centre, you pass the **Stelea Church** complex (Complexul Biserica Stelea), founded as a monastery by Moldavian prince Vasile Lupu (1634-53) in 1645 as a peace offering to Wallachian ruler Matei Basarab. The Gothic-style complex, closed during the communist era, was under renovation at the time of writing. Few archaeological relics of interest are displayed at the small **Archaeological Museum** (Muzeul de Arheologie), Str Stelea 4. Apart from a few blocks bearing funerary inscriptions outside, the main building is filled with contemporary paintings by local artists. The museum is open daily, except Monday, from 9 am to 5 pm. Admission is free.

Continue west along Str Stelea, then turn left along Str Raudiţei onto Blvd Libertăţii. In **Central Park** a marble cross crowned by three arches stands outside a **small chapel** dedicated to the victims of the December 1989 revolution. The 18th century **Metropolitan Church** (Biserica Mitropolie) is in

WALLACHIA

the park. For a short time following the closure of the press at the 16th century **Dealu Monastery**, this church housed a small printing press in its monks' quarters on a hill 3km north-east of the centre. The head of the great Wallachian prince Mihai Viteazul, who was beheaded on the orders of the Habsburg general George Basta on 3 August 1601, is buried in the monastery.

A few blocks north is the partially frescoed **Târgu Church** (Biserica Târgului), opposite the central post office on Str Ion Rădulescu. The church, which dates from 1654, was painted during the 17th and 18th centuries but heavily destroyed during an earthquake in 1940. Extensive renovations followed in 1941 and again in the 1970s. Inside is a memorial plaque to local priest and teacher, Professor Georgescu (1928-52), who was among the thousands to die while toiling under communist forced labour to build the Danube-Black Sea Canal in Dobruja.

Testament to Romania's thousands of abandoned children is Marin Răducu's mural painting entitled **Wall of Childhood** (Zidul Copilariei în Imagini). The mural – made up of 115 panels, each 4sq metres large – decorates the concrete wall surrounding Târgovişte's largest orphanage. The painter, who spent his own childhood in an orphanage in Siliştea Gumeşti in the south of Dâmboviţa county, embarked on the project in the early 1990s in a bid to brighten up the lives of those who lived inside the grey compound. Many of the 150 children in the orphanage helped Răducu paint the 230m long, 2m-high wall. Visitors are welcome to visit the orphanage; the orphans will gladly show you which part of the kaleidoscope they painted. The orphanage (Casă de Copii; ☎ 612 327) is in a run-down housing area in the western suburbs at Str Moldoviei 5, close to the **Wallachian State University**.

Heading out of town north along Str Brezişeanu, you pass the small **Gheorghe Petreşcu House Studio** (Casă atelier Gheorghe Petreşcu). The Romanian still-life, landscape and portrait painter (1872-1949) spent the last 20 years of his life in Târgovişte where he captured most of the town's major sights on canvas. Some 50 pieces are exhibited in the house where he lived.

Places to Stay

Accommodation is not cheap. Providing you speak basic Romanian or are an expert at wild gesticulations, you should be able to secure yourself a bed for the night in a private house with BTT (☎ 634 224, 213 776), Str Victoriei, block H1. The staff here are not yet accustomed to dealing with independent travellers but are keen to please. A private room should cost no more than US$10. The agency has no fixed price list, however, so negotiate.

The main hotel in town is the *Hotel Valahia* (☎ 634 491; ☎ & fax 01-312 5992) overlooking the central square at Blvd Libertăţii 7. Spacious single/double rooms with private bath cost US$32/43 a night, including breakfast. The hotel is popular with business travellers.

At the time of writing the *Hotel Dâmboviţa* (☎ 613 961) at Blvd Libertăţii 1 was closed for renovation.

Out of town, 20km south of Târgovişte on the main road to Piteşti (Şoseaua Târgovişte-Gaeşti), you will find the *Hanul Dragodana* (☎ 045-711 109), a large inn with double rooms with private bath (cold water only) for US$20 a night. The inn has a large terrace restaurant, open 24 hours and popular with truckers.

Places to Eat

The top place in town to eat is the jolly *Di Di El* (☎ 213 789), a five minute walk from Hotel Valahia, at Str Nicolae Bălcescu (Calea Domnească), block A. It serves huge, well topped pizzas and great spaghetti for no more than US$5 a head with a bottle of wine thrown in. It has an outside terrace, takeaway service, and is open daily from 9 am to 1 am.

Casă Domnească, behind BANCOREX on Str Victoriei, is a small, cheap restaurant frequented by locals, with an outside terrace and a playing-cards club upstairs which is open until late. The terrace is a good spot for coffee and light snacks.

Recommended for its local cuisine is *Casă Dâmboviteana*, opposite the History Museum on Str Nicolae Bălcescu and open daily from noon to whenever it feels like closing.

Getting There & Away

Bus Major daily services include 13 to Bucharest, five to Câmpulung Muscel (73km), two to Ploieşti (52km) and Braşov (90km), and one to Râmnicu Vâlcea (267km) and Craiova (171km).

Train Advance tickets are sold at the Agenţie de Voiaj CFR (☎ 611 554), just north of the train station at Blvd Castanilor 2. It is open weekdays from 7 am to 7 pm.

From Târgovişte there are 14 local trains daily to Ploieşti-Sud (1¾ hours). To get to Târgovişte from other cities, you have to change trains at Ploieşti-Sud.

PITEŞTI
• *area code ☎ 048, pop 185,475*

Piteşti is a large, industrial, heavily polluted town that most Romanians will tell you to avoid. They're right. Nevertheless, the city is one of Romania's great commercial centres with the country's only stretch of motorway (*autostrada*) bringing motorists the 114km west from Bucharest. Since 1966 Dacia cars – modelled on the old Renault 12 and the butt of endless jokes – have been produced here, creating work for some 29,000 people.

During the early communist era the town was more ominously known as the home of Piteşti prison, a high-security prison dating from 1900 and used by the communists in the late 1940s and early 1950s as the site of a horrific experiment in which imprisoned dissident students were forced to torture each other, hence breaking down all barriers between 'victim' and 'torturer'. This grotesque 're-education programme' was brought to an abrupt halt in 1952 after details of the horrors leaked out, and the prison was later closed and demolished.

Orientation

Confusingly, Piteşti has two bus stations and two train stations but most travellers only use the stations in the south. Buses to/from Bucharest and other major cities in Romania all arrive/depart from the southern bus station (Autogară Sud), off the southern end of Blvd Bratianu on Str Abatorului Târgul din Vale. All Bucharest and Curtea de Argeş trains stop at the southern train station (officially Piteşti-Sud but known as Piteşti) on Blvd Republicii, . Bus Nos 2, 4 and 8 run between the train station and town.

Blvd Republicii leads west from the train station to the town centre. The main pedestrianised street, Str Victoriei, where all the hotels, restaurants and tourist offices are, runs parallel to Blvd Republicii.

Maps The commercial *Municipiul Piteşti* map (1997) includes a detailed city map (including the suburbs) and a map of Argeş county. It is sold for US$1.20 at the tourist office and at the reception of Hotel Argeş.

Information

Tourist Offices The only tourist office (☎ 625 450) adjoins Hotel Muntenia (separate entrance on Str Victoriei). It arranges excursions to Curtea de Argeş, sells maps and arranges car rental. It is open weekdays from 9 am to 5 pm.

Money There is a currency exchange inside Hotel Muntenia. You can cash travellers cheques and get cash advances on Visa/MasterCard at BANCOREX, at the southern end of Str Victoriei on the corner of Blvd Republicii and Str Craiovei. A couple of doors south at Blvd Republicii 83 is the Bancă Comercială Română. Both are open weekdays from around 8 to 11 am.

Post & Communications The central post office is opposite the church at the southern end of Str Victoriei. It is open daily from 7 am to 9 pm; the post office section is only open weekdays. There is a small telephone office at Blvd Victoriei 8.

WALLACHIA

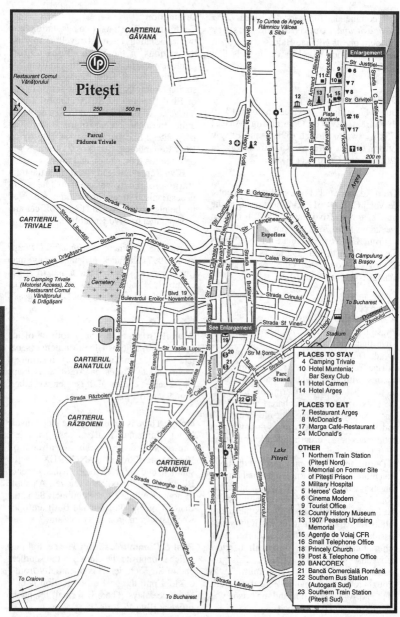

Piteşti

0   250   500 m

PLACES TO STAY
4 Camping Trivale
10 Hotel Muntenia;
   Bar Sexy Club
11 Hotel Carmen
14 Hotel Argeş

PLACES TO EAT
7 Restaurant Argeş
8 McDonald's
17 Marga Café-Restaurant
24 McDonald's

OTHER
1 Northern Train Station
   (Piteşti Nord)
2 Memorial on Former Site
   of Piteşti Prison
3 Military Hospital
5 Heroes' Gate
6 Cinema Modern
9 Tourist Office
12 County History Museum
13 1907 Peasant Uprising
   Memorial
15 Agenţie de Voiaj CFR
16 Small Telephone Office
18 Princely Church
19 Post & Telephone Office
20 BANCOREX
21 Bancă Comercială Română
22 Southern Bus Station
   (Autogară Sud)
23 Southern Train Station
   (Piteşti Sud)

Cultural Centres For a touch of the west visit the French Cultural Centre (Alliance Française de Roumanie; ☎ & fax 212 927) at Str Vasile Milea 4.

Things to See

After WWII, **Piteşti prison**, just north of the centre on Str Negru Vodă (between Nos 32 and 34), was selected by the communist government as the site for its so-called 'Student Re-education Centre' because of its high-security measures and its isolation from any private homes at the time. Operational since 1900, it was not until 1949, following the arrest of some 1000 anti-communist students in 1948 on charges of belonging to the National Peasant Party, the Iron Guard, or the Zionist movement, that psychiatric abuse became a major feature of the already harsh prison regime. The experiment was part of a crackdown during which an estimated 180,000 people were rounded up and sent to labour camps and prisons. More than 30 prisoners Piteşti died and hundreds were tortured during the four years the experiment was in place.

Today a tall, mosaic-tiled column in memory of those who died in Piteşti marks the spot where the prison stood. It stands between the first two, of three, apartment blocks built on the site after the prison was destroyed. A **military hospital** (*spitalul militar*), dating from 1881, still stands opposite.

The existence of the prison and the atrocities committed inside are completely ignored in the county **history museum** (Muzeul Judeţean de Istorie) overlooking the small central park at Str Armand Călinescu 4. At the time of writing the museum was

---

From Victim to Torturer

In 1949-52 a unique and experimental 'student re-education programme' was introduced in Piteşti, Gherla and Aiud prisons as a means of torturing political prisoners. The programme was implemented by Eugen Ţurcanu, an inmate at Piteşti prison, acting on the orders of the Securitate. Ţurcanu rounded up a core team of torturers from among his fellow inmates.

Re-education induced tortured prisoners to become torturers themselves. The first stage of this grotesque process involved the prisoner confessing all his crimes and 'anti-state' thoughts that he'd failed to earlier reveal to Securitate interrogators. He then signed a declaration in which he consented to his 're-education'. Scrubbing floors with a rag between the teeth, eating soup hog-like with both hands tied behind the back, licking toilets clean and being beaten to unconsciousness were just some of the persuasive methods used.

Religiously inclined prisoners, dubbed 'Catholics', were baptised each morning with a bucket of urine. Others were forced to don a white sheet in imitation of Christ and wear a penis carved from soap around their necks. Fellow prisoners kissed the soap pendant and the prisoner was flogged by other inmates in imitation of Christ's ordeal on the road to Golgotha.

Next, the victim was forced to disclose the names of fellow inmates who'd shown him kindness or sympathy. He then had to renounce his own family, 'reviling them in such foul and hideous terms that it would be next to impossible ever to return to natural feelings towards them', according to former political prisoner Dimitru Bacu in his novel *The Anti-Humans*.

In the final stage of the programme, victims had to prove their successful 'regeneration' – by inflicting the same mental and physical abuse on new prison recruits. If they refused they were driven through the programme again. Those who slackened in their new role as re-educator spent time in the prison's incarceration cell, black room, or isolation cell.

The incarceration cells were 1.8m-long upright coffins with a small hole for ventilation. One or two prisoners had to stand in these cells for eight to 15 days. The black room was 2.7sq metres and windowless. Up to 30 prisoners were detained here for a maximum of three weeks without water. Isolation cells were reserved for sentences of three months or more, and many prisoners kept in these cells died of tuberculosis.

In 1954 Eugen Ţurcanu and 21 other prisoners were secretly tried and sentenced to death for the murder of 30 prisoners and the abuse of 780. The Securitate denied all knowledge of the programme. ■

closed and under renovation. When open, its hours are 10 am to 6 pm (closed Monday). Crossing the park towards Blvd Republicii you pass the **monument** in memorial to those who died in the 1907 peasant uprising.

On Str Victoriei, the unusual Saint George's Church (Biserica Sfântul Gheorghe), also known as the **Princely Church** (Biserica Domnească), was built by Prince Constantin Şerban and his wife Princess Bălas between 1654 and 1658. The steeple, supported by brick columns on top of the church porch, is really quite unique. The church housed a school in the 18th century.

West of the centre in the Trivale district is a large **forest and park** (Parcul Pădurea Trivale). Approaching the park along Str Trivale from the centre, you pass **Heroes' Gate** (Poarta Eroilor), erected between 1916 and 1918 in memory of those who died during WWI. The paved street running through the gate leads to nothing more than a few ramshackle houses and a dead end. Further into the forest, 1km west of Camping Trivale, is a **zoo**, open daily, except Monday and Tuesday, from 10 am to 7 pm. Admission costs US$0.20. In summer, a daily bus runs from Autogară Sud every hour between 8.30 am and 7.30 pm.

Places to Stay

Camping The town's major campsite, *Camping Trivale* (☎ 276 190), is 4km west of the centre at the western end of Str Trivale in the forest. Double wooden cabins cost US$3 a night; wash facilities are basic and only equipped with cold water. To get there walk west along Str Trivale. If you've got a car, hostel signs (marked with a picture of a hut and a tree) lead you from the centre along Calea Drăgăşani to the site; you cannot access it by car from Str Trivale. Camping Trivale is open from mid-May to the end of August.

Hotels Piteşti's hotels are within spitting distance of one another. The two-star, family-run *Hotel Carmen* (☎ 222 699; fax 215 297) at Blvd Republicii 84 is the small-est of the trio. It has 15 double rooms, all with private bath, costing US$25 a night, including breakfast.

The towering, three star *Hotel Muntenia* (☎ 625 450; fax 214 556) overlooking Piaţa Muntenia on Blvd Republicii has over 500 beds, with double rooms ranging in price from US$16 to US$30, depending on how recently the room was refurbished. The hotel has all the facilities including a billiard room, conference hall, bar, restaurant and adjoining Bar Sexy nightclub.

The more intimate, one star *Hotel Argeş* (☎ 625 450), opposite the Muntenia on Piaţa Muntenia, is the friendliest of the lot. It is also the only hotel to have single rooms with private bath at US$10 a night, as well as doubles at US$20.

Places to Eat

Choice is limited. One of the most hip places in town is the *Marga Café-Restaurant*, next door to the small telephone office at Blvd Victoriei 8. It has an outside terrace for people-watching on the busy pedestrianised street. Its inside is practically filled by a table-tennis table – always busy! *Restaurant Argeş* at the northern end of Str Victoriei, next to Cinema Modern at Str Victoriei 20, is your regular pork cutlet-and-fries type of place. It adjoins the *Salon Euro Bingo*, open 24 hours.

The *Restaurant Cornul Vănătorului*, next to Camping Trivale, is a large, terraced restaurant in the forest. It serves traditional Romanian dishes and is a popular drinking hole for merry-making campers in summer; it is closed in winter.

Fast-food kiosks and burger vans are dotted along pedestrianised Str Victoriei. *McDonald's* has pride of place, opposite Piaţa Muntenia; it is open daily from 7 am to midnight. It has a second drive-in and sit-down outlet opposite Autogară Sud on Blvd Republicii.

Getting There & Away

Bus All major services use Autogară Sud. Daily services include two to Alexandria

(272km) and Braşov (136km); five to Bucharest (108km); and one to Craiova (142km), Sibiu (260km), Râmnicu Vâlcea (75km) and Târgu Jiu (174km).

There is also a daily, early-morning bus from Autogară Sud to Istanbul. Tickets are sold by the Öz Murat travel agency (☎ 221 151) at the bus station.

Train The Agenţie de Voiaj CFR (☎ 630 565) is at Str Domniţa Bălaşa 13. All major train services arrive at/depart from the southern train station, simply listed on timetables as Piteşti. Travellers heading from Bucharest to Curtea de Argeş have to change trains at Piteşti.

SCORNICEŞTI
● *area code ☎ 048*

Some 38km south-west of Piteşti, off the main E70 highway to Craiova, lies Scorniceşti, one of the most publicised villages in Romania, not least because it was the birthplace and childhood village of Nicolae Ceauşescu. The communist dictator actually only spent the first 11 years of his life in the small rural village, before he moved to Bucharest to serve as an apprentice cobbler. The village first hit the national headlines in 1976 when the remains of the first homosapiens in Europe were allegedly found here by scientists.

In 1988, Scorniceşti gained further notoriety when, as part of the president's systemisation scheme, the centre of the village was bulldozed and rebuilt with characterless apartment blocks. A gigantic football stadium was consequently added to the concrete montage – a present from Ceauşescu to his home town. Scorniceşti was among the first villages to be razed under the scheme, although the ornate street lamps and grandiose flowerbeds which run the length of the central street somehow failed to make their way to other systemised villages.

Ceauşescu's childhood home was spared. Prior to 1989, the small whitewashed cottage housed a museum dedicated to the Conducator. Following the December revolution the

---

Systemisation

Ceauşescu's systemisation plan condemned thousands of villages to being bulldozed off the country map in a bid to curb private farming and create more state agricultural land. Displaced villagers were to be uprooted to soul-less purpose-built communal apartment blocks where – according to the propaganda – a new life utilising the 'experience of the peasant with the efficiency of the Marxist worker' awaited them.

The grand plan was approved in 1974 but not implemented until 1988. Out of Romania's 13,123 villages, all but 5000 were destined to be destroyed by the year 2000. Some three million people would have to abandon their homes, cattle and traditional rural lifestyle in the process.

Stupidly, Ceauşescu ignored the fact that it was these small, privately owned farmsteads – comprising just 6% of Romania's total arable land – that produced 20% of the country's milk, 25% of its fruit, and 14% of its meat. All his greedy eyes could focus on was the additional 4.5% of agricultural land the state would acquire by squeezing the rural population into a smaller geographical area.

The first villages to be systemised in August 1988 were Buda, Demieni, Odoleanu and Vladiceasca in the Ilfov district north of Bucharest, and Scorniceşti (Ceauşescu's home village). Villagers were given just a few days notice to evacuate their condemned homes which were flattened to make way for new 'agro-industrial complexes'. Few accommodation blocks had running water, while cramped kitchens were shared by up to 10 families. Despite being assured otherwise, there was no opportunity for villagers to grow their own fruit and vegetables or keep livestock, leaving many in dire financial straits. Villagers in some regions were forced to demolish their own homes.

Widespread hostility from the west forced Ceauşescu to abandon systemisation in 1989. Immense pressure was also exerted on the Romanian government by the authorities in Hungary who perceived the scheme as a tool for destroying the last remaining strongholds of Hungarian culture in Transylvania and assimilating ethnic minorities. For the thousands sentenced to a life of misery confined within four grey walls devoid of their ancestors' warming spirits, the damage had already been done. ∎

WALLACHIA

museum was closed. Today, it is possible to visit the two room house, tended by Ceauşescu's sister who lives in a small house opposite. A photograph of Ceauşescu at his mother's funeral in 1977 and another of him and Elena admiring corn in a field are displayed on the chimney breast in the hallway. In the bedroom, there is a painting of his parents and, above the bed, a tapestry portrait of Ceauşescu.

The house is not officially open to visitors but the women in the kiosk on the main road opposite will happily sell you a 'ticket' for US$0.15, escort you down the path to the house and then scuttle away, leaving stunned tourists to tackle Ceauşescu's formidable sister alone! Act humble and she will invite you inside.

Ceauşescu's mother Alexandra (1889-1977) and father Andruta (1890-1972) are buried in the family grave in the village cemetery, next to the white church further north along the main road; continue past the Ceauşescu house and turn left at the junction. The expensive white marble tombstone was laid in 1993 by the Ceauşescu family.

Scorniceşti is signposted west off the main Piteşti-Craiova road. The Ceauşescu house is at the northernmost end of the village. Drive through the unsystemised outskirts of the village, past the systemised centre, and continue along the main road until you cross a small bridge. The house is the first on the left, immediately after the bridge, opposite a small kiosk and well.

CURTEA DE ARGEŞ
• *area code ☎ 048*

Curtea de Argeş, a princely seat in the 14th century after the capital of Wallachia was moved here from Muscel Câmpulung, is a welcoming place for visitors. The church is considered to be the oldest monument preserved in its original form in Wallachia, while the monastery (or episcopal cathedral), made from polished, sculpted stone on the fringe of the town, is unique for its chocolate-box architecture and the host of royal tombs it hides.

Orientation & Information
The train station, a 19th century architectural monument, is 100m north of the bus station (☎ 712 685) on Str Albeşti. To get to the centre – a 10 minute walk – turn left along Str Albeşti, then bear right at the fork up the cobbled Str Castanilor. Cross the small square and turn left along Str Negru Vodă. At the crossroads continue straight, past the Disco Club Castel, until you reach a statue of Basarab I, where the road forks in three directions. All the major sights, campsite and hotels (signposted) are a short walk from here. Continue walking straight ahead, past the princely court on the left, for Calea Basarabilor.

Curtea de Argeş does not have a tourist office. The currency exchange inside the Hotel Posada, at the northern end of Calea Basarabilor, is open daily from 9 am to 4 pm. The post office at Calea Basarabilor 121 is open weekdays from 7 am to 8 pm. The telephone office, in the same building, is open weekdays from 7 am to 9 pm, and at weekends from 8 am to 2 pm. There is a small pharmacy next door.

You can change money and cash travellers cheques at the Bancă Comercială Română, next to the prefecture further north along Calea Basarabilor (open weekdays from 8 am to noon).

Things to See
The ruins of Curtea de Argeş's **Princely Court** (Curtea Domnească), an ensemble originally comprising a church and palace, are in the centre. The church was built in the 14th century by Basarab I, whose statue stands in the small square outside the main entrance to the court. It was built to commemorate his victory over the Hungarian army on the Posada pass, close to the Wallachian-Transylvania border. Basarab died in Târgovişte in 1352, but it was not until 1939 that his burial place near the altar in the princely church at Curtea de Argeş was discovered. The princely court was rebuilt by Basarab's son, Nicolae Alexandru Basarab (1352-68) and completed by Vlaicu Vodă (1361-77).

While little remains of the palace today, the 14th century church built on the ruins of a 13th century church in the shape of an inscribed Greek cross, is almost perfectly intact. Some 14th century frescoes are still clearly defined. The church is lovingly tended by a dedicated, French-speaking caretaker who guides visitors around against a background of prerecorded classical and choral music. It is open daily from 9 am to 5 pm. Admission is US$0.75.

Opposite the main entrance to the court is the **County Museum** (Muzeul Orasenesc; ☎ 711 446), housed in a white and blue painted building at Str Negru Vodă 2, open daily, except Monday, from 9 am to 4 pm. Rising on a hill behind the small park opposite are the ruins of the 14th century **Sân Nicoară Church** (Biserica Sân Nicoară). Also signposted from here is the tiny, 17th century **Olari Church** (Biserica Olari), tucked away at the end of a dirt track amid small cottages. The 'church of the potters' is painted with frescoes on the outside.

Back in the centre, walk past the Princely Court and head north along Str Basarabilor for 1km until you reach **Curtea de Argeş Monastery** (Mănăstirea Curtea de Argeş). The episcopal cathedral – which is a fantastic 'chocolate-box' piece of architecture topped with several stone-carved towers decorated with spiralling whorls – was built in 1514 by Neagoe Basarab (1512-21) with marble and mosaic tiles from Constantinople. In 1526 the church was finished and painted inside. Legend has it that the wife of the master stonemason, Manole, is embedded in the stone walls of the church, in accordance with a local custom which obliged the mason to bury a loved one alive within the church to ensure the success of his work. When the church was complete, Manole could not bear to continue life without his wife and killed himself.

The current edifice dates from 1875 when French architect, André Lecomte du Nouy, was brought in to save the 16th century monastery, which was in near ruins, from demolition.

The white marble tombstones of Carol I (1839-1914) and his poet wife Elizabeth (1853-1916), who wrote under the pen name Carmen Sylva, lie on the right in the monastery's pronaos, the first room you enter. On the left of the entrance are the tombstones of King Ferdinand I (1865-1927) and the British-born Queen Marie (1875-1938) whose heart, upon her own request, was put in a gold casket embellished with the Romanian coat of arms and buried in her favourite palace in Balcic in southern Dobruja. Following the ceding of southern Dobruja to Bulgaria in 1940 however, her heart was moved to a marble tomb in Bran. Today, it rests in Bucharest's National History Museum. Neagoe Basarab and his wife Stâna are also buried in the pronaos.

In the park opposite the monastery lies the legendary **Manole's well** (fontaine de maître Manole), a natural spring where pensioners fill their plastic water bottles. The story goes that the doomed Manole fell to the ground from the roof of the monastery when, during the building process, his master, Neagoe, removed the scaffolding. With the aid of miraculous wings made from roofing tiles, he made it as far as the park before coming down to earth with an almighty bump. The natural spring marks his landing pad.

Places to Stay

Camping Sân Nicoară (☎ 713 726), behind Sân Nicoară church at Str Plopis 34, is a small, friendly site with wooden chalets with double beds for US$8 a night. The communal showers are clean but there is no running hot water. Turn right at the Basarab I statue along Str Sân Nicoară. The site is 100m up the hill on the right.

Decidedly shady and not recommended for lone travellers is the dirt-cheap *Hotel Cumpăna* at Str Negru Vodă 36. A bed in one of its eight shared rooms costs US$3 a night. It has no bath or shower – only a shared toilet and sink – and there is no hot water. From the train station, turn left along Str Albeşti, right onto Str Castanilor, cross the small square then turn right along Str Negru Vodă. The entrance is in a courtyard off the main road.

The *Hotel Posada* (☎ 711 800; fax 711 802; email posada@starnets.ro), at Calea Basarabilor 27-29, has decent doubles with private shower for US$20 and doubles with cable TV and bath for US$35.

Six kilometres north of Curtea de Argeş in Albeşti de Argeş, is the *Hanul Albeşti*. The large inn is only open in summer.

Places to Eat

The *Black & White Café* at Calea Basarabilor 123 is a modern, air-conditioned café which serves light snacks during the day and is transformed into a busy bar at night. It is open daily from 9 am to 4 am.

Further north along the same street, opposite the prefecture, is the *New York Bar*, a flashy restaurant with the New York skyline plastered on one wall. You can eat here too; it is open daily from 8 am to 10 pm.

More traditional dishes are served in the *Fântâna lui Manole* restaurant, in the park opposite Curtea de Argeş Monastery. It has a great terrace and is open late in summer.

After hours, *Disco Club Castel*, close to the museum on Str Negru Vodă, is *the* place to hang out. It rocks Sunday to Thursday from 9 pm to 2 am, Friday and Saturday from 9 am to 3 am. Admission is free.

Getting There & Away

Major daily bus services include one to Bucharest (4½ hours), Câmpulung Muscel (1½ hours), Râmnicu Vâlcea (50 minutes) and Sibiu (three hours); and two to Braşov (four hours) and Poienari (26km, 40 minutes).

There are eight trains daily to Piteşti (38km, one hour) and one train daily in summer to Bucharest (3½ hours).

POIENARI & AREFU
• *area code ☎ 048*

From Curtea de Argeş, most Dracula fiends head north up the Argeş valley to Poienari citadel (Cetatea Poienari). In 1459, tens of Turks captured by Vlad Ţepeş in revenge for killing his father and brother three years previously, also marched along this route. At the end of the march, the Turks built the defensive fortress for the bloodthirsty prince. The result – a castle strategically positioned to guard the entrance from Transylvania into the Argeş valley – is considered by Dracula buffs to be Romania's 'real' Dracula's castle.

Some 1480 steps (this author counted 1449 but the castle-keeper swears there are 1480) lead up from the side of a hydroelectric power plant to the castle ruins. A substantial amount of the castle, which towers on a crag above the village, fell down the side of the mountain in 1888. Tickets to the castle costing US$0.50 are sold by the castle-keeper at the top of the steps.

Six kilometres south of Poienari citadel is Arefu, a tiny village inhabited solely by descendants of the minions who served Vlad Ţepeş – or at least that is the line upon which Arefu markets itself! Tourists following the Dracula trail come here in their droves to sit around camp fires, sing folk songs and listen to tales told by villagers whose great-great-great grandfathers mingled with the notorious Impaler. Legend has it that in 1462 when the Turks besieged Poienari citadel, the Arefians helped Vlad Ţepeş to escape into the mountains. His wife, convinced they would not escape alive from the surrounded castle, had already flung herself from the turret. As an expression of gratitude to his loyal serfs, Ţepeş gave the Arefians their pasture lands. A document signed by Mircea Ciobanul (1545-52) in 1540 attests to the people of Arefu having earlier been granted 16 mountains and 14 sheepfolds by Ţepeş.

Just 1km north of the fortress lies **Lake Vidraru**. It is an artificial lake dammed between 1961-66 to feed the hydroelectric power plant. The platform at the top of the viewing tower offers magnificent views of the Argeş valley. From here the **Trans-Făgăraşan highway**, a mountain pass which peaks at 2034m, leads you across the Carpathians into Transylvania. The tunnel cutting between the Negoiu and Moldoveanu peaks is 845m long. Note that the pass, allegedly built by the army as a training exercise, is only open for some three months of the year. There is a sign telling you

The Dracula Myth

Fifteenth century Wallachian prince Vlad Ţepeş is all too often credited with being Dracula, the vampire-count featured in the classic Gothic horror story *Dracula* (1897) written by Anglo-Irish novelist Bram Stoker.

This madcap association of these two diabolical figures – one historical, the other fictitious – is nothing more than a product of the popular imagination.

Vlad Ţepeş, ruler of Wallachia in 1448, 1456-1462 and 1476, was outrageously bloodthirsty. But he was not a vampire. The Romanian name Drăculea (literally 'son of Dracul') was bestowed on him by his princely father, Vlad III, who was called Vlad Dracul after the chivalric Order of the Dragon accredited to him by Sigismund of Luxembourg in 1431.

Vlad Ţepeş gained the name 'Ţepeş' meaning 'impaler' after the primary form of capital punishment he used to punish his enemies – impaling. A wooden stake was carefully driven through the victim's backbone without touching any vital nerve, ensuring at least 48 hours of conscious suffering before death.

Ţepeş rarely ate without a Turk writhing on a stake in front of him. Contrary to popular belief, this torture was not unusual at the time. Ţepeş's first cousin, Ştefan cel Mare, is said to have 'impaled by the navel, diagonally, one on top of each other' 2300 Turkish prisoners in 1473.

'Can't I even enjoy my meal in peace without you lot whingeing?'

Bram Stoker's literary Dracula by contrast was a bloodsucking vampire – an undead corpse reliant on the blood of the living to sustain his own immortality. Until 1824 in Stoker's adopted England a wooden stake was commonly driven through the heart of suicide victims to ensure the ill-fated corpse did not turn in its grave into a vampire. In Romania, vampires form an integral part of traditional folklore. The seventh born child is particularly susceptible to this evil affliction, identifiable by a hoof as a foot or a tail at the end of its spine.

Stoker set *Dracula* in Transylvania, a region the novelist never set foot in. The novel was originally set in Austria and was entitled *The Undead*. Following critics' comments however that it was too close a pastiche of Sheridan le Fanu's *Camilla* (1820) – a vampire novel set in southern France – Stoker switched titles and geographical settings. Count Dracula's fictitious castle on the Borga pass was inspired by Cruden Bay castle in Aberdeenshire where Stoker drafted much of the novel. The historical facts were uncovered at the British Museum in London.

Kitsch as it may be, Dracula continues to sustain an extraordinary subculture. The novel itself has never been out of print (first translated into Romanian in 1990), while movie-makers have remade the film countless times, kicking off with Murnau's silent movie *Nosferatu* in 1922 followed by Universal Pictures' *Dracula* in 1931.

Dracula fan clubs have been set up around the globe. The New York club alone attracts over 5000 hungry members, many of whom meet up with fellow fans at the annual Dracula World Congress. Worthy members of the Transylvanian Dracula Society meanwhile can lay claim to a noble title within the House of Dracula or, more prestigious still, to a knighthood of the Count Dracula Order. Ironically the society, set up in 1971, only came out of the closet in 1990: Ceauşescu, known as everything from the 'genius of the Carpathians' to the 'anti-Christ', was too closely compared to both Vlad Ţepeş and Dracula for society members to pursue their vampish activities without being persecuted. ∎

whether it is open or closed at the side of the road south of Poienari citadel.

Places to Stay

Villagers in Arefu are accustomed to having tourists stay in their homes. Ask for a room in the shop in the centre of the village or go to the school director who coordinates the local agrotourism set-up. The director's house is the large house on the right as you enter the village. Accommodation can also be arranged in advance through the Transylvania Society of Dracula (☎ 01-222 6195; fax 01-313 3056; ☎ & fax 01-679 5742), Blvd Primăverii 47, Bucharest, which arranges guided tours to Poienari with overnight stays in Arefu.

Two kilometres south of Poienari in Căpătâneni is the *Popasul Drumeţul* which has basic double wooden huts for US$7 a night. Showers are communal and there is no running hot water. The campsite is just off the main Curtea de Argeş-Poienari road, on the side road to Arefu.

The large, chalet-style *Cabana Câmpâna*, on the western side of Lake Vidraru, runs a small campsite and has double/triple/five-bed rooms in its main building for US$30/40/75 a night, including breakfast. It costs US$1.50 per person to pitch a tent. Advance bookings can be made through the Hotel Posada in Curtea de Argeş. Some 50m north of the cabana is the *Cabana Foriestier*, run by the Forestry Union, from which various hiking trails are marked.

On the eastern side of the lake is the small *Casă Argeşean* (☎ 730 309) which has a handful of double rooms for US$10 a night. Continue north towards Lake Bilea and Sibiu, to find the popular *Hotel Bilea Cascadă* (see Transylvania – Around Sibiu).

WEST TO TÂRGU JIU

Poienari village proper lies 5km south of the main road which leads west from Curtea de Argeş to the industrialised town of **Râmnicu Vâlcea** (formerly spelt Rîmnicu Vîlcea). ANTREC (☎ 050-732 901, 739 236; 050-fax 738 498) has an office and there is a campsite 2km north of the town next to *Hotel*

Capela; both are run by the same company which manages *Hotel Alutus* (☎ 050-736 601; fax 050-737 760) in the town centre at Str General Praporgescu 10.

From Râmnicu Vâlcea you can head north up the **Olt valley** to **Călimăneşti-Căciulata**, a jaded twin-spa resort which has lost much of its appeal since the days when it was among Europe's most fashionable resorts. It was a favourite haunt of Napoleon III and was awarded a gold medal for its mineral waters at Vienna in 1873. The old Roman town comes to life during the first week of August, when it hosts a large folk music and crafts festival. Accommodation can be arranged through Călimăneşti-Căciulata SR (☎ & fax 050-750 270, 750 990), Calea lui Traian 413. Just a couple of kilometres north lie the **Cozia & Turnul monasteries**. The monastery at Cozia was built by Mircea cel Bătrân in the late 14th century and today shelters the Wallachian prince's tomb. The original fountain dates from 1517, to which another was added by Constantin Brâncoveanu in 1711. A museum is also sheltered in the complex.

Costeşti

Fifty-one weeks of the year, the mountain village of Costeşti in the southern Carpathians, 2km north along a dirt track signposted off the main Râmnicu Vâlcea-Târgu Jiu road, is a sleepy village. During the first week of September, it buzzes with flamboyant dancing and music-making, copper-pot selling and horse-trading, as Romania's minority Roma community flocks to Costeşti by horse and cart (or expensive Mercedes as the case may be!) to celebrate Romania's largest **Roma festival**.

Thousands of Roma attend the Costeşti fair during which lucrative business deals are struck and marriages arranged. The festival is also attended by the two rival figureheads of Romania's Roma community – the self-proclaimed Emperor of Roma worldwide Iulian Rădulescu, and Romanian Roma king Florin Cioaba – who both hold court during the week of celebrations (see the Sibiu section in the Transylvania chapter for more details).

The village of Costeşti is 82km east of **Cem Romengo**, a symbolic 'Roma State' declared in an outlying district of Târgu Jiu by emperor Iulian Rădulescu in March 1997. The Cem Romengo, which has no official frontiers, was proclaimed after 40 Roma were arrested for building houses on state-owned, agricultural land.

The emperor, who made it clear that his state, modelled on that of the Vatican, did not 'endanger the sovereignty or unity of Romania', hoped the move would force the local authorities to recognise the land ownership rights of the arrested Roma.

Bistriţa & Arnota Monasteries

Bistriţa Monastery (Mănăstirea Bistriţa), one of Romania's most impressive monasteries, is 6km north of Costeşti. The current Brâncoveanu-style building (1856) was built on the site of a former 15th century monastery. The first book printed in Wallachia (1508) is preserved in the monastery. Until 1982 the monastery sheltered one of the country's largest schools for handicapped children. The school is now housed in a separate building at the entrance to the monastery estate. Some 800m from the main monastery building is the **Peştera Sfântul Gheorghe**, a small, hillside chapel, hidden in the 'St George' cave in the hillface and previously used to keep the monastery's treasures safe. One of the 35 nuns who live here today gives 20 minute guided tours; ask the attendant in the main chapel.

From Bistriţa Monastery a forest road leads 4km north to the smaller **Arnota Monastery** (Mănăstirea Arnota). Ancient crosses are carved in the sheer rock face lining the southern end of this road. Wallachian prince, Matei Basarab, who had the monastery begun in 1636 (it was completed in 1706), is buried here.

Horezu Monastery

Equally splendid in riches and magnitude is the fortified Horezu monasterial complex, 7km further west along the Târgu Jiu road.

The monastery was built during the reign of Constantin Brâncoveanu and is considered one of Romania's most remarkable examples of the unique synthesis of western and oriental architectural styles for which he became famed. The twin-towered, trefoil-shaped main church has an unusually large pronaos and open porch supported by 10 ornate stone-carved columns. Its doors are made from pearwood. During the 17th and 18th centuries Horezu housed the country's most prestigious fresco painting school.

Three kilometres south of the turn-off for Horezu Monastery is the village of **Măldăreşti**, home to an ethnographic museum housed in a traditional *cula* dating from 1688. Culas – small, square, two-floored houses with an outside porch supported by two pillars – were built in Romania until the end of the 18th century.

Places to Stay Horezu Monastery is signposted off the main road 1km east of Horezu village. There is a small *Popas Turistic* with simple wooden huts at the western end of the village.

ANTREC, which has an office in Târgu Jiu (see that section), arranges rooms in private houses for US$5 to US$10 a night. You can also contact the families involved in the agrotourism scheme direct. In Horezu village contact the Figura family (☎ 050-860 113), the Bălasa family (☎ 050-860 375) or the Dăscălete family (☎ 050-860 094).

Polovragi & the Women's Cave

From Horezu a dirt road heads west to the 18th century **Polovragi Monastery** (Mănăstirea Polovragi), founded by Radu the Handsome (1474-75) in 1470. Every year in June the monastery hosts a folk craft fair. Close to the monastery is a small cave.

The **Women's Cave** (Peştera Miuerilor), at the gateway to the Galbenul Gorges, 3km from Baie de Fier, was named following the discovery of bones on the cave's upper floor which archaeologists believe to be those of women who used to retreat into the cave for safety during invasions in the Middle Ages. The cave is one of the few in Romania to be properly lit and equipped with guides, who show tourists around part of the 10km-long caves.

TÂRGU JIU
• *area code ☎ 053, pop 98,342*

Târgu Jiu is home to the internationally famed modernist sculptures of Constantin Brâncuşi (1876-1957).

It also lies in the heart of the Jiu valley mining region. Frequent strikes in this region from the 1980s onwards paralysed industrial activity, forcing the communists to give in to the miners' militant demands. Their mass descent upon Bucharest in 1990 ended in bloodshed and their 1991 rampage led to the fall of Petre Roman's first post-revolution government.

In mid-1997 the might of the miners was broken. As part of its grand plan to close the country's unprofitable pits, the government offered lucrative pay-offs (up to 20 monthly salaries – US$7200) to miners prepared to take voluntary redundancy. Some 42,000 out of Romania's total 175,000 miners grabbed the money and ran. A mass exodus of miners and their families from the Jiu valley's industrial towns then followed as miners sold up and headed back to their home villages in the countryside. One, so desperate to leave, sold his apartment for a crate of beer!

During WWII, Târgu Jiu prison was home to communist leader Gheorghe Gheorghiu-Dej. Other prominent communists interned in Târgu Jiu during WWII included Ceauşescu, then secretary-general of the Union of the Communist Youth, who spent four years (1940-4) in prison fitting electric cables; and Ion Iliescu who replaced Ceauşescu as president in 1990.

Orientation

Târgu Jiu centre, east of the river Jiu, is a 15 minute walk from the bus and train stations. Exit the station and turn right along Str Nicolae Titulescu, which becomes Blvd Republicii, until you reach Str Unirii, the main thoroughfare which cuts across town from east to west. Head 500m west along Str Unirii then turn right onto Calea Victoriei.

The main hotels, shops and restaurants are dotted along the pedestrianised section of this street.

Maps The prerevolution *Judeţul Gorj Hartă turistică* map is sold at the reception of Hotel Gorj for US$0.50. It includes a detailed map of Gorj county as well as a small city map of Târgu Jiu.

Information

Tourist Office The official tourist office, OJT Gorj (☎ 214 814; fax 214 010), adjoining the Hotel Gorj, is actually quite helpful although its staff appear to speak no English. It is an agent for ANTREC and can arrange rooms in private homes in Horezu, Tismana, Novaci, Padeş and Polovragi (see Places to Stay later). Through ANTREC the office also provides a guide for the day for US$15 and arranges picnics in the countryside for US$15.

The ACR (☎ 214 563; fax 212 593) has an office on Calea Victoriei.

Money There is a currency exchange inside the ACR office, open weekdays from 9 am to 5 pm. You can change travellers cheques and get cash advances on Visa/MasterCard at the BANCOREX in the centre on the corner of Calea Victoriei and Calea Eroilor. It is open weekdays from 8 to 11.30 am.

Post & Communications The post office at the southern end of Str Vasile Alecsandri is open weekdays from 7 am to 8 pm, Saturday from 8 am to noon. The central telephone office, just around the corner of Str Stadion, is open daily from 8 am to 8 pm. There is a second, smaller post office on Str Unirii.

Things to See

Târgu Jiu's 'Brâncuşi tour' starts in the central park at the western end of Calea Eroilor with three of the four sculptures which Brâncuşi built between 1937 and 1938 in memory of those who died during WWI. The entrance to the park is marked by Brâncuşi's *Gate of the Kiss (Poarta Sărutului)*, an archway reminiscent of

WALLACHIA

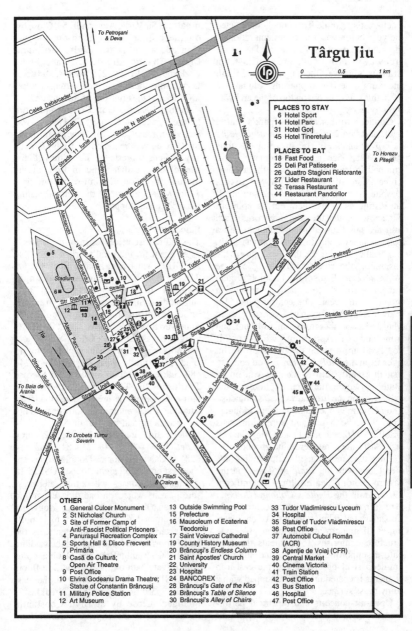

Târgu Jiu

0   0.5   1 km

PLACES TO STAY
6 Hotel Sport
14 Hotel Parc
31 Hotel Gorj
45 Hotel Tineretului

PLACES TO EAT
18 Fast Food
25 Deli Pat Patisserie
26 Quattro Stagioni Ristorante
27 Lider Restaurant
32 Terasa Restaurant
44 Restaurant Pandorilor

To Petroşani & Deva
To Horezu & Piteşti
To Baia de Arania
To Drobeta Turnu Severin
To Filiaşi & Craiova

WALLACHIA

OTHER
1 General Culcer Monument
2 St Nicholas' Church
3 Site of Former Camp of Anti-Fascist Political Prisoners
4 Panuraşul Recreation Complex
5 Sports Hall & Disco Frecvent
7 Primăria
8 Casă de Cultură; Open Air Theatre
9 Post Office
10 Elvira Godeanu Drama Theatre; Statue of Constantin Brâncuşi
11 Military Police Station
12 Art Museum
13 Outside Swimming Pool
15 Prefecture
16 Mausoleum of Ecaterina Teodoroiu
17 Saint Voievozi Cathedral
19 County History Museum
20 Brâncuşi's *Endless Column*
21 Saint Apostles' Church
22 University
23 Hospital
24 BANCOREX
28 Brâncuşi's *Gate of the Kiss*
29 Brâncuşi's *Table of Silence*
30 Brâncuşi's *Alley of Chairs*
33 Tudor Vladimirescu Lyceum
34 Hospital
35 Statue of Tudor Vladimirescu
36 Post Office
37 Automobil Clubul Român (ACR)
38 Agenţie de Voiaj (CFR)
39 Central Market
40 Cinema Victoria
41 Train Station
42 Post Office
43 Bus Station
46 Hospital
47 Post Office

Bucharest's 'Arc de Triomphe' constructed the year before, also in commemoration of the reunification of Romania. The stone archway bearing folk art motifs from Brâncuşi's native Oltenia, stands 5.3m tall and 6.6m wide. The supporting columns are 1.7m thick. Flip a coin on top of the archway for good luck!

Continue further along the park's central mall, and you come to the *Alley of Chairs (Aleea scaunelor)*. The dwarf-sized stone stools – each 55cm high and 45cm wide – are grouped in trios either side of the avenue. Three are missing at the alley's western end. Despite their minuscule size, one's immediate instinct is to test them out for comfort. Note however that the stools are works of art. You are not allowed to sit on them and a policeman is on duty to ensure tourists don't.

The alley leads to the third sculpture in the ensemble, the riverside *Table of Silence (Masa tăcerii)*. Each of the 12 stools around the large round stone table represents a month of the year. The central park, also known as the Brâncuşi park, is open between May and December from 6 am to 10 pm, and from January to April from 7 am to 8 pm. If you head north along the banks of the Jiu river from the *Table of Silence*, you come to a small **Art Museum** (Muzeul de Artă) on Str Stadion, which includes a photographic exhibition on the life and works of Brâncuşi. The museum is open daily, except Monday, from 9 am to 5 pm and admission costs US$0.30. If the door is locked, ring the bell or look for the caretaker in the grounds.

Brâncuşi's most famed sculpture lies on a direct axis with the *Table of Silence*, at the eastern end of Calea Eroilor. A magnificent 29.35m tall, the *Endless Column (Coloana fără sfârşit)* is visible from the central park. Considered as much a triumph of engineering as of modern art, the totem pole-style structure comprises 15 elements threaded onto a supporting steel core and sits on a 3m-deep steel base. Each of the cast-iron elements is coated in zinc and topped with a shiny brass surface.

Open-air concerts and theatrical performances are held in summer at the **open-air theatre** at Str Vasile Alecsandri 53. Close by, on the corner of Str Stadion and Str Confederaţiei, is the **Elvira Godeanu Drama Theatre** (Teatrul Dramatic Elvira Godeanu; ☎ 213 209, 213 498). A **statue** of Constantin Brâncuşi, armed with his sculpting chisel, stands in front of the theatre.

In mid-1997 the **Gorj County Museum** (Muzeul Judeţean Gorj) at Str Geneva was closed for renovation. Str Geneva, formerly Str Griviţa, was renamed in 1996 after the city of Geneva presented Târgu Jiu with Nicolae **trio of clocks** that stand in front of the **statue of Tudor Vladimirescu** on Piaţa Tudor Vladimirescu. At the time of writing the clocks had stopped.

Places to Stay

The OJT tourist office (see Information) acts as an agent for the rural tourism specialist, ANTREC, which has a small office (☎ & fax 216 964) at Str Crişan 2. It arranges nightstays in private homes in Târgu Jiu's surrounding villages; guests can also experience delicious home-made cooking. Single/double/triple rooms start at US$5/8/9 a night. Breakfast is an extra US$2.

Undiscriminating backpackers should head for the grotty *Hotel Tineretului* (☎ 244 683), close to the train station at Str Nicolae Titulescu 26. The reception are unfriendly but rooms are cheap at US$10 for a double. Clean communal showers and hot water are a hit-and-miss affair.

Târgu Jiu's main hotel is the 12-storey *Hotel Gorj* (☎ 214 148, 214 815; fax 214 828) at Calea Eroilor 6. Double/triples are cheapest on the top eight floors – US$15/18 including breakfast – where the water pressure is at its worst (on bad days expect no more than a dribble from the tap). Hot water is programmed (6 to 8 am, and 7 to 11 pm).

The cheapest hotel in the centre is the *Hotel Sport* (☎ 214 402) behind the stadium off Blvd Constantin Brâncuşi. Double rooms with private bath on the 1st and 2nd floors are US$12 a night while those on the less-appealing 3rd floor cost US$7. Breakfast is included. Close by at Blvd Constantin Brâncuşi 10 is the expensive *Hotel Parc*

Constantin Brâncuşi

Constantin Brâncuşi (1876-1957) shaped modern abstract sculpture, carving out a name for himself as one of the 20th century's greatest sculptors.

Brâncuşi was born into a peasant family in Hobiţa near Târgu Jiu. His parents died when he was 10 years old, forcing him to give up his pastoral existence tending to the family sheep flock for a job in a shop in Craiova.

Here he taught himself to read, write, and carve everything from soap dishes and brush holders to drums and violins out of scrap wooden crates. On the strength of his extraordinary woodworking skills local draper, Ion Georgescu Gorjan, sponsored Brâncuşi's subsequent studies at art school in Craiova then Bucharest between 1898 and 1902.

In 1904 the impoverished Brâncuşi won a scholarship to the School of Fine Arts in Paris, making the greater part of the journey from Romania to the French capital on foot. He sold his watch so he could buy a ferry ticket across Lake Constance.

Brâncuşi later studied under French sculptor Auguste Rodin and painters Arnedo Modigliani and Henri Rousseau under whom he explored his fascination with African art. His early works included *The Kiss* – two primitive figures entwined in an embrace – and *The Beginning of the World* – a polished marble egg which Brâncuşi dubbed a 'sculpture for a blind man'.

In 1937 the Romanian sculptor returned to his homeland to create a sculptural ensemble in Târgu Jiu as a WWI memorial. Its 'piece de resistance' was to be an endless column – a theme that had always obsessed Brâncuşi. In 1918 he carved a 2m-tall column comprising four threaded, truncated pyramidal elements. Yet it was not until his return to Romania that he fulfilled his ambition of creating a monstrous, 29.35m-tall column threaded with 15 steel 'beads'.

The Endless Column which took three months to assemble was engineered by Ştefan Georgescu Gorjan, the son of the Craiova draper who'd been Brâncuşi's beneficiary more than three decades before. During the communist crackdowns of the 1950s, the young engineer was imprisoned for alleged 'anti-state activities' while Brâncuşi, still based in Paris, was declared persona non grata. Subsequent attempts to tear down the endless column failed and it was only after the sculptor's death in exile in 1957 that the true genius of his column was recognised. ■

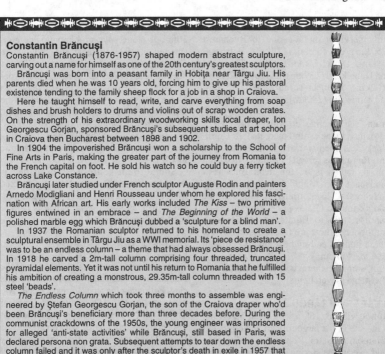

(☎ 215 981) which charges US$50/65 for a double/triple room, including breakfast.

Places to Eat

Most eating places are clustered around the Hotel Gorj and along the pedestrianised end of Calea Victoriei. Immediately opposite the hotel on Calea Eroilor is the cheap and cheerful *Lider Restaurant* which serves mainly pizza. Next door is the more upmarket *Quattro Stagioni Ristorante*, a funky Italian restaurant which is also packed. Third in line is the *Deli Pat Patisserie*, handy for a quick cup of coffee and a creamy cake; it is open daily from 9 am to 9 pm.

There's a clean, modern *Fast Food* on the corner of Str Traian and Str General Magheru. Hamburgers and salamiburgers are less than US$1; mini-pizzas are a mere US$0.30. It's open daily from 9 am to 11 pm.

Great mititei (spicy meatballs) are cooked while you wait at the *Terasa Restaurant*, behind the Hotel Gorj on Calea Victoriei. Wash them down with local beer served on tap. The terrace is open pretty much nonstop in summer. The *Restaurant Pandorilor*, close to the train and bus stations on Str Nicolae Titulescu, is open 24 hours.

Stock up on fresh fruit and vegetables at the *central market*, south of the stadium park on Str Unirii.

Getting There & Away

Bus The bus station is 100m south of the

train station off Str Nicolae Titulescu. Major daily services include one to Bucharest (257km) via Piteşti (174km), Petroşani (57km), Deva (150km), Sibiu, Timişoara and Hunedoara (137km); and two to Craiova (102km), Drobeta-Turnu Severin (82km) and Timişoara (280km).

Train The Agenţie de Voiaj CFR (☎ 121 924), next to the central market at Str Unirii, block 2, is open weekdays from 9 am to 7 pm. Târgu Jiu is served by a branch line from Filiaşi, which is on the main Bucharest-Timişoara line. Major daily train services include five local trains to Filiaşi (three hours); four to Craiova (2¾ hours); and an express train to Bucharest (4¾ hours). Northbound, there are five trains to Simeria (three hours), and eight trains to Petroşani (1¼ to 1¾ hours).

In summer there is one train daily to Constanţa (seven hours).

WEST FROM TÂRGU JIU

Runcu village, 16km west from Târgu Jiu, is the site of the large folk art and crafts fair (Simpozion Satul Românesc traditional), held every year during the last weekend in August. Continuing west, turn left 1km before Peştişani and follow the dirt track for a couple of kilometres until you reach **Hobiţa**, the birthplace of Constantin Brâncuşi. The sculptor, who was an orphan, lived in the village until the age of 10 when he moved to Craiova to work as an errand boy in a local grocery store. The tiny ramshackle cottage in which he spent his childhood years now houses a small museum dedicated to the artist.

Some 20km further west is **Tismana Monastery** (Mănăstirea Tismana), one of Romania's oldest monasteries, dating from 1375, and an important centre of Slavonic writing. The original monastery was founded by monk and calligrapher Nicodim in a small stone church, later to be grandly rebuilt in 1508 by Wallachian prince, Radu cel Mare. The region west beyond Tismana is a major karst area in the south-western Carpathians, providing intrepid explorers

with countless caves. In **Padeş**, there is a 10m-tall stone, pyramid monument constructed in 1921 to mark the spot where Craiovan-born revolutionary Tudor Vladimirescu (1780-1821) issued his 'Proclamation of Padeş' on 4 February 1821, just four months before he was captured by the Turks and executed. In his proclamation, Vladimirescu called for the 'evil ones' ruining the country to be disposed of, leading to a series of uprisings against Ottoman rule in 1821.

Some 10km south-west of Padeş is **Ponoare Nature Reservation**, a protected lilac forest stretching for some eight hectares. Each spring, a folk festival is held to mark the blossoming of the trees.

DROBETA-TURNU SEVERIN
• *area code ☎ 052, pop 118,114*

Drobeta-Turnu Severin is on the bank of the Danube river. Yugoslavia lies on the opposite side. Following the first Roman-Dacian War between 101-102 AD, the Roman Emperor Trajan built a bridge across the Danube at Drobeta, the remains of which can still be seen. It was this bridge that Trajan's army then used to cross into Dacia at the start of the second Roman-Dacian War (105-106 AD) which led to the final conquest of Dacia by the Romans.

Though of ancient origin, the present town of Drobeta was laid out during the 19th century when its port was built. In 1524, Drobeta was besieged and destroyed by the Turks who dominated the town until 1829. A three hour stop is enough to see the best of Drobeta-Turnu Severin. Eleven kilometres from Drobeta is Topolniţa Cave (Peştera Topolniţa), which at more than 10,000m long on four levels, ranks among the largest caves in the world.

From Drobeta, there are local buses to Yugoslavia.

Orientation

From the train station, walk straight up the steps immediately opposite the main station building to Blvd Republicii (Blvd Carol I). Follow this road east for 1.5km to the Hotel

MATTHIAS LÜFKENS

MATTHIAS LÜFKENS

NICOLA WILLIAMS

NICOLA WILLIAMS

Top: Sunrise, Black Sea coast, Northern Dobruja
Middle: Mila 23, Danube Delta, Northern Dobruja
Bottom left: Băile Herculane, Crişana & Banat
Bottom right: One of the 1989 Revolution memorials, Timişoara, Crişana & Banat

COLIN D SHAW

COLIN D SHAW

MATTHIAS LÜFKENS

Top: Mountain scenery near Turda, Crişana & Banat
Bottom left: Festival of St Maria, Moisei Monastery, Maramureş
Bottom right: Merry Cemetery, Săpânţa, Maramureş

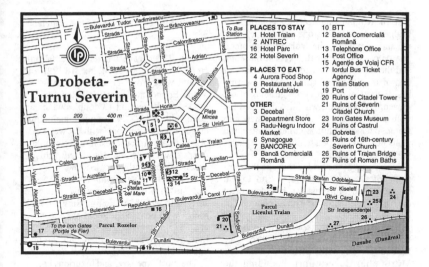

PLACES TO STAY
1 Hotel Traian
2 ANTREC
16 Hotel Parc
22 Hotel Severin

PLACES TO EAT
4 Aurora Food Shop
8 Restaurant Juil
11 Café Adakale

OTHER
3 Decebal
   Department Store
5 Radu-Negru Indoor
   Market
6 Synagogue
7 BANCOREX
9 Bancă Comercială
   Română

10 BTT
12 Bancă Comercială
   Română
13 Telephone Office
14 Post Office
15 Agenţie de Voiaj CFR
17 Iordul Bus Ticket
   Agency
18 Train Station
19 Port
20 Ruins of Citadel Tower
21 Ruins of Severin
   Citadel Church
23 Iron Gates Museum
24 Ruins of Castrul
   Dobreta
25 Ruins of 16th-century
   Severin Church
26 Ruins of Trajan Bridge
27 Ruins of Roman Baths

Parc, at the intersection of Str Coştescu. The town centre lies one block north of here. The bus station is out of town at the eastern end of Str Brânceveanu.

Some of the staff at the amazingly helpful information desk (☎ 311 244, 315 251) inside the left-luggage room at the train station speak English. It is open 24 hours. The Hala Radu-Negru indoor market (open weekdays from 6.30 am to 8 pm, Saturday from 7 am to 2.30 pm, Sunday from 7.30 am to noon) is at the northern end of Str Coştescu. The Decebal department store is a block further north.

Information

Money You can change money, cash travellers cheques or get cash on Visa/MasterCard at BANCOREX, on the corner of Str Bibiescu and Str Unirii; or at the Bancă Comercială Română, two blocks south on the corner of Str Coştescu and Str Aurelian. It is open weekdays from 8.30 am to 2 pm; the Commercial bank is open weekdays from 8.30 to 11.30 am and 1.30 to 6.30 pm, Saturday from 10 am to noon.

Post & Communications The post office,

open weekdays from 7 am to 9 pm, Saturday from 8 am to noon, is adjacent to the telephone office, at Str Decebal 41. The telephone office is open weekdays from 7.30 am to 8 pm, weekends from 8 am to 2 pm.

Things to See

At the eastern end of Blvd Republicii, at Str Independenţiei 1, is the highly recommended **Iron Gates Museum** (Muzeul Porţile de Fier; ☎ 312 177), open daily, except Monday, from 9 am to 5 pm. Housed in the former Trajan school for girls, dating to 1922, the museum was appropriately opened on 15 May 1972, the day before the official unveiling of the mammoth Porţile de Fier hydroelectric power station (see the following section). It contains a fine exhibition on the natural history of the Danube (Dunărea) river.

Other sections of the museum cover history, ethnography, popular art, astrology, the evolution of man, and archaeology. Particularly impressive is the scale model of the Roman bridge constructed across the Danube in 103 AD by the Syrian architect Apollodor of Damascus, on the orders of the Roman emperor Trajan. Considered a major feat of Roman engineering, Apollodor's bridge comprised 24 stone pillars, each 45m tall and 18m wide. The **Trajan bridge** stood just below the site of the present museum, and the ruins (ruinele pedului lui Traian) of two of its pillars can still be seen towering beside the Danube from the grounds of the museum. Apollodor, who also designed the Forum in which Trajan's column stands in Rome, later killed himself after architectural plans he drew up for a temple did not please the emperor Hadrian.

North-east of the bridge ruins lie the remnants of **Castrul Drobeta**, a 2nd to 6th century Roman fort that was built to protect the bridge following the Roman conquest of Dacia in 106 AD.

East of the castle ruins, also in the museum grounds, are the ruins of the 16th century medieval **Severin Church** (Biserica Mitropoliei Severinilui), including the remains of the crypt which lie protected beneath glass today.

In the museum basement there is an **aquarium**, in which various fish species prevalent in the Danube swim around in small glass tanks, much to the delight of the hordes of schoolchildren who fill the museum at weekends. Particularly noteworthy is the giant Somnul fish, said to be the largest freshwater fish to exist in the Danube and weighing in between 20kg to 30kg, as well as various types of carp (which amusingly translates as 'crap' in Romanian!).

Close to the indoor market, at the northern end of Str Coştescu, is a red-brick **synagogue** in a grand state of dilapidation.

Places to Stay & Eat
Private Rooms There is no campsite at Drobeta-Turnu Severin. BTT (☎ 315 131, 314 651), at Str Coştescu 4, sometimes arranges private rooms (US$9 per person). The office is open weekdays from 9 am to 6 pm.

ANTREC (☎ & fax 220 833) specialises in arranging rooms in private houses, both in Drobeta and along the Danube river. A bed for the night starts at around US$10, including breakfast. Its office is at Str Avram Iancu 38.

Hotels The cheapest hotel is the friendly *Hotel Severin* (☎ 212 074; fax 318 122), a 15 minute walk from the train station, at Str Mihai Eminescu 1 near Blvd Republicii. It has seven singles and 13 doubles which are good value at US$12/20 a night, including a clean, private bathroom (with hot water) and breakfast. Its in-house restaurant, a couple of doors down Str Mihai Eminescu, grills an excellent pork cutlet for US$2.80.

Staff at the *Hotel Traian* (☎ 311 799; fax 311 749) at Blvd Vladimirescu 74, are rude, surly and worth avoiding. Single/double rooms with private bathroom are expensive at US$25/33 a night. The hotel has a restaurant, tacky summer garden and 24 hour billiard bar.

The most expensive and luxurious hotel is the modern, three-star *Hotel Parc* (☎ 312 851, 312 852; fax 316 968) at Blvd Republicii 2, boasting clean, comfortable single/double rooms with private bathroom and breakfast for US$51/79 a night. It also has a handful of apartments costing US$115. Its restaurant is considered to be the best in town and its outside terrace in the park the most delightful.

Getting There & Away
Bus Major daily bus services include two to Târgu Jiu (82km) and Craiova (111km), and three buses on weekdays to Porţile de Fier.

There are no public buses from Drobeta-Turnu Severin across the border into Yugoslavia. There are private local buses however, departing daily from outside Drobeta's train station, to Negotin and to Pojarevat.

Single tickets costing US$7 to either destination are sold by the Iordul ticket agency (☎ 319 939) opposite the train station at Str Dunării 3. This bus serves local traders who regularly make the short journey back and forth across the border to buy and sell their wares. Theoretically, the buses are scheduled to leave daily at 10 pm. In reality, they leave when they're full, meaning you can wait until 4 am for the bus to depart. Expect to wait between two and four hours at the Porţile de Fier-Kladova border crossing.

Return buses from Negotin and Pojarevat likewise depart for Drobeta-Turnu Severin when they are full.

Train The Agenţie de Voiaj CFR (☎ 313 117) at Str Decebal 43 is open weekdays from 7 am to 7 pm.

Two daily Bucharest-Belgrade trains depart from Drobeta-Turnu Severin at 1.18 am and 3 pm, arriving in Belgrade (8¼ hours) at 9.23 am and 8.18 pm. On the return journey, trains depart from Belgrade at 7 am and 8 pm, arriving in Drobeta-Turnu Severin at 4.11 pm and 5.31 am.

There is also one train daily to Budapest (10½ hours), departing from Drobeta at 1.45 am. The return train leaves Budapest at 7.30 pm, arriving in Drobeta at 6 am, and continues east to Constanţa.

All express trains between Bucharest and Timişoara stop here. Local trains make slower, more frequent trips in both directions. Services include 16 trains daily to/from Bucharest (five hours), Craiova (1½ to 2½ hours) and Timişoara (3½ hours); and 13 trains daily to Băile Herculane (40 minutes to 1¼ hours) and Orşova (25 minutes).

In summer there are two trains daily to Constanţa (5¾ hours).

Boat At the time of writing, no river services ran from Drobeta-Turnu Severin port (☎ 315 296, 311 459), 2km from the centre at the southern end of Str Portului behind the Hotel Parc. River boats – by special arrangement only – depart from Orşova (see next section).

PORŢILE DE FIER, ORŞOVA & THE KAZAN GORGES

Ten kilometres west of Drobeta-Turnu Severin, the road and railway run along the northern bank of the Danube passing the famous **Iron Gates** (Porţile de Fier) at Gura Văii, a monstrous, concrete hydroelectric power station. On top of the dam wall runs the road linking Romania to Yugoslavia. The

view of the Iron Gates from the train window is quite spectacular.

Construction work first started on the power station – a Romanian-Yugoslav joint venture – in 1960. The mammoth project, which took 12 years to complete, involved the two countries each building a 1010 MW turbine plant; the gates on the Romanian side are 310m long and 34m wide.

The Iron Gates at Gura Văii stand on the site of **Old Orşova** (Orşova Veche), one of 13 settlements on the banks of the Danube to be swallowed up by the artificial lake (105 sq km was flooded in total), created to curb this treacherous stretch of the Danube. A Roman colony under the name of Tierna or Dierna, Orşova was an important port that was later to be dominated by the Turks. Prior to 1918, it marked the border into Hungarian-controlled Banat.

New Orşova lies 15km upstream of Gura Văii. Between Gura Văii and **Comarnic**, a village 2km north of New Orşova, the railway is said to cross 56 viaducts and bridges and go through nine tunnels. A further 15km upstream are the spectacular **Kazan Gorges** (Cazanele Mici and Cazanele Mari).

Places to Stay
The *Motelul Porţile de Fier* (☎ 052-326 778), 15km east of Drobeta-Turnu Severin on the E752 to Băile Herculane, is a convenient stopping point for those heading by car into Yugoslavia or further north to Banat.

Getting There & Away
Bus Three buses depart on weekdays from Drobeta-Turnu Severin to Porţile de Fier, departing at 6.15 am, and 1 and 3.30 pm (10km, 25 minutes). There are no buses from Drobeta-Turnu Severin to Porţile de Fier on weekends.

Train Most major trains to/from Drobeta-Turnu Severin stop at Orşova. Between Gura Văii and Orşova (15km, 30 minutes) there are five local trains daily.

The Constanţa-Budapest train also stops at Orşova. Eastbound, it departs from Orşova at 5.34 am, arriving in Constanţa (eight hours) at 1.25 pm. Westbound, it leaves Orşova at 2.16 am. Twice daily Bucharest-Belgrade trains pass through Drobeta, at 3.44 pm and 2.03 am.

Boat It is possible to arrange a boat trip along the Danube from Orşova port (☎ 361 295) to Porţile de Fier. The 20km trip has to be arranged well in advance however and will only be taken seriously by the harbour master if it involves a group of at least 10 people. Those lucky enough to get a trip off the ground can expect to pay about US$50 an hour for the privilege. It is a purely sightseeing exercise; no boats cross the Romanian border into Yugoslavia.

CRAIOVA
• *area code ☎ 051, pop 310,838*

The university town of Craiova, founded on the site of the Dacian stronghold of Pelendava, midway between Drobeta-Turnu Severin and Piteşti, prides itself on its strong academic tradition and the wealth of prominent characters who have passed through on their journey to stardom: Wallachian prince, Mihai Viteazul was born here and the world-famous sculptor Constantin Brâncuşi carved his first sculptures from scrap wooden crates here. Craiovan-born Petrache Poenaru (1799-1875) invented the first cartridge fountain pen.

Today Craiova is better known as the source of Craiova beer; the producer of diesel locomotives; and the home of the Rodae car factory which produced the Oltcit (the Romanian version of the Citroën Axel) and the sporty Cielo car. The South Korean investors, Daewoo Heavy Industries, who have pumped US$210 million into the plant since construction started in 1994, plan to invest a total of US$1 billion by 2000. In mid-1997, hundreds of the company's 5000 Craiova employees were temporarily laid off following a sharp drop in car sales.

Prior to the war in Yugoslavia, IAR93 sub-sonic jet fighter-bombers were manufactured in Craiova for the Romanian and Yugoslav airforces. Production ground to a halt in 1992, however, after the UN imposed trade sanctions against Yugoslavia. Workers at the plant blocked the Craiova-Piteşti highway with a military plane in mid-1997 in a desperate bid to get their jobs guaranteed.

At the same time, Craiova was mourning the deaths of 16 people who were killed when an 'experimental bomb' exploded at the military base on the town's outskirts.

Orientation
The northern bus station (Autogară Nord) from which buses to/from most other towns arrive/depart, is next to the train station, 1km north-east of the centre on Blvd Carol I (Blvd Republicii). Bus No 1 runs from the train station to the centre and Autogară Nord. There are no buses to the southern bus station (Autogară Sud); a taxi from the centre should cost no more than US$0.75.

Information
Tourist Offices The Mapamond Agenţie de Turism (☎ 415 071; fax 415 173) overlooks the central square on the corner of Str Oltet and Calea Unirii. All its staff speak English and are happy to assist lost tourists. It is open weekdays from 8 am to 8 pm, Saturday from 8 am to noon.

TAROM (☎ 411 049) has an office inside the Complex Comercial Unirea, opposite the Hotel Jiul. It is open Monday to Thursday from 8 am to 4 pm, and Friday from 8 am to 1 pm. The ACR office (☎ 187 000), opposite the Alliance Française on Str Ion Marinescu, is open Monday to Thursday from 8 am to 4 pm, Friday from 8 am to 1 pm.

Money The TTC currency exchange at Str Oltet, block 1, offers competitive rates. It is open daily, except Sunday, from 8 am to 8 pm. You can cash travellers cheques and get cash advances on Visa/MasterCard at BANCOREX, close by on the corner of Str Oltet and Str Nicolaescu Plopsor. Alternatively, try the Bancă Comercială Română, on the corner of Calea Unirii and Str Alexandru

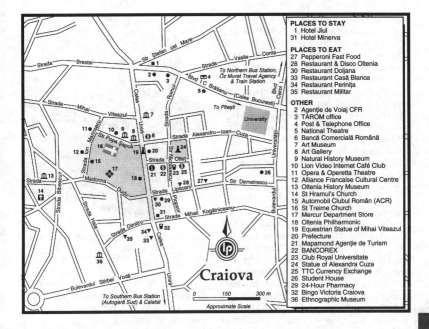

PLACES TO STAY
1 Hotel Jiul
31 Hotel Minerva

PLACES TO EAT
27 Pepperoni Fast Food
28 Restaurant & Disco Oltenia
30 Restaurant Doljana
33 Restaurant Casă Blanca
34 Restaurant Perinița
35 Restaurant Militar

OTHER
2 Agenție de Voiaj CFR
3 TAROM office
4 Post & Telephone Office
5 National Theatre
6 Bancă Comercială Română
7 Art Museum
8 Art Gallery
9 Natural History Museum
10 Lion Video Internet Café Club
11 Opera & Operetta Theatre
12 Alliance Francaise Cultural Centre
13 Oltenia History Museum
14 St Hramul's Church
15 Automobil Clubul Român (ACR)
16 St Treime Church
17 Mercur Department Store
18 Oltenia Philharmonic
19 Equestrian Statue of Mihai Viteazul
20 Prefecture
21 Mapamond Agenție de Turism
22 BANCOREX
23 Club Royal Universitate
24 Statue of Alexandra Cuza
25 TTC Currency Exchange
26 Student House
29 24-Hour Pharmacy
32 Bingo Victoria Craiova
36 Ethnographic Museum

Craiova

Ioan Cuza (open weekdays from 8.30 to 11.30 am and 1.30 to 8.30 pm).

Post & Communications The central post and telephone office is opposite the National Theatre on Blvd 1 C Brătianu. It is open daily, except Sunday, from 8 am to 7 pm. DHL Worldwide Express (☎ 417 171; fax 415 500) has an office inside the Hotel Jiul, open weekdays from 8.30 am to 5.30 pm.

The highlight of Craiova for any email addict has to be the Lion Video Internet Café Club (☎ 410 930; email lionvideo @topedge.com) on Str Popa Șapcă. Online access costs US$1/2 for 30 minutes/one hour and you can set up your own private email account for US$5 a month (see Places to Eat for more details). It is open daily from 11 am to 7 pm.

Bookshops The Librărie Thalia, inside the National Theatre, sells a decent range of English and French-language novels. It is open weekdays from 10 am to 7 pm, Saturday from 10 am to 5.30 pm.

Cultural Centres The best information source for French-speakers is the Alliance Française (☎ & fax 412 345) at Str Ion Marinescu 10. The centre arranges three or four cultural events – exhibitions, plays, films and so on – every month and is open weekdays from 9 am to 4 pm, Saturday from 9 am to 1 pm.

Things to See
Overlooking Calea Unirii, in the central square in the pedestrianised part of town, stands a **statue of Mihai Viteazul** who was born in Craiova. To the eastern side of the prince is the **prefecture** which bears a memorial plaque to Craiova's victims of the 1989 revolution. Some 25 names are honoured, the average age of which is 20. The youngest victim was 19; the oldest 65.

Close by at Str Popa Șapcă 4 is a small

Natural History Museum (☎ 419 435), open daily, except Monday, from 9 am to 5 pm. Services are held in the red-brick **St Treime Church** (Biserica Sfânt Treime) in the park opposite on Wednesday and Friday at 6 pm, Sunday at 8 am. The church is locked at all other times. Behind the church on Str Ion Marinescu is the city's **Opera & Operetta Theatre**, a former school which was a revolutionary hideout between 13 and 15 June 1848.

Heading north from the square up Calea Unirii, you come to Craiova's **Art Museum** (Muzeul de Artă), considered by most to be a definite highlight of a visit to the town. The museum is housed in the Dinu Mihail Palace, built between 1900 and 1907 by the wealthy Romanian nobleman, Constantin Dinu Mihail. It was home to former Polish president, Ignacy Moscicki, in 1939 and later to Ceauşescu. Its numerous rooms take you through the history of art in Romania – including some wonderful 18th century frescoes originating from Creteşti Monastery – and the rest of Europe. The exhibition crescendos with the Constantin Brâncuşi cabinet in which some early works of the sculptor are displayed, including the magnificent *Kiss*, the *Thigh* and *Miss Pogany*. The orphaned Brâncuşi lived in a house with two friends at Str CA Rosetti 14 until 1895 when he became a boarder at the Craiova Trade School. The museum is open daily, except Monday, from 9 am to 5 pm. Admission for foreigners is US$1.10.

Craiova's old town – of which little evidence remains today – lies east of Calea Unirii around Piaţa Veche (Old Square). An excellent **Ethnographic Museum** (Muzeul olteniei Secţia de Etnografie), housed in a former governor's house dating from 1699, stands at the intersection of Str Dimitru and Str Hala. In its rose-bedded grounds is **St Dimitru Church**, Craiova's oldest, dating from 1652. Further north, at Str Madona-Dudu 44, is a **History Museum** (Muzeul Olteniei istorie; ☎ 418 631), housed in a wonderful, ivy-clad 19th century building. The street on which the museum stands is named after the Madona-Dudu icon dis-

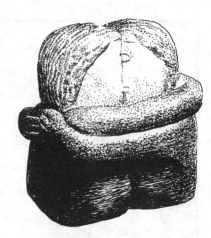

Constantin Brâncuşi's early sculpture *Kiss* can be seen in Craiova's Art Museum.

played inside the towering **St Hramul's Church** (1928) opposite the museum. The icon is said to perform miracles for those who pray in front of it.

Places to Stay

Private Rooms ANTREC (☎ & fax 413 785) has an office in the Complex Unirea at Calea Dumbrăvii 2. It arranges rooms in private houses in Craiova and villages around the town. A bed for the night costs around US$12 including breakfast.

University Rooms It is worth asking if there are any rooms going in the student dorms at the main *university* building, on the corner of Blvd Republicii and Calea Bucureşti. Alternatively, try the *student house* (casă de studentilor), a couple of blocks south of the main building on Blvd Universităţii.

Hotels The cheapest rooms in town can be found at the gloriously crumbling *Hotel Minerva* (☎ 413 300, 412 531) in the centre at Str Mihail Kogălniceanu 1-3. The grand old building – today protected as an architectural monument – has barely had any renovations done to it since it first opened as a hotel in 1902 and while facilities inside are poor, the decor is a sight to behold. Single/double rooms, complete with all the original furnishings, have a handbasin in each and cost US$20/31 a night, including breakfast. The communal bathroom has no bath or shower – only a toilet and handbasin. Hot water is limited to a few hours in the morning and evening.

The same company also runs the most expensive hotel in town, the three-star *Hotel Jiul* (☎ 414 166, 565 541; fax 412 462) at Str Ştefan cel Mare 1-3. The large concrete block has 204 rooms, with singles/doubles costing US$55/72 a night, including breakfast. A matrimonial room (ie a room with a 'real' double bed), is also US$72.

Out of Town Six kilometres east of Craiova on the road to Piteşti (E70) is the *Hanul Doctorului* (☎ 144 013), a modern inn with 41 double rooms with private bathroom costing US$39 a night. Some 20km south of Craiova on the road to Bechet, the *Staţiunea Victoria* at Bratovieşti offers accommodation in seven small rooms which overlook a lake.

Places to Eat
Eating options are limited in Craiova and tracking down a full meal can be tough. If you do not have an aversion to uniforms, a good place to go is the *Restaurant Militar*, adjoining the hotel reserved for the military on Str Dimitru. Traditional caşcaval (pressed, breaded cheese) and pork cutlets are served in the Craiova beer garden outside which specialises in the local golden beer brewed in the town. All the waiting staff are military personnel!

Close to the Hotel Minerva there are a couple of places worth a nibble: the *Restaurant Periniţa* at the southern end of Calea Unirii serves Craiova beer for US$0.30 a bottle and cooks up şaşlik `on a barbecue when there are enough customers to warrant the effort. Next door is the *Restaurant Casă Blanca*, an open-air terrace tucked away in a courtyard off the main street. Both are open daily from 10 am to around 11 pm.

Fast food is served in a clean, modern stand-up bar at *Pepperoni Fast Food*, at Str Lipscani. It is open weekdays from 8 am to 8 pm, Saturday from 8 am to 2 pm. A block west on the same street is the less flash *Restaurant & Disco Oltenia* which hosts occasional live bands.

The place to go to surf the Net is the massively popular *Lion Video Internet Café Club* (see Post & Communications earlier), ironically packed, not with Web geeks, but with 10-year-old boys smoking and playing computer games. The whole experience is a bit like sitting in a war zone, given the violent sound effects and childish shrieks emanating from the surrounding computers. But once you have managed to fight your way past all the kids clamouring for a computer, it is a fun place to be. It is open daily from 11 am to 7 pm and soft drinks cost US$0.35.

Entertainment
Theatre, Opera & Classical Music Craiova has an active cultural scene which is well worth seeking a glimpse of if you have an evening spare. Highly recommended is a play at the *National Theatre* (Teatrul Naţionale), a large impressive building on Blvd 1 C Brătianu. Tickets are sold at the Agenţie de Teatrală (☎ 413 755), adjoining the main theatre building, open daily from 10 am to 12.30 pm and 4 to 6.30 pm. Tickets are also sold here for performances held at the *Opera & Operetta Theatre* (Teatrul de opera şi operată) at Str Ion Marinescu 12. Classical concerts are performed by the *Oltenia Philharmonic* (Filarmonic Oltenia) on Calea Unirii. The ticket office (☎ 411 284), open daily from 10 am to 1 pm and from 4 to 7 pm, is inside the main Philharmonic building. Tickets cost US$0.75/0.35 for adults/students.

Bars & Bingo The *Club Royal Universitate*, on the corner of Str Oltet and Str Nicolaescu Plopsor, is a dimly lit trendy bar where students tend to hang out; it is open daily from 10 am to midnight. And you can play bingo 24 hours a day at *Bingo Victoria*, which overlooks the Hotel Minerva on Str Mihail Kogălniceanu.

Getting There & Away

Air Craiova has a small airport (☎ 116 860, 178 126) out of town. No flights arrived or departed from it in 1997.

Bus Craiova has two bus stations: the northern bus station (Autogară Nord), from which buses to/from most other towns arrive/depart, is next to the train station, 1km north-east of the centre on Blvd Carol I (Blvd Republicii). Major daily bus services include one to Calafat (87km), Câmpulung Muscel (172km), Târgovişte (171km), Horezu (111km), Piteşti (142km) and Râmnicu Vâlcea (180km); and two to Drobeta-Turnu Severin (111km) and Târgu Jiu (102km).

The Öz Murat travel agency (☎ 418 780) has an office outside Autogară Nord. It runs a daily bus to Istanbul via Bucharest, departing at 8 am. The price of a return ticket is US$57.

The southern bus station (Autogară Sud), 5km south of the centre, serves pinprick-sized villages south of Craiova.

Train Advance train tickets are sold at the Agenţie de Voiaj CFR (☎ 411 634), opposite the Hotel Jiul in the Complex Comercial Unirea. The office is open weekdays from 7 am to 7.30 pm.

CALAFAT

• *area code ☎ 051*

The small town of Calafat, 87km south-west of Craiova on the Danube opposite Vidin, Bulgaria, makes a convenient entry/exit point to/from Bulgaria. Car ferries cross the river hourly and there are frequent local trains to/from Craiova (where you can catch an express train to Bucharest or Timişoara). Apart from the **Muzeul de Artă** on Str 22 Decembrie and a monument to the 1877-78 war of independence against the Turks, there isn't much to see or do in Calafat.

Orientation & Information

The ferry landing is right in the centre of Calafat, about four blocks from the train station. To use the left-luggage office at the train station, first buy a baggage ticket at the ticket window, then look for the baggage room *(bagaje de mână)* in a small building just down the track.

It's impossible to change travellers cheques in Calafat. As you get off the ferry you'll see several exchange kiosks near customs. Commissions vary from 3% to 5%, so shop around. People on the street can exchange Romanian lei for Bulgarian leva, but it is not recommended (rip-offs are common). The Bancă Agricola, opposite the post office on the way from the ferry to the train station, changes cash at the official rate with no commission.

Places to Stay & Eat

The *Hotel Dunărea Calafat* (☎ 231 303), on a slight hill near the ferry terminal, is US$24/37 for a single/double with bath. The accommodation situation is better in Vidin, so continue on if it's not too late.

Getting There & Away

There is one daily bus and six local trains a day to/from Craiova (2½ hours). If you're continuing through to Bucharest or elsewhere, buy a ticket to your final destination and, as soon as you reach Craiova, go into the station and purchase a reservation for your onward express train.

Bulgaria The car ferry crosses the Danube hourly year-round (30 minutes, US$3.50 or DM6 in cash only). Bicycles are sometimes US$2, sometimes free.

The queue of southbound cars waiting at Calafat to board the ferry to Bulgaria is often pretty horrendous. Northbound it's not so bad and pedestrians can just walk past all the queues in both directions. Cars can spend several hours in the queue on the Romanian side. There are small 24-hour cafés along the line where you can buy drinks, though one person will have to remain sober to move the car along.

GIURGIU
• *area code* ☎ *046*

The main route from Bucharest to Bulgaria is via the border town of Giurgiu, 64km south of the capital on the north shores of the Danube river. The *Bulgaria* and *Istanbul Expres* trains both rumble across Giurgiu's 4km-long bridge across the Danube on their journeys south, while lumbering lorries and other heavy vehicles favour the road route as the main bridge between Bulgaria into the west.

For motorists and foot passengers there are three ways of crossing from Giurgiu into Ruse, Bulgaria – the small Bac ferry (the cheapest option), the larger Ro-Ro boat, or the road bridge. Backpackers, note that you cannot cross the bridge on foot; a line of taxis waits at its northern end to motor individual travellers the 4km south for US$29.

Giurgiu town itself is ugly, with nothing to see or do.

Orientation & Information

Giurgiu train and bus stations are a five minute walk from the centre of town at the end of Str Gării. Exit the station and walk straight up Str Gării until you reach the main street. Giurgiu's northern train station (Giurgiu Nord) is 5km out of town; local trains run between the two stations. Most trains to Bulgaria depart from Giurgiu Nord.

The post office and central market are on Str Constantin Brâncoveanu. Turn right at the bridge crossing, then turn right onto Str Constantin Brâncoveanu. To get to the centre from here, turn left onto the main street.

Places to Stay & Eat

The three-star *Hotel Steaua Dunării* (☎ 217 270), next to the main ferry terminal at Str Mihai Viteazul 1, is a large, well-illuminated block that is generally half-empty. It has single/double rooms with private bath for US$30/40 a night. The restaurant is huge and empty with a very limited menu (one dish). It has a currency exchange inside.

Motel Prietenia (☎ 221 971), or *Motel Vamă* (literally 'Customs Motel') as it is known locally, is no more than 100m from the road bridge into Bulgaria. Double rooms with private bath are well priced at US$20 a night; a good little restaurant serving home-made dishes adjoins it. If the queue at the bridge is long, pop in here for a strong coffee and *Euronews* on cable TV.

A five minute walk from the train and bus stations is the *Hotel Victoria* (☎ 212 569) at Str Gării 1. It is pretty shabby and run-down. Singles/doubles are US$11/16. To get to the hotel from Str Gării, walk under the arches next to the lotto shop and cross the small play area; the hotel is around the corner above the Elvila shop.

Five kilometres from the centre on the northbound Şoseaua Bucureşti road to Bucharest is the small and friendly *Mini-Motel* (☎ 210 150). Clean single/double/triple rooms with private bath are US$11/20/25 a night.

Getting There & Away

Bus & Train There are no buses from Giurgiu to Bulgaria.

Most Giurgiu-Ruse trains depart from Giurgiu Nord train station (☎ 215 106). The daily *Istanbul Expres* from Bucharest passes through Giurgiu Nord at 2.22 pm (12 hours). On its return journey it leaves Istanbul at 8.05 pm, arriving in Giurgiu at 11.15 am. The daily *Bulgaria Expres* stops at Giurgiu at 6.15 am.

There are also two daily local trains to Ruse, departing from the Central Giurgiu train station (☎ 211 098) at 8.35 am and 3.10 pm (4km, 15 minutes).

Car & Motorcycle The main E70 highway from Bucharest to Giurgiu leads directly to the bridge crossing, signposted 'Punctul de frontiera Giurgiu'. Toll tickets are sold from the row of kiosks marked 'casă' on the right as you approach the customs control zone. A single crossing for a car/motorbike is US$10/3.

Ferry The main ferry terminal from which the Ro-Ro boat arrives/departs is close to the centre next to Hotel Steaua Dunării. Approaching Giurgiu from Bucharest, turn left at the bridge crossing (see Car & Motorcycle previously). It is also signposted from the main street in town. The crossing takes 20 minutes and ferries depart daily every two hours (on the hour) between 1 am and 11 pm. The return ferry from Ruse to Giurgiu follows the same schedule. A single ticket for a car/foot passenger is US$17/1, plus an additional US$3.50 ecological tax (*serviciul taxe ecologice*) levied by the Bulgarian authorities. Lorries and larger vehicles generally favour this crossing.

Cheaper and quicker, with smaller or no queues at all, is the Bac ferry boat which departs from a smaller port 2km out of town; it is clearly signposted 'BAC ferry boat' from the centre of town. Tickets for the 10 minute crossing cost US$6/1 for a car/foot passenger, plus the US$3.50 ecological tax. The ferry operates 24 hours.

CĂLĂRAŞI
* *area code* ☎ 042

The surreal entry by road from the northwest into Călăraşi, beneath an ungainly 'bridge' of rusting conveyor belts which lumber in an intricate maze to the city's steel works, says it all about this city. Largely industrial with a heavily systemised centre, the town offers absolutely no reason to come here except to catch the next ferry out – across the Danube to Ostrov from where you can cross into Bulgaria.

For travellers without private transport, crossing the Danube into Bulgaria at Giurgiu (see the Giurgiu section) would be much simpler. This Călăraşi crossing is not served by public transport and is only suitable for motorists. From the centre of Călăraşi, you have to hike 8km south to the port from where you catch a make-shift ferry across the Danube to Ostrov (still in Romania).

The Călăraşi-Ostrov ferry crossing operates 24 hours. It takes cars, lorries and foot passengers. Tickets for the 20 minutes cross-

ing are sold on board. A single ticket for a car and passengers is US$1.20; foot passengers cost US$0.15. Nonswimmers should note that the ferry is a highly precarious affair – vehicles and people are piled on board a large raft which is then pushed across the water by a small, motorised boat.

OSTROV & BEYOND
* *area code* ☎ 042

Once in Ostrov you can continue east to the Black Sea coast, or cross the border into Silistra, Bulgaria. Coming off the ferry a one-way street leads you directly to the customs control point. Continuing past the border control, the eastbound road to Dobruja follows a barbed-wire fence marking the Romanian/Bulgarian border for a further 200m. All the towering apartment blocks you see form part of **Silistra**. The abandoned, Soviet-made Ilyushin plane parked on the Bulgarian riverbank was originally intended to house a bar. The attempt failed. This part of Bulgaria (Southern Dobruja) was part of Romania from 1919 until 1940.

Ostrov village proper is 5km east of the ferry terminal and border crossing. There is a small **Popas Turistic** immediately on the right when you enter the village. From here, for some 15km the eastbound road gracefully follows the twists and turns of the magnificent Danube river, making it one of the most beautiful drives in Romania. This majestic riverside stretch peaks at the **Dervent Monastery** (Mănăstirea Dervent) which overlooks Lake Dervent, south of the Danube. Bus loads of tour groups stop here to be fed and to listen to the monks calling the faithful to worship: two large bells are rung while intricate rhythms are beaten out with wooden hammers on a plank of wood.

The road continues east into Northern Dobruja.

Northern Dobruja

Dobruja (Dobrogea) is the squat neck of land between the Danube River (Râul Dunărea) and the Black Sea (Marea Neagră). Although the rest of Romania declared independence from the Ottoman Empire in 1877, northern Dobruja wasn't joined to Romania until 1878 when a combined Russo-Romanian army defeated the Turks in Bulgaria. Southern Dobruja was ceded to Bulgaria. This relatively recent accession of northern Dobruja by the Turks accounts for the many mosques in the area.

In antiquity the region was colonised first by the Greeks who called the Black Sea Pontus Axeinos, meaning 'inhospitable sea'; then by the Romans. Both left behind much for visitors to admire. Histria, 70km north of Constanţa, is the oldest ancient settlement in Romania, founded by Greek merchants in 657 BC. From 46 AD, Dobruja was the Roman province of Moesia Inferior. At Adamclisi (Tropaeum Traiani) the Romans scored a decisive victory over the Geto-Dacian tribes, which made possible their expansion north of the Danube. Dobruja later fell to Byzantium, and in 1418 it was conquered by the Turks.

Orientation & Information

Dobruja's 245km stretch of Black Sea coast (*litoral* in Romanian) is Romania's hottest tourist spot. Practically every tourist agency in Romania sells package deals to the Black Sea resorts which are jammed with concrete-block hotels overlooking packed beaches. There are better facilities here than in most other parts of Romania, and in midsummer the Black Sea coast resembles a massive outdoor party, with beachfront barbecues and plenty of beer.

The high season runs from mid-May to mid-September. From October to late April, the beaches are eerily quiet, few hotels are open, and the weather is downright cold.

There are nine main resorts, most of them named after mythical gods: Mamaia, Eforie

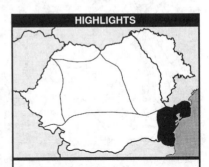

HIGHLIGHTS

- Discover Roman Tomis in Constanţa's archaeological museum and adjoining mosaic museum
- Bathe in black mud at Eforie Nord
- Be a beach bum on Mamaia's golden sands
- Explore the ancient Greek and Roman cities of Histria
- Study pelicans on Lake Furtana
- Tour the Danube Delta's narrow waterways by boat with a local fisherman

Nord, Eforie Sud, Costineşti, Neptun-Olimp, Jupiter-Aurora, Venus, Saturn and Mangalia. Mamaia, on the northern fringe of Constanţa, and the ancient Greek coastal town of Mangalia (Callatis), offer wide, sandy beaches and attract an older, more sedate crowd. Eforie Nord is famous for its curative black mud while Neptun-Olimp is a former Communist Party playground where days merge with nights in an orgy of blasting beach music and flashy nightclubs. Costineşti, previously reserved for youth, is pretty hot if you're looking for action. Eforie Sud, Jupiter-Aurora, Venus and Saturn – all purpose-built concrete jungles from the late 1960s – are dilapidated, dying resorts.

At the south end of the coast, close to the Bulgarian border, are the small fishing villages of Doi Mai and Vama Veche which hold a unique charm all of their own.

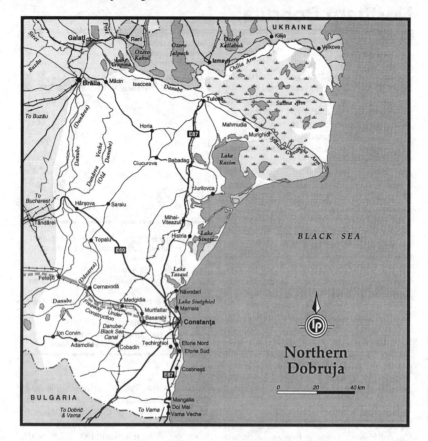

Cheap accommodation is rare. Expect to pay US$30 and up for a comfortable hotel room. Private rooms are only widely available in Costineşti, Doi Mai and Vama Veche. Advance hotel reservations are a good idea from mid-June to August. If you can't find a room head for the Centrul de Cazare, a central accommodation office which keeps tabs on vacancies and bookings.

In summer it's easy to walk from one resort to another along the shore. Private minibuses shuttle beach-hoppers along the coast, stopping at all the resorts between Constanţa and Mangalia. Maps are widely available despite the fact that most of the resorts do not have street names.

Organised Tours & Courses

If you intend staying more than a couple of days the most cost-effective way to travel is on a package tour. These are sold by travel agents both in Romania and abroad.

Most travel agencies along the coast organise day trips to other resorts on the Black Sea, wine-tasting trips to the Murfatlar winery, as well as two and three-day excursions to Istanbul and Bulgaria. None of these tours are geared to individual travellers; sign up at one of the larger hotels if you want to be sure that the trip will actually take place.

The Black Sea University Foundation (☎ & fax 01-222 4118), Blvd Primăverii 50, Bucharest, arranges short summer courses covering a wide range of technical, historical and cultural subjects on the Black Sea coast. Accommodation is usually in two-star hotels.

CONSTANŢA
• *area code* ☎ *041, pop 350,476*

Constanţa, halfway between Istanbul in Turkey and Odessa in Ukraine, is Romania's largest port and second-largest city. In ancient times Constanţa was the Greek-controlled town of Tomis. The Romans renamed it Constantiana after the emperor Constantine (306-337 AD) who fortified the city, had the streets paved, thermal baths built and rich mosaics laid – all of which had been destroyed by Slav and Avar attacks by the 8th century AD.

After Constanţa (known as Küstendje under Turkish rule) was taken by Romania in 1877, the town grew in importance, with a railway line being built to it from Bucharest. By the early 1900s it was a fashionable seaside resort frequented by European royalty.

Despite the dirty, crowded beaches, the picturesque old town has a peaceful Mediterranean air. There are a few excellent museums, which you can easily see in an afternoon while waiting for the Constanţa-Istanbul ferry. The city is the main transport hub on the Black Sea coast and the gateway to other resorts.

Constanţa hosts a national folk music festival each year during the last weekend in August.

Orientation

Constanţa's train station and main southern bus station (Autogară Sud) is some 2km west of the old town. The left-luggage office (open 24 hours) at the train station is downstairs inside the passageway from the main hall to the tracks. To reach old Constanţa, exit the station, buy a ticket (US$0.20) from

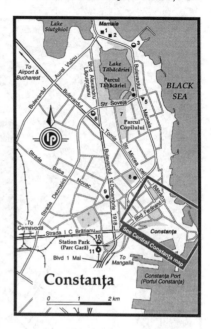

1   Hotel Perla
2   Hotel Parc
3   Pescărie Bus Stop
4   Planetarium; Dolphinarium
5   China Restaurant
6   Autogară Nord (Northern Bus Station)
7   Stadionul 1 Mai; Childrens' Park
8   Automobil Clubul Român
9   Culture House
10 Autogară Sud (Southern Bus Station)
11 Train Station

the kiosk to the right and take trolleybus No 40, 41 or 43 down Blvd Ferdinand to Victoria Park (four stops from the station). From here walk south along Blvd Tomis to Piaţa Ovidiu. Trolleybus No 40 continues to the southern edge of Mamaia; No 41 continues to Mamaia centre (see Getting Around). The less-frequented northern bus station (Autogară Nord) is 3km north of the centre on Str Soveja.

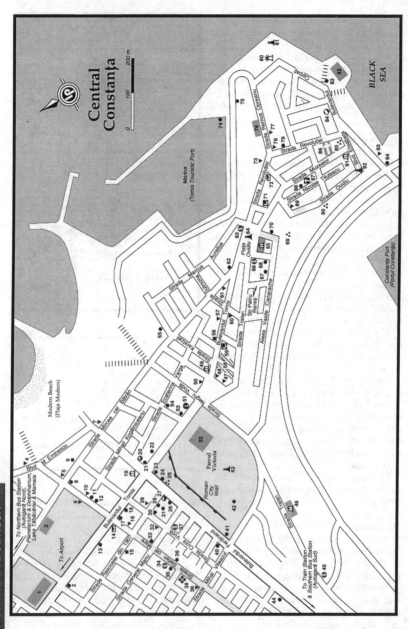

Central
Constanţa

0   100   200 m

BLACK
SEA

Marina
(Tomis Touristic Port)

Modern Beach
(Plaja Modern)

Constanţa Port
(Portul Constanţa)

To Northern Bus Station
(Autogară Nord),
Planetarium & Dolphinarium,
Lake Tăbăcăriei & Mamaia

To Airport

To Train Station
& Southern Bus Station
(Autogară Sud)

Parcul
Victoria

Roman
City Wall

PLACES TO STAY
6   Hotel Sport
15 Hotel Guci
56 Hotel Tineretului
76 Hotel Palace
88 Hotel Intim

PLACES TO EAT
4   Restaurant Zorile
    Mării
5   Pizzeria Coral
7   Privat Club
9   Beta Fast Food
10 Quick Restaurant
16 Au Coq Simpa
29 Market Expo; Fast
    Food
32 Restaurant Sport
39 McDonald's
47 Nur Restaurant
48 La Strada Club Bar
50 Restaurant Erzurum
57 Pelican Pizza Italiana
60 Patisseria Unister
61 Royal Club
    Restaurant
73 Cantină
77 Casă Tomis
78 Palace Café
89 Casă cu Lei
93 Vraja Marii Café

OTHER
1   Sports Hall
2   Sidis Supermarket
3   Metamorfoze State
    Drama Theatre &
    Opera
8   Kodak Films
11 TAROM; Avis
12 Galeriile de Artă
13 Metamorfoze State
    Drama Theatre;
    Opera Ticket Office

14 Central Post Office
17 Autori Dobrogeni
    Bookshop
18 Agenţie de Turism
    Intern
19 Art Museum & Gallery
20 Bus Stop for Mamaia
21 Grand Supermarket
22 Romar Travel Agency
23 Farmacie
24 British Council Library
25 Old City Wall
26 Danubius Exchange
27 Bus Stop for Train
    Station
28 Oleg Danovski Ballet
    Theatre
30 Nouvelles Frontières/
    Simpa Turism
31 Market
33 Cinema Progresul
34 Bancă Comercială
    Ion Ţiriac (BCIT)
35 Ballet Theatre Ticket
    Office (Agenţie de
    Bilete)
36 Librărie Mihai
    Eminescu
37 Bancă Agricola
38 Tomis Department
    Store
40 Danubius Travel
    Agency
41 Fantasio Musical
    Theatre
42 Cinema Grădină
    Tomis
43 Victory Monument
44 Cinema Republica
45 Bancă Comercială
    Română
46 Naval History
    Museum
49 Folk Art Museum

51 Agenţie de Turism
    Intern
52 Prefecture
53 Farmacie
54 Fundaţia Actionea
    Ciuica Bookshop
55 Elpis Puppet Theatre
58 Galeriile Comerciale
    Voicules
59 Geamia Hunchiar
    Mosque
62 Fuji Film Centre
63 Bancă Agricola
64 Statue of Ovid
65 History &
    Archaeological
    Museum
66 BANCOREX
67 Agenţie de Voiaj CFR
68 Contur Agenţie de
    Turism
69 Roman Mosaic
70 Danubius Travel
    Agency
71 Mahmudiye Mosque
72 Post Office
74 *Condor* Cruise Boat
75 Yacht Club
79 Farmacie Ovidius
80 Genoese Lighthouse
81 Mihai Eminescu
    Statue
82 Casino
83 Aquarium
84 Chinese Consulate
85 Archaeological Site
86 Orthodox Cathedral
87 Roman Catholic
    Church
90 Roman Baths
91 Ion Jalea Museum
92 Saligny Monument
94 Main entrance to
    Constanţa Port

Most facilities are on the pedestrianised Str Ştefan cel Mare, at the south-western end of which is the Tomis department store. Most travel agencies and information points are on Blvd Tomis, the main axis running from the new town in the north to the old town and port in the south.

Maps The best city map, *Constanţa Tourist Map* (Amco Press, 1997) includes a map of the city centre and suburbs, the port and Mamaia, and shows all the public transport routes. It costs US$1.20 in major hotels,

kiosks and travel agencies. The *Hartă turistică a Municipiului Constanţa* (Publirom, 1996) is less comprehensive.

If you are visiting the rest of the coast, a good buy is the bilingual *Romanian Seashore Guide/Ghidul Litoralului* (Publirom, 1997) which also lists hotels and restaurants in Constanţa and along the coast. It costs US$4.

Information
Tourist Offices The Agenţie de Turism Intern (☎ & fax 611 429), Blvd Tomis 46, is

NORTHERN DOBRUJA

utterly useless (except for the maps it sells), treating individual travellers as a nothing less than a severe nuisance. Tourist groups are accorded slightly more respect. It's open weekdays from 8 am to 5 pm, Saturday from 8 am to noon.

Money Most hotels, supermarkets and travel agencies have exchange outlets. The Danubius Exchange at Blvd Ferdinand 44, Balcan at Str Ştefan cel Mare 64, and the not so Nasty Change at Str Ştefan cel Mare 46, all offer good rates.

Bancă Română de Comerţ Exterior (BANCOREX), Str Traian 1, changes travellers cheques and gives cash advance on Visa/MasterCard on weekdays from 8.30 am to 2 pm. Bancă Agricola, at Piaţa Ovidiu 9 and on the corner of Str Cuza Vodă and Str General Manu, offers identical services. Both branches are open weekdays from 8 to 11 am. Bancă Comercială Ion Ţiriac (BCIT), Str Ştefan cel Mare 32-34, is open weekdays from 9 am to 2.30 pm.

Bancă Comercială Română at Str Traian 68 has an ATM outside which accepts Visa/MasterCard. The bank is open weekdays from 8 to 11.30 am.

Post & Communications The central telephone and post office is at Blvd Tomis 79 on the corner of Str Ştefan cel Mare. The telephone section is open daily from 7 am to 10 pm, the post office weekdays from 9 am to 5 pm. There is a smaller post office in the old town at the south end of Str Revoluţiei.

Travel Agencies The Danubius travel agency is among the most efficient in Constanţa. Its English-speaking staff sell tickets for ferries to Istanbul and arrange day trips to the Danube Delta, Murfatlar and other resorts on the coast. It has an office next to the Roman mosaic museum at Piaţa Ovidiu 11 (☎ 613 103, 619 039; fax 615 836, 619 041) and another at Blvd Ferdinand 36 (670 129, 615 836; fax 618 010). Both are open weekdays from 9 am to 7 pm, Saturday from 9 am to 2 pm.

For advance hotel bookings in other resorts try Contur Agenţie de Turism (☎ 613 192), next to BANCOREX on Piaţa Ovidiu. You can usually get a hotel room cheaper through here than through the hotels direct.

Romar travel agency (☎ & fax 672 144) at Blvd Tomis 66 sells TAROM air tickets. Nouvelles Frontières/Simpa Turism (☎ 60 468; fax 664 403) at Str Răscoaiei 1907, 9, sells tickets for charter flights to Paris.

Bookshops The best bookshop in town for English and French-language novels is the Fundaţia Actionea Civica bookshop on the corner of Str Dragoş Vodă and Str Ecaterina Varga (open weekdays from 10 am to 6 pm).

Libraries & Cultural Centres The British Council (☎ & fax 618 365) runs a small library on the 2nd floor of Constanţa district library (Biblioteca Judeţeana Constanţa) at Blvd Ferdinand 7. It's open Monday, Wednesday and Friday from 4 to 8 pm, Tuesday and Thursday from 9 am to 3 pm.

The French Institute (Institut Francais de Constanţa; ☎ & fax 619 438), Blvd Ferdinand 78, hosts music, theatre and film festivals.

Online Services Log into *Virtual Constanţa* at www.cycor.ca/fix-ok/romain.html for an online tourist guide.

Medical Services The Farmacie Ovidus is just off Str Remus Opreanu on Str Revoluţiei (open weekdays from 8 am to 7 pm, Saturday from 8 am to noon). Approaching the old town, there is a pharmacy next to the Agenţie de Turism Intern on Blvd Tomis (open weekdays from 7 am to 8 pm, Saturday from 9 am to 5 pm and Sunday from 9 am to 2 pm).

Walking Tour
Constanţa's most renowned attraction is the **History & Archaeological Museum** (Muzeul de Istorie Naţionale şi Arheologie; ☎ 614 582, 618 763) at Piaţa Ovidiu 12. Originating from a small private collection set up by the city mayor in 1879, the museum houses exhibits which trace the history of Dobruja from ancient times to the end of

WWII. Among the most prized pieces are 24 2nd century Roman statues discovered under the old train station in 1962. The most unusual statue is that of the serpent Glykon – the god of good, guardian of the family and of the house – which is carved from a single block of marble. Also displayed in the treasury are pieces of gold jewellery from the 4th century AD, discovered in the tomb of a four-year-old girl in Mangalia. The museum is open in summer daily from 9 am to 8 pm, and in winter daily, except Monday, from 9 am to 6 pm. Admission is US$0.75. Pick up a copy of the excellent, English-language guide to the museum for US$1.20.

The archaeological fragments of Roman Tomis spill over onto the surrounding square. Of particular interest are the eight, 2nd century altars on stone pillars, all of which bear funerary inscriptions in Greek or Latin. To the side of these is another museum, which shelters a gigantic 3rd century, paved **Roman mosaic** (Edificiul Toman cu Mozaic) discovered in 1959 and left *in situ*. It covers an area of 850m2. This is just a small section of the original 2000m2 mosaic which 'carpeted' the floor of the imperial hall in Roman times.

Walking down the steps from the mosaic, you come to the lower terrace of the museum, overlooking the modern port, where the storerooms were. Of particular interest are the statues of Bacchus, the god of vegetation and wine, and of Hermes, the winged messenger of the Roman deities and the god of commerce. From this lower terrace, a staircase led to the Roman public thermal baths, at the southern end of the cliff. Parts of these remain today. The mosaic museum is open in summer daily from 9 am to 8 pm, and in winter daily, except Monday, from 9 am to 6 pm. Admission is US$0.90. The English-language guide, *The Roman Paved Mosaic from Tomis*, sold at the ticket office for US$1.20, is worth every cent.

The **statue of Ovid** (1887) commemorates the outlaw-poet who was exiled to Constanţa in the 8th century. His grave is believed to lie below the statue. During his exile here he wrote numerous poems and

Glykon was one of several Roman statues found beneath Constanţa's train station.

much prose, including *Tristia (Poems of Sadness)*, *Ibis* and four books of *Ex Ponto (Letters from the Black Sea)*, in which his life in exile is featured.

A block south of this square, on Str Muzeelor, is the large **Mahmudiye mosque**, a testament to the period when Constanţa fell under Turkish rule. The mosque – the first steel, concrete and brick construction to be built in Romania – was known as the King Carol I mosque when it was built in 1910 to serve Constanţa's Muslim merchants. Today it remains the seat of the spiritual head of Dobruja's modest Muslim community. The mosque has a 140-step minaret which you can climb when the gate is unlocked. Two blocks further down the same street is the **Orthodox cathedral** (1885). A small **archaeological site** lies south of it, displaying some walls of houses dating from the 4th to 6th centuries. Constanţa's **Roman Catholic church** (Biserica Romano-Catolica Sfântul Anton) is one street west of the

Orthodox cathedral at Str Nicolae Titulescu 11. Sunday services are held at 9 and 10.30 am, noon, and 6 pm; with additional services at 8 am and 6 pm on Monday and Wednesday.

Continuing south along Str Muzeelor you come to the small **Ion Jalea museum** (Muzeul Ion Jalea) in a pretty, Moorish-style house at Blvd Elisabeta 26. One block west of the museum is the **Saligny monument**. The Romanian engineer Anghel Saligny (1854-1923) designed the Cernavodă bridge across the Danube in 1895 and constructed Constanţa's modern port between 1899 and 1910.

From the monument, meander along the peaceful waterfront which offers sweeping views of the placid Black Sea. On summer evenings this is a popular hangout for kids, entwined couples and old men playing chess. Have a beer or coffee on the terrace of Constanţa's French-style Art-Nouveau **casino** (1910). Opposite, in the casino's old beer house, is an **aquarium** (☎ 611 277) – a dismal affair displaying various fish in cramped quarters. It is open daily from 9 am to 8 pm; admission is US$0.60. Further along the promenade is the **pier** with a fine view of old Constanţa, and the **Genoese**

lighthouse. The 8m-tall lighthouse was built between 1858 and 1860 in memory of 13th century merchants from Genoa who helped to revive Constanţa's then-ailing port. It functioned until 1913 and was restored in 1948. Behind the lighthouse, a tragically poised **statue of Mihai Eminescu** (1934) looks out to the sea.

For other worthwhile sights return to Piaţa Ovidiu and follow Blvd Tomis north-west to the grand supermarket. Halfway up Blvd Tomis you pass the **Geamia Hunchiar mosque**, built in 1868 with stones from the old gate of the former Ottoman fortress which was destroyed during the Russian-Turkish war in 1828. Further along Blvd Tomis is the worthwhile **Folk Art museum** (Muzeul de Artă Populară) at No 32. When you reach the supermarket, turn left and explore Victoria Park, which has remains of the 3rd century **Roman city wall** and the 6th century Butchers' tower, pieces of Roman sculpture and the modern **Victory monument** (1968). If you continue north-west along Blvd Tomis you come to the **art museum** (Muzeul de Artă; ☎ 616 133) at No 84. Wacky contemporary art exhibitions are held in the adjoining **small art gallery** (galeriile mica). Both open daily from 9 am

---

Street Kids, Child Prostitution & AIDS

An estimated 2000 children live on Romania's city streets, many of them squatting in sewers and other unsavoury 'homes' in Constanţa. Iaşi, Galaţi, Oradea and Bucharest's train stations are other street-kid hotspots.

AIDS, tuberculosis and syphilis are just some of the scourges threatening these children. By the end of 1996, 4446 cases of AIDS had been reported in Romania, 75% of them children (comprising more than half of all paediatric AIDS cases in Europe). Unofficial Health Ministry estimates put the number of HIV cases at 20,000. Syphilis affected 653 children and adolescents under 18 years in mid-1997. Social workers believe 95% of all sexually active youngsters living on the streets have the disease.

Child prostitution, pornography and paedophilia have penetrated Romania at an alarming speed since the collapse of communism. In September 1997 an Anglican vicar was charged with having unlawful sex with a minor after being caught in bed with a 14-year-old in an apartment near Bucharest's Gara de Nord. He was the fifth foreigner to be arrested on these grounds since October 1996. Aid workers reckon some 50 western European paedophiles pay regular visits to the Romanian capital to prey on its street children. Trafficking of children to brothels abroad is not unheard of either.

Aid organisations are doing their utmost to help street children. Perhaps the most eye-catching approach is being made by the local charity PARADA. Clowns, jugglers, stilt walkers and other members of the group – many of them reformed street children themselves – parade the street-kid ghettos, luring Romania's desperate youngsters out of the gutter and into their circus act. ■

to 8 pm; in winter the museum and gallery are closed on Monday.

The **Naval History Museum** (Muzeul Marinei Române; ☎ 619 035) is housed in the old Navy high school at Str Traian 53. The captions are all in Romanian, but the illustrations are informative. It is open daily in summer from 9 am to 8 pm.

Heading north towards Mamaia, you pass Constanţa's **Planetarium & Dolphinarium** (Planetarium şi Delfinariu; ☎ 647 055) at Blvd Mamaia 255, on the south-eastern shores of Lake Tăbăcăriei. Both are open daily in summer from 9 am to 8 pm. There are dolphin shows and the planetarium hosts informative demonstrations of the planets' activities throughout the day. Tickets for both shows cost US$0.50 and are sold at the *casă* 30 minutes before the show starts. Both shows last between 20 and 30 minutes. The planetarium also has an observation tower. Trolleybus No 40 stops directly outside the Dolphinarium.

Sailing

You can sail aboard the *Condor*, moored at the marina at the east end of Str Remus Opreanu, for US$2.50 an hour. Look for the *Plimbări pe mare* sign opposite the yacht club. The boat sails daily from May to September from 10 am to 6 pm. The marina is also known as the Tomis Tourist Port (Portul Turistic Tomis).

Rent paddle and rowing boats from the beach attendants on the *plaja modern* (modern beach), north of the marina. Steps lead down to the beach from Str Negru Vodă and Str Ştefan cel Mare.

Language Courses

The British Council sponsors the CLASS (Constanţa Language Association; ☎ 612 877) at Blvd Mircea cel Bătrân 103.

Places to Stay

Camping The nearest *campsites* are in Mamaia, 6km north of Constanţa. Don't let the 20 minute trolleybus ride deter you however – Mamaia is a much calmer, more tranquil place to stay after a day's sightseeing.

Hotels Constanţa's hotels are large, soulless blocks with zero appeal. Even if you're only overnighting in the city, consider taking a trolleybus to Mamaia where accommodation is better value.

The cheapest hotel in Constanţa is the not-cheap, two-star *Hotel Tineretului* (☎ 613 590, 618 855; fax 611 290), Blvd Tomis 20-26. It's a five-storey hotel with neat double rooms/apartments with private bath for US$30/50.

Romanian poet Mihai Eminescu stayed for 10 days at the *Hotel Intim* (☎ 618 285, 617 814) – then called Hotel d'Angleterre – when he visited Constanţa in 1882. Single/double rooms at this historic hotel at Str Nicolae Titulescu 7-9 cost US$32/45, including breakfast. The hotel has an elegant indoor dining room and terrace.

Equally fine is the three-star *Hotel Palace* (☎ 614 696; fax 617 532), dating from 1914, in the old town overlooking the marina at Str Remus Opreanu 5-7. The view costs: single/double rooms with all the mod cons cost US$60/80. The hotel has some two-star doubles which are less expensive at US$30 a night, including breakfast.

Sport enthusiasts should opt for *Hotel Sport* (☎ 617 558; fax 611 009) at Str Cuza Vodă 2. This modern hotel has a gym and small sports complex. Single/double rooms with private bath are US$35/40, including breakfast. The hotel is actually on Str Mircea cel Bătrân, overlooking the sea.

Constanţa's top hotel is the three-star *Hotel Guci* (☎ & fax 638 426), behind the central post office at Str Răscoaiei 1907, 23. Rooms are luxuriously decked out with modern furnishings. Incredibly, despite the price – US$100 for a double and US$130 for a two-room suite – and western style of service, none of the rooms has a real double bed; they all have two tiny single beds. Other facilities include an expensive restaurant, jacuzzi, sauna and gym.

At the time of writing, the three-star *Hotel*

Continental was closed for extensive renovations.

Another cluster of hotels lies around Lake Tăbăcăriei, 4km north of the centre and just a km or so short of Mamaia. The two-star *Olt* (☎ 655 556) and *Holidays* (☎ & fax 616 137) are both in the Satul de Vacanţa (Satellite Holiday Village) on the north-western side of the lake. Take trolleybus No 40 from the train station or city centre to the Pescărie bus stop.

Places to Eat

Restaurants For dirt-cheap food – quality not guaranteed – head for the *Cantină* on the corner of Str Remus Opreanu and Str Revoluţiei. Leave with a full stomach for around US$1. The canteen is open daily from 9 am to 7 pm. Another budget option is the locally frequented *Restaurant Erzurum*, one block north-west of the folk art museum on Blvd Tomis. It serves soups for less than US$1, and has the finest čay (tea) this side of Istanbul. It's open daily from 10 am to 6 pm. The authentic Turkish *Nur Restaurant* is opposite Erzurum, at the north-western end of Str Traian.

For Italian-inspired delights try *Pelican Pizza Italiana* (☎ 615 976) at Str Sulmona 9. It has a fine terrace garden and serves cocktails. Eat before 9 pm if you don't want to be subjected to a cabaret comprising half-naked women prancing around a small stage. It is open daily from noon to midnight. For those who prefer something more modest, there is the French *Au Coq Simpa* (☎ 614 797) at Str Ştefan cel Mare 19. It's open daily from 11 am to midnight.

Constanţa's modest splurge is the *Casă Cu Lei* – named 'House of the Lions' after the stone lions that majestically welcome diners from their rooftop perch – at Str Dianei 1. Even if you're not eating, the bar here is an agreeable oasis. It's open daily from 10 am to 1 am. Extravagant splurge-seekers should opt for the flashy *Royal Club Restaurant* (☎ 617 390) at Str Mircea cel Bătrân 5.

Around the beach there is a variety of places. The *Privat Club* serves a small selection of traditional Romanian dishes for US$3

a head. The restaurant – an ugly, circular concrete tower overlooking the beach on the corner of Blvd Ferdinand and Str Mircea cel Bătrân – is open daily from noon to midnight. Close by is the more attractive *Pizzeria Coral* (☎ 611 911), housed in a glass conservatory above the beach at Str Mircea cel Bătrân 94. It serves a good range of pastas and pizzas and is open from 10 am to past midnight. *Restaurant Zorile Mării*, at the top of the steps on Str Ştefan cel Mare, is a popular lunch spot for restless sunbathers.

The *China Restaurant* (☎ 655 311), almost opposite the Dolphinarium at Str Zorelelor 67, is good. The special fried rice is of the Romanian variety but the meat and fish dishes are good. It's open daily from noon to midnight and usually crammed with expats. Next door is a large billiard hall.

Cafés & Fast Food Last-minute and late-night snacks can be grabbed at the *Vraja Marii* café, adjacent to the main port entrance at the southern end of Blvd Elisabeta.

Light snacks and copious amounts of beer are served in the *Constanţa Yacht Club* café and snack bar, overlooking the marina at the east end of Str Remus Opreanu. This is the place to meet the city's sailing elite. Heading back into town from the marina along Str Remus Opreanu, you pass the cheap and cheerful *Casă Tomis* and the *Palace Café*.

The place to 'be seen' is the trendy, Italian-style *La Strada Club Bar*, named after the classic Fellini film at Str Vasile Alecsandri 7. It has a funky, modern interior, serves outrageously creamy cappuccinos, and is open 24 hours.

Fast-food outlets serving kebabs, burgers and hotdogs are dotted all over town. There are some inside the modern *Galeriile Comerciale Voicules*, behind La Strada off Blvd Tomis. There is also a fast-food outlet inside the *Market Expo*, in the new town opposite the ballet theatre on Str Răscoaliei 1907.

Beta Fast Food in the central park opposite the TAROM office on Str Ştefan cel Mare has a terrace where you can drink beer and munch on traditional Romanian mititei (spicy meat balls) with mustard. It is open daily from 10 am until dusk. The *Quick Restaurant* opposite has quick service but tasteless dishes. It's open from 10 am to 8 pm.

McDonald's adjoins the Tomis department store on Str Ştefan cel Mare.

Self-Catering The central market is between the train station and southern bus station. In the centre there is another market, just behind the bus stop for the train station, off Str Răscoaiei 1907.

Everything under the sun is sold at the *Sidis Supermarket* at Blvd Ferdinand 99. It is open Monday to Saturday from 8 am to 9 pm, Sunday from 9 am to 3 pm. The *Coral alimentar*, on the corner of Str Mircea cel Bătrân and Str Ştefan cel Mare, is open 24 hours; as is the *Grand Supermarket* at Blvd Tomis 57 on the corner of Blvd Ferdinand. Both are old-style shops where you point at the item you want. The Grand has an excellent choice of cakes and biscuits.

Freshly baked breads, pastries and cakes are sold at the *Patisseria Unister*, on the corner of Blvd Tomis and Str Sulmona; it is open daily, except Sunday, from 8 am to 6 pm.

Entertainment
There is plenty to do in Constanţa after sunset. Foreign films are presented in the original languages (with Romanian subtitles) at *Cinema Progresul* (☎ 664 411), Str Ştefan cel Mare 33, and *Cinema Republica* (☎ 616 287), Blvd Ferdinand 58. Tickets are less than US$1. In summer, films are also screened at the *Cinema Grădină Tomis* (also known as *Cinema Panoramic*), an outside cinema in Victoria park. Tickets are sold one hour before the film starts (usually around 9.30 pm).

Colourful cabarets, pantomimes and musicals are performed at the *Fantasio Musical Theatre* (Teatrul de Revista Fantasio; ☎ 616 036, 618 843; fax 616 607), behind Cinema Grădină Tomis at Blvd Ferdinand 11. The spectacles on at the *Elpis Puppet Theatre* (Teatrul de Păpuşi Elpis;

☎ 618 992; fax 611 744), Str Karatzali 16, are fun too. Tickets cost US$0.20. Daily performances usually start at 11 am.

The more literary should head to the *Metamorfoze State Drama Theatre & Opera* (Teatrul Dramatic Metamorfoze şi Opera; ☎ & fax 611 744) in the central park at Str Mircea cel Bătrân 97. Tickets are sold in the ticket office at Blvd Tomis 97 (open weekdays from 9 am to 3 pm and from 4 to 6 pm, Saturday from 9 am to noon, Sunday from 5 to 6.50 pm). Performances start at 7 pm. The theatre is also home to the Black Sea Philharmonic (Filharmonica Marea Neagră; ☎ & fax 617 522).

Ballets are performed at the *Oleg Danovski Ballet Theatre* (☎ Teatrul de Balet Oleg Danovski; ☎ 665 219) in the old town at Str Răscoaiei 1907, 5. Tickets for all performances are sold at the Agenţie de Bilete (☎ 664 076) at Str Ştefan cel Mare 34, open daily from 10 am to 5 pm.

Spectator Sport
FC Farul Constanţa – the city's cherished football team, has its home ground at Stadionul 1 Mai in Parcul Copilului (literally 'children's park'), in the northern suburbs of town at Str Primăverii 2. Tickets for games are sold at the stadium (☎ 616 142; fax 644 827).

Getting There & Away
Air In summer there are international flights to/from Constanţa's Mihail Kogălniceanu airport (☎ 662 582, 663 093), 25km from the centre. See Getting There & Away at the front of this book for details.

Between May and September TAROM (☎ 662 632, 614 066), Str Ştefan cel Mare 15, runs daily flights, except Sunday, from Constanţa to Bucharest; single/return is US$50/100. Its office is open weekdays from 9 am to 5 pm, Saturday from 9 am to 1 pm.

Bus Constanţa has two bus stations: private buses to Istanbul (via Bulgaria) depart from the southern bus station (Autogară Sud), next to the train station on Blvd Ferdinand. There is a daily bus to Istanbul (17½ hours; US$17/23 single/return), departing from Autogară Sud at noon. Tickets are sold in advance from Özlem Tur (☎ 662 526) in the bus station.

From Constanţa's northern bus station (Autogară Nord) daily services include one to Histria (52km), Mahmudia via Tulcea (145km), and Brăila in Moldavia (277km); two to Măcin (218km); five to Tulcea (125km); and six to Hârşova (84km).

If you're travelling south along the Black Sea coast, buses are more convenient than the slowpoke trains. Exit Constanţa's train station, turn right and walk 50m to the long queue of private minibuses. One leaves every 30 minutes for Mangalia, stopping at Eforie Nord, Eforie Sud, Neptun-Olimp, Venus and Saturn. Pay the driver (US$0.40). City buses Nos 10, 11, 12 and 20 also travel south along the coast.

Train Constanţa's train station is near the bus station at the west end of Blvd Ferdinand. The Agenţie de Voiaj CFR (☎ 614 960), Aleea Vasile Canarache 4, is open weekdays from 7.30 am to 7 pm, Saturday from 7.30 am to 1 pm. You can also buy advance tickets for departures from Constanţa at the CFR office in Mamaia.

From Constanţa there is a daily train to Chişinău in Moldova (13¾ hours): the *Bessarabia* departs from Constanţa at 9.10 pm.

The *Ovidius* train to Budapest also runs overnight (17 hours), departing Constanţa at 6.45 pm. The return train leaves Budapest at 7.30 pm.

In winter there are reduced services to other cities in Romania. Services to most major towns in Transylvania and Banat only run in summer. All trains to Mangalia stop at Eforie Nord, Eforie Sud, Costineşti and Neptun.

Ferry Istanbul is the only city served by ferry from Constanţa port (☎ 611 540, 618 240). This ferry runs from 1 May to 1 September only.

The timetable is changeable. In summer 1997, there were two ferries a week to Istan-

bul (20 hours). A single/return ticket for a simple deck seat cost US$40/55. A single cabin with private bathroom cost US$110/170 and a double cabin was US$200/320. Double cabins with shared bath were cheaper at US$140/200. Four-deck cabins with shared bath cost US$240/320. The single/return fee for a car was US$50/80; for a motorcycle US$25/40.

Tickets can be bought in advance from the Danubius travel agency (see Travel Agencies). You can also buy tickets two hours before departure from the ticket office on the ferry. Boats do fill up. Danubius runs a free shuttle bus for its passengers from its office on Piaţa Ovidiu to the port (*poarta*), at the southern end of Blvd Elisabeta from where the ferry departs. The main entrance, signposted 'Portul Constanţa', is next to the customs point (*vamă*).

Getting Around

To/From the Airport Mihail Kogălniceanu airport (☎ 662 58, 663 093) is 25km north-west of the centre on the road to Hârşova. If you are flying with TAROM, take the free shuttle from its office at Str Ştefan cel Mare 15, 1½ hours before flight departures. All public buses to Hârşova stop at the airport. Allow yourself a good hour for the journey.

Bus & Trolleybus Public transport runs daily from 5 am to 11.30 pm. A ticket valid for two journeys costs US$0.20. You can also buy a day-ticket for US$0.50, or a weekly/10 day pass for US$3/4. Trolleybus No 100 links the train station and Autogară Sud with Autogară Nord. Trolleybus Nos 40, 41 and 43 go from Autogară Sud to the old town. No 43 continues to the stadium south of Lake Tăbăcăriei; No 41 goes to Mamaia, and No 40 goes to the Pescărie bus stop at the southern edge of Mamaia. From here you can catch trolleybus Nos 41 or 47 to the centre of Mamaia or opt for a 20 minute stroll along the beach to the centre.

Bus No 12 goes from the train station to Mangalia. To get to Eforie Nord and Tech-irghiol take bus No 11 from the train station.

Bus No 42 departs from the Fantasio bus stop on Blvd Ferdinand to Autogară Nord.

Car & Motorcycle Avis (☎ & fax 616 733) shares an office with TAROM at Str Ştefan cel Mare 15, open weekdays from 9 am to 5 pm, Saturday from 9 am to 1 pm. Hertz (☎ 665 123) is at Blvd Tomis 106.

The Automobil Clubul Român (ACR; ☎ 611 849; fax 691 220), has an out-of-town office at Blvd Tomis 141, building T-1, between Constanţa and Mamaia. The Peco station at the northern end of Lake Tăbăcăriei between Constanţa and Mamaia at Blvd Mamaia 160 is open 24 hours.

MAMAIA
* *area code* ☎ *041*

Mamaia, an 8km strip of beach between the freshwater Lake Mamaia (or Siutghiol) and the Black Sea, just north of Constanţa, is Romania's version of Palm Beach. The statistics speak volumes: 61 hotels line this heady strip, with 27,000 beds that actually fill up in the high season (mid-June to August). Mamaia is an above-average example of the Black Sea resorts you'll find further south, with fine, golden sands, abundant greenery and a festival atmosphere. According to legend, the resort gained its name from the desperate cries of a fair maiden, who, during the time of the Ottoman Empire, was kidnapped by a Turk and taken out to sea in a boat. As the wind howled her frantic cries for her mother – 'Mamaia! Mamaia!' – could be heard for miles around.

Orientation
The resort lines both sides of the Constanţa-Năvodari road which runs along the coast. Some hotels and restaurants are on the promenade which is parallel to this road. The Pescărie bus stop is at the southern end of Mamaia.

From Constanţa, take trolleybus No 41 or 47 to the Staţia Cazino bus stop.

Information
Tourist Offices The tourist office inside the Centrul de Cazare in the Cazino complex

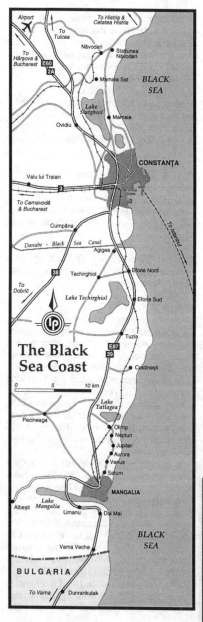

The Black Sea Coast

NORTHERN DOBRUJA

arranges guided tours, as does the tourist office inside Hotel Bucureşti. The Litoral tourist office (☎ 831 334) close to the Pescărie bus stop arranges car rentals and guided tours. It is open from April to October 15, weekdays from 9 am to 3 pm.

Money Every hotel has a currency exchange, but to change travellers cheques and get cash advance on Visa/MasterCard you have to go to Constanţa. Most of the large hotels accept credit cards.

Post & Communications The telephone and post office is 200m south of the Cazino complex on the promenade. It's open weekdays from 8 am to 8 pm. There is a larger post office 1km short of the northern end of Mamaia.

Medical Services SALVAMAR operates medical huts on the beach between 15 June and 15 September.

Things to See & Do
Mamaia's number one attraction is its wide, golden **beach** which stretches the entire length of the resort. Unlike other resorts along the coast, the loudspeakers, from which pop music usually blares, do not work.

From the Cazino complex a **pier** (1935) leads out to sea. The concrete construction doesn't entirely withstand the assault of the waves but this doesn't seem to deter fishermen from casting their rods off the end. Little remains of the water slides either side of the pier.

In summer, the *Luceafarul* and *Steluta* ferry tourists across the freshwater Lake Mamaia to **Ovidiu Island** (Insula Ovidiu), departing every hour (on the hour) between 11 am and 8 pm from the wharf directly opposite the Staţia Cazino bus stop which is next to the taxi rank on the main road to Constanţa. The wharf is signposted 'Debarcaderul Cazino: Mamaia – Insula Ovidiu'. A return ticket costs US$2.

Some 50m north of the Hotel Bucureşti is a **watersports** school, offering waterskiing, yachting, windsurfing and rowing on Lake Mamaia. Also near the Bucureşti is a small mini-golf course. You can hire paddle boats outside Hotel Perla.

The tennis courts at Grăvina Boema, on the highway between the Doina and Victoria hotels, cost US$7 per hour including equipment rental.

Places to Stay
A basic hotel room starts at US$5. In high season head straight to the Centrul de Cazare Cazino (☎ 831 209), on the 1st floor of the Cazino complex. The entrance is close to the rusty old waterslide; follow the faded signs. Staff here have lists of available accommodation. The office is open daily from 10 June to 10 September, from 10 am to 9 pm.

Camping The *Popas Tabăra Turist* (☎ 831 534) is at the northern end of Mamaia's 8km strip. It's small and always full in summer. It costs US$1 per person to pitch a tent and US$4 per person for a bed in a wooden hut. Take bus No 23 from Mamaia's Pescărie bus stop to the Staţia Tabăra Turist bus stop, 300m north of the Hotel Comandor. Adjoining the site is the *Enigma Party Zone* disco.

Popas Mamaia (☎ 831 534), 2km further north from the Tabăra campsite, is a larger complex. You must pass a control point to get in. It costs US$2 to pitch a tent, and a bed in a wooden hut is US$3.50 per person. Rates drop by 50% between September and April. Bus No 23 stops outside the site.

One kilometre further north is *Popas Hanul Piraţilor* (☎ 831 454) with double/triple wooden huts for US$6/10. It also has a two-room villa to let for US$20. Again, take bus No 23.

Beach Chalets The *Cazino Delta Pensiune* (☎ 831 665), inside the Cazino complex on the south side of the main building, offers white-washed, terraced chalets overlooking the beach. A double chalet with shared bathroom and cold water costs US$6 a night. Don't expect more than four bare walls and a mattress on the floor.

The *Mini-Hotel* (☎ 831 878; fax 831 562), also in the Cazino complex but on the north side of the main building, has identical, sea-view chalets to let. Its five triple rooms and 50 doubles cost US$3.50 per person in May, US$5 in June and September and US$6 in July and August. Look for the sign 'Bunga-low, Snack Bar, Cazino' outside the Cazino building.

Hotels The *Hotel Victory* (☎ 831 153; fax 831 253) is 300m north of the Cazino along the promenade. This small, family-run hotel is the only hotel in Mamaia which stands on the beach. Watching the sun rise above the sea while you lie in bed is a real treat. Incred-ibly, the Victory is also the cheapest hotel, offering 10 double rooms with private bath for US$15 a night. Book in advance in peak season.

The friendly, three-star *Hotel Albatros* (☎ 831 381; fax 831 346), 50m south of the Victory, is the next best option. Single/doubles with bath are US$20/35. From the Staţia Cazino bus stop turn; the hotel is 20m further on the left.

Next door to the Albatros is the cheaper, two-star *Hotel Condor* (☎ 831 142; fax 831 906). Doubles with private bath (it has no singles) are US$20 a night. A large restau-rant, currency exchange and snack bar are also in the complex.

The *Hotel Perla* (☎ 831 670) and the *Hotel Parc* (☎ 831 670) are two high-rises at the most southern end of Mamaia, close to the Pescărie bus stop. Both have standard rooms with mid-range prices; single/double/triple rooms cost US$22/35/40.

Unique in design is the three-star *Hotel Bucureşti* (☎ 831 025; fax 831 360). For-merly the most fashionable hotel in Mamaia, it has not yet lost its charm. Double rooms are US$25 a night, including breakfast. The Bucureşti is in the northern half of the resort.

Mamaia's most exclusive beach-front hotel is the four-star *Hotel Rex* (☎ 831 595; fax 831 690); a large, pre-WWII white build-ing some 200m north of the Bucureşti. It has a picture-postcard swimming pool on a terrace above the beach. Single/double rooms cost US$90/110 and a luxury apart-ment is US$150. English, French and

German-language newspapers are sold at reception. The pool is exclusively for hotel guests.

Places to Eat
Almost every hotel has an adjoining restau-rant serving the usual pork and grilled meatballs. *Fast-food stands* along the busy pedestrianised street suffice for lunch and hot snacks. The eating scene is generally uninspiring though; stock up on fresh fruit and vegetables in Constanţa or rely on a diet of biscuits and bananas from the small food store in the Cazino complex (open daily in summer from 9 am to 9 pm).

The Cazino's *Delta Restaurant* has slow staff but the traditional Romanian food served on wooden platters is worth the wait. Be sure to try the pastrami with mămăligă (salted meat with corn mush) at least once during your stay; swill it down with a bottle of Murfatlar wine for no more than US$5 a head. Folk bands play most evenings in summer; it is open daily from 10 am to midnight.

In the northern part of the resort, the tour-isty *Hanul Piraţilor Restaurant*, across the road from the Popas Hanul Piraţilor hotel, is the place to enjoy a good mixed grill and plenty of wine. Ovidiu Island's thatched-roof *Rustic Restaurant* is famous for seafood and worth a visit.

Getting There & Away
Bus Travelling between Constanţa and Mamaia by trolleybus is quick. Trolleybus No 40 runs from the train station to the centre of Constanţa down Blvd Ferdinand, then on to the Pescărie bus stop near Hotel Parc, at the southern end of Mamaia. In summer a shuttle runs up and down Mamaia's 8km boardwalk.

To get to Constanţa's northern bus station, take the southbound bus No 23 from the Staţia Cazino stop in Mamaia to the bus stop outside Restaurant Boulevard on the south-western shore of Lake Tăbăcăriei. The northbound bus No 23 goes to the neighbour-ing resort of Năvodari.

Train Tickets for trains departing from Constanţa can be bought in advance at the Agenţie de Voiaj CFR (☎ 617 930) adjoining the post and telephone office on the promenade.

Getting Around

Trolleybus tickets valid for two journeys cost US$0.20 and are sold at the kiosk next to the central bus stop, Staţia Cazino. In low season the kiosk shuts, so stock up on tickets before you leave Constanţa or buy them at the Pescărie bus stop. Buy tickets for the shuttle bus to Constanţa from the driver (US$0.20 for a single journey).

The main taxi rank is directly opposite the Staţia Cazino bus stop. To call a taxi dial ☎ 953 or ☎ 831 331.

EFORIE NORD & LAKE TECHIRGHIOL

Eforie Nord, 17km south of Constanţa, is the first large resort south of the city. The beach is below 30m cliffs. Tiny **Lake Belona**, just behind the southern end of the beach, is a popular bathing spot.

South-west of Eforie Nord is Lake Techirghiol, once a river mouth and famous for its black sapropel mud, effective against rheumatism. Mud-covered sun-worshippers strutting along the beach are not an uncommon sight in Eforie Nord. Lake Techirghiol's waters are four times as salty as the sea; the lake is 2m below sea level.

In mid-1997, Eforie Nord gained international notoriety as the site of a controversial memorial statue to the Romanian fascist movement, the Iron Guard. Opposition by a US Jewish civic rights organisation, the Anti-Defamation League, resulted in the Romanian president, Constantinescu, ordering the statue's removal.

Eforie Nord has 80 hotels, villas and inns providing accommodation for some 19,000 sun-seeking, mud-loving tourists every year. Avoid the town if you have an aversion to crowded beaches and blaring pop music.

Unlike its sister resort, Eforie Sud, 3km south of Eforie Nord, is as dead as a dodo.

Orientation & Information

The train station is only a few minutes' walk from the post office and main street, Blvd Republicii. Exit the train station and turn left. Turn left after Hotel Belvedere and then right onto Blvd Republicii. Large city maps are posted at the train and bus stations, and around town. Buses from Mangalia and Constanţa stop in the centre of town on Blvd Republicii.

Most hotels and restaurants are on Str Tudor Vladimirescu which runs parallel to Blvd Republicii along the beach. The actual beach is a good 10m drop from this promenade road.

The Agenţie de Turism Intern (☎ 741 188), Blvd Republicii 4, 50m north of the bus stop, arranges private rooms for US$10 per person (open April to September, Monday to Saturday 8 am to 4 pm). There is a currency exchange in practically every hotel, supermarket and on every street corner. The telephone office inside the central post office at Blvd Republicii 11 is open daily from 7 am to 10 pm; the post office is open weekdays from 9 am to 6 pm.

Mud Baths

Wallow in black mud! Popas Şincai (see Places to Stay) offers the cheapest bath in town. Its mud baths (baia de nămol), on the northern shores of Lake Techirghiol, are open from mid-June until the beginning of September daily from 8 am to 8 pm. Pay US$0.30 to the staff at reception, strip off in the male or female changing rooms, then strut out to the lakeside beach (separate beaches for men and women). Slap mud from the bathtub over your body then wait for it to dry in the sun. At the first signs of cracking, rinse off in the showers. Repeat this procedure until your body can't take any more.

Most of the major hotels offer mud baths at more extortionate prices. There are public thermal baths (băi termale) at the northern end of Blvd Republicii, close to the Nunta Zamfirei folklore restaurant. Most tour groups seeking extensive pampering head straight for the băza de tratament adjoining the Delfinul, Meduza and Steaua de Mare hotels.

Places to Stay
Camping The low-budget traveller's first stop should be *Popas Şincai* (☎ 741 621), a few hundred metres west of Eforie Nord's train station. Walk west to the far end of the railway platform, cross the tracks and follow a path to a breach in the wall. As well as camping space (US$0.30 per person), there are five two-room huts at US$5 per person and a lovely but dilapidated old villa by the lake (US$5 per person).

There are better facilities at *Camping Meduza* (☎ 742 385), behind Hotel Minerva and Hotel Prahova at the northern end of the beach. Walk north along Str Tudor Vladimirescu and turn immediately left after Club Maxim. This site is closer to the beach but much further from the train station. Tent spaces are US$1.50 per person.

There are three grotty, run-down camp sites in Eforie Sud. They are dirt-cheap however, charging no more than US$1 a night to pitch a tent or US$5 to sleep in a wooden hut. *Camping Cosmos* is close to the beach, at the southern end of the resort, while *Camping Olt* and *Camping Rusalca* are closer to the train station at the northern end of the resort (from the train station turn left along Blvd Republicii, and take the second major turn-off on the right).

Hotels Eforie Nord has 42 hotels. The *Hotel Europa* (☎ 742 990), Blvd Republicii 19, is the resort's most upmarket address. It costs US$30/45 for a single/double with bath.

The two-star *Hotel Delfinul*, *Hotel Meduza* and *Hotel Steaua de Mare* are concrete high-rises, side-by-side at Str Tudor Vladimirescu 39-43, at the northern end of the resort. The hotels, owned by the same company (☎ 742 884; fax 742 980), specialise in natural cures, mud baths and other self-pampering delights, and are generally filled with package tour groups. Single/double rooms in all three hotels start at US$20/35.

Places to Eat
The *Cofetăria Pescărus* opposite the post office has great pastries. The adjacent restaurant of the same name is loud and crowded in summer. *Restaurant Berbec*, Str 1 Mai, near the Hotel Union at the northern end of the beach, is famous for its folk-dancing shows. It costs US$10 for a meal and music.

Nunta Zamfirei is a Romanian restaurant famed for its folk song-and-dance shows. Most tour groups come here. Walk north along Blvd Republicii and turn left onto the small track opposite the public thermal baths. It is open daily from 10 am to midnight.

Marginally more tranquil is the *Vraja Mării* restaurant, nestled between the shores of Lake Belona and the Black Sea.

Getting There & Away
The Agenţie de Voiaj CFR (☎ 617 930) is inside the post office building at Blvd Republicii 11.

All trains between Bucharest and Mangalia stop at Eforie Nord, but you're better off on a private bus (see Getting There & Away under Constanţa). Slower and only slightly cheaper are city bus Nos 10 and 11, which leave for Eforie Nord from the street just south of Constanţa's train station.

COSTINEŞTI
Costineşti, 9km south of Eforie Sud, is a small fishing village where horse-drawn carts still rattle along the pot-holed roads while pensioners observe the world from doorsteps or street benches. Until 1989 the village-resort, which hosted a pioneer youth camp in 1949 and the first international student camp in 1956, was only open to young people. Today, anyone can stay here.

Costineşti buzzes in July and August when the holiday radio station Radio Vacanţa broadcasts from the beach, blasting music across loudspeakers. Party-lovers rock till they drop on the outside disco floor close to the beach or in Disco Voz Maris behind Hotel Forum. A national film festival, a young actors' festival and a jazz festival are all key events in July and August.

NORTHERN DOBRUJA

For the rest of the year Costineşti reverts to being a simple, sleepy village.

Orientation & Information

Costineşti is 4km east of the Constanţa-Mangalia highway. The post office and Agenţie de Voiaj CFR (☎ 617 930) are north-west of the beach, just off the main road into the resort.

Places to Stay & Eat

There is a large *campsite* off the main road to the beach; a double wooden hut costs US$5 a night. More upmarket are the luxury wooden bungalows equipped with shower, toilet and hot water at the *2 x 1 Complex Turistic* (☎ 734 230, 734 202), immediately on the left as you enter Costineşti from the north. A double wooden hut is US$15 a night and a two-room apartment for four people is US$30. The complex is only open from June to the end of August.

Most houses have a sign outside advertising *cazare* (rooms). The *Vila Claudia* (☎ 734 341) charges US$6 per person a night. Home-cooked meals are extra. Follow the signs from the centre of the village.

The *Complex Junona* (☎ 734 454; fax 734 315) at Str Principală 82 has wooden chalets to let and can arrange accommodation in private homes. So can *BTT* (☎ 734 000; ☎ & fax 734 077) inside the *Hotel Forum*, overlooking the southern end of the beach.

Getting There & Away

From Constanţa there are 17 trains daily between 4.31 am and 8.18 pm to the Costineşti Tabără train halt (40 minutes), 2km south of Costineşti train station proper. Get off at Costineşti Tabără for the beach and resort.

From Costineşti Tabără, trains continue south to Neptun (10 minutes) and Mangalia (20 minutes).

NEPTUN-OLIMP

Prior to the collapse of communism, Neptun-Olimp, 6km south of Costineşti, was an exclusive resort controlled by the Communist Party with facilities reserved for party officials, foreign tourists and a handful of elite Romanians deemed sufficiently 'important' by the party. Ceauşescu, had his own luxury villa, fit for a king, built here.

Today, the 'party' is well and truly alive here. The resort is open to all and sundry, most hotels have been privatised, and Romanians flock here in droves.

Orientation

Olimp, by rights a separate resort built in the 1960s, lies on the northern fringe of Neptun, overlooking Lake Tatlageac. To its south, handsome villas and luxury hotels, bathed in the shade of the Comorova forest (pĂdurea Comorova), overlook the artificial lakes of Neptun I and Neptun II which separate the resort from the sea. Together the two resorts form a vast expanse of hotels and discos.

Information

Tourist Offices Most hotels have tourist desks with English-speaking staff who are more than happy to help you with organised tours along the coast.

The travel agency Touring ACR (☎ 731 873) has an office inside Olimp's Hotel Belvedere, open June to mid-September only. The friendly, English-speaking staff will do their best to help out.

Money Bancă Română de Comerţ Exterior (BANCOREX), next to Hotel Decebal on the main street in Neptun, changes travellers cheques for a US$3 commission. It is open weekdays from 10 am to 1 pm. Cash travellers cheques at the Bancă Comercială Română next door, open weekdays from 8.30 to 11.30 am.

Post & Communications The post office and telephone centre is one block north of Hotel Decebal on the main street in Neptun.

Activities

The number one activity is to hang out on the beach until the dulcet tones of Radio Vacanţa blasting from the loudspeakers get too much, then thank your stars it's not a Ceauşescu speech you're being forced to digest (as was the case until 1989).

After that, restless sunbathers have a choice: ride through town in a traditional **horse-drawn cart** – (US$3 for 10 minutes); play **mini-golf** – at the course opposite Hotel Mioriţa on the main street in Neptun or close to Hotel Arad heading towards Olimp; play **tennis** – at the court next to the Mioriţ mini-golf course; or hire a side-by-side **tandem** – US$1.50 an hour from the kiosk outside Disco Rainbow, opposite Disco Why Not?, on the main street.

Windsurfing fans can hire a sail and board (with instructor) to surf on Neptun's lakes from Bar Siesta in Neptun for US$3.50 an hour. The bar is on the path between Lake Neptun I and II and the beach. Along this path you can also book a **sail** on the *Dragunas*, an old-style, wooden fishing boat. **Jet skis** can be hired from the northern end of Neptun beach or from the jetty in Neptun. There is also a **yacht club** (☎ 752 395) on the beach in Neptun. Both resorts have a **bowling** alley: *Bowling Neptun* (☎ 731 258) is immediately on the right, almost opposite Camping Neptun, as you enter Neptun from the south. *Bowling Olimp* (☎ 731 222) is behind the beachfront Hotel Amfiteatru.

Billiard halls and **amusements malls** line both beach fronts. Excited motorists keen to try out the widely advertised 'Sexy Car Wash' in Neptun should note that there is nothing sexy whatsoever about this run-of-the-mill car wash.

Places to Stay

A bed for the night in a two or three-star hotel (Neptun-Olimp has no one-star hotels) starts at around US$11/18, not including breakfast.

The Dispecerat Cazare (literally 'room dispatcher') can give you information on hotels and take bookings. It can also arrange campsites and sometimes rooms in private houses. The office (☎ 701 300) is inside the main commercial complex (signposted Levent Market) on the main street. It is open 24 hours between June and September.

Camping Both of Neptun-Olimp's camp-sites are packed in summer. *Camping Neptun* (☎ 731 220; fax 731 447) – also known as Neptun Holiday Village – at the southern end of Lake Neptun II, is open all year round. In July and August, a double room in the main building is US$10; a double hut with running water is US$8 per person; a triple hut with/without running water is US$7.50/6 per person; and camping is US$4 per person.

Camping Olimp (☎ 731 314; fax 731 447) at the northern end of Olimp's tourist strip, charges similar prices for its 140 wooden, more basic huts.

Hotels Hotel accommodation in Neptun-Olimp is not for the budget traveller. The twin resort has some 40 two and three-star hotels. Expect to pay at least US$22 a night for a double room in a two-star hotel and US$36 a night in a three-star hotel. If you have not booked in advance you will generally end up paying more. Breakfast is not included in the nightly rate.

Neptun's hotels are along the main street. The hotels at its southern end overlook the two Neptun lakes. Lined up along Lake Neptun I you'll find *Hotel Midia* (☎ 731 915; fax 731 47), *Hotel Tomis* (☎ 731 121; fax 731 447), *Hotel Histria* (☎ 731 819; fax 731 447), *Hotel Callatis* (☎ 731 619; fax 731 447), and *Hotel Traian* (☎ 731 122; fax 731 447), all of which are two-star. These names draw upon the coast's ancient Greek and Roman roots. Another cluster of hotels – including *Hotel Apollo* where the Agenţie de Voiaj CFR is based – lies north-west of Lake Neptun II; none of them have lake views.

Most of the hotels in Olimp look out to sea. The main hotels are *Hotel Panoramic* (☎ 731 235; fax 731 356), *Hotel Amfiteatru* (☎ 731 456; fax 731 447) and *Hotel Belve-dere* (☎ 731 952; fax 731 447), all three-star hotels housed in one large semi-circular block with steps to the beach. North of this lie the sky-rise *Hotel Transilvania* (☎ 731 350; fax 731 123), *Hotel Moldova* and *Hotel Muntenia* (☎ 731 917; fax 731 447), *Hotel Oltenia* (☎ 731 021; fax 731 447) and the *Hotel Crişana* and *Hotel Banat* (☎ 731 618;

fax 731 447), all named after regions in Romania.

Places to Eat

In this heaving resort crammed with fast-food joints, one of the most beautiful places to eat is the tranquil *Restaurant Insula* (☎ 731 722), comprising a series of floating wooden rafts moored on Lake Neptun I. Traditional Romanian dishes are served here. It's open daily from noon until well past midnight.

Also known for their local cuisine and colourful folklore shows are the *Calul Bălan* (☎ 731 524), on the left as you enter Neptun's main street from the south, and *Popasul Căproarelor* (☎ 731 824), at the north-west end of Neptun in Comorova forest.

Getting There & Away

Bus Private buses from Constanţa and Mangalia will drop you on the main highway, 2.5km from Neptun-Olimp's hotels (for further information on private buses see Getting There & Away under Constanţa).

From the same highway, city bus Nos 15 and 20 travel south to Mangalia, while city bus No 20 runs 38km north to Constanţa.

Train Tickets for trains can be bought in advance from the Agenţie de Voiaj CFR (☎ 617 930) inside Neptun's Hotel Apollo (see Places to Stay). Halta Neptun station is within walking distance of the Neptun-Olimp hotels, midway between the two resorts. All trains travelling between Bucharest, Constanţa and Mangalia, local and express, stop at Halta Neptun.

JUPITER, AURORA, VENUS & SATURN

The uninspiring confetti resorts of Jupiter, Aurora, Venus and Saturn run along the 10km stretch of coast between Neptun-Olimp and Mangalia. Unlike their larger, neighbouring fun spots, these purpose-built resorts dating from the late 1960s and early 1970s hold little appeal. Rusty carousels and water slides decay on the beach while flag-ging discos desperately try to pull in the punters with tacky wet T-shirt and beach-beauty competitions.

The upside is that hotel accommodation is cheaper. Most hotels in the twin resort of Jupiter-Aurora are named after semiprecious stones while local architects in Venus pride themselves on the dimensions of their rounded, high-rise hotels, all of which bear women's names.

Information

There are post offices in Venus and Saturn; the Venus post office also houses an Agenţie de Voiaj CFR (☎ 617 930) where you can buy train tickets in advance. None of the resorts has a train station.

Activities

Horse-lovers can race and ride at the **Mangalia Stud Farm** (Herghelia Mangalia; ☎ 751 325), 3km from Mangalia at the southern end of Venus. The stud dates from 1928. It has a small racecourse and experienced riders can ride for US$6 an hour.

Across the street from Hotel Adriana at the southern end of Venus, there is a **thermal bath** (signposted 'Băi Mezotermale'), with hot, sulphurous water and medicinal mud. It's open daily from mid-May to September, with separate entrances for women and men. Admission is US$3.

Saturn is – at a push – the most lively of the resorts. You can rent **paddleboats** on the beach, there is an indoor **bowling** alley and **cinema**, and there are a couple of fun discos which still rock, such as Disco Why Not? opposite Hotel Mureş on Str Rozelor.

Places to Stay

Jupiter-Aurora's two campsites, *Complex Vile Liliacul* (☎ 731 402; fax 731 484) and *Camping Zodiac* (☎ 731 192; fax 731 484) are around Lake Tismana. Liliacul is south of the lake and Zodiac is north. *Popas Venus*, next to the Mangalia stud farm, was closed at the time of writing.

Camping Saturn (☎ 751 380; fax 755 559), at the northern end of the resort behind the Minerva restaurant, has double wooden huts for US$2.50 a night. A four-person tent costs US$1 a night to pitch. The site has communal showers but no hot water. It has tennis courts too (bring your own racquet and balls).

There are some 55 hotels spread between the four resorts: a double room with private bath in a one-star hotel costs no more than US$5 a night or US$10 a night in a two-star hotel.

Getting There & Away

Private buses shuttle beach-hoppers along the coast from Mangalia, through Saturn, Venus and Jupiter-Aurora, to Neptun-Olimp and Eforie Nord. The small minibuses stop in the centre of Saturn, Venus and Jupiter-Aurora (see Getting There & Away).

MANGALIA
• *area code ☎ 041, pop 43,832*

Ancient Greek Callatis (now Mangalia) contains several minor archaeological sites. It is well equipped with facilities and attracts many elderly German, Belgian and French tour groups (it's not a place for partying). Mangalia is the second most important harbour of Romania, although mainly military. Special permits were needed at one time to enter the town. Most of the Romanian naval power is harboured there.

Orientation

Mangalia's train station (☎ 751 026) is 1km north of the centre. Turn right as you exit and follow Şoseaua Constanţei (the main road) south. At the roundabout, turn left for Hotel Mangalia and the beach or continue straight for the pedestrianised section of Şoseaua Constanţei where most facilities are. Buses between resorts stop in front of the train station and at Staţia Stadion, the central bus stop just south of the roundabout on Şoseaua Constanţei.

Information

Tourist Offices Your best bet for information is the reception of the Hotel President. Staff speak English, French and German and sell a good selection of maps for Mangalia

and other resorts on the coast. Alternatively take a peek at the information boards (English, French, German) in the Hotel Mangalia which are updated regularly. The tourist office inside the hotel organises day trips to the Danube Delta (US$60) and Murfatlar vineyards (US$23), and a two day trip to Istanbul (US$195).

Money There are currency exchanges in most hotels. The Nasty Change at Şoseaua Constanţei 15 is open daily from 8 am to 8 pm. Cash travellers cheques and get cash advance on Visa/MasterCard at the Bancă Comercială Română, Şoseaua Constanţei 25 (open weekdays from 8 to 11 am); or at Bancă Agricola on the beach front at Str Teilor 7 (open weekdays from 8 to 11.30 am, 1 to 5 pm, Saturday from 8 am to noon). There is an ATM accepting Visa/MasterCard outside the Bancă Comercială Română.

Post & Communications The telephone and post office is at Str Ştefan cel Mare 16. The post office is open weekdays from 7 am to 8 pm; the telephone section is open daily from 7 am to 10 pm.

There is an Internet café (☎ 755 861) inside the Hotel President, open weekdays from noon to midnight.

Things to See & Do

Mangalia's sights can be seen in two to three hours. At the south side of Hotel Mangalia (see Orientation), along Str Izvor, are the ruins of a 6th century **Palaeo-Christian basilica** and a fountain (Izvorul Hercules) dispensing sulphurous mineral water. The numerous apartment blocks around Hotel Mangalia were built towards the end of the Ceauşescu era. Some 50m north of the Hotel Mangalia, on the promenade, is a small white building which houses the **Mangalia laboratory** (1994). Studies have been made here on the 32 new species found in Movile cave in Limanu, 9km south of Mangalia (see Limanu, Doi Mai & Vama Veche). The laboratory is open upon request.

Return to the roundabout and continue south along Şoseaua Constanţei. You'll soon reach the **Callatis Archaeological Museum** (Muzeul de Arheologie Callatis; ☎ 753 580) on the left at No 21. It has a good collection of Roman sculptures and is open daily in summer from 9 am to 8 pm; admission is US$0.75. Adjacent to the museum is the **Farul outdoor cinema** (grădină de vară Farul) where films are screened daily in summer around 8 pm. Just past the high-rise building next to the museum are some remnants of a 4th century **Roman-Byzantine necropolis**.

Continue south another 500m on Şoseaua Constanţei to the centre of town. On most summer evenings cultural events take place in the **Casă de Cultură**, which has a large mural on the façade; the **Disco Galaxy** adjoins it. At the end of Şoseaua Constanţei turn right onto Str Oituz where you pass the Turkish **Sultan Esmahan Mosque** (Moscheea Esmahan Sultan), dating from 1460. Women visiting the mosque should be dressed decently and have their shoulders covered.

From here, head east down Str Oituz to the beachfront where, in the basement of the Hotel President, remains of the walls of the ancient Greek Callatis citadel dating from the 2nd to 7th centuries are exhibited in the **Callatiana Archaeological Reservation** (Muzeul Poarta Callatiana). It is open 24 hours.

There is a **market** specialising in beachwear just north of the food market on Str Vasile Pârvan.

Places to Stay

Camping The nearest *campsites* are in Jupiter-Aurora and Saturn. To get to Camping Saturn from Mangalia, follow Şoseaua Constanţei 1km north from Mangalia's train station to the Art Deco Saturn sculpture, turn right, walk 50m then turn left. You could also take bus Nos 14, 15 and 20 from the train station to the Saturn sculpture (two stops).

Private Rooms ANTREC (☎ 750 473; fax 754 711) has an office at Str Aurora 13, block D, apartment 21. It arranges rooms in private

homes in Mangalia and other resorts along the Black Sea coast. Prices start at US$10 a night.

Hotels Mangalia has fewer hotels than its neighbouring resorts. The popular choice is *Hotel Mangalia* (☎ 752 052, 752 053; fax 632 650, 753 510) at Str Rozelor 35. Tour groups flock here for the week-long intensive spa treatments it offers which cost between US$150 and US$200. Single/double rooms cost US$25/35 in high season. It is one of the few hotels on the coast with full wheelchair access; there are ramps onto the beach.

Surprisingly pleasant are the three two-star hotels on the promenade: the *Hotel Zenit* (☎ 751 645; fax 632 650) at Str Teilor 7, the *Hotel Astra* (☎ 751 673; fax 632 650) at Str Teilor 9) and the *Hotel Orion* (☎ 751 156; fax 632 650) at Str Teilor 11, all charge US$20 a night for a double with private bath.

Mangalia's luxury, four-star *Hotel President* (☎ 755 861, 690 212; fax 755 695), overlooking the beach at Str Teilor 6, is the top place to stay on the coast. Single/double rooms with all the perks are US$70/90 and the penthouse suite is US$140.

Places to Eat

Hotel restaurants are the main dinner option. Get fresh pastries and superb coffee at *Patisserie Peach-Pit* on Şoseaua Constanţei close to the archaeological museum. *Four Seasons*, next door to the museum, closes at 6 pm, so fill up on pizza, sandwiches and ice cream while you can. For fast food, salads and soups try the self-service *Fast Food* outlet, beneath the *Terasa President* on the beach in front of Hotel President; it is open daily from 9 to 3 am.

For a splurge try the *Café Jolly* inside the Hotel President's business centre; it has five-course set menus for around US$10. For a stiff pint of local bere la halba with the locals go to the *Restaurant Casino*, immediately north of the Hotel President.

Stock up on packed-lunch delights at the *food market* (Piaţa Agroalimentară) behind Hotel Zenit on Str Vasile Alecsandri.

Getting There & Away

Bus Private buses from Constanţa stop at Mangalia's train station and near the roundabout at the central Staţia Stadion bus stop (see Getting There & Away under Constanţa). City bus No 12 also travels the main highway to Constanţa.

Bus No 14 runs from Mangalia's train station to the Bulgarian border at Vama Veche, 10km south of Mangalia, six times a day.

Train The Agenţie de Voiaj CFR (☎ 752 818) adjoins the central post office at Str Ştefan cel Mare 16. It is open weekdays from 9 am to 5 pm.

Mangalia is at the end of the line from Constanţa. From Constanţa there are 18 trains daily in summer to Mangalia (43km, one to 1½ hours). In winter the service is reduced to just five a day. Many of these trains are direct to/from Bucharest's Gara de Nord (269km, 4½ hours). In summer there are also express trains to/from Arad, Iaşi, Oradea, Sibiu, Suceava and Timişoara.

LIMANU, DOI MAI & VAMA VECHE

Limanu, 9km south of Mangalia, gained international fame following the fantastic discovery of **Movile Cave** (Peştera Movile) by Romanian speleologist Cristian Lascu in 1986. The 200m-long cave, uncovered 3.5km from Limanu, contained 32 new speciesof flora and fauna and two new genuses – previously unknown to scientists – dating from the Upper Miocene period five million years ago. These creatures energise themselves via chimosynthesis, feeding on a thick layer of sulphur-consuming bacteria formed on top of the water in the vacuumed cave. Besides Movile, this unique phenomenon is only known to exist some 5000m below sea level. Romanian speleologists say NASA is interested in carrying out research here. The cave is a research area and closed to the public. You can visit the laboratory in Mangalia however.

The Lipovani fishing village of **Doi Mai** (literally '2 May'), 5km south of Limanu, attracts Romania's most bohemian sunseek-

ers. Its pot-holed roads and tumble-down houses remain untouched by the rest of the coast's tourist mania. The few travellers who make their way spend starry nights around camp fires on the beach. In the 18th century a handful of Lipovani – descendants of the Old Believers, a schismatic sect of the Russian Orthodox church persecuted for its rejection of church reforms in the 17th century – settled in Doi Mai. Their descendants today are characterised by a hardy nature and heavy vodka-drinking habits.

Equally tranquil is the border village of **Vama Veche** (literally 'old custom point'), 4km south of Doi Mai. The beach here is wide with fine golden sands. Some people bathe nude. Camping is permitted on the beach in both villages. In Vama Veche there are cold showers on the beach and a small café where breakfast is served. Neither village has a hotel. In Doi Mai ask at the village shop to stay in a private home for the night. In Vama Veche ask at the *Scoica Snack Bar*. You should pay no more than US$5 for a double in either place. Note that sanitary facilities in the village are poor; many houses have no running water and have unlit, outside toilets.

Getting There & Away

Bus The private minibuses serving the coast stop short of Doi Mai and Vama Veche. From Mangalia, bus No 14 runs six times a day from the train station to Vama Veche.

Bulgaria From the south end of Vama Veche you can walk or drive across the border into Bulgaria. The crossing is open 24 hours. If you cross on foot, be prepared for a 6km hike to Durankulak, the first settlement inside Bulgaria. Alternatively hitch a ride, although few cars pass.

Motorists can also cross into Bulgaria at Negru Vodă, 15km west of Mangalia on the main Constanţa-Dobrič highway (38). Kardam, the first village inside Bulgaria, is 5km from the border crossing. The Constanţa-Varna bus which used this crossing was suspended at the time of writing (see

Getting There & Away under Constanţa for details of buses to Bulgaria).

THE DANUBE-BLACK SEA CANAL

The Danube Canal (Canal Dunăre) runs for 64km from Cernavodă in the west to Agigea on the eastern coast. The canal, which opened in 1984, shortens the sea trip from Constanţa to Cernavodă by 400km. There are two 310m-long locks (at Cernavodă and Agigea), and water from the canal is used for irrigation.

Cernavodă

The train from Bucharest crosses the Danube at Cernavodă on a great 571m-long **iron bridge** designed by Romanian engineer Anghel Saligny (1854-1923) and erected in 1895. The railway follows the canal for most of its journey from Cernavodă to the coast.

Cernavodă has the dubious distinction of housing Romania's only **nuclear power plant**, inaugurated in April 1996. It's on the eastern side of town.

The Death Canal

The Danube-Black Sea canal took 30,000 people nine years to construct. Some 300 million cubic metres of land were manually excavated and 4.2 million cubic metres of rein-forced concrete shifted by workers. This canal was only part of a centuries-old dream to build an inland waterway linking the North and Black seas, which was finally realised in 1992 when a 171km canal between the Main and Danube rivers in Germany was opened.

Thousands of lives were lost during the communists' first attempt at building the canal – or 'death canal' *(canalul mortii)* as it was known – between 1949 and 1953. During the communist purges of this period some 180,000 political prisoners were interned in forced-labour camps in Romania; 40,000 of them were worked to death on the project. Ironically the project was abandoned in 1953 and not resumed again until 1975 when a more suitable and properly researched route was followed.

Together with the House of the People in Bucharest, the canal has gone down in history as one of Ceauşescu's most costly follies – and not just financially. ∎

To date, just one of its five 700MW reactors is live. The Candu reactor, a Canadian design, is the first to be built in Europe and the first western-designed reactor to be built in eastern Europe. Cernavodă's nuclear power plant is constructed on a recognised earthquake zone. Three quakes have occurred in this region since 1979.

Using Canadian technology, construction work started on the plant in 1978. Speedy workmanship under Ceauşescu's guidance was allegedly so shoddy the plant's foundations started to crack and it was only following the Canadian partners' direct intervention that the plant closed until international safety standards were met. Guided tours of the plant have to be arranged well in advance with the plant's public relations unit (☎ 041-238 339, ext 1312/1202).

Murfatlar

As they approach Constanţa, the canal and railway pass through the Murfatlar area, where Romania's best dessert wines are produced. The profitable Murfatlar vineyards are west of the small town of Basarabi, some 14km west of Constanţa. Wine-tasting and guided tours of the factory are possible – but only for groups of 20 or more. Individual travellers can try their luck at the *punct turistic*, 3km from the main entrance to the factory, which is signposted. It is open daily from 8 am to 3 pm. Most travel agencies arrange group wine-tasting tours to Murfatlar.

ADAMCLISI

In the south-western part of Adamclisi, 45km from Basarabi, archaeologists have uncovered remains of the Roman city of Traian Tropaeum which sprang up following Traian's conquest of the Dacians. Like other Roman colonies in Dobruja, the city was heavily destroyed during Goth attacks in the 3rd century and not rebuilt until the reign of Constantine I (306-337 AD). Following the domination of Dobruja by the Turks in 1418, the settlement was renamed Adamclisi, meaning 'man's church'.

There is also a giant triumphal Roman

monument. The original **Tropaeum Traiani monument** – 161m above sea level – was built by Emperor Traian between 106 and 109 AD in honour of his victory against the Dacian King Decebal (87-106 AD) in Adamclisi. Thirty metres tall, it was dedicated to Mars, the god of war, and contained the mausoleum of one of Traian's high-ranking officers who was killed in the battle. The names of 3800 other legionaries who died were carved on its sides.

Today's monument is a replica of the original. The sides of the base are decorated with 54 pictorial scenes (metopes), depicting the Roman battle at Adamclisi and another fought against the Dacians in southern Dobruja (now a part of Bulgaria). Figures at the top of the base represent Traian's captured enemies. A dead-straight, 1.5km-long avenue carves from the east through the fields to the foot of the Tropaeum Traiani.

Pillars, friezes and other fragments of the original monument are displayed in the **Tropaeum Traiani Museum** (Muzeul Tropaeum Traiani).

To get to the museum head west from the monument into Adamclisi. Turn right at the 'Muzeul Adamclisi' signpost in the centre of the village, then turn left. The museum is at the end of this road. The remains of the fortress and the Tropaeum Traiani are visible from the lookout point here. To get the best view, however, continue west out of Adamclisi for a couple of kilometres until the hillside complex rises magnificently into view in the north. The museum and Tropaeum Traiani monument are open daily, except Monday, from 9 am to 5 pm.

Getting There & Away

Adamclisi is difficult to reach by public transport. Buses departing daily from Constanţa's northern bus station (Autogară Nord) to Daeni via Ostrov pass through Adamclisi, so ask the driver to drop you off.

From Constanţa's southern bus station (Autogară Sud), the one daily bus daily to Băneasa, departing at 11.05 am, stops at Adamclisi.

HISTRIA

Heading into the Danube Delta, you can make a small detour to Histria (formerly spelt Istria), 70km north of Constanţa. This is one of Romania's oldest settlements, founded by Greek merchants in 6th century BC. Approaching Histria along the coastal road from the south you pass through the seaside resort of **Năvodari**, an industrial town designated as a youth resort in 1959 and home to the state-run **Petromidia oil refinery**. Despite being Romania's most modern refinery (built in the 1980s), Petromidia is included on the government's 1997 shortlist of loss-making state enterprises to be closed.

Histria was settled in 657 BC by Greek traders who contributed to the town's rapid growth as one of the key commercial ports on the Black Sea coast, even superseding Constanţa. Subsequent Goth attacks coupled with the gradual sandlocking of the harbour, however, led to its equally rapid decline. By the 7th century AD, the town was abandoned.

Citadel

If you've seen the lost city of Pompeii you may leave Histria Citadel (Cetatea Istria) disappointed. If you haven't, you will find the walls, baths and paved roads left *in situ* at the **Histria Archaeolgical Complex** (Complexul Arheologic Histria) quite superb. Visitors are free to walk around the original streets of the ancient fortified city.

Archaeological relics uncovered at the site are displayed in the well-arranged **Muzeul Histria** (Histria Museum) at the entrance to the site. From the *casă* at the entrance, marked paths lead visitors through the remains of the ancient city, and pass by the big tower (*turnul mare*) into the main western sector (*cartierul economic*) where most of the public buildings, thermal baths (*băilor romane*) and the civil basilica (*basilica civilă*) were. Many of the original foundations remain and some of the original mosaic floor is visible in the baths. Close by is the Christian basilica (*basilica creştină*), built with stones from the old theatre in the

6th century AD. Cart tracks grooved in the marble-slabbed floor are evident at the main entrance (*poarta mare*) to the city.

On the cliffs in the eastern sector is the 'sacred zone' (*zona sacră*). This is the only part of the citadel where archaeologists have removed the Roman remains to uncover remains of a **Greek temple** (*tempele greceşti*) dedicated to the ancient Greek deities Zeus and Aphrodite. Archaeologists believe the temple was built at the end of the 6th century BC.

The ruins of Histria Citadel fall under the protection of the Danube Delta Biosphere Reserve (see the Danube Delta section of this chapter). If you have your own transport the citadel is a good trip from Mamaia or Constanţa. The reedy marshes spreadeagled along the road to the citadel are popular with birdwatchers. At dusk look out for clouds of pelicans.

The complex, 4km south of Histria village, is open daily from 8 am to 7 pm. Admission is US$0.75. From Constanţa, turn east off the main road at the signpost for 'Cetatea Histria'. The complex is a further 7km along this road. Wear closed shoes when visiting here as grass snakes lurk in the ruins.

Places to Stay

There are no hotels or campsites in Histria but you can get a bed for the night if you ask people in the village.

The campsites in Năvodari are only for the downright crazy or desperate. *Camping Năvodari*, adjoining the petrol station on the right as you enter the resort, charges an outrageous US$4 a night to pitch a tent on the scrap of wasteland behind the main building. It has no wash facilities. Further north along the coast road is the *Tăbara de Copii*. It overlooks the Petromidia oil refinery.

Getting There & Away

Getting to Histria is tough without private transport. One bus departs daily at 3.20 pm for Histria from Constanţa's northern bus station (Autogară Nord) – useless if you only want to make a day of it.

Danube Delta

The triangular 5800sq km Danube Delta (Delta Dunării), just south of the Ukrainian border, is Europe's youngest land geologically. Amid this wetland of reed beds and waterways, lily-covered lakes and shifting sand dunes, the Danube river ends its fantastic journey. Having ploughed its way 2860km from Germany's Black Forest (Schwarzwald) across 10 countries, picking up more than 8% of Europe's waterways, the Danube spills into three main channels – the Chilia, Sulina and Sfântu Gheorghe arms – as its final crescendo into the Black Sea.

The Danube Delta is an everchanging environment of marshes, reeds, floating islets and sand bars, constantly replenished by over two tonnes of silt per second, making Romania 40m longer each year. Reed marshes cover 156,300 hectares and constitute one of the largest single expanses of reed beds in the world.

Just over 14,500 people live on the Delta. Traditional wooden kayaks and rowing boats (*barcă cu rame*) are the primary means of accessing its 27 fishing villages.

The Danube Delta is protected under the Danube Delta Biosphere Reserve (DDBR), 273,300 hectares of which are strictly protected or buffer zones, off limits to tourists and fishermen. The Delta is also included in UNESCO's world heritage list.

The DDBR was set up in response to the ecological disaster that befell the Delta during the communist regime when there was a greedy attempt to transform it into an agricultural region. In 1983 Ceauşescu approved plans to reclaim 38% of the Danube Delta for fish farming, forestry and agriculture. Vast expanses of seasonally flooded areas were artificially drained. Virgin reed beds – natural filters for the 70 million tonnes of alluvium water swept into the Delta each year – were cut down and ploughed. Water channels were engineered to enable 15,000 tonne cargo ships to transport industrial freight between ports.

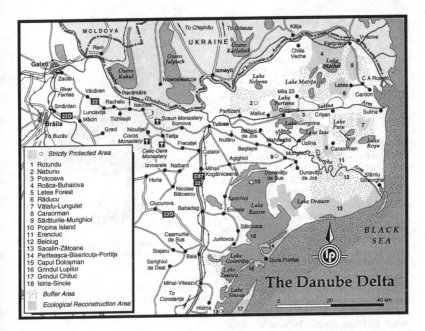

The Danube Delta

Strictly Protected Area
1 Rotundu
2 Nebunu
3 Potcoava
4 Roăca-Buhaiova
5 Letea Forest
6 Răducu
7 Vătafu-Lunguleţ
8 Caraorman
9 Sărăturile-Murighiol
10 Popina Island
11 Erenciuc
12 Belciug
13 Sacalin-Zătoane
14 Periteaşca-Bisericuţa-Portiţa
15 Capul Doloşman
16 Grindul Lupilor
17 Grindul Chituc
18 Istria-Sinoie

Buffer Area

Ecological Reconstruction Area

Following Ceauşescu's downfall, Romanian president Iliescu called an immediate halt to the project.

Many of the DDBR's 18 strictly protected areas – 50,000 hectares including a 500-year-old forest and Europe's largest pelican colony – had been protected as national parks under communism. But Ceauşescu's meddling in the natural water flow of the reclaimed areas affected the entire ecological balance of the Delta, and DDBR scientists acknowledge that the original ecosystem of this region can never be fully restored. However, with US$4.5 million in aid from the World Bank combined with a disciplined approach to tourism, the DDBR is making strides towards the revival of this wonderful wetland.

You need time and patience to explore the Danube Delta. All three main channels are easily accessible. Commercial traffic coupled with the NAVROM passenger ferries which serve the larger villages in the Delta have driven birds deeper into the wetland, however. So if it's exotic wildlife you're seeking, your best bet is to explore the smaller waterways in a weather-beaten kayak, rowing boat or motorboat with a local fisherman.

Wherever you intend to go in the Delta, stock up on supplies: village shops are an alien concept. Stock up on mosquito repellent even before you hit Tulcea.

Finally, no trip to the Delta is complete without sampling some local Danubian cuisine. Pickled fish, fresh fish, fish kebabs or fishermen's borsch – a pert, sour soup brewed in a black pot over an open fire – are on the menu of the day, every day.

History

In 1940, Romania was forced to relinquish the 340sq km delta area north of the Danube to the Soviet Union.

The Delta's population incorporates large Ukrainian (24%) and Lipovan (13%) communities. Lipovans are descendants of the Old Believers who, refusing to recognise Russian Church reforms of 1653, fled Russia and sought refuge in the Delta. They are scattered in Mila 23, Sfântu Gheorghe, Jurilovca and Periprava. The Delta population is mainly elderly. Young people leave the remote wetland for large cities as soon as they can.

Climate

The Danube Delta is the most humid region in Romania, particularly during the summer months (maximum 22.2°C). In spring around 70% of the region is flooded. Winters are mild (minimum -1.2°C) and it is an extremely rare occurrence for the main channels to ice over. Even the smaller waterways rarely freeze.

Birdwatching

Halfway between the North Pole and the Equator, the Danube Delta is a major migration hub for thousands of birds. Prime times are mid-April to mid-May and late October when half the world's population of red-breasted geese winter here. Long-tailed ducks, whooper swans, black-throated divers and clouds of white storks are equally abundant at this time.

Some 280 bird species have been recorded in the Delta. Europe's largest white pelican and Dalmatian pelican colonies are also here. Protected species typical to the Delta include the roller, white-tailed eagle, great white egret, mute and whooper swans, falcon and bee-eater.

Protected zones shield the largest bird colonies. Large green signs in most villages show visitors where these zones are and what birds can be found there. Most of the signs are in Romanian. There are 65 observation towers dotted throughout the Delta. Birdwatchers usually congregate around Lake Furtuna, Murighiol, the brackish areas around Lake Razim and Lake Babadag, and Histria.

The Romanian Ornithological Society and Ibis Tours (see Organised Tours later in this section) in Tulcea arrange birdwatching

The red-breasted goose heads for the Danube Delta in winter.

trips as do specialist travel agencies abroad (see Getting There & Away at the front of this book).

Fishing

Sport fishing is allowed in designated areas year-round, except during the spawning period from 1 April to 1 June. You must have a permit from the Fishing & Hunting Association (Asociaţia Judeţeana a Vanatorilor) in Tulcea (see Information under Tulcea). There are some 75 fish species in the Delta's waters including pike, Danubian herring and Black Sea sturgeon. The most common catch is carp.

Getting Around

Most hotels and travel agencies in Tulcea arrange day trips in the Delta on small private motorboats. You can also approach the boatmen direct and arrange your own tailor-made trip at a more competitive price (see Travel Agencies under Tulcea). This is the best way to sample the Delta if your time is limited.

In the Delta proper it's easy to hire rowing boats from fishermen. This is the only way to penetrate the Delta's exotic backwaters. Allow yourself at least three or four days.

Permits All visitors need a permit to travel in the Delta. Only scientists are allowed to enter strictly protected zones with special permits issued by the DDBR. As a tourist, you're fined US$100 if you enter a protected zone without a permit. They cost US$1 and are sold in Tulcea at travel agencies and at hotel receptions in Crişan, Sulina and Murighiol. Permits are automatically included in tours organised by travel agencies. You also need a permit to fish or camp.

NAVROM Ferries The government subsidised NAVROM operates two types of passenger ferries – the *nave clasice* is your typical, time-consuming chug-chug ferry, and the *nave rapide* is a speedier hydrofoil. Tickets are sold at the NAVROM ferry terminal between 11.30 am and 1.30 pm. Buy your ticket in advance. Delta residents get an 80% discount *(tarif subvenţionat)*. Tickets are more expensive for the hydrofoils.

Hydrofoils Hydrofoils only sail along the Sulina arm (braţul Sulina) from Tulcea to Sulina, Crişan and Mila 23. There are reduced services in winter.

From Tulcea there is a hydrofoil to Sulina on Tuesday and Thursday, departing at 4.30 pm and arriving at 6 pm. Return hydrofoils depart from Sulina on Wednesday, Friday and Sunday at 7.30 am. The Friday ferry continues to Galaţi (see Getting There & Away under Tulcea). A single Tulcea-Sulina fare is US$13.

On Monday, there is a hydrofoil departing from Tulcea at 2 pm to Crişan and Mila 23. The ferry returns from Mila 23 to Tulcea via Crişan on Sunday at 7 am, arriving in Tulcea at 10 am. A single Tulcea-Crişan/Mila 23 fare is US$8/10.

Ferries The ferries serve all three channels. You can travel 1st or 2nd class and they operate year-round.

A Sulina ferry departs from Tulcea on Monday, Wednesday, Friday and Saturday at 1.30 pm (four hours). The return ferry departs from Sulina on Tuesday, Thursday, Saturday and Sunday at 7 am. They stop at Partizani, Maliuc, Gorgova and Crişan. A single 1st/2nd class ticket to Sulina costs US$9/7. Tulcea-Crişan costs US$6/4.50; Tulcea-Maliuc costs US$5/4.

The Sfântu Gheorghe ferry departs from Tulcea on Monday, Wednesday and Friday at 1.30 pm (five hours). The return boat departs on Tuesday, Thursday and Saturday at 6 am. These boats stop at Balteni de Jos, Mahmudia and Murighiol. A single Tulcea-Sfântu Gheorghe 1st/2nd class fare is US$10/7.50.

Ferries to Chilia-Veche from Tulcea depart on Monday, Wednesday, Friday and Saturday at 1.30 pm (four hours). The Monday and Friday ferries continue to Periprava (another 1½ hours). Return ferries depart from Chilia-Veche on Tuesday, Thursday, Saturday and Sunday at 5.45 am. The Tuesday and Saturday ferries start out in Periprava, departing at the ungodly hour of 4.15 am. These ferries stop at the tiny villages of Patlageanga, Ceatalchioi, Plaur, Pardlina and Tatanir – all of which are not marked on most maps. A single Tulcea-Chilia-Veche 1st/2nd class fare is US$9/7. A Tulcea-Periprava 1st/2nd class ticket costs US$13/10.

Organised Tours Tulcea's hotels and travel agencies offer day trips between mid-May and September (see Travel Agencies under Tulcea).

Independent travellers with more than a day to see the Delta should link up with a local guide. This is the best way to catch a glimpse of the Delta's most spectacular side, including its fantastic birds.

The Romanian Ornithological Society (Societata Ornitologică Română; ☎ & fax 040-515 438), Str Gării 11, block I G5, apartment 2, Tulcea, arranges birdwatching trips.

Ibis Tours (☎ & fax 040-511 261; email psolca@tlx.ssitl.ro), Str Grivitei 1, block C1, apartment 9, Tulcea, arranges wildlife tours in the Delta and Dobruja led by professional ornithologists. A guide for the day plus accommodation in a private home costs around US$25.

TULCEA
• *area code ☎ 040, pop 90,000*

Tulcea ('tool-chee-a') is a modern industrial city and the gateway to the Delta paradise. The town itself offers few attractions so tourists generally head out on the first available ferry into the Delta. Wandering along Tulcea's riverfront – cleaned up and remodelled under Ceauşescu's much maligned systemisation of the 1980s – is pleasant enough despite the polluting aluminium smelter close by.

Tulcea was founded on the Roman city of Aegyssus dating from the 1st century AD. By the 17th century Tulcea was a flourishing port town, guarded by seven towers. Following the city's liberation from Turkish rule in 1878, it became a leading commercial centre.

Tulcea hosts the International Folk Festival of Danubian Countries each year in August.

Orientation

The Tulcea arm (braţul Tulcea) of the Danube loops through Tulcea, cutting off the northern part of town from the main part of Tulcea where all the facilities are. The northern part of Tulcea is known as Tudor Vladimirescu.

The bus and train stations and ferry terminal are on Str Portului, overlooking the river at the western end of town. The left-luggage office at the train station is open 24 hours. Lake Ciuperca lies west of the stations.

Central Tulcea focuses on the promenade which stretches along the southern banks of the river. A tall angular monument on the riverfront is a good landmark; private boats for hire are moored here. One block south of the promenade is Piaţa Unirii (formerly Piaţa Civică). The Diana department store is here.

Maps

An adequate city map is included in the *Tulcea* guide, sold for US$1.20 in all the museums.

A small map of the Delta with various

sailing routes marked on it is included in the quality *Cartea Deltei* (1997), a detailed book in Romanian about the Delta.

The best map of the Danube Delta is the green-covered *Hartă Turistică Delta Dunării*. Incredibly it doesn't appear to be sold in Tulcea. This author only saw it in Bucharest!

Information

Tourist Offices The DDBR (☎ 550 950; fax 550 498) has a tourist information centre 3km from the centre at Str Taberei 32. It's open weekdays from 10 am to 4 pm and sells maps of the Delta and travel permits. From the centre head west along Str Isaccea and turn right after the railway tracks. Go up the hill; the centre is behind the school on the left. The DDBR plans to open a central tourist office behind the culture house (*casă de cultură*) on the riverfront by 1999.

The Danube Delta Research Institute (☎ 524 2422, 524 546; fax 524 547), 1km south of the centre at Str Babadag 165, has a small information centre. It's open weekdays from 10 am to 4 pm.

The Automobil Clubul Român (ACR; ☎ 515 151, 512 345) has an office on the waterfront, close to the angular monument. ACR organises boat trips for an expensive US$20 an hour and takes bookings for its floating hotel.

Fishing and hunting permits are sold at the Fishing & Hunting Association (Asociaţia Judeţeana a Vanatorilor; ☎ 511 404; fax 514 055) at Str Isaccea 10. The office is open Monday, Tuesday and Thursday from 7 am to 2 pm, Wednesday and Friday from 7 am to 2 pm and from 5 to 8 pm, and Saturday from 7 am to 1 pm. A map in the window highlights the areas where tourists are allowed to fish and hunt.

Money All the hotels have currency exchanges. You can get cash advances on Visa/MasterCard and cash travellers cheques at the Bancă Comercială Română, near the Delta Research Institute on Str Toamnei. It is open weekdays from 8 to 11 am. Bancă

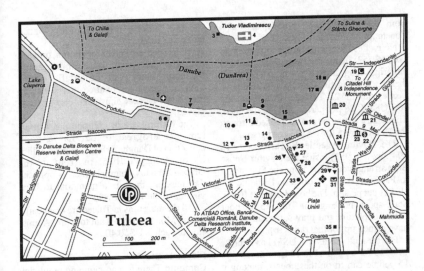

Tulcea

0   100   200 m

PLACES TO STAY
3 ACR Boat Hotel
15 Navitur House Boat;
    Café; Agenţie de
    Turism
16 Hotel Delta;
    NouvellesFrontières
    Simpa Turism
17 ATBAD Floating
    Hotels
18 BTT
24 Hotel Egreta
35 Hotel Europolis;
    Danubius Travel
    Agency

PLACES TO EAT
7 Comandor Boat
   Restaurant
12 Furtuna Bursa Café &
    Patisserie
25 Café Bar Club

26 Union Visa Café &
    Supermarket
28 Lux Bar &
    Mini-Market
29 Restaurant Select
30 Bread & Food Shop
    (Pâine Alimentar)

OTHER
1 Train Station
2 NAVROM Ferry
   Terminal; Bus
   Station
4 Tudor Vladimirescu
   Church
5 Floating Ambulance
6 Culture House
8 Ferry Boat to Tudor
   Vladimirescu
9 Gomoescu Boat Hire
10 Automobil Clubul
    Român (ACR)

11 Monument
13 Fishing & Hunting
    Association
14 TAROM
19 Azizie Mosque
20 Art Museum
21 History &
    Archaeology
    Museum
22 Bancă Agricola
23 Ethnographic
    Museum
27 Bookshop
31 Post & Telephone
    Office
32 Diana Department
    Store
33 Agenţie de Voiaj
    CFR
34 Natural History
    Museum &
    Aquarium

Agricola has a branch on Str 9 Mai, next to the ethnographic museum.

Post & Communications The post office and telephone centre is at Str Păcii 6. It's open weekdays from 7 am to 8 pm, Saturday from 8 am to noon.

Travel Agencies The Danubius Travel Agency (☎ 517 836), inside the Hotel Europolis, arranges boat trips on Sunday along the Sulina arm to Maliuc and Mila 23 and then back via Lake Furtuna along the narrower channels. The trip departs at 11 am and returns at 7 pm. The agency is open daily from 8.30 am to 6.30 pm. It also sells Constanţa-Istanbul ferry tickets.

Nouvelles Frontières/Simpa Turism (☎ & fax 515 753) inside the Hotel Delta arranges day trips along the Sulina arm to Crişan and then back along the Old Danube (Dunărea Veche) via Mila 23. Trips depart at 10 am and cost US$20/26 per person for 1st/2nd class. The same excursions can be booked through the Hotel Egreta for US$25 per person.

The Navitur Agenţie de Turism (☎ 518 894; fax 518 953) inside the Navitur House Boat arranges day trips along the Sulina arm to Partizani, Lake Furtuna and Maliuc for US$11 per person. The boat departs at 10 am. Staff speak no English. Turn up an hour before departure and pray sufficient people have signed up for that day's trip.

Private motorboats cost US$11 an hour, or US$110 for a good 11 to 12 hour day. Up to 15 people can fit on these boats, making it remarkably cost-effective. The boatmen will suggest routes for you. SC Gomoescu (☎ 526 616; fax 520 779), moored opposite the ACR office, is one of the many boats in this part of the harbour to do day trips.

Emergency A floating ambulance station (staţia de ambulanţa; ☎ 511 170) is moored in front of the culture house on the riverfront. The station is staffed 24 hours and some of its crew speak English. The station operates an emergency rescue service with the aid of small medically equipped motorboats.

Things to See

As you stroll along the river note the **Independence Monument** on Citadel Hill, at the far eastern end of town. It was erected in 1904 in honour of those who died during the 1878-88 war of independence against the Turks and stands on the site of the old Roman fortress. You can reach the monument by following Str Gloriei from behind the Hotel Egreta to its end. Some ruins of the citadel can be seen in the **archaeological site** at the foot of the monument, next to the **History & Archaeology Museum** (Muzeul de Istorie şi Arheologie; ☎ 513 676).

On Str Independenţei to the east, you'll see the Turkish minaret of the **Azizie Mosque** (1863).

At the southern end of Str Gloriei, turn left onto Str 9 Mai. At No 2 is the **Ethnographic Museum** (Muzeul de Etnografie; ☎ 515 628) in which traditional costumes, fishing nets, rugs, carpets and much else are displayed.

The **Natural History Museum & Aquarium**, Str Progresului 32, has a good collection of Danube fish and detailed exhibits on delta wildlife. In front of the Greco-Orthodox church, which is opposite the museum, there is a memorial to local victims of the 1989 revolution.

All the museums in Tulcea are open daily, except Monday, from 8 am to 6 pm. Admission to each is US$0.40.

Places to Stay

Camping There is a no-camping regulation within Tulcea's city limits which is apparently enforced by police. Backpackers still pitch their tents on the shores of Lake Ciuperca behind the train station. Seek local advice from BTT (☎ 512 426) at Str Babadag 2. BTT operates a campsite at Lake Roşu, south of Sulina in the Delta.

Private Rooms ANTREC (☎ & fax 515 753), Str Isaccea 2, arranges accommodation in private homes in and around Tulcea for around US$10 a night, including breakfast. It also arranges local guides for US$10 a day.

Hotels Rooms in Tulcea are expensive and there is little choice. The cheapest is the Hotel Europolis (☎ 512 443), Str Păcii 20: US$21/29 for a single/double with private bath and cable TV. Breakfast is an extra US$2. The staff smile here.

Then there is Tulcea's two high-rise hotels: the Hotel Egreta (☎ 517 103) at Str Păcii 1 has singles/doubles for US$28/37, and the Hotel Delta (☎ 514 710) across the road at Str Isaccea 2 offers the same for a completely overpriced US$43/56. Foreign tour groups lurk here.

Boatels Moored opposite Hotel Delta, is the

Navitur House Boat (☎ 518 894; fax 518 953). The boat is not the cleanest and staff speak no English but double cabins with shared bath are cheap at US$10 a night. There is no hot water. There is a small bar/café aboard.

ACR's *Sfântul Constantin* floating hotel is at Tudor Vladimirescu. Doubles and triples cost US$18 per person. ACR arranges for rowing boats across the river.

Nouvelles Frontières/Simpa Turism takes bookings for luxury three-star rooms aboard the *Cormoran Floating Hotel*, moored close to Murighiol (Sfântu Gheorghe arm) at Uzlina. Double cabins cost US$66 and bathrooms are shared between two cabins. There is a restaurant, bar, disco and sunbathing terrace on board. For an extra charge, guests can water ski, windsurf, and hire small rowing boats or motorboats to explore the Delta. The agency also arranges accommodation in the cheaper *Cormoran Boarding House* in which a bed for the night costs only US$25 per person.

Top of the range are the four luxury floating hotels run by ATBAD (☎ 514 114; fax 517 6225), Str Babadag 11. Nightly rates aboard the three-star *Delta 1* and four-star, air-conditioned *Delta 2*, *Delta 3* and *Delta 4* depend on the number of guests. For a group of six they start at US$89 per person a night, dropping to US$55 for groups of 16 or more. Rates include full board and transfer from Tulcea. ATBAD arranges equally expensive cruises around the Delta.

Places to Eat
Topnotch for the choice it offers is *Restaurant Select* at Str Păcii 6. It serves great fish, frog legs, tonnes of pizza and the local speciality, tochitura Dobrogeana, which is chopped meat swamped in a spicy sauce and served with corn maize (mămăligă), salty sheep cheese and a fried egg. It's good value at US$2. The menu is in six languages. The Select is open daily from 10 am to midnight.

For fresh fish afloat try the large *Restaurant Comandor*, moored halfway between the Hotel Delta and the train station. It is air-conditioned and open daily from 10 am to 10 pm.

Tops for a nightcap is the trendy *Lux Bar*, in a courtyard off Str Unirii. Walk under the arches next to the clothes shop adjoining the bookshop. The club has outside seating and is open until late. After closing, most drinkers frequent the seedy but seething *Café Bar Club*, on Str Unirii and open 24 hours.

Stock up on picnic supplies at the *Pâine* counter, next to the post office on Str Păcii. There is an *Alimentar* next door selling fruit, vegetables and dried products. Both are open daily from 8 am until dusk. Fresh bread is also sold at *Placinta* on Str Isaccea. The *Union Visa* café and old-style supermarket on Str Unirii is also OK for groceries. It's open daily from 8 am to 10 pm.

Things to Buy
There is a fishing tackle shop which carries a good stock of sleeping bags, jackets, maps, gas stoves and other survival gear next to the Fishing & Hunting Association office on Str Isaccea. It is open weekdays from 10 am to 6 pm, Saturday from 7 am to 1 pm.

Getting There & Away
Air Tulcea's airport (☎ 519 210, 511 581) is 12km south of the centre in Cataloi. At the time of writing all TAROM flights between Bucharest and Tulcea were suspended. TAROM has an office in Tulcea (☎ 511 227) at Str Isaccea, block M1.

Bus The bus station (☎ 513 304) adjoins the NAVROM ferry terminal on Str Portului. There's one direct daily bus from Tulcea to Măcin via Isaccea (93km); from Măcin you can then hitch to Smârdan where you can catch a ferry across the Danube to Brăila in Moldavia. Alternatively, take one of the five daily buses from Tulcea to Zaclău (110km) where there is a ferry crossing to Galaţi (Moldavia).

There are four buses daily to Constanţa (125km), two of which continue to Costineşti on the Black Sea coast. The one daily bus to Bucharest (263km) departs from Tulcea at 5.30 am.

From Tulcea there are three buses daily to Murighiol, via Mahmudia, departing at 6.30 and 11 am, and at 1 pm. The 11 am bus stops at Beştepe too, from where a connecting bus departs at 1.20 pm to Dunavăţu de Jos. Upon arrival, buses immediately make the return journey.

Train The Agenţie de Voiaj CFR (☎ 511 360) at Str Babadag 4 is open weekdays from 9 am to 4 pm. From the train station (☎ 513 706) on Str Portului there are four trains daily to/from Constanţa via Medgidia (four hours). The daily express train from Bucharest takes five hours. The overnight local train to/from Bucharest is bearable if you go 1st class; arrive early to get a seat.

Boat The NAVROM ferry terminal (☎ 511 552) adjoins the bus station on Str Portului.

There is a speedy hydrofoil to Galaţi on Friday, departing from Sulina at 7.30 am, passing through Tulcea at noon, and arriving in Galaţi at 1.30 pm. A single Tulcea-Galaţi ticket costs US$13. There is another boat from Tulcea to Galaţi on Saturday, departing at 12.15 pm and arriving in Galaţi at 5 pm.

From Galaţi, there is a boat on Monday at 8.30 am, arriving in Tulcea at noon. A second boat departing on Monday at noon arrives in Tulcea at 1.30 pm, then continues to Crişan (3 pm) and Mila 23 (5 pm).

Getting Around
A small motorboat departs every half-hour from the riverfront to Tudor Vladimirescu. The crossing takes five minutes and costs US$0.08. Look for the sign 'Dunărea Tulcea-Tudor Vladimirescu' on the riverfront.

TULCEA TO SULINA
The Sulina arm – the middle and shortest channel of the Danube – stretches 63.7km from Tulcea to Sulina, the Delta's largest village. This channel is used by commercial traffic. The canal, 247m wide in places, was straightened in the 19th century for this traffic and was widened in the 1960s to make it accessible to larger freighters.

Ironically, since 1991, a shipwreck has blocked more than half the width of the canal between Partizani and Maliuc, cutting off the 15,000-tonne freighters which frequently chugged the length of the strait. Since the capsizing of the Greek-owned *Rostock* cargo boat, only 7000-tonne ships can use the Sulina arm.

The Tulcea-Sulina ferry's first stop is **Partizani**, a small fishing village. Get off here for the *Ilgani de Sus Cabana*. The ferry's next stop is **Maliuc**, a popular stopping point for organised tours which have lunch at the *Hotel Salcia* (☎ 511 515). Single/double rooms here cost US$9/14, including breakfast. Ask at reception about camping behind the hotel. From Maliuc you can hire fishing boats for tours of smaller waterways to the north. The rate is US$10 to US$15 per hour.

North of Maliuc is **Lake Furtuna**, a snare for birdwatchers. The smaller **Lake Nebunu**, east of Furtuna along Gârla Sontea, is a strictly protected zone.

The ferry halts briefly at **Gorgova**, a typical Danubian village, before making its way to Crişan.

Crişan, Mila 23 & Caraorman
The Sulina arm gracefully wields its way through Lake Obretinu, sliced in two into Obretinu Mare (big) and Obretinu Mic (small), and then arrives at the junction with the Old Danube (Dunărea Veche). Although it is not Crişan proper, most organised boat tours stop here.

Perched on the junction's tip is the 1st class *Hotel Lebăda* (☎ 543 778). The large, thatched-roof hotel decked out in a traditional rustic style costs US$40 a night. The wooden camping huts outside the hotel are for the hotel staff. The hotel has an excellent restaurant and arranges boat hire. A six person rowing boat is US$0.50 per person an hour. Hotel Lebăda is open from 1 March to 1 November.

Next door is the DDBR's excellent **Information & Education Ecological Centre** (Complex pentru Instruire Informare Ecologica Crişan), well worth a visit. It features well-presented displays on wildlife, birds, and flora and fauna common in the Delta. The centre's library has a large selection of publications. You can watch videos (Romanian only) about the Delta in the audio-visual room. The centre is open weekdays from 8 am to 4.30 pm.

One kilometre upstream is the main Crişan ferry stop. Get a local fisherman to take you on a tour of the nearby waterways.

From Crişan, there are ferries to Mila 23 and Caraorman. The **Caraorman forest** is a strictly protected zone, being home to two rare species of oak found elsewhere only in southern Italy.

SULINA
• *area code* ☎ *040, pop 8000*

Just over 50% of the Delta's population lives in Sulina. As the ferry sails through the centre you'll pass derelict dredges and freighters – many noble ships have ended their careers at Sulina's scrapyard.

A canal dug between 1880 and 1902 shortened the length of the Tulcea-Sulina channel from 83.3km to 63.7km, ensuring Sulina's future as the Danube Delta's main commercial port. After WWI Sulina – founded on an ancient Byzantine port dating to 950 AD – was declared a 'free port' and trade boomed. Greek merchants dominated business here until their expulsion in 1951. The Sulina arm has now been extended 8km into the Black Sea by two lateral dykes.

But business is not booming today. Since the opening of the Danube-Black Sea Canal freighters no longer need to steer their way through Sulina's backwaters. Furthermore, in 1988 the Soviet Mir space station sighted radiation leakage from a dump Ceauşescu built close to the port for Europe's chemical and nuclear waste in an effort to obtain hard currency. Following enormous international pressure, the Romanian government was forced to invest millions of US dollars to clean the site up.

Although not as good a base as Maliuc or Crişan for seeing wetland wildlife, Sulina is a romantic spot on the extreme edge of Europe. Its riverfront promenade is evoca-

tive at sunset. Sulina is not connected to a road network so there are few vehicles. It has a beach, a 19th century lighthouse, and a crumbling cemetery with Romanian, Ukrainian, Turkish, Greek, Jewish and British graves – testimony to the colourful ethnic mix that once passed through its docks.

Orientation & Information
Sulina is easy to navigate. The ferry dock is in the centre of town, with a few shops and bars to the west, the Hotel Sulina and Black Sea to the east. There are no banks. The DDBR plans to open a tourist information centre in Sulina.

Things to See
Sulina's sparse attractions include a few old **churches** and the defunct 18.5m-tall **lighthouse** dating from 1870. On the way to the beach you pass an overgrown 19th century **British cemetery**. Villains, bandits, pirates and exiled lovers who sought refuge in remote Sulina during the 18th and 19th centuries are said to lie here.

The beach, 2km from town, has an accumulation of Danube silt. This has required the creation of a channel out into the Black Sea. You'll also see a long line of Romanian radar installations among the dunes, pointed out to sea.

Places to Stay
Camping You can camp in the cow pasture opposite the Hotel Sulina. People also camp on the beach.

Private Rooms As you get off the ferry, watch for people offering private rooms. The going rate is around US$6 per person.

Hotels The three storey *Hotel Europolis*, next to the Sulina Cinema, is US$8 per person for a spacious but plain room with shared bath. A few hundred metres west along the riverfront from the Europolis, past the bookshop, is a small sign pointing to the *Hotel Ochiş*, which you enter from the rear. Rooms are US$6 per person. Government-owned *Hotel Sulina* (☎ 543 017), Str Deltei 207, charges foreigners US$20 per person.

Getting There & Away

For information on ferries and hydrofoils see Getting Around at the start of this chapter and Getting There & Away under Tulcea.

TULCEA TO SFÂNTU GHEORGHE

The Sfântu Gheorghe arm (braţul Sfântu Gheorghe) is the most southern channel of the three, stretching 109km south-east from Tulcea to the fishing commune of Sfântu Gheorghe. Centuries ago Sfântu Gheorghe stood on the Black Sea. Today it is barraged inland by a wall of shifting sand dunes and marshland.

This is also the Delta's oldest, windiest, and widest channel, stretching 300m to 400m across in parts. A road runs along more than half of the Sfântu Gheorghe arm, making it more accessible to travellers.

From Tulcea, a potholed road leads 13km south-east to **Nufăru**, a village boasting archaeological finds from the 12th and 13th centuries. The ferry's first stop is at **Balteni de Jos**, 3km south-east of **Victoria** which is accessible by road. The sweeping views of the Delta from **Beştepe**, 6km further south by road, are superb.

The ferry's second stop is at **Mahmudia**, 28km from Tulcea. Mahmudia was developed on the site of the ancient Roman walled city of Salsovia, meaning 'sun city'. Inscriptions on tombstones dating from 322 BC suggest Salsovia gained its name from pagan sun worship practised here. Appropriately Mahmudia has one hotel, the *Hotel Plaur*, next to the NAVROM ferry. Doubles/triples cost US$7/10 and apartments cost US$10. Ask here about hiring rowing boats.

Murighiol & Uzlina

Ferries stop at Murighiol, 45km from Tulcea, which is also accessible by road. Murighiol ('violet lake') was named by the Turks. It was renamed 'Independenţa' under the communist regime. Murighiol was a Roman military camp in the 2nd century BC. Some remains of the fortifying walls, intersected

with 15 towers and two gates built during this period, can still be seen today.

Murighiol is centred on a large purpose-built hotel, campsite and boat-rental complex – the *Camping & Hotel Pelican*, adjacent to the NAVROM ferry port. A bed in a hotel room/wooden hut is US$8/3 a night. You can pitch your tent for US$2 a day. Staff speak English and French. To get to the hotel by road, follow the battered 'Han, Motel, Hotel' signs.

Local fishermen waiting to take tourists out on the water hang out in the hotel bar. Expect to pay around US$17 an hour. From Murighiol, the most popular day trip is east to Uzlina, a 1½ hour journey by motorboat. Uzlina was exclusively reserved as a hunting ground for Ceauşescu until 1989. Today his private hunting lodge houses a DDBR **Information & Education Ecological Centre** (Complex pentru Instruire Informare Ecologica Crişan). It's open weekdays from 8 am to 4.30 pm. The protected zones of Lake Uzlina and Lake Isac to the north-east of the village are home to large pelican colonies. **Lake Sărăturii** (87 hectares), immediately west of Murighiol, is also a birdwatcher's paradise and is a protected zone.

From Murighiol, the road continues 5km south to **Dunavăţ de Sus** where it comes to an abrupt end. For places to stay see Boatels under Tulcea.

Sfântu Gheorghe

From Murighiol the ferry continues downstream, past Ivancea – one of the Delta's largest geese nesting areas – to the ancient fishing village of Sfântu Gheorghe ('sfant-u gore-gay'). This is one of the best villages in the Delta to sample traditional cooking although few travellers get the chance to taste the black caviar for which Sfântu Gheorghe is famed. This is a delicacy reserved strictly for religious feasts. Sfântu Gheorghe is the only village in the Delta where Black Sea sturgeon are caught. According to village records, in 1880 a sturgeon weighing 880kg was hauled in, from which 129kg of black caviar was extracted. Most caviar is exported.

There is no hotel in Sfântu Gheorghe but you can stay in private homes. You can book in advance at the *Vila Visconti* (☎ 040-524 7320), Str Mircea Vodă 6. Gicu Constantin in Niculiţel (see Upriver from Tulcea) also arranges private accommodation in Sfântu Gheorghe. The DDBR plans to open a tourist information centre in Sfântu Gheorghe.

Getting There & Away
For details on buses and ferries to/from Murighiol, Mahmudia and Balteni de Jos see Getting Around at the start of this chapter.

TULCEA TO PERIPRAVA
The Chilia channel (braţul Chilia), 120km in length, snakes along Romania's border with Ukraine before fanning out into some 40 tiny rivers forming a mini-delta of its own.

This northern arm is the longest and largest of the three but is the least used.

NAVROM ferries only call at **Chilia-Veche** and **Periprava**. Between these two confetti settlements, seldom visited by foreigners, the river passes between two islands, **Babina** (Ostrovul Babina) and **Cernovca** (Ostrovul Cernovca). These islands were dyked by Ceauşescu in the late 1980s as part of his drive to turn the Delta into agricultural land.

Cutting off these islands from the Delta's natural flooding regime was disastrous for fishermen in Chilia-Veche who found their main source of income had dried up. Prior to the dyking, Babina and Cernovca had served as one of the Delta's most important feeding spots for migratory birds and sheltered numerous bird breeding and nesting places. They were one of the few spots where grey willows, buttercups, gypsy-wort and the rare 'bittersweet nightshade' grew in abundance.

Since 1994 the DDBR has attempted to ecologically reconstruct these two islands by reflooding them. Part of the dam in the northern part of Babina was opened in 1994, followed by openings made to the circular channel around Cernovca in 1996.

South-east of Babina and Cernovca islands, close to Periprava, lies the Delta's extremely impressive forest, **Letea forest** (Pădurea Letea) covering 2825 hectares. It has been a national park since 1938 and is protected by the DDBR today. A large buffer zone surrounds it to ensure illegal woodcutters remain well away from the oak and ash trees, some of which are 500 years old. The trees are unusual because their roots, embedded in sandy earth, are extraordinarily shallow. Tourists can visit Letea village nearby and spend a few days touring the surrounding waterways. Expect to pay local fishermen US$45 to US$60 a day.

Getting There & Away
For information on ferries to/from Chilia-Veche and Periprava see Getting Around at the beginning of this chapter.

AROUND LAKE RAZIM
Lake Razim which flows into Lake Goloviţa at its southern end, is the largest permanent water expanse in the Delta. Between 1969 and 1978 the western shores of both these lakes were empoldered for fish farming.

On Lake Razim's eastern shores, the **Holbina** polder's natural vegetation remains preserved, including pockets of oak forest.

From Tulcea a dirt road leads south to **Agighiol** on the north-western tip of Lake Razim. From here the road snakes further south. Houses in all the villages along this route are crowned with thatched-reed roofs, typical to the Delta. Reeds are cut by hand in winter and used to weave baskets, thatch roofs and insulate walls. Under communism, reed was harvested in vast amounts and transported to paper and cellulose factories in Brăila, and during the Stalinist era reed-cutting constituted hard labour for political prisoners. The DDBR discourages the large-scale cutting of reed for commercial use as reed beds act as a natural filter for the water passing through the Delta. Since 1990 reed cutting has been reduced by 90%.

Continuing south from Agighiol you pass through **Sarichioi**, a small village overlooking the protected **Popina Island** (Insula Popina). This 98 hectare island is the most important nesting area in the Delta for shelduck who rest in abandoned fox holes. From

1981-90 the island was used as pastureland for cattle which led to its rapid degeneration into a barren, overgrazed piece of land.

In the centre of **Enisala**, 8km south, is a **peasant museum** (Muzeul Gospodăria Tărăneasca) inside a 19th century cottage. It's open daily, except Monday and Tuesday, from 10 am to 6 pm. On a hill above the village are remains of a 13th century **citadel** commanding staggering views of Lake Razim. Also visible from the hilltop is Lake Babadag. The marshes between the Babadag and Razim lakes lure many birdwatchers.

Babadag (population 10,000) is on the south-western edge of Lake Babadag. The forests surrounding the village are popular with birdwatchers. The **Mosque Ali Gazi Pasha**, built at the start of the 17th century, is Romania's oldest architectural Muslim monument. It houses a small oriental art exhibition. At the time of writing the mosque was being renovated. It is opposite the bus station on Str Mihai Viteazul. From here head north to Babadag's one hotel, the *Hotel Dumbrava* (☎ 047-561 302) at Str Republicii. Singles/doubles cost US$7/14.

From Enisala the road continues to run parallel with Lake Razim's shores, passing through **Sălcioara**. The stretch of road from Enisala to Sălcioara is occasionally closed and used as a practise target range for the Romanian army. Six kilometres further south is **Jurilovca**, a fishing village where most houses are built from dried peat bricks. Adjoining **Lake Goloviţa** is a fish farm. From here you can hire a boat to take you across to **Gura Portiţei** (1½ hours), on the eastern shores of Lake Goloviţa. Camping is forbidden. From here, Lake Goloviţa spreadeagles out to the south into Lake Zmeica and Lake Sinoie.

On the eastern shores of Lake Sinoie at Histria are the remains of a Greek colony dating from 657 BC (see Histria in Northern Dobruja).

Getting There & Away

Few buses from Tulcea head this far south, making this part of the Delta almost impossible to explore without private transport. See Getting There & Away for details.

Hitching is tough; few motorised or horse-powered vehicles pass.

UPRIVER FROM TULCEA

The ferry trip between Tulcea and Galaţi is especially fun since this part of the Danube marks the boundary between Romania and Ukraine. You get a fine view of Reni, perhaps the best free peek possible into Ukraine. Reni is the second most important Ukrainian Danube port (the most important being Izmayil). At the time of writing the border into Giurgiuleşti (Moldova) and further to Reni (Ukraine) was closed.

By road the route is equally interesting. Stop to pick walnuts from the trees, and take time to see Niculiţel's paleo-Christian basilica. This region is also home to Europe's only known leper colony.

Celic-Dere & Cocoş Monasteries

From Tulcea, head west along the main Tulcea-Smârdan road for 29km, then turn left for Celic-Dere. Some 5km south along this dirt-track road lies the Celic-Dere Monastery (Mănăstirea Celic-Dere) built in 1838. A collection of medieval art is housed in its **religious ethnographic museum**.

Cocoş Monastery (Mănăstirea Cocoş), 38km west of Tulcea, was built in 1838 on the site of a 17th century hermitage. Today it houses a **medieval book and icon museum**, open daily, except Monday, from 10 am to 4 pm. To get here from Celic-Dere, get back onto the Tulcea-Smârdan road and continue west for 7km. Turn left at the signpost for Niculiţel and continue, past the village, for another 7km. There is one bus daily from Tulcea to Cocoş.

Niculiţel

The ruins of a 4th century **paleo-Christian basilica** (Basilica Martirică Niculiţel) are in Niculiţel, 31km west of Tulcea. It was only uncovered in 1971 following heavy storms which left part of the martyrs' crypt exposed. Bones of four martyrs were later discovered in the crypt.

The paleo-Christian basilica was probably built under the Emperor Valentian II, following a Christian-Roman form. It was modified by Theodosius II in the 5th century.

A modern building shields the remains where archaeologists work today. Parts of the church walls have been reconstructed, and the centre of the church is still to be excavated. The complex is open daily from 10 am to 2 pm, and from 3 to 7 pm.

North of Niculiţel, **swamps** stretch for some 10km to the Danube. Bargain with a local fisherman to take you out to explore them in a kayak.

Places to Stay & Eat Local French and English teacher Gicu Constantin runs a small B&B scheme for US$8 per person a night from his home (☎ 040-516 166) in Niculiţel at Str Gurgoaia 746. He is an excellent local guide (US$10 a day) and arranges birdwatching tours, swamp rides and boat trips on the Delta. Gicu Constantin often meets guests at Tulcea train and bus stations and provides transport to his house.

Isaccea to Măcin

In 514 BC the Persian king Darius' fleet crossed the Danube river at Isaccea during his war with the Scythes. Isaccea is 8km west of the Niculiţel turn-off on the main Tulcea-Smârdan highway. The settlement was later fortified by the Romans who named it Noviodunum and based their Danube naval fleet here. The Ottomans conquered Dobruja in 1418 but it was not until 1484 that they gained control of Isaccea along with the Danubian fortress downstream at Chilia.

Just a few kilometres west of Isaccea, between the pinprick villages of Revărsăre and Rachelu, is a small dirt-track road leading to **Tichileşti**. This village is home to Europe's last remaining hospital for leprosy sufferers. A wooden bar cuts Tichileşti off from the outside world.

The ruins of the Roman wall built around the ancient city of Arrubium can be seen in Măcin, 40km west of Isaccea on the Dobruja-Moldavia border. For an aerial view, hike 11km south to **Greci** and climb Ţuţuiatul peak (467m). On a clear day, the views of the Danube, the Delta and the Black Sea are absolutely superb.

You can cross the Danube into Brăila at **Smârdan**, 13km west of Măcin (see Brăila in the Moldavia chapter). The small ferry, which makes the short 10 minute crossing every half-hour, is suitable for cars and foot passengers. A single fare for a car/foot passenger is US$2/0.75.

Europe's Only Leper Colony

The leprosarium in Tichileşti is the only known leper colony remaining in Europe. The village, home to 43 patients, is conveniently isolated in Romania's backwaters in the Danube Delta. Its existence was wholly denied during the Ceauşescu regime and even today few Delta residents know of, or admit to, its chilling presence.

The colony was founded in 1929 when 180 lepers were banished from northern Bucovina (present-day Ukraine). Orthodox monks from Tichileşti monastery gave the lepers shelter and in 1931 a hospital was established in the small village. Queen Marie, known for her work with cholera sufferers in the Balkan wars, financed the building of two pavilions at Tichileşti in the 1920s.

Between 1952-57 there were over 280 leprous exiles in Tichileşti, the only specialist sanatorium in Romania which provided its leprosy victims with medical care and moral support. Traditionally lepers were shunned and reviled by society, being forced to wear distinctive clothing and rattle a wooden clapper to warn others of their 'filthy' approach.

The leprosarium is funded by the state. In mid-1997 it received US$1.50 per patient per day. In 1991 it received substantial aid from the German Maltese Cross charity which helped build a new bathhouse. The patients today, ranging in age from 30 to 86, require continual treatment and lead a semi-independent life in small cottages in the 'leper village'. They are cared for by a staff of 33.

Tichileşti is a closed village. Only friends and relatives are allowed to enter it. ■

NORTHERN DOBRUJA

Crişana & Banat

The plains of Crişana and Banat, divided in two by the Mureş river, merge imperceptibly and stretch into Yugoslavia's Vojvodina and Hungary's Great Plain. Until 1918 all three regions were governed jointly, and although Subotica (Yugoslavia), Szeged (Hungary) and Timişoara now belong to three different countries, all three cities bear the unmistakable imprint of the Habsburg Empire.

Oradea, Arad and Timişoara all had large military fortresses intended to defend Austria-Hungary's south-eastern flank. All three were handed to Romania following WWI, despite their predominantly Hungarian populations. The Hungarian element is still strong throughout the region, especially in terms of architecture. In Banat you'll also see the Slavic influence of the Serbs.

It's logical then that the 1989 revolution should have begun in the west, where the ethnically mixed population had always been at the margin of communist economic development. Drained of food and resources to finance Ceauşescu's great projects around Bucharest, facing increasing marginalisation of national minorities and better informed through Hungarian and Yugoslav TV coverage of the political changes in East Germany, Czechoslovakia etc, the western part of the country exploded in December 1989. Visitors making a pilgrimage along the 'freedom trail' will want to visit the small Hungarian church in Timişoara where it all began.

Crişana and Banat are the door to Romania from the west. All trains from Hungary and Yugoslavia pass through Timişoara, Arad or Oradea. They're all good places to get your bearings.

History

Historical Banat is today divided between western Romania, eastern Hungary and northern Yugoslavia. The Agathyrsi people, a Thracian or Illyrian tribe, first settled the region in the 6th century BC. By 106 AD it was incorporated in the Roman province of

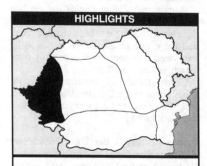

HIGHLIGHTS

- Marvel at stalactites and stalagmites up to 55,000 years old in the magnificent Bears' Cave, Peştera Urşilor
- Descend into the depths of the surreal Scarişoara ice cave
- Follow the trail of the 1989 revolution in Timişoara
- Enjoy a night at the opera in Timişoara
- Wallow in a health-giving thermal bath in Băile Herculane

Dacia. From the end of the 9th century until the Ottoman conquest of Banat in 1552, the region fell under Hungarian rule.

Under the Treaty of Karlowitz in 1699, the Turks relinquished Hungary to Austria but Banat remained in Ottoman hands until 1716 when Habsburg forces led by Prince Eugene of Savoy finally conquered the region. Under the Treaty of Passarowitz, signed in July 1718, Banat became part of the Austro-Hungarian empire. Following this Swabian colonists from south-west Germany left their homeland for Banat.

Following the Treaty of Trianon in 1920 when the region was split among Romania, Hungary and Yugoslavia, Banat's current borders were set. At the outbreak of WWII there were 130,000 Germans in this region. Both WWII and the collapse of communism in 1989 saw a mass exodus of Germans from this region.

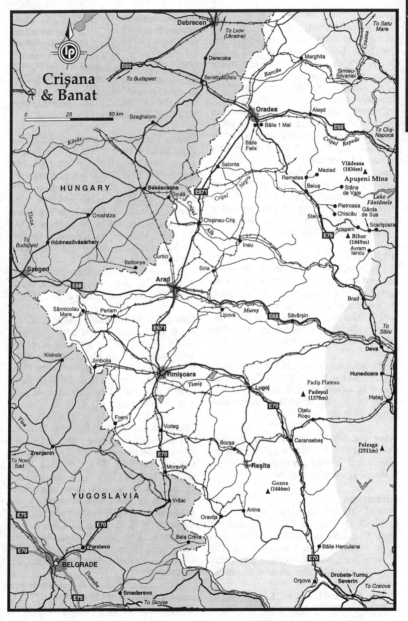

ORADEA
• *area code* ☎ *059, pop 325,000*

Oradea, only a few kilometres east of the Hungarian border, is the seat of Bihor County. It's also the centre of the Crişana region, a fertile plain drained by the Alb, Negru and Repede rivers at the edge of the Carpathian Mountains.

Of all the cities of the Austro-Hungarian Empire, Oradea best retains its 19th century elegance. When Oradea was ceded to Romania in 1920, this example of Habsburg majesty became the backwater it remains today, a time capsule preserved for romantics in search of a simpler world. Băile Felix with its thermal springs is close by. Oradea is a great place to stop, spend your remaining Romanian currency and prepare yourself for a return to the ruthless west.

Orientation

The train station is a couple of kilometres north of the town centre: tram No 1 runs south from Piaţa Bucureşti (outside the train station) to Piaţa Unirii, Oradea's main square. Tram No 4 runs from Piaţa Bucureşti to the northern end of Str Republicii – a five minute walk to the centre – and to Piaţa Unirii.

The main square north of the river is Piaţa Republicii (also known as Piaţa Regele Ferdinand I), around which most facilities lie.

The left-luggage office at the train station is open 24 hours.

Maps The *Ghidul Practic Al Municipului Oradea* (1996) includes a public transport scheme and detailed city maps. It is sold for US$1.20 in some bookshops.

Information

Tourist Offices The Agenţie de Turism Crişul (☎ 130 737; fax 133 323), inside the Hotel Crişul Repede at Str Libertăţii 8, is open weekdays from 9 am to 4 pm. The tourist office inside the Hotel Dacia (☎ & fax 411 280) offers similar services as well as city tours of Oradea.

The Automobil Clubul Român (ACR; ☎ 130 725; fax 130 415), next to the Bancă

Română de Comerţ Exterior (BANCOREX) at Piaţa Independenţei 31, is open weekdays from 8 am to 3 pm, and Saturday from 8 am to 1 pm. Dac Air has an office (☎ & fax 135 098) at Piaţa Independenţei 47, open weekdays from 9 am to 7 pm, Saturday from 9 am to noon. It also sells tickets for TAROM, MALEV, JAT Yugoslav airlines, Air France, KLM and British Airways.

Money The currency exchange inside the Hotel Dacia is open weekdays from 7 am to 8 pm, weekends from 9 am to 1 pm. BANCOREX at Piaţa Independenţei 31 cashes travellers cheques and gives cash advance on Visa/MasterCard. It's open weekdays from 8.30 am to 2 pm. The Bancă Comercială Română, at the northern end of Piaţa Independenţei, offers the same services and has an ATM accepting Visa/MasterCard outside. The bank is open weekdays from 8.30 am to 6.30 pm, Saturday from 9 am to 1 pm. In the centre of town is the Bancă Agricola at Str Avram Iancu 2.

Post & Communications The post office at Str Roman Ciorogariu is open weekdays from 8 am to 8 pm. To get to the telephone office walk down the alley next to the Salon Bingo Billiard Restaurant (next to the Hotel Parc) at Str Republicii 5. The telephone office – at the end of the alley – is open daily from 7 am to 9 pm.

Things to See & Do

Oradea's most imposing sights are on the two city centre squares, Piaţa Unirii and Piaţa Republicii. The Orthodox **Moon Church** (Biserica cu luna; 1784) on Piaţa Unirii, has an unusual lunar mechanism (1795) on its tower, comprising black and gold semispheres which adjust position automatically in accordance with the moon's movement. The other churches and civic palaces on this square are an interesting mix of rococo, baroque, Renaissance and Art Nouveau.

In the centre of the Piaţa Unirii stands an equestrian **statue of Mihai Viteazul** (1994). This ruling prince of Wallachia (1593-1601)

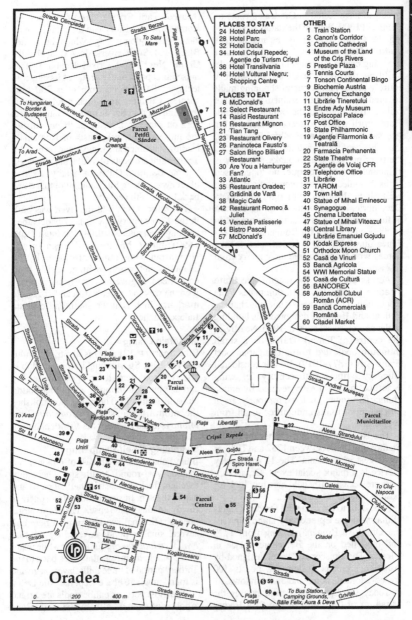

PLACES TO STAY
24 Hotel Astoria
28 Hotel Parc
32 Hotel Dacia
34 Hotel Crişul Repede;
   Agenţie de Turism Crişul
36 Hotel Transilvania
46 Hotel Vultural Negru;
   Shopping Centre

PLACES TO EAT
8 McDonald's
12 Select Restaurant
14 Rasid Restaurant
15 Restaurant Mignon
21 Tian Tang
23 Restaurant Olivery
26 Paninoteca Fausto's
27 Salon Bingo Billiard
   Restaurant
30 Are You a Hamburger
   Fan?
33 Atlantic
35 Restaurant Oradea;
   Grădină de Vară
38 Magic Café
42 Restaurant Romeo &
   Juliet
43 Venezia Patisserie
44 Bistro Pascaj
57 McDonald's

OTHER
1 Train Station
2 Canon's Corridor
3 Catholic Cathedral
4 Museum of the Land
   of the Criş Rivers
5 Prestige Plaza
6 Tennis Courts
7 Tonson Continental Bingo
9 Biochemie Austria
10 Currency Exchange
11 Librărie Tineretului
13 Endre Ady Museum
16 Episcopal Palace
17 Post Office
18 State Philharmonic
19 Agenţie Filarmonia &
   Teatrală
20 Farmacia Perhanenta
22 State Theatre
25 Agenţie de Voiaj CFR
29 Telephone Office
31 Librărie
37 TAROM
39 Town Hall
40 Statue of Mihai Eminescu
41 Synagogue
45 Cinema Libertatea
47 Statue of Mihai Viteazul
48 Central Library
49 Librărie Emanuel Gojudu
50 Kodak Express
51 Orthodox Moon Church
52 Casă de Vinuri
53 Bancă Agricola
54 WWI Memorial Statue
55 Casă de Cultură
56 BANCOREX
58 Automobil Clubul
   Român (ACR)
59 Bancă Comercială
   Română
60 Citadel Market

Oradea

is said to have rested in Oradea en route to Vienna in 1600. West of the statue, overlooking the Crişul Repede, is the magnificent **Vulturul Negru** ('Black Vulture') hotel and shopping centre, an unusual secession-style building dating from 1908 and almost entirely preserved. A quaint shopping mall, covered by a fantastic stained-glass dome ceiling, runs through the building, linking Piaţa Unirii with Str Independenţei and Str Alecsandri. A **statue of Mihai Eminescu**, the 19th century romantic poet, overlooks the river on its southern banks. Close by is an abandoned **synagogue**, no longer used by its dwindled Jewish community. Heading west along the river, turn right onto Piaţa Decembrie. In front of the **Casă de Cultură** in the central park is a large **monument** to soldiers who fought for Romanian independence during WWI. It is dedicated to 'the heroes who fought to free the country from fascism'.

Across the bridge the magnificent **State Theatre** (Teatrul de Stat), dominates Piaţa Republicii. The famous Viennese architects, Fellner and Hellmer, designed this building in the neo-classical style in 1900. Nearby, in the centre of Parcul Traian, is a small **museum** dedicated to the Hungarian poet Endre Ady (1877-1919). He was considered Hungary's finest 20th century, left-wing lyric poet and is greatly revered by ethnic Hungarians today. He lived for four years in Oradea, prior to his undignified death from syphilis.

The **Roman Catholic cathedral** on Str Stadionului, built between 1752 and 1780, is the largest in Romania. The 11 am Sunday service is a major social event. Organ concerts are occasionally held here too; look for posters outside the cathedral.

Next door to the cathedral Oradea's sights climax with the **Episcopal Palace** (Episcopia Ortodoxă Română), dating from 1770 and modelled on the Belvedere Palace in Vienna. The Episcopal Palace, designed by Austrian architect Hillebrand, boasts 100 fresco-adorned rooms and 365 windows.

Today the Episcopal Palace houses the **Museum of the Land of the Criş Rivers**

(Muzeul Ţarii Crişul), one of the best in Romania, with history and art exhibits relevant to the region through which the White, Black and Swift rivers flow (Crişul Alb, Crişul Negru and Crişul Repede). The museum is particularly proud of its egg collection: 10,000 eggs from over 700 bird species. Contemporary rock bands play in the bandstand in the beautifully landscaped park on summer days. Immediately outside the museum entrance, busts of Romania's leading statesmen and kings stand on parade. To the right are busts of Wallachia's princes.

Note **Canon's Corridor** nearby, a series of archways along Str Stadionului that dates back to the 18th century.

The **citadel**, south of the river, was built in the 13th century. It was later bequeathed to Hungarian ruler Matthias Corvinus (1458-1490) during his iron-fist reign of the Hungarian kingdom. Unfortunately the citadel is not worth visiting, as it's been converted into government offices. You pass it on the way to Oradea's fruit and vegetable **market**, which is at the south end of Piaţa Independenţiei.

Mountain Biking

Bike Sport (☎ 121 745) is at Str Nufărului 39. The Bike Sport mountain-biking club is also run from here. It arranges trips locally and can put you in touch with other biking clubs in Romania. The club also publishes the monthly newsletter *Mountain Bike Mania* (see the Facts for the Visitor chapter).

Swimming & Self-Pampering

Băile Felix, 8km south-east of Oradea, is a famous year-round health spa where city dwellers flock to splash in thermal pools and nap in the sun. In summer the atmosphere is rowdy in the best sense. There's a large, open-air, thermal swimming pool here and several smaller ponds covered by the rare *Nymphea lotus thermalis*, a giant white water lily (50cm in diameter) that dates back to the Tertiary period of three million years ago and is found nowhere else except the Nile Delta.

The most popular public pools are Strand Apollo and Strand Felix, by the Staţia Băile

Felix bus stop. Both are open daily from 7 am to 6 pm (closed from November to April) and charge US$1 for day use. Bring your own bathing suit and towel.

Places to Stay

Camping From May to mid-September you can camp at *Camping 1 Mai*, Băile 1 Mai, 9km south-east of Oradea. It has 32 cabins at US$4 per person. If it's full, walk 500m further along the road, past the bus terminus to *Camping Venus* (☎ 261 507). Take a southbound tram No 4 (black number) from the train station or an eastbound tram No 4 (red number) from Piaţa Unirii to the end of the line, then bus No 15 to the last stop. There's a large thermal swimming pool near these camping grounds, and Băile Felix is a mere 30 minute walk.

Hotels The best bet for budget-conscious backpackers is the *Hotel Parc* (☎ 418 410, 411 699) at Str Republicii 5-7. Spacious and spotlessly clean singles/doubles with shared bathroom are US$7/13 a night. Breakfast is an extra US$2. The staff speak French and go out of their way to help.

Next in line is the unfriendly *Hotel Crişul Repede* (☎ 132 509) at Str Libertăţii 8. The rooms are worn but the hotel offers the one advantage of having the only low-budget singles with private bath in town. A single/double with shower is US$7/11 a night. A double with bath/shared bath is US$12/11.

Marginally more upmarket is the two-star *Hotel Astoria* (☎ 131 663) close to the theatre at Str Teatrului 2. It has a handful of cramped singles for US$6 a night; the rest are doubles/triples with private bath at US$21/19 a night. The *Hotel Transilvania* (☎ 130 508, 131 663) at Str Teatrului 1 was closed for renovation at the time of writing.

South of the river at Str Independenţei 1 stands the fantastically preserved Art-Nouveau building in which the musty but friendly *Hotel Vulturul Negru* (☎ 135 417) is housed. Dating to 1908, the 'Black Vulture' is a hotspot with local students and foreign backpackers, despite its sinister name and

'haunted house' atmosphere! It offers simple single/double rooms with shared bathroom for US$6/13 a night. Doubles with private bath are US$16.

Business travellers usually opt for the soulless *Hotel Dacia* (☎ & fax 411 280), overlooking the river at Aleea Ştrandului 1. Singles/doubles with private bath, minibar and all the mod cons cost US$49/78 a night and luxury suites are US$92. The hotel has a casino, 24-hour bar with cabaret show, and thermal pool which is open to non-guests (admission US$1).

Out of Town Băile Felix, 8km south-east of Oradea by tram (see Getting Around), boasts a host of concrete block hotels, most of which get packed with sun-worshippers and local holidaymakers in summer.

Some of the cheapest rooms can be had at *Hotel Felix* (☎ 059-136 532; fax 059-261 321), behind the *Hotel Lotus* (☎ 059-261 361, 059-134 355) in the centre of the resort. Singles/doubles at the Felix are US$20/26 a night and the disco here rocks from 6 pm to 6 am. The *Hotel Someş* (☎ 134 222), in the north-western corner of the resort, is the only hotel in Băile Felix that has triple rooms (US$34). Singles/doubles are US$22/31.

If you're into partying, avoid the bargain-basement *Hotel Padis* (☎ 261 549, 261 540; fax 134 373) and the *Hotel Muncel* (☎ 261 334; fax 134 373), both on the south-eastern edge of the resort. The Padis has been a hang-out for rheumatism sufferers since 1971 and its clientele remains elderly today. Staff at the Muncel, meanwhile, are quick to tell you that their hotel is 'for health, *not* entertainment'. Singles/doubles in both cost US$13/17.

Places to Eat

Restaurants & Cafés The least prominent of Oradea's restaurants but worth tracking down is the *Restaurant Oradea & Grădină de Vară Promesse*, tucked behind the Hotel Parc in a courtyard at Str Republicii 5-7. The tender grilled beefsteak topped with a fried egg is delicious, as are its many other grilled meats, all for no more than US$1.50. Live bands often play in the summer garden and the dance floor gets packed with young lovers smooching as night falls. It is open daily from 5 pm to midnight.

A couple of doors down at Str Republicii 3 is *Paninoteca Fausto's*, Oradea's other popular hangout. A cross between a café and restaurant, its terrace on the main street is packed from morning to night. It serves a small selection of Romanian dishes and lots of beer and is open daily from 8 am to midnight.

With three pages of Romanian dishes and one paragraph of Chinese on the menu, *Tian Tang*, opposite the Hotel Parc, is an overpriced letdown. Still, the 'pork cu China mor' is a fair rendition of garlic pork with mushrooms. It is open daily from 10 am to 11 pm.

Restaurant Mignon, Str Roman Ciorogariu 1, is the city's most elegant – and expensive – choice, serving quality continental cuisine. A full meal including wine is about US$7 a head. The restaurant is open daily from 10 am to midnight.

Select at Str Republicii 15 serves traditional caşcaval (pressed cheese) for US$1 and 'Gordon Bleu' for US$2. It is open daily from 10 am to 11 pm. *Restaurant Olivery*, Str Moscovei 12, is an unpretentious cellar restaurant with quality food at reasonable prices. It is open daily until 10 pm.

Heading towards the river bank, the *Atlantic* at Str I Vulcan has various fish dishes – not tested, but not raved about locally either! It is open daily from noon to 11 pm. West of Piaţa Republicii on the riverbank is the *Magic Café* where you can sip on locally produced *Frutti-Fresh* fizzy drink and watch fishermen catch their dinner. Always packed – if only for the prime views it offers of daring youths leaping from the bridge into the swirling Swift river – is *Restaurant Romeo & Juliet* on Str Română. It mainly serves pizza and is open daily from noon to midnight.

Fast Food The *Rasid Restaurant*, on the corner of Str Republicii and Parcul Traian, is a modern fast-food outlet serving burgers

and fries at a self-service counter for US$1. It is open daily from 10 am to midnight.

Close by on Str Aurel Lazăr is the hip *Are You a Hamburger Fan* – a fast-food takeaway. It's open weekdays from 9 am to 10 pm, Saturday from noon to 11 pm, Sunday from 3 to 10 pm.

South of the river, on the corner of Piaţa Decembrie and Str Spiro Haret, is *Venezia Patisserie* which has an excellent selection of fresh cakes, pastries, apple strudels and gooey chocolate cakes for around US$0.15 a piece. The *Bistro Pascaj*, next to the Vultural Negru shopping centre on Str Independenţei, is another small, clean fast-food joint worth a bite.

Aura, on the way to the bus station at Str Dimitrie Cantimir 9-11, serves Romanian fast food and a small selection of vegetarian takeaways; it's open Monday from 8 am to 3 pm, Tuesday to Friday from 8 am to 4 pm. *McDonald's* has an outlet at Blvd Republicii 30 and another, south of the centre on Str Dimitrie Cantemir.

The slick *Tonson Continental Bingo* complex, close to the train station at the north end of Str Republicii has a few snacks on offer to munch while you play bingo or wait for your train. It is open 24 hours.

Self-Catering The central market *Piaţa Cetate*, is next to the citadel on Piaţa Independenţei. Oradea's only western-style supermarket, selling everything from fresh fish to white chocolate, condoms and tampons, is inside the *Prestige Plaza* on the corner of Blvd Dacia and Str Menumont. It is open Monday to Saturday from 8 am to 8 pm, Sunday from 8 am to 4 pm.

Entertainment
Cinema Highly atmospheric is the grand old *Cinema Libertăţii* (☎ 134 097), in the Vultural Negru building at Str Independenţei 1. Films shown in their original language with Romanian subtitles are screened daily at noon, 3 and 6 pm. Tickets cost US$0.30.

Bars Most of Oradea's terrace cafés and restaurants double as bars by night; the

Grădină de Vară at Restaurant Oradea has the largest terrace. At the traditional *Casă de Vinuri* (literally 'wine shop') just off Piaţa Unirii on Str Avram Iancu, you can get your empty water bottle, beer bottle or mug filled with quality local wine at a bargain price! It's open Monday to Saturday from 8 am to 8 pm, Sunday from 9 am to 1 pm.

Theatre & Classical Music The *State Philharmonic* (Filharmonica de Stat; ☎ 130 853) at Str Moscovei 5 and the *State Theatre* (Teatrul de Stat; ☎ 130 835) at Str Madach Imre 3-5 on Piaţa Republicii are both well worth a visit. Tickets are sold at the Agenţie Filarmonia & Teatrală (☎ 417 864) at Str Republicii 6, open weekdays from 10 am to 4 pm, Saturday from 10 am to 1 pm. Tickets cost between US$3 and US$10. Students and pensioners get discounts. The ticket office inside the theatre is open daily from 10 am to 1 pm, and from 5 to 7 pm.

Big kids will enjoy the shows at Oradea's *Puppet Theatre* (Teatrul de Păpuşi; ☎ 133 398) at Str Vasile Alecsandri 8.

Getting There & Away
Air TAROM operates two daily flights on weekdays and one on Saturday from Oradea to Bucharest (one hour; US$55/$110 single/return). Tickets are sold at the TAROM office (☎ & fax 131 918) at Piaţa Republicii 2, open weekdays from 6.30 am to 8 pm, Saturday from 11 am to 2 pm.

Bus From Oradea bus station there are two daily services to Beiuş (63km) and Deva (190km); and one to Satu Mare (133km).

Hungary Most of the travel agencies arrange bus excursions to Budapest at competitive rates. There are also public buses to Budapest and Debrecen. A daily bus departs for Budapest at 6 pm from outside the train station (10 hours). Tickets (US$6/11 single/return) are sold at the bus station, inconveniently located at Str Războieni 81 on the south-eastern side of town (bus No 12 from Piaţa Unirii). If the bus is not full you can purchase a ticket from the driver before departure.

A daily bus also departs from Oradea bus station for Debrecen in Hungary at 5 am. Single/return tickets cost US$4/7.

Train The Agenţie de Voiaj CFR (☎ 130 578), Str Republicii 2, is open weekdays from 7 am to 8 pm. International tickets cannot be purchased at Oradea's chaotic train station; pick them up at the CFR office in advance.

There are plenty of trains to Hungary from Oradea. Among the express trains are the *Claudiopolis* which departs for Budapest at 3.15 am, and the *Corona* which departs at 6.30 pm. These trains arrive in Budapest 3¾ hours later.

Trains shuttle twice daily between Budapest-Nyugati (the train station) and Oradea (four hours). Fares from Oradea are US$7 to Püspökladány or US$16 to Budapest. These unreserved trains are known as the *Varadinium* (departs at 7.15 am) and the *Partium* (departs at 3.15 pm). If you don't already have a ticket, take bus No 11 from Oradea's train station or take a local train to the border at Episcopia Bihor (eight minutes), where you can easily buy a train ticket to Hungary with lei.

Car & Motorcycle The border crossing into Hungary for motorists at Borş, 16km west of Oradea, is open 24 hours.

Getting Around
To/From the Airport Oradea airport (☎ 413 985, 413 951) is 6km west of the centre on the Oradea-Arad road. TAROM runs a shuttle bus to/from the airport. It leaves from the TAROM office one hour before flights are scheduled to arrive or depart.

Tram & Bus To get to Băile Felix take tram No 4 (red or black number) east from Piaţa Unirii or tram No 4 (black number) south from the train station or from outside McDonald's to the end of the line at Nufărul. From here bus No 14 runs to the spa (US$0.30; pay the driver). On the way back, it's quickest to board at Staţia Strand Apollo, 50m south of Staţia Băile Felix.

Car Rental Hertz (☎ 132 888) has an office at Str Mihai Viteazul 2. Prices charged are the same throughout Romania (see Getting Around at the front of the book).

PEŞTERA MEZIAD
Sixty-three kilometres south of Oradea, approaching the western fringe of Transylvania's vast Apuseni mountains, is the small market town of **Beiuş** from where the Meziad Cave (Peştera Meziad) can be easily reached. The cave is not among the most spectacular in Romania but it is one of the few freely accessible, with guides to show visitors around. It was discovered in 1859 and, until its more impressive neighbouring caves opened, attracted thousands of visitors.

To reach the cave from Beiuş, follow the signpost for Peştera Meziad from the town centre (11km). When you get to the village of Remetea, bear right at the fork next to the Camin Cultural building and continue for 9km until you reach Meziad. Turn left at the first fork, then cross the small white bridge to a gravel road. The main office for the cave is 4km along this road. The entrance to the cave is a further 1.5km.

Local shepherds guide tourists around the cave although it is a hit-or-miss affair as to when the shepherds are at home. Officially, the cave administration office is open daily, except Tuesday, between 9 and 11 am, and from 2 to 4 pm. Admission is US$1. If you intend to explore the cave alone, bring a torch.

Places to Stay
At the time of writing the *Cabana Meziad*, opposite the cave administration office, was closed for renovation. Wild camping is permitted around the cave and in the cabana grounds.

There is no hotel in Beiuş. The nearest, nameless *hotel* adjoins a petrol station, 5km north-west of the town on the Beiuş-Oradea road. If you are travelling by car, consider staying at Stâna de Vale, 23km east of Beiuş.

Getting There & Away
The train and bus stations adjoin each other on the southern edge of town. Travellers will find little use for Beiuş's train services which include only a few trains daily to Holod, 20km north, and Vaşcău.

Buses are marginally more useful. Services include three daily to Meziad (24km); one to Chişcău (21km) and Pietroasa (20km); two to Deva (127km) and Oradea (63km); and six to Ştei (21km). If the ticket office in the bus station is closed, pay on board.

STÂNA DE VALE
Stâna de Vale is a small alpine resort (1300m) in the Pădurea Craiului mountains in the Bihor Massif. It lies at the end of a forest road 23km east of Beiuş. Between December and February it is transformed into a bustling ski centre. In summer, it is a pitifully quiet hiking resort luring few visitors other than rowdy kids on summer camp.

The ski lift is next to the campsite. It is possible to hire skis and have lessons. A couple of hiking trails lead into the Apuseni mountains. A trail marked by red stripes (5½ to six hours) takes you to the **Cabana Padiş** in the heavily karstic Padiş zone (see Padiş Plateau in the Transylvania chapter). Another more challenging trail, marked by blue triangles (six hours), leads to the Cabana Meziad. Don't attempt it in bad weather or in winter.

Places to Stay
In summer, your best bet is to bring your own tent and pitch it outside the derelict wooden bungalows in the campsite at the western end of the resort. At the time of writing the resort's main hotel, *Hotel Iadolina* (☎ 052-211 601), was closed for renovation. There are a limited number of rooms at the *Stâna de Vale Brăserie*, next to the Iadolina. A bed in a double/triple – with a grotty shared bathroom – is US$3.50 per person a night. You can eat in the downstairs restaurant.

The *Cerbal Vila & Restaurant*, opposite the Iadolina, is only open in winter.

Getting There & Away

There are no buses or trains to/from Stâna de Vale. If you don't have your own private transport, hitch or hike.

PEŞTERA URŞILOR

Although it's not easy to reach, Peştera Urşilor (Bear Cave) is one of Romania's finest caves and well worth a day trip from Oradea, 82km north-west. The cave, named after the bear skeletons found there, is in a former marble quarry 1km from Chişcău, a small village featured on few road maps.

The galleries of Peştera Urşilor (482m), accidentally uncovered by quarry workers in 1975, extend over 1000m on two levels. Skeletons of the extinct cave bear *(Ursus spelaeus)* found in the first gallery suggest that 190 bears became trapped in the cave – their den – by an earthquake.

The magnificent cave – a constant cold 10°C – resembles a set from the film *Raiders of the Lost Arc*. Stupendous stalactites and stalagmites loom from every angle, creating uncanny shapes in the half-darkness against a backdrop of continually dripping water. The stalactites, many of which scientists believe to be 22,000 and 55,000 years old, grow 1cm every 20 years. The ceilings of the five galleries are saturated in a sea of baby, spaghetti-like stalactites.

Guided tours of the cave are compulsory. Guides only speak Romanian but allow you plenty of time to explore. The pretty melody that guides tap out on the larger stalactites should not be missed. Admission to the cave is US$2.20 and an additional US$3.50/7 fee is charged if you want to take a camera/video camera. The site is open from May to September only, Tuesday to Sunday from 10.30 am to 5 pm.

Various ethnographic exhibits are displayed in the small **Ethnographic Museum** (muzeul etnografie), opposite Camping Fluturi. It is open 24 hours; if you cannot find the person with the key, ask at the campsite bar. Admission is US$0.15.

Places to Stay & Eat

Camping Fluturi, in the centre of Chişcău, has a dozen wooden cabins with bedding and shared bathrooms for US$3.50 a night. The site has no running hot water.

Getting There & Away

Oradea's Agenţie de Turism Crişul charges US$20 per person for a return trip to the cave. Expensive it may be, but it is the most hassle-free way of getting to Peştera Urşilor, particularly if time is short.

Otherwise there is one daily bus from Beiuş to Chişcău. Check with Oradea's Agenţie de Turism Crişul before heading out.

By private transport, head south from Oradea, through Beiuş. Follow the road for a further 10km along the Crişul Negru, then turn right at the turn off for Pietroasa and Peştera Urşilor. Continue along this road; the cave is signposted on the right.

PEŞTERA GHEŢARUL DE LA SCĂRIŞOARA

From Chişcău, cave buffs should head straight to the fantastic ice cave (Peştera Gheţarul), commonly known as the Scărişoara ice cave. If coming from Beiuş, head south to **Ştei**. This town is still marked on many maps by its former name, Dr Petru Groza, in memory of Romania's first postwar communist prime minister. His memorial statue is today dumped on wasteland near Bucharest.

Two kilometres further south, turn left, following the signs for **Arieşeni**, a village renowned for its traditional folk customs and wooden church, and for Gârda de Sus. From Gârda de Sus, a dirt track leads to the ice cave, 18km further east in the Arieş valley. It is impossible to access the cave from Scărişoara village.

Exploring the Cave

The cave was first documented in 1863 by Austrian geographer Arnold Schmidt, who wrote up his findings, accompanied by detailed maps of its numerous chambers. His early documentation enabled the Romanian scientist and speleologist Emil Racoviţa (1868-1947) to pursue further explorations between 1921-3. In 1927 he published a comprehensive account of how the extraordinary ice cave was formed. Believed to be among 10 of its kind in Europe, the cave is filled with 7500 cubic metres of ice. The ice, at an altitude of 1150m, dates to the ice age when the Apuseni mountains were shrouded in icebergs (*gheţar*). A few centimetres of ice close to the cave's entrance does melt each summer, but the remainder of the 15m-thick bergs inside remain solidly frozen.

Descending the 201 wooden steps leading down to the cave's entrance, the temperature drops noticeably. The steps halfway down are iced over and rain turns to snow before it hits the ground around the cave entrance. The maximum temperature inside the cave in summer is 1°C; in winter it drops to -7°C. Safety precautions inside the cave are not up to western standards and lighting is non-existent. Bring your own torch or ask the keeper for an oil/carbon lamp (*lampă cu carbid*). Even with a torch it's difficult to see the full wonders of the cave, although once your vision adjusts to the darkness, it is possible to make out the numerous stalagmites.

Tickets cost US$1.20. Officially it is open daily, except Monday, from 10 am to 4 pm, although opening hours tend to be haphazard. Lone travellers are forbidden from visiting the cave; you have to go in groups of two or more.

GÂRDA DE SUS & AROUND

Two kilometres west of Arieşeni on the border of Bihor and Alba counties is a small **ski slope** (753m long), signposted 'Teleschii Virtop'. It is open daily from 9 am to 6 pm, between December and May.

The village of Gârda de Sus lies in the Arieş river valley in the Apuseni mountains. Until 1932 it was classified as part of Scărişoara. Traditional folk costumes, resembling those worn by early Dacian tribes, are still worn in the village where logging has always been the main activity.

Three days of festivities follow a death in the village in accordance with the village *mioriţa*. As the legend goes, two shepherds named Muntenia and Moldavia plotted to kill fellow shepherd Transylvania whose flock was greater than theirs. Transylvania's sheep told their master of Muntenia and Moldavia's plans, following which the wise shepherd told his flock 'If I die, lay three flutes by my head, one made from bone, another from birch and the third from a different type of wood'. He also asked them to tell his mother 'I am not dead but I married nature and am rejoicing with my wife through the mountains and forest, singing as wind with my flutes'. Transylvania was murdered soon after. Ever since, for three days and three nights, the villagers of Gârda join the bereaved in their celebration of the mioriţa whereby death is but a pipe song

Some 20km south of Gârda de Sus is the village of **Avram Iancu**. Formerly known as Vidra de Sus, it was renamed after the great revolutionary leader who was born here. This village is also a good access point for the colourful Girls' Fair held each year on top of Mount Găina. See the Apuseni Mountains in the Transylvania chapter.

Places to Stay

Camping The *Popas Turistic Gherda*, at the western end of Gârda de Sus, has small wooden bungalows for rent in the summer for US$3 per person. It also has a small restaurant and bar.

Private Rooms The Belgian charity Opération Villages Roumains has helped local people in Gârda de Sus establish their own agro-tourism scheme whereby tourists can stay in their homes. The local representative in Gârda de Sus is Ioan Stefanut who lives at house No 31. Alternatively you can make bookings in advance through the central office in Cluj-Napoca (see Transylvania). There is also a representative in Arieşeni, 8km west. Ask for Marta Maghiar at house No 13.

Hotels Eight kilometres west of Gârda de Sus is the more modern *Complex Turistic*

Arieşeni. A bed in a comfortable wooden cabin with a shared bathroom is US$3.50/2.50 in summer/winter. It also has a number of double rooms in modern, heated villas equipped with a kitchen, dining room and TV. A bed in a villa starts at US$4/3 in summer/winter. The restaurant and bar is open 24 hours. Advance bookings can be made through the Complex Hotelier Cetate (☎ 058-811 780; fax 058-815 812, 831 501), Str Unirii 3, Alba Iulia.

Getting There & Away

From Gârda de Sus, hikers can head north to the Padiş Plateau. A trail marked by blue stripes (five to six hours) leads from the village to the Cabana Padiş (see the Padiş Plateau section in the Transylvania chapter).

ARAD
* *area code* ☎ *057, pop 190,114*

Arad, 57km north of Timişoara, sits in wine-making country on the banks of the Mureş River, which loops around Arad's 18th century citadel before flowing west to Szeged in Hungary. Arad developed as a major trading centre during Turkish occupation of the city between 1551 and 1687. There's not much to see here except elegant turn-of-the century architecture, commissioned while the town was part of the Austro-Hungarian empire.

Arad is the main gateway into Hungary. Consider stopping, if only to spend your remaining lei before crossing the Hungarian border.

Orientation

The train station is a few kilometres north of the centre. Take tram Nos 1, 2 or 3 south down the main drag, Blvd Revoluţiei, into town. The bus station is two blocks west of the train station on Blvd Revoluţiei. The left-luggage office at the train station in the main building is open 24 hours. Locally Blvd Revoluţiei is simply known as 'the boulevard'.

Maps Detailed city maps are included in the 1995 *Hartă Comercială a Aradului* city guide; the multilingual *Arad Ghidul Municipiului* (1995) in English, French, German, Hungarian and Italian; and the 1997 *Best of the West* city guide. All three are sold in most hotels and travel agencies for no more than US$2.

Information
Tourist Offices The Agenţie de Turism Zârandul (☎ 257 279), opposite the town hall at Blvd Revoluţiei 76, sells town maps and guides (US$3) as well as tickets for buses to Germany, the Czech Republic and Austria (see Getting There & Away). It is open weekdays from 8 am to 5 pm. BTT (☎ 280 776; fax 281 556) has an office at Blvd Revoluţiei 16, off Piaţa Avram Iancu.

The Automobil Clubul Român (ACR; ☎ & fax 281 445) is Piaţa Independenţei. It is open daily, except Sunday, from 8 am to 5 pm. You can buy a copy of *The Best of the West* city guide here – useful for its city maps if nothing else.

The Soros Foundation for an Open Society (Fundaţia Soros pentru o Societate Deschisă; ☎ & fax 284 000) runs an information centre at Blvd Decebal 2-4. It is open weekdays from 9 am to 5 pm.

Money People on the street change lei into Hungarian forints and vice versa, but be extremely careful. There is a currency exchange inside the TAROM office at Str Unirii 1, open weekdays from 8 am to 4 pm.

The Bancă Comercială Română, Blvd Revoluţiei 72, changes travellers cheques and gives cash advance on Visa/MasterCard (open weekdays from 9 am to noon and 3 to 6 pm, Saturday from 9 am to noon). Bancă Agricola on Piaţa Avram Iancu does too (open weekdays from 8 am to 7 pm, Saturday from 8 to 11 am). West Bank has an office at Blvd Revoluţiei 88, open weekdays from 8.30 am to 12.30 pm and 1.30 to 5.30 pm, Saturday from 8.30 to 11.30 am.

There is an ATM accepting Visa/MasterCard outside the Banc Post, close to the train station on Blvd Revoluţiei.

Post & Communications You'll find the

post and telephone office at Blvd Revoluţiei 44. It is open daily, except Sunday, from 7 am to 8 pm. After hours, there are public cardphones outside as well as an automatic phonecard dispenser.

Things to See

After crushing the liberal revolution of 1848, the Habsburgs had 13 Hungarian generals hanged outside Arad's large, star-shaped **citadel**. A monument to these men stands in front of the Sub Cetate camping ground outside the southern walls of the citadel. Beneath the monument lies the ashes of 11 of the 13 generals, buried here to mark the 125th anniversary of their execution.

The citadel houses a military base today and is closed to the public. It was built under the orders of the Habsburg Queen Marie Theresa between 1763 and 1783. Austrian architect and military general Filip Ferdinand Harsch was commissioned to design the Vauban-style, six-pointed star. It stands on the site of an old fortress built in 1551 by the Turks.

The U-shaped, neo-classical **town hall** (primăria) on Blvd Revoluţiei is Arad's most impressive building. The clock ticking on the 54m-tall tower topping the 1876 building was purchased in Switzerland in 1878. Framing the town hall right and left is the steepled **Cenad Palace** (Palatul Cenad), constructed in an eclectic style by the Arad Cenad railway company at the end of the 19th century; and the **Aurel Vlaicu University** building, decorated in Viennese Rococo motifs and built in the same period to house the local administration's treasury.

Behind the town hall, on Piaţa George Enescu, is the local **History Museum** (Muzeul de Istorie), inside the Palace of Culture, built 1911-13, which also houses Arad's **philharmonic orchestra**. Busts outside pay homage to leading literary figures including Romanian poet George Coşbuc (1866-1918), and post-Romantic historian Alexandru Xenopol (1847-1920).

To the east of the museum, along the Mureş river, lies the **Youth Park** (Parcul Copiilor). The military band is kind enough

to hold its rehearsals in the bandstand in the park on summer afternoons. You'll find a statue of 19th century teacher Elena Ghiba Birta (1801-64) close to the main entrance to the park.

At the southern end of Blvd Revoluţiei is the neo-classical **State Theatre** (Teatrul de Stat), dating from 1874. On a corner at Piaţa Plevnei, two blocks beyond the theatre, is a **tree stump** into which apprentice blacksmiths used to hammer a nail to symbolise their acceptance into the guild. The house – known as the 'House with the Padlock' (Casă cu Lacăt şi Însemnele Calfelor) after the padlocked metal bar which keeps the stump in place – was built in 1815 by local tradesman Joseph Winkler.

South of the theatre, off Piaţa Avram Iancu, at Str Cozia 12 is the Jewish community's **synagogue**, still very much in use today. Jews first settled in Arad in the early 18th century. The town became a centre of reform following the appointment of Aaron Chorin as rabbi of Arad in 1789. Arad's 600-strong Jewish community, which numbered 10,000 prior to WWII, remains one of the largest Jewish communities in Romania outside Bucharest.

Places to Stay

Camping The well run *Sub Cetate* campsite, Str 13 Generali, is 1.5km from the centre. No public transport passes this way but it's a pleasant walk. Cabins and tent sites each cost US$5.50 per person. The on-site restaurant/bar is open from March until mid-October.

Private Rooms ANTREC (☎ & fax 254 046), Str Vasile Milea 7, arranges rooms in private homes in and around Arad for around US$12, including breakfast. Bookings can be made in advance through its Bucharest office, or abroad through Eurogîtes (see the Facts for the Visitor chapter).

Hotels The *Bază Sportiva UTA* (☎ 281 354), overlooking the Mureş river at Str Teiului 1, has a few four-bed rooms above the sports club for US$7 a night (for the whole room).

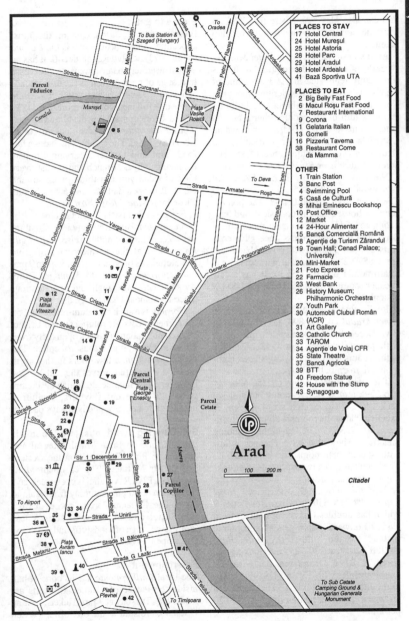

PLACES TO STAY
17 Hotel Central
24 Hotel Mureşul
25 Hotel Astoria
28 Hotel Parc
29 Hotel Aradul
36 Hotel Ardealul
41 Bază Sportiva UTA

PLACES TO EAT
2 Big Belly Fast Food
6 Macul Roşu Fast Food
7 Restaurant International
9 Corona
11 Gelataria Italian
13 Gornelli
16 Pizzeria Taverna
38 Restaurant Come da Mamma

OTHER
1 Train Station
3 Banc Post
4 Swimming Pool
5 Casă de Cultură
8 Mihai Eminescu Bookshop
10 Post Office
12 Market
14 24-Hour Alimentar
15 Bancă Comercială Română
18 Agenţie de Turism Zărandul
19 Town Hall; Cenad Palace; University
20 Mini-Market
21 Foto Express
22 Farmacie
23 West Bank
26 History Museum; Philharmonic Orchestra
27 Youth Park
30 Automobil Clubul Român (ACR)
31 Art Gallery
32 Catholic Church
33 TAROM
34 Agenţie de Voiaj CFR
35 State Theatre
37 Bancă Agricola
39 BTT
40 Freedom Statue
42 House with the Stump
43 Synagogue

Arad

0   100   200 m

Citadel

To Sub Cetate & Camping Ground & Hungarian Generals Monument

You can also play tennis here for US$1 an hour; the canoes are apparently only for club members.

Arad's best-value hotel is *Hotel Mureşul* (☎ 280 766) at Blvd Revoluţiei 88. It was completely renovated in 1993 but some of the rooms leave you wondering otherwise. Nevertheless the crumbling old building retains a turn-of-the century charm and its hotel rooms are the cheapest in town at US$15/24 a night for a single/double with shared shower, including breakfast. The hotel entrance is on Str Vasile Alecsandri.

Not bad value either is *Hotel Ardealul* (☎ 280 840; fax 281 845), close to the State Theatre at Blvd Revoluţiei 98. The hotel is actually housed in a neoclassical building, dating to 1841, with a music room where Brahms, Liszt and Strauss once gave concerts. Singles/doubles with private bathroom are US$20/27 a night and a room with a 'matrimonial bed' is US$30. It has a few cheaper rooms with shared bath for US$11/13 a night.

Really smelly and grotty is the miserable *Hotel Aradul* (☎ 280 894; fax 280 691) at Blvd Decebal 9. Single/double/triple rooms with private shower cost US$22/27/35 a night; rooms with a disgusting shared bathroom are marginally cheaper.

The quiet *Hotel Central* (☎ 256 636; fax 256 629), a modern five-storey building set back off Str Horia in a small garden, is excellent value. Its rooms with private bathroom are US$35/65/68 a night including breakfast. They also have cheaper rooms with shared bathrooms for US$15/25/32. The hotel has a lovely terrace café overlooking its summer garden.

Skip the shockingly overpriced *Hotel Astoria* (☎ 216 650) at Blvd Revoluţiei 9 which has doubles (luxury of course) from US$120 onwards. Splurgers should plump instead for the nine-storey *Hotel Parc* (☎ 280 820; fax 280 725) overlooking the river at Blvd Dragalina 25. Singles/doubles/triples with TV cost US$40/51/60 a night including breakfast. The hotel can arrange a chauffeur taxi service for US$0.20 per km.

Places to Eat

Restaurants & Cafés One of the most appealing restaurants in town is the *Corona* (☎ 231 073) at Blvd Revoluţiei 40. It has an almost Mediterranean terrace and serves a fair range of meat as well as the usual salads and soups. Diners inside watch TV while they eat. A full meal costs no more than US$4 a head. More upmarket is the glittering *Restaurant International* a few blocks north up Blvd Revoluţiei. The complex includes a fast food joint and brasserie serving English, Romanian, Greek, French and almost every kind of salad you can think of for around US$1. It is open daily from 9 am to 11 pm. Close by is *Macul Roşu Fast Food*.

For pizza and pasta the hot choice is *Pizzeria Taverna*, Blvd Revoluţiei 73. Great for its choice of name if nothing else, is *Big Belly Fast Food*, at the northern end of Blvd Revoluţiei. It's open daily from 8 am to 9 pm.

Restaurant Come da Mamma, Piaţa Avram Iancu, is a small and unpretentious place for standard Romanian dishes.

Gornelli is a slick café-cum-restaurant, on the corner of Blvd Revoluţiei and Str Crişan. Decked out Italian-style, it's open daily from 10 am to 11 pm; it's best just for coffee. The *Gelateria Italian*, a few doors further north on Blvd Revoluţiei, serves the real McCoy however when it comes to Italian ice cream. It has 28 different flavours, including bubble-gum and cola, and is always packed.

Self-Catering Arad has two open-air *markets*, one on Piaţa Mihai Viteazul and another on Piaţa Catedralei, at the western end of Str Meţianu. The excellent *Mini-Market* on Blvd Revoluţiei is open weekdays from 7 am to 10 pm, Saturday from 8 am to 6 pm. The *Alimentar*, on the corner of Blvd Revoluţiei and Str Cioşca, sells a less impressive range of foodstuffs and junk food but is open 24 hours.

Entertainment

The local *Philharmonic* has its concert hall inside the Palace of Culture. Concerts are held every Tuesday at 7 pm. Tickets, costing US$0.50, are sold at the box office (☎ 280

519) inside the culture palace two hours before performances begin.

Arad's Agenţie de Teatrala, which sells tickets to local theatre performances, is at the back of the *State Theatre*, open Tuesday to Sunday from 11 am to 1 pm.

Getting There & Away

Air Business Jet (☎ & fax 284 010), inside Hotel Parc, operates international flights from Arad (see Getting There & Away at the front of this book). Its office is open weekdays from 9 am to 5 pm.

TAROM (☎ 254 440), Str Unirii 1, has daily flights, except Sunday, to Bucharest. Single/return tickets cost US$65/130. Its office is open weekdays from 8 am to 4 pm.

Bus A number of buses to Hungary depart from the bus station, two blocks west of the train station. Buses go daily to Szeged (US$3), three times a week to Békéscsaba (US$2) and four times a week to Budapest (seven hours, US$7). Tickets for Budapest and Békéscsaba are available at the ticket window but for Szeged you pay the driver directly. Don't go by the times posted at the station – ask.

Agencies along Blvd Revoluţiei sell bus tickets to Hungary, so shop around for a good price. A dependable choice is Marco Polo (☎ 254 473), Blvd Revoluţiei 59. It also has bus services to Budapest (five hours, US$5), Austria, Poland and Germany.

The Armin Mayer Reisebüro (☎ 285 611, 456 175), Str Fantanele 44, and the Agenţie de Turism Zârandul (see Information) both sell tickets for the twice-weekly buses to Germany.

Train Tickets for trains to Hungary and Poland have to be bought in advance from the Agenţie de Voiaj CFR (☎ 280 977) which shares an office with TAROM at Str Unirii 1, open weekdays from 8 am to 8 pm.

Arad is a major railway junction. Trains for Budapest (3¼ hours) depart from Arad eight times a day. These trains cross the border at Curtici, 17km north-west of Arad.

There is also one daily train to Warsaw (15½ hours).

Alternatively, take a daily commuter train from Arad to Nădlac (1½ hours) then walk, hitch or take a taxi 6km to the border crossing and catch one of the seven daily trains from Nágylak, Hungary, to Szeged (1¼ hours).

To get to Hunedoara from Arad, you have to get a train to Deva and then take a bus from there to Hunedoara.

Arad is well served by trains to other destinations in Romania.

Car & Motorcycle The border crossing into Hungary is 52km west of Arad in Nădlac. This is the major road crossing from Romania into Hungary and it can get congested. It is open 24 hours. Nădlac has one hotel, the *Hotel Nădlac* (☎ 057-474 833) on the main road at Str Independenţei 32.

Getting Around

To/From the Airport TAROM operates a free shuttle bus from its office to Arad airport (☎ 255 706, 254 440). It departs one hour before flights are scheduled to take off.

Car Rental Hertz (☎ 192 211) has an office on Str Piatra Craiului (see Getting Around at the front of this book for prices).

TIMIŞOARA
• *area code* ☎ *056, pop 350,000*

Geographically out on a limb, Timişoara (pronounced 'Ti-mi-shwar-re'; known as Temesvár in Hungarian, Temeschburg in German) is often bypassed by travellers, yet for no good reason. Romania's fourth largest city has a soothing Mediterranean air, with outdoor cafés and regal, Habsburg-era buildings fronting its two main squares. Opera and drama thrive here, thanks in part to Timişoara's 10,000 university students.

Unlike other cities in the country, few Romanians have a bad word to say about Timişoara, dubbed the 'city of flowers' or the 'city of gardens' after the ring of pretty parks which surround it. Locals view themselves as being residents of Romania's 'Primul Oraş Liber' ('First Free Town'), for it was

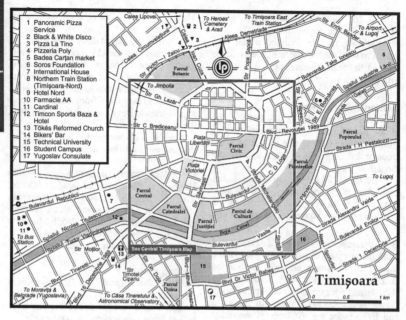

1	Panoramic Pizza Service
2	Black & White Disco
3	Pizza La Tino
4	Pizzeria Poly
5	Badea Carţan market
6	Soros Foundation
7	International House
8	Northern Train Station (Timişoara-Nord)
9	Hotel Nord
10	Farmacie AA
11	Cardinal
12	Timcon Sporta Baza & Hotel
13	Tökés Reformed Church
14	Bikers' Bar
15	Technical University
16	Student Campus
17	Yugoslav Consulate

Timişoara

here that protests in December 1989 ignited countrywide uprisings that eventually toppled Ceauşescu.

In part due to its proximity to Hungary, Timişoara is one of Romania's most developed cities. Timiş County, of which Timişoara is the administrative centre, is the richest agricultural area in Romania.

Orientation

Timişoara's northern train station (Timişoara-Nord) is just west of the city centre on Blvd Republicii. The left-luggage office at the train station is at the entrance to the underground passageway to the tracks, and is open 24 hours.

Timişoara's bus station is beside the Idsefin Market, three blocks from the train station. Take Str General Dragalina south to the canal, cross the bridge and head west to the next bridge.

Confusingly, some street names have changed although locals – and some street

signs and maps – still refer to them by their former names. Blvd C D Loga was formerly called Blvd Victoriei, and Piaţa Romanilor was formerly Piaţa Traian (the square is still marked on all trams as Piaţa Traian).

Maps There is a tourist map in the city guide *What, When, Where Timişoara*. The guide is published every two months with text in English, German, French, Italian and Hungarian, and is sold in kiosks and hotels for US$1.20.

Information

Tourist Offices Cardinal (☎ 191 911), at Blvd Republicii 6, is Timişoara's unofficial tourist office. It is open weekdays from 8 am to 6 pm, Saturday from 9 am to 1 pm; it has a second office around the corner from Hotel Nord on Str General Dragalina.

The Agenţie de Turism Banatul (☎ 191 907, 191 909; fax 191 913) at Str 1 Mai 2 arranges regional tours and stocks a stack of

Timişoara Trivia
- Timişoara will be briefly blacked out by a solar eclipse on 11 August 1999.
- MGM's original 'Tarzan the Apeman' was born in a Timişoara suburb.
- Frenchman Gustave Eiffel, who engineered Paris's Eiffel Tower, built a bridge over the city's Bega canal.
- Timişoara was the first European city to introduce horse-drawn trams (in 1869), and the first to sport electric street lighting (in 1889).
- The world record for drawing 'speed cartoons' is held by Romanian artist Ştefan Popa from Timişoara (he can draw 131 cartoons in one minute).
- Every October Timişoara hosts Romania's week-long, national beer festival. ■

free 1983 city maps. The office is open weekdays from 9 am to 5 pm, Saturday from 9 am to 1 pm.

The Automobil Clubul Român (ACR; ☎ 115 819) is at Str Hector 1.

Money Change money in any of the numerous currency exchanges or at Bancă Bucureşti (open weekdays from 10 am to 6 pm), next to the Expo complex on Str Popa Şapcă.

At Blvd Revoluţiei 1 opposite the Hotel Continental is Bancă Comercială Română where you can cash travellers' cheques and get cash advance on Visa/MasterCard. It is open weekdays from 8.30 am to noon and from 2 to 7 pm, Saturday from 9 am to 1 pm. The same services are offered by: Bancă Comercială Ion Ţiriac (BCIT) at Piaţa Unirii 3 (open weekdays from 8.30 am to 2.30 pm); BANCOREX opposite the Humanitas bookshop on Str 9 Mai (open weekdays from 8.30 am to 1.30 pm); and Bancă Agricola, close to Vila International on Blvd CD Loga (open weekdays from 9 am to noon). The currency exchange inside the Hotel Continental also gives cash advance on major credit cards; it operates weekdays from 8 am to 6 pm, Saturday from 8 am to 3 pm, and Sunday from 8 to 11 am.

Post & Communications The central post office is two blocks east of the Hotel Continental on Blvd Revoluţiei. It is open weekdays from 7 am to 8 pm, Saturday from 8 am to noon. If there are huge queues, try the smaller post office near the Hotel Banatul. It is open the same hours.

The central telephone office is just off Piaţa Victoriei on Blvd Mihai Eminescu. Faxes can also be sent and received here (fax 190 953): it costs US$0.50/1.50 per A4 page to send a fax within Romania/abroad and US$0.30/1 per A4 page to receive a fax from within Romania/abroad. The office is open daily from 7 am to 1 pm, and from 2 to 9 pm.

TNT Express (☎ 191 637, ext 2138, 2238; fax 191 637, ext 2238) has an office at Timişoara airport. For a downtown express mail service, try DHL (☎ 203 030, 195 408; fax 195 609) at Blvd Revoluţiei 21.

Emails can be sent free of charge from the Soros Foundation for an Open Society (Fundaţia Soros pentru o Societate Deschisă; ☎ 199 960, 221 471; fax 221 469; email staff @office.sorostm.ro; www.sorostm.ro) at Str Semenic 10. It is open weekdays from 10 am to 4 pm. You can get online access from the Internet provider, RC Team (☎ 201 271; fax 201 128; email rcteam@online.ro; www.online.ro) at Str Argeş 13.

Bookshops The Humanitas bookshop, Str Mercy 1, sells an outstanding range of English-language books about Romania, including a translation of the complete works of national poet Mihai Eminescu. The shop is open Monday to Saturday from 10 am to 7 pm, Sunday from 10 am to 2 pm.

The Librărie Universitatea, close by on Blvd Revoluţiei (open Monday to Thursday from 10 am to 6 pm, Friday from 9 am to 6 pm, Saturday from 9 am to 1 pm), and the Librărie Mihai Eminescu on Piaţa Victoriei (open weekdays from 9 am to 6 pm, Saturday from 9 am to 1 pm) stock a less exhaustive range.

English-language novels and reference books are also sold at Librărie Noi, open weekdays from 10 am to 6 pm, Saturday from 10 am to 2 pm.

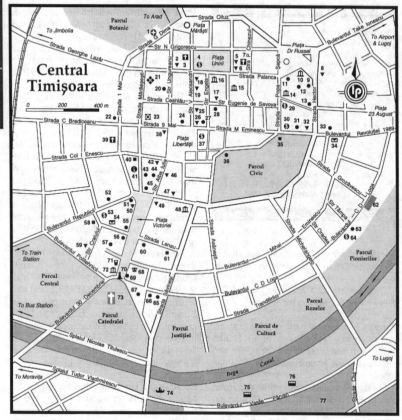

Central Timişoara

Libraries & Cultural Centres The following centres may be useful to visitors.

French Cultural Centre (Centrul Cultural Francez)
   Blvd C D Loga 46 (☎ 190 544, 190 445; fax 190 543)
British Council
   Str Paris 1 (☎ & fax 197 678)
International House
   Blvd Republicii 9 (☎ 193 886, ☎ & fax 190 593; email rodica@ihlctim.sorostm.ro)
German Democratic Forum (Demokratisches Forum der Deutschen)
   Str Gheorghe Lazăr 10-12 (☎ & fax 199 222)
Bulgarian Banat Unit
   Piaţa Unirii 14 (☎ & fax 190 697)

Democratic Union of Serbs
   Blvd Victor Babeş 14 (☎ & fax 191 754)

Medical Services The Farmacie on the corner of Piaţa Libertăţii and Str Vasile Alecsandri is open weekdays from 7.30 am to 7.30 pm, Saturday from 8.30 am to 1.30 pm. Farmado, at the southern end of Piaţa Victoriei is open every day from 9 am to 11 pm.

Opposite the central post office on Blvd Revoluţiei is Farmacie Remedia, open weekdays from 7 am to 7.30 pm, Saturday from 8 am to 3 pm.

PLACES TO STAY
35 Hotel Continental
40 Hotel Timişoara
58 Hotel Banatul
61 Hotel Central
62 Vila International

PLACES TO EAT
2   BM Croissant
5   Restaurant Unirea
6   Tiffany Restaurant
8   Crama & Berăria
    Bastion
17 Bochoris
18 Hamburger Plus
19 Extra Plus
25 Marele Zid Chinezesc
26 Aroma Cafea
32 Mike's
38 Restaurant Militar
42 N & Z
46 Universal Fast Food
47 Brasserie Opera
49 McDonald's
50 Restaurant Bulevard
59 Cina Restaurant

OTHER
1   Hospital
3   Serbian Church
4   Bancă Comercială
    Ion Ţiriac (BCIT)
7   Catholic Cathedral
9   Automobil Clubul
    Român (ACR)
10 Galerie Buzovar
11 Librărie Noi
12 Complex Expo
    Bastion
13 Dac Air; AIR MALEV
14 Ethnographic Museum
15 Galerie First
16 Art Museum;
    Prefecture Palace
20 Executăm Foto Grafi
21 Stil Supermarket
22 Central Market
23 Synagogue
24 Farmacie
27 Humanitas Bookshop
28 Yugoslav Airlines
    (JAT)
29 Bancă Bucureşti
30 Bancă Comercială
    Romnă
31 TAROM
33 Farmacie Remedia
34 Central Post Office
36 Librărie Universitaţea
37 BANCOREX
39 Greco-Catholic
    Church
41 Agenţie de Turism
    Banatul
43 Agenţie de Teatrala
44 German State Theatre
45 National Theatre &
    Opera
48 Huniades Palace;
    Banat Museum
51 Agenţie de Voiaj CFR
52 Cardinal
53 Currency Exchange
54 Post Office
55 Librărie Mihai
    Eminescu
56 Farmado
57 Kodak Express
60 Cinema Studio
63 French Cultural
    Centre
64 Bancă Agricola
65 Cinema Capitol
66 State Philharmonic
    Theatre
67 Outside Cinema
    (Cinema de Vară)
68 Telephone Office
69 Cinema Timiş
70 Memorial to Victims
    of 1989 Revolution
71 Violeta Bar
72 Galerie Helios
73 Metropolitan
    Cathedral
74 Clubul Dan
75 Terasa Eminescu
76 Strand
77 University

Piaţa Unirii

Lined with blue, amber and blazing-red buildings, Piaţa Unirii, in the heart of the old town, is Timişoara's most picturesque square. The east side of the square is dominated by the baroque 1754 **Roman Catholic Cathedral** (Catedrală Episcopală Romano-Catolică; ☎ 190 081). The main altar painting was completed by Michael Angelo Unterberger, director of the Fine Art Academy in Vienna. Competing for pride of place on the opposite side of the square is a **Serbian Orthodox Cathedral** (Biserica Ortodoxă Sârbă; ☎ 135 490), built the same year as its Catholic counterpart; the interior was painted by local Banat artist Constantin Daniel. People come from afar to fill their water bottles at a spring in front of the church. Sunday services are held in German, Hungarian and Romanian in the Catholic cathedral, and in Serb in the Orthodox one.

The **Trinity Column**, surrounded by a fountain in the centre of the square, was erected by the people of Timişoara at the end of the 18th century in thanks to God for allowing them to survive the plague which hit the town between 1738 and 1739. Overlooking the square to the south is the baroque **old prefecture palace** *(palatul vechii prefecture)*, also built in 1754 and currently being renovated to house an **art museum**.

From Piaţa Unirii, take a small detour and walk east down Str Palanca to the **Banat Ethnographic Museum**, Str Popa Şapcâ 8, housed in part of the city's remaining 18th century **bastion**, built by the Habsburgs. It is open daily, except Monday, from 10 am to 5 pm. Trade fairs and exhibitions are hosted at the **Bastion Exhibition Centre** (Expo complex) every month. In October a national beer festival is held here.

Two blocks west of the square at Str

Mărăşeşti 6 is Timişoara's **Great Synagogue**. It is one of three still functional in the town which has the second largest Jewish community in Romania.

Piaţa Libertăţii to Piaţa Victoriei

Walk south past the **town hall**, a monumental Baroque structure built in 1734 on the site of 17th century Turkish baths, to Piaţa Libertăţii. It was in this square that the leader of the 1514 peasant revolt, Gheorghe Doja, was tortured with red hot irons before being executed. Doja's peasant army, following an initial victory against a noble army led by Timişoara governor Stephen Báthory, was quickly quashed, captured and killed. Legend has it that upon Doja's public execution, his followers were forced to eat parts of his mutilated body as an appetiser before their own executions.

Continue along Str Lucian Blaga to the 14th century Huniades Palace, which houses the **Banat History Museum** (Muzeul Banatului; ☎ 191 339) at Piaţa Huniade 1. The significance of many of the exhibits is lost on foreigners as only Romanian captions are provided, but it's still worth visiting. Sadly there is no formal exhibition on the 1989 revolution but if you wander through the maze of corridors, you'll find boards, entitled 'Libertăţii', featuring a few photographs of people crowded around the opera house. The museum is open daily, except Monday, from 10 am to 4.30 pm. Admission is US$0.10.

The fortified **Huniades Palace** was built by the Hungarian king Carol Robert, Prince of Anjou, between 1307 and 1315. It was redesigned under the Habsburgs in the late 18th century.

From here head west to the marble 18th century **Opera House & National Theatre**, which looks straight down Piaţa Victoriei, a colourful pedestrian mall lined with shops and cafés. It was immediately in front of the opera house on this square that thousands of demonstrators gathered on 16 December 1989, following the siege on László Tökés' house the previous day. The 17 December marked Operation Timiş, which set out to crush the uprising that had begun the day before. Tanks rolled into Opera Square and fired on the crowd of thousands until it was reduced to no more than a few hundred. A memorial plaque on the front of the Opera house today reads: 'So you, who pass by this building, will dedicate a thought for free Romania'.

In attempts by Ceauşescu to hide the Timişoara bloodbath, many of the bodies of the revolution's early victims were smuggled from Timişoara mortuary to Bucharest where they were burnt. Striking factory workers joined bereaved relatives on **Piaţa Victoriei** in their demands for the government to return the bodies and publish lists of the hundreds arrested. Orders were once more issued to fire on the crowd. By 20 December the 100,000-strong crowd had taken over some tanks, and the army retreated. The bloodshed then spilled over to Bucharest.

At the south end of Piaţa Victoriei, there is a large wooden cross adorned with wreaths and flowers – a **memorial** to the victims of the 1989 revolution who died between 16 and 22 December. Behind the memorial cross towers the exotic Romanian Orthodox **Metropolitan Cathedral** built between 1936 and 1946. Eleven ornate spires decorated with green and yellow tiles in geometrical patterns top the majestic building which stands 83m tall. Unique to the church are its electrical bells, weighing 8000 kg and cast from iron imported from Indonesia. A collection of 16th to 19th century icons on wood and glass are displayed in the basement.

South of the Centre

The 1989 revolution began on 15 December 1989 at the **Tökés Reformed Church** (Biserica Reformată Tökés; ☎ 129 992), just off Blvd 16 Decembrie 1989 at Str Timotei Cipariu 1. Following attempts made by the Securitate to physically remove László Tökés and his wife from their family home above the church, several hundred ethnic Hungarians from the town formed a human chain around the building, joined over the next few days by several thousand ethnic

Romanians. Despite the human barrage outside, Securitate troops broke into the building, arrested the pair, and took them to the village of Mineu, 40km north of Zalău in Transylvania.

Daily services in Hungarian are still held here. The church upstairs on the 2nd floor is usually locked but someone in the office below may open it for you (leave a donation). The rest of the building is now apartments. Tökés' own small apartment is likewise privately inhabited.

Heading back into the centre, turn right at Blvd Vasile Pârvan along the south bank of the Bega canal. The **University of West Timişoara** (UWT; ☎ & fax 201 105) at Blvd Vasile Pârvan 4 is a vast modern complex, first established in 1944 and attracting some 10,000 students.

Two kilometres south of the centre, close to Casă Tineretului on Calea Martirilor, is Timişoara's **Astronomical Observatory** (Observatorul Astronomic). Hundreds are expected to gather here on 11 August 1999 to witness a total eclipse of the sun by the moon, an event that last occurred in 1961 and will not occur again until the year 2081. To get to the observatory, take tram No 8 from the northern train station to Calea Martirilor.

The **Banat Village Museum**, 6km from the centre in the Green Wood forest, exhibits some 20 monuments and more than 30 traditional peasant houses dating from the 19th century. The 43-acre open-air display, created in 1917, is on the site of an abandoned pheasant farm. It is open daily, except Monday, from 10 am to 6 pm. Take tram No 1 (black number) from the train station.

Timişoara's Martyr Memorials

Numerous memorial slabs for those from Timişoara who died in the 1989 December revolution are encrusted in walls on streets throughout town. Eight years on, most are still honoured with fresh flowers and lavish bouquets.

With the aid of public and private donations, a series of haunting sculptures has been built in Timişoara to create a memorial to the Timişoara martyrs.

Outside the Hotel Continental on Blvd Revoluţiei, stands the modernist bronze sculpture, **Evolution** (*Evoluţie*), symbolising an eternal knot.

On the corner of Str C Brediceanu and Str 9 Mai, outside Timişoara's Greco-Catholic church, is **The Target Man** (*Omul Ţintă*), a life-size bronze sculpture of a skeleton writhing in pain.

Opposite the entrance to the Hotel Central are **The Martyrs** (*Martirii*). A pile of faceless bodies lie stacked up, squashed to death. The larger-than-life corpses lie on a granite pedestal.

More conventional sculptures include the **Martyrs Fountain** (*Fântâna Martirilor*) behind Cinema Capitol on Blvd C D Loga near the Mihai Viteazul bridge; the **Young Heroes' Monument** (*Monumentul eroilor tineri*) in the small square opposite BANCOREX off Piaţa Libertătaţii; and the **Crying Church** (*Biserica plângătoare*) on Piaţa Kütti.

East of the centre, on Piaţa Traian, is **Freedom's Bell** (*Clopotul Libertăţii*), a massive stone bell. Take trolleybus No 11 or bus No 26 to Piaţa Traian (formerly Piaţa Romanilor).

Painfully haunting is **The Winner** (*Învingătorul*), sculpted by Bucharest artist Constantin Popovici. The angular bronze statue features the skeleton of a man, standing tall, with his right arm raised to the sky in victory. But his left arm and leg have been amputated, leaving the left side of his bottom resting on a crutch. A sculptor from Munich carved the minimalist **Opening** (*Deschidere*), comprising a doorway of two large, upright steel plates on which two simple crosses are embedded. It stands in the grounds of the youth palace (*casă tineretului*), 2km south of the centre on Calea Martirilor. Take tram No 8 from the northern train station.

Immediately following the first outbreak of violence in Timişoara on 16 December 1989, the press reported that 70,000 people had been killed and buried in mass graves in Timişoara's outskirts. Foreign journalists in Timişoara at the time were given guided tours of these supposed mass graves by army officers who claimed the bodies were revolution victims. It was clear however that the 21 corpses exhibited had undergone lengthy autopsy prior to burial, and it was later proven that the corpses displayed to journalists were those of simple peasants buried months before in what turned out to be a poor peoples' cemetery.

Many of the victims of the 1989 revolution are buried in the **Heroes' Cemetery** (Cimitirul Eroilor), inside the main city cemetery north of the centre on Calea Lipovei. The lines of graves are marked by identical black granite tombstones, each engraved with the name and age of the victim. Opposite the main entrance to the cemetery stands a giant mausoleum, made from white marble and granite, sheltering an **eternal flame to the unknown soldier**. It is open weekdays from 8 am to 8 pm, weekends from 8 am to 5 pm. Take trolleybus No 14 from Piaţa Mărăşti to the Cimitirul Eroilor stop on Calea Lipovei.

Activities

City dwellers make the most of the Bega canal which flows through the town to the south. Luxury swimming pools with landscaped sunbathing terraces and beer gardens line the length of the grubby black canal waters which are definitely no good for swimming in. Top of the range is the Strand complex (☎ 203 663), opposite the university at Str Vasile Pârvan 3. Entrance to the swimming pool is US$0.30; a bottle of beer and a cushioned sun lounge is less than US$1. The complex is open 24 hours; after 9 pm buy a pool ticket from the administration bureau – the white door on the left as you enter. The Terasa Eminescu (☎ 197 150) complex next door is a similar set-up except that it has pop music blaring at the poolside, attracting a younger crowd. Entrance is US$0.25 and it is open daily from 9 am to 7 pm. Close by is the elitist Clubul Dan canoeing club.

You can play tennis for US$1.20 an hour and swim at the Timcon Sporta Baza (☎ 193 089), adjoining the hotel at Splaiul Tudor

Vladimirescu 15a. The centre has canoes too, officially only for club members, but competent canoeists should be able to persuade the staff otherwise.

Language Courses

International House, Blvd Republicii 9 (☎ 193 886, ☎ & fax 190 593; email rodica @ihlctim.sorostm.ro) runs four and eight-week Romanian language courses. Hourly rates range from US$3.60 to US$8, depending on the number of students in the class. Private tuition is also available.

The university foreign language faculty (☎ & fax 201 105; email relint @mb.sorostm.ro) runs eight-week summer schools which include basic accommodation on the student campus.

Places to Stay

Camping The *Pădurea Verde* campsite is in the Green Wood forest on the opposite side of town from the northern train station (Timişoara-Nord). From the station catch tram No 1 (black number) and ask to be let off at the 'camping'. The route from the tram stop is unmarked – follow one of the trails leading through the forest. The site has 50 small cabins for US$3 per person, and tent camping is US$2 for two people. There's a small restaurant on the premises. It's open from June to mid-September.

Hotels – bottom end Timişoara's cheapest hotel is *Casă Tineretului* (☎ 162 419), the 'Youth House'. It's a large, modern building on Str Arieş about 2km south of the centre. Rooms with shared bath are US$6 per person. From the northern train station take tram No 8 to Calea Martirilor.

Timişoara's best value city-centre hotel is the surprisingly comfortable *Hotel Banatul* (☎ 191 903) which you pass on your approach from the train station to the centre at Blvd Republicii 5. First-class rooms in the adjoining annex were partially renovated in 1995 and are spotlessly clean, with a balcony overlooking the street, private modern bathroom with shower, and continuous hot water. Renovated singles/doubles are US$7/9 a

Tarzan

MGM's original *Tarzan the Ape Man* (1932) was born in Timişoara. Billed by the movie-makers as 'the only man in Hollywood who's natural in the flesh and can act without clothes', Johnny Weissmüller (1904-84) was a box-office hit.

The Romanian-born actor went on to make 11 more Tarzan movies which featured the not-so-bionic Jane, and the yodelling jungle-cry (not really Weissmüller but a mix of recorded animal sounds). MGM allegedly paid Weissmüller's wife US$10,000 to divorce him in a bid to appease lovestruck fans (Weissmüller married five times in all). In 1940 he was dropped by MGM and went on to shoot 16 *Jungle Jim* movies with Columbia before retiring in the 1950s.

Weissmüller was hot in the swimming stakes too. He was an Olympic gold medallist five times over in 1924 and 1928, and won 76 world and 52 national swimming titles during a sporting career that spanned five years. He later modelled swimwear.

Throughout his life, Timişoara's Tarzan never declared himself Romanian. His family left Romania in 1907 for the US and he consequently claimed Pennsylvania as his birthplace to ensure his eligibility for the Olympics. ■

night. The 'old' second-class rooms are also OK for US$5/7 a night. Staff at the reception speak English.

Hotel Nord (☎ 197 504), around the corner from Timişoara's northern train station at Str General Dragalina 47, has over-priced single/double rooms with shared bathrooms for US$14/23 a night; singles/doubles with private shower at US$15/25 a night. However heavy your pack is, don't be tempted to stay here; the trek into town is worth it!

The run-down *Timcon Hotel & Sporta Baza* (☎ 193 089), south-east of the centre at Str Tudor Vladimirescu 15a, has very basic rooms with shared bathrooms and cold water for US$2 a night.

Hotels – middle & top end The cheapest of the more expensive hotels is the small, 87-room *Hotel Central* (☎ 190 091; fax 190 096) at Str Lenau 6. It costs US$17/26 for a double room/apartment with private bath.

The modern, 11-storey *Hotel Timişoara* (☎ 198 854/56/57/58; ☎ & fax 199 450), behind the opera house at St 9 Mai 2, offers all the mod cons including a public relations/tourist office, casino, currency exchange, hairdresser, top class restaurant etc. Two/three-star doubles – which simply translates as older/more modern furnishings – are US$44/62.

Equally well adorned with facilities is the towering three-star *Hotel Continental* (☎ 134 144; fax 130 481), overlooking the Parcul Civic at Blvd Revoluţiei 3. It has 167 rooms and singles/doubles are US$53/65. It has a disco, casino, large terrace restaurant and café and American-style saloon.

Set on an attractive tree-lined avenue south of the centre is the four-star *Vila Inter-national* (☎ 199 339, 190 193; fax 190 194, 199 338) at Blvd C D Loga 4. It was origi-nally built as a villa for Ceauşescu and even today tends to attract a pretty elitist crowd. Its luxury three-room/two-room apartments cost US$91/80 for one person, followed by an additional US$3 for each additional guest. The restaurant is highly recommended if you can afford to pay western prices.

Places to Eat

Restaurants *Restaurantul Bulevard*, on Piaţa Victoriei opposite the opera, has an elegant indoor restaurant and less-formal terrace restaurant. It has long been considered one of the most distinguished places in town; if its delicious 'crisp on the outside and gloriously runny on the inside' caşcaval is anything to go by, then it well deserves its reputation. It is open daily from 10 am to 11 pm.

The *Restaurant Militar*, on the corner of Piaţa Libertăţii and Str 9 Mai, is run by the adjoining military academy. *N & Z*, just off Piaţa Libertăţii on Str Alba Iulia, serves typical Romanian dishes. Its menu is displayed in pictures outside. A typical meal costs US$2. It is open daily from 10 am to 10 pm and is always packed.

The *Restaurant Unirea* and the *Tiffany Restaurant* are next door to each other at Piaţa Unirii 14. Both have tables and chairs and there is little to choose between the two. For a fully fledged dinner, Tiffany has the upper edge. Both are open daily from 9 am to after midnight.

Crowded with foreign tourists in summer is the *Crama Bastion* and *Berăria Bastion*, in a section of the city's 18th century fortifications on Str Popa Şapcă. The menu is nothing special but the interior is a real blast from the past and the beer garden is idyllic in summer. The restaurant is open daily from 10 am to midnight.

Restaurants specialising in international cuisine are also starting to sprout: highly recommended is the *Marele Zid Chinezesc* (Great Wall Chinese; ☎ 132 188), just off Piaţa Libertăţii at Str Alecsandri 2. If you go for one of the set menus, it's good value.

Leaning more towards Italy in its choice of cuisine is the *Horse Pizzeria*, tucked inside the bastion walls on Str Popa Şapcă. Its 17 different types of pizza come in two sizes – regular or mini. The salami and

caşcaval pizza for US$2 is excellent. Spaghetti and salad are also available. The restaurant is open daily from 10 am to midnight.

North-west of the centre on Calea Lipovei there is a cluster of pizza places. The *Pizzeria La Tino* next to the Black & White disco, and the *Pizzeria Poly* next to the railway bridge, are both upmarket restaurants serving a huge variety of pizzas starting at US$1. The Poly pizzeria has a number of vegetarian choices as well as a 'pizza dessert', topped with nuts, cherries, bananas and other fruits. Both are open until late. The *Panoramic Pizza Service* (☎ 127 776, 195 157), on the corner of Calea Lipovei and Calea Torontalului has a delivery service.

South of the centre, overlooking the Bega canal along Str Vasile Pârvan, is the luxury *Restaurant Cessena* (☎ 203 663), inside the Strand swimming pool complex. It is open daily from 9 to 1 am.

Cafés There are plenty of terrace cafés to choose from in the centre. The *Aroma Cafea*, on the corner of Str Alecsandri and Piaţa Libertăţii, stocks a good range of pizzas, pastries and other lights snacks (open weekdays from 8 am to 10 pm, and weekends from 10 am to 8 pm).

The *Brasserie Opera*, close to the opera house on the corner of Blvd Republicii and Str Alba Iulia, is an upmarket terrace café with a fine view of McDonald's opposite. It has a small menu offering pizzas for US$2 and is open daily from 10 am to 11 pm.

If you want to get into the local student scene, try hanging out at the *university café*, next to the library in the main university building, south of the river at Blvd Vasile Pârvan 4.

For dirt-cheap food try the *Cantină Complex CFR*, near the bus station at Str General Dragalina 37a. It is open daily from 8 am to 9 pm.

Fast Food *Hamburger Plus* and *Extra Plus* are next to each other on Str Alecsandri. Both sell a variety of mushroom, Mexican, cheese and enchilada burgers, starting at US$0.50.

They are open daily, except Monday, from 9 am to 9 pm.

Mike's, opposite the Hotel Continental on Blvd Revoluţiei, doles out shakes, burgers and fries 24 hours a day. It has a café and takeaway patisserie next door and a little play area for the kids.

McDonald's is on Piaţa Victoriei. At Str Alba Iulia 7 is *Universal Fast Food*, serving an inspiring range of salads and sandwiches. It's open weekdays from 8 am to 9 pm, Saturday from 10 am to 9 pm.

Self-Catering The 24-hour *Stil* supermarket at Str Mărăşeşti 10 stocks an impressive array of imported and local products. It even has western-style trolleys. The smell alone recommends nearby *BM Croissant*, at Str Ungureanu 10, an honest-to-goodness bakery with fresh pastries and delicious fruit-filled croissants. Many items sell out by 10 am. It is open weekdays from 7 am to 8 pm, Saturday from 8 am to 2 pm.

Timişoara has a colourful produce *central market* on Str Brediceanu near the intersection of Str 9 Mai. The *Badea Carţan market*, east of the centre on the corner of Piaţa Badea Carţan and Blvd Take Ionescu, sells domestic products and lots of fruit.

Entertainment

Cinema Timişoara has no less than seven or eight cinemas, all of which screen films in their original language (generally English) with Romanian subtitles. Cinemas in the centre include the *Cinema Studio*, next to Hotel Central at Str Lenau; *Cinema Timiş* on Piaţa Victoriei; and the popular *Cinema Capitol*, next to the state philharmonic theatre on Blvd CD Loga. Tickets for all the cinemas cost US$0.70. Most have four or five screenings a day.

The city sports an outside cinema too – the *Cinema de Vară* – which is far more fun! Its entrance – two large green wooden gates – is on the corner of Blvd CD Loga and Str 20 Decembrie 1989. Tickets for the daily screening at 9.30 pm are US$0.70.

Bars & Clubs Most people hang out at night in the terrace cafés on Piaţa Victoriei, downing bottles of the local *Timişoreana Pils* beer for around US$0.50 a bottle. The *Violeta Bar* at the south end of the square is particularly popular.

The Greek bar *Bochoris* at Str Eugeniu de Savoya 8 has to be one of the coolest bars in town. Its modern, minimalist decor attracts students in droves, most of whom seem to play cards here during the day then drink awesome amounts of ouzo at night. It is open daily from 9 am until well into the morning; ouzo is only served after 11 pm.

Equally cool is the *Bikers' Bar*, close to the Tökés church at Str Moţilor 6. Its painted black walls are heavily decorated with bike parts, Iron Maiden posters and Harley Davidson shields brilliantly painted in fluorescent paint. Thankfully the music is not quite so 'in-your-face'. It is open daily from 2 pm to 4 am.

Discos From October to May there's a disco in the *Casă de Cultură a Studenţilor*, Blvd Tineretii 9. It's near the corner of Str General Dragalina, three blocks south of the train station. Tram No 1 passes this way.

North-west of the centre at the junction of Calea Lipovei and Calea Circumvalaţiunii is the hi-tech *Black & White* disco. It is open Monday to Thursday from 9 pm to 6 am, Friday and Saturday from 4 pm to 6 am. Trolleybus No 14 from Piaţa Mărăşti stops outside the disco, opposite the taxi rank.

Theatre & Classical Music Highly regarded throughout Romania is the repertoire of Timişoara's *National Theatre & Opera* (Teatrul Naţional şi Opera Română) on Piaţa Victoriei. Make sure you take a peek at Timişoara at night from the balcony during the interval. Tickets are sold at the Agenţie de Teatrală (☎ 134 660) at Str Mărăşeşti 2. It's open weekdays from 10 am to 1 pm, and at weekends from 5 to 7 pm. Tickets start at US$0.60.

Close by is the *German State Theatre* (Teatrul German de Stat; ☎ 201 291). The box office is inside the theatre on Str Alba Iulia, open weekdays from 10 am to 7 pm.

Classical concerts are held most evenings at the *State Philharmonic Theatre* (Filharmonia Banatul; ☎ 192 521, 195 012). Tickets costing US$1/0.50 for adults/students can be bought at the box office inside the philharmonic theatre on Blvd CD Loga or from the Agenţie de Teatrală on Str Mărăşeşti.

Some classical music concerts, folk dances and other traditional festivities are held on the *open air stage* in the beautiful, rose garden park, Parcul Rozelor, south of the town. The main entrance is one block south of Blvd CD Loga. These one-off events are generally advertised in the local press and on posters around town.

Getting There & Away

Air The TAROM office (☎ & fax 190 150, 132 876) is opposite Hotel Continental at Blvd Revoluţiei 3-5. It is open weekdays from 7 am to 1 pm and 3 to 7 pm, Saturday from 7 am to 1 pm, Sunday from 8 to 11 am. It has domestic flights daily, except Sunday, from Timişoara to Arad (US$50) and Bucharest (US$100).

DAC Air/MALEV fly twice daily on weekdays to Bucharest (US$40/80) and once daily on weekdays to Cluj (US$30/60). Tickets are sold at the DAC Air office (☎ 221 555; fax 221 556), Str Popa Şapcâ 1. It's open weekdays from 9 am to 8 pm, Saturday from 9 am to 1 pm.

Austrian Airlines has its office (☎ 190 320, 194 600; fax 194 605) inside the Vila International at Blvd C D Loga 44. It is open weekdays from 9 am to 5 pm.

Banat Air has an office inside the Hotel Timişoara (☎ 194 486, 194 487).

Bus Daily buses connect Timişoara to Békéscsaba, Baja and Szeged in Hungary, and Belgrade. Tickets are sold from window No 2 inside the bus station (☎ 194 411, 193 447) at the west end of Str Tudor Vladimirescu. There is also a weekly service to Budapest (eight hours, US$8).

Few towns within Romania are served by bus from Timişoara. Daily services include two buses to Târgu Jiu and one to Brad via Deva, and to Câmpeni.

From Timişoara, there are two buses weekly to Germany. Tickets are sold at the Erna Mayer Reisebüro (☎ 191 903) inside the Hotel Banatul.

Train All major train services depart from Timişoara's northern train station (Timişoara-Nord; ☎ 112 552, 193 806) at Str Gării 3. The Agenţie de Voiaj CFR office (☎ 191 889) for advance ticket sales is at Piaţa Victoriei 2, open weekdays from 8 am to 8 pm. International tickets are not sold at the train station.

Two daily express trains connect Timişoara with Belgrade (3¾ hours). It's also possible to reach Yugoslavia by taking a local train to the Romanian town of Jimbolia (one hour) and then a connecting train to Kikinda (19km). Two unreserved local trains also run daily from Timişoara to Vršac.

There are two daily trains from Timişoara to Budapest (4¾ hours).

Getting Around

To/From the Airport Timişoara airport (☎ 191 637) is 12.5km north-east from the centre on Calea Lugojului. TAROM runs a shuttle bus from its office on Blvd Revoluţiei. Bus No 26 which stops outside the Hotel Continental also goes to the airport.

Tram, Trolleybus & Bus Tickets costing US$0.11 for one journey are sold at kiosks next to tram and bus stops. All public transport runs between 4.45 am and 11.15 pm. Tram No 1 runs from the northern train station (Timişoara-Nord) to Piaţa Libertăţii, the Hotel Continental and the eastern train station (Timişoara-Est). Tram No 4 runs from the Hotel Continental to Piaţa Traian (Piaţa Romanilor). Trolleybus No 11 goes from Str Tineretului to the Metropolitan cathedral and the northern bus station.

Car Rental Avis (☎ 203 233) shares an office with TAROM at Blvd Revoluţiei 3-5.

Avis has a second office at Timişoara airport (☎ 203 234).

ACR (☎ 133 333; fax 201 200) at Str Hector 1 provides advice for motorists and is an agent for Eurodollar Rent-a-Car. The office is open daily, except Sunday, from 9 am to 7 pm.

BĂILE HERCULANE
* *area code ☎ 055, pop 6000*

Legend has it that Hercules bathed in the curative natural springs, still flowing today in the mountain spa resort of Băile Herculane. The first baths were built here by Roman legions following their invasion of Dacia. Inspired by the incredible healing powers of the springs, they named the resort *Ad Aquas Herculi Sacras*, meaning the 'Holy Water of Hercules'.

During the early 19th century Băile Herculane developed as a fashionable resort, attracting royal visits from the Habsburg Emperor Franz Joseph. Sadly, most of the grand hotels and baths dating from the Austro-Hungarian empire stand empty and neglected. Their regal exteriors have been given a lick of paint in recent years, creating the illusion of a thriving resort, but inside fungus grows on the damp-ridden walls. It remains doubtful whether sufficient cash will ever be found to restore the resort to its former glory.

Mount Domogled (1100m) towers over Băile Herculane to the west, dominating the Cerna valley in which the resort lies. The extensive forest reservation includes rare trees, turtles and butterflies, and has been protected since 1932.

Orientation
Băile Herculane lies either side of a road which follows the Cerna river. The train station is at the junction of the main Drobeta-Turnu Severin-Timişoara highway and the Băile Herculane turn-off.

The resort is split into three parts: the residential area is at the western end of the resort on Str Trandafirilor; the concrete blocks of the newer satellite resort are 2km east of the residential area, and the historic

centre is at the resort's most eastern end (8km from the train station).

Information
Tourist Offices The official Bîrou de Turism (☎ 560 454) is opposite the Hotel Apollo at Piaţa Hercules 5 but it's useless if you don't speak Romanian. Try the tourist office inside the Hotel Roman instead, where some of the staff speak English.

Money The currency exchange on the 3rd floor of the Hotel Roman is open weekdays from 10 am to 7 pm. You can cash travellers cheques at the Bancă Comercială Română, which is opposite the Hotel Apollo at Piaţa Hercules 4. It is open weekdays from 8 to 11.30 am and 1.30 to 8 pm, Saturday from 9 am to 1 pm.

Post & Communications There is a small post office in the historic centre at Str Cernei 14, open weekdays from 9 am to 5 pm. The central post and telephone office is next to the bus station on Str Izvorului, open weekdays from 8 am to 8 pm. There are no public cardphones in Băile Herculane.

Things to See
All the sights lie in the historic centre. Most of the Roman baths were destroyed during the Turkish and Austrian-Hungarian occupations. Some ancient Roman baths stand well preserved, however, in the **Roman Bath Museum** (Terma Română), inside the Hotel Roman at Str Română 1. The 2000-year-old baths were served by a natural spring in the side of the mountain. Today, the flow of the natural spring is channelled into the hotel's 2nd floor swimming pool instead. Hanging on the walls in one of the baths are replicas of engravings made by the Romans in praise to the Gods for curing their ills. The original stone engravings are displayed in a museum in Vienna. An original carving of Hercules in the rock face of one of the walls is thought to have formed an **altar to Hercules**.

Natural springs from which drinking water flows – believed to be good for stomach problems – are dotted throughout the historic centre. To the side of the hotel flows the **Hercules II spring** (Izvorul Hercules).

At Str Cernei 14 stands the resort's **central pavilion**, built during the 1800s by the Habsburgs as a casino and restaurant. Today it houses a few small shops and a **History Museum** (Muzeul de Istorie), open weekdays from 10 am to 8 pm, and at weekends from 10 am to 1 pm. Beside the steps leading up to the museum entrance stands a 200-year-old **Wellingtonia Gigantea tree**, famed for its enormous size. On the opposite side of the river stand the derelict **Austrian baths**.

Self-Pampering

Wallowing in a thermal bath or being pummelled into oblivion by a not-so-sexy masseur is all part and parcel of a stay in Băile Herculane. The crumbling old baths dating to 1821 inside the Hotel Apollo are officially only for those with a doctor's recommendation but it's worth asking anyway.

Seven kilometres east from the centre, along Str Română, there is an outside pool and thermal spring. The scenery alone along this road makes the hike worthwhile. In summer the pool is packed.

The Hotel Roman and the Hotel Afrodite both have thermal swimming pools which are open to non-guests (admission US$1).

Hiking & Climbing

Directly behind the Hotel Roman stands the **Brigands' Cave** (Peştera Haiducilor), overlooking the site of an old Roman road. It is named after the thieves who would hide in the cave, waiting for their prey to roll by. A path leads up to the cave from the hotel. A second path, marked by blue stripes, leads to the Grota cu Aburi, a 2.5km slog uphill. East of the cave, lies the **Munk natural spring** (izvorul Munk); from the centre a 3km trail marked by red stripes starting at the Brasseria Central at Str Izvorului 1 leads to it.

South-east of the resort, the **White Cross** (Cruca Alba) is a popular hike; the trail to the cross on the top of the hill is marked by

yellow stripes. It starts from Str 1 Mai next to the Hotel Cerna.

The rock face behind the Hotel Roman is popular with climbers in summer.

Places to Stay

Practically all the hotels in Băile Herculane have a costly, short-stay rate (one to three days) and a cheaper, long-stay rate (three to 21 days). All the prices listed below are short-stay rates. If you plan to stay longer, negotiate! Some of the top hotels get full in July and August; the resort dies from mid-September to mid-May.

Camping The *Sera de flori* campsite (☎ 560 929), at Str Castanilor 25, strategically located between the old and new resorts and close to the bus station, has two and four-bed bungalows overlooking the Cerna river. A bed costs US$4 a night; there are communal showers (cold water only) and toilets. It is open between May and October. It is also possible to pitch your tent by the *Motel Arjama*, a yellow-canopied building 3km north of the resort on the Băile Herculane-Caransebeş road.

Historic Centre Excellent value is the wonderfully regal *Hotel Apollo* (☎ 560 688, 560 494), built in 1824 to serve the prosperous Apollo baths dating to 1821. Basic but clean single/double rooms with private bathroom and TV cost US$5/8 a night. Hot water flows daily, except Sunday, from 7.30 to 8.30 am and 7 to 8 pm. The hotel overlooks the statue of Hercules at Piaţa Hercules 4.

Equally grand and slightly more upmarket is the two-star *Hotel Roman* (☎ 560 394, 560 390; fax 560 410), built in the side of the mountain on the site of a natural spring at Str Română 1 (see Things to See). Single/double rooms with cable TV, private bathroom and hot water daily from 7 am to midnight cost US$16/23. Traditional Romanian bands play in the hotel restaurant on Saturday evenings. Tickets cost US$1.20 at reception. Other facilities include a bowling alley, pool tables, swimming pool (US$1), sauna and gym.

Prior to 1989, Ceauşescu and his Party

friends stayed at the elitist *Vila Belvedere* (☎ 560 885; fax 560 884), close to the 19th century Austrian baths at Str Nicolae Stoica Hateg 46. The state protocol villa, as it was known then, is now a privately run, intimate hotel, open to anyone. It has three beautifully furnished doubles with private bathrooms for US$28, including breakfast. Its six apartments are huge and cost US$37.

The *Hotel Cerna* (☎ 560 436) at Str 1 Mai 1 has cheap single/double rooms for US$4/9. Bus No 1 from the train station stops outside. At the concrete-block *Hercules Hotel* (☎ 560 880; fax 560 454) at Str Izvorului 7, singles/doubles with private bathroom are US$9/11 a night.

Satellite Resort There is little difference between the three concrete monsters in the newer part of Băile Herculane. The 218-room *Hotel Afrodite* (☎ 560 730) at Str Complexelor 2 offers single/double rooms with private bathroom for US$9/11. A colour TV is an extra US$1 a night and hot water runs between 8 am and 8 pm. Identical prices are charged at the *Hotel Diana* (☎ 560 550) at Str Complexelor 1, although at the time of writing it was closed for repairs. The 210-room *Hotel Minerva* (☎ 560 770; fax 560 768) charges US$16/32 for singles/doubles.

The cheapest of the bunch is *Hotel Dacia* (☎ 560 819, 560 817), also at Str Complexelor 1. Double rooms cost US$12 and are often fully booked.

Places to Eat & Entertainment
Băile Herculane has few restaurants beyond those inside its hotels. The in-house restaurants of the Hotel Roman and the Villa Belvedere serve the best food – US$3 for a main meal without alcohol.

The *Brasseria Central*, next to the Diana III natural spring (izvorul Diana III) at Str Izvorul 1, is a small terrace café which plays

traditional music and gets packed in summer. There is a 24-hour *mini-market*, opposite the Dacia hotel in the new centre. Next door to it is the popular *Bar Cezar*. Further along Str Castanilor, towards the train station, is the *Restaurantul Bimbu*, serving a variety of Romanian dishes including its speciality, tripe soup.

The hottest nightspot in town is the *Brigand's Cave Club*, overlooking the river on Str Română. Youngsters also hang out at the *discoteca*, in the basement of the old central pavilion at Str Cernei 14.

Getting There & Away
Bus The small bus station (☎ 560 595) is between the old and new resorts on Str Castanilor. The only daily service is to Orşova; buses depart at 9 am, 1, 3 and 4.30 pm (40 minutes).

Train The train station is 5km south-west of the new resort. The Agenţie de Voiaj CFR (☎ 560 538) at Piaţa Hercules 5 is open weekdays from 8 am to 3 pm.

The two daily Bucharest-Belgrade trains stop at Băile Herculane which is on the main Timişoara-Bucharest line. Services from Băile Herculane include 12 trains daily to Orşova (35 minutes); 13 to Drobeta-Turnu Severin (40 minutes to 1¼ hours); 16 to Craiova (two to three hours) and Timişoara (3¼ hours); and 10 to Bucharest (five to six hours).

In summer there are two daily trains to Constanţa (6¾ hours).

Getting Around
Bus No 1 runs every half-hour from the train station to the new resort, stopping outside the mini-market, to Hotel Cerna (Str Cernei) and Hotel Apollo (Piaţa Hercules) and to the historic centre. Tickets costing US$0.10 are sold on the bus.

Maramureş

Maramureş, actually part of Transylvania, shares the same history as its southern neighbour, the major difference being that Dacian Maramureş was never conquered by the Romans, earning the region the title, 'land of the free Dacians'. This, coupled with its mountainous terrain which was unsuitable for agriculture, meant it remained unscathed by collectivisation in the 1940s and by systemisation in the 1980s. This accounts for Maramureş' unique ethnographical standing today.

The region, cut off by a natural fortress of mountains, remains largely untouched by the 20th century. Traditional gender roles are deeply embedded in family life where contraception, abortion and divorce are scarcely acknowledged. Social activities revolve around the tall-steepled, wooden village churches, dating from the 15th and 16th centuries. In Orthodox and Greco-Catholic churches alike, men still take their pews in front of the altar *(pronaos)*, while the wives take a backseat in the *naos*. Little boys sit on a balcony above the pronaos, peering down at their sisters lined up on benches in front of the men. At 16 years of age the girls are relegated to the back of the church along with other unmarried women, often outside in the cold. As in all Orthodox churches in Romania, women are not allowed at the altar. Many villages in the region have abandoned their ancestors' traditional places of worship for ungainly new concrete churches.

Traditional folk costumes are worn in most villages, although it is only on Sunday and special holidays that the colourful costumes, each bearing motifs typical to each village, are donned. The rest of the year, men set off for the fields in their sober-coloured, wide-bottomed trousers decorated with 30cm-wide leather belts, while women do their chores in coarse linen navy-blue or black skirts, and cardigans.

Industrialisation has touched some parts of Maramureş however, so travellers in

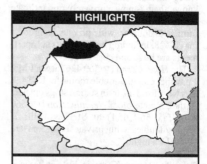

HIGHLIGHTS

- Drink *ţuică* (plum brandy) and eat strawberries at Ţurţ
- Tour the wooden churches: those in Surdeşti and Budeşti are among the best
- Visit the fascinating Merry Cemetery in Săpânţa
- Ride with lumberjacks on a steam train up the Vaser valley, and stay overnight in a forest cabana
- Learn about the communist purges of the 1950s at the museum inside the former communist prison at Sighetu Marmaţiei

search of days gone by may be disappointed. It is only further afield, in the Mara and Izei valleys, that medieval Maramureş truly comes alive.

Baia Mare and Satu Mare, the two main towns, offer few attractions and serve mainly as stepping stones to the region's more remote spots. Maramureş is practically impossible to explore without private transport.

History

Maramureş, with Sighetu Marmaţiei as its capital, was first attested in 1199. Hungary gradually exerted its rule over the region from the 13th century onwards. Tartar invasions of the Hungarian-dominated region continued well into the 17th and 18th centuries, the last battle being documented on the

Prislop pass in 1717. Numerous churches sprang up in Maramureş around this time to mark the Tartars' final withdrawal from the region.

Maramureş was annexed by Transylvania in the mid-16th century. In 1699 the Turks ceded Transylvania to the Austrian empire and it was not until 1918 that Maramureş, with the rest of Transylvania, was returned to Romania.

Between 1940 and 1944 the Maramureş region – along with the rest of northern Transylvania – fell under pro-Nazi Hungarian rule.

SATU MARE
* *area code ☎ 061, pop 130,000*

Satu Mare, meaning 'big village', has a large ethnic Hungarian population. Many shop signs are written in both Hungarian and Romanian, and many people still refer to the town by its former Hungarian name, Szatmar.

Orientation
Satu Mare can easily be covered on foot. The train and bus stations are adjacent to each other at the north end of Str Griviţei.

South of the centre, the Someş river crosses the town from east to west.

Maps The small map shop inside the BTT travel agency sells an excellent city map, published in 1994 in Romanian, Hungarian and German, with a comprehensive street register, for a mere US$0.11. Also worth picking up is its 1993 map of Satu Mare district *Judeţul Satu Mare* which includes a brief lowdown of the town's historic and tourist sights in Romanian, Hungarian and German, each described from a different historical perspective.

Information
Tourist Offices The BTT travel agency (☎ 737 915; fax 717 069) at Blvd Traian 7 is as good as – if not better than – any official tourist office. It sells maps, arranges tours and can also rent you a Dacia for around US$0.17 per km (it has other cars too). BTT

is also the official agent for ANTREC and arranges private accommodation in rural homes.

The efficient Agenţie de Turism inside the Hotel Dacia sells tickets for international buses from Bucharest and arranges tours of the region. It is open weekdays from 9 am to 5 pm.

Money The currency exchange inside the BTT office is open weekdays from 8 am to 5 pm, as is the Cambio currency exchange on the corner of Piaţa Libertăţii and Str Ţibleşolui. You can cash travellers cheques at the currency exchange inside the Trans-Europa travel agency next to the Hotel Aurora at Piaţa Libertăţii 11. It is open weekdays from 9 am to 5 pm, Saturday from 9 am to 1 pm.

For cash advance on Visa try Bancă Română on Str 25 Octombrie, open weekdays from 8.30 am to 1 pm. If you only have MasterCard go to BANCOREX on the corner of Piaţa 25 Octombrie and Str Mareşal Ion Antonescu; it is open weekdays from 8.30 am to 2 pm. Out of hours, get cash on Visa/MasterCard from the ATM outside the Bancă Comercială Română at Str Horea 8. The bank is open weekdays from 8 am to noon, Saturday from 9 am to 1 pm.

Post & Communications The central post office, at the southern end of Str 25 Octombrie, is open weekdays from 7 am to 8 pm. There is another post office on the corner of Str Mihai Viteazul and Str M Averescu, open weekdays from 7 am to 8 pm, Saturday from 8 am to noon. The telephone office, opposite BTT on Blvd Traian, is open the same hours as the central post office.

Medical Services There is a well stocked pharmacy, opposite the Hungarian Reformed church on the corner of Piaţa Păcii and Str Ştefan cel Mare, open weekdays from 8 am to 8 pm.

Things to See
Satu Mare's sights are centred on Piaţa Libertăţii. There is a large **art museum** on

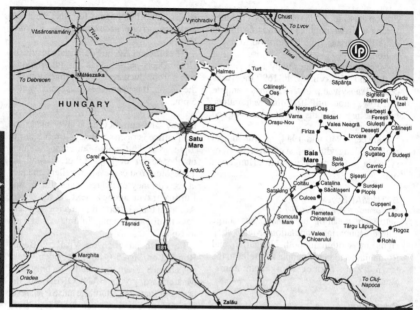

the corner of Str Cuza Vodă and Piaţa Libertăţii, open weekdays, except Monday, from 11 am to 6 pm, and weekends from 10 am to 2 pm.

From Piaţa Libertăţii, walk through the alleyway next to the Hotel Dacia, housed in the former **city hall and royal court** on the northern side of the square. Opposite the entrance to the **State Philharmonic** is the **Casă Memorială Erdós**, in which contemporary art and photographic exhibitions are hosted. It is open daily, except Monday, 9 am to 5 pm. Continuing north down the alley, you come to a small courtyard, in the centre of which stands a 45m-tall **fire tower** (turnul pompierilor), dating from 1904.

A **Roman Catholic Cathedral** lies on the east side of Piaţa Libertăţii. Building began on the cathedral in 1786; its two towers were added in 1837. It was badly damaged during WWII, and remained closed until 1961 when restoration was completed. Churchgoers are particularly proud of the cathedral's organ,

made in Budapest and bearing 57 registers and 4122 pipes. On Piaţa Pacii is the town's large **Hungarian Reformed Church**. In front of the church is a statue of Kölcsey Ferenc who founded the Hungarian school next door. Satu Mare's Orthodox community worship at the **Orthodox church** at the eastern end of Str 1 Decembrie 1918.

Prior to WWII, some 13,000 Jews lived in Satu Mare which boasted eight synagogues and a school. Most Jews were deported to death camps in 1944 and their synagogues destroyed, although the **Great Synagogue**, dating from 1920, is still in use today, serving Satu Mare's 200-strong Jewish community. A school – and seat of the community – (Comunitatea Eureilor; ☎ 711 823, 711 164) adjoins the synagogue.

In front of the Magazin Universal on Piaţa 25 Octombrie there is a **statue of Corneliu Coposu**, former president of the National Peasant Democratic Party (PNTCD) who spent 17 years as a political prisoner in com-

Maramureş

UKRAINE

▲ Farcău (1961m)

Bârsana
Strâmtura
Rozavlea
Bogdan Vodă   Vişeu de Sus
Botiza   Dragomireşti Moisei   Borşa
Ieud   Complex
                                  Turistic Borşa
Pietrosul
(2305m) ▲   Prislop
Tibleşu   Pass   To Vatra
(1840m) ▲   Dornei

Mountains

Someşul

munist prisons, including the one in Sighetu Marmaţiei. He died in 1995, one month after being awarded the Légion d'Honneur at the French embassy in Bucharest.

Satu Mare has a local **history museum** (☎ 737 626) at Blvd Vasile Lucaciu 21, open daily, except Monday, from 10 am to 5 pm. Admission is US$1.30.

Ardud Hungarian poet Petőfi Sándor (1823-49) married his wife Júlia Szendrey on 8 September 1847 in a small palace-chapel in Ardud, 18km south of Satu Mare. His wife was widowed less than two years later when Petőfi was killed during the battle of Albeşti.

One ruined pillar remains of the **Károlyi Palace** where the couple wed. Dating from 1730, it was destroyed in WWII. A monument in memory of the revolutionary poet has since been put up in the village.

Places to Stay
Camping *Steaua Nordului* (literally 'north

star'; ☎ 740 655), 6km north of Satu Mare on the road to Vama at Str Botizului 30, has two-bed cabins for US$5 a night. The restaurant and bar is open 24 hours. Bus No 32 runs here from Satu Mare centre.

Private Rooms BTT arranges accommodation in private rooms and dormitories in and around Satu Mare for around US$10 a night. Call in advance if you want a room.

Hotels The two-star *Hotel Sport* (☎ 712 959), a five minute walk from the centre at Str Minelului 25, has the cheapest rooms in town. Double rooms with shared bathroom are US$16 a night including breakfast. Unfortunately the hotel has no single rooms and is often fully booked.

The *Hotel Dacia* (☎ 714 276, 714 277; fax 715 774), at Piaţa Libertăţii 8, is a stylish building with rooms to match. Comfortable single/double rooms cost US$15/30 a night including breakfast. Its luxury apartments are US$42. The hotel reception rents out board games for bored guests and there is a casino which is open to non-guests.

Less prestigious, less luxurious, and more expensive is the modern, 201-room *Hotel Aurora* (☎ 714 199; fax 714 946) at Piaţa Libertăţii 11. Singles/doubles are US$18/28 a night and an apartment is US$42.

Out of Town The *Motel La Mircea* (☎ 761 847), 5km south of the centre at Str Lucian Blaga 330b, has a handful of double rooms to let for US$11 a night. It is primarily a 24 hour restaurant and cabaret, complete with topless dancers. Its rooms are mainly reserved for clients seeking more than a peaceful night's sleep. Avoid!

Places to Eat
Restaurants & Cafés Satu Mare's eating scene is yet to take off and it is the hotel restaurants that draw most diners. The *Restaurant Corso*, next to the Hotel Dacia on Piaţa Libertăţii, offers the typical soup, pork cutlet and salad menu. It accepts credit cards and is open daily from 7.30 am to 11 pm. Also serving local cuisine but in a sunny,

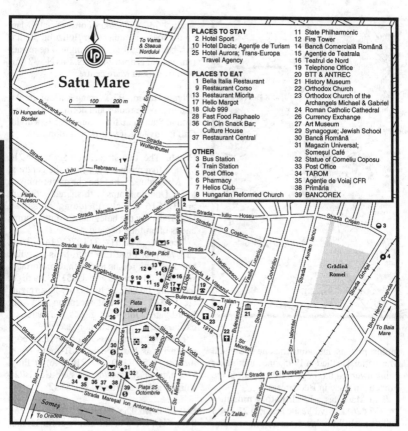

PLACES TO STAY
2 Hotel Sport
10 Hotel Dacia; Agenţie de Turism
25 Hotel Aurora; Trans-Europa Travel Agency

PLACES TO EAT
1 Bella Italia Restaurant
9 Restaurant Corso
13 Restaurant Mioriţa
17 Hello Margot
18 Club 999
28 Fast Food Raphaelo
36 Cin Cin Snack Bar; Culture House
37 Restaurant Central

OTHER
3 Bus Station
4 Train Station
5 Post Office
6 Pharmacy
7 Helios Club
8 Hungarian Reformed Church
11 State Philharmonic
12 Fire Tower
14 Bancă Comercială Română
15 Agenţie de Teatrala
16 Teatrul de Nord
19 Telephone Office
20 BTT & ANTREC
21 History Museum
22 Orthodox Church
23 Orthodox Church of the Archangels Michael & Gabriel
24 Roman Catholic Cathedral
26 Currency Exchange
27 Art Museum
29 Synagogue; Jewish School
30 Bancă Română
31 Magazin Universal; Someşul Café
32 Statue of Corneliu Coposu
33 Post Office
34 TAROM
35 Agenţie de Voiaj CFR
38 Primăria
39 BANCOREX

green environment is the outside *Moiriţa* terrace restaurant at Str Mihai Viteazul 5. Live bands play most nights; it is open daily from 8 am to 10 pm.

If you want to go Italian try the not-very-Italian *Bella Italia Restaurant* (☎ 712 053) at Str Ady Endre 10, open daily from 10 am to 10 pm. The Italianish *Cin Cin* snack bar, inside the culture house on Piaţa 25 Octombrie, serves pizza, pasta and good cappuccinos. It is open 24 hours.

Fast Food *Hello Margot* (☎ 716 691) at Str G Doja 1 sells fast food delights at stagger-ingly cheap prices. It is open daily from 10 am to midnight. Impressively clean and offering a fine array of lush pastries and ice cream is *Fast Food Raphaelo*, just off Piaţa Libertăţii on Str Cuza Vodă.

Entertainment
Posters advertising what's on where in the city – including discos, rave parties and the like – line the walls outside the state philharmonic building.

Bars & Discos The hippest spot in town at the time of writing was the *Helios Club*

(☎ 761 351) at Str Ştefan cel Mare 18. Music tends to be house and the club is open on Thursday, Friday and Saturday from 9 pm to 5 am.

Club 999, overlooking Piaţa Libertăţii on the corner of Blvd Traian and Str G Doja, is another popular spot; it has a restaurant and an outside café on the square.

Theatre & Classical Music The *State Philharmonic* (☎ 712 666, 712 616) is beside the Hotel Dacia, tucked in an alleyway at Piaţa Libertăţii 8. Plays in Romanian are performed at the *Teatrul de Nord* (☎ 715 876) at Str Horea 5. Tickets for both are sold opposite at the Agenţie de Teatrală (☎ 712 106), Str Horea 6. It's open weekdays from 10 am to 4.30 pm.

Getting There & Away

Air TAROM operates four weekly Satu Mare-Bucharest flights. Single/return tickets costing US$68/136 are sold at the TAROM office (☎ 721 785) at Piaţa 25 Octombrie 9. It's open Monday, Wednesday and Friday from 7 am to 6.45 pm, Tuesday and Thursday from 8 am to 6 pm.

Bus The bus station (☎ 732 039) is a 10 minute walk from the centre.

Buses to Hungary depart from outside the train station. Tickets are sold in the bus station. Buses to Budapest depart on Monday and Thursday at 6.30 am (single/ return US$7/12); to Nyíregyháza on Wednesday, Friday and Saturday at 4 am (single/return US$5/7); and to Debrecen on Tuesday at 4 am (US$6/8).

Trans-Europa sells tickets for buses from Bucharest to western Europe.

Local buses include 13 daily to Baia Mare (59km), one to Negreşti Oaş (50km), Oradea (133km) and Turţ (35km); and two to Sighetu Marmaţiei (122km).

Train The Agenţie de Voiaj CFR (☎ 731 240) at Piaţa 25 Octombrie, block 9, is open weekdays from 7 am to 7 pm.

The daily Baia Mare-Budapest train stops at Satu Mare at 2.05 am and arrives in Budapest at 8.13 am. In summer, the Constanţa-Kraków train departs from Satu Mare at 3.15 pm and arrives in Kraków at 4.56 am.

There are frequent trains to other destinations including Arad, Baia Mare, Braşov, Constanţa (summer only), Oradea and Timişoara.

Getting Around

To/From the Airport Satu Mare airport (☎ 730 990, 734 844) is 9km south of the city on the main Oradea-Satu Mare road. TAROM runs a shuttle bus to/from the airport. It leaves from the Str Mareşal Ion Antonescu bus stop, close to the TAROM office, one hour before flights are scheduled to leave.

Bicycle The Mountain Bike Shop, close to the philharmonic on Piaţa Libertăţii, has not yet caught onto the idea of bicycle rental but does repairs and sells spare parts. It is open weekdays from 10 am to 4 pm, Saturday from 10 am to 1 pm.

ŢARA OAŞULUI
area code ☎ 061

Ţara Oaşului, literally 'Land of Oaş', refers to the depression in the eastern part of Satu Mare district. The origin of the name is unclear although some say that Oaş is derived from the Hungarian word, 'vos', meaning 'iron', named after the supposed brutish, iron-like nature of the region's inhabitants.

Turţ

The northern village of Turţ (pronounced 'turts'), 27km north-east of Satu Mare, is home to Romania's finest **pălincă factory**, Fabrika Capşun. Since 1376, the factory has produced *pălincă* – a fiery plum brandy almost identical to traditional Romanian *ţuică* except that it is distilled more than three times. It also produces *capşun*, a marginally milder, strawberry liqueur. You can visit the factory and fill your empty bottle with *casă pălincă* – 52% proof – at the grey house, behind the blue house, 200m from the factory. Expect to pay about US$1 for half a

MARAMUREŞ

litre. If you visit the village in mid-June you can join in the strawberry harvest.

The factory is opposite strawberry fields (and the Peco petrol station which was being built at the time of writing), at the southern end of the village. To get to Turţ from Satu Mare, follow the northbound Budapest road to Turulung village. Turţ is signposted on the right just after the village.

Negreşti-Oaş & Around

Heading south-east from Turţ, through the lakeside **Călineşti-Oaş**, you come to Negreşti-Oaş. The main reason for stopping in this small village is to visit the **Open-Air Museum** (Muzeul satalui Oşenesc), signposted down a small street next to the Hotel Oşanul. Its small collection includes a traditional farm and pig sty from Moişeni, a wine press from Oraşu Nou, and a washing whirlpool and felting mill. Some people from the village freely use the water-powered whirlpool in the museum to wash their clothes. The museum is open week-days, except Monday, from 9 am to 5 pm, on Saturday from 9 am to 2 pm, and Sunday from 9 am to 5 am. Admission is US$0.30.

There is also a small **Oaş History Museum** (Muzeul Ţarii Oaşului) in the village, opposite the Hotel Rebecca on Str Victoriei. The museum was closed for reno-vation at the time of writing.

You can change money and get cash advance on Visa/MasterCard in Negreşti-Oaş at the Bancă Agricola, Str Victoriei 67, open weekdays from 8.30 am to noon; or at the Bancă Comercială Română opposite.

Four kilometres south of Negreşti-Oaş is **Vama**, traditionally a ceramics and pottery centre of which little evidence remains today. The village 'ceramika' store is now a 'magazin mixt' selling everything from second-hand coats to tins of canned vegeta-bles. **Valea Măriei**, 2.5km west of Vama is a small alpine resort offering accommodation.

Places to Stay & Eat

BTT in Satu Mare can arrange accommoda-tion in private homes in some villages in the Satu Mare district.

Accommodation in Călineşti-Oaş is the most idyllic. The *Popas Turistic Lacul Albastru*, 1km south-west of Călineşti-Oaş opposite Lake Albastru, has eight small four-bed bungalows for US$4 per person. It has communal showers and a small restau-rant/café/bar.

More upmarket is the luxurious *Cabana Călineşti-Oaş* (☎ 850 750), signposted on the right as you approach Lake Albastru from the south. It offers overpriced but clean, double and triple rooms for US$14 per person. Make sure you ask for a room with a lake view and balcony. The cabana does not serve breakfast and has no hot water.

Negreşti-Oaş has two hotels: the two-star, 102-bed *Hotel Oşanul* (☎ 851 162) at Str Victoriei 89 has shabby doubles for US$11 including breakfast. It also has luxury apart-ments for US$19. At the other end of the scale is the new, German-owned *Hotel Rebecca* (☎ 851 043, 851 411; fax 850 250) at Str Victoriei 75. A double room with private bathroom, TV, fridge and telephone costs US$30 a night, breakfast not included.

Heading north from Negreşti-Oaş towards Săpânta, you can pitch your tent at the *Cabana Sâmbra Oilor*, just south of the Huta pass on the border of the Satu Mare and Maramureş districts.

In Valea Măriei, 2.5km west of Vama, is the modern *Complex Pirita* (☎ 853 545). Double/triple/quad rooms with shared bath cost US$5.50/7/7 a night. Double rooms with private bath are US$7 and luxury apart-ments cost US$17. The complex has a restaurant and billiard bar. To reach the more attractive *Cabana Teilor* (☎ 851 329) and *Cabana Valea Măriei* (☎ 850 750), turn right along the forest track, immediately opposite the Complex Pirita. The Cabana Teilor, at the end of the left fork, has a tennis court, excel-lent restaurant and double rooms for US$10. The Cabana Valea Măriei, at the end of the right fork, has dirt-cheap doubles for US$1.40 a night per person. BTT in Satu Mare takes bookings for both cabanas.

Getting There & Away

There is one daily bus from Satu Mare,

departing at 6.30 am and arriving in Negreşti Oaş 1½ hours later, from where it continues to Turţ. The return bus heads back to Satu Mare immediately, making it impossible to visit these villages in a day by public transport.

BAIA MARE
• *area code* ☎ *062, pop 127,000*

Baia Mare (literally 'big mine'), at the foot of the Gutâi mountains, is the seat of Maramureş County. The town gained notoriety during Ceauşescu's regime as home to the Romplumb and Phoenix metallurgic plants which released more than five billion cubic metres of residual gases into the atmosphere each year, smothering the town with a permanent sulphur-dioxide/metal powder smog. In the early 1990s, a new smoke stack was built in an attempt to alleviate air pollution. The toxic smog might no longer be evident but smoke continues to belch from the chimneys on the outskirts of what remains the largest non-ferrous metal centre in the country.

Baia Mare was first documented in 1329 and developed as a goldmining town in the 14th and 15th centuries. In 1446 the town became the property of the Iancu de Hunedoara family. In 1469, under the rule of Hungarian king Matthias Corvinus (Iancu de Hunedoara's son), the town was fortified.

Orientation
The train and bus station, west of the centre on Str Gării, are a 15 minute walk from Piaţa Libertăţii, Baia Mare's central square. The Şasar rivers flows across the south of the town.

Maps The excellent *Ghidul Turistic al Judeţului Maramureş* (1997) is written in Romanian but includes a city map as well as a quality map of the Maramureş district. It costs US$3 and is sold at the Hotel Mara and at the mineral museum.

The map in the 1996 *Baia Mare Ghid Turistic* is larger and easier to follow. Its hotel, restaurant and useful addresses listings

are good too. It costs US$1 from the Nord Vest Agenţie de Turism at Hotel Carpaţi.

Information
Tourist Offices The Nord Vest Agenţie de Turism (☎ 414 812; fax 415 461) inside the Hotel Carpaţi at Str Minerva 16, arranges tours, sells maps and guides and is generally helpful. It is open weekdays from 9 am to 5 pm.

BTT (☎ & fax 412 162) has an office at Blvd Traian 8; none of its staff speak English.

Post & Communications The central post and telephone office at Blvd Bucureşti 9 is open weekdays from 7 am to 8 pm.

Money You can change money in the currency exchange opposite the Oaza Italiana restaurant on Str 22 Decembrie; it is open weekdays from 8 am to 9 pm. The currency exchange inside the TAROM office at Blvd Bucureşti 5 is open Monday to Thursday from 8 am to 5 pm, Friday from 2 to 6 pm.

You can cash travellers cheques and get cash advance on Visa/MasterCard at BANCOREX, Blvd Unirii 8; Bancă Agricola, Blvd Unirii 16; or Bancă Comercială Română, which is directly opposite at Blvd Unirii 15.

Laundry Bizarrely, Baia Mare has a dry cleaners. The Spălătorie Cicetib on Str Decebal is open weekdays from 9 am to 5 pm, Saturday from 8 am to 4 pm. It charges US$0.35 per shirt and US$1 per pair of trousers.

Things to See
Despite the town's largely industrial suburbs, charming quarters in the old town have been retained. Transylvanian prince Iancu de Hunedoara (János Hunyadi in Hungarian), who served as royal governor of Hungary between 1446 and 1453, lived in what is now a crumbling, 15th century house at Piaţa Libertăţii 18. In 1456 he successfully hammered the Turks on the banks of the Danube close to Belgrade, winning praise

MARAMUREŞ

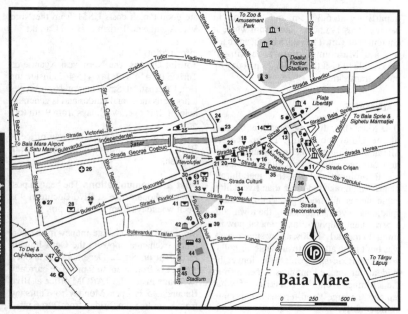

from Pope Pius II for his unearthly efforts. Hunedoara died of the plague in Belgrade that same year. His house, **Casă Iancu de Hunedoara**, today houses temporary exhibitions arranged by the local history museum.

Hunedoara's life story and that of Baia Mare is told in the local **History Museum** (Muzeul de Istorie; ☎ 411 927), just off the north-eastern end of the square at Str Monetăriei 1. The museum is open daily, except Monday, from 9 am to 5 pm.

Towering above the square is a 50m-tall stone tower, known as **Stephen's Tower** (Turnul Ştefan). The 14th century Gothic-style tower was initially topped with a bell which was replaced by a mechanical clock in 1628. Behind the tower, on Str 1 Mai, is the **Cathedral of the Holy Trinity** (Catedrală Sfântul Treime), close to the local **Art Museum** (Muzeul de Artă; ☎ 413 964) at Str 1 Mai 8.

If you continue south from the museum to

Str 22 Decembrie, you come to the **central market** around which lies the only remaining part of the 15th century city walls – the **Butchers' Tower** where famous brigand Gregore Pintea Viteazul was shot in 1703.

Heading north from Piaţa Libertăţii across the footbridge over the Şasar river, walk past the **Dealul Florilor Stadium** (Stadionul Dealul Florilor) where the Baia Mare football club plays and pop concerts are held. Open-air masses are often held on Sunday next to the WWI **Ostaşilor Română Monument** in the park. East of the stadium is the **Ethnographic Museum** (Muzeul Ethnografic; ☎ 412 845) in which all the traditional trades of the Maramureş region are represented.

An absolute must if you do not intend exploring Maramureş proper is the excellent **Village Museum** (Muzeul Satalui), behind the ethnographic museum. Tens upon tens of traditional wooden houses and churches for which the region is famed are exhibited in

PLACES TO STAY	OTHER	
13 Hotel Minerul	1 Village Museum	25 Agenţie de Voiaj
17 Hotel Maramureş	2 Ethnographic	CFR; Automobil
21 Hotel Bucureşti	Museum	Clubul Român
23 Hotel Carpaţi;	3 WWI Ostaşilor	(ACR)
Nord VestAgenţie	Română	26 Hospital
de Turism	Monument	27 Dry Cleaner
35 Motel Laguna	4 History Museum	28 Central Post Office
39 Hotel Mara	5 Puppet Theatre	30 Farmacie; Foto
45 Hotel Sport	6 Agenţie de Teatrul	Express
	7 Casă Iancu de	31 TAROM; Currency
PLACES TO EAT	Hunedoara	Exchange
16 Elite	8 Stephen's Tower	32 Post Office
18 Cofetăria Crinul	9 Cathedral of the	36 Market
20 Oaza Italiana	Holy Trinity	38 BANCOREX
24 Pizza Bar	10 Art Museum	40 BTT
29 Cocuşal de Aur	11 Butchers' Tower	41 Post Office
33 Restaurant	12 Teatrul Dramatic	42 Mineral Museum
Select	14 Post Office	43 Olympic Swimming
34 Cofetăria	15 Butoiasul cu Bere	Pool
Hollandeza	19 Statue of a Miner	44 Dacia Sports Hall
37 Perla Centre	22 Prefecture	46 Train Station
		47 Bus Station

MARAMUREŞ

this open-air museum, open between 15 May and 15 October daily, except Monday, from 10 am to 6 pm. Admission is US$0.30.

Baia Mare has a small **zoo** (☎ 416 998) adjoining an **amusement park** at Str Petőfi Sándor 28. It is open daily from 10 am to 7 pm; admission is US$0.40.

The city's uninspiring **Mineral Museum** (Muzeul de Mineralogie; ☎ 437 651) is at Blvd Traian 8. Close by is the **Jewish Cemetery**. There is a monument here to the Jews deported from Baia Mare to Auschwitz during WWII. Up until 1848, Jews were not allowed to live in the city because of a 17th century law forbidding them from settling in Hungarian mining towns.

Language Courses
The Fiatest Centru Educational (☎ & fax 437 050), Blvd Unirii 16, organises Romanian language courses. A one hour lesson for up to five people is around US$10 (for the whole class). The school also has branches in Bucharest, Braşov, Sibiu and Cluj-Napoca.

Places to Stay
Private Rooms ANTREC (☎ 433 593; fax 417 028) has a representative at Blvd Decebal, block 3, apartment 25. It can arrange rooms in private homes in Baia Mare and its surrounding villages for around US$10 a night, including a yummy home-cooked breakfast. Bookings can be made in advance through ANTREC's Bucharest office or abroad, through the Eurogîtes reservation system (see Facts for the Visitor at the front of this book).

Hotels Bang in the centre and cheap is the *Hotel Bucureşti* (☎ 416 301) overlooking Piaţa Revoluţiei at Str Culturii 4. Single rooms with TV and a private bathroom are US$13. Doubles – only available with shared bathrooms – are US$13. A luxury apartment with private bath and TV is US$22.

Overlooking Piaţa Libertăţii at No 7 is the equally run-down *Hotel Minerul* (☎ 416 056; fax 416 059). Overpriced single/double rooms are US$22/25.

The cheapest is *Hotel Sport* (☎ 434 900; fax 430 777), behind the southern stadium at Blvd Unirii 14a. A bed in a room is US$6 per person. The hotel has no baths or showers – just smelly communal toilets and sinks – and no hot water.

The most comfortable hotel in town is the

Romania's Robin Hood

Gregore Pintea Viteazul (literally 'the brave') is Romania's most famous *haiduc* (brigand). The unscrupulous outlaw who prowled the country's highways in the 17th century was a nobleman by birth who accumulated his wealth by robbing the poor. However, he fell in love with a simple peasant woman, and following her tragic death he was so broken-hearted he gave away all his riches and, henceforth, stole only from the rich to give to the poor.

In 1701 Austrian king Leopold I issued a reward for the capture of Pintea – dead or alive. But the cunning outlaw continued to slip through the authorities' fingers until 1703 when he was shot by nobles who, on the advice of a local witch, used a gold coin cut in quarters as bullets.

Romania's Robin Hood died instantly, leaving nothing but his undershirt, now housed in a simple Maramureş church in Budeşti, as testimony to his wilful ways. ■

three-star *Hotel Maramureş* (☎ 416 555; fax 432 582) at Str Gheorghe Şincai 37. Doubles with private bathroom, cable TV, lots of hot water and balcony are US$35. Larger, less atmospheric and not as well located is the *Hotel Mara* (☎ 436 660; fax 431 100) at Blvd Unirii 11. Single/double rooms with private bathrooms, TV and programmed hot water (check the hours at reception) are US$28/37 including breakfast. The hotel has a restaurant and bingo hall. Completely over-the-top in price is *Hotel Carpaţi* (☎ 414 8112; fax 415 461) at Str Minerva 16. Single/double rooms are US$65/75 a night including breakfast; doubles with 'matrimonial beds' cost more.

Motel Laguna (☎ 416 079) at Str 22 Decembrie 13 is a small, family-run hotel. It has 13 places in single and double rooms with private bathroom, costing US$8 per person. A nonstop nightclub is in the basement.

Out of Town Three kilometres north of the centre at Str Malinului 22 is the luxurious seven-room *Hotel Minion* (☎ & fax 417 056). Single/double rooms are US$15/30

including breakfast. To get to the hotel, follow the signs from Str Victoriei.

The *Baza Sportiva Apa Sărăte Simarad*, 7km north-west of Baia Mare, has disgustingly dirty double and four-bed rooms for US$4 per person. It also has a tennis court. Follow the signposts off the main road to Satu Mare. Cleaner and friendlier is *Apa Sărăte*, an attractive wooden house 200m further on. Double rooms here are US$7.

Places to Eat

Restaurants & Cafés *Oaza Italiana*, behind Hotel Bucureşti on Piaţa Revoluţiei, is one of the most popular restaurants in town. Its pizzas, starting at US$1.50, lack cheese and tomato sauce but are still a refreshing change from pork cutlet! Varieties include Hawaii, Deutschland and a 'you and me' pizza for two. The flashy *Pizza Bar* next to Hotel Carpaţi on Str Minerva is not as good; it's open daily from 8 am to 8 pm.

Next door to Oaza Italiana is the equally busy *Bucureşti Restaurant* which has a great terrace overlooking the fountains on Piaţa Revoluţiei. It serves spaghetti, soups and salads as well as scanty meat options. Its mămăligă is recommended. To the east end of Piaţa Revoluţiei is the old state establishment-style *Cofetăria Crinul* – dirt-cheap, quality not guaranteed. It's open daily from 7 am to 8 pm.

Elite, close to the Laguna motel at Str 22 Decembrie 20, is a small family-run restaurant; open daily from 10 am to 9 pm.

The southern end of Piaţa Libertăţii offers a couple of reasonable choices: the *Boema Café* is open daily from 7 am to 8 pm and serves soups, salads and the like. Next door is the *Restaurant & Patisserie Dunărea*, best for coffee and cakes. Behind this block, overlooking the cathedral, is a popular *Pizza Bar*.

Heading towards the bus and train stations, the *Cofetăria Hollandeza*, at the western end of Str Progresului adjoining a shop which sells goods imported from Holland, serves a small choice of snacks on its pretty terrace. A couple of blocks further west is *Restaurant Select*, a cheap place serving typical Romanian dishes. It is open daily from 9 am to 10 pm. *Cocuşal de Aur*, close to the bus and train stations on Blvd Bucureşti, is a modern, upmarket restaurant serving vaguely European cuisine.

Fast Food The *Perla Centre*, on the corner of Str Culturii and Str Progresului, sports a brightly lit, purple fast-food bar with 'point-and-order' service. Burgers and hot dogs cost around US$1. It's open daily from 10 am to 10 pm.

Self-Catering The central market is beneath the Butchers' Tower on the corner of Str 22 Decembrie and Str Vasile Alecsandri.

Entertainment
Cinema Baia Mare has two cinemas, both screening films in their original languages with Romanian subtitles. The *Minerul* (☎ 413 269) in the same block as the Hotel Minerul at Piaţa Libertăţii 6 has daily showings at 10 am, noon and 2 pm. Tickets are US$0.50. The *Dacia* (☎ 414 265) at Piaţa Revoluţiei 7 shows one film daily. There is a billboard advertising what's on where, next to the Cofetăria Crinul at the eastern end of Piaţa Revoluţiei.

Beer Bars The *Butoiasul cu Bere*, down a small alleyway at Str Gheorghe Şincai 9, is a traditional beer bar. The entrance is through the iron gates with part of a beer barrel embedded in them.

Theatre Plays are performed in Romanian at the *Teatrul Dramatic* (☎ 411 124) at Str Crişan 4. Tickets can be bought in advance at the Agenţie de Teatrul on the corner of Piaţa Libertăţii and Str Podul Viilor; it's open daily, except Monday, from 9 am to noon and from 4 to 6 pm.

Getting There & Away
Air TAROM operates four flights weekly between Baia Mare and Bucharest. The TAROM office in Baia Mare (☎ 411 624), at Blvd Bucureşti 5, is open weekdays from 7 am to 7 pm.

Bus The bus station (☎ 431 921) is next to the train station at Str Gării 2. The outlying villages are served by few buses from Baia Mare and your best bet is to head to Satu Mare or Sighetu Marmaţiei where buses are more frequent.

Daily bus services from Baia Mare include 13 daily to Satu Mare (59km); six to Sighetu Marmaţiei (65km), stopping at Baia Sprie (10km); one to Cluj-Napoca (152km); and two to Zalău (100km).

Train The train station (☎ 432 369) is 1km west of the centre at Str Gării 4. Advance tickets are sold at the Agenţie de Voiaj CFR (☎ 421 613), Str Victoriei 5-7.

There is one direct train daily between Baia Mare and Budapest (seven to eight hours) which departs from Baia Mare at 1.10 am.

Major train services include 10 trains daily to Satu Mare (one to 1¼ hours); one to Cluj-Napoca (5¼ hours); four to Braşov (8½ hours); two to Gheorgheni (5½ hours).

Getting Around
To/From the Airport The airport (☎ 412 299, 433 394), is 9km west of the centre at Tăuţi Măgherăus. TAROM runs a shuttle from its office. It departs from town 1½ hours before flights are scheduled to leave. It also meets incoming flights.

Car Rental The Nord Vest Agenţie de Turism inside Hotel Carpaţi rents self-drive and chauffeur-driven cars (see Information). There is also an Automobil Clubul Român (ACR) in the same office as the Agenţie de Voiaj CFR at Str Victoriei 5-7.

AROUND BAIA MARE
Baia Sprie
Baia Sprie, 10km east of Baia Mare, is a small mining town first chronicled in 1329. The mine still operates today, employing some 3000 people and mining approximately 156,000 tonnes of copper, lead and zinc ore annually.

A **roadside cross** stands at the foot of the track which leads to the mine. The modest cross is in memory of political prisoners who died in the mine during the communist purges of 1950-56. During this period hundreds of thousands of people were arrested for alleged anti-state activities. An estimated 180,000 people were interned in hard-labour camps such as those by the Danube-Black Sea canal, or in high-security prisons such as Piteşti, Gherla and Sighetu Marmaţiei. Between 1947 and 1964 some 200 to 300 political prisoners were committed to forced labour at the Baia Sprie mine, including Corneliu Coposu, secretary to National Peasant Party leader Iuliu Maniu who was himself imprisoned at Sighetu.

Entering from the west, Baia Sprie mine is signposted 'Exploatarea Minera' off Str Montana as you enter the centre of the village. The village church, bearing a traditional Maramureş tiled roof dating from 1793, is next to a monstrous new church in the centre. The church warden will happily unlock the new church for guests. A Chestnut Festival is held in the village each year.

Şurdeşti & Around

The towering **church** at Şurdeşti is one of the most magnificent in the Maramureş region and well worth the hike.

The tiny church's disproportionately giant church steeple is considered the tallest wooden structure in Europe – if not the world. The church was built in 1724 as a centre of worship for followers of the Greco-Catholic faith. It remains a Uniate church today, serving the 400 families who live in the village. Mass is held daily at 9 am. The entire interior of the church is original, down to the little boys' naughty etchings and names scratched in the church balcony especially reserved for them. The priest and his wife live in the house below the church; the priest's wife speaks a little French and will gladly open the church for you. The church is signposted 'monument' from the centre of the village.

Approaching Şurdeşti from Baia Sprie, you pass through **Şişeşti** village, home to the Vasile Lucaciu Memorial Museum (Muzeul Memorial Vasile Lucaciu). Vasile

Lucaciu (1835-1919) was appointed parish priest in 1885 and built a church for the village supposedly modelled on St Peter's in Rome (impossible to tell by looking at it). The church was ceremoniously named, and dedicated to, the Union of all Romanians (Unirii Tuturor Românilor).

The last wave of nomadic Tartar tribes from the Eurasian steppe settled in the mining town of **Cavnic**, 8km north of Şurdeşti, as late as 1717. A monument known as the Tartar stone stands in the centre of the small town, which was first documented in 1445. In 1952 and 1955, political prisoners were sent to the gold and silver mine here.

Heading north from Cavnic along the mountainous **Neteda Pass** (1040m) towards Sighetu Marmaţiei, you pass a small memorial plaque to those who died under the communist purges in the mines.

Two kilometres south of Şurdeşti in **Plopiş** is another fine church with a towering steeple crowned by four miniature spires. This is a feature of many of the churches in Maramureş. Ask for the key at the lone house nearby. Fourteen kilometres further south is **Lăschia**. Its church dates to 1861, and has a bulbous steeple. Note the motifs carved on the outer walls, which are like those traditionally used in carpets.

Baia Mare to Izvoare

North-east of Baia Mare a dirt road twists and turns its way through the remote villages of **Firiza**, **Blidari** and **Valea Neagră**, culminating 25km north of Baia Mare at Izvoare, where there are natural springs. Viewing churches is not on the agenda here; wallowing in the mountainous rural countryside dotted with delightful wooden cottages and ramshackle farms is.

Izvoare is dominated by pine forests and the rather ugly Statiunea Izvoare complex. The complex is closed between mid-June and mid-September when it is taken over by local schools as a summer holiday camp. The rest of the year it is business as usual. In winter a **ski lift** offers stunning aerial views of the fun **sculpture park** spread throughout the extensive grounds of the Izvoare cabana.

This route is not served by public transport, while hitching is a mission, simply because of the few vehicles that pass by. A five to six hour **hiking trail** marked by red triangles leads from Baia Mare to Izvoare; it starts some 3km north of Baia Mare along the Baia Mare-Izvoare road.

Places to Stay & Eat
Baia Sprie has one hotel in town, the upmarket *Motel Giesswein* (☎ 062-462 219) behind the Peco petrol station. It has two singles and eight doubles costing US$11/17 a night.

Out of town, the *Cabana Mistreţu*, overlooking a small lake amid trees, has three double rooms for US$3 per person. It also has a restaurant and bar which apparently hosts raunchy cabaret shows every so often – be warned! In summer, sunbathers swarm to the cabana and lake. To get to the cabana, follow the signposts to Chiuzbaia. It is 3km along this road.

Equally popular in summer – and winter – is the highly recommended *Staţiunea & Cabana Mogoşa* (☎ 062-460 800; fax 062-462 771), overlooking Lake Bodi at 731m. The cabana has single, double, triple or four-bed rooms with private bath and hot water costing US$6.50 per person. Campers can pitch their tents by the lake. In summer you can hire boats and swim in the lake. In winter you can rent skis; the chairlift and two ski lifts are open daily, except Monday, from 9 am to 4 pm. Cabana Mogoşa is 6km northeast of Baia Sprie. Follow the road to Sighetu Marmaţiei and turn right at the signpost for Mogoşa.

Less fancy is the *Complex Turistic Şuior* (☎ 062-460 842) about 1km further from the Cabana Magoşa along the same road. A bed in a basic double or four-bed room with shared bathroom is US$10. The complex has no running hot water, but it does have tennis courts, a ski lift, a handball court, bar and restaurant.

From Cavnic, the *Cabana Gutin Mina* is signposted 2.4km from the village. It has

seven rooms, costing US$7 per person a night.

In Firiza there is the clean and friendly *Motel Căprioara* (☎ 062-416 000, 437 676) which overlooks the lake. Double rooms with shared bath are US$9 a night; its one triple room costs US$10 and it has two luxury apartments with private bath for US$28.

ŢARA CHIOARULUI
The Ţara Chioarului in the south-west part of Maramureş county takes in the area immediately south of Baia Mare. The numerous villages, most of which boast traditional wooden churches, form a convenient loop – ideal for a two hour driving tour by private transport. Travellers relying on public transport will run out of patience long before they have visited even a quarter of Ţara Chioarului's ethnographic treasures.

Things to See
Follow the main road south from Baia Mare to Cluj-Napoca for 14km to **Satalung**. Three kilometres south of Satalung, take the unmarked turning on the left opposite the Cabana Stejarul to Finteuşu Mare and continue for 5km until you reach the village of **Posta**. At the top of the hill towers a small wooden church dating to 1675. Its surrounding cemetery is beautifully kept.

Şomcuta Mare, 24km south of Baia Mare, is the scene of the Stejarul ('oak tree') festival which takes place every year in July. The festival attracts bands, choirs and other music-makers from all over the region. The small **Vălenii Şomcutei Cave** (Peştera de la Vălenii Şomcutei), 4km away, is signposted from the centre of the village.

Nine kilometres south of Şomcuta lies **Valea Chioarului**, the most southern village in Ţara Chioarului. Its delightful and tall church stands next to the bus stop and a small café/bar in the centre of the village. Beside the church there is a bust of Mihail Viteazul looking like a Turkish sultan, put up by the village in 1994.

From Şomcuta a minor road winds its way to **Remetea Chioarului**, 12km north-east.

The tiny church, which dates to 1800, is the highlight of Ţara Chioarului. It stands majestically beside the village's extraordinarily ugly, seven-spired, modern church (built in 1996).

Culcea, some 5km north-west of here, has an unremarkable plastered church built in 1720 and extensively renovated in 1939. The church in **Săcălaşeni**, 2km further north, has a small church built in 1442, but sadly a modern church dominates the village. The traditional, wooden bell tower behind it is a nice touch.

From **Catalina**, head west 2km to the predominantly Hungarian village of **Coltău** (Koltó in Hungarian). Signs in the village remain bilingual. Hungary's most celebrated poet Petőfi Sándor (1823-49) lived in the village in 1847, prior to his leading the revolution against Habsburg domination of Hungary (1848-1849). He was killed in a battle at Albeşti, 4km north-east of Sighişoara in Transylvania. There is a small memorial house in the centre of Coltău where the revolutionary poet spent a few months. In the garden stands the giant 300-year-old cypress tree under which he sought inspiration.

Places to Stay & Eat

The rambling old *Motel Două Veveriţe*, 11km south of Baia Mare on the road to Cluj-Napoca, has an excellent terrace restaurant. At the time of writing its rooms were closed for renovation. The motel is 3km off the main road amid pine trees; it is signposted from the main road. Many campers pitch their tents for free next to the lake beside the main road, opposite the motel turn-off.

The *Cabana Stejarul* (☎ 062-481 245) 3km south of Satalung has old, wooden cabins for rent; the price is negotiable. The restaurant inside the main building – built to resemble a tree stump – is open 24 hours.

In Valea Chioarului, the *Popasul Mesteacăn* (☎ 062-483 295) has double and four-bed wooden cabins for US$10. Its large terrace restaurant and bar is also open 24 hours.

SIGHETU MARMAŢIEI
* *area code ☎ 062, pop 40,000*

Sighetu Marmaţiei is the northernmost town in Romania, lying on the confluence of the Tisa, Iza and Ronişoara rivers. Its name is derived from the Thracian and Dacian word *seget*, meaning 'fortress'.

Sighet (as it is known locally), a couple of kilometres from the Ukrainian border, is famed for its vibrant winter festival, and the peasant costumes notable in everyday life. Its dusty streets bustle with colourful markets, tucked beneath church domes of all denominations. Once a month families from the outlying villages make the long trip into town – piled high in horse-drawn carts with bottles in hands and playing violins – to wave off their boys to the army for one year's compulsory military service. Amid a sea of tears and drunken embraces, the young 18-year-olds clamber aboard the Bucharest train. Their spartan wooden suitcases are threaded through the train's windows as it lumbers out of Sighet station.

Sighetu Marmaţiei's former maximum-security prison is now open as a museum. Although little evidence remains today of the true horror it housed, it is a definite highlight of any visit to northern Romania.

Information

Tourist Offices The official tourist office (☎ 315 484; fax 312 815), Piaţa Libertăţii 21, runs a currency exchange and can – unofficially – rent you a car; price negotiable. The office is open weekdays from 8 am to 4 pm, Saturday from 9 am to 1 pm. For information about the area, however, the office is pretty useless. Your best bet is to hike 6km south to Vadu Izei where there is an excellent Agro-Tur office run by a young, dynamic and extremely knowledgeable team.

Post & Communications The post and telephone office is opposite the Maramureş Museum on Str Ioan Mihaly de Apşa (Str Bogdan Vodă). You can send faxes, email and access the Internet from the privately run Sighetu Business Centre (☎ & fax 313 887; email lazin@sintec.ro) in an apartment block

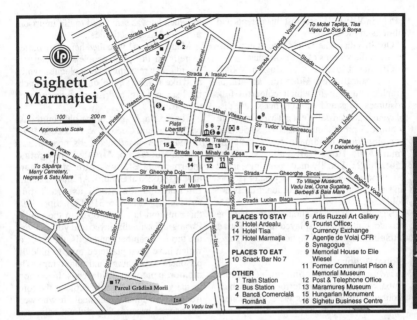

Sighetu Marmației

0   100   200 m

Approximate Scale

To Motel Teplița, Tisa
Vișeu De Sus & Borșa

To Săpânța
Merry Cemetery,
Negrești & Satu Mare

To Village Museum,
Vadu Izei, Ocna Șugatag,
Berbești & Baia Mare

Parcul Grădina Morii

To Vadu Izei

PLACES TO STAY	5 Artis Ruzzel Art Gallery
3 Hotel Ardealu	6 Tourist Office;
14 Hotel Tisa	Currency Exchange
17 Hotel Marmația	7 Agenție de Voiaj CFR
	8 Synagogue
PLACES TO EAT	9 Memorial House to Elie
10 Snack Bar No 7	Wiesel
	11 Former Communist Prison &
OTHER	Memorial Museum
1 Train Station	12 Post & Telephone Office
2 Bus Station	13 Maramureș Museum
4 Bancă Comercială	15 Hungarian Monument
Română	16 Sighetu Business Centre

at Str Independenței, block 2, stairway A, apartment 23. It costs US$0.75 to send an email or US$3 for 30 minutes online access. The centre opens weekdays from 7 am to 7 pm; weekends from 8 to 10 am.

Money There is a currency exchange inside the tourist office which is generally besieged by black market money changers. Ignore them. The Bancă Comercială Română, Str Iuliu Maniu, offers a better exchange rate and gives cash advance on Visa. The bank is open weekdays from 8.30 am to 12.30 pm.

Piața Libertății & Around
Sighet, first documented in 1328, was a strong cultural and political centre, being the birthplace of the Association for the Romanian Peoples' Culture, founded in 1863. On Piața Libertății is the **Hungarian Reformed Church**, built during the 15th century on the site of an 11th century Gothic-style church.

Close by is the **Roman Catholic Church**, constructed in the 16th century.

Just off the square at Str Bessarabia 10 is Sighet's only remaining **synagogue**. Prior to WWII there were eight synagogues serving a large Jewish community which made up 40% of the town's population, the highest proportion of any Hungarian town. Jews first settled in Sighet in the 17th century. A century later it became a centre for the Frankist sect which incorporated elements of Judaism, Islam and Catholicism in its religion.

The Jewish writer and 1986 Nobel Peace prize winner, Elie Wiesel, who coined the term 'Holocaust' was born in and later deported from Sighet. His house, on the corner of Str Dragoș Vodă and Str Tudor Vladimirescu, is now a **memorial museum**. Dubbed 'the survivor of the century', Wiesel wrote an autobiography, *La Nuit (The Night)*, which was the first account ever published of the horrors of the Nazi concentration camps in WWII. Wiesel lost his parents and siblings in the camps.

On Str Gheorghe Doja there is a **monument** to the victims of the Holocaust.

Off Piaţa Libertăţii at Str Bogdan Vodă 1 is the **Maramureş Museum**, an ethnographic museum in which colourful folk costumes, rugs and carnival masks are displayed. It is open daily, except Monday, from 9 am to 5 pm. Admission is US$0.50. For contemporary, handmade crafts visit the small **Artis Ruzzel** art gallery at Piaţa Libertăţii 21. Locally made paintings, icons on wood and glass, rugs, sheepskin jackets and other garments of traditional dress are sold here.

Serious art lovers should also visit the private collection displayed in the **Pipaş Museum**, 2km east of Sighet in Tisa Village.

Sighet Prison

In May 1947 the communist regime embarked on a reign of terror during which thousands of Romanians were imprisoned, tortured, killed or deported. While many leading figures from the prewar republic were sent to hard-labour camps, the regime's most feared intellectual opponents were interned in the maximum-security prison in Sighet. Between 1948 and 1952, about 180 members of Romania's prewar academic and government elite were rounded up and imprisoned here. Two-thirds of them were over the age of 60. It became known as the Ministers' Prison (Închisoarea Miniştrilor).

Today 12 white marble plaques cover the barred windows of the prison as testament to the prisoners' internment. The first four list the 51 prisoners who died in the Sighet cells, notably academic and head of the National Liberal Party (PNL) Constantin Brătianu; historian and leading member of the PNL Gheorghe Brătianu; the governor of the National Bank, Constantin Tătăranu; and Iuliu Maniu, president of the National Peasants' Party (PNT). Maniu's opposition party was outlawed in August 1947, following which the president was arrested. Maniu was – unlike most others interned at Sighet – tried in a spectacular communist show trial

in which he was sentenced to life imprisonment for 'fascist activities'.

Many of the 51 who died here were buried secretly in the poor people's cemetery in Cearda. The remaining eight plaques, which read like a 'Who's Who' of the former republic, list those Sighet prisoners who survived the torture.

The prison, housed in the old courthouse on Str Corneliu Coposu, was closed in 1974. In 1989 the abandoned cells opened as a private **Museum of Arrested Thoughts & International Study Centre of Totalitarianism** (Muzeu al Gândirii Arestate şi Centru Internaţional de Studii asupra Totalitarismului; ☎ 315 516, 314 480). Since 1997 this museum has been open to the public. Photographs are displayed and you can visit the torture chambers and cells, the walls of which have been plastered over to hide the prisoners' scratchings and engravings. The **memorial plaque** outside reads 'In memory of the young, intelligent people at the forefront of Romanian intellectual life who were imprisoned because they did not believe in communism and died, through torture, in this odious prison'. The museum is open daily, except Monday, from 9.30 am to 1 pm, and from 3 to 5 pm.

Village Museum

The traditional occupations of hunting, fishing, berry-picking – and, later, agriculture, forestry and sheep farming – are vividly portrayed in Sighet's outstanding open-air Village Museum (Muzeul Satului), signposted on the right as you approach the town from the south.

Traditional peasant houses from all over the Maramureş region have been reassembled in the museum, including the 17th century dwelling of the noble Berciu family from Călineşti. The three-room house, representative of peasant architecture, comprises a living room, an entrance hall and a cold room used for storing food. Constructed entirely from wood, the main structure is made from wide fir beams and the door and window frames are carved from ash wood. The wooden walls remain bare

Road through the Bicaz Gorges, Moldavia

Moldavia
Top: Autumn colours, eastern Carpathians
Bottom: Winter landscape, eastern Carpathians

inside with only the floor covered with clay. Most of the other typical houses displayed in the museum are made from oak. By the 19th century houses in the region had become larger with a fourth room being added. This enabled two brothers from Vadu Izei, upon inheriting their father's house, to saw it in half, right down the middle!

The museum is open daily, except Monday, from 10 am to 6 pm. Admission costs US$0.50 with an additional US$1.20 fee for cameras.

Places to Stay & Eat
Sighet has one central hotel, the *Hotel Tisa* (☎ 312 645) at Piaţa Libertăţii 8. It has 40 doubles, most of which have been renovated recently. A double with private bathroom, TV and telephone is US$21 a night, including breakfast.

The grotty *Hotel Ardealu* (☎ 312 172) opposite the train station on Str Iuliu Maniu, has a handful of basic single and double rooms with no bath, no shower and no hot water. There is a communal toilet and sink however. Beds cost US$3.

A short walk from the centre, overlooking Eminescu Park is the *Hotel Marmaţia* (☎ 512 241, 511 540; fax 515 484) at Str Mihai Eminescu 54. Singles/doubles with private bath are US$10/16 a night.

The upmarket, two-star *Motel Tepliţa* (☎ 513 174; fax 515 484), slightly out of town on the road to Borşa at Str Tepliţei 56, has four double rooms with private bath, TV and telephone for US$28 a night, including breakfast.

Cheap snacks and light meals are served at the fun *Snack Bar No 7* on Str Traian, a real eye-opener into the local scene.

Getting There & Away
Bus The bus station is opposite the train station on Str Gării. Local buses include six daily to Baia Mare (65km); two to Satu Mare (122km), Borşa and Ocna; five to Budeşti; three to Vişeu de Sus; and one to Bârsana, Botiza, Călineşti, Coştiui, Glod, Ieud, Mara, Săpânţa and Târgu Lăpuş.

Train Train tickets are sold in advance at the Agenţie de Voiaj CFR (☎ 512 66), close to the tourist office at Piaţa Libertăţii 25. It is open weekdays from 8 am to 6 pm. There are five trains daily to Vişeu de Jos (two hours), stopping at Petrova, Bocicoi and Tisa.

There are also two daily trains to Cluj-Napoca (six hours); and one to Bucharest (12 hours).

SĂPÂNŢA
• *area code* ☎ *062, pop 5000*
Săpânţa village, 12km north-west of Sighetu Marmaţiei, lies just 4km south of Ukraine. Locals pop across the border to shop but this border crossing is not open to foreigners.

The history of this strongly Orthodox, frontier village is brilliantly illustrated in the church cemetery, unique for the colourfully painted, wooden crosses – each bearing a humorous epitaph – that adorn the tombstones. Săpânţa's crosses have been shown in art exhibitions in London and Paris and attract coachloads of tourists every year. Yet this peasant village – so far – remains untouched by its fame. Villagers sit outside their cottages, fenceposts strung with colourful rugs and handwoven bags for sale, yet there is no hard sell.

Merry Cemetery
Săpânţa's Merry Cemetery (Cimitirul Vesel) was the creation of Ioan Stan Pătraş, a simple wood sculptor who, in 1935, started carving crosses from oak to mark graves in the church cemetery. He painted each cross in blue – the traditional colour of hope and freedom. On top of each he wrote a short, witty poem as an epitaph to the deceased. He composed these humorous and often cutting poems during the merrymaking which embraced the ritual three day wake.

Prior to his own death (aged 69) in 1977, Pătraş carved and painted his own cross, complete with a portrait of himself and a lengthy epitaph, covering both sides of the wooden cross, in which he speaks of the 'cross' he bore all his life, working to support his family since his father's death when he was 14 years old. Pătraş's grave is directly opposite the main entrance to the church.

Every cross tells a different story, and the painted pictures and inscriptions illustrate a wealth of traditional occupations. Shepherds tend their sheep, mothers cook for their families, barbers cut hair, and weavers bend over looms. An alcoholic is pictured swigging from a bottle, while others mark the grave of Ion Salflic, shot and decapitated by a 'bad Hungarian', and that of a soldier captured and imprisoned in a concentration camp during WWII and later shot and buried in a nearby forest in 1946. Newer crosses in the cemetery are distinguished by illustrations of car accidents.

Since Pătraş's death, Dumitru Pop, an apprentice under Pătraş since the age of nine, has carried on the colourful cross tradition. He lives and works in Patraş' former house and studio, using the same traditional methods of carving and painting. He makes about 10 each year depending on the mortality rate in the village. It is not yet known who will inherit the task after him; tradition demands that it is a man's job and Pop only has daughters.

The house and workshop where Pop lives and works is also a **museum**. In one small room, various pictures carved in wood and painted by Pătraş are displayed. These include portraits of members of the Executive Committee of the Communist Party, and a portrait of Nicolae and Elena Ceauşescu carved in honour of Ceauşescu's visit to Săpânţa in 1974.

Places to Stay

Camping Poieni, 3km south of Săpânţa, has two-bed wooden cabins for US$3 per person a night, including breakfast. Tents can also be pitched. The campsite is only open in summer.

MARA VALLEY

The Mara Valley (Valea Mara) lies in the heart of Maramureş proper. It takes its name from the Mara river which runs south-west through the valley from Sighetu Marmaţiei

to Baia-Mare. Villages here are famed for their spectacular churches.

Berbeşti

South of Sighetu Marmaţiei, and 6km south of Vadu Izei (see Izei Valley), you pass through the tiny village of Berbeşti. At the northern end of the village is a traditional *troiţă* (literally 'crucifix'); a large, Renaissance-style monumental cross carved with solar emblems which stands by the roadside. It is over 300 years old. Traditionally travellers prayed by the cross to ensure a safe journey, crossing themselves as they passed in their horse-drawn carts. During the 16th and 17th centuries, a troiţă was planted by most roadsides, a tradition that is today evident only in more rural areas. The belief that travelling is dangerous still remains and even in cities it is common for passengers to cross themselves for protection as the bus or train pulls out of the station.

Giuleşti

Continuing south from Berbeşti, bear right after **Fereşti** to Giuleşti, the main village in the Mara valley. It was to Giuleşti, in 1918, that the revolutionary poet Ilie Lazăr summoned delegates from all over Maramureş, prior to their signing Transylvania's Union agreement with Romania. Ilie Lazăr's house, built by Greco-Catholic priest Vasile Mihalyi in 1826, is preserved and open to tourists as a memorial museum. During the communist crackdown in the early 1950s, Ilie Lazăr was arrested for alleged anti-state activities and imprisoned at Sighet prison.

Delightfully untouched by the 20th century, Giuleşti is notable for its crumbling wooden cottages adorned with 'pot trees' in their front yards, on which a colourful array of pots and pans are put out to dry. Comically, cooking pots likewise adorn fences and gateposts and everything else that branches out.

Dwellings are simply numbered one to one hundred. Traditional sheepskin waistcoats, and jackets, handwoven rugs, saddlebags and tablecloths are sold at house No 9 (the small house adorned with the most pots and pans), tucked in the first bend on the right as you enter Giuleşti from the north. A heavy sheepskin jacket costs around US$42, a coarse saddlebag US$15, and a typical working waistcoat US$28.

Sat-Şugatag & Around

Seven kilometres south of Giuleşti is Sat-Şugatag, home to a recently repaired church dating from 1642, with interior paintings from 1783. A small altar around which services are held in summer stands in the large cemetery grounds. The church is famed for its fine, ornately carved wooden gate which appears on most promotional leaflets about Maramureş. Sat-Şugatag was first documented in 1360 as the property of Dragoş of Giuleşti.

One kilometre east of Sat Şugatag, is **Mănăstirea**. The church here was built by monks in 1633. By 1787 just one monk and four servants remained, and during the reign of Austro-Hungarian king Joseph II the monastery was closed. The original monks' cells lie on the northern side of the church, and a monk's grave is embedded in rock inside the church. Several 18th century icons on glass and wood have been preserved, as have some of the frescoes on the outside western wall of the church.

Three kilometres south of Mănăstirea is the small spa resort of **Ocna Şugatag**, built on top of a hill in 1321. The village is named after the former salt mine in the village which was exploited until the 1950s (*ocnă* translates as 'salt-mine').

Places to Stay Ocna Şugatag is the ideal base for exploring the Mara Valley. The large *Hotel Ocna Şugatag*, on the right as you enter the village from the north, has 35 double rooms with shared bath and no hot water for US$3 a night. It also has a handful of unheated wooden bungalows.

Better value are the modern, beautifully carved wooden bungalows in the centre of Ocna Şugatag at *Camping Trust Miron*. A four-bed bungalow is US$4 a night; the restaurant and summer garden are open daily from 10 am to 10 pm. The same company

also runs the modern *Trust Miron Restaurant & Motel* (☎ 062-436 015), signposted some 200m further along the road from the campsite. It has a swimming pool, sauna, restaurant and six comfortable double rooms with private bathrooms for US$10 a night.

Opposite the campsite, hidden behind trees, is the *Hotel Crăiasa* complex, complete with thermal pools, but at the time of writing the hotel was closed.

Hoteni

Nine kilometres south-east of Ocna Şugatag is Hoteni, famed for its Tânjaua de pe Mara Festival, a traditional folk festival held every year from 1 to 14 May to celebrate the first ploughing of spring. Twelve to 16 young men, known as *flăcăi*, put on their finest clothes then decorate the village bulls with flowers, leaves, ribbons and bells. They then lead them to the village's chosen ploughman whose duty it is to plough the first field. Once completed, the flăcăi take the ploughman home from the fields on their shoulders, circling his house three times before taking him to the *dărasca* – the nearest river or well – where they ritually bathe him. This is believed to stimulate the earth's fertility and ensure a good crop. The partying continues for two weeks.

Harniceşti

Four kilometres south of Ocna Şugatag is Harniceşti, home to a marvellous church dating from 1770. At the time of writing the Orthodox church, serving the 300 families living in the village, was under restoration. A footpath, signposted 'Spre Monument', leads from the primary school in the centre of the village to the hillside church.

Deseşti

This village is just a few kilometres south-west of Giuleşti on the road to Baia-Mare. In 1925 the tiny Orthodox church serving the 270 families in Deseşti was struck by lightning, destroying much of the outer walls and the steeple. It has since been repaired and fitted with a lightning conductor. The church was built in 1770 and its interior paintings, featuring biblical scenes and floral motifs, were painted by Radu Munteanu in 1780. At the time of writing the paintings were being restored.

Close to the church is an oak tree, hundreds of years old and measuring 6m in diameter. It has been preserved as a monument to the extensive oak forest that once covered the area before people felled the trees to build their homes.

Places to Stay & Eat At the time of writing, an agro-tourism scheme similar to that already operating in Vadu Izei, was being set up here. Contact the Vadu Izei branch to arrange accommodation in the Mara valley. A bed in a private home costs around US$10 a night, including a breakfast of eggs, jam, and milk straight from the cow.

Mara

Mara, just a couple of kilometres south of Deseşti, is best known for its elaborate wooden fences. Porches, architecturally unique to the Maramureş region, were originally designed to protect the dwellers of the house from evil. Positioned a short distance away from the house on the roadside, the porch marked the boundary between the sacred space of the house and the untidy public space. The pillars of the gate are carved with solar images and the tree of life (pomul vieţi), ensuring the house dwellers a long life.

In more recent times, the spiritual importance of the outside porch has been overridden by the increasing social status attached to it. In Vama, older porches dating from the 1770s are evident, but plenty of brashly decorated, modern gates have been built in the last 10 years. The tradition of carving the construction date, as well as the sculptor's name, into the gate still remains today.

Eastern Mara Valley

Heading south from Sighetu Marmaţiei, bear left at **Fereşti** along the dirt track leading to Maramureş' least accessible villages. Coming from Baia Mare, you can also approach this area through Cavnic, across the Neteda Pass. Unlike many other villages in Maramureş which are gradually abandoning their original churches and investing in modern, concrete ones, parishioners in these off-the-beaten-track spots remain staunchly faithful to the wooden churches where their ancestors also worshipped.

Corneşti, the first village along this stretch, has a small church dating from the 18th century with interior paintings by Hodor Toador.

Continuing 7km further south you come to **Călineşti**. In 1862 archaeologists uncovered a cache of bracelets and ankle chains here, believed to date from Roman times. Călineşti has two churches, known as Susani (sus meaning 'upper') and Josani (jos meaning 'lower'). Susani church, dating from 1683, is on the left side of the road as you enter the village from the north. However, the 'lower' church, built 20 years previously and dedicated to the birth of Christ, is more spectacular. To get to the church, turn right at the road for Bârsana and continue until you reach house No 385. A small path opposite this house twists and turns its way through apple orchards and across muddy fields to the church; follow the upper path when you come to the fork.

From Călineşti a mud track leads to **Sârbi**, inhabited since 1402. Its two churches are built from oak, as are most churches in Maramureş. The Susani church dates from 1667 with interior paintings by Al Ponehachile. Sârbi's Josani church dates from 1665.

Budeşti, 4km south of Sârbi, is one of the most untouched, beautiful villages in Maramureş. There is little to do or see except absorb the local scene but this alone makes a trip here rewarding. Josani church, built in 1643, features four small turrets surrounding the main steeple. Inside the church is a small collection of icons on glass and wood, dating from 1766. Its prize piece however is the painting of the Last Judgement, preserved in its entirety. This, and the other frescoes, were painted around 1762. The church also houses the undershirt of its most famous 17th century inhabitant, Gregore Pintea Viteazul.

The church allegedly bought the shirt from the local Romanian community in Budapest for 1000 forint. Outside the church there is a **memorial** to victims of the 1989 revolution.

IZEI VALLEY

The Izei Valley (Valea Izei) follows Iza river eastward from Vadu Izei, the main village in the valley, through to Moisei. Unlike other rural areas in Maramureş, tourism is gradually developing in this region, providing tourists with ample opportunity to indulge in some traditional cuisine, or try their hand at wood carving, wool weaving and glass painting.

In mid-July, Vadu Izei, together with the neighbouring villages of Botiza and Ieud, hosts the Maramuzical Festival, a lively four day international folk music festival. Guests stay in local homes or in tents.

Vadu Izei
* *area code ☎ 062, pop 6000*

Vadu Izei is situated on the confluence of the Iza and Mara rivers 6km south of Sighetu Marmaţiei. The village museum is in the oldest house in the village (1750). If you visit a private home in this region, you will quickly realise that little has changed since the 18th century.

Since the early 1990s, Vadu Izei has been supported by the Belgian charity Opération Villages Roumains, which originally started out as an international pressure group against Ceauşescu's systemisation program. Clothing, books and other supplies for the village school were donated to the tiny village which is today twinned with its Belgian sponsor village, Braine-le-Comte. More recently, the village gained financial backing from the EU's PHARE program to develop infrastructure.

The highly efficient village tourism society, Fundaţia Turistică Agro-Tur (☎ & fax 330 171), set up in 1994 with the help of Opération Villages Roumains, sells maps and guides of the region and can arrange for a local French or English-speaking guide to show you around for US$10 a day. It also sells local crafts. Its office, house No 161 at

the northern end of the village, is open irregular hours. If it's closed, contact Denisia Covrig (☎ 330 076) at house No 58 (English and French-speaking) or Petru Negrea (☎ 330 083) at house No 319 (French-speaking). Agro-Tur also arranges guided tours of Maramureş's wooden churches; picnics in the countryside; wood carving, icon painting and wool weaving workshops; traditional folk evenings; and fishing trips.

Places to Stay & Eat Agro-Tur (see above) also arranges accommodation in private homes. Some 20 families are involved in the scheme which offers bed and breakfast for US$10 a night. Half/full board is US$13/15 a night. Bookings can be made either through the Agro-Tur office in the centre of the village at house No 161, or directly at the homes involved. Some homes, such as that of Ana Iurca at No 333 (☎ 330 365), immediately on the left as you enter the village, are clearly signposted and welcome guests knocking at their door.

Bârsana

From Vadu Izei, bear left and continue for 12km through the village of **Onceşti**, whose 18th century church is today displayed in the village museum in Sighetu Marmaţiei, to Bârsana (formerly spelt Bîrsana). Dating from 1326, the village acquired its first church in 1720, the interior paintings of which were done by Hodor Toador from Vişeu de Jos and Ion Plohod from Dragomireşti. The Orthodox **Bârsana Monastery** (Mănăstirea Bârsana) is a popular pilgrimage spot in Maramureş. It was the last Orthodox monastery to be built in the region before Serafim Petrovai – head of the Orthodox church in Maramureş – suddenly converted to Greco-Catholicism in 1711. Following his declaration, a wave of conversions to Greco-Catholicism ensued in the region.

Rozavlea

Continuing south you pass through **Stâmtura** whose church (1661) was actually built in the neighbouring village of

Rozavlea, 11km south, and then transported to Stâmtura.

Rozavlea was first documented under the name of Gorzohaza in 1374. Its fine church, dedicated to the archangels Michael and Gabriel, was constructed between 1717 and 1720. It was built in another village then erected in Rozavlea on the site of an ancient church destroyed by the Tartars.

Botiza

From Rozavlea continue south for 3km to **Sieu**, then take the turn-off for Botiza. Botiza's old church, built in Vişeu de Jos and erected in Botiza in 1694, is today overshadowed by the giant new church constructed in 1974 to serve the 500 or so devout Orthodox families. The weekly Sunday morning service (9 am) is very much the major event of the week in Botiza. The entire village flocks to the church to partake in the religious activities which continue well into the afternoon. In the church calendar, however, Orthodox Easter is the most important feast of the year. In the pitch-black darkness of Easter Sunday morning, villagers file through the village to the church, each bearing a lit candle which continues to burn until dawn breaks a few hours later.

As in most remote villages in Maramureş, few children attend Botiza's local primary school. Most fail the final exam needed to enter secondary school in Sighetu Marmaţiei, simply because they spend the greater part of the school year helping their parents in the fields. The privileged few make it to Sighetu Marmaţiei, and later to university in Cluj-Napoca, Timişoara or Bucharest.

Places to Stay & Eat Villagers in Botiza, with the help of Belgian charity Opération Villages Roumains, have formed their own agro-tourism scheme. Half/full board in a local home is US$10/23 a night. The society is led by wealthy weaver, schoolteacher and wife of the local priest, Viktoria Berbecaru (☎ 062-334 991; ext 7 'casă preotului') who runs a small office from her home, the large white house next to the new church in the centre. She also sells bottles of home-made ţuică for US$1.20 and, if you ask politely, she is more than happy to give you some fresh bread and cheese for your onward journey.

Poienile Izei

From Botiza a track leads west to Poienile Izei, home to the most dramatic **frescoes** of hell you are ever likely to encounter. The church, with its 50cm-wide oak beams and thatched roof, was built in 1604. Its interior frescoes date from 1783 and remain magnificently intact today. They depict hell, symbolised by a ferocious bird waiting to swallow up sinners. Aboriginal-style paintings depict the various torments inflicted by the devil on sinners who fail to obey the extensive set of rules represented in the frescoes. The church is no longer in use but it is possible to visit; ask for the key at the priest's house – a large wooden house in the centre of the village with an ornately carved terrace and a 'status-symbol' porch. Four kilometres further north along the same dirt track is the village of **Glod**, the birthplace of the popular Maramureş folksinging duo, the Petreuş brothers.

Places to Stay A local agro-tourism scheme is still in its teething stages. Ask for the home of Ion Petreuş (not a band member) who heads the local agro-tourism group. Alternatively, approach the agro-tourism group in Botiza, staffed by French speakers who have details of the Poienile Izei scheme.

Ieud

The oldest wooden church in Maramureş (dating from 1364) is in Ieud, 6km south off the Sighetu Marmaţiei-Vişeu de Sus road. Children fill the dirt streets of this fervently Orthodox, highly traditional village in which century-old customs are still firmly intact today. Abortion is forbidden, divorce is a rare occurrence, and six to eight-children families are the norm. Between 1787 when the first marriage was registered and 1980, there were no divorces in the village.

Ieud (population 1200) was first documented in 1365 but evidence suggests the village was inhabited as early as the 11th century by Balc, Dragoş Vodă's grandson and later prince of Moldavia, who built himself a castle. In 1364 Ieud's fabulous Orthodox 'Church on the Hill' (Biserica de lemn din dal) was built on the castle ruins. Made from fir wood, it housed the first document known to be written in Romanian (1391-2), in which the catechism and church laws pertaining to Ieud were coded. The *Zborhicul de la Ieud* is now in the National Museum in Bucharest. The church was restored in 1958 and more recently in 1997. It is generally locked but you can get the key from the porter's house, distinguishable by a simple wooden gate opposite the *textile incaltaminte* in the centre of the village.

Ieud's second church *(Biserica de lemn din şes)*, today Greco-Catholic in denomination, was built in 1717 after Tartar troops withdrew from the region. The church is modelled on a cathedral, meaning it has no porch, unlike most other churches in the region. Few of its frescoes remain but it does house one of the largest collections of icons on glass found in Maramureş. The church is at the southern end of the village.

In 1945, some 250 young people from Ieud marched in protest through the region, prompted by fears that Maramureş would be annexed by Ukraine. Their banners read 'Ieud este în România' ('Ieud is in Romania').

Places to Stay Opération Villages Roumains runs a small agro-tourism scheme in Ieud. You can make advance bookings through the tourist office in Vadu Izei or go straight to the local representative, Gavrila Chindris, who lives at house No 665. A bed for the night starts at US$10, including breakfast.

Bogdan Vodă
The former village of Cuhea, 11km southwest of Vişeu de Jos, was renamed Bogdan Vodă in 1968 in honour of the Moldavian prince (1359-65) from Maramureş who marched south-east from Cuhea to found the

state of Moldavia in 1359. A statue of the great *voievode* (prince) is to be erected outside the village church, which was built in 1718. Some of the interior paintings in the pine wood church draw upon the traditional method of painting on linen, while others – Baroque in style – are painted directly on wood. A rope carved in wood is wrapped around the four sides of the church.

The church, dedicated to St Nicholas, is on the left as you enter the village from the north, opposite the *alimentara*.

Dragomireşti
Four kilometres south of Bogdan Vodă lies Dragomireşti, a village whose church (1722), in fine Maramureş fashion, was uprooted in 1936 and moved to the Village Museum in Bucharest.

At the time of writing, the churchless villagers were industriously building a new wooden church, on the same site. The new church is immediately on the left as you enter the village.

A further 4km east is **Săliştea de Sus**, which was first documented under the name Keethzeleste in 1365. It has two old churches, which date from 1680 and 1722, along with two new multi-spired, concrete churches.

Places to Stay Two kilometres east of Săliştea de Sus is the *Cabana Popasul Izei* which has 14 rooms and a campsite. A bed in the main building is US$8 a night. Rooms have a shared bathroom and there is no hot running water.

VIŞEU & VASER VALLEYS
The Vişeu valley (Valea Vişeu) which tracks the Vişeu river on its journey south is considered among the most picturesque in Maramureş, although there are few wooden churches along this route. A railway line also links this stretch, from Rona de Jos in the north to Borşa in the south, making it more accessible for travellers without private transport.

The twin villages of **Rona de Jos** and **Rona de Sus**, 19km south-east of Sighetu

Marmaţiei, lie just a couple of kilometres apart. Both boast churches, dating from 1793 and 1685 respectively. Continue south through the unremarkable **Petrova** and **Leordina**, and you eventually come to the spectacular logging village of Vişeu de Sus.

Vişeu de Sus

Vişeu de Sus is the main gateway to the Vaser valley through which the Vaser river flows. First chronicled in 1363, the town has always had a strong logging tradition.

Since the 1940s, following the construction of a narrow gauge railway from Vişeu de Sus into the Vaser valley, the wood has been brought down the mountain by steam train. Today, some 4000 cubic metres of fir wood *(brad)* is felled each month by the lumberjacks at the Vişeu de Sus logging plant. Each day at 7 am, a team of burly men is transported 43km up the valley to the logging camp in the forests at **Comanu**, close to the Ukrainian border. The felled wood is carted down the mountains by animals then loaded onto the train. Bears, stags, lynx and mountain cocks run wild here.

It is possible to ride with the lumberjacks along the forestry line which covers the 43km in around eight hours. The steam train stops at **Făina**, 32km north of Vişeu de Sus; **Halta Valea Babii** 6km further along the line; and **Comanu**.

At the time of writing the only hotel in Vişeu de Sus was closed, but there are basic cabanas where you can spend the night in Făina and Valea Babii. Further information is available from the Vişeu forest office (☎ 062-360 533, 360 534; fax 069-359 520) in Vişeu de Sus on the corner of Str 22 Decembrie and Str Iuliu Maniu (look for the sign with the green fir tree logo).

Getting There & Away The steam train departs from the depot at Gara CFR Vişeu weekdays at 7 am and returns with its load at around 8 pm.

Tickets costing US$0.50/0.75 to Făina/Comanu or Valea Babii are sold, an hour before departure, from the ticket office next

to the bright-green building at the Station CFR Fabrica, some 200m down the tracks from Gara CFR Vişeu. Photo passes valid for one week are also sold here for 20 DM, the proceeds of which go towards buying the workers' children Christmas presents.

To get to the wood factory and train station (☎ 052-353 533), turn left opposite the Vişeu forest office on the corner of Str 22 Decembrie and Str Iuliu Maniu and continue along this stone road for 2km. The wood factory *(fabrica de lemn)* and train station are on your left.

Moisei

Moisei lies 9km south-east of Vişeu de Sus, at the foot of the Rodna massif. A small town known for its traditional crafts and customs, Moisei gained fame in 1944 when retreating Hungarian (Horthyst) troops gunned down 31 people before setting fire to the entire village.

In 1944 following the news that the front was approaching Moisei, villagers started to flee, including those forced labour detachments stationed in the village. Occupying Hungarian forces organised a manhunt to track down the deserters. Thirty-one were captured and detained in a small camp in Vişeu de Sus without food or water for three weeks. On 14 October 1944 – just nine days before the region was freed from Hungarian occupation after the liberation of Satu Mare – Hungarian troops brought the 31 prisoners to a house in Moisei, locked them inside, then shot them through the windows. Before abandoning the village, the troops set it on fire, leaving all 125 remaining families homeless.

Only one house in Moisei survived the blaze; the one in which the prisoners were shot. Today, it houses a small **museum** (Expoziţia Documentar – Istorica Martirii de la Moisei 14 Octombrie 1944), in tribute to those who died in the massacre. Photographs of the 29 who died as well as the two who survived the bloodbath adorn its walls. Opposite the white cottage, on a hillock above the road and railways line, is a circular **monument** to the victims. The 12 upright columns symbolise the sun and light. Each column is decorated with a traditional carnival mask, except for two which bear human faces based on the real-life features of the two survivors.

The museum and monument are at the most eastern end of the village. If the museum is locked knock at the pink house next door and ask for the key.

Borşa

Ore has been mined at Borşa, 12km east of Moisei, since the mid-14th century. The area was colonised in 1777 by German miners from Slovakia; eight years later, Bavarian-Austrian miners known as 'gold washers' moved to Baia Borşa, 2km north-east of the town, to mine copper, lead and silver.

The Complex Turistic Borşa, a small ski resort and tourist complex 10km east of Borşa town proper, is a main entranceway to the **Rodna mountains**, part of which form the Pietrosul Rodnei Nature Reservation (5900 hectares). Hiking trails leading into the massif are listed inside the two-star *Hotel Ştibina* (☎ 062-343 466), Str Fântâna 23. Double rooms with private bath here cost US$24 a night.

In winter, you can ski down the 2030m-long ski-run in the complex. The ski lift (☎ 343 703, 344 442), Str Brâdet 10, is open daily from 7 am to 6 pm; ski hire is not available.

PRISLOP PASS

Hikers who do not wish to traverse the Rodna mountains into Transylvania can always opt for a trek from Borşa to the east across the Prislop Pass. Famed for its magnificent remoteness, the Prislop Pass is the main route from Maramureş into Moldavia. From Moldavia you can bear north-east to Câmpulung Moldovenesc and on to the monasteries of southern Bucovina; or south to the natural mineral water of Vatra Dornei and through to the fantastic Bicaz Lake (see Moldavia).

At 1416m, immediately before the pass proper, a roadside monument honours the site of the last Tartar invasion prior to their final flight from the region in 1717. Close to the monument stands the *Hanul Prislop*, site of the Hora de la Prislop, the major Maramureş festival, held every year in mid-August. The festival has its origins in a *nedeie*, a traditional sheep market. Today the *hora* – a round dance – is just another excuse for merrymaking with old friends from the surrounding villages. In keeping with the strong Maramureş tradition of folk dancing, the hora dancers stamp their feet, swing their upper body, and clap vigorously to the rhythm of a *ţâpurituri*, a chanted rhyme drummed out by three musicians on a traditional *zongora* (viola tuned in the key of A minus the C sharp), a *cetera* (shrill violin), and a *doba* (bongo made from fir or maple wood, covered with goat or sheep hide).

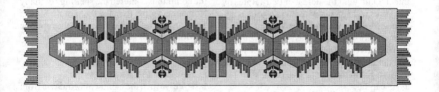

Moldavia

With its forest-clad hills and tranquil valleys, Moldavia rivals mighty Transylvania when it comes to rich folklore, natural beauty and turbulent history. Prince Bogdan won Moldavian independence from Hungary in 1359, after which the central part of the medieval principality, tucked away in the easily defended Carpathian foothills, became known as Bucovina (which means beech wood),

Only the southern part of Bucovina belongs to Romania today. It is famed for its fantastic medieval painted monasteries and attracts lots of tour groups.

History

Moldavia was the second medieval Romanian principality to secure independence from the Hungarians, providing refuge during the 18th century for thousands who were persecuted in neighbouring Transylvania which was still under Hungarian rule.

In 1359 disgruntled Maramureş prince, Bogdan of Cuhea, after years of conflict with the Hungarians, moved his centre of resistance to this region east of the Carpathians. A bloody battle against Hungarian forces in 1364-65 further secured Moldavian autonomy.

From Suceava, Ştefan cel Mare (Stephen the Great), called the 'Athlete of Christ' by Pope Pius VI, led the resistance against the Turks from 1457 to 1504. This prince and his son, Petru Rareş, erected more than 50 fortified monasteries and churches throughout Bucovina during their reign. Many have miraculously survived five centuries of war, often with their stunning exterior frescoes intact. Only with the defeat of Petru Rareş by the Turks in 1538 did Moldavia's golden age wane. Moldavia regained a measure of its former glory after it was united with the principality of Wallachia by Prince Alexandru Ioan Cuza in 1859 – when the modern Romanian state was born, with Iaşi as its capital.

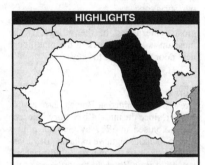

HIGHLIGHTS

- Trail the homes and meeting places of Romania's greatest literary heroes in Iaşi
- Hike through the Bicaz gorges; beware the 'neck of hell'
- Watch Nicolae Grigorescu's eyes watching you at Agapia monastery
- Marvel at the *Last Judgement* fresco at Voroneţ monastery, famed for its vibrant blue
- See how salt miners live and work in Cacica

Medieval Moldavia was much larger than the portion incorporated into Romania in 1859. It also included Bessarabia, the area east of the Prut River, which was conquered and claimed by Russia in 1812. Despite being recovered by Romania from 1918-40 and again between 1941-44, Bessarabia is now split between Ukraine and the republic of Moldova (see the Moldova chapter).

Confusingly, many Romanians refer to Moldavia as Moldova (the Slavic form of Moldavia), a legacy of the Stalinist era when the communists altered the spellings of many Romanian words to make them more Slavic. They always refer to Moldova as the republic of Moldova.

IAŞI
- *area code ☎ 032, pop 346,613*

Iaşi ('ee-yash'), the capital of Moldavia from

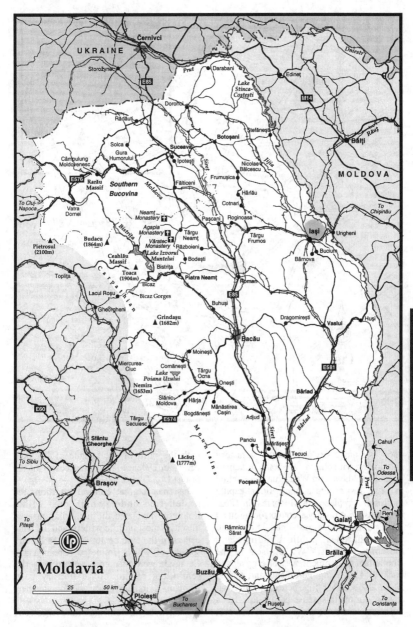

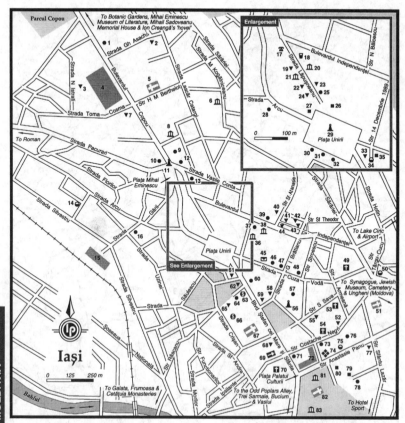

1565, is a university city, steeped in history and oozing with charm. When the principalities of Moldavia and Wallachia were united in 1859, Iaşi served as the national capital until it was replaced by Bucharest in 1862. This illustrious history accounts for the city's great monasteries, bust-lined streets and parks, churches, public buildings and museums. During WWI, the seat of the Romanian government was briefly moved back to Iaşi. King Ferdinand and Queen Marie also sought refuge here during the war. It was during this same period that Iaşi's notorious history of anti-Semitism took root

with the birth of the League of National Christian Defence – the predecessor of the fascist Iron Guard.

Iaşi has a great cultural tradition: the linden tree under which poet Mihai Eminescu meditated, the memorial houses of the city's most prolific writers, and the wine cellars of the 19th century Junimea literary society of which Eminescu, Creangă and Caragiale were members, remain powerful reminders of this city's literary past. Romania's first university was founded here in 1860.

Modern Iaşi is Romania's third largest city

PLACES TO STAY
26 Hotel Unirea
27 Hotel Traian
35 Hotel Continental; ANTREC
79 Hotel Orizont; BTT
80 Hotel Moldova

PLACES TO EAT
2 Monte Carlo
3 Cantină Titu Maiorescu
7 Casă Universatilor
19 Terasa Corsu
22 Grădină Iaşul; Brasserie
23 Ad Hoc
24 Restaurant Iaşul
33 Restaurant Select
40 Summertime & Anita Restaurants
41 Golden Sheep
42 Balta Reche
43 Sahla
44 Gülistan Mini-Restaurant
52 Pizzeria Italiana Cucina Casă Linga
55 Le Flagrant Délice
58 EuroParadis
59 Cofetăria Opera
61 Metro Restaurant
62 Gelaterie Bar Archelino; Centre Fast Food Brasserie
65 New Yorker
68 Metro Pizza
77 Scala Restaurant Complex; Disco

OTHER
1 French Cultural Centre
4 Alexandru Ioan Cuza University
5 Forty Saints Church
6 Mihail Kogălniceanu Museum
8 Pogor House Literary Museum; Club Junimea
9 Voievodes Statuary
10 University Library; British Council Library
11 Statue of Mihai Eminescu
12 Student Cultural House
13 University Library (Corpus B)
14 Bus Station
15 Train Station
16 Automobil Clubul Român (ACR)
17 Telephone Centre; Farmacon
18 Escape Jazz & Folk Club
20 Museum of the Union
21 Galerie de Artă
25 Cinema Republica
28 TAROM
30 Agenţie de Voiaj CFR
31 Cinema Victoria
29 Statue of Prince Alexandru Ioan Cuza
32 Junimea Bookshop
34 Taxi Rank
36 Theatre Museum
37 House of Vasile Alecsandri
38 Natural History Museum
39 Costache Ghica House
45 Post Office
46 Quick Foto
47 Pharmacy
48 Philharmonic
49 Golia Monastery
50 Bus to Lake Ciric
51 Bărboi Monastery
53 Armenian Church
54 Saint Sava's Monastery
56 Statue of Vasile Alecsandri
57 Vasile Alecsandri National Theatre
60 Central Supermarket
63 BANCOREX
64 Agenţie Opera
66 Bancă Comercială Ion Ţiriac (BCIT)
67 Moldavian Metropolitan Cathedral
69 Roman Catholic Church
70 Church of the Three Hierarchs
71 Apicola Shop
72 Civic Centre; Mayor's Palace
73 Icar Tours
74 Moldova Department Store
75 Taxi Rank
76 Central Market
78 Luceafărul Theatre
81 Dosoftei House; Museum of Old Moldavian Literature
82 Saint Nicolas' Royal Church
83 Palace of Culture

and its streets bustle with student life, a better-than-average choice of restaurants, bars and hot night spots. Each year the university hosts the National Mihai Eminescu Symposium. If you are coming to/from the republic of Moldova, Iaşi is an ideal place to break your journey en route to the monasteries of southern Bucovina or south to Galaţi and the Black Sea coast. The original town is said to have been built on seven hills, drawing on associations with Rome.

You will need at least two full days to see the main sights.

Orientation

To reach Piaţa Unirii from the train station, walk north-east along Str Gării two blocks, then turn right onto Str Arcu. From Piaţa Unirii, Blvd Ştefan cel Mare şi Sfânt runs south-east past the Moldavian Metropolitan Cathedral to the Palace of Culture. Or take tram Nos 3, 8, 9 or 11 to Piaţa Unirii.

To reach the left-luggage office at the train station (open 24 hours), turn right as you leave the station and walk to the adjacent 11-storey apartment building. Left luggage is below it, facing the parking lot.

Maps *Municipiul Iaşi* (Helios Publishing House, 1996) is the best city map. Some street names have since changed but it includes English texts on all the main sights. It is sold for US$0.50 in the shop inside the Palace of Culture.

Information

Tourist Offices Iaşi has no official tourist office but the tourism department (☎ 135 060) at Iaşi County Council plans to open an Info-Turism centre by summer 1998. In the meantime, visitors are welcome to call into their office, inside the Civic Centre (Centru Civic) at Blvd Ştefan cel Mare şi Sfânt 69; it is open weekdays from 9 am to 3 pm. Icar Tours (see Travel Agencies) is another good information source.

The Automobil Clubul Român (☎ 112 345), two blocks from the train station at Str Gării 13-15, assists motorists and sells a small selection of road maps of the region.

Money The IDM exchange inside the Select Restaurant, opposite Hotel Continental on Str Cuza Vodă, gives cash advance on Visa/MasterCard and cashes travellers cheques. It is open weekdays from 8 am to 8 pm, Saturday from 9 am to 1 pm. IDM also has exchanges inside the Victoria and Republica cinemas (see Entertainment – Cinema), in the Supercopou supermarket opposite Copou park on Blvd Copou, and at Iaşi Central Market.

There's a 24 hour currency exchange inside the Scala Restaurant complex (see Entertainment).

BANCOREX, at Blvd Ştefan cel Mare şi Sfânt 6, changes travellers cheques and gives cash advance on Visa/MasterCard weekdays from 8.30 am to 12.30 pm. BCIT, a couple of doors away at Blvd Ştefan cel Mare şi Sfânt 12, offers identical services and is open weekdays from 8.30 am to 1.30 pm.

Post & Communications The post office, close to Hotel Continental on Str Cuza Vodă, is open weekdays from 7 am to 8 pm, Saturday from 8 am to noon. Phonecards are sold at the telephone centre, opposite the Escape

jazz bar on Str Alexandru Lăpuşneanu. It's open daily from 7 am to 9 pm.

Emails can be sent and the Internet accessed from DNT Iaşi (☎ 252 936; fax 252 933; email info@dntis.ro; www.dntis.ro), a computer and communications centre set up by the Open Society Foundation (☎ 252 920; fax 252 926; email office@sorosis.ro; www.sorosis.ro/) at Str Moara de Foc 35, 7th floor. It costs US$1 for one hour online.

Travel Agencies Prospect Meridan (☎ 217 376; ☎ & fax 211 060), room 106, Hotel Continental, Str Cuza Vodă 4 arranges city tours around Iaşi and one/two day trips to Cotnari and the Bucovina monasteries. It also arranges accommodation in rural homesteads (see Places to Stay), fishing trips and picnics in the countryside.

The Agenţie Studenteasca de turism Totem, inside the Student Cultural House at Str Vasile Conta 30 (northern end of Piaţa Mihai Eminescu), is open weekdays from 9 am to 4.30 pm, Saturday from 9.30 am to noon. BTT (☎ 112 700; fax 215 037), inside the Hotel Orizont at Str Grigore Veche 27, is open weekdays from 8 am to 6 pm.

Icar Tours (☎ & fax 216 319), Str Costache Negri 43, sells tickets for international buses (departures only from Bucharest) and is an agent for Air Moldova International. Its staff are friendly, speak English and French and are the driving force behind the county council's bid to set up a real tourist office in town.

Bookshops The top bookshop in Iaşi (and Romania?) is the Junimea bookshop (☎ 114 664), Piaţa Unirii 4. It stocks an excellent range of maps, dictionaries and novels in English and French. It also sells Romanian history books and English-language journals covering social, political and cultural issues in Romania published by the Romanian Cultural Foundation (see Facts for the Visitor).

Most news kiosks on Piaţa Unirii sell the latest issues of *Time*, *The Economist* and *Newsweek*.

Libraries & Cultural Centres The main

building of the Mihai Eminescu University Library (Biblioteca Centrală Universitara Mihai Eminescu) is on the corner of Str Pacurari and Blvd Copou. At Str Pacurari 4 is the British Council library (☎ & fax 116 159).

The French Cultural Centre (Centre Culturel Français de Iaşi; ☎ 147 900; fax 211 026; email equipe@ccf.tuiasi.ro; www.ccf.tuiasi.ro), Blvd Copou 26, arranges film evenings, theatre workshops, and musical evenings. The library in the centre is open Monday to Thursday from 1 to 6 pm, Friday from 10 am to 6 pm, Saturday from 10 am to 1 pm. Opposite, at Blvd Copou 21, is the German Cultural Centre, closed for renovation.

A World Trade Centre will open on Str Anastasie Panu in 1999.

Media The *Iaşi Romania Tourist Guide* is a pocket-sized city guide. Its major shortcoming is that it fails to list a single address for any of the hotels and restaurants featured; it is sold for US$0.50 at the reception of the Hotel Unirea.

Tune into Radio Iaşi on 105.3 FM.

Piaţa Unirii to Piaţa Palatul Culturii

Start your city tour on Piaţa Unirii with a trip to the 13th floor of **Hotel Unirea** for a bird's eye view of Iaşi. The streets radiating out from the square can clearly be seen and on a good day you can see the three monasteries across the valley in the Nicolina district to the south.

Walk back down onto Piaţa Unirii, the main square in the centre of Iaşi. In front of Hotel Unirea stands a bronze **statue of Prince Alexandru Ioan Cuza** (1820-73) who achieved the union of Wallachia and Moldavia. The statue marks the spot where the Union Hora (traditional Romanian dance) was danced in 1859 to celebrate the union. Opposite is the **Hotel Traian**, a neo-classical building designed in 1882 as a performance hall by French engineer Gustave Eiffel, father of the Eiffel tower in Paris. Walk up the pedestrian street beside Hotel Traian to Cuza's former residence, a

large neo-classical building (1812) at Str Alexandru Lăpuşneanu 14. King Ferdinand and Queen Marie stayed here between 1916 and 1918. In 1948 it was transformed into the **Museum of the Union** (Muzeul Unirii). A large number of household and personal belongings of Cuza and his wife Elena (1825-1909) are displayed, including numerous tea sets and ornate ivory fans. Of more interest are the displays on the leaders of the 1848 revolution. The museum is open daily, except Monday, from 10 am to 5 pm. Admission is US$0.20. Contemporary works by local artists are exhibited in the **Galerie de Artă** at Str Alexandru Lăpuşneanu 7-9. It is open Monday to Saturday from 9 am to 9 pm, Sunday from 9 am to 3 pm.

Continue north along Str Alexandru Lăpuşneanu then bear right along Blvd Independenţei. The 18th century Roset house at Blvd Independenţei 16 which served as the seat of Physicians and Naturalists' Society in 1844, is now a **Natural History Museum** (Muzeul de Istorie Naturală). Alexandru Ioan Cuza was elected prince here in 1859. The museum is open Tuesday, Thursday and Saturday from 9 am to 3 pm, and Wednesday, Friday and Sunday from 9 am to 4 pm. Admission is US$0.15. Opposite the museum at Str Universităţii Vechi 16 is the baroque **Costache Ghica House**. The seat of the first university in Romania was founded here in 1860. Today it is the university faculty of Medicine and Pharmacy. From 1934 until his death, the poet Mihail Codreanu (1876-1957) lived one block north of the old university at Str Rece 5.

East at Blvd Independenţei 33 is the **St Spiridon's Monastery** (Mănăstirea Sfântul Spiridon; 1804). The beheaded body of Grigore Ghica III lies inside a tomb in the church in the monastical complex. His head was sent to the Sultan after the Turks killed him in 1777.

Back-track west along Blvd Independenţei and turn left down Str 14 Decembrie 1989 (formerly Str Vasile Alecsandri) to Piaţa Unirii. This side street

MOLDAVIA

is steeped in history. The poet Vasile Alecsandri lived in the house at No 3. Today it is a **Theatre Museum** (Muzeul Teatrului). No 6 was built in 1920 to house the literary group, Viața Românească. At No 8 is the **Lascăr Cantacuzino-Pașcanu House** where a printing press operated from the 18th century onwards. No 13 housed the printing press and bookshop of the Junimea literary society.

The broad, tree-lined Blvd Ștefan cel Mare și Sfânt leads directly south-east from Piața Unirii to the monumental Palace of Culture. Along the way you pass the giant **Moldavian Metropolitan Cathedral** (Mitropolia Moldovei). With four spires and a cavernous interior painted by Gheorghe Tattarescu, it was built between 1833 and 1839. Worshippers will tell you it is the largest Orthodox church in Romania. In mid-October thousands of pilgrims flock here to celebrate the day of St Paraschiva, the patron saint of the cathedral and of Moldavia. Inside the cathedral lies a coffin said to contain the bones of St Friday.

Opposite is the central park, lined with bronze busts of eminent literary figures, where local artists try to sell their masterpieces. At the north-eastern end of the park is the **National Theatre**. In front of it is a majestic statue of its founder Vasile Alecsandri (1821-90), a poet who single-handedly created the theatre's initial repertoire with his Romanian adaptation of a French farce. The theatre was built between 1894-96 according to the designs of Viennese architects Helmer and Fellner. Attend at least one performance here if only to admire the richly designed interior.

The cement block next to the park in front of the theatre is the former **Communist Party headquarters**.

Continuing along Blvd Ștefan cel Mare și Sfânt, you pass the fabulous **Church of the Three Hierarchs** (Biserica Sfinților Trei Ierarhi), unique for its rich exterior which is covered in a wealth of intricate decorative patterns in stone. This stone embroidery duplicates the traditional ornamental motifs found on the shirtsleeves of a Moldavian folk costume. In its original form, the exterior was covered in gold.

The Three Hierarchs' church was built between 1637 and 1639 by Prince Vasile Lupu. It was badly damaged by Tartar attacks in 1650 but later restored.

Inside the church, on either side of the first chamber *(pronaos)* are the marble tombs of the Prince Vasile Lupu and his family (left); Prince Alexandru Ioan Cuza (right); and Moldavian prince Dimitrie Cantimir. Inside the Gothic hall – an unmarked white stone building, reconstructed beside the church – is a **museum of 17th century frescoes**. In 1994 the church reopened as a monastery, with seven monks. The Sunday services here are beautiful, song-filled events.

Close to the church outside the **Iași School Museum** at Blvd Ștefan cel Mare și Sfânt 64 is a **statue of Gheorghe Asachi** (1788-1869), the son of a wealthy Orthodox priest and a teacher of algebra and geometry at the Greek academy from 1812. The house at Str Theodor Codrescu 2 in which he lived from 1846 until his death is now a **memorial museum**, dedicated to his life and works. Asachi's tomb is inside the 18th century **Forty Saints Church**, opposite the university on Str Henri Matthias Berthelot.

At the southern end of Blvd Ștefan cel Mare și Sfânt stands the giant neo-Gothic **Palace of Culture** (Palatul Culturii), formerly the administrative seat of the town. The palace was built between 1906 and 1925 on the ruins of the **old princely court**, founded by Prince Alexandru cel Bun (1400-32) in the early 15th century. Some remains of the ruined princely court have been preserved underneath the concrete flooring of the Summer Theatre (see Entertainment – Theatre & Classical Music).

The main attraction of the 365-room building today, however, is the **Gheorghe Asachi library** and the four first-class museums it houses: the **Ethnographic Museum** (Muzeul de Etnografie) is one of the best in the country. Each of its nine halls is devoted to a different theme ranging from agriculture, fishing and hunting, to wine making. A further four colourful halls, guaranteed to raise the spirits, exhibit traditional national costumes and rugs from Romania's different regions. The **Art Museum** (Muzeul de Artă) is split into two galleries – *the galerie de artă românească* containing works by Romanian artists, and the *galerie de artă universală* exhibiting works by foreign artists. The Romanian art gallery has works by artists including Nicolae Grigorescu and Moldavian-born Petre Achiţemie, renowned throughout Romania for his 2000sq metre memorial painting at Mărăşeşti.

Highlights of the **History Museum** (Muzeul de Istorie) include portraits of all of Romania's rulers dating from 81 AD. Various mechanical creations and musical instruments are displayed in the less colourful **Technical Museum** (Muzeul Ştintei şi Technicii).

Admission to all four museums and the temporary exhibitions held in other halls in the palace costs US$0.50/0.25 for adults/students. You can also buy separate tickets costing US$0.10 for each of the museums – a good idea since a tour of all four museums in one stint can be a bit brain-numbing. The palace is open daily, except Monday, from 10 am to 5 pm.

In front of the palace on Piaţa Palatul Culturii is an **equestrian statue** of Ştefan cel Mare, unveiled in 1883 to the sound of a 21 cannon salute. A memorial to Iaşi's 16 heroes who died in 1989 stands by the entrance to the palace grounds. Opposite, at Str Anastasie Panu 69, is the **Museum of Old Moldavian Literature**, housed inside the 17th century Dosoftei House (Casă Dosoftei). Dosoftei served as metropolitan of Moldavia between 1670 to 1686 and was responsible for printing the first church liturgy in the Romanian language (1679). The museum is open daily, except Monday, from 10 am to 5 pm.

Behind Dosoftei House is **St Nicolas' Royal Church** (Biserica Sfântul Nicolae Domnesc), one of Iaşi's oldest buildings founded by Ştefan cel Mare in 1492. Little remains however of the original church, restored and extended by Prince Antonie

Roset in 1677, only to be pulled down and rebuilt by French architect André Lecomte de Noüy in 1884.

Monasteries & Churches

Find your way a few blocks north, past the central market, to fortified **Golia Monastery** (Mănăstirea Golia), built in late-Renaissance style on the north-eastern limits of medieval Iaşi on Str Cuza Vodă. The monastery's walls – 1.2 to 1.5cm thick – and the 30m-tall Golia tower at the entrance shelter a 17th century church. The church is noted for its vibrant Byzantine frescoes and intricately carved doorways. The bastions of the surrounding wall were added in 1667 by Prince Gheorghe Duca (1668-72). The monastical complex was damaged by fire in 1822 and by 1863 the church was practically in ruins. Between 1900 and 1947 it was closed. It regained monastery status in 1992.

Inside the Golia tower is a Turkish fountain. East of the tower is a **memorial house** to Ion Creangă. The writer (1837-89), renowned for his short stories based on Moldavian folklore, lived here between 1866 and 1871. There is a museum dedicated to his life and works in his inspirational hovel close to the university on Ţicău Hill (see later in this section).

From Golia monastery, head south along Str Armeană. On the right at No 22 you pass a small stone and brick **Armenian Church** (Biserica Armeană), dating from 1395 and considered the oldest church in Iaşi. A succession of extensive renovations has meant that little of the original Armenian architecture remains today. At the southern end of Str Armeană, turn right to **St Sava's Monastery** (Mănăstirea Sfântul Sava), a small red-washed church (1625) at Str Costache Negri 41. If you turn left along Str Costache Negri you come to the 19th century **Bărboi Monastery** (Mănăstirea Bărboi). The church was built in 1841 on the site of a 17th century Bărboi church. Apart from a few 19th century icons there is little of extraordinary worth inside the church today; its *trompe l'oeil* painted interior is worth a look. A block south at Str Grigore Ghica Vodă 26 is

MOLDAVIA

Barnovschi Monastery (Mănăstirea Barnovschi) dating from the rule of Prince Miron Barnovschi-Movilă (1626-9).

University & Around

From Târgu Cucu (formerly Tîrgu Cucu) take bus No 35 westbound and get out when you see a building marked *Stadionul Emil Alexandrescu* on the left. Iaşi's 80-hectare **Botanic Gardens** (Grădină Botanică), on the far side of Parcul Expozitiei from this stop, are Romania's largest by far. Dating from 1856, they have 21km of shady lanes to explore, rose and orchid gardens, as well as numerous greenhouses in which some 30,000 species of tropical and subtropical plants quietly grow.

Follow the bus route back a few blocks to **Copou park**, a nice place to sit and write postcards or update your diary. The park was laid out between 1834 and 1848 during the princely reign of Mihail Sturza. It is famed as being a favourite haunt of poet Mihai Eminescu (1850-89) who allegedly wrote some of his best works beneath his favourite linden tree in this park. The tree still stands – just about – behind a 13m-tall **monument of lions** opposite the main entrance to the park. The branches of the sagging tree, over 100 years old, are held up with metal supports and bandaged with green belts. A bronze bust of Eminescu stands in front of it.

To the right of the lion monument is the **Mihai Eminescu Museum of Literature** (Muzeul Mihai Eminescu – Muzeul Literaturi Română), housed in an ugly, white, modern building which is still partly under construction. The museum recalls the life and loves of Eminescu who was born in northern Moldavia. His great love, Veronica Micle, lived in Iaşi (at Str Nicolae Gane 4 with her vicar husband Ştefan) so he consequently spent a lot of time here. A bust of Veronica faces the bust of her lover and his favourite lime tree at the end of **Junimea alley** in the park. The museum is open daily, except Monday, from 10 am to 5 pm. Admission is US$0.12.

Walk back down Blvd Copou, past the huge neo-classical **Alexandru Ioan Cuza**

University at No 11. The founder of the fascist Iron Guard, Corneliu Codreanu (1899-1938), studied at this university. Just before the statue in the middle of the street, turn left to the 1850s mansion at Str Vasile Pogor 4. It was here in the house of Junimea founder, Vasile Pogor (1833-1906) that meetings of the literary society were held from 1871. The building is currently being renovated; by 1999, it should be reopened as the **Pogor House Literary Museum** (Casă Pogor; ☎ 145 760). There is a statue of Pogor outside the main entrance of the building which is on the left of the building. In its grounds stand **rows of busts** of some of the more eminent members of the society, including dramatist Ion Luca Caragiale (1852-1912), poet Vasile Alecsandri (1821-90), and historian Alexandru Xenopol (1847-1920).

The foundation stone of the house (1850) is exhibited in the **Club Junimea** (☎ 145 760, 213 210), an outbuilding in the grounds. If you want to know the real inspiration behind Romania's greatest poets, ask for a tour of the recently restored wine cellars beneath the club. They're vast!

One block south of the Pogor house behind the **Student Cultural House** on Piaţa Mihai Eminescu is the Students' House park, the centrepiece of which is the **Voievodes Statuary**. Perched on a small hillock, these fantastic, crumbling statues of Moldavia's princes were moved here from the university courtyard in the 1960s. In pairs stand Moldavia's first prince, Dragoş (1352-53), and Alexandru cel Bun (1400-32); Moldavia's greatest prince Ştefan cel Mare (1457-1504) and Mihai Viteazul (1600); Petru Rareş (1527-38) and Ion Vodă cel Viteaz (1572-74); Vasile Lupu (1634-53) and Dimitrie Cantemir (1693).

North of the university at Aleea Mihail Sadoveanu 12 is the 19th century **Mihail Sadoveanu Memorial House** (Casă Memorială Mihail Sadoveanu). The storyteller lived here between 1918 and 1936.

The attractive **Ţicău district** rises to the east of Blvd Copou. At Str Simion Bămuţiu 4 is the 19th century *bojdeucă* (literally

Mihai Viteazul is among various Moldavian princes remembered in Iaşi's Statuary.

'hovel'), dating to 1842, where short story writer Ion Creangă (1837-89) lived and spent many a brainstorming session with his close friend and mentor Mihai Eminescu.

The politician Mihail Kogălniceanu (1817-91) lived for a short time in the 19th century mansion at Str Mihail Kogălniceanu 11. Today it houses a **museum** devoted to the life of the Moldavian activist who published numerous papers on the Moldavia National Party during the 1848 revolution. Kogălniceanu went on to serve under Alexandru Ioan Cuza as foreign minister after Moldavia and Wallachia were united in 1859.

Close by at Str Henri Matthias Berthelot 18 is the house where the French general, Henri Matthias Berthelot, lived between 1916 and 1917. The intervention in October 1916 of the 1500-strong French military mission led by Berthelot clinched Romania's survival in WWI. The general was later awarded Romanian citizenship. Iaşi was also the birthplace of Romanian biologist, Antarctic explorer and speleologist, Emil Racoviţa (1868-1947). He was born at Str Lascăr Catargui 36, in the west of the Ţicău district.

South of the Centre

Heading out of town along Şoseaua Bucium (DN 224) towards Vaslui, you pass the **Odd Poplars alley**, lined with 25 poplar trees marking the spot where poet Mihai Eminescu also sought inspiration.

South-west of the centre in the Nicolina district are three of Iaşi's most tranquil monasteries, all of which make for a pleasant day's hike. Perched on top of Miroslavei hill is the 16th century, fortified **Galata Monastery** (Mănăstirea Galata), founded by Prince Petru Şchiopul in 1582 who is buried in the church alongside his daughter. The ruins of the monks' living quarters and a Turkish bath are all that remain today. The new church was built in 1847.

East of Galata at the northern end of Str Cetăţuia are the ruins of **Frumoasa Monastery** (Mănăstirea Frumoasa). It was built between 1726 and 1733 by Prince Grigore Ghica II and served as a royal residence in the 18th century. From here, head south along Str Cetăţuia and follow the steep, narrow road to the top of Dealul Cetăţuia. On the top of 'castle hill' is the impressive 17th century **Cetăţuia Monastery**, preserved in its original form. The monastery was founded by Prince Gheorghe Duca in 1669. Between 1682 and 1694 a Greek printing press was housed here.

Jewish Iaşi

Under 17th century Turkish rule, the headquarters of the Hacham Bashim was in Iaşi and in the 19th century the city was one of the great centres of Jewish learning in Europe. The world's first professional Jewish theatre opened in Iaşi in 1876. A **statue** of its founder, Polish composer and playwright Avram Goldfaden (1840-1908), stands in the central park on Blvd Ştefan cel Mare şi Sfânt. More than one third of the city's population at this time was Jewish, served by 127 synagogues.

Only one synagogue remains today – the **Great Synagogue**, built in 1671, is no longer used, and is barely visible amid the concrete apartment blocks surrounding it at Str Elena Doamna 15. There is a small

MOLDAVIA

The Iron Guard

The militant Legion of the Archangel Michael, better known as the Iron Guard or the Greenshirts, was communism's arch enemy.

The extreme-right fascist group believed that its fanatical commitment to ridding Romania of all its Jews and communists was embedded in Orthodox doctrine. The Legion was established in June 1927. Its founder and 'captain', Corneliu Codreanu (1899-1938), created it after God called him to task in the prison where he was serving a five year sentence for compiling a list of Jews to be murdered. Upon his release from prison, Codreanu killed the police chief of Iaşi because of his alleged sympathy with Jews.

The Iron Guard was divided into *cuibs* (nests) comprising 13 'brothers'. To be initiated into a cuib, a new recruit had to suck blood from slashes cut into the arms of each of his future brothers. From his own blood, he was compelled to write an oath pledging his willingness to murder if the Legion commanded it. Prior to embarking on a mission, members each contributed blood to a goblet from which they all drank. They anointed themselves with holy water and hung packets of soil around their necks.

The Iron Guard was not a political party but it did figure greatly in the political arena of the 1930s. This dynamism climaxed with King Carol II briefly installing the Iron Guard-affiliated League of the National Christian Defence in government in 1937. Following the declaration of a royal dictatorship, Codreanu and 13 other legionaries were arrested, imprisoned and shot. Their deaths were avenged by the Iron Guard murder of Armand Călinescu – one of four prime ministers to be killed by the Legion. Over 250 legionaries were then assassinated on the king's orders, their corpses strung up in public squares throughout the country.

Iron Guardists held key positions in Marshall Antonescu's pro-Nazi regime. Their first move was to dig up the remains of Corneliu Codreanu and rebury them in a ceremony attended by over 150,000 people. The public funeral ended with a tape recording of Codreanu's voice booming out: 'You must await the day to avenge our martyrs'.

In June 1941 the Iron Guard embarked on a three day killing spree in Bucharest in an attempt to overthrow Antonescu. In one incident, 200 Jews were arrested and slain in the city's slaughter house. Days later Hitler ordered Antonescu to rid Romania of its murderous element. The Iron Guard was squashed, its leaders fled into exile in Nazi Germany and fascist Italy. Horia Simia, who took over as 'captain' after Codreanu's death, was interned in Buchenwald concentration camp and remains in exile today. ■

museum inside the synagogue but you have to contact the Iaşi Jewish community (☎ 114 414) in advance to visit it. On the unkempt scrap of lawn in front of the synagogue is a **monument** to the victims of the 1941 pogrom.

Many of the victims of the Iron Guard's pogroms were buried in four concrete bunkers in the **Jewish cemetery** (Cimitirul Everesc) on Mountain Hill (Dealul Munteni), which is east of the centre off Str Păcurari.

Language Courses

Romanian language classes are held at the International Language Centre on the 8th floor of DNT Iaşi (☎ 252 936; fax 252 933; email info@dntis.ro; www.dntis.ro), at Str Moara de Foc 35.

Places to Stay

Camping There is budget accommodation at Lake Ciric, 6km north-east of town. The campsite here has closed but the *Baza Sportiva şi de Agrement Ciric* (☎ 179 304), across the dam and to the right, offers simple *casuţa* (cabins) at US$2, and is open from mid-May to August. To reach the lake, take a tram to Târgu Cucu and then wait for bus No 25 to Lake Ciric, which leaves hourly from the stop opposite the building marked 'Complexul Târgul Cucului'.

Private Rooms ANTREC (☎ 217 376; ☎ & fax 211 060), in room 106, Hotel Continental, Str Cuza Vodă 4, arranges private rooms in villages around Iaşi. A bed is between US$10 and US$15 a night, and this price includes a hearty, home-cooked breakfast.

Hosts charge an extra US$4 to US$6 for an evening meal.

Hotels Most of Iaşi's hotels are within spitting distance of each other in the centre of town. Best value for backpackers is the *Hotel Continental* (☎ 114 320) at Piaţa 14 Decembrie 1989. Single/double rooms with a squeaky-clean shared bathroom are US$8/10. Rooms facing the street are noisy. The hotel has a small café and currency exchange on the ground floor and some of the staff speak basic French.

Similar prices are charged at the grotty *Hotel Sport* (☎ 232 800; fax 231 540), south of the centre in the Nicolina district at Str Sfântu Lazăr 76.

The modern, three-star, 13-storey *Hotel Unirii* (☎ 142 110; fax 117 854), at Piaţa Unirii 2, is a characterless concrete block. Single/double rooms with private bathroom are expensive at US$34/78, including breakfast. It has a casino, cabaret show, restaurant and panoramic café on the 13th floor.

At Piaţa Unirii 1 is the more elegant *Hotel Traian* (☎ 143 330; fax 212 187). If you're a foreigner, the staff at reception will offer you the most expensive room. The cheapest rooms are on the top floors where water pressure is at its lowest. Single/double/triple rooms with a private shower on these floors cost US$11/15/21.

The 14 storey, three-star *Hotel Moldova* (☎ 142 225; fax 117 940), Piaţa Palatului 1, is overpriced at US$28/51 for a single/ double room with private bath. It is one of the few hotels in Romania to have wheelchair access. The hotel has an adjoining indoor swimming pool, sauna and tennis court, open to non-guests too.

Behind the Moldova is Hotel Orizont (☎ 112 700; fax 215 037) at Str Grigore Ureche 27. Singles/doubles are US$14/23 or US$17/30 if you want a room with a balcony. The staff will tell you that the balconies overlook the Palace of Culture – they don't. The hotel's disco-bar is open daily from 5 pm to midnight.

The World Trade Centre to open on Str Anastasie Panu in 1999 will house a five-star hotel.

Places to Eat
Restaurants Traditional Romanian food is served at the *Balta Reche* (☎ 112 567), dating to 1799 at Str Reche 10. Try the caşcaval (fried cheese) for US$1, or the house speciality, feteasca neagră (black pudding served with mămăligă and topped with salty sheep cheese). The restaurant is open daily from 8 am to midnight.

Also popular is the *Trei Sarmale* (☎ 132 832), inside a 17th century inn out of town at Str Bucium 42. Check before you head out here as the restaurant is often booked by tour groups. Take bus Nos 30 or 46 from Piaţa Mihai Eminescu and get off at the Bucium bus stop, directly outside the restaurant.

The grey old days are more evident at the *Iaşul* on Str Alexandru Lăpuşneanu. Typical Romanian dishes are served and there is a live folk band some evenings; it's open daily from 9 am to 10 pm. Close by, opposite the Hotel Continental is *Restaurant Select*, favoured mainly for its bingo hall and casino. Its terrace in the sun overlooking a taxi rank remains unrivalled for breakfast. It is open daily from 8 am to midnight.

The Italian *Metro Restaurant* (☎ 213 502) at Str Grigorie Veche 1-3, has flashy decor but prices are reasonable and the food is wholesome. Carbonara and lasagna are around US$2 and wine is US$1.70 a bottle. The restaurant is open daily from 9.30 to 2 am. Good pizzas are served at the *Pizzeria Italiana Cucina Casă Linga*, Str Costache Negri.

Metro Pizza (☎ 117 520) at Blvd Ştefan cel Mare şi Sfânt 18 serves excellent, 26cm-round pizzas for US$1 to US$1.70. The 'metro special', topped with cheese, salami, mushrooms and a fried egg is particularly satisfying; it's open daily from 8 am to midnight and has a takeaway counter too. The *Metro Café*, Blvd Ştefan cel Mare şi Sfânt 6, is equally popular. The same team runs the *Café Milano*, opposite the train station at Str Silvestru 12, open daily from 9 to 1 am.

The stylish French restaurant, *Le Flagrant*

Délice (☎ 216 377) at Str Sfântul Sava 10, offers set menus for US$8 to US$14. Typical French delights listed on the giant-sized A3 menu include frog legs, salade niçoise and salade de foie volailles (chicken liver salad). It is open daily from noon to midnight and serves the best cappuccino in town.

Cafés There's an abundance of outside cafés along Str Anastasie Panu. More fun is the cluster of summer cafés-cum-bars spilling out over the pavements around Piaţa Mihai Eminescu. Students run a good café outside their cultural house at the northern end of Piaţa Mihai Eminescu.

Favoured by Iaşi's Greek student community is the Greek café-cum-restaurant, *Monte Carlo*, Str Gheorghe Asachi 1. It has a great terrace shaded by rambling vines, and traditional Greek music spouts from speakers. A full meal will set you back no more than US$2; it is open daily from noon to 11 pm.

The *Grădină Iaşul & Brasserie* (open daily from 10 am to 10 pm), next door to the Iaşul restaurant on Str Alexandru Lăpuşneanu, and the *Terasa Corsu* (open daily from 9 am to midnight), opposite the Union Museum, are other hot spots on sunny days. For a cup of coffee inside, try the glittery, modern *Ad Hoc*, bang next door to the Union Museum.

Not exotic but sympathetic to the wallet is the university canteen, *Cantină Titu Maiorescu* behind the main university building. Walk up Blvd Copou, turn left along Str Toma Cosma, then follow the small path immediately to the right after the university building. Walk past the water tower and follow the path through the park until you reach the canteen on your left. It is open daily, except Sunday, from 8 am to 3 pm and slaps out vegetable soup and pork cutlet for a bargain US$0.50.

Close by on Str Toma Cosma, is the popular *Casă Universatilor* (☎ 140 029). The terrace café around the back is packed from June onwards, if only for the wonderful scent of its many lime trees. A meal here costs about US$0.75; getting 'high' on lime is free. It is open daily from 8 am to 11 pm.

Numerous outside cafés are also dotted along Blvd Ştefan cel Mare şi Sfânt. Favoured for its delicious Italian ice cream is the *Gelaterie Bar Arlechino*, almost opposite the central park. Overlooking the park at Str Brătianu 30 is *EuroParadis* (☎ 147 661). At No 32 is the *Cofetăria Opera*, open daily from 8 am to 9.30 pm.

The city's kebab alley runs alongside the eastern side of the Medical University. The Syrian *Sahla* café at Str Sfânt Theodor 22 is open daily from 9 am to 11 pm. For US$0.75 worth of falafel, pop into the *Golden Sheep*, a few doors down from Sahla. Lebanese fast food is slapped out with care at *Summertime* in the former Armanda building at Str Sfânt Theodor 30. It is open 24 hours and has water pipes for those wanting to smoke the traditional way. The Turkish *Gülistan Mini-Restaurant*, on Str Independenţei, dishes out döner kebabs for US$0.75, as does *Anita*, another döner joint on the corner of Str Rece.

Fast Food For pizza delivery, call *Metro Pizza* (☎ 112 883) – another one – at Str Silvestru 10. It is open daily from 9 to 1 am. After hours, try *D'oro* fast food (☎ 210 082), at Blvd Ştefan cel Mare şi Sfânt 11, open 24 hours. The *Centre Fast Food Brasserie*, next door to the Gelateria Bar Arlechino, serves pork for US$1.20, soups for US$1 and pizza slices for US$1.50; it's open daily from 8 am to midnight.

Brilliant-yellow *Nest* fast-food kiosks, open 24 hours and serving hot dogs and more hot dogs (and public transport tickets), are dotted all over town.

Self Catering The indoor *central market* is great for fresh fruit and veg. It has entrances on Str Costache Negri and Str Anastasie Panu and is open daily.

The *Central Supermarket*, on the northern end of Blvd Ştefan cel Mare şi Sfânt, is open daily, except Sunday, from 8 am to 8 pm. An excellent range of imported and local products are sold at the 24 hour *Rodex Supermarket*, next door to the TAROM office on Str Arcu.

Entertainment

Cinemas Cinemas show the latest box office hits in English with subtitles in Romanian. Evening screenings start at 8 pm. Try the *Victoria*, Piaţa Unirii 4; the *Republica*; Str Alexandru Lăpuşneanu 12; the *Dacia*; Piaţa Voievozilor 14; or the *Copou* on Blvd Copou 48.

Bars & Clubs The top club is the alternative jazz and folk club *Escape* (☎ 116 027), open 24 hours at Str Alexandru Lăpuşneanu 18. Bright turquoise outside and lit with blue inside, this funky bar with a 'hole-in-the-wall' stage attracts a cool crowd. There is live jazz on Thursday and traditional folk on Sunday.

Also popular is the *New Yorker* billiard bar at Blvd Ştefan cel Mare şi Sfânt 10. It has nine pool tables, one snooker table and a small café and restaurant, all open daily from 10 to 1 am.

Discos Cheap and tacky is the *Scala Restaurant Disco*, on the corner of Str Anastasie Panu and Str Sfântu Lazăr. *Cocktail Night Club*, behind Luceafărul Theatre, has plenty of flashing lights and loud music. It's most fun on Friday and Saturday (closed Monday).

Iaşi's best student disco is *Metro Pizza* (yet another one) at the Complexul Studentesc 'Tudor Vladimirescu' east of town (five stops from Piaţa Unirii on tram No 8). It's closed on Monday and Tuesday and from July to mid-September.

Theatre & Classical Music On the eastern side of Blvd Ştefan cel Mare şi Sfânte, is the neo-baroque *Vasile Alecsandri National Theatre* (Teatrul Naţional Vasile Alecsandri; ☎ 115 108). More alternative shows and performances are held in the smaller studio hall *(sală studio)* upstairs which has its entrance on Str Cuza Vodă. Tickets for all performances are sold at the box office in the theatre one hour before the performance begins. For advance bookings go to the Agenţie de Opera (☎ 116 070), Blvd Ştefan cel Mare şi Sfânt 8. It is open weekdays from

9 am to 1 pm, and from 3 to 5 pm. Tickets cost around US$0.60; students are half-price.

Massively popular – and cheap – are the Tuesday and Friday evening concerts held inside the *Philharmonic* (Filharmonica; ☎ 114 601) at Str Cuza Vodă 29. Tickets costing US$0.20 to US$0.50 are sold from the box office inside, open weekdays from 10 am to 1 pm, and from 5 to 7 pm. Performances generally start at 7 pm.

There is a youth theatre – the *Luceafărul Theatre* (Teatrul Luceafărul) on Str Grigore Ureche; performances are rarely held at the *Summer Theatre* (Teatrul Vară) inside the Palace of Culture at Str Palatului 1. When they are, details are advertised in the local press.

Getting There & Away

Air TAROM operates twice daily flights on Monday, Wednesday and Thursday between Iaşi, Suceava and Bucharest. A single fare from Iaşi to Bucharest/Suceava is US$55/28. TAROM (☎ 115 239) has an office in Iaşi at Str Arcu 3-5, open weekdays from 7 am to 7 pm, Saturday from 7 am to noon.

Bus Staff at the information booth at the central bus station (☎ 146 587), Şoseaua Arcu, speak English.

There are four buses daily to Chişinău in the republic of Moldova, departing at 7 am, 2, 5 and 8.15 pm. Tickets for the private bus to Istanbul departing 8 am are sold at the Toros Excursii office (☎ 214 920) in the bus station ticket hall.

Train The Agenţie de Voiaj CFR (☎ 147 673, 145 269), Piaţa Unirii 4, is open weekdays from 8 am to 8 pm. Express train tickets to Bucharest and Timişoara are sold from window Nos 8, 6 and 3. International train tickets are sold from windows Nos 11, 14 and 15 on the 2nd floor.

Iaşi is on the main line between Bucharest and Kiev, which goes via Chişinău. The Ungheni border crossing is only 21 km away. Reservations are required on the four daily trains from Iaşi to Chişinău.

For Galaţi you may have to change trains at Bârlad or Tecuci. If you are planning to visit the monasteries in southern Bucovina, take a train to Suceava then change trains, or take a train bound for Vatra Dornei or Oradea and get off at the Gura Humorului stop. To get to Târgu Neamţ from Iaşi you often have to change at Paşcani.

Getting Around
To/From the Airport TAROM operates a free shuttle bus service between its office at Str Arcu 3-5 and Iaşi airport (☎ 174 058, 271 590). It leaves 1½ hours before flight departures.

Bus, Tram & Trolleybus Public transport tickets costing US$0.22 for a two-journey ticket are sold at the silver-coloured kiosks next to the bus stops, news kiosks, and most of the numerous, canary-yellow Nest fast-food kiosks. Bus No 35 runs between Piaţa Eminescu and Copou park, making a stop outside the university en route. Tram No 3 runs between the bus and train stations and the centre.

AROUND IAŞI
Rolling hills, lush vineyards and pretty villages surround Moldavia's 'town of seven hills'. At the **Bucium winery**, 7km south of Iaşi, you can taste a variety of sweet wines as well as Bucium champagne. At weekends, Iaşi residents picnic in **Bârnova forest**, 16km south of the city and accessible by train.

Cotnari
Cotnari is 54km north-west of Iaşi. Its **vineyards**, dating from 1448, are among the most famed in Romania, producing four to six million bottles of sweet white wine a year. Many are exported. Legend says Ştefan cel Mare (1457-1504) described it as 'wine given by God'. Cotnari wine is also known as the 'flower of Moldavia'.

There was a Geto-Dacian stronghold on Cătălina hill (280m) in Cotnari from the 4th century BC. In 1491 Ştefan cel Mare built a small church in the village and in 1562 a

Latin college was founded. During this period French monks arrived bringing grape stocks which they planted in the village. By the end of the 19th century Cotnari wine had scooped up prizes at international exhibitions in Budapest (1889), Vienna (1873) and Paris (1889). In 1947 King Michael I started building a small **royal palace** here, abandoning it half-complete in 1947. It was not restored until 1966. Today it houses the administration of the Cotnari Winery.

Following the fall of communism, 800 hectares of the winery's 2000 hectare estate were returned to local farmers whose land had been confiscated under Ceauşescu. The winery produces some 40,000 hectolitres of wine a year, employing 3000 pickers during the September harvest (paid US$1.50 a day plus free food and lodging in 1996). Its most popular wines include white table wines such as *frâncuşa* (classified as dry but more on the medium side) and *cătălina* (semi-sweet), and the sweet, golden *grasa* and *tâmăioasa* dessert wines.

The Cotnari Winery (☎ 032-730 393, 730 396; fax 032-730 205, 730 303) arranges wine tasting sessions and tours of its wine cellars and factory, which was equipped with the latest German technology in 1996. Every year on 14 September wine connoisseurs flock to Cotnari to celebrate the harvest.

To get there, continue past the village shop on the road towards Botoşani and Hârlau. The factory is 200m further on the left.

Places to Stay & Eat ANTREC (see Iaşi – Travel Agencies) arranges private rooms in Cotnari – in the home of the general director of Cotnari factory, next door to King Michael's palace! From the centre of the village, turn left at the shop and continue up the hill until you reach the palace on your left. The Bilius family home is next door. The Bilius family are excellent hosts and rooms are beautifully furnished with large windows or a balcony overlooking Cătălina hill. A bed for the night is US$10 to US$15, including breakfast. Other meals, washed down with house wine, can also be provided.

Getting There & Away Three local trains daily from Iaşi to Hârlau stop at Cotnari (54km, 1¾ hours). Trains depart from Iaşi at 5.40 am, 4.48 and 8.20 pm. Return trains leave Cotnari at 4.19 am, 3.50 and 7.24 am.

Botoşani, Ipoteşti & Liveni

Botoşani is 50km north of Cotnari. Poet Mihai Eminescu (1850-89) was born in Ipoteşti, 8km north-west. His family home is today a **Memorial House** (Casă Memorială). In the village cemetery and in the centre of Ipoteşti is a **Mihai Eminescu National Centre of Studies** (Centrul National de Studii Mihai Eminescu; ☎ 517 602) housing a library and museum.

Bucovina Estur (see Suceava – Places to Stay) arranges accommodation in homes in Ipoteşti. There are a handful of run-down hotels in Botoşani: The *Hotel Rapsodia* (☎ & fax 518 054) at Str Cuza Vodă 4, *Hotel Rareş* (☎ 512 667) at Calea Naţională 315, and *Hotel Tineret* (☎ 525 725) at Blvd Mihai Eminescu.

To get to Ipoteşti (called Mihai Eminescu on some maps), head north out of Botoşani on the road to Dorohoi. At the north end of Cătămareşti-Deal village turn left at the signpost for Ipoteşti.

The composer George Enescu (1881-1955) was born in **Liveni**, 35km north of Ipoteşti. His childhood home is now a **Memorial House**. Liveni is marked as George Enescu on many maps.

Getting There & Away There are two daily buses to Botoşani from Iaşi (117km) and Târgu Neamţ (113km); and eight daily from Suceava (40km) in southern Bucovina.

TÂRGU NEAMŢ
* *area code ☎ 033*

Târgu Neamţ (literally 'German Market Town') offers tourists little except the ruins of a 14th century citadel and a cluster of pre-1989 museums which are always closed. It can, however, serve as a stepping stone to Neamţ Agapia and Văratec monasteries. Târgu Neamţ is poorly served by public transport.

Orientation & Information
The bus station (☎ 636 74) is at the end of Str Cuza Vodă 32. Turn right out of the bus station, then right along Blvd Mihai Eminescu to Blvd Ştefan cel Mare. The hotel and citadel are signposted from here. The train station is signposted from the bus station.

There is a currency exchange inside the Bancă Post on Piaţa Mihai Eminescu, open weekdays from 8 am to noon. The post and telephone office is at Blvd Mihai Eminescu 154, open weekdays only from 7.30 am to 8.30 pm.

Things to See
Neamţ Citadel (Cetatea Neamţului), considered Moldavia's finest ruined fortress, is on a hill above the town. It was attacked by Hungarians in 1395, by the Turks in 1476, and finally conquered by Polish forces in 1691. It fell into ruin in the 18th century.

Follow the signs for the 'Cetatea Neamţului' along Blvd Ştefan cel Mare. At No 37 there is a **History and Ethnographic Museum** (Muzeul de Istorie şi Etnografie), apparently always closed. Opposite is the **Memorial House** to Veronica Micle (1850-89), always closed too.

A **statue** of writer Ion Creangă stands on Piaţa Mihai Eminescu. The storyteller attended secondary school in Târgu Neamţ.

Places to Stay & Eat
The only hotel is the *Casă Arcasului* (☎ 662 615) at the foot of the citadel. Double/triple rooms cost US$22/34. The similarly priced *Hotel Oglinzi* (☎ 662 590), is 4km north of Târgu Neamţ on the Suceava road.

Pizza Orient (☎ 661 297), in Piaţa Mihai Eminescu park, slaps out pizza for US$1. It is open daily from 7.30 am to 11 pm.

Getting There & Away
Bus Between 5.15 am and 6.15 pm buses depart hourly from Târgu Neamţ bus station to Piatra Neamţ (43km). There are seven buses to Agapia (Complex Turistic Agapia) between 5 am and 6.15 pm (11km). Buses leave for Văratec at 7.10 am, 2 and 6.30 pm.

There is a daily bus to Bacău (93km), Braşov (280km), Gheorgheni (160km), Iaşi (100km), Miercurea Ciuc (217km), Sfântu Gheorghe (315km), Slănic Moldova (164km) and Suceava (71km). There are two daily buses to Botoşani (113km), Durău (61km) and Rădăuţi (258km).

Train From Târgu Neamţ take one of five daily local trains to Paşcani (50 minutes) from where you can get trains to Iaşi, Suceava and other cities in Moldavia. There is one direct train a day from Târgu Neamţ to Iaşi (2½ hours).

AROUND TÂRGU NEAMŢ

Târgu Neamţ is ringed by monasteries, noted not for their outstanding artistic treasures but rather as Romania's most active religious centres. Agapia and Văratec are called monasteries even though they house nuns.

Neamţ Monastery

Neamţ monastery (Mănăstirea Neamţ) is Romania's largest and oldest monastery. Some 70 monks live in the fortified compound which includes a **medieval art museum** and a **memorial house** to novelist Mihail Sadoveanu (1880-1961). It was built during the same time as Neamţ citadel as a fortified refuge for local people. Just one of its original frescoes dating from 1497 remains intact today.

The monastery, 15km west of Târgu Neamţ, is not served by public transport. Hitch a ride west along the road to Ceahlău and Topliţa.

Agapia Monastery

Heading 4km south from Târgu Neamţ towards Piatra Neamţ, you hit the turn-off for **Agapia Monastery** (Mănăstirea Agapia) in the Topliţa valley. Within the confines of the monastery walls, its 400-plus nuns lead a simple life oriented around prayer, toiling in the fields, tending their vegetable garden and weaving carpets and embroideries for the few tourists who succeed in making their way to this remote spot.

Agapia comprises two monasteries: the upper 'monastery on the hill' (Agapia din Deal) was founded by Lady Elena, the wife of Petru Rareş, in 1527. The more spectacular 'monastery in the valley' (Agapia din Vale) was built by Gavril Coci (brother of Vasile Lupu) between 1642 and 1644. It was badly damaged by the Turks in 1821, its current neo-classical façade dating to 1823. Between 1858 and 1860, the young Nicolae Grigorescu (1838-1907) was commissioned to paint the interior of the church, the result of which is a fantastic mural of directionless eyes which stare at you whichever way you turn. The collection of icons inside the monastery dates to the 16th and 17th centuries.

It is occasionally possible for tourists to stay at the monastery (☎ 033-6622 136). Bookings have to be made in advance. Book through Bucovina Estur in Suceava (see Suceava – Information). It does not charge commission.

Getting There & Away All buses between Târgu Neamţ and Piatra Neamţ stop in Sacaluseşti village, from where it is a 3km hike along a narrow road to the lower monastery; the upper monastery is a further 30 minute walk uphill.

There are also seven direct buses from Târgu Neamţ to the lower monastery, listed on bus timetables as 'Complex Turistic Agapia'. Some people visit Agapia from Piatra Neamţ, from where there are two buses daily to the complex (40km).

Văratec Monastery

Six hundred nuns live at Văratec monastery (Mănăstirea Văratec), 7km south of the Agapia turn-off. The complex houses an **icon museum** and a small embroidery school. The **grave** of poetess Veronica Micle, Mihai Eminescu's great love, lies within the monastery walls. Micle translated Edgar Allan Poe's novel *Morella* into Romanian. She committed suicide on 4 August 1889, two months after Eminescu's death.

You can hike to Văratec from Agapia (1½ hours); trails are clearly marked. Other hiking trails lead to the tiny **Secu**, **Sihăstria** and **Shila** monasteries, founded in the Secu

Brook Valley by Moldavian boyars between 1602 and 1813.

Getting There & Away There are three buses daily from Târgu Neamţ to Văratec, departing from Târgu Neamţ at 7.10 am, 2 and 6.30 pm (11km). If it's sunny, walk.

PIATRA NEAMŢ
* *area code ☎ 033*

Piatra Neamţ (literally 'German Rock'), 43km south of Târgu Neamţ, is a picturesque town, dramatically sunken in a valley and surrounded on all sides by sheer mountain faces. Perched above the town to the east is the rocky Pietricica mountain. To the southwest stands the Cernegura mountain, flanked by the artificial lake, Lacul Bâtca Doamnei, at its eastern most foot. The Cozla mountain which towers over Piatra Neamţ to the north is a national park. Ştefan cel Mare founded a princely court here in the 15th century.

Every year at the end of May, Piatra Neamţ hosts a week-long, international theatre festival, attracting theatre companies from all over Europe.

Orientation
The Bistriţa river runs from east to west along the southern edge of the town. The train station is on the north bank of the river at Piaţa Mareşal Ion Antonescu 50. The bus station is next door at Str Bistriţei 1.

Blvd Republicii leads north from Piaţa Mareşal Ion Antonescu to Piaţa Ştefan cel Mare where most facilities are. The old town is immediately north-west of this square, at the foot of Cozla mountain.

Information
Tourist Offices All the hotels have tourist offices which arrange trips to the monasteries. RomSteam-Aldo (☎ & fax 231 431; email romsteam@decebal.ro), Str Plevnei 2, block L2, apartment 58, and the Ronedo Tourist Agency (☎ 231 870; fax 231 306), 1km west of the centre at Blvd Decebal 59, apartment 1, both specialise in steam train adventures around Romania (see Facts for the Visitor – Activities).

TAROM (☎ 214 268) is opposite the Hotel Ceahlău at Piaţa Ştefan cel Mare 1. It operates no flights from Piatra Neamţ.

Money The Nasty Change inside the Magazin Elegant shop on Piaţa Ştefan cel Mare offers the best rates. Get cash advance on Visa/MasterCard, and change travellers cheques at BANCOREX at Blvd Traian block A4 (open weekdays from 8.30 am to noon), or at the Bancă Comercială Română, Blvd Traian 19 (open weekdays from 8 am to 7 pm, Saturday from 8 am to 2 pm). There is an ATM outside which accepts Visa/MasterCard.

Post & Communications The post and telephone office on Str Alexandru cel Bun is open daily from 7.30 am to 9 pm. Faxes can also be sent from here.

Things to See & Do
Walk along Blvd Republicii to the central square, Piaţa Ştefan cel Mare. On the western side of the square is a small **park**, prettily laid out with a wooden pavilion and a **statue** of Ştefan cel Mare in its centre. Steps from the park lead to Piaţa Libertăţii, a small pedestrianised square where the remains of Piatra Neamţ's historic heart lie.

The quaint **Princely Court museum complex** (Muzeul Curtea Domnească) was founded in 1497 by Ştefan cel Mare. It comprised a 10m-tall **bell tower** and **St John's Church** (Biserica Sfântu Ioan; 1498). Some ruined foundations of the princely court have been unearthed in the courtyard of the Petru Rareş school (Liceul Petru Rareş), opposite the pedestrianised square on Str Ştefan cel Mare. An **Art Museum** (Muzeul de artă) and small **Ethnographic Museum** (Muzeul de etnografie) are next to the bell tower. Both are open daily, except Monday, from 10 am to 4 pm.

The local **History Museum** (Muzeul de Istorie), Blvd Mihai Eminescu 1, is open daily, except Sunday, from 9 am to 5 pm. There is a **Natural History Museum** (Muzeul de Ştinţe Naturale) at the northern end of Str Petru Rareş.

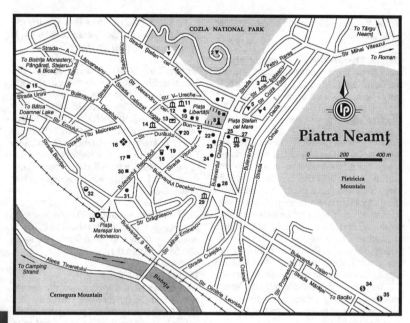

Piatra Neamţ

PLACES TO STAY	7	Petru Rareş School;	22	TAROM
6 Hotel Ceahlău		Remains of	23	Agenţie de Voiaj
17 Hotel Central		Princely Court		CFR
30 Hotel Bulevard	8	Statue of Ştefan cel	24	Kodak Express
		Mare	25	Pharmacy
PLACES TO EAT	9	Tineretului Theatre;	26	Lascăr Vorel Art
1 Colibele Haiducilor		Agenţie de Teatrală		Gallery
2 Cercul Gospodinelor	10	Bell Tower	27	Cinema Panoramic
4 Non-stop Billiard Bar	11	Ethnographic Museum		Prezinta
5 Restaurant Chic	12	Art Museum	28	Cinema Pietricica
19 Terasa	13	Post Office	29	History Museum
20 Patisserie	14	Calistrat Hogaş	31	BTT
21 Restaurant Cozla		Memorial Museum	32	Bus Station
	15	Ronedo Tourist	33	Train Station
OTHER		Agency	34	BANCOREX
3 Natural History	16	Department Store	35	Bancă Comercială
Museum	18	Little Las Vegas		Română

Three kilometres east of the centre of town is **Lacul Bâtca Doamnei**, an extremely popular spot during summer weekends. It is possible to swim in the lake (everyone else does!) and you can rent paddle and rowing boats.

Places to Stay

Camping Pitch your tent or hire a little wooden cabin at *Camping Strand* (☎ 217 835), overlooking the Bistriţa river and within spitting distance of the lake at Aleea Tineretului 1. A tent/wooden hut for two costs US$7/8 a night. To get to the campsite from the train station, turn right along Blvd 9 Mai and walk 50m until you come to a small bridge on the right. Cross the bridge and turn right along Aleea Tineretului.

Private Rooms Staff at the BTT tourism agency (☎ & fax 214 686), opposite the Hotel Bulevard at Blvd Republicii block A2, do not speak English but can find you a private room to stay in if you can get the message across. The office is open weekdays from 8 am to 4 pm.

Top Tours (☎ & fax 234 204), Str Ştefan cel Mare 17, takes bookings for ANTREC accommodation in private rooms in villages around Piatra Neamţ, in Durău and Ceahlău.

Hotels The cheapest is the one-star *Hotel Bulevard* (☎ 218 011; fax 218 111), a five minute walk from the bus station at Blvd Republicii 38. A bed in a cramped single/double room with shared bathroom is US$12/14. Bring your own toilet paper.

Close by is the 132-room *Hotel Central* (☎ 216 412, 216 414; fax 214 532) at Blvd Republicii 26. It is a huge concrete tower and as dreary inside as it is outside. Single/double rooms are US$27.50/28.50, including breakfast. Some staff speak pidgin French.

Top of the range is the 11-storey *Hotel Ceahlău* (☎ & fax 233 559) which towers in all its ugliness beneath the picturesque Pietricica and Cozla mountains at Piaţa Ştefan cel Mare 3. Two-star single/double rooms cost US$28.50/57 a night, including private bathroom, TV and breakfast.

Places to Eat
The restaurant *Cozla*, on Piaţa Ştefan cel Mare, is a large, glass-domed building, its interior smothered inside with hanging ivy and other green plants. The chicken liver for US$2 is passable but nothing to rave about; it is open daily from 9 am to midnight.

A 15 minute hike, but worth it, is the *Colibele Haiducilor* (☎ 213 909), in a traditional old Romanian house halfway up Cozla mountain. Strictly local cuisine is served

here. Steps lead up to the restaurant from Str Ştefan cel Mare; alternatively, from Str Ştefan cel Mare turn on to Str Ion Creangă and continue up the stone road. Further up the mountain, at the end of Str Ion Creangă, is *Cercul Gospodinelor* (☎ 223 845), another Romanian restaurant located inside a more modern building but favoured for its panoramic views. Colibele Haiducilor is open daily from 8 am to midnight; Cercul Gospodinelor is open from 8 to 2 am.

Numerous cafés and bars are dotted on Piaţa Ştefan cel Mare. Particularly popular are the *Panoramic Café* outside Hotel Ceahlău, and *Buon Gusto*, a 24 hour snack bar and café at the square's eastern end. *Restaurant Chic* is tucked in a huge courtyard off Piaţa Ştefan cel Mare and is glorious in summer. It is open daily from 10 to 1 am.

The *Patisserie*, on the corner of Blvd Republicii and Str Calistrat Hogaş, is a pleasant, airy café serving good cakes and coffee; open daily from 10 am to 9 pm.

Entertainment
Bars & Discos *Little Las Vegas* dares you to risk all in a round of American poker at Blvd Republicii 9. The games bar is open weekdays from 10 am to 11 pm, weekends from 10 am to 11 pm.

For the cheapest local brew in town try a pint of homemade beer or yeast drink for US$0.21 at the very local *Terasa*, a few doors away from Little Las Vegas. It is constantly filled with a flow of veteran drinkers from 10 am to 6 pm daily.

There is a non-stop *billiard bar*, opposite the history museum on Piaţa Kogălniceanu, in the same building as the Democratic Party headquarters.

Theatre Performances in Romanian are held every Friday, Saturday and Sunday at 7 pm at the *Tineretului Theatre* (Teatrul Tineretului; ☎ 211 472; fax 217 159) at Piaţa Ştefan cel Mare 1. Tickets costing US$0.35 are sold in advance at the Agenţie de Teatrală adjoining the theatre.

MOLDAVIA

Getting There & Away

Bus The bus station (☎ 211 331) is next to the train station, at Str Bistriţei 1. Hourly buses run to/from Târgu Neamţ (43km) between 5.30 am and 6 pm. There are two buses a day to Agapia, departing at 8 am and 7.30 pm.

Train The Agenţie de Voiaj CFR (☎ 210 034), at Piaţa Ştefan cel Mare 10, is open weekdays from 7.30 am to 8 pm.

BICAZ & THE BICAZ GORGES

Bicaz, on the confluence of the Bicaz and Bistriţa rivers, is 26km west of Piatra Neamţ. The town is famed for **Bicaz lake** (Lacul Izvorul Muntelui; Mountain Spring Lake) which sprawls over 3000 hectares north of Bicaz. The hydroelectric dam *(baraj)*, closing the lake at it's southern end, was built in 1950 with several villages being submerged and relocated in the process. Taking photographs of the footbridge crossing the dam wall is forbidden; soldiers patrol the dam from a wooden hut at the western end of the bridge.

On the eastern side of the lake is **Grozăveşti**, a village with a wooden church typical of those in Maramureş. The church was built this century after the old church, on the same site, fell into the lake. Apparently the day the church drowned, the local village priest received a postcard from Maramureş. The postage stamp featured a wooden Maramureş church, thus inspiring him to build his new church in that style.

You can rent **boats** at the Munteanu port (☎ 671 350) on the western side of lake. Turn right immediately after the bridge at the *Port Munteanu* sign. Paddle boats cost US$0.75 per person an hour and a cruising boat for up to 50 people is US$23 an hour. There is a small café here and a sunbathing deck on the lake shores. Boats can also be hired on the eastern side of Bicaz lake from the Boatel Utea Libada (☎ 671 036; see Places to Stay). Rowing and paddle boats here come equipped with life jackets and cost US$0.75 per person an hour.

From the southern end of Bicaz lake you can follow the road north along the lake shores to Vatra Dornei (see The Ceahlău Massif section), or continue west to Lacul Roşu and Gheorgheni into Transylvania, via the **Bicaz Gorges**. Hot tip: both routes are among the most remarkable in Romania!

The **Bicaz Gorges** (Cheile Bicazului) are 21km from Bicaz town. The gorge steeply twists and turns uphill for 5km, cutting through sheer, 300m-high limestone rocks on its journey through the mountains. Around the 'neck of hell' (Gâtul Iadului) the narrow mountain road runs directly beneath the overhanging rocks. Dozens of artisans sell locally made crafts from open-air stalls set up beneath the rocks. This entire stretch is protected under the Hăşmaş-Bicaz Gorges National Park (Parcul Naţional Hăşmaş-Cheile Bicazului). Ambitious plans in the 1980s to build a tunnel between Lacul Roşu and Bicaz to enable lorries to bypass this hazardous stretch remain on hold. Continuing along this road, you cross into Transylvania.

Places to Stay

Campers can pitch their tents for free on the patch of grass outside the *Cabana Bicaz Baraj* (430m) at the foot of the dam wall. The cabana has no rooms but serves snacks in its small café. The *Cabana Izvorul Muntelui* (797m) in Izvorul Muntelui, 12km from Bicaz town on the eastern side of the lake, has a few basic rooms.

The *Popas Turist Motel* at the southern end of the gorges has 46 beds costing US$2 a night. Bathrooms are shared and there is no hot water.

Around Bicaz lake the cheapest spot to stay is aboard the *Utea Libada* (☎ 671 036), moored at the southern end of the lake. It has 13 cabins costing US$5/7 for doubles/triples with a shared shower. Str Barajului leads from the main road to the boatel.

Next to the Str Barajului turn-off on the main road, is the *Motel complex* (☎ 671 456) which has double rooms in its main building for US$17 with shared bath and two-bed huts for US$6 a night. The complex has a small shop.

A couple of kilometres further north on the eastern side of the lake in Potoci village is the two-star *Motel Potoci* (☎ 672 236). Double rooms with private bath cost US$28 and a night in a cabana is US$6 per person.

Getting There & Away

Bicaz is on a branch line between Bacău (1½ to 2¼ hours) and Piatra Neamţ (25 to 40 minutes). There are nine trains daily in each direction, most of which stop at Bicaz.

DURĂU & THE CEAHLĂU MASSIF

From the south-eastern end of Bicaz lake, a road leads north through pine forests to the mountain resort of Durău (800m), a convenient base for hiking in the Ceahlău Massif . The story goes that Ceahlău's 'magic mountain' spells eternal friendship for those who hike up it together.

From here you can head east into Transylvania or north to Vatra Dornei (see Southern Bucovina). The Vatra Dornei road closely follows the Golden Bistriţa river (Bistriţa Aurie) for much of the way and is one of the country's great scenic delights.

Durău & Ceahlău

In the 19th century climbers sought shelter at **Durău Monastery** (Mănăstirea Durău) (1830), a complex comprising two churches and quarters for 35 nuns who inhabit the monastery today. Visitors are welcome.

The annual **Ceahlău Folk Festival** takes place in Durău on the second Sunday in August. Shepherds come down from the mountains and locals don traditional dress.

In **Ceahlău** (550m), 6km north of Durău, there are the remains of a princely palace built between 1639 and 1676 and an 18th century wooden church. The museum is in the centre of the village, 500m up a dirt track off the main road. Various hiking trails lead from Durău and Ceahlău into the Ceahlău Massif (see below).

Places to Stay The nuns at *Durău monastery* (☎ 033-678 383) still take in the weary and blistered. The monastery has six modern cabanas where travellers can stay for US$7 a night.

The *Cabana Paulo*, the first cabana you pass on the main road to Durău, has 16 places in a wooden, chalet-style house costing US$7 per person a night. Some 50m further is the family home of Igor Ghinculor (☎ 033-678 288). He has five double rooms with shared bathroom and hot water heater to let for US$7 per person and can arrange accommodation in private homes elsewhere in Durău and Ceahlău.

The *Hotel Cascada* opposite the monastery is a large, but not unattractive, concrete block, which has 81 single/double rooms for US$14/21 a night.

Hiking up the hill by the side of the Cascada, you come to Durău's main cluster of hotels: the 20-room *Hotel Bistriţa* is the smallest and friendliest of the lot. It has double rooms for US$14, and wooden bungalows which you can rent for US$4 a night. Bathrooms are shared and hot water is limited to a couple of hours in the morning and evening. The two-star *Hotel Durău* at the top of the hill has 80 double rooms for US$6 per person a night. The hotel has a bowling centre and disco.

The Ceahlău Massif

Moldovan Olympus (Olimpul Moldovei), the name given to Moldavia's most awe-inspiring mountain range proves just how much Moldavians prize the Ceahlău massif. The supreme God of the Dacians, Zamolxe, is said to have sought shelter in these mountains, making the 'magic mountain' his home and sacrificing the daughter of King Decebal on the altar of Dochia, hence creating the Dochia peak (1790m). The highest peak, Ocolaşu Mare, is 1907m. The 5200-hectare area is protected under the Ceahlău Massif National Park (Parcul Naţionale Muntele Ceahlău; 1941).

Hiking trails lead from Durău, Ceahlău village, Bicaz, Bicazul Ardelean (10km west of Bicaz towards the Bicaz Gorges), and Neagră (5km west from Bicaz Ardelean), into the Ceahlău massif. Most trails culminate at the Cabana Dochia, topping Dochia

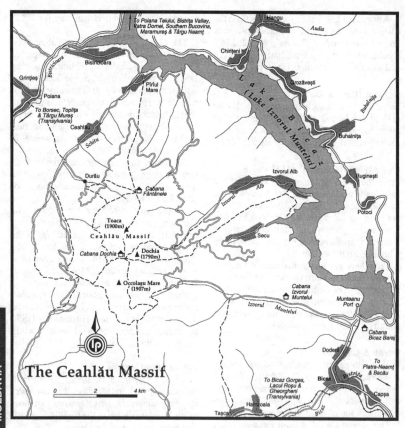

The Ceahlău Massif

Peak. The mountain rescue team, SALVAM-ONT, has rescue points at Cabana Dochia and Cabana Izvorul Muntelui (see Bicaz – Places to Stay). You can also SOS the team via Bicaz hospital (☎ 671 970).

The hiking map *Masivul Ceahlău Hartă turistică* (Publiturism, 1990) is difficult to find. It is easiest to buy in Bucharest. Popular marked hiking trails are best tackled in summer.

INTO THE DANUBE DELTA
From Moldavia there is no through road into northern Dobruja and the Danube Delta; any

trip west involves a short ferry crossing across the Danube river (Râul Dunărea). The alternative is to head south towards Bucharest then head east and cross the Danube at Cernavodă (see the Northern Dobruja chapter). For foot passengers there are direct ferries from Galaţi to Tulcea.

Galaţi
Galaţi ('ga-lahts'), on the confluence of the Danube, Siret and Prut rivers, is Moldavia's main gateway to the Danube Delta. It is home to Romania's largest steel mill with shabby shipyards scattered for kilometres

COLIN D SHAW

NICOLA WILLIAMS

MATTHIAS LÜFKENS

MATTHIAS LÜFKENS

Top left: The fresco-covered Suceviţa Monastery, Moldavia
Top right: The *Last Judgement* fresco, Voroneţ Monastery, Moldavia
Bottom left: Wam fast food, Chişinău, Moldova
Bottom right: City Hall, Tiraspol, Moldova

MATTHIAS LÜFKENS

MATTHIAS LÜFKENS

Moldova
Top: All Saints' Church, Chişinău, Moldova
Bottom: Equestrian Statue, Tiraspol, Moldova

along the riverside. During WWII, Galaţi was heavily bombed. Massive housing complexes fill the centre and cover entire hillsides of this ugly, industrial town today.

A funky **sculpture park** lies on the western outskirts of the town, on the road to Brăila. Further west is the **Galaţi Steel Works**, inaugurated in 1968 as part of Ceauşescu's grand five year plan under which Romania would be transformed into a great, heavy-industrial machine. Today the works, which employ thousands of people, are just one of the many thorns in the government's side. The plant is loss-making yet its closure would have a devastating economic effect on Galaţi's population, not least because the town's entire heating system is generated by the plant.

In mid-1997 the Romanian government declared part of Galaţi a ZLG – a free trade zone (Zona Libera Galaţi) – in an attempt to lure foreign investors.

Romania's naval fleet is paraded in Galaţi in all its glory every year on Marine Day on the second weekend in August.

Orientation & Information Galaţi has two ports, passenger ferries to Tulcea sail from the main port at Str Portului 34. To get to the centre from here, exit the main port building and turn left along Str Portului, continue for 1km, then turn right onto Str Domnească – the main street. Galaţi's main hotels are 200m north on this street.

Little tug boats – suitable for cars and lorries – depart from the smaller port to cross the Danube to the small village of IC Brătianu (formerly called '23 August' and marked on some maps as Zaclău) on the river's southern banks. The boat landing is 2.5km east from the centre along Str Portului.

The bus and trains station are adjacent to each other on Str Gării. Exit the station and head straight up the hill along Str Gării. Turn left along Str Domnească, past the university, until you reach the hotels. Continue south along Str Domnească to get to the main port.

Change money in the hotel currency exchange or head 1.5km west along Str Brăila, past the Hotel Dunărea, to the Bancă Comercială Română where you can change travellers cheques and get cash advance on credit cards.

Places to Stay & Eat Galaţi has two main hotels – the *Hotel Galaţi* (☎ 036-460 040) at Str Domnească 12, and the *Hotel Dunărea* (☎ 036-418 041) immediately opposite on the corner of Str Domnească and Str Brăila. The 'Danube' is cheaper at US$21/34 for singles/doubles with private bath. The Galaţi charges US$31/40.

The towering *Hotel Regina* (☎ 036-468 362) is 2.5km west of the centre at Str Gheorghe Coşbuc 1. Single/double/triple rooms are US$17/30/38 a night, including breakfast. To get to the hotel, turn right off Str Domnească along Str Brăila, then turn right after passing the Bancă Comercială Română.

Str Domnească is clustered with eating places, including the large *Restaurant Olympic*, with a terrace; the more funky *Sydney Restaurant*, open daily from noon to 6 am; and *Pizzeria Emporio*. From the centre, take the first left off Str Brăila to get to Galaţi's *Chinese Restaurant*.

Getting There & Away There are boats, trains and buses. Useful daily buses include one to Iaşi (255km) and one to Bucharest (212km).

The Agenţie de Voiaj CFR (☎ 036-435 121) is at Str Brăila, block 1. Daily train services from Galaţi include 15 trains to Brăila (30 to 40 minutes); and five to Bârlad (three hours) where you can change for Iaşi.

Ferry From Galaţi, a boat departs on Monday at 8.30 am, arriving in Tulcea at noon. A second boat departing on Monday at noon arrives in Tulcea at 1.30 pm, then continues to Crişan (arriving at 3 pm) and Mila 23 in the Danube Delta (arriving at 5 pm).

From Tulcea there is a speedy hydrofoil to Galaţi on Friday, departing from Sulina at 7.30 am, departing from Tulcea at noon, and arriving in Galaţi at 1.30 pm. The cost of a

MOLDAVIA

single Galaţi-Tulcea ticket is US$13. There is another boat from Tulcea to Galaţi on Saturday, departing at 12.15 pm and arriving in Galaţi at 5 pm. It is possible to buy a ticket straight through to Sulina or Sfântu Gheorghe in the Danube Delta; you have to change ferries however in Tulcea.

The two small tug ferries, *Poinari I* and *Poinari II*, depart every hour from the eastern boat landing, which is signposted *Trecere Bac* from the centre. A single ticket costs US$1 for a car and US$0.14 for a foot passenger. The crossing to IC Brătianu takes five minutes.

Southern Bucovina

Southern Bucovina embraces the north-western region of present-day Moldavia; northern Bucovina is in Ukraine. In 1775, the region was annexed by the Austro-Hungarian empire. It remained in Habsburg hands until 1918 when Bucovina was returned to Romania. Northern Bucovina was annexed by the Soviet Union in 1940 and incorporated into Ukraine.

The painted churches of southern Bucovina are among the greatest artistic monuments of Europe – in 1993 they were collectively designated a World Heritage Site by UNESCO. If your time is limited, the Voroneţ and Moldoviţa monasteries, both quite accessible by bus and train, provide a representative sample of what Bucovina has to offer. To do a complete circuit on your own will require three days. You can save time by renting a car in Suceava for US$50 per day – travelling the rugged mountain road between Moldoviţa and Suceviţa alone is worth the expense.

Apart from the religious art and monasteries, southern Bucovina is well worth visiting for its folklore, picturesque villages, bucolic scenery and colourful inhabitants, all as good as anything you'll find elsewhere in Romania.

SUCEAVA
• *area code ☎ 030, pop 117,571*

Suceava was the capital of Moldavia from 1388 until 1566. During the 15th century the town flourished as a commercial centre, due in the main to its great strategic location on the Lviv-Istanbul trading route. By the end of Ştefan cel Mare's reign in 1504 Suceava had some 40 churches. In 1675, Suceava fortress, which had never surrendered or been conquered, was blown up by the Turks, symbolising the decline of the town as a commercial and spiritual centre.

During the Ceauşescu regime in the 1980s, Suceava became notorious for its toxic pulp and paper works which churned out 20 tonnes of cellulose and fibre waste a day. By 1990, hundreds of local people were reported to be suffering from respiratory and nervous disorders known as 'Suceava syndrome'.

The colourful Moldavian Furrier Fair is held every year in Suceava in mid-August.

Orientation
Suceava has two train stations. Trains which originate or terminate in Suceava arrive/depart at Gara Suceava Nord. Trains which transit Suceava arrive/depart from Gara Suceava in the Burdujeni district. Both stations – 2km apart – are a few kilometres north of Piaţa 22 Decembrie, the centre of town. The left-luggage office at Gara Suceava is at the information window on the main platform (open 24 hours).

The department store (universal magazin) is close to the Hotel Bucovina, south of Piaţa 22 Decembrie, on Str Ştefan cel Mare (open weekdays from 7 am to 8 pm, Saturday from 8 am to 2 pm). In front of it is a small flower market.

Maps The *Judeţul Suceava Hartă Turistică* (Publiturism, 1983) includes a small city map of Suceava; many street names have since changed however. If you speak French, the *Suceava* county guide (1981) has good historical and cultural information. It's sold for US$0.25 at the Bucovina History Museum.

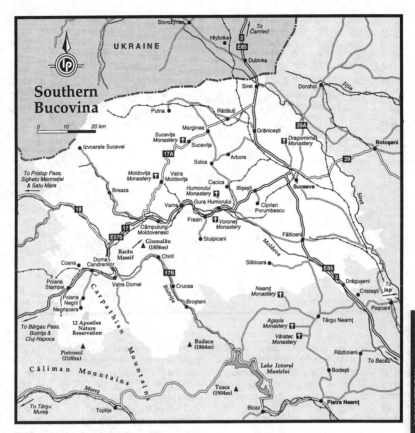

Information

Tourist Offices The ONT Carpaţi tourist office (☎ 221 297), Str Nicolae Bălcescu 2, is an utter disaster. Avoid. Staff are rude and have the cheek to sell you promotional brochures freely distributed elsewhere. It arranges monastery tours, guides for US$18 a day, and rents chauffeur-driven cars. It is open weekdays from 7.30 am to 7.30 pm, Saturday from 8.30 am to 1.30 pm.

For service with a smile from people who are as much in love with their work as they are with their country, head straight for Bucovina Estur instead (see Travel Agencies later). Nothing is too much effort for staff here.

The Automobil Clubul Român (☎ 210 997), Str Nicolae Bălcescu 8, sells road maps. It's open weekdays from 8 am to 4 pm.

Money The Platinum currency exchange office inside Bucovina Estur (see Travel Agencies) is open weekdays from 9 am to 5 pm, Saturday from 9 am to 1 pm.

BANCOREX, on the corner of Str Curtea Domnească and Str Firmu, gives cash advance on Visa/MasterCard and changes travellers cheques. It is open weekdays from

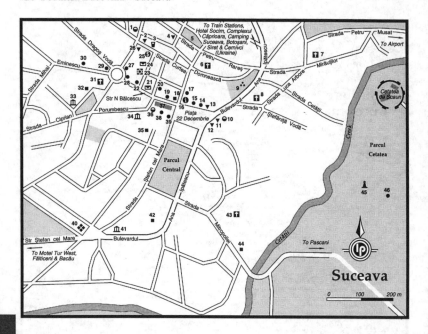

8.30 am to noon. Travellers cheques can also be cashed at the Bancă Comercială Română at Str Ştefan cel Mare 31; open weekdays from 8.30 am to 1.30 pm and 3 to 7 pm, weekends from 10 am to 1 pm. Outside the bank is an ATM which accepts Visa/MasterCard.

Post & Communications The telephone centre, inside the post office on the corner of Str Firmu and Str Nicolae Bălcescu, is open weekdays from 7 am to 8 pm, Saturday from 8 am to noon.

Travel Agencies Unbeatable for the service and friendly smiles it offers is Bucovina Estur (☎ & fax 223 259), on the western side of Piaţa 22 Decembrie at Str Ştefan cel Mare 24. Its English-speaking staff arrange accommodation in private homes in Suceava and villages around the painted monasteries, sell maps, rent cars with or without a driver, have English-speaking guides, and arrange

tours to the monasteries and the Cacica salt mine. The office is open weekdays from 9 am to 8 pm, Saturday from 9 am to 11 am.

BTT (☎ 215 235, 214 389; fax 520 438) at Str Meseriasilor 10, offers monastery tours and arranges accommodation in private homes in Câmpulung Moldovenesc, Vama, Humor and Ciocăneşti. The office is open daily, except Sunday, from 7.30 am to 6.30 am.

Things to See
The foundations of the 15th century **princely palace** are near the bus stop at Piaţa 22 Decembrie. To the north of the square is **St Dimitru's Church** (Biserica Sfântu Dimitru). This church was built between 1534-35 by Petru Rareş in a clubbed Byzantine style typical of Moldavian churches in the 16th century. Its interior frescoes were painted in 1535 and the exterior was originally painted too; traces of the Jessy tree, the acatiser hymn and the siege of Constantino-

PLACES TO STAY		6	St Dimitru's Church	31	St Nicholas Church
18	Hotel Suceava;	7	Mirăuţi Church		& Monument
	Restaurant	8	Domniţelor Church	33	Simeon Florea
	Suceava	9	Princely Palace Ruins		Memorial House
32	Hotel Arcaşul	10	Buses to/from	34	Hanul Domnesc;
35	Hotel Gloria		Train Station		Ethnographic
42	Hotel Bucovina	14	Pharmacy Nr 1		Museum
44	Hotel Balada	15	TAROM	36	Taxi Rank
		16	ONT Office	37	Culture House
PLACES TO EAT		17	Supermarket	38	Artizant Souvenir
2	Café Olmasil	19	Agenţie de Voiaj CFR		Shop
4	Toscana Pizza &	20	BTT	39	Bucovina
	Burger House	21	Post Office		Estur
11	Poftă Bună Patisserie	22	ACR	40	Universal Department
12	Poftă Bună Fast Food	23	Synagogue		Store
13	Café-bar Bucureşti	24	Post Office	41	Bucovina History
26	Restaurant Aida	25	BANCOREX		Museum
		27	Kodak Express	43	Monastery of St John
OTHER		28	Bookshop		the New
1	Bus Station; Hotel	29	Cinema Modern	45	Statue of Ştefan cel
3	Club Amsterdam	30	Eurostela 24-hour		Mare
5	Central Market		Shop	46	Cemetery

ple can still be faintly seen on the eastern wall.

At Str Ciprian Porumbescu 5, just west of Piaţa 22 Decembrie, is **Hanul Domnesc**, a 16th century guesthouse that now houses an **ethnographic museum** (closed Monday). Its collection of folk costumes is quite good.

Close by at Aleea Simeon Florea Marian 2 is the **Simeon Florea Marian Memorial House** (☎ 227 297), dedicated to the life and works of the folk song poet, Simeon Florea Marian (1847-1907) whose bust stands in the small park in front of the museum. The museum is open daily, except Sunday, from 9 am to 6 pm. If the door is locked, knock, and someone should answer.

Next to the post office on Str Firma is the town's only surviving **synagogue** dating from 1870. It still serves the small Jewish community numbering no more than 200 today. Prior to WWII, some 18 synagogues served the local Jewish community. There is an **old Jewish Cemetery** with graves dating to the 1700s on the corner of Str Ştefan Tomşa and Str Alexandru cel Bun. It is completely overgrown and you can only enter it by the backyard of a private house. The **new Jewish Cemetery**, on the opposite side of the road to the central Orthodox cemetery,

close to the citadel on Str Parcului, is a lavish affair in contrast.

Return to Piaţa 22 Decembrie and follow Str Ştefan cel Mare south past the **Central Park** (Parcul Central) to the surprisingly informative **Bucovina History Museum** (Muzeul naţionale al Bucovinei) at Str Ştefan cel Mare 33. The presentation comes to an abrupt end at 1945 and old paintings now hang in rooms that formerly glorified the communist era. The museum is open daily, except Monday, from 10 am to 6 pm.

Backtrack a little to the park and take Str Mitropoliei south-east to the **Monastery of St John the New** (Mănăstirea Sfântu Ioan cel Nou; 1522) at Str Ioan Vodă Viteazul 2. The paintings on the outside of the church are badly faded, but give you an idea of the churches for which Bucovina is famous.

Continue on Str Mitropoliei, keeping left on the main road out of town, till you see a large wooden gate marked *Parcul Cetăţii* on the left. Go through it and, when the ways divide, follow the footpath with the park benches around to the left to the huge **equestrian statue** (1966) of the Moldavian leader, Ştefan cel Mare. Twenty metres back on the access road to the monument is another footpath on the left, which descends towards the

MOLDAVIA

MOLDAVIA

Bucovina's Monasteries

The painted churches of southern Bucovina were erected at a time when northern Moldavia was threatened by Turkish invaders. Great popular armies would gather inside the monasteries' strong defensive walls, waiting to do battle. To educate, entertain and arouse the interest of the illiterate soldiers and peasants who were unable to enter the church or understand the Slavic liturgy, well known biblical stories were portrayed on the church walls in cartoon-style frescoes.

Most amazing in these vast compositions is the realistic manner of portraying human figures against a backdrop not unlike the local landscape (the forested Carpathian foothills). Some frescoes have been damaged by centuries of rain and wind, but more often than not the intense colours have been duly preserved, from the greens of Suceviţa, to the blues of Voroneţ and the reds of Humor. Natural dyes are used to colour the walls – sulphur for yellow, madder for red, and cobalt or lapis for blue.

All Orthodox monasteries face the east in keeping with the traditional belief that the light of God shines in the image of the rising sun. An outside porch, likewise tattooed with frescoes, is typical of the Bucovina monasteries. Within, they are divided into three rooms – the *pronaos*, the tomb room, and the *naos*. Women are not allowed to enter the altar, shielded from public view by an iconostasis – a beautifully sculpted, gilded partition in the naos. The church domes are a peculiar combination of Byzantine pendentives and Moorish crossed arches with larger-than-life paintings of Christ or the Virgin peering down.

Each monastery is dedicated to a saint, whose patron day is among the most important feast days for the monastery inmates. The nuns or monks are required to fast – no meat, eggs or dairy products – for several days leading up to any religious feast. Wednesday, Friday, Lent, the six weeks after Easter, and the days preceding Christmas are likewise fast days.

Novices are required to serve three to seven years in a monastery before being ordained. Numerous penances have to be observed during this training period: many have to stand motionless in the street for several consecutive days, bearing a plaque indicating that they are 'waiting' for cash donations towards the 'spiritual furthering' of their monastery.

Following the Habsburg occupation of Bucovina in 1785, most monasteries were closed and their inhabitants forced to relinquish their spiritual lives for a civilian one. The monasteries were equally persecuted under communism, and it is only since 1990 that the inner activity of these holy sanctuaries has matched the dynamism of their outer façades.

Most monasteries are open daily from 8 am to 6 pm and provide free guided tours in English or French. An additional entrance fee is charged for cameras/camcorders. Smoking and wearing shorts is forbidden and women are required to cover their shoulders. ■

Cetatea de Scaun (City of Residence), a castle dating from 1388 that in 1476 held off Mehmed II, conqueror of Constantinople (Istanbul). The original fortress, known as Muşat's fortress was built by Petru I Muşat. It had eight square towers and was surrounded by defensive trenches. Ştefan cel Mare developed it further, building 4m-thick, 33m-tall walls around it so it was impossible to shoot an arrow over. From 1775 following the occupation of Bucovina by the Austrians, the fortress was dismantled and the stones used to build houses in Suceava town. Restoration work started on the fortress in 1944. It is open daily, except Monday, from 10 am to 6 pm. Admission costs US$0.15.

On the hillside opposite the fortress is **Mirăuţi Church** (1390), the original Moldavian coronation church, which was rebuilt in the 17th century. It was to this church that Petru I Muşat moved the Metropolitan cathedral in the 16th century. Get here by taking the path down through the park on the west (left) side of the fortress.

Places to Stay

Camping Near the Suceava River, between Gara Suceava Nord and Suceava in the district of Iţcani, is *Camping Suceava* (☎ 214 958) on Str Cernăuţi. It has been privatised but is in bad shape, with two-bed wooden huts that could use a good cleaning. A bed in a hut is US$3.50 a night.

Private Rooms *Bucovina Estur* (see Travel Agencies) arranges private rooms for US$10 per person. The agency can also arrange private rooms in Vatra Dornei, Vatra Moldoviţa, Humor or Dragomirna Monasteries and Gura Humorului.

Hotels The cheapest, seediest and dodgiest joint in town, only recommended for groups of die-hard backpackers (lone travellers, avoid!) is the *Autogară Suceava* (☎ 216 089) hotel above the bus station ticket hall on Str Armenească. A bed in a simple, smelly double room with shared bathroom is US$4. Reception? The bus station information booth.

Cleaner is *Hotel Socim* (☎ 257 675; fax 522 662) in a converted block of flats, some 200m walk from Gara Suceava at Str Jean Bart 24. A bed in a double/triple/four-bed room with shared shower and toilet is US$2.80/2.80/3.50 a night. Breakfast is not included and the air is foul-smelling in some of the rooms. Hot water is only available between 6 and 9 am, and 4 and 9 pm.

Better value for the comfort and security it offers is the central *Hotel Gloria* (☎ 521 209; fax 520 087) at Str Mihai Vasile Bumbac 4. Singles/doubles for US$11/15 are good value. A scrambled egg and salami breakfast is included.

The state-run, two-star *Hotel Suceava* (☎ 222 497; fax 521 080) at Str Nicolae Bălcescu 2 is a modern hotel in the centre of everything. Staff are friendly but rooms are over-rated at US$45 for a single or US$62 /57 for a double with private bath/shower. Breakfast is included.

Single/double rooms are offered for identical prices at its sister hotel, the *Hotel Arcaşul* (☎ 210 944; fax 227 598), close to the Simeon Florea Marian Memorial House at Str Mihai Viteazul 4-6. Breakfast costs an extra US$3.

The last in the state trio is the *Hotel Bucovina* (☎ 217 048) at Str Ana Ipătescu 5. Singles/doubles with private bathroom are US$45/90 a night, including breakfast.

Book through Bucovina Estur for the privately run *Hotel Balada* (☎ 223 198; fax 520 087) at Str Mitropoliei 3. The agency gets 10% discount. Double/triple rooms cost US$45/64 (without discount).

Out of Town Eight kilometres north, in a forest on the road to Dorohoi, is the *Complexul Căprioara* (literally 'deer complex'; ☎ & fax 520 708), a private motel, disco and bar which draws a large crowd. A bed in one of its six double rooms is US$7. There are also a dozen wooden camping huts on the complex which cost US$6 a night. Tents can be pitched for a US$2 fee.

Some 4km from the centre, on the road to Humor Monastery, is the *Motel TurWest* (☎ 210 485) on Str Rulmantului. Doubles/four-bed rooms cost US$20/40 a night without breakfast. It also has a small bar with a billiard table and a disco.

Places to Eat
Restaurants & Cafés Eating options in Suceava are limited. The soups served at the *Restaurant Suceava* at Str Nicolae Bălcescu 2 are greasy but the charcoal-grilled beef steak for US$2 is tasty and fairly fat-free. The restaurant is open daily from 10 am to 10 pm but is often booked by tour groups.

Favoured locally is *Country Pizza*, not far from the stadium at Blvd 1 Decembrie 1918. Its small selection of pizza slices, with a variety of generous toppings ranging from salami to seafood, cost a mere US$1.20 – although if you want to do what everyone else does, you should pay an extra US$0.05 for 1g of ketchup which you douse thickly over your pizza. It is open daily from 10 am to midnight.

Toscana Pizza & Burger House, close to the bus station on Str Petru Rareş, is a clean, modern establishment with large windows overlooking the street and a reasonable choice of pizzas. It is open daily from 10 am to 11 pm.

There is a smoky *fast food* outlet next to the BTT office at Str Meseriasilor 10, open daily from 8 am to midnight. The *Café Olmasil* on Str Curtea Domnească has billiard tables and is open daily from 8 am to 10 pm. The *Restaurant Aida*, opposite the café on the same street has the usual plates of pork and potatoes, and has really seen better days. The place is open daily from 8 am to 9 pm.

MOLDAVIA

Cunningly located smack next to the central bus stop on Piaţa 22 Decembrie is the excellent *Poftă Bună Patiserie* and adjoining *fast food* outlet. The cakes, pastries and pain au chocolat for US$0.14 are heavenly and the best bet for a delicious breakfast. It has a standup counter where you can drink juice or dunk your pastry in your coffee. Hot dogs for US$0.50 and hamburgers for US$0.75 are sold in the adjoining fast food outlet, open 24 hours.

Self-Catering There is a *supermarket* opposite the Suceava restaurant on Str Ştefan cel Mare. It opens weekdays from 10 am to 8 pm, Saturday from 7 am to 9 pm. *Eurostela*, almost opposite St Nicholas Church on Str Mihai Eminescu, opens 24 hours. The *central market* is close to the bus station, on the corner of Str Petru Rareş and Str Avram Iancu.

Entertainment

Cinema *Cinema Modern*, facing the roundabout on the corner of Str Mihai Eminescu and Str Dragos Vodă, screens films in English. There is also a small cinema inside the *Cultural House* (Casă de Cultură) on Piaţa 22 Decembrie.

Bars & Clubs The private *Club Amsterdam* on Str Curtea Domnească charges a US$28 yearly membership fee for entrance to the cheap-thrills nightclub. One-time guests can pay US$3, providing you manage to pass the hefty security on the door. A cheaper bet is *Club 33*, inside the Cultural House, which is open daily from noon to midnight.

The top spot in summer is the outside disco at the out-of-town *Complexul Căprioara*, surrounded by forests 8km north of Suceava (see Places to Stay – Out of Town). The disco rocks 24 hours.

Getting There & Away

Airport TAROM has two flights on Monday, Wednesday and Thursday from Suceava to Iaşi and Bucharest. A single fare from Suceava to Bucharest is US$55 and a single Suceava-Iaşi ticket is US$28. The TAROM

office (☎ 214 686) at Str Nicolae Bălcescu 2, is open Monday to Wednesday from 7 am to 6.30 pm, Thursday and Friday from 7 am to 5 pm, Saturday from 7 am to 10 am.

Bus The bus station (☎ 216 089) is in the centre of town at Str Armenească. Tickets for international destinations to Chişinău in Moldova and Cernăuţi (Chernivtsi) in Ukraine are only sold from ticket window No 4. Tickets for buses in transit can only be bought half an hour before the bus departs from Suceava.

Services to other Romanian destinations include eight buses daily to Gura Humorului (47km), Piatra Neamţ (120km), and Siret (43km); 10 daily to Rădăuţi (62km) and Botoşani (42km); and one daily to Satu Mare (358km), Iaşi (141km) and Târgu Neamţ (71km).

Train Tickets for trains can be bought 24 hours or more before departure at the Agenţie de Voiaj CFR (☎ 214 335) at Str Nicolae Bălcescu 8. It is open weekdays from 7 am to 8 pm.

The main routes served by local trains include Suceava-Ilva Mică (from where some trains continue to Cluj-Napoca), via Ciprian Porumbescu, Gura Humorului, Vama, Câmpulung Moldovenesc and Vatra Dornei. Another route is Suceava-Păltinoasa, via Cacica. You can go to Putna by train. Suceava is on the main Bucharest-Suceava railroad, so is well served by express trains to other cities in Romania.

Getting Around

To/From the Airport Suceava airport is 16km east of the centre in the Salcea district. TAROM operates a free shuttle bus from its office at Str Nicolae Bălcescu 2 to the airport. It departs one hour before flights. Local buses also run every 25 minutes between 5.35 am and 11 pm from Suceava bus station to the airport.

Bus & Trolleybus Buses and trolleybuses run between 5 am and 11 pm. The central bus and trolleybus stop is at the western end of

Piaţa 22 Decembrie from which all buses and trolleybuses to/from the two train stations arrive/depart. Trolleybus Nos 2 and 3 and bus Nos 26 and 30 run between the centre and Gara Suceava. To reach Gara Suceava Nord, take trolleybus No 5 or bus Nos 1, 7, 8, 10, 11, 13 or 29. The buses and trolleybuses for both train stations stop directly outside the station.

Local buses to villages within a 15km radius of the city depart from the Autogară Burdejeni, a small red-brick building close to Gara Suceava at Str Nicolae Iorga 24. Take trolleybus No 4 and bus Nos 12, 15, 21 and 31 from the central bus stop.

Car Rental Bucovina Estur (see Information – Travel Agencies) rents cars with/without a driver for US$70/60 a day, including unlimited kilometres. It can also provide English or French-speaking guides for US$15 a day. The ONT Carpaţi tourist office (see Tourist Offices) rents a car with a driver for around US$55 a day with unlimited kilometres. For those who plan to tour the monasteries, it can provide a guide for an additional US$18 a day.

AROUND SUCEAVA

Not vital but interesting if time allows are the sights around Suceava: Dragomirna Monastery can be easily incorporated into any trip north to Arbore and Putna. The villages of Illişeşti and Ciprian Porumbescu are en route to Humor and Voroneţ monasteries.

Dragomirna Monastery

Dragomirna monastery (Mănăstirea Dragomirna), 12km north of Suceava in the village of Mitocul Dragomirna, was founded between 1608-9 by the scholar, calligrapher, artist and bishop Anastasie Crimca who joined the Putna monastery as a novice monk in his teenage years.

The splendidly stone-carved turret on the top of the main church (1627) incorporates some 2000 different motifs. The intricate rope lacing around the side of the church represents the unity of the Holy Trinity and the short-lived unification of the principalities of Moldavia, Wallachia and Transylvania in 1600. The church tower is 42m tall.

Dragomirna's treasures that survived Cossack attacks in 1653 are displayed in a **museum of medieval art** in the monastery grounds. Exhibits include a beautifully carved candle made by the Bishop Crimca; ornamental carved cedar crosses featuring 32 miniature biblical scenes mounted in silver-gilt filigree; and a large number of missals and religious scripts written in Slavic and illustrated by Crimca.

Dragomirna remained inhabited during the Habsburg and later communist purges on the Orthodox church. Crimca's dying wish was that a day should not pass without prayers being said in his monastery. Thus seven elderly nuns defied communist orders and remained alone at the monastery throughout the 1960s and 1970s. Today, 60 nuns live here. Admission to the complex is US$0.30.

Places to Stay & Eat Bucovina Estur (see Suceava – Travel Agencies) arrange accommodation for up to six people at Dragomirna monastery. Male and female guests sleep in separate rooms. Both sexes are allowed to join the nuns for a vegetarian dinner in the evening. The mother superior does not charge guests but she expects a 'small donation'.

Getting There & Away Buses from Suceava to Dragomirna depart every 15 minutes between 5.50 am and 8.30 pm (45 minutes, US$0.45) from Suceava bus station.

Illişeşti & Ciprian Porumbescu

Illişeşti, 20km south-west of Suceava, was home to a wealthy evangelist priest who had a daughter called Berta. In the neighbouring village of Ciprian Porumbescu, 6km south, lived the Romanian composer Ciprian Porumbescu (1853-83) who fell wildly in love with the priest's beautiful daughter. Being poor and of the Orthodox faith however, the composer was not considered a suitable match for Berta, inspiring him to compose the well-known *Ballad of Ciprian*.

MOLDAVIA

In 1873, Porumbescu was imprisoned in Austria for alleged anti-state activities. Until his sudden death at the age of 30 in 1883, he taught music in Braşov where he composed Romania's first operetta, *Crai Nou (New Prince)*.

The **Memorial House** (Casă Memorială) to Ciprian Porumbescu in which the composer lived for most of his life, remains in the village of Ciprian Porumbescu. The key for the house is available from the **Ciprian Porumbescu Museum** (Muzeul Ciprian Porumbescu; ☎ operator 991; ask for ☎ 338), at the western end of the village. Concerts are held in the museum which displays various relics from Porumbescu's life. The bed in which Berta slept is also exhibited here. The museum is open daily, except Monday, from 9 am to 6 pm. Admission is US$0.25/0.15 for adults/students.

To get to Ciprian Porumbescu from Illişeşti, continue for 4km west along the Suceava-Gura Humorului road, past the Hanul Illişeşti. Turn left at the signpost for Ciprian Porumbescu and continue for 6km along the forest road until you reach the village. At the southern end of the village, next to a well, the road forks; turn left for the memorial house or right for the museum complex.

Places to Stay & Eat Wild camping is permitted in Illişeşti forest which surrounds the village to the west. You can buy fresh milk and cheese from the shepherds who live in small wooden huts in the valley of the Stupca brook which you pass before entering the forest.

There are cabanas in the forest and rooms at the *Hanul Illişeşti* (☎ operator 991; ask for Illişeşti Hanul 4), 3km west of Illişeşti on the road to Gura Humorului. Double/triple rooms with private shower at the inn cost US$7/11 a night. A night's stay in an unheated cabana is US$3.50. Hot water can be arranged if you call in advance.

Getting There & Away Two buses daily, departing from Suceava at 1.30 and 7.30 pm, stop at Illişeşti village from where it is a good 6km hike through forest to Ciprian Porumbescu.

There are also four local trains daily to Ciprian Porumbescu (40 minutes). Trains depart from Gara Suceava Nord at 5.29 am and 3.36 pm; from Gara Suceava trains leave at 7.20 am and 7.17 pm.

GURA HUMORULUI
• *area code* ☎ *030, pop 14,000*

This small logging town, 36km west of Suceava on the main railway line to Cluj-Napoca, is an ideal centre for visiting the monasteries. Most trains stop here and the adjacent train and bus stations are a seven minute walk from the centre of town. There is an **Ethnographic Museum** (Muzeul Etnografie) at Blvd Bucovinei 21. The central post office is close to Restaurant Select, on the corner of Str Bucovinei and Str 9 Mai. The Agenţie de Voiaj CFR, Str Republicii 10, is opposite the Cinema Lumina.

A popular trip is to catch a train to Gura Humorului then trek 4km south to Voroneţ monastery; walk back to Gura Humorului and then hike 6km north to Humor where you can stay the night before visiting the monastery the following day. If you plan to bus it from Gura Humorului to Voroneţ and Humor monasteries, check the bus schedule immediately when you arrive in town; bus times change fairly regularly and it is usually quite difficult to make it to both monasteries in a day.

From Gura Humorului you can continue following the main Suceava-Vatra Dornei road west to Câmpulung Moldovenesc and the Rarău mountains, turning off the main road 16km before Câmpulung Moldovenesc at Vama where a road leads north to the Moldoviţa and Suceviţa monasteries.

Alternatively you can head directly north from Gura Humorului to the Solca and Arbore monasteries making a small detour to the Cacica salt mines en route; from Arbore you can then continue north to Rădăuţi where you can continue north to Putna monastery or head west to Suceviţa and Moldoviţa.

Places to Stay

Private Rooms More and more families in Gura Humorului are organising their own agro-tourism scheme, inviting guests to stay in their own homes for around US$15 a night. They have no official office but staff at Restaurant Select (see Places to Eat) have a list of families who rent rooms. The Bolac family at Str Ana Ipătescu 13 and the Rusu family at Str Victoriei 6 (☎ 231 220) both do.

Also excellent hosts are the Andrian family (☎ 238 863) at Str Câmpului 30. They have three modern double rooms which they rent out for US$25 a night in high season, including breakfast. Guests share one bathroom which has a hot water boiler.

Bucovina Estur (see Suceava – Places to Stay) takes bookings for rooms here.

Hotels The four-storey *Hotel Carpaţi* (☎ 231 103), Str 9 Mai 9, has grotty single/double rooms with primitive communal showers for US$7/11 a night per person. The hotel has no hot water.

Otherwise, try *Cabana Ariniş* at the foot of the wooded hills, 1km south of town (US$5 per person). If you are coming from the station on foot, don't cross the river and enter town but follow the right embankment downstream till you reach a bridge at the entrance to Parc Dendrologic. Go through the park to a suspension bridge that leads directly to the cabana. By car the cabana is accessible from the Voroneţ road (turn left just south of the bridge). You could easily walk from here to Voroneţ in under an hour. Meals are served at the cabana and in the large terrace restaurant by the suspension bridge.

Places to Eat

Basic places for pork and soup include *Restaurant Moldova*, on the left just after the bridge as you come from the stations, and the *Bucovina*, on the right behind the cinema.

Topnotch is *Restaurant Select* (☎ 320 968) at Str Bucovinei 1. Specialities on its Romanian/English/French menu include trout for US$1.20 and a fine selection of soups. It is open daily from 10 am to midnight. Next door to the restaurant is a well stocked *Mini-Market*, ideal for getting in supplies if you intend hiking to the monasteries.

Getting There & Away

From Gura Humorului bus station (☎ 230 707), Str Ştefan cel Mare 37, there is one bus daily to Arbore (36km); two to Rădăuţi (40km) and Piatra Neamţ (261km); three to Solca (21km) and Cacica (15km); four to Voroneţ (4km); five to Botoşani (64km) via Illişeşti (15km); seven to Humor monastery (6km); nine a day to Câmpulung Moldovenesc (33km); and eight to Suceava (47km). On weekends the service is greatly reduced. If you have limited time, you can bargain with taxi drivers here for tours to the monasteries.

Gura Humorului is on the main railway line between Suceava and Ilva Mica, with some eight daily trains covering this route which continues west to Cluj-Napoca in Transylvania. From Gura Humorului there are four trains daily to Iaşi (2¾ hours).

VORONEŢ

The walled monastery of Voroneţ (Mănăstirea Voroneţ), famed for its vibrant fresco of the Last Judgement, has deservedly been dubbed the 'Sistine Chapel of the East'. Note the vibrant, matchless blue used throughout the frescoes here – it's a unique pigment known worldwide as 'Voroneţ blue'.

The *Last Judgment,* which fills the entire western wall is perhaps the most marvellous and dramatic Bucovine fresco. At the top, angels roll up the signs of the zodiac to indicate the end of time. The middle fresco shows humanity being brought to judgement. On the left, St Paul escorts the believers, while on the right Moses brings forward the nonbelievers. From left to right the latter are Jews, Turks, Tartars, Armenians and Africans – a graphic representation of the prejudices of the time. Below is the Resurrection.

At the top of the northern wall is *Genesis,* from Adam and Eve on the left to Cain and

MOLDAVIA

Abel on the right. The southern wall features another tree of Jesse with the genealogy of some 100 biblical personalities featured in its eight registers. In the vertical fresco to the left of this is the story of the martyrdom of St John of Suceava (who is buried in the Monastery of Sfântu Ioan cel Nou in Suceava).

The tomb of Daniel the Hermit, the first abbot of Voroneţ monastery, lies in the narthex. His portrait is above the main entrance to the church. It was upon the worldy advice of Daniel the Hermit, who told Ştefan cel Mare that he should not give up his battle against the Turks, that the Moldavian prince went on to win further victories against the Turks and then to build Voroneţ monastery out of gratitude to God. In 1785 the occupying Austrian administration forced Voroneţ's monks to abandon their monastic life and it was not until 1991 that the monastery became inhabited once more, this time by a small community of nuns.

Admission to the monastery is US$0.75 plus US$1.40/2 for cameras/video cameras. Voroneţ also has a very good souvenir shop, with a wide range of postcards and books about the painted monasteries, including the beautifully illustrated, A4-size *The Moldavian Mural Painting in the 15th and 16th Centuries*, published in hardback by the National Commission of Romania as part of a UNESCO-funded project in 1996. It costs US$28.50 with texts in Romanian, English, French and German.

Places to Stay & Eat

Private rooms are available at the Nistru family home (☎ 230 551). The family has four double rooms, costing US$25/21 a night in summer/winter, including breakfast. There are two bathrooms, each kitted out with an electric water heater. To reach the house from the monastery, continue past the main entrance, turn right along a dirt track, and continue for 50m.

Getting There & Away

There are four buses daily from Gura Humorului to Voroneţ, departing at 7 am, 12,

2.45 and 4.40 pm. A sunny option is to walk the 4km along a narrow village road to Voroneţ. The route is clearly marked and it is impossible to get lost.

Bucovina Estur (see Suceava – Travel Agencies) arranges private transport to Voroneţ; if you want to stay the night, they can organise transport there too.

HUMOR

Of all the Bucovina monasteries, Humor monastery (Mănăstirea Humorului) – the smallest of the painted monasteries – has the most impressive interior frescoes. It was founded by Chancellor Theodor Bubuiog in 1530 under the guidance of Moldavian prince Petru Rareş, Ştefan cel Mare's illegitimate son. Unlike the other monasteries, Humor has no tower and is surrounded by ramparts made from wood; its traditional Moldavian open porch was the first of its kind to be built in Bucovina.

Its exterior frescoes, dating from 1535, are predominantly red. The red is derived from a pure madder dye made from a herbaceous climbing plant with yellow flowers. Paintings on the church's southern exterior wall are devoted to the Holy Virgin, the patron saint of the monastery. There's a badly faded depiction of the 1453 siege of Constantinople, with the parable of the return of the prodigal son beside it to the right. St George, the traditional protector of warriors, is depicted on the northern wall. On the porch is a painting of the *Last Judgment*: the long bench on which the 12 apostles sit, the patterned towel on the chair of judgement, and the long, horn-like bucium used to announce the coming of Christ, are all typical Moldavian elements. In Humor the bucium is played during funerals to symbolise the mourners' crying for the dead.

Humor's fan-shaped roof shelters five chambers, the middle one of which – the tombs' room – has a lower ceiling than the others. This hides a treasure room *(tainiţa)* where the riches of the monastery were traditionally kept safe. The wooden door leading up to the room used to be concealed with painted bricks. On the right wall as you enter the tombs' room is a votive painting depicting the founder, Toader Bubuiog, offering, with the help of the Virgin Mary, a miniature replica of the monastery to Christ. The tomb of Bubuiog, who died in 1539, and his wife, lie on the left side of the room; a painting of his wife praying to the Virgin Mary is above her grave.

The paintings in the first chamber (pronaos) depict various scenes of martyrs, all wearing traditional, wide-sleeved Moldavian shirts. The decorative, metre-high border which runs around the base of the four walls duplicates the decorative borders and geometric patterns typical of traditional Moldavian carpets. Above this decorative border is a pictorial representation of the first three months of the Orthodox calendar (synaxary), with each day represented by an icon. The calendar starts with 1 September on the eastern wall and runs clockwise around the room. Unlike the other interior paintings which were restored by UNESCO in the early 1970s the paintings in the altar room (naos) have never been restored.

During the Austrian occupation the monastery served as a boys' school; many of the children's etchings written in Slavic can still be seen above the tomb of Bubuiog's wife in the tombs room. Humor monastery was later used as a store house and a museum before the nuns came in 1991.

Admission to the monastery is US$0.70; a US$1.40/3.50 fee is charged for the use of cameras/video cameras. Nuns provide free guided tours in French.

Places to Stay & Eat

Don't be deceived by the sign outside the monastery advertising 'rooms free' at the *Maison de Bucovine* (☎ operator 991; ask for ☎ 172 Mănăstirea Humor), 50m from the monastery; it simply means it has rooms available. The US$11.50 nightly fee, which includes a hearty breakfast cooked up by host Maria Albu, is well worth it. Shared bathrooms in a separate outbuilding are clean and have hot water heaters. Maria

speaks French and cooks evening meals for an additional fee.

The Butucea and Gheorghiţă families both provide accommodation in their homes. Ask in the village for directions. Bucovina Estur and the BTT travel agency in Suceava arrange accommodation in private rooms in Humor. Bucovina Estur's nightly rates start at US$10; BTT's at US$18. Both include breakfast.

It is possible to stay at the monastery (☎ via operator 991; ask for ☎ 140 Mănăstirea Humor) but it cannot be arranged in advance. Nuns providing the guided tours will occasionally invite you to spend a night or two at the monastery; this does not happen during peak season when the monastery is flooded with tourists.

Getting There & Away

There are seven daily buses from Gura Humorului to Humor, departing from Gura bus station at 7.40, 11 am, and 12.30, 2.30, 4 and 5 pm. You can also hike the 6km north from Gura Humorului to Humor or hitch a ride on a horsecart (forget cars; few pass by).

Bucovina Estur (see Suceava – Travel Agencies) also arranges private transport and guided tours to Humor.

MOLDOVIŢA

Moldoviţa monastery (Mănăstirea Moldoviţa) is in the middle of a quaint village. As at Suceviţa, Moldoviţa consists of a fortified quadrangular enclosure with three towers and brawny gates, with a magnificent painted church at its centre. Moldoviţa is in the care of nuns and has undergone careful restoration in recent years. Its frescoes are predominantly yellow.

The fortifications here are actually more impressive than the badly faded frescoes dating from 1537. On the church's southern exterior wall is a depiction of the defence of Constantinople in 626 AD against Persians dressed as Turks, a prayer to the Holy Virgin, and Jesse's Tree, all of which are painted on a dark blue background. On the porch is a representation of the Last Judgement. Inside the sanctuary, on a wall facing the original

MOLDAVIA

carved iconostasis, is a portrait of Prince Petru Rareş, the monastery's founder, offering the church to Christ. All of these works date from 1537. The vast throne with its 2m-high back on which Rareş would hold court is displayed in the small museum at Moldovița Monastery, housed in a worshipping room built on the complex in 1612. The museum is open daily, except Monday, from 10 am to 6 pm. Admission to the monastic complex is US$0.60.

The ruins of a former church dating from the reign of Alexandru cel Bun (1400-32) on which Moldovița was built in 1532 can still be seen in the grounds of the monastery.

Places to Stay & Eat

Popas Turistic, between the train station and the monastery, has small cabins at US$4.50 per person. It's open from mid-June to mid-September. You can also camp here. There's no running water, but you can draw water from the caretaker's well on his farm next door. A simple restaurant in the *Complex Commercial*, near the campsite on the road to Vama, serves *mititei* (grilled meatballs) and draught beer.

You can also stay in **Vama**, a small village 14km south of Moldovița, between Gura Humorului and Câmpulung Moldovenesc on the main Suceava-Vatra Dornei road. The *Cabana Vama* is signposted on the left as you enter the village from the east; follow the dirt track for 1km. In the centre of the village at Str Victoriei 7 is the *family home of Lucan Viorel*; the family has three double rooms to rent costing US$11 per person, US$15 per person including breakfast. The hosts speak some French; ask for some fresh milk from their cow during your stay. The *Mihai Nicorescu family*, next door at Str Victoriei 5, also has rooms to let for the same prices.

The agro-tourist agency, *Opération Villages Roumains*, set up by the Belgian charity of the same name, also arranges rooms in private homes in Vama and around for US$10 to US$12 a night. It has a small 'biroul de informații' signposted in the centre of the village where you can arrange a bed for the night. Alternatively advance bookings can be made through its central office in Cluj-Napoca, Transylvania. Opération Villages Roumains also arranges English and French-speaking tour guides for US$10 a day.

Bucovina Estur and the BTT travel agency in Suceava both arrange accommodation in private rooms here. Estur's nightly rates start at US$10; BTT's at US$18. Both include breakfast.

Getting There & Away

Moldovița monastery is right above Vatra Moldoviței's train station (be sure to get off at Vatra Moldoviței, not Moldovița). From Suceava there are seven daily trains to Vama (1½ hours), and from Vama two daily trains leave for Vatra Moldoviței (50 minutes) at 7.09 am and 2.51 pm, returning to Vama at noon and 5.57 pm.

SUCEVIȚA

Sucevița (Mănăstirea Sucevița) is the largest and finest of the Bucovina monasteries. The church inside the fortified quadrangular monastic enclosure, built between 1582 and 1601, is almost completely covered with frescoes. Mysteriously, the western wall of the monastery remains bare of any impressive frescoes. Legend has it that the artist fell off the scaffolding while attempting to paint the wall and was killed, leaving artists of the time too scared to follow in his footsteps. Beneath one of the arcs of the buttress looms the head of a woman carved in black stone in memory of the legendary woman who toiled for 30 years to build the monastery, carrying a stone a day in her ox-drawn cart to the site where the grand edifice stands today. The exterior frescoes – predominantly red and green – date from around 1590.

As you enter you first see the *Virtuous Ladder* fresco covering most of the northern exterior wall, which depicts the 30 steps from Hell to Paradise (one step for each year of Christ's life). The frescoes inside the arches above the open porch depict the apocalypse and the vision of St John. On the southern exterior wall is the Jesse tree symbolising the continuity of the Old and New

Testaments. The tree grows from the reclining figure of Jesse, who is flanked by a row of ancient philosophers. King David stands in the middle of the tree whose branches ascend to the Virgin Mary and Christ at its top. On either side, scenes from the Old Testament are depicted. To the left is the Virgin as a Byzantine princess, with angels holding a red veil over her head.

Inside the church, in the second chamber, the Orthodox calendar is depicted with the same symbolic icons for each day as seen at Humor monastery. Here, however, all 365 days of the calendar are featured. The tombs of the founders, Moldavian nobles Simion and Ieremia Movilă, lie in the tombs' room. The last of the painted monasteries to be built, this is the only one not to have been built by Ştefan cel Mare or his family. Ieremia Movilă, who died in 1606, appears with his seven children on the western wall inside the naos.

Suceviţa monastery was first inhabited by monks in 1582. During the communist era, only nuns over 50 were allowed to stay at Suceviţa.

Apart from the church, there's a small museum at Suceviţa Monastery in which various treasures and art pieces from the monastery are displayed. It is open daily from 8 am to 8 pm. The nuns offer free guided tours of the complex in French.

Places to Stay & Eat
It's worth spending a night here and doing a little hiking in the surrounding hills, which are forest-clad and offer sweeping views. Wild *camping* is possible in the field across the stream from the monastery. Otherwise, *Hanul Suceviţa* (☎ operator 191; ask for Hanul Suceviţa ☎ 141), a restaurant about 1km back towards Rădăuţi, has 23 double rooms with private bath in the grotty, two storey building at US$4.50 per person a night. The hotel only has hot water if 14 or more of its rooms are occupied; hot water then flows between 7 and 10 am, and 8 and 11 pm. The restaurant has basic meals and is open year-round.

Don't leave Suceviţa without eating at the *Popasul Bucovinean* (☎ operator 191; ask for Suceviţa ☎ 165), an excellent traditional Moldavian restaurant which also has private rooms to let in a building that used to be exclusively reserved for members of the Communist Party's central committee. Double rooms cost between US$8.50 and US$11 depending on the size of the room and bed (some have some real double beds). Triples are US$13 a night, and an egg, cheese, ham and jam breakfast is an extra US$2. Some rooms have private bathrooms. There are also 10 wooden double huts on the site which cost US$4.20 per hut. The Popasul Bucovinean is 5km south of Suceviţa on the road to Vatra Moldoviţei.

Getting There & Away
Suceviţa is the most difficult monastery to reach by public transport. There are four buses from Rădăuţi (17km), one in the morning and three in the afternoon. Two daily buses connect Suceviţa to Moldoviţa (36km), one in the early morning and another around mid-afternoon. The road connecting the two monasteries winds up and over a high mountain pass (1100m), through forests and small alpine villages. The road is stunning and offers unlimited freelance camping opportunities, but you need a car to explore it fully (hiking up would be madness). It's possible to hike the 20km north to Putna in about five hours.

CACICA SALT MINE
Fifteen kilometres north of Gura Humorului, on the road to Solca, is the small village of Cacica, home to Moldavia's largest salt mine (Salină Veche Cacica). The mine was discovered in 1445 but was not exploited until 1791 under the Habsburg regime. By the end of the 19th century, the Cacica mine was a thriving enterprise with hundreds of miners from Bulgaria, Hungary, Poland, Yugoslavia and Ukraine. The village earned the nickname 'little Austria' for its harmonious, multiethnic population.

It was during this same period that the miners discovered a large salt cross in one of the galleries 26m underground. In 1904 the miners dug by hand a small Orthodox church in the mine, lit by oil lamps when it first opened. They dedicated it to St Varvara (Sfântu Varvara), the traditional protector of miners. To this day, miners still celebrate 9 December – their patron saint's day – with a church service followed by merrymaking in the village. Separate altars were also built in the chapel to serve local Roman and Greco-Catholics. The church – the first to be built in Cacica – is still in use today. On the right wall as you enter, there is an icon of the Holy Virgin to which believers come to pray, light candles and plead for their troubles to be resolved. Locally, it is believed that this icon is miracle working.

Every year on 15 August, the Holy Virgin's Assumption, Roman Catholic pilgrims from all over Romania flock to Cacica to celebrate the holiday. The parish priests from each of the three churches in the village are invited to the chapel in the salt mine where an ecumenical mass is celebrated. A congregation of thousands gathers for this unique religious event.

Guided tours in Romanian are available of the mine. Its other features include a natural salt 'lake of wishes', a dancing hall large enough to host a tennis court and a vast array of fantastic salt sculptures. The history of the mine is explained in the small **Salt Museum** (Muzeul Salinei Cacica), next to the main entrance. The mine and museum (π operator 191; ask for Salină Veche Cacica) is open daily from 9 am to 5 pm. Admission is US$0.30/0.15 for adults/students.

Getting There & Away

From Gura Humorului there are three buses daily to Cacica (30 minutes), departing daily at 6.30 and 11.45 am, and 4.30 pm. Get off at the main bus stop in the village opposite the red-brick Roman Catholic Church; the old salt mine (Salina Veche Cacica) is immediately opposite the church. If you are driving by car be sure to ask for the 'old' salt mine; the 'new' salt mine dating from 1986, is some 9km from Cacica village. From Suceava there are six local trains daily to Cacica (3/4 hours).

SOLCA & ARBORE MONASTERIES

Few tourists make their way to the tiny monasteries of Solca and Arbore; those who do leave disappointed. Arbore has a handful of scarcely visible frescoes on its outside walls while the monastery at Solca, located next door to a beer factory, has none at all. Neither monastery is inhabited today and both are often closed; tracking down the person in the village who has a key can prove problematic.

Solca Monastery

The walled monastery of Solca, 21km north of Gura Humorului, is little more than a village church today and rarely used. The monastery was built in 1612 as a defence for the village as well as for religious worship. It has cellars for storing gunpowder and narrow windows in the wall through which arrows could be shot. Following the occupation of Bucovina by the Austrians, it was stripped of its monastic status. The iconostasis inside the church dates from 1895.

The beer factory next door to the monastery was opened by the monks in the 17th century. By 1810, the Austrian administration had opened a larger factory on the same site. This factory – the present-day Solca Beer Factory (Fabrica de Bere Solca) – still uses gunpowder cellars of the monastery for storing beer kegs.

Getting There & Away Getting to Solca by public transport is tiresome. Theoretically there are three buses daily from Gura Humorului to Solca, departing from Gura bus station at 6.30 and 11.45 am, and 4.30 pm. At Solca, buses turn around and head back to Gura, making it difficult to see much else except Solca in one day. From Rădăuţi there is one bus daily to Solca, via Arbore, departing at 6.45 am.

Arbore

Arbore monastery is 15km east of Solca and 33km north of Suceava. It was built in 1503 by Suceava's chief magistrate Luca Arbore (he owned the entire village) who raised the small church next to his private residence as a family chapel and cemetery. His Gothic-style tomb lies inside the first chamber (*pronaos*) of the church, beneath a beautiful stone-carved canopy. The village cemetery across the street from the monastery is adorned with colourful wreaths and flowers.

Arbore's predominantly green frescoes date from 1541. Bad weather has left most of the walls bare, and it is only the impressive frescoes protected by the protruding walls and large overhanging eaves on the western wall that are of any interest: scenes from the *Lives of the Saints* and Genesis run along the wall in eight registers and faint traces of the Last Judgement are evident in the upper right-hand corner.

Getting There & Away From Gura Humorului there is one bus a day, departing at 4.30 pm, which makes it practically impossible to get to Arbore and back in one day. Arbore is easier to access from Suceava if you are prepared to hike the final couple of kilometres from the main bus stop next to the Arbore turn-off on the main Suceava-Siret road. Take any bus from Suceava heading to Siret or Rădăuți (see below). From Rădăuți to Arbore there are five buses daily departing at 6.30 am, noon, and 3.30, 5.30 and 8 pm.

RĂDĂUȚI
• *area code ☎ 030*

Rădăuți ('rah-dah-oots') is a large and boring market town. The only reason to come is to catch a train to Putna or a bus to the monasteries in Arbore, Solca and Sucevița.

The bus station (☎ 464 430) is on Blvd Ștefan cel Mare, a block north from Rădăuți's train station (☎ 461 849), which is on Str Gării. From the bus station, head east along Blvd Ștefan cel Mare until you reach the central square, Piața Unirii. The left-luggage office at the train station is open 24 hours.

Nine kilometres west from Rădăuți towards Sucevița, you pass through the village of **Marginea**, famed for its black earthenware and pottery. Some 12km south of Rădăuți on the main Suceava-Siret road,

you pass through **Grănicești**, a completely systemised village comprising towering concrete apartment blocks which sprung up under Ceaușescu's regime in the 1970s and 1980s. Opposite the ugly block, on the left side of the road if you are approaching from the north, is an abandoned **white fox farm and fur factory**, formerly owned by the Communist Youth organisation. White foxes were bred here and then slaughtered for their furs. It was closed down after the December 1989 revolution.

Places to Stay & Eat
The only hotel open at the time of writing was the 16-room *Hotel Azur* (☎ & fax 464 718), a good 10 minute walk from the centre at Calea Cernăuți 29. Doubles and four/five-bed rooms with private bath are US$6 per person a night.

Getting There & Away
Bus Buses from Rădăuți include eight a day to Suceava (62km) seven a day to Sucevița (17km); two daily to Câmpulung Moldovenesc (77km) and Târgu Neamț (258km) via Suceava; three to Botoșani (89km) via Siret; two to Gura Humorului (40km); and one to Iași (215km) via Siret. Somewhat bizarre is the bus schedule to Putna – one weekly bus, departing on Friday at 3 pm. It is wise to check all departure times with the clerk at the ticket window as the times posted up cannot always be trusted. Bus tickets are sold only an hour prior to departure.

From Rădăuți, there are also three daily buses to Cernăuți, (Chernovitsi).

Train Rădăuți is on the Putna-Dorneşti branch line. There are eight trains daily from Rădăuți to Putna (one hour) and Dorneşti (11 minutes). From Dorneşti there are direct trains to Siret (26 minutes), Suceava (1½ hours), and all other stops on the Bucharest-Suceava line. Some trains from Rădăuți go direct, via Dorneşti, to Suceava.

PUTNA
Legend has it that Ștefan cel Mare, in celebration of his conquest of the fortress of

nearby Chilia against the Turks, climbed to the top of a hill overlooking Putna village, 28km north-west of Rădăuţi, and fired his bow and arrow. Where the first arrow landed in the valley below became the site of Putna monastery's holy well, the second arrow decided the site where the altar was to be and the third landing was the site of the bell tower. As you approach Putna monastery (Mănăstirea Putna), you can see the spot where Ştefan cel Mare stood, marked by a large white cross. The monastery, built by the great prince between 1466 and 1481, is still home to a very active religious community with groups of monks chanting mass just before sunset.

The emblem of Moldavia – an auroch's head with the sun between its horns and the moon and stars either side – rests above the entrance to Putna monastery. In the large building behind the monastery (formerly the Abbot's house) is the **Putna museum** where a wealth of treasures from the monastery and surrounding regions are displayed, including medieval manuscripts, rare textiles, the Holy Book that Ştefan cel Mare used to carry with him when he went to battle, and a miniature bronze bell brought to Putna by pilgrims from the republic of Moldova in commemoration of the 486th anniversary of Ştefan cel Mare's death.

Ştefan cel Mare himself is buried in the church tombs' room. Two years prior to his death, the prince oversaw the creation of his tombstone carved in Italian Carrara marble. His tomb lies on the right as you enter. Below is the grave of his third wife, Maria Voichiţa,. On the left is the grave of their two children, Bogdan and Petru. Above the children's grave is that of Ştefan cel Mare's second wife, Maria of Mangop from Greece, who died 'from the cold' in 1472.

Outside the church are three bells, cast on the order of Ştefan cel Mare and inscribed in Slavic. The largest of the three, dating from 1484 and reserved strictly for heralding royal deaths, was among the many treasures of the monastery that were stashed away in its tower and thus never plundered during the continuous attacks on Putna during the 16th

and 17th centuries. Following the Austrian occupation in 1775, the Roman Catholic creed was imposed on the monastery and various restoration works which took place during this time reflect the conversion to Catholicisation of Putna at this time.

Some 60 monks live at Putna today. Under communism the monastery was condemned by the authorities as a 'corrupt and outdated institution' with 75% of its inhabitants being forced into secular life (some of the older monks were allowed to stay). The monks today practise icon painting, shepherding, wood sculpturing and agriculture.

In Chilia, 2km from the monastery, is **Daniel the Hermit's cave**. Inside is a humble wooden table and memorial plaque to the hermit, Daniel Dimitru, born in a village near Rădăuţi in the 15th century. He became a monk at the age of 16 and later moved to Chilia where he dug himself a cave in a rock. In 1451, Ştefan cel Mare came to Chilia to seek advice from the wise hermit. Daniel told him he would rule Moldavia one day. Ştefan again sought his advice in 1476 at Voroneţ monastery where Daniel told him he had to continue his fight against the Turks. Following the building of Putna monastery, Daniel moved to Voroneţ monastery where he died in 1596.

To get to Chilia from the monastery, turn right off the main road following the sign for Cabana Putna. Bear left at the fork and continue until you reach a second fork in the road; turn right here, cross the railway tracks, and continue over a small bridge, following the dirt road until you see the rock, marked by a stone cross on its top, on your left.

Places to Stay & Eat

Some people camp freelance in the field opposite Daniel's cave at Chilia near the train station.

The *Cabana Putna* (☎ operator 191; ask for Putna ☎ 123), signposted 50m off the main road through the village leading to the monastery, has three and four-bed cabins with shared bathrooms for US$20 per person, including breakfast. The restaurant is open when it has clients.

Almost opposite the turning for the cabana is the *Complex Turistic Putna* (☎ operator 191; ask for Putna ☎ 104), a shabby hotel and wooden hut complex with a grotty in-house restaurant. Double/triple/four to eight-bed rooms with shared bath are US$11/10/6 per person, including breakfast. A bed in one of its eight wooden huts is US$4.50. Parties of four or more get 70% discount!

Getting There & Away

Local trains travel to Putna from Suceava eight times daily (two hours). The large monastic enclosure is at the end of the road, just under 2km from the station. From Putna there is also one direct train a day to Iaşi (5¾ hours).

You can hike the 20km from Putna to Suceviţa monastery in about five hours. Follow the trail marked with blue crosses in white squares that starts near the hermit's cave. About 4km down the road you turn off to the left.

VATRA DORNEI
● *area code* ☎ *030, pop 17,000*

A fashionable spa resort during Habsburg times, Vatra Dornei today is a study of decaying elegance. Grand baroque-style buildings stand neglected and forlorn either side of the Dorna river (Râul Dorna) which cuts across the town from east to west. Treatment bases *(baza de tratament)*, once all the rage, now struggle to sell their mind-boggling array of mud, electric and other types of 'baths'. Today the town is home to Romania's largest sparkling mineral water bottling plants, namely *Dorna*.

Hikers still frequent this quiet, unassuming town nestled at the confluence of Dorna and Bistriţa rivers in the Dornelor depression (Ţara Dornelor). Between December and March, skiers ski on the snow-topped Dealul Negrii (1300m).

Orientation & Information

The train station is in the centre of Vatra Dornei, on the main street, Str Republicii. The post office, cinema and some museums are on the north banks of the Bistriţa, accessible by bridge from Str Republicii.

Vatra Dornei has no tourist information office but hotel staff can answer simple questions. The post and telephone office is in the old centre at Str Mihai Eminescu 1; it is open weekdays from 8 am to 8 pm. You can change money and get cash advance on Visa at Bancă Agricola, on the river's southern bank at Str Vladimirescu 10; it's open weekdays from 8.30 am to 12.30 pm.

Things to See & Do

Vatra Dornei's **park** is beautifully laid out with sprawling avenues, well groomed lawns and neatly arranged flower beds. Bronze busts of national poet Mihai Eminescu, composers George Enescu and Ciprian Porumbescu gaze out from beneath the trees. A new **church** is currently being built in the centre of the park.

You can taste Vatra Dornei's natural **spring waters** at the drinking fountain in the basement of the fairytale single-turreted castle in the west of the park. The water – not tasty – is bicarbonated, good for curing stomach ills and not recommended for those with heart and liver problems, stomach ulcers or high blood pressure. Adjoining the park on Str Republicii is a grandiose, baroque mansion, home to a bustling **casino** in Habsburg times. It is empty today. At Str Parcului 3 is a small **Natural History Museum** (Muzeul de Ştinţe Naturale şi Cinegetică) in which flora and fauna from the surrounding Câliman and Rarău mountains are exhibited. It is open daily, except Monday, from 10 am to 6 pm.

North of the river, opposite the post office on Str Mihai Eminescu is an **Ethnographic Museum** (Muzeul de Etnografie); open daily, except Monday, from 10 am to 6 pm.

There is a **skilift** (telescaun) at the south end of Str George Coşbuc which takes you to the top of Vatra Dornei's main 1300m high slope on Negrii Hill (Dealul Negrii). Steps lead to the station from the street; it is open daily, except Monday, from 9 am to 4 pm. Bring your own boots and skis.

MOLDAVIA

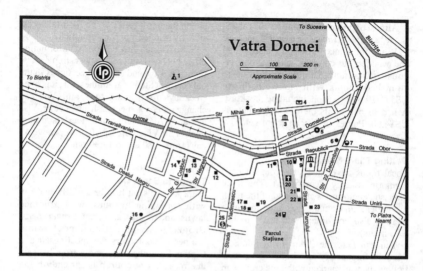

Vatra Dornei

PLACES TO STAY
 1 Camping Runc
12 Hotel Bar
13 Hotel Bucovina
    & Restaurant
15 Hotel Informatica
17 Hotel Căliman
18 Hotel Dorma
19 Hotel Bradul
21 Hotel & Lucer Bar
22 Vila Zimbrul
23 Vila Căprioara

PLACES TO EAT
 9 Miorița 24-hour
    Restaurant
14 Camy-Lact
    Restaurant & Shop

OTHER
 2 Cinema
 3 Ethnographic Museum
 4 Post Office
 5 Train Station; Agenţie
    de Voiaj CFR

 6 Market
 7 Bus Station
 8 Natural History
    Museum
10 Salon Felix
11 Former Casino
16 Ski Lift
20 New Church
24 Drinking Fountain;
    Un-named Bar
25 Bancă Agricola

Places to Stay
Camping There is a clean, private campsite, *Camping Runc* (☎ 371 466), in a forest-covered hill overlooking the town from the north-east. It has 43 wooden double cabins costing US$4 a night with communal showers and toilets; and you can pitch your tent here too. There is also a restaurant and bar on the site. To get to the campsite, head west along Str Mihai Eminescu until you see a sign on the right for 'Camping Runc'.

Private Rooms ANTREC (☎ 374 238; fax 374 308), Str Nicolae Bălcescu 9, arranges rooms in private homes in Vatra Dornie and

around, starting at US$8 per person a night, including breakfast. Call in advance.

Villas The friendly *Vila Zimbrul* (☎ 372 405), overlooking the park at Str Parcului 5, comes highly recommended. First-class doubles with lots of space are a bargain US$10 a night with private bath and US$7 with shared bath. The tariff includes a delicious home-made breakfast consisting of fresh bread, cheese and ham, with coffee in a vodka bottle and fresh flowers tucked in the linen napkins served in your room if you order it the night before. Nothing is too much for the family who runs it; backpackers seeking some good old-fashioned home pampering should head straight here.

Avoid the *Vila Căprioara* (☎ 372 643; fax 373 844) directly opposite the Zimbrul at Str Parcului 29 if you can't speak German; the management seems to have an aversion to non-German speaking foreigners.

A new villa is to open by 1998 next to the steps leading up to the telescaun station on Str George Coşbuc.

Hotels The *Hotel Informatica* (☎ 373 534) at Str George Coşbuc 6 still sports a two-tier pricing system, charging foreigners US$10 a night for a bed in a musty double, triple or seven-bed room. Romanians pay US$4.

Round the corner is the smart *Hotel Bucovina* (☎ 374 205; fax 374 207) at Str Republicii 35. It has 100 rooms, many with wooden balconies overlooking the spa's main street. Single/double/triple rooms are US$27/47/60 a night, including breakfast.

Heading south along Str Republicii, you'll find the cheap five-room *Hotel Bar* (☎ 373 728) at No 10. Rooms are good value at US$5 for a double room with real double beds. The place is rough and solo women should avoid it.

Str Republicii 5 is home to Vatra Dornei's two-star concrete block hotels where tour groups generally stay: the *Hotel Căliman* (☎ 373 921; fax 371 778) has 155 rooms with hot water between 7 and 9 am, noon to 1 and 7 to 9 pm. The six storey *Hotel Bradul* (☎ 373 921; fax 371 778) has 140 rooms, a sauna, swimming pool and nightclub. The *Hotel Dorna* (☎ 371 021; fax 371 025) is the last in line. Doubles in all three hotels cost US$40 with breakfast.

Ravers should head straight for the flash *Hotel* (☎ 371 251) bang in the park with its entrance at Str Parcului 3. Downstairs is the town's trendiest *Lucer Bar* disco packed full with teens every night (open daily from 8 pm to midnight; admission US$0.70); upstairs is the hotel with six doubles and one triple – all with private bath – for US$10 per person a night. Rooms are furnished with traditional Romanian rugs and wall hangings.

Places to Eat

Vatra Dornei has few eating places, but those it does have offer quality Romanian cuisine at unbeatable prices: the *Camy-Lact* restaurant, adjoining the shop by the same name at Str George Coşbuc 1, specialises in dairy products (the shop stocks a wonderful array of homemade cheeses, yoghurts etc). Meat is served in its restaurant, as well as delicious chocolate pancakes (clătite cu ciocolată) for US$1. It's open daily from 10 am to 10 pm.

The crispiest-on-the-outside, runniest-in-the-inside caşcaval pâine (breaded cheese) in the whole of Romania is served at *Miorita*, on the corner of Str Parcului and Str Republicii. Soups start at US$0.75 and salads from US$0.30. It is open 24 hours and has a 24-hour shop on its the ground floor.

Salon Felix, a few doors away at Str Republicii 3, is good for a drink and boogie; it's open daily from 9 pm to 3 am.

Getting There & Away

The bus station (☎ 371 252) is at the eastern end of town on Str 22 Decembrie. There are two buses daily to Piatra Neamţ (148km); and Bistriţa (83km); and one a day to Iaşi (237km), Botoşani (155km) and Bacău (219km). Train services are slightly more useful. Tickets are sold in advance at the Agenţie de Voiaj CFR (☎ 371 039, 371 781), which is inside the train station (☎ 371 197) on Str Republicii 1.There is one direct daily train to Iaşi (4¾ hours).

A 24 hour petrol station selling some car accessories and handling minor car repairs is 1km out of town on the road north to Câmpulung Moldovenesc.

AROUND VATRA DORNEI

Vatra Dornei stands in the middle of Romania's most dramatic mountain passes, steeped in legend and famed for their wild beauty and savage landscapes. If you head south-west into Transylvania you cross the **Bârgau Pass**, otherwise known as the Tihuta Pass or, if you've read Bram Stoker's novel *Dracula*, the Borgo Pass! (See the Transylvania chapter.)

MOLDAVIA

In Dorna Candrenilor, 8km west of Vatra Dornei, you can access the **Căliman Mountains**. The highlight of these volcanic mountains is the anthropomorphic rocks which form a nature reservation called the **12 Apostles Nature Reservation** (Stîncile Doisprezece Apostoli). A trail is marked by blue triangles then red circles from Vatra Dornei to its peak at 1760m. Only attempt to tackle this tough climb if you are experienced and have a map and the right gear!

A less challenging route if you have a car is to drive to Dorna Candrenilor, turn left along the road to Poiana Negrii and continue for 14km along road and dirt track until you reach Negrişoara. From here it is a three hour walk (4km) along a path to the foot of the geological reservation.

Heading north you cross from Moldavia into the Maramureş region via the **Prislop Pass** which peaks at 1416m. See the Maramureş chapter.

The road north-east from Vatra Dornei leads, via Câmpulung Moldovenesc, to Gura Humorului from where the trail to southern Bucovina's monasteries begins.

CÂMPULUNG MOLDOVENESC
• *area code ☎ 030, pop 18,586*

The small logging town and 14th century fair town, tucked in the Moldavia valley at an altitude of 621m, is popular with hikers heading 15km south to the **Rarău mountains**. In winter, Câmpulung attracts cross-country skiers. There is also a short 800m ski slope served by a chair lift at the foot of the resort. Between 1786 and 1809 many German miners settled in the region at the invitation of the Habsburg authorities.

A winter sports festival takes place in Câmpulung Moldovenesc every year on the last Sunday in January.

Orientation & Information
The main street, Calea Transilvaniei, which runs into Calea Bucovinei, cuts across the town from west to east. The bus (☎ 312 551) and train stations (☎ 311 440) are a five minute walk west of the centre at Str Gării 8. To get to the centre from the main Câmpu-

lung Moldovenesc train station (don't get off at Câmpulung Moldovenesc Est train station), turn left along Str Gării and then right along Str Dimitrie Cantimir until you reach the post office on the corner of Calea Bucovinei. Câmpulung Moldovenesc's main hotel, the Zimbrul, is a couple of blocks from the post office on Calea Bucovinei.

The currency exchange inside the Hotel Zimbrul is open daily from 7 am to 3 pm. You will also find a tourist office of sorts here, open weekdays from 8.30 am to 3 pm. The Agenţie de Voiaj CFR (☎ 311 102) is opposite the hotel at Calea Transilvaniei 2.

Things to See
The highlight of Câmulung Moldovenesc is its bizarre **wooden spoon collection**, displayed in a small house at Str Gheorghe Popovici 3. Love spoons, jewellery made from spoons and a host of other cutlery delights collected by Ioan Ţugui are exhibited in the museum Other fun wooden objects are displayed at the **wood carving museum** at Calea Bucovinei 10. Both museums are open daily, except Monday, from 9 am to 4 pm. If either museum is locked, ask around until you find someone who has a key.

Places to Stay & Eat
There is no hot water in the town between 9 am and 3 pm. Bucovina Estur and the BTT travel agency (see Suceava – Places to Stay) arrange accommodation in private rooms in Câmpulung Moldovenesc. BTT charge US$18 a night including breakfast; Bucovina Estur US$10 a night. BTT (☎ 311 049; fax 311 250) has a branch office in Câmpulung Moldovenesc at Str Pinului 35.

The *Complex Turistic Semenic* (☎ 311 714) at Str Nicu Dracea 6, is a small, family run hotel with 12 simple doubles and three singles, most of which have old ceramic stoves for added warmth in winter. A bed for the night is US$1.50. The restaurant, serving local dishes including wild mushrooms from the forest, is open daily from 8 am to 8 pm.

The *Hotel Zimbrul* (☎ 312 441; fax 311

890), on the main street at Calea Bucovinei 1-3 is your typical state-run, 10 storey concrete block. Characterless singles/doubles with private bath are US$27/35 a night. A single room with a larger bed is US$1 extra, and breakfast is an additional US$1.50.

Top of the range in character and luxury is the small, three-star *Minion Pensiune* (☎ 312 028; ☎ & fax 311 581), a pretty red-and-white, wooden-shuttered cottage overlooking the river at Str Dimitrie Cantemir 26b. The four single and two double rooms costing US$25 per person are beautifully furnished with wooden floors, private showers (hot water 24 hours) and cable TV. The French-inspired restaurant (open daily from 8 am to 11 pm) serves typical Bucovina delights such as hot cheese bread (delicious!) and trout with garlic sauce and mămăligă (corn mush). The pension also arranges car rental with a local guide (French, Italian or English-speaking) for US$0.40 akm.

THE RARĂU MOUNTAINS

The Rarău mountains, forming part of the eastern Carpathians, are a popular hiking spot despite the sense of doom they engender. The mountains take their name from the Romanian word 'ră', meaning 'evil', 'harm' or 'a fated place'. Optimists claim that the name is derived from the old Latin adjective, 'rarum', meaning 'rare'.

In summer (May to October) you can access the Rarău mountains and the Cabana Rarău (1400m) from Câmpulung Moldovenesc by car. As you enter Câmpulung Moldovenesc from the east, a road is signposted on the left 'Cabana Rarău 14km'. Note, however, that this road is narrow and extremely pot-holed and rocky in places. If you do not have a four-wheel drive do not attempt it in wet weather. Hikers note that this same route is marked by red circles (three to four hours).

A second mountain road – slightly less pot-holed – leads up the Cabana Rarău from the village of **Pojorâta**, 3km west of Câmpulung Moldovenesc. This road is not marked on maps. Turn left at the fork after the village post office, cross the railway

tracks, then turn immediately left along the dirt road. Yellow crosses mark this trail (four to five hours). Note the large stones of **Adam and Eve** as you enter the village.

Cabana Rarău can also be accessed from the south in the village of **Chiril**, 24km east of Vatra Dornei on the main Vatra-Dornei-Durău road. This is the best of the three road options for those determined to drive. The route is marked by blue circles (3¼ hours to 3¾ hours) for hikers.

The Lady's Stones

Towering majestically above Cabana Rarău are Rarău's most prized rocks, the Lady's Stones (Pietrele Doamnei), otherwise known as the Princess's Rocks. A clutter of crosses crown the highest (1678m) of the three 70m-tall Mesozoic limestone rocks, in memory of the climbers it has claimed (the last accident was in 1978). Legend has it that it was on top of these rocks that Moldavian prince Petru Rareş (1527-38) commanded his family to hide after he was driven from the throne by the Ottomans in 1538 and imprisoned in Transylvania. But Rareş' wife, fearing an attack by the Turks on Moldavia, climbed to the top of the highest stone, hid all her jewels here, and then flung herself from the top.

A trail (30 minutes), marked by a simple footpath, leads from the Cabana Rarău to the foot of the three stones. From the top of the highest stone you can see Pietrosul Bistriţei, the name given to the highest point of the Bistriţa mountains. The volcanic tip of Giumalăului is also visible on a clear day.

The Slătiora Forest Reservation

Some 320 plant species, including the 'lady's shoe' orchid (cypripedium calceolus) and the edelweiss (*floare de colt*; literally 'flower of stone'), grow in the Rarău mountains. Many can be found in the Slătiora forest reservation (Codrul secular de la Slătiora, 790 to 1350m) on the eastern side of the mountain range. The reservation, protected by law since 1913, covers an area of 408 hectares in which virgin woods, more than 100 years old, stand. Much of it is out

The Rarău Massif

0   4   8 km

gles, leads from the Slătiora forest reservation to the flower reservation. In summer it is easy to access the village of Slătiora by car. From Câmpulung Moldovenesc, head east towards Gura Humorului. Some 25km along this road there is a turn-off on the right to the mountain village of Stuplicani; turn right and follow the dirt track for 13km. Immediately after Stuplicani, turn right to Slătiora (9km).

Places to Stay & Eat

The *Cabana Rarău*, in the heart of the Rarău massif at 1400m, is the main base for hikers. It has 12 doubles, most with private bathrooms; seven triples, four four-bed rooms, one five-bed room, two six-bed rooms and one room with seven beds. A bed in any of them is US$3.50 a night, including breakfast. It only has hot water when it is completely full; at other times staff will let you boil a pan of water in the kitchen. The cabana has a restaurant and small shop selling basic provisions.

About 1km east of Cabana Rarău is the smaller, less frequented *Cabana Pastoral*. It has five doubles and three triples costing US$2.50 per person a night. The cabana does not have running water but there is a well outside. Guests are woken each morning by the dulcet tones of host Sorin Avasiloaie beckoning the neighbouring shepherd on the hillside on his *trâmbiţă*, a bugle-style musical instrument traditionally used by mountain folk to communicate with other inhabitants living in the mountains. If you want a mountain guide, Sorin is your man!

If you plan to access the mountains from Chiril in the south, then the *Cabana Zugreni* (☎ 373 581, 211 628), 4km west of Chiril, close to Sunători village on the road to Vatra Dornei, is your best bet. It has five doubles, two triples, three four-bed rooms and three five-bed rooms, all with shared bath. A night's sleep costs US$5.50 including breakfast. There are cheaper wooden huts here, on the banks of the Bistriţa river; they cost US$4 per person. Tents can be pitched for around US$0.10. Traditional Moldavian food is dished up in the adjoining restaurant.

of bounds and only a small part can be freely explored.

A trail marked by red stripes and red triangles (five hours) leads from Cabana Rarău to the forest reservation.

The Todirescu Flower Reservation

Rarău's 100-year-old forest reservation is crowned by the glorious Todirescu flower reservation (Fineţele montane de la plaiul Todirescu) which sprawls for 44 hectares across Todirescu mountain on the southern edge of the Slătiora reservation. The best time to visit it is in July when its meadows are ablaze with colour. Tulips, bluebells, daffodils, daisies, chrysanthemums, and the poisonous omagul (aconitum anthora) are just some of the floral delights to be found here. The reservation has been protected under law since 1933 and can be easily accessed from Slătiora village. The westward trail (one hour) is marked by blue crosses. Another trail, marked by red trian-

Moldova

The former Soviet republic of Moldova, independent since 1991, is a country in limbo. Historically, it is partly Romanian, partly Russian, united by force under the Soviets to form one country, but not one people. After the demise of the USSR, the question of reunification with neighbouring Romania was raised, fuelling ethnic tensions in the predominantly Russian-speaking regions. Moldova's inherent ethnic mix exploded into civil war in 1992, killing more than 500 people. In late 1997, the country was on the brink of de facto federalisation.

A sliver of land jammed between Romania and Ukraine, Moldova's borders are roughly marked by the Prut river on the west and the Dniestr river on the east.

Despite being one of the most densely populated areas in the former USSR, Moldova has few cities. Its capital, Chişinău, was heavily bombed during WWII but in recent years has made something of a comeback. Funky bars and fun eating places are starting to sprout as the country gets back on track towards a market economy.

Take a step into provincial realms however and there's no escaping the tremendous poverty that prevails. Shop shelves are bare, battered buses rumble along dusty streets, and pensioners try to survive on US$7 a month. Many employees do not get paid for months at a time.

On the eastern banks of the Dniestr lies the self-proclaimed republic of Transdniestr. This last bastion of Soviet socialism in eastern Europe is a must for any traveller who never saw the USSR. The predominantly Russian-speaking population yearns for the revival of the Soviet Union. And while their attempts to win independence from Moldova have yet to yield results, their efforts at recreating Soviet life have produced USSR-style rampant inflation, food rationing, hellish bureaucracy and curfews.

Southern Moldova is populated by one of the world's smallest ethnic minorities, the

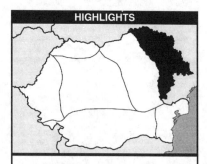

HIGHLIGHTS

- Stroll Chişinău's tree-studded avenues and discover a touch of the Orient in its colourful markets
- Tour the Cricova underground wine town if your wallet can take the pinch
- See how 13th century monks lived by visiting caves at Orheul Vechi
- Visit the self-styled republic of Transdniestr, the only place in the world where the Moscow *putsch* succeeded

Gagauz ('ga-ga-ooze'). While initially declaring a Gagauz Soviet Socialist Republic in 1991, the 153,000 Turkic-speaking population settled for large autonomy in regional affairs in 1994 and enjoy parliamentary presentation in Chişinău today. The Gagauz even have their own university in their capital, Comrat.

In both regions the Organisation for Security and Co-operation in Europe (OSCE) is closely monitoring the respect of minority rights and administering conflict control.

Facts about the Country

HISTORY
Bessarabia & Transdniestr
Moldova today straddles two different historic regions divided by the Dniestr river.

Historic Romanian Bessarabia incorporated the region west of the Dniestr, while Tsarist Russia governed the territory east of the river (Transdniestr) since its defeat of the Turks in 1792.

Bessarabia, part of the Romanian principality of Moldavia, was annexed in 1812 by the Russian empire. After the October revolution, Bessarabia declared its independence in 1918. Two months later this newly formed Democratic Moldavian Republic decided to unite with Romania, angering Moscow. Russia never recognised this union.

In 1924, the Soviet Union – to make up for its loss of the Bessarabian Moldavian Republic – created the Moldavian Autonomous Oblast on the eastern banks of the Dniestr, incorporating Transdniestr within the Ukrainian Soviet Socialist Republic (SSR). A few months later the Soviet government renamed the Oblast the Moldavian Autonomous Soviet Socialist Republic (Moldavian ASSR). In 1929 it moved the capital from Balta (present-day Ukraine) to Tiraspol.

WWII

In June 1940 Romanian Bessarabia was occupied by the Soviet army in accordance with the secret protocol attached to the Molotov-Ribbentrop Pact. The Soviet government immediately joined Bessarabia with the southern part of the Moldavian ASSR – namely, Transdniestr. This newly united territory was named the Moldavian Soviet Socialist Republic (Moldavian SSR). The remaining northern part of the Moldavian ASSR was given back to the Ukrainian SSR (present-day Ukraine). Bessarabia underwent Stalinist terror and Sovietisation, marked by the deportation of some 300,000 Romanians. On 13 June 1941, 5000 families from Bessarabia were deported to Siberia.

In 1941 allied Romanian and German troops attacked the Soviet Union. Bessarabia and Transdniestr fell into Romanian hands. Thousands of Bessarabian Jews were rounded up in labour camps in Transdniestr from where they were deported to Auschwitz.

In August 1944 the Soviet army reoccupied Transdniestr and Bessarabia. Under the terms of the Paris Peace Treaty of 1947, Romania had to relinquish all of the region and Soviet power was restored in the Moldavian SSR.

Sovietisation & Nationalism

The Soviet authorities continued where they had left off in 1940. An immediate Sovietisation programme was enforced in the Moldavian SSR. The predominantly Russian and Ukrainian population in Transdniestr – only in Romanian hands between 1941-44 – was little affected by this programme.

Ethnic Moldovans (Romanians) in the Bessarabia suffered worse. On the night of 5 July 1949, 25,000 Moldovans were deported to Siberia and Kazakhstan. The Cyrillic alphabet was imposed on the Moldovan language (a dialect of Romanian) and Russian became the official state language. Street names were changed to honour Soviet communist heroes, and patronymics were included in people's names as done in Russian. All nationalist sentiments were squashed. In 1950-2 Leonid Brezhnev, then first secretary of the central committee of the Moldovan Communist Party, is said to have personally supervised the deportation of a quarter of a million Moldovans. Ethnic Russians and Ukrainians were encouraged to settle in the region in order to dilute the Moldovan population further.

Gorbachev's policies of *glasnost* (openness) and *perestroika* (restructuring) from 1986 onwards paved the way for the creation of the nationalist Moldovan Popular Front in 1989. Under the leadership of communist Mircea Snegur as chairman of the Moldova's Supreme Soviet, Moldovan written in the Latin alphabet was reintroduced on 31 August 1989 as the official state language. In February-March 1990 the first democratic elections to the Supreme Soviet (parliament) were won by the Popular Front who gained an overwhelming majority. On 27 April 1990 the Supreme Soviet reinstated the Moldovan national flag (the Romanian tricolour with the Moldavian coat of arms in its centre). In

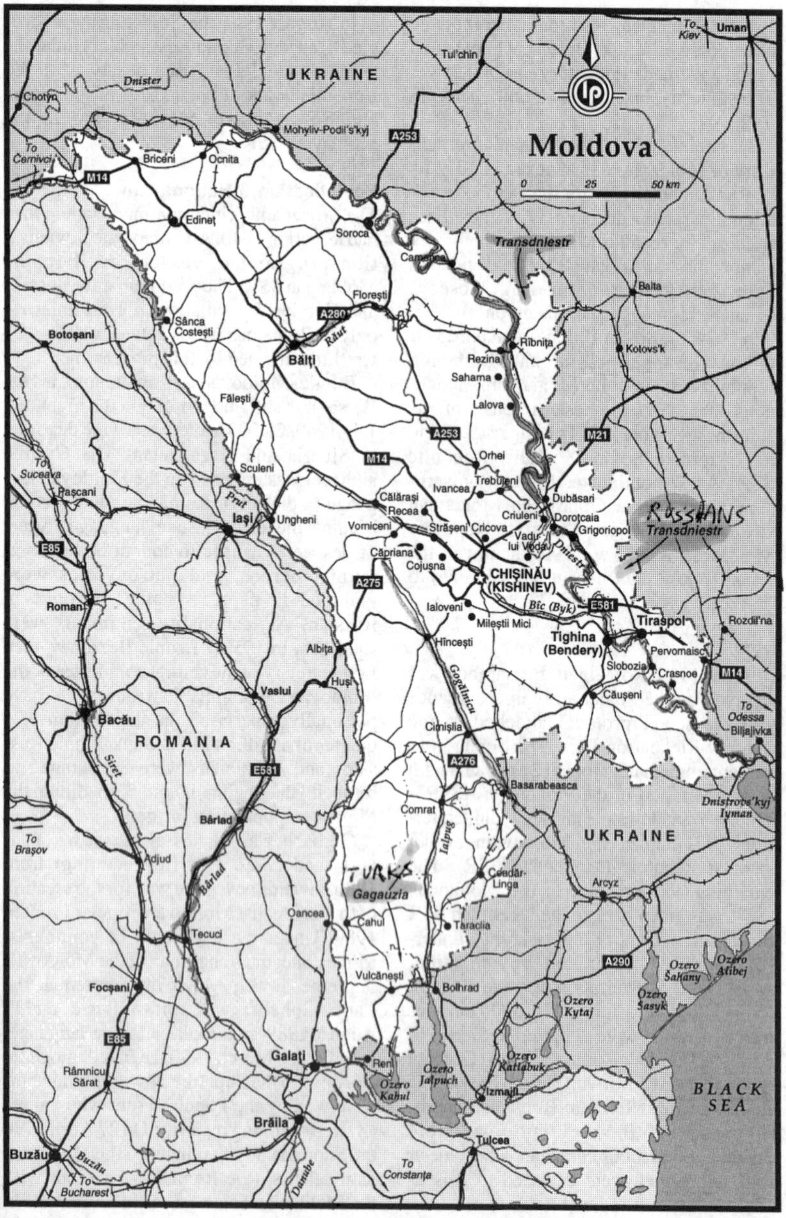

Moldova
0 25 50 km
UKRAINE
ROMANIA
UKRAINE
BLACK SEA
Dnister
Chotyn
Mohyliv-Podil's'kyj
Tul'chin
To Kiev
Uman
A253
To Černivci
M14
Briceni
Ocnita
Edineț
Soroca
Camenca
Transdniestr
Balta
Florești
A280
Răut
Sânca Costești
Botoșani
Bălți
Ribnița
Rezina
Saharna
Kotovs'k
Lalova
Fălești
A253
M21
M14
Orhei
To Suceava
Sculeni
Trebujeni
Ivancea
Dubăsari
Pașcani
Prut
Călărași
Recea
Criuleni
Dorotcaia
RUSSIANS
Iași
Ungheni
Vorniceni
Strășeni
Cricova
Vadu lui Vodă
Grigoriopol
Transdniestr
Dniestr
E85
Căpriana
Cojușna
CHIȘINĂU (KISHINEV)
A275
Roman
Ialoveni
Bîc (Byk)
E581
Tiraspol
Rozdil'na
Mileștii Mici
Tighina (Bendery)
Hîncești
Albița
Pervomaisc
Slobozia
Crasnoe
M14
Gogâlnicu
Huși
Vaslui
Căușeni
Bacău
To Odessa
Biljajivka
Cimișlia
Siret
A276
E581
Basarabeasca
Dnistrovs'kyj lyman
Comrat
Bârlad
Ialpug
To Brașov
Adjud
TURKS
Ceadâr-Linga
Gagauzia
Arcyz
Bârlad
Oancea
Cahul
Tecuci
Taraclia
A290
Ozero Šahany
Ozero Alibej
Focșani
Vulcănești
Bolhrad
Ozero Kytaj
Ozero Šasyk
E85
Ozero Katlabuk
Galați
Reni
Râmnicu Sărat
Ozero Kahul
Ozero Jalpuch
Izmail
Brăila
Tulcea
Buzău
Buzău
To Constanța
To Bucharest
Danube

predominantly Russian-speaking Transdniestr, local councils refused to adopt the new state symbols and stuck to the red banner.

In June 1990 the Moldovan Supreme Soviet passed a declaration of sovereignty. Following the failed coup attempt against Mikhail Gorbachev in Moscow in August 1991, Moldova declared its full independence. Romania was the first country, quickly followed by the US in December 1991, to recognise Moldova's independence.

In December 1991 Mircea Snegur was democratically elected president. The same month he signed the Alma-Ata Declaration to become a member of the newly established Commonwealth of Independent States (CIS). However, Moldova's full CIS membership was only ratified by the Moldovan parliament in April 1994 after lengthy discussions over the ethics of Moldova joining a political grouping dominated by Russia.

Moldova was granted 'most favoured nation' station by the US in 1992, qualifying for IMF and World Bank loans the same year. In March 1994 Snegur signed NATO's Partnership for Peace agreement. Moldova's neutrality is inscribed in its constitution however, meaning it has no intention of joining NATO and is not signatory to the CIS collective security agreements.

Ethnic Tensions

Moldovan nationalists' race along the road to independence in the late 1980s sparked off equally strong nationalist sentiments among ethnic minority groups. In the Russian stronghold of Transdniestr, the Yedinstivo-Unitatea (Unity) movement was formed in 1988 to represent the interests of the Slavic minorities, keen on keeping the Soviet Union alive. This was followed in November 1989 by the creation of the Gagauz Halki political party in the south of Moldova where the Turkic-speaking Gagauz minority was centred. Both ethnic groups' major fear was that the first move of an independent Moldova would be to reunite with Romania, its historic ancestor.

Following the pursuit of nationalist policies by the Supreme Soviet from early 1990, the Gagauz went on to declare a separate Gagauz Soviet Socialist Republic on 21 August 1990. Their nationalist claims were silently backed by the Turkish government and also by Russians in Transdniestr sympathetic to their 'persecuted' ethnic brothers.

A month later the Transdniestrans also declared independence from Moldova, establishing the Dniestr Moldovan Republic on the eastern banks of the Dniestr river. Transdniestran militia and Moldovan armed forces clashed at Dubăsari after Transdniestrans took over the local police station. Three people were killed and dozens injured.

Both self-declared republics went on to hold presidential elections in December 1991. Igor Smirnov came out as head of Transdniestr, Stepan Topal of Gagauzia.

Sporadic outbursts of violence ensued as the Moldovan government categorically refused to accept separatists' claims. In March 1992 President Mircea Snegur declared a state of emergency in the country. Two months later full-scale civil war broke out in Transdniestr when Moldovan police clashed with Transdniestran militia in Tighina (Bendery), on the western bank of the Dniestr. The Moldovan army initially succeeded in pushing separatist forces back across the Dniestr, but in a memorable comeback, Transdniestran troops with logistical help from the Russian 14th army and Cossacks, fought their way back across Tighina bridge to take control of Tighina. An estimated 500 to 700 people were killed and thousands wounded.

A cease-fire was signed by Moldovan and Russian presidents Snegur and Boris Yeltsin in July 1992. Provisions were made for a Russian-led, tripartite peacekeeping force comprising Russian, Moldovan and Transdniestran troops to be stationed in the region. Troops remain here today, maintaining an uneasy peace in the region.

Russia continues to play a pivotal role in the Moldovan-Transdniestran conflict. Its 14th army, then led by Alexander Lebed (contender against Yeltsin in Russia's 1996

MOLDOVA

presidential elections) and headquartered in Tiraspol since 1956, covertly supplied Transdniestran rebels with weapons. Lebed became a champion of Russian interests abroad although he later strongly accused the Transdniestran authorities of corruption, arms trafficking and money laundering. The continued presence of the 5000-strong Russian 'operational group' in Transdniestr today is seen by local Russian speakers as a guarantor of their security.

In October 1994, Russia and Moldova signed an agreement for the withdrawal of the Russian 14th army from the region. However, troops have not been pulled out despite their presence undermining Moldova's independent constitution: the Russian Duma has not yet ratified the troop withdrawal accord; the Russian government does not know where to relocate the 5000 troops; and does not know how to dispose of the vast amounts of arms and ammunition it stockpiled in Transdniestr during the Cold War. In 1997 the removal of Russian army material was vigorously opposed by the Transdniestran separatists who would like to keep these handy war deposits for themselves. This development soured their relations with Moscow.

In May 1997 representatives of Moldova and Transdniestra representatives signed a memorandum in Moscow. Under the auspices of Russia, Ukraine and the OSCE both sides agreed to resolve their conflict 'within the framework of a single state'. However the implementation of the accord has been hampered by the stubborn attitude of the rebel republic reluctant to give up its hard fought independence.

At a CIS summit in Chişinău in October 1997 Transdniestr formally asked in vain to be accepted as a full-fledged member. And there was no breakthrough in peace talks because Igor Smirnov failed to show up for his prearranged meeting with the presidents – Moldova's Petru Lucinschi, Russia's Boris Yeltsin and Ukraine's Leonid Kutchma.

Reports about a looming 'de facto' federalisation of Moldova have likewise triggered strong opposition in Chişinău.

GEOGRAPHY

Landlocked Moldova covers an area of 33,700sq km, consisting almost entirely of steppe – gently rolling, partially wooded plains cut through with rivers and streams. Some 75% of land is rich in chernozem (black) soils making it among the most fertile lands in the former Soviet Union. Wine and sunflower production are large industries here.

The centre of the country is more forested and home to Moldova's highest mountain, 430m Mount Balaneşti.

Moldova's 450km-long western boundary with Romania is marked by the Prut river, a tributary of the Danube which kisses Moldova at its most south-western tip. The Dniestr river lies within a few kilometres of its eastern border with Ukraine, crossing the country from north to south on its way to the Black Sea. Moldova also shares northern and southern borders with Ukraine.

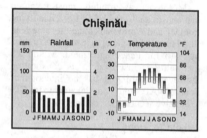

GOVERNMENT & POLITICS

At the end of 1997 Moldovan political parties were gearing up for parliamentary elections scheduled to be held in 1998.

President Petru Lucinschi, elected in November 1996, was set to establish a firm reform-minded powerbase in the 104-seat parliament with the creation of the Movement for a Democratic and Prosperous Moldova. Since taking office the 'neo-communist' who boasted his good ties with Moscow has turned out to be 'the closest Moldova has to a western-style reformist'. With his prime minister Ion Ciubuc and under pressure from international financial institutions, he has launched some urgently needed reforms, too often blocked by a recalcitrant parliament. By mid-1997, just two out the 27 reform bills presented to a parliament split among the Agrarians, the Communists and the Nationalists had been adopted.

Former president Mircea Snegur is expected to take the lead of the nationalist opposition which has united as the Democratic Convention of Moldova. It advocates a closer relationship with Romania and more distance from Moscow.

ECONOMY

In the Soviet Union Moldova was the sixth-largest agricultural producing country, its main export being wine and champagne. Its transition from a centralised to a market economy has seen the country's overall economy drop to barely one third of its size in 1989. Today its economy is the size it was in 1966.

The most influential factor of Moldova's economy is the weather. Agriculture, the country's main industrial sector, representing 43% of GDP, has suffered two consecutive poor harvests since 1996. The International Monetary Fund (IMF) forecast a slight GDP growth in 1997 and a possible further growth of three to five per cent in 1998, depending on implementation of structural reforms.

Annual inflation stood at 8% in mid-1997 down from 15.1% in 1996 (105% in 1994, 415% in 1993, 1500% in 1992). The Moldovan leu introduced in November 1993 has been remarkably stable. The IMF has linked further loans to the government speeding up privatisation, reforming the tax system and raising the pension age to 65 years. In June 1997 parliament approved a privatisation programme under which 580 state enterprises will be sold off.

In March 1997 the government hiked up electricity prices by 60% prompting thousands of protesters demanding wage increases to take to the streets in Chişinău. The government refused to back down.

Moldova is heavily dependent on Russia

Moldova's coat of arms

for its energy supply. In late 1997 Moldova's debts to the Russian Gazprom company totalled US$238.7 million while the Transdniestr separatist republic owed US$241.3 million. Moldova was rumoured to pay the outstanding bills by giving Gazprom shares in the state energy companies Moldenergo and Moldovagas. Plans to link Moldova to Romania's power supply seem unviable.

To attract foreign investment parliament passed a law in July 1997 allowing foreigners to buy land despite heavy protest from communist deputies declaring the law to be tantamount to 'a national betrayal'.

Mikhail Gorbachev's anti-alcohol campaign in the mid-1980s led to a sharp fall in local liquor production. The demise of the former USSR led to a collapse of the large distribution network. Today the wine industry – with its 200,000 hectares of vineyards, 150 winemaking and 23 bottling facilities – is a priority development sector. The European Bank for Reconstruction and Development (EBRD) has granted Moldova a loan to modernise 10 wineries and a glass bottle production factory.

MOLDOVA

The economic situation in the rebel republic of Transdniestr, which does not receive any IMF loans, is dismal.

POPULATION & PEOPLE

Moldova is the most densely populated region in the former Soviet Union (29 inhabitants per square kilometre).

. The total population is 4.4 million. Moldovans comprise 64.5% of this, Russians 13%, Ukrainians 13.5%, Gagauz 3.5%, Bulgarians 2%, Jews 1.5%, and other nationalities such as Belarusians, Poles and Roma, 2%. More than two-thirds of Russians live in cities.

Most Gagauz and Bulgarians live in southern Moldova. In Transdniestr Ukrainians and Russians total 53% of the region's population; Moldovans comprise 40%.

RELIGION

Just over 98% of the population is Orthodox. The Moldovan Orthodox Church, subordinated to the Moscow Patriarchate, is the only church recognised by the state.

Even in religious worship Moldova fails to be united! An increasing number of Moldovan Orthodox believers want to switch sides to the breakaway Bessarabian Orthodox Church which looks to the Romanian Orthodox Patriarchate in Bucharest for guidance. The Bessarabian Church was set up by dissident priests from the Moldovan Church in 1992.

In mid-1997 the Moldovan supreme court ruled that the state had to legalise the Bessarabian church in Moldova. The government consequently said it would appeal the decision while the metropolitan of the Moldovan Orthodox Church warned of a 'war among Orthodox Christians' in Moldova.

LANGUAGE

Moldovan is essentially Romanian. It is a dialect politically manufactured by the Soviet regime from 1924 onwards in a bid to create a 'new' language for its newly created Moldavian ASSR and to pave the way for the incorporation of Bessarabia in 1940.

The introduction of the Cyrillic alphabet created a distinction from Romanian and Russified the Romance language. New words were consequently invented by the authorities, lists of Romanian words 'polluting Moldovan' drawn up and circulated, and all words or neologisms of Latin origin decisively scrapped.

Moldovan is the predominant language spoken today, except in Transdniestr where Russian is the main language and where Moldovan continues to be written in the Cyrillic script. Elsewhere it is written in the Latin alphabet.

Facts for the Visitor

VISAS & DOCUMENTS

All western travellers need a visa to enter Moldova.

Invitations & Tourist Vouchers

To get a visa, *everyone* (except US citizens) needs an invitation or proof of prebooked accommodation (tourist voucher) from a company or organisation. Unless you already have contacts in Moldova it is *very* difficult to get an invitation.

In Bucharest tourist vouchers for Moldova are issued on-the-spot for US$5 from Moldova Tur (☎ 01-312 7070, extension ☎ 2310), Str Luterană 2-4, apartment 10, Bucharest. This voucher confirms a reservation at the Hotel Naţional, run by Moldova Tur in Chişinău. However, you are not obliged to stay at this hotel. Treat the voucher as nothing more than a piece of paper enabling you to get a visa (if you actually want to stay at the Hotel Naţional, you have to make a separate booking!).

Visas can be bought on arrival at Chişinău airport. You still need an invitation or tourist voucher in support of your visa application.

An HIV/AIDS test is required for foreigners intending to stay in Moldova longer than three months. Certificates proving that applicants are HIV negative have to be in Russian and English.

Types of Visa & Costs

A single transit visa is valid for three days and costs US$20. You can also get double transit visas (US$40) which enable you to enter the country twice (maximum stay three days each entry).

Single entry tourist visas costing US$40 are valid for one month from the date of issue. Multiple entry visas valid for one/two/three months cost US$70/100/120 and have to be supported by an invitation from a registered company or organisation in Moldova. You cannot get a multiple entry visa on the strength of a tourist voucher.

Visas take five to seven days to process, except single transit visas bought on arrival at the airport. An additional US$20 fee is charged for 'rush' visas normally issued in 24 hours.

Other Documents

Upon entering Moldova you have to fill in a declaration form stating how much foreign currency you have. Do not lose this form. You are obliged to show it when you leave the country. You are not allowed to leave with more money than you declared on arrival. Any excess will be confiscated. Keep all receipts when you change money to prove you obtained it legally.

EMBASSIES

Moldova has embassies and consulates worldwide. Diplomatic missions in-country are listed in the Chişinău section. Moldovan missions abroad include:

Bulgaria
   Frederic Juliot Curie 19, bloc 1, B-1113 Sofia (☎ 02-739 962, 701 470; fax 02-730 367)
Germany
   An der Elisabethkirche 24, D-53113 Bonn (☎ 0228-910 9411, 910 9415; fax 0228-855 4831); Kennedyallee 119a, D-60596 Frankfurt (☎ 069-636 4212; fax 069-636 4220)
Hungary
   Str Karinthy Fr. ut. 17, fsz 5-6, Budapest (☎ 1-209 1191; fax 209 1195, 1-186 8373; email armrung@mail.elender.hu)

Romania
   Aleea Alexandru 40, RO-71273 Bucharest (☎ 01-230 0474, 312 9790; fax 01-312 9790)
   Consulate: Str Câmpina 47, RO-713 26 Bucharest (☎ 01-666 5720, 312 8631; fax: 01-312 8631)
Russia
   18 Kuznetskii most, RUS-103031 Moscow (☎ 095-924 6342, 924 6342; fax 095-924 5353; email moldemb@online.ru)
Turkey
   St Kaptanpasha 49, Gaziosmanpasha, Anhara, Istanbul (☎ 446 5527; fax 446 5816; email moldova@tr-net.tr)
Ukraine
   Blvd Kutuzova 8, UA-252011 Kiev (☎ 044-295 6703, 295 3292; fax 044-295 6703; email moldovak@sovamn.com)
USA
   2101 S Street NW, Washington, D.C. 20008 (☎ 202-667 1130/31; fax 202-667 1204; email 103714.2137@compuserve.com; www.moldova.org)

CUSTOMS

Exiting Moldova, you are only allowed to import 400 cigarettes and 2L of hard liqueur or wine. The customs office in Chişinău (☎ 2-569 460; fax 2-263 061) is at Str Columna 65.

MONEY

Moldova introduced its own currency, the Moldovan leu (plural lei) to replace the Soviet rouble in November 1993. One leu equals 100 bani. Its initial exchange rate to the US$ was 3.85 lei and it has remained fairly stable ever since.

Travellers cheques and credit cards are only accepted at a couple of banks in Chişinău. Banks charge around 4% commission to cash cheques or give cash advance on Visa/MasterCard. There are no ATMs in Moldova.

Note that the self-styled Transdniestran republic has its own currency – good for a laugh if nothing else. See Money in the Transdniestr section.

Most hotels still adhere to the old Soviet three-tier pricing system, meaning foreigners pay twice as much as CIS citizens and

MOLDOVA

three times as much as Moldovans for the same room.

Candies are a sweet form of currency at bus and train stations. Ticket prices are never rounded up to a sensible figure, meaning ticket sellers do not give the correct change. Boiled sweets or sticks of gum are doled out instead.

Currency Exchange

In mid-1997 the Moldovan leu was worth:

Australia	A$1	=	L2.82
Canada	C$1	=	L2.60
France	FF1	=	L0.70
Germany	DM1	=	L2.60
Japan	¥100	=	L3.05
Romania	L10,000	=	L5
Russia	R10,000	=	L7
UK	UK£1	=	L5.88
USA	US$1	=	L4.58

POST & COMMUNICATIONS

Avoid mailing letters from Moldova; the post is wildly erratic and letters invariably get lost. It costs US$0.19 to send a postcard/letter under 20g to western Europe, and US$1.50 to Australia and the USA.

In Chişinău there are public cardphones from which international calls can be made. Chipcard phonecards costing US$7.50 (35 lei) are sold at the central post and telephones offices. Only local and national calls can be made from the old Soviet, token-operated phones. Tokens cost 15 bani and are also sold at post and telephone offices. To make an international call, dial 8, wait for a dial tone, then dial 10, followed by the country code, city code and number.

Outside of Chişinău, you have to book international calls via an operator from telephone centres. Give the operator the name, city and number of the person you want to call, put down a minimum three minute call deposit, then sit and wait for your number to be announced over a loudspeaker. If no connection is made (nobody home, line busy, no connection etc), a service charge (about US$1) is deducted from your deposit. Since

it can take up to two hours to make a connection, this can be very frustrating.

To call Moldova from the former Soviet Union, you can use the former USSR regional code for Moldova which is still intact: dial ☎ 8, then the Soviet regional code (☎ 042), followed by the city code (ie, to call Chişinău from Moscow dial ☎ 8-0422).

BOOKS

Belarus & Moldova Country Studies, part of the Area Handbook Series, edited by Helen Fedor and published by the Federal Research Division of the Library of the Congress provides the most comprehensive analysis of Moldova up to 1995 you're likely to find.

For the Soviet period, try *Nationalism in the USSR and Eastern Europe* edited by George Simmonds and containing an excellent chapter entitled 'The Moldavian SSR 1964 – 1974' by Sherman David Spectator; or *Nations, Nationalities, People: A Study of the Nationalities Policy of the Communist Party in Soviet Moldova* by Michael Bruchis.

Contemporary politics is tackled in *Romania after Tyranny* edited by Daniel Nelson which focuses on current relations between Romania and Moldova. *From Moldavia to Moldova: The Soviet-Romanian Territorial Dispute* by Nicholas Dima; and *The Nationalities Question in the Soviet Union*, edited by Graham Smith, are also good.

Available locally (Chişinău only) is the picture book, *Chişinău* (Editura Uniunii Scriitorilor, Chişinău, 1996). It is packed with photographs of the city with captions in Moldovan and Russian and costs US$15. French speakers will appreciate the cheaper *Chişinău 1941* (Scrieri Despre, Chişinău, 1995), costing US$2 and containing black & white photographs of the Moldovan capital before WWII.

Engleza de gata – Off-Pegged English by Violeta Wăstăsescu and Fuluia Turu (Editura Uniunii Scriitorilor, Chişinău, 1994) is a valuable pocket-size Moldovan-English phrase book written for Moldovans heading overseas but easy to use the other way round.

It contains every conceivable sentence you'll ever need to utter. It costs US$0.50 in most bookshops in Chişinău.

MEDIA

Locally, little is published in foreign languages. The English-language 12-page broadsheet, *Welcome*, costing US$0.30 provides a much-appreciated update of local news and a 'what's on' listing. It's published fortnightly but can be difficult to find: try the kiosk opposite Government House on Blvd Ştefan cel Mare.

Radio France International (RFI) can be picked up on 102.3 FM. Sun TV is a joint Moldovan-American venture which utilises the best of all the cable channels including CNN, Euronews, and the popular private Romanian channel, Pro TV.

Since Transdniestran militia took over the Moldovan radio transmitter at Grigoriopol, Radio Moldova International has to broadcast from transmitters in Bucharest. The Grigoriopol transmitter remains under the control of the separatists who use it to transmit Radio Dniestr in their self-styled republic.

ELECTRICITY

Moldova runs on 220 V, 50 Hz AC. Most appliances that are set up for 240 V will handle this happily. Sockets require two-pin Russian plugs, identical to European plugs except the pins are thinner. Some sockets you can jam a European plug into. Others you can't.

TOILETS

In Moldova most toilets bear Russian signs: : for women and **M** for men. Hygiene standards are as low as in Romania (see Facts for the Visitor at the front of this book).

GAY & LESBIAN TRAVELLERS

Moldova repealed its Soviet anti-gay law in 1995, thereby legalising homosexuality. It is still not a good idea to be too 'out' in Moldova however.

DANGERS & ANNOYANCES

Getting an invitation to visit Moldova is a major hassle. In-country, Soviet bureaucracy can be a trial.

Simply getting around is a pain in the neck. Patience, tolerance and a low expectation of service are key factors in keeping down stress levels. Most trams, buses and trolleybuses are fit for the scrapheap. The lingering Soviet legacy of train personnel speaking only Russian can be a trifle frustrating to non-Russian speakers.

Don't flash your wealth about, beware of pickpockets, and stick to the same street rules as in any city. Street crime against foreigners has not yet hit the heady heights it has in Romania – simply because the country attracts so few of them! Likewise few beggars plague the street, simply because there's no market. This will undoubtedly change as more western travellers make their way here.

Travelling in the self-declared republic of Transdniestr is safe providing you stay away from military objects and installations. If in doubt, check with the Moldovan consulate in Bucharest or abroad, or with the OCSE.

PUBLIC HOLIDAYS & SPECIAL EVENTS

Moldova national holidays include:

New Year's Day	1 January
Russian Orthodox Christmas	7 & 8 January
International Women's Day	8 March
Orthodox Easter	March/April/May
Victory (1945) Day	9 May
Independence Day	27 August
National Language Day	31 August

Transdniestrans boycott the Moldovan independence day and celebrate their own independence day on September 2.

Getting There & Away

Moldova is way off the beaten tourist track. Few trains and even fewer buses (and tourists) come here while flight routings from the west are still in their infancy. Most flights are eastbound.

AIR

All international flights to Moldova use Chişinău (Kishinev) airport. The only direct flights into Moldova from the west are from Berlin and Paris.

Moldova has three national airlines: Moldavian Airlines is a private airline set up in 1994. It offers direct flights to Budapest, Prague, Moscow and Rostov, and flights with one stopover to Vienna, Rome and Warsaw. It has no offices abroad but some specialist travel agencies sell tickets for its flights.

Air Moldova International is another private airline dating from 1995. It flies direct to Berlin, Kiev, Dnepropetrovsk, Donetsk, Odessa and Warsaw. Again, it has no offices abroad.

Air Moldova is the state carrier for Moldova with direct flights to Istanbul, Larnaca, Minsk, Moscow, Paris, St Petersburg, Sofia and Yekaterinburg. Offices abroad include:

Austria
  Hilton Top Centre 1742, Landstrasse Haup Str 2, A-1030 Vienna (☎ 01-713 4051; fax 01-713 4036)
Belarus
  Karla Marksa 28, BY-220050 Minsk (☎ 017-227 6234; fax 017-227 7597)
Bulgaria
  Stambolijski 156, Sofia (☎ & fax 02-222 604)
France
  19, rue St Roch, F-75001 Paris (☎ 01 42 96 10 40; fax 01 42 96 18 77)
Germany
  Kennedy Allee 119a, D-60313 Frankfurt/Main (☎ 069-963 6420; fax 069-963 64220)
Romania
  Batiştei 5, Bucharest (☎ 01-312 1258; fax 01-312 0822)
Turkey
  Istanbul International airport, Terminal 2, TR-34830 Istanbul (☎ 212-663 0879; fax 212-663 0856)
Russia
  Vnukovo airport, Moscow (☎ 095-436 7539; fax 095-924 4661); Nevsky Prospekt 7/9, St Petersburg (☎ 812-311 8093)

Ukraine
  ulitsa Karla Marxa, Kiev (☎ 044-271 2636)

Be wary of travel agents who try to convince you the *only* way to the republic is by plane via Bucharest: any honest agent will advise you to only fly as far as Bucharest and then get a train from there to Chişinău.

For further information about air travel in the region, see the Getting There & Away chapter at the beginning of this book.

LAND

For information on travelling to Moldova by land, see the Getting There & Away chapter at the beginning of this book.

Getting Around

For general information on travel within Moldova, see the Getting Around chapter at the beginning of this book.

Border Crossings Within Moldova

Since the 1992 civil war, several army control posts have been set up on the Dniestr river which marks the 'unofficial' border between Moldova and the self-declared Republic of Transdniestr. These posts are set up by the Moldovan army, Transdniestr's self-declared border guards, and a Russian-led tripartite peacekeeping force.

Before entering Tighina from Chişinău, you have to stop at a control post. Vehicles are searched by the Transdniestrians. Spot checks on your car papers and driving licence by all three forces are frequent. Peacekeeping forces are stationed throughout the self-styled republic, including across the bridge between Tighina and Tiraspol.

The bridge along the main eastbound road (M21) from Chişinău to Dubăsari (and to Kiev) is closed to all vehicles. Despite a sign at the western end of the bridge reading 'Stop: Trespassers will be shot', locals cross the bridge next to the hydroelectric power plant on foot. Foreigners are strongly advised not to try this.

To get to Kiev from Chişinău you have to follow a minor road east to Vadu lui Vodă where the bridge across the Dniestr was still open at the time of writing. From Doroţcaia, bear north to Dubăsari and the M21. Before embarking on this route, it is a good idea to check in Chişinău if this is still possible.

If you are crossing into Ukraine at the Pervomaisc border you also have to drive through the republic of Transdniestr.

Chişinău & Around

Chişinău is strategically placed in the centre of the country. It is surrounded by fertile plains which, for centuries, have been renowned as a rich wine-producing region.

North of the capital lie two of Moldova's most unique treasures – the underground wine kingdom at Cricova and the fabulous 13th century monastery carved in a cliff-face at Orhei.

CHIŞINĂU
• *area code ☎ 2, pop 735,229*

Chişinău, Moldova's capital, is a surprisingly green city on the banks of the Bîc (Byk) river. It is circled by a ring of parks and lakes and, despite being the transport hub of the country, its pretty, tree-lined avenue and refreshingly quiet streets bear more resemblance to a provincial town in Romania than a nation's capital.

Chişinău was first chronicled in 1420. It became known as a hotbed of anti-Semitism in the early 20th century: in 1903 the murder of 49 Jews sparked protests from Jewish communities worldwide, and in 1941 during WWII the notorious Chişinău pogrom was executed.

Chişinău served as the headquarters of the USSR's south-western theatre of military operations during Soviet rule. Between 1944 and 1990 the city was called Kishinev, its Russian name still used by the handful of travel agents abroad who actually know where this unassuming city is.

More than half of Chişinău's population

today is Moldovan; Russians comprise 25% and Ukrainians 13%.

Orientation
Chişinău's street layout is a typical Soviet one comprising of straight streets in a grid system.

The train station is a five minute walk from the centre on Aleea Gării. Exit the train station, turn right along Aleea Gării to Piaţa Negruzzi, then walk up the hill along Blvd Negruzzi to Piaţa Libertăţii. From here the main street, Blvd Ştefan cel Mare (formerly Lenina prospekt), crosses the town from the south-east to north-west. At its northern end is the central square, Piaţa Marii Adunarii Naţionale (Great National Assembly Square), dominated by the government building, cathedral and Chişinău's very own Arc de Triomphe.

The central bus station (Autogară centrală) is behind the central market (piaţa centrală) on Str Mitropolit Varlaam. Buses to/from destinations south of Chişinău use the south-western bus station (Autogară Sud-vest), 2km from the city centre.

Street names are still changing and in many cases, both old and new names are used simultaneously. Hence, Str Hînceşti is sometimes signposted Str Vasile Alexsandrii too.

Maps The *Chişinău Map*, published in Bucharest in 1993, costs US$2.50 in most bookshops. Hotels sell it too but charge at least double the price. Avoid.

Information
Tourist Offices The state tourist office, Moldova Tur (☎ 266 100), is on the ground floor of Hotel Naţional, Blvd Ştefan cel Mare 4. The staff need a push to answer questions but will eventually do so. The office arranges 2½-hour city tours by car or mini-bus for an extortionate US$35 an hour. Avoid. It also arranges day trips to Cricova wine cellars for US$55, can get bus or train tickets for a US$5 commission, and rents out chauffeured cars for US$5 an hour plus an extortionate fee per kilometre which they

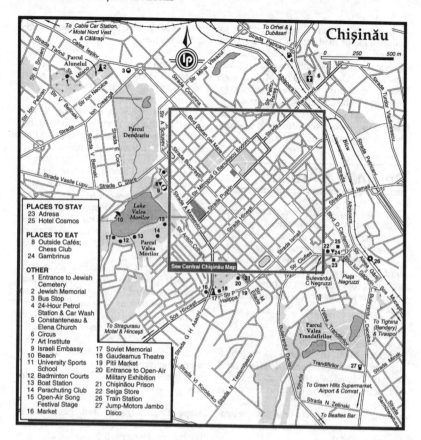

To Cable Car Station,
Motel Nord Vest
& Călăraşi

To Orhei &
Dubăsari

Chişinău

0   250   500 m

PLACES TO STAY
23 Adresa
25 Hotel Cosmos

PLACES TO EAT
8   Outside Cafés;
    Chess Club
24 Gambrinus

OTHER
1   Entrance to Jewish
    Cemetery
2   Jewish Memorial
3   Bus Stop
4   24-Hour Petrol
    Station & Car Wash
5   Constanteneau &
    Elena Church
6   Circus
7   Art Institute
9   Israeli Embassy
10 Beach
11 University Sports
    School
12 Badminton Courts
13 Boat Station
14 Parachuting Club
15 Open-Air Song
    Festival Stage
16 Market

17 Soviet Memorial
18 Gaudeamus Theatre
19 Piţii Market
20 Entrance to Open-Air
    Military Exhibition
21 Chişinău Prison
22 Seiga Store
26 Train Station
27 Jump-Motors Jambo
    Disco

Parcul Alunelul

Parcul Dendrariu

Lake Valea Morilor

Parcul Valea Morilor

See Central Chişinău Map

To Straguresu
Motel & Hineşti

Bulevardul
C Negruzzi

Piaţa Negruzzi

Parcul Valea Trandafirilor

To Tighina
(Bendery)
& Tiraspol

To Green Hills Supermarket,
Airport & Comrat

To Beatles Bar

refuse to reveal. Faxes can be sent for a scandalous US$10 per A4 page to Russia/CIS or US$20 per page to Europe.

The Cricova Tour excursion bureau (☎ 221 419; fax 243 544) is at Str Mitropoli G Banulescu Bodoni 45 (see Cricova section).

The only printed information Moldova Tur has is dusty brochures featuring Hotel Naţional and a guidebook to the Moldovan SSR dating from 1985.

The information desk (☎ 264 157) inside Hotel Cosmos, Piaţa Negruzzi 2, is more right-on. Staff here smile. Unfortunately

prices are similar to those extortionate ones at Moldova Tur.

Foreign Consulates Diplomatic missions in Chişinău include the following:

Bulgaria
    Embassy: Str 31 August 127 (☎ 223 282, 237 983; fax 237 908)
France
    Consulate: Str Sfatul Ţării 18 (☎ 237 234, 237 017; fax 234 781)
Germany
    Embassy: Str Maria Cibotari 37 (☎ 234 607, 232 872; fax 234 680)

Hungary
    Embassy: Blvd Ştefan cel Mare 131 (☎ 228 353, 227 786; fax 28 594)
Romania
    Embassy: Str Bucureşti 66/1 (☎ 233 434, 237 583; fax 233 469)
    Consulate: Str Vlaicu Parcalab 39 (☎ 237 622)
Russia
    Embassy: Str A Mateevici 80 (☎ 248 225, 224 046; fax 248 226)
    Consulate: Blvd Ştefan cel Mare 151 (☎ 228 573, 224 046)
Ukraine
    Embassy: Str Sfatul Ţării 55 (☎ 232 563, 732 382; fax 232 562)
USA
    Embassy: Str A Mateevici 103 (☎ 233 772, 233 476; fax 233 044)

Money Travellers cheques are impossible to cash in Chişinău.

Moldindconbank gives cash advance in Moldovan lei on Visa/MasterCard for a 4% commission. The branch inside the international ticket hall at the train station is open weekdays from 9 am to 1 pm, 2 to 7 pm. The city-centre branch inside the Air Moldova office, Blvd Negruzzi 8, is open weekdays from 8 am to 8 pm, Saturday from 8 am to 7 pm. Another branch, open similar hours, is at Blvd Renaşterii 7. The Petrol Bank on the corner of Blvd Ştefan cel Mare and Str Ismail gives cash advance on Visa (open weekdays from 9 am to 12.50 pm, 3.15 to 4.30 pm).

If you want to get cash advance in US$ on Visa/MasterCard go to the Bancă de Export Import a Moldovei, Blvd Ştefan cel Mare 6.

There is a 24 hour currency exchange at Blvd Ştefan cel Mare 6.

Post & Communications The central post office (☎ 261 228, 261 116) is at Str Bulgariă 10. Post restante letters can only be collected from the post office at Blvd Ştefan cel Mare 134 on the corner of Str Puşkin (open weekdays from 8 am to 7 pm and on Saturday from 8 am to 6 pm).

The central telephone, fax & telegraph office is on the corner of Blvd Ştefan cel Mare and Str Tighina. Book international calls inside the hall marked *Convorbir Inter-brurbarie* (the entrance overlooking Str Tighina). Faxes and telegrams can also be sent from here. This hall is open 24 hours but faxes can only be sent between 8.30 am and 10 pm.

A simpler solution is to buy a US$7.50 (35 lei) phonecard from the desk marked *Reteaua telefoane Chişinău* inside the second hall (entrance overlooking Blvd Ştefan cel Mare). Tokens costing 15 bani for the token-operated public phones from which only local and national calls can be made are also sold here. This hall is open weekdays from 8 am to 7 pm, Saturday from 9 am to 5 pm.

Travel Agencies The Voiaj travel agency (☎ 546 464; fax 262 741), Blvd Negruzzi 8, sells plane tickets and is the most customer-friendly agency in town. The Agenţie de Turism (☎ 277 738, 227 646), Str Renaşterii 13, arranges tours at a price – Cricova for US$70 per person and wine tasting in Cojuşna for US$35 including dinner.

Bookshops English-language books – mainly dictionaries and text books – published by Oxford University Press can be found at the Educational Centre (☎ 229 910), Str Mihai Eminescu 64, apartment 5. The entrance is in a courtyard off the main street. The centre is open weekdays from 9 am to 6 pm. Staff speak English.

Cartea Librărie, Blvd Ştefan cel Mare 6, stocks the best range of country and city maps as well as three-month-old copies of the British *Daily Telegraph*, *Daily Express*, *Times* and other national dailies. These cost around US$1. The shop is open daily, except Sunday, from 10 am to 7 pm. Local maps are also sold at the Cartea Universal, Blvd Ştefan cel Mare 54, and at the Cartea Academica on the northern side of the Arc de Triomphe at Blvd Ştefan cel Mare 148.

Cultural Centres The French Cultural Centre (Alliance Française; ☎ 234 510, 237 236; fax 234 781; email alfrmd @mdearn.cri.md) which is inside the Ginta Latina Theatre, Str Sfatul Ţării 18, screens French films on Saturday at 10 am, holds

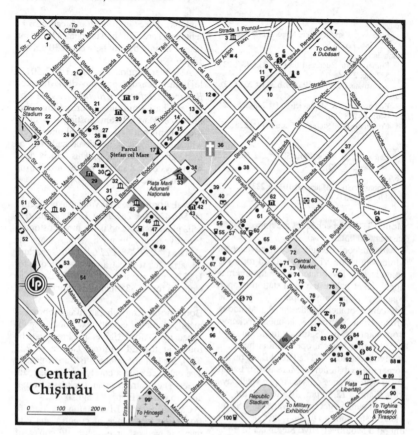

Central Chişinău

0   100   200 m

French language courses, has an extensive library for public use, and hosts regular cultural events.

Photography & Video The Kodak outlet inside the Seiga Store, Blvd Negruzzi 6/2, sells and develops film. It is open daily from 9 am to 9 pm. There is another Kodak store inside the Unic Magazinul Centur, Blvd Ştefan cel Mare 8, and another at Blvd Ştefan cel Mare 136. Film processing costs US$1 plus an additional US$0.30 per print.

Media Tune into Radio Nova on 105.9 FM.

Medical Services There is a small pharmaceutical booth selling basic medicines like aspirin inside the train station's main hall; open daily from 9 am to 4 pm. The pharmacy close to the Hotel Naţional on Blvd Negruzzi is open daily from 8 am to 8 pm. The Centrală on Blvd Ştefan cel Mare, close to the Cartea Librărie bookshop, is open similar hours. Farmacie Ninervia opposite the flower market on Str Mitropoli G Banulescu Bodoni is open 24 hours.

Emergency The emergency suite on the 4th floor of the Hotel Naţional provides health

PLACES TO STAY
4 Hotel Zarea
6 Hotel Turist
21 Hotel Casă
24 Hotel Dacia
27 Hotel Seabeco
    Moldova
28 Hotel Codru
79 Hotel Meridan
88 Hotel National;
    Moldova-Tur
90 Hotel Chişinău

PLACES TO EAT
7 Sănătate
9 Café Fortus
10 Indian Tandoori
22 Belde Company
41 Restaurant Caragoli
42 La Tour Eiffel
59 Consar Express
67 La Brunel
69 Cactus Café & Bar
71 Belluno
75 Alimentara Sfânta
    Maria
76 Cafenea Mămăliguta
82 Cantină
93 Wam Fast Food
96 Oraşul Vechi
98 El Paso

OTHER
1 Russian Consulate
2 Hungarian Embassy
3 Pushkin Museum
5 Agenţie de Turism
8 Jewish Memorial
11 Cocktail Bar
12 Fedesco Supermarket
13 Victoria Supermarket
14 Cricova Tour
15 24-Hour Pharmacy
16 Cartea Academia
    Bookshop
17 Statue of Ştefan cel
    Mare

18 Opera & Ballet
    Theatre
19 Presidential Palace
20 Parliament
23 Main Entrance to
    Stadium
25 French Cultural
    Centre; Ginta
    Latina Theatre
26 German Embassy
29 Republic Palace
30 Bulgarian Embassy
31 Belarusian Embassy
32 Archaeology
    Museum
33 Government House
34 Arc de Triomphe
35 24-Hour Flower
    Market
36 Cathedral
37 Old Jewish School
38 Chekhov Drama
    Theatre
39 Kodak Express
40 Post Office
43 National Palace
44 National Library
45 National History
    Museum
46 Licurici Puppet
    Theatre
47 National Art Museum
48 Admiral Club
49 Press House
50 National Natural
    History &
    Ethnographic
    Museum
51 Russian Embassy
52 US Embassy
53 Water Tower
54 University
55 Iorc Beach Bar
56 Organ Hall
57 Mihai Eminescu
    National Theatre
58 Kodak Express

60 Ialoveni Sherry
    Factory Shop & Bar
61 Bookshop
62 Philharmonic
    Concert Hall
63 Synagogue
64 24-Hour Petrol
    Station
65 Bucuria Sweet Shop
66 Magazinul de Firm
    Cricova
68 Luceafarul Theatre;
    La Luceafarul Club
70 Moldindconbank
72 Main Entrance to
    Market
73 Notus Magazin
74 Cartea Universal
77 Bus Station
78 Main Entrance to
    Market
80 Unic Magazinul
    Centur
81 Central Telephone,
    Fax & Telegraph
    Office
83 Petrol Bank
84 Bancă de Export
    Import
85 Cartea Librărie
    Bookshop
86 24-Hour Currency
    Exchange
87 Centrală Farmacie
89 Air Moldova; Voiaj
    Travel Agency
91 Exhibition Hall;
    Galeria Brancuşi
92 Moldavian Airlines
94 TAROM
95 Satirical Theatre
97 Turkish Embassy
99 Entrance to Civil
    Cemetery
100 Megapolis Bar &
    Disco; University
    Cultural House

care. Contact the US embassy for a list of English-speaking doctors.

Things to See & Do

Chişinău was heavily bombed during WWII and little remains of its historic heart. Walk north-west along Blvd Ştefan cel Mare to the **Arc de Triomphe**, built in 1846 and restored in 1973. Buskers often play under the arches. To its east sprawls **Cathedral Park** (Parcul Catedralei), dominated by the city's main **Orthodox Cathedral** (1836). In the north-western side of the park, on Str Mitropoli G Banulescu Bodoni, there is a colourful 24 hour **flower market**.

The area immediately west of the Arc de Triomphe on Blvd Ştefan cel Mare is dominated by **government house** where Prime Minister Ion Ciubuc's cabinet meets. The parliament convenes in **parliament house**,

MOLDOVA

at Blvd Ştefan cel Mare 123. Further north is the contemporary **Opera & Ballet Theatre** (Opera Naţionale de Moldavia).

Ştefan cel Mare Park (Parcul Ştefan cel Mare) dominates this western flank of Blvd Ştefan cel Mare. The park entrance is guarded by a statue of Ştefan cel Mare. The medieval prince of Moldavia is Moldova's greatest hero today, bearing testimony to their pre-Soviet roots. Violent clashes between Moldovan nationalists and pro-Soviet supporters took place in 1990-1 here. Just outside the park is the large **Cinema Patria**, built by German prisoners of war in 1947.

From the Arc de Triomphe bear west along Str Puşkin. The **National Art Museum** (Muzeul de Arte Plastice; ☎ 245 245) is along this street on the corner of Str 31 August. It is currently closed for restoration but its main exhibits are displayed in the **National History Museum** (Muzeul Naţional de Istorie al Moldavia; ☎ 226 614, 226 619) at Str 31 August 121a. In the hall, left of the ticket office, is an incredible life-size rendering of the Soviet army's attack on

Ştefan cel Mare launched 1000 street names throughout Moldova as well as Romania.

Chişinău in 1945. The locally produced furniture displayed in the hall to the right of the ticket office is not part of the museum; it's a furniture shop! The history museum is open daily, except Sunday and Monday, from 9 am to 5 pm. A **statue** of Lupoaica Romei (the wolf of Rome) and the two abandoned children, Romulus and Remus, stands in front of the museum. The words of Romanian poet Mihai Eminescu pay homage to Moldova's Dacian roots. At Str 31 August 121 is the **Licurici Puppet Theatre**. Opposite is the **National Library**.

Continuing west along Str Puşkin you come to the **state university** at Str A Mateevici 6. The **water tower** *(turnul de apă;* ☎ 241 648) outside its main entrance dates from 1892 and hosts temporary historical exhibitions. It's open daily, except Friday, from 10 am to 6 pm. Temporary art exhibitions are held in the **Art Gallery L** inside the **Republic Palace** (Palatul Republicii; ☎ 232 615) on the corner of Str Bucureşti and Str Maria Cibotari.

Walk north along Str A Mateevici then bear east one block to the excellent **National Natural History & Ethnographic Museum** (Muzeul Naţional de Etnografie şi Istorie Naturală; ☎ 221 916) at Str M Kogălniceanu 82. The museum is housed in an unusual Turkish-style complex built 1903-5 and includes a well presented display of Moldova's evolution from the Jurassic age to contemporary computing times. Its highlights include a life-size reconstruction of a mammal skeleton, 5m tall and 6m long, which was discovered in the Rezine region in 1966. The museum is open every day, except Sunday and Monday, from 10 am to 6 pm.

The **Archaeology Museum** (Muzeul de Arheologie; ☎ 222 574), on the corner of Str 31 August and Str Mitropolit G Banulescu Bodini, displays reconstructions of traditional houses from Moldova's different regions and has a colourful exhibition of traditional handwoven rugs, carpets and wall hangings. It is open daily, except Sunday, from 9 am to 1 pm, 2 to 5 pm.

From the university head south along Str

A Mateevici, past a small park, to Str Ismail. On the corner is a small **open-air military exhibition**. It displays various models of Soviet-made tanks, fighter planes and other military toys inherited by Moldova's armed forces. Highlights include a SM-90 rocket launcher (1960) and a couple of MIG-17s and 21s which local kids now use to scramble on. The exhibition is open daily, except Monday, from 10 am to 6 pm.

Opposite, on the corner of Str Mircea Eliade and Str A Mateevici, is **Chişinău Prison**. Relatives of the inmates stand on the pavement next to fighter planes shouting to the inmates behind the boarded-up prison windows. Prisoners shout back. It's a real circus. The military exhibition is flanked to the east by **Pitii Market**, Str P Halippa. Old men sell spare car parts and other mechanical gadgets here.

The small park straddled by Str A Mattevici is dominated by a **victory memorial** to the Soviet army in 1945. An eternal flame burns in the centre of the five-edged pyramid in memory of Chişinău's unknown soldiers who died in WWII. Soldiers' graves line the boundaries of the park and there is a small **military cemetery** at its northern end. In the centre of the park is a **memorial** to those who died during the fight for Moldovan independence in 1991.

The entrance to the adjoining **civil cemetery** (cimitrul central), known locally as the Armenian cemetery, is on the corner of Str A Mateevici and Str Armeneasca. The graves of civilians who died in WWI are on the right as you enter. The blue and silver-domed **All Saints Church** in the centre of the cemetery dates from 1830.

Heading south of the cemeteries, at the junction of Str P Halippa and Str Hînceşti, is another typically monstrous **Soviet memorial**. The Russian inscription has been painted over on this one. There is a small **market** close by on Str Lacului where you can taste the local brew at dirt-cheap prices.

North-east of the centre on the corner of Str Anton Pann and Str I Pruncul is the **Pushkin Museum** (Muzeul Puşkin; ☎ 240 440), housed in a cottage where Russian poet

Alexandr Pushkin (1799-1837) spent an exiled three months in the 1820s. The house remains as it would have been then. The museum is open daily from 10 am to 5 pm. A half hour excursion in broken English costs US$2.50.

The entire southern end of Str Varlaam is dominated by a huge **bazaar** which should not be missed. Local traders flog carpets from Turkey while wrinkled pensioners desperately clutch a bizarre collection of bras, T-shirts and not-so-kinky knickers. Porters scurry around with trolleys to carry goods away, cars honk like crazy as they stupidly try to squeeze through the bustling crowds, women spit out sunflower seeds and old men huddle in groups haggling for the best bargain.

Close by at the south of Blvd Ştefan cel Mare opposite the Hotel Naţional is an **Exhibition Hall** (Sala de Expozitii; ☎ 229 331), with a permanent exhibition of contemporary Moldovan art. It is open weekdays from 10 am to 6 pm, weekends from 11 am to 4 pm. The **Galeria Brancuşi**, inside the hall, has some nice pieces for sale.

Parks & Lakes City dwellers' favoured haunt is **Lake Valea Morilor**, covering an area of 141.47 hectares east of the city. Steps lead to the lake and surrounding park from Str A Mateevici (opposite the university at its western end).

The beach on the north-western shores gets packed with sunbathers and swimmers at weekends. Hire canoes, rowing and paddle boats for US$1 an hour from the boat station *(staţia de bărci)* on the lake's southern shores. The boat house is open weekdays from 10 am to 9 pm, weekends from 10 am to 8 am. There are **badminton courts** (☎ 721 753) close to the university sports school on the western shore. High flyers should hike up to the **parachuting club** (☎ 515 795), above the open-air song festival stage. An eight day parachuting course costs US$55. Bus No 29a from the city centre stops outside the university entrance to the park.

South of the park is the **Expo-Business**

MOLDOVA

Chişinău (☎ 627 416; fax 628 263), a free enterprise zone where VAT-exempt goods are sold. Locals flock here for cheap alcohol. Next to the entrance stand Chişinău's disgraced heroes – communists Lenin, Karl Marx and Fredrich Engels. The complex is open daily from 10 am to 9 pm.

North-west of the centre on the road to Cojuşna and Ungheni is Chişinău's largest park, **Izvor de la Sculeni Elena Parcul**, Calea Eşilor. It is dominated by three interconnecting lakes which you can explore with rented canoes and rowing boats. Opposite the parks' southern entrance is a **cable car** station; you can make a three minute journey across the valley for US$0.25. The station is open daily, except Sunday, from 7 am to noon, 1 to 7 pm. To get to the park, take trolleybus No 1 or 23 to the last stop. Microbus No 11 runs from Str Studenţilor in the centre to Calea Eşilor.

Jewish Chişinău North-east of the Central bus station is a maze of run-down, dusty streets filled with hopscotch-playing children and old women sitting on doorsteps. Few cars or city dwellers make it to these parts and a stroll through the calm, crooked streets is worthwhile.

Many of these streets formed the **Chişinău ghetto**. On the street leading east from Blvd Renaşterii to Str Fantalului, is a **memorial** to the martyrs and victims of the Chişinău ghetto, inscribed in Hebrew, Moldovan and Russian. At Str Rabbi Ţirilson 4 is the remains of a **Yeshiva**, Chişinău's Jewish school which functioned until WWII. Chişinău's only remaining working **synagogue** (☎ 221 215, 226 131; www.kishinev.org.il) is close by at Str Habad Lubavia 8. Before WWII, there were over 70 synagogues in Chişinău, each serving a different trade. Glassblowers worshipped at the one on Str Habad Lubavia. Today about 120 believers attend the Saturday service.

Since independence Chişinău's Jewish community has seen a massive revival. The active community runs an adult education program at its small secondary school, operates a meals-on-wheels service for elderly

Jews, and prints a newspaper in Hebrew. It also runs a soup kitchen in Chişinău and in Tiraspol. An estimated 30,000 Jews live in Moldova today. The community is lent support by the US-based Friend of Kishinev Jewry (☎ & fax 718-756 0458), 720 Lefferts Ave 2, Brooklyn, NY-11203.

The city's **Jewish cemetery** is north-west of the centre, next to Alunelul park on Str Milano. Most graves are unkempt and overgrown. There are ruins of an old synagogue next to the cemetery's surrounding stone wall. In Alunelul park there is a **memorial** to the 49 Jews killed in the 1903 pogrom. The remains of the victims were moved here after the cemetery in which they were buried was destroyed by the communists in the 1960s. To get to the park and cemetery take bus No 1 from Blvd Ştefan cel Mare and get off at the Parcul Alunelul stop. Cross the road and walk up the hill to the southern end of Str Milano. The cemetery entrance is on the left.

Places to Stay – bottom end
Camping The nearest *campsite* is 12km north-east of Chişinău in Vadul lui Vodă forest. It is a popular weekend spot for locals. Take bus No 31 from the centre.

Private Rooms The best bet for budget travellers is *Adresa* (☎ 266 414, 264 698; ☎ & fax 262 096), a five minute walk from the train station at Blvd Negruzzi 1. It rents out apartments and rooms in the city centre for short and long-term stays.

A clean apartment for two people in an apartment block in the centre costs US$19 a night, or US$15 a night if you stay more than two nights. Lower rates are charged for one/two-week stays. Most apartments have a well-equipped kitchen and a bathroom with a small water heater. You have to pay in advance and leave a US$1 deposit for the key. Adresa is open weekdays from 9 am to 9 pm, Saturday from 9 am to 6 pm. Staff do not speak English.

Hotels The *Hotel Turist* (☎ 229 512, 229 639), overlooking the giant Soviet memorial to communist youth at Blvd Renaşterii 13a, has cheap singles/doubles for US$21/24 a night. Rooms have a private shower but hot water is variable. Reception staff speak no English and are a touch hostile.

Of equal standing is the cheap, 120-bed *Hotel Zarea* (☎ 227 625), Str Anton Pann 4. Singles/doubles with shared bathroom cost US$11/24 and triples are US$22. The hotel has a bar and billiard club. Staff are surly.

Opposite the central bus station at Str Tighina 42 is the *Hotel Meridan* (☎ 260 620). Singles/doubles with TV and private shower are US$13/19 a night and singles/doubles with shared bathroom are US$11/15. Hotel staff only speak Russian. The entrance to the hotel is through the Foto Express kiosk.

Places to Stay – middle

Hotels The *Hotel Cosmos* (☎ 264 457; fax 264 300), Piaţa Negruzzi 2, is a tall and ugly concrete block. It has reasonably priced rooms, friendly staff, and a 24 hour bar serving morning coffee for weary travellers arriving on the night train from Bucharest. The hotel also has a handy left-luggage room open to non-guests too. Singles/doubles with private bathroom and TV are US$31/35 plus an additional US$0.40 'registration tax'. One/two room apartments cost US$37/63.

The towering, 17-storey *Hotel Naţional* (☎ 266 083, 266 144) at Blvd Ştefan cel Mare 4 is run by Moldova Tur. Singles with/without TV cost US$28/22 with an ominous US$18 rate for those who only want the rooms for 12 hours. Doubles with/without TV are US$40/34. Rooms for Romanians and Moldovans are cheaper. Everyone also has to pay a registration tax totalling 50% of the minimum salary – US$2 in mid-1997. The hotel has a post office, left-luggage room, café and restaurant.

Close by is the attractive *Hotel Chişinău* (☎ 266 341; fax 266 406), Blvd Negruzzi 7. Singles/doubles with private bath cost US$15/24. The hotel restaurant is reputed to be good for traditional Moldovan cuisine.

Out of Town Following major renovation in 1996, the *Motel Nord Vest* (☎ 639 828; fax 624 931), 3km from the centre at Calea Eşilor on the main Chişinău-Cojuşna highway, is now a pleasant, 100-bed motel. Singles/doubles with TV, fridge and shower cost US$28/56. The motel has a tennis court, sauna and excellent restaurant and bar.

Places to Stay – top end

The three-star *Hotel Dacia* (☎ 232 251; fax 234 647), Str 31 August 135, is a large block close to parliament in the heart of the city's 'embassy land'. Foreigners pay a hefty US$80/120 for a single/double with private bath.

Hotel Codru (☎ 225 506; fax 237 902), Str 31 August 127, charges an the same ridiculous US$80/120 for a single/double. The hotel decor is dark and gloomy.

Considered the best in town is the could-be-anywhere-in-the-world *Hotel Seabeco Moldova* (☎ 232 875, 232 896; fax 232 870), next to the German embassy at Str Maria Cibotari 37. The enticing sofas in the reception are enough to make you want to check in immediately. Single/double rooms go for US$150/200, a junior/senior suite is priced US$210/270 while an executive suite costs US$320. The hotel has a restaurant, said to be excellent, and a casino.

At the time of writing building work was taking place at *Hotel Casă*, behind parliament at Str A Corobeceanu 7a.

Places to Eat

Restaurants *Sănătate* (☎ 243 622), Blvd Renaşterii 24, is the best place to sample authentic Moldovan cuisine. Staff are kitted out in traditional costume and the decor definitely veers towards the 'rustic'. Local delicacies on the menu, written in Romanian, Russian and English, include boiled sturgeon for US$4 and a huge variety of mămăligă dishes for around US$1. In the adjoining terrace bar overlooking the street, you can eat şaşlik, cooked to order, for no more than US$2. Restaurant and terrace are open daily from noon to midnight.

The *Gambrinus* restaurant, next to the Seiga store at Blvd Negruzzi 4/2, is one of Chişinău's more modern restaurants with a bright decor and even brighter terrace. The menu is in Russian only and garnishes cost extra. The seiga chicken for US$2.50 is tasty. It is open daily from noon to midnight.

The Italian-inspired *Belluno* (☎ 260 342), Blvd Ştefan cel Mare 124, is one of Chişinău's better restaurants with prices that won't break the bank. The picture book menu touts delicious-looking Italianish dishes for around US$3. It is open daily from 10 am to 2 am and has a floor show at weekends.

For authentic Turkish cuisine look no further than the *Belde Company* restaurant and bar (☎ 233 451), popular with Chişinău's diplomatic crowd, at Str Lazlo 139. The iskender kebab, costing US$3, served on a bed of fried toast, topped with a spicy yoghurt is delicious, as is the US$1 baclava. The restaurant is open daily from 10 am to 10 pm and has an outside terrace.

Equally good value is the Jewish restaurant *La Bunel* (literally 'at Grandpa's'; ☎ 222 219), Str Mihai Eminescu 50. Main dishes like chicken fillet stuffed with cheese, pelmeni (Russian meat dumplings) in mushroom sauce or Jewish stew cost around US$1.50 and service is impeccable. In summer bands play outside.

Monte Nelly (☎ 244 394), which is inside the opera & ballet theatre on Blvd Ştefan cel Mare, serves pricey food in an elegant, air-conditioned setting. It is open daily from noon to midnight. Equally expensive and not particularly authentic is the Indian cuisine served at the *Indian Tandoori* (☎ 227 516), Blvd Renaşterii 6. Portions are small and not spicy. Avoid the aloo ghoba unless you're into watery, over-boiled potatoes and mushy cauliflower. Main dishes range to US$5 to US$10. The restaurant is open daily from noon to 3 pm, 6 to 11 pm.

Restaurant Caragoli and *La Tour Eiffel* in the same block at Str Puşkin 26 are two uninspiring, expensive restaurants touting a European-style menu and attracting the city's young 'n vulgar nouveau riche. Caragoli is open daily from noon to midnight. The Eiffel – nothing French about it – is open daily from 10 am to midnight.

Three of the city's coolest restaurants – in decor and cuisine – are on Str Armeneasca. The *Cactus Café* on the corner of Str 31 August and Str Armeneasca is kitted out 'wild west' style with swinging saloon doors and chairs suspended from the ceiling. Its mind-boggling menu includes chicken with chocolate sauce for US$2.50, turkey with bananas for US$3 and spicy pork with chicken liver and cheese sauce for US$4. Its salads – 20 varieties – are equally adventurous. Cactus is open daily from 10 am to 10 pm.

El Paso (☎ 50 4100) at No 10 serves excellent Mexican cuisine. Don't miss the fried pork with chocolate-almond sauce! Book in advance if you want to guarantee a table – especially under the arches on the candle-lit terrace. It is open daily from 11 am to midnight.

Third in line is the elegant and elitist *Oraşul Vechi* (Old City; ☎ 225 063, 262 035) where government ministers hang out. Don't be intimidated by the overdressed doormen – prices are reasonable and the mix of classical and traditional folk music played by the piano and violin duo is top notch. Local dishes include mămăligă with skrob and shkvaski for US$2.50, mushroom tokana for US$3 and stuffed sheep cheese tomatoes for US$1. It's open daily from noon to 11 pm.

South of centre, the *Valentia Cafe* (☎ 729 154) serves traditional Moldavian food at above-average prices. It is open daily from noon until 1 am and has a pleasant terrace in a pretty, landscaped garden.

Cafés When the sun shines, outside cafés *(cafenele)* sprout like mushrooms after the rain. Many serve food; most serve Moldovan wine. Chişinău's top terrace is outside the opera & ballet theatre on Blvd Ştefan cel Mare (open daily from 9 am to midnight). There are also some good outside cafés opposite the main entrance to the university on Str A Mateevici 6 and in the opposite courtyard leading to Valea Morilor park. At the western end of Str A Mateevici is another courtyard filled with outside cafés and chess fiends. The chess club is in the same courtyard.

More permanent fixtures include *Cafenea Mămăliguta*, slightly north of the central telephone office on Blvd Ştefan cel Mare, and *Alimentara Sfânta Maria*, a few doors north along the main street. In summer, it has a terrace with cane chairs and tables overlooking Blvd Ştefan cel Mare's flower sellers and lively kiosks.

Consar Express, Blvd Ştefan cel Mare 130, serves pelmeni, pasties and other light snacks. It's open daily from 10 am to 10 pm. The video café-bar *Café Fortus*, on Blvd Renaşterii, has a terrace and shows videos six times daily on two regular TV screens positioned back to back!

A more humbling experience is a meal in one of the city's Soviet-style *Cantină* (canteen). The best of the bunch is opposite the telephone office on Blvd Ştefan cel Mare.

Fast Food Popcorn is sold for US$0.10 from *stands* dotted the length of Blvd Ştefan cel Mare.

Wam, on the corner of Blvd Ştefan cel Mare and Str Ismail, is an absolute delight to visit, just for the sheer cheek of its marketing technique. The fast-food joint is an upside-down copy of McDonald's, sporting red and yellow flags with the letter W and staff touting upside-down Ms on their uniforms. Fish burgers cost US$3, regular meat burgers US$2 and pizza slices US$1. It is open 24 hours and hosts occasional rave parties. There is a second Wam outlet in the central market.

For fast Turkish food go to *Quickie* (☎ 265 563) at Str Ismail 46 (entrance on Str 31 August). Tasty şaşliks cost US$2 and salads start at US$0.20. It is open daily from 9 am to 11 pm.

The genuine McDonald's is set to open on Str Ştefan cel Mare between Str Puşkin and Str Vlaicu Pircâlab in early 1998. A second outlet will open opposite the Greenhills supermarket on Blvd Decebal – despite repeated arson attacks on the site!

Self Catering The *central market* (piaţa

centrală) is well worth a visit for its glorious choice of fresh food. Don't expect any bargains unless you can speak Romanian or Russian. The indoor meat and dairy produce hall is pretty gruesome, particularly in summer, but it's here you'll see the real side of Chişinău. The main entrance to the market is close to the central bus station on Str Tighina and Str Armeneasca. It is open daily 7 am to 5 pm.

Western-style supermarkets are taking off. The most central is *Fedesco* which has an outlet next to the Hotel Naţional and Blvd Ştefan cel Mare and one at Str Banulescu Bodoni 51. Both are open daily from 9 am to 9 pm. A few doors further at No 47, opposite the 24 hour flower market, is the *Victoria Supermarket*, open daily from 9 am to 8 pm. Slightly out of town is the *Green Hills Market* at the junction of Blvd Decebal and Blvd Dacia. It is open Monday to Saturday from 9 am to 9 pm, Sunday from 9 am to 8 am. It has a bar and restaurant on the second floor and an excellent range of locally produced wines, champagnes and cognacs in the ground floor shop.

Entertainment

Posters listing what's on where are pasted up on the 'teatrul concerte' notice board outside the opera & ballet theatre on Blvd Ştefan cel Mare. The English-language newspaper, *Welcome*, runs a fortnightly calendar of cultural events.

Discos Boppy discos are held nightly at the *Teresa Nica* disco, bowling and billiard club, Str P Halippa 3. Entrance is US$0.25/1 for women/men on weekdays and US$0.50/2.50 at weekends. The billiard and bowling club is open daily from 11 to 3 am, the disco from 8 pm to 3 am. A calmer teenage disco rocks at weekends from 7 to 10 pm in the *Megapolis* bar and disco inside the university cultural house *(casă de cultură a universităţii)* at the southern end of Str A Kogălniceanu.

The *Jump-Motors Jambo disco*, on the south-eastern edge of Valea Trandafirilor Park on the corner of Str Trandafirilor, is open daily from noon to 2 am. Admission is US$1/2 weekdays/weekends.

Theatre The *Opera & Ballet Theatre*, one block north of Pushkin park, on Blvd Ştefan cel Mare, is home to the Moldovan national opera & ballet company. The box office (☎ 245 113, 244 181) is open daily from 10 am to 2 pm, 5 to 7 pm.

Satirical plays are staged at the *Satirical Theatre* (Teatrul Satiricus; ☎ 224 034) on the corner of Str Tighina and Str 31 August.

Contemporary Romanian productions can be seen at the *Mihai Eminescu National Theatre* (Teatrul Naţional Mihai Eminescu) at Blvd Ştefan cel Mare 79. The box office (☎ 250 258, 224 536) is open daily from 10 am to 1 pm, and from 3 to 6 pm.

Plays in Russian are performed at the *Chekhov Drama Theatre* (Teatrul Dramatic A Cehov, ☎ 233 062) sited where the Chişinău choral synagogue used to be until WWII. The theatre is on the corner of Str Mitropolii Varlaam and Str Pircaleb.

The Poetic Star youth theatre, *Luceafărul Theatre* (Teatrul Luceafărul; ☎ 226 520) at Str Veronica Micle 7 stages more alternative productions.

Productions in Moldovan and Russian are held at the *Licurici Puppet Theatre* (Glow Worm; ☎ 245 273, 241 338) at Str 31 August 121. Performances start daily at 5 pm and the box office is open daily from 9 am to 2 pm. Tickets cost US$0.50.

Various cabarets, musicals and local theatre group productions take place at the *National Palace* (Palatul Naţional), Str Puşkin 24. Performances start daily at 7 pm and the box office is open daily from noon to 7 pm.

Classical Music Classical concerts and organ recitals are held at the *Organ Hall* (Sala cu Orgǎ; ☎ 225 404), a protected building dating from 1911 next to the Teatrul Naţional Mihai Eminescu at Blvd Ştefan cel Mare 79. Performances start at 6.30 pm and tickets are sold at the box office in the Eminescu theatre.

Moldova's National Philharmonic is based at the Philharmonic concert hall (☎ 224 016) at Str Mitropolii Varlaam 78.

Bars & Clubs A must is the rustic drinking hole in the basement of the *Ialoveni sherry factory shop* on the corner of Blvd Ştefan cel Mare and Str Hînceşti. Swill a tumbler of Moldovan sherry with drunken locals for less than US$0.25. Staff wear traditional costume and speak absolutely no English. Given they only serve one thing however it is easy to make yourself understood! Bottles of the potent sherry, dessert wines and brandies are sold in the shop on the ground floor. It is open weekdays from 8 am to 2 pm and 3 to 8 pm, and on Saturday from 8 am to 2 pm.

The equally racy *Admiral Club* (☎ 226 548), Str Bucureşti 68, is lined with one-armed bandits and card players and is open daily from noon to midnight. If this is your scene, you'll find another outlet (open daily from noon to 5 am), behind the Mihai Eminescu theatre.

Topping the charts as the funkiest bar in town is *La Luceafărul Club*, a popular jazz club inside the Teatrul Luceǎfarul at Str Veronica Micle 7. Entrance costs US$1.50.

Slightly out of town at Blvd Dacia 25 is the *Beatles' Bar*, a theme bar of sorts revolving around the UK's Liverpool four. The bar is decked out with posters galore but the management has not yet invested in their music! The bar is open daily from 11 am to midnight. It is one of the few drinking holes in town to serve locally brewed Chişinău beer.

Circus Bus No 27 from Blvd Ştefan cel Mare or bus No 24 from Str A Mateevici goes to the circus (☎ 244 094) across the river at Str Renaşterii 33. The box office (☎ 228 638) is open daily from 9 am to 6 pm. Performances are held on Friday at 6.30 pm, and on Saturday and Sunday at noon, 3 and 6.30 pm. Tickets cost US$2 to US$4.

Spectator Sport
Moldovans are big football fans and they have two stadiums to prove it. The main

Republic Stadium (Stadionul Republican), south of the centre, has floodlighting. The main entrance – a 1950s Stalinist structure – is on Str Ismail with a smaller entrance on the southern end of Str Bucureşti. The entrance to the smaller Dinamo Stadium (Stadionul Dinamo) is north of the centre on the corner of Str Bucureşti and Str S Lazo.

Things to Buy

Don't leave Chişinău without visiting the Magazinul de firm Cricova (☎ 222 775), the commercial outlet of the Cricova wine factory on Blvd Ştefan cel Mare. It stocks 10 types of wine and seven champagnes produced in Cricova. The oldest – and most expensive at around US$5 – date to 1983 and are quite divine. The shop is open weekdays from 10 am to 2 pm, 3 to 7 pm. The outlet of the Ialoveni sherry factory is close by on the corner of Blvd Ştefan cel Mare and Str Hînceşti (see Entertainment – Bars & Clubs).

Just a couple of doors down at Blvd Ştefan cel Mare 126 is the heavenly Bucuria sweet shop – open Monday to Saturday from 8 am to 9 pm and on Sunday from 8 am to 5 pm.

The Salon Teatrul Benefits inside the Opera & Ballet Theatre on Blvd Ştefan cel Mare sells unique theatre costumes and beautifully handmade block ballet shoes for US$5 to US$7. It is open weekdays from 10 am to 7 pm.

Chişinău's Soviet-style department store, Unic Magazinul Centru, is at Blvd Ştefan cel Mare 8; open weekdays from 9 am to 6 pm, Saturday from 8 am to 6 pm.

Local artists and crafters sell their wares in the small plaza next to the Mihai Eminescu theatre. Bargains!

Getting There & Away

Air Moldova's only airport is in Chişinău, 14.5km from the centre. It has only international flights. Airline offices selling tickets include:

Air Moldova
  Airport (☎ 525 506)
  Blvd Negruzzi 8 (☎ 264 041, 264 358; fax 264 587)

Moldavian Airlines
  Airport (☎ 525 064, 529 365; fax 525 064)
  Blvd Ştefan cel Mare 3 (☎ 549 339, 549 340; fax 549 341)
Air Moldova International
  Airport (☎ 262 347; fax 525 058)
TAROM
  Blvd Ştefan cel Mare 3 (entrance on Str Ismail) (☎ 212 424, 262 618)
Transaero
  Airport (☎ 266 103)
  National Hotel, Blvd Ştefan cel Mare 4 (☎ 266 052, 524 403)

Bus Chişinău has two bus stations. Most buses within Moldova depart from the Central bus station (Autogară Centrală) which you'll find behind the central market on Str Mitropolit Varlaam. Tickets for local buses to Străşeni, Capriăna and beyond are sold at ticket window Nos 40 and 41. Window Nos 42 and 43 sell tickets for buses to Orhei and beyond. Tickets cannot be bought in advance.

Bus services to/from Comrat, Hînceşti and other southern destinations use the less crowded South-western bus station (Autogară Sud-vest), 2km from the city centre on the corner of Şoseaua Hînceşti and Str Spicului. The destinations for which ticket windows sell tickets are listed above each window. No 9 sells tickets for buses in transit.

Buses to Turkey depart from the train station. Tickets to Istanbul are sold at the Eskicioğlu Meridian InterTrans office (☎ 549 835, 549 813) next to Autogară Centrală. Buses leave Chişinău daily at 9 and 11 am, and 6 pm. A single fare is US$29. In Istanbul, tickets are sold by the Eskicioğlu Meridian InterTrans office (☎ 212-511 8682, 520 8182), Hotel Büyük Levent Alti, Gençtürk Caddesi 58, Laleli.

At the time of writing, Eskicioğlu Meridian InterTrans were hoping to operate weekly buses from Chişinău to Berlin by 1998.

Gülen Tur (☎ 263 748, 265 424), also at the train station, runs daily buses to Istanbul. Three to seven daily buses leave on the hour from the train station. A single ticket also costs US$29. In Istanbul, tickets are sold by

MOLDOVA

Öz Gülen Turizm (☎ 212-511 9724, 212-526 5332; fax 212-520 6986), Vidinli Tevfik Paşa Caddesi 13/1, Laleli.

Local services from Chişinău's Autogară Sud-vest include five buses daily to Comrat in Gagauzia and six buses daily to Hînceşti.

Services from Autogară Centrală include one daily to Recea, three daily to Căpriana and Tiraspol via Tighina, 11 daily to Străşeni, and 16 daily to Tighina. There are also daily buses to Bălţi, Edineţ and Briceni and buses every half hour between 9.15 am and 10 pm to Orhei and to Bălţi.

Train The train station is at Aleea Gării. Far from being seedy, dirty and teeming with pickpockets, it's clean and well sign-posted, and bears a greater resemblance to a station in the provinces rather than a capital city.

The timetables are outside the train station. They are in Moldovan and Russian, and easy to comprehend. You are not allowed on the platform without a valid train ticket. The information booth (☎ 252 735, 252 736) is in the ground floor ticket hall. It costs US$0.05 per question (Moldovan and Russian only). The currency exchange inside this hall is open daily from 8 am to 1 pm, 2 to 8 pm.

Tickets for international trains for same-day departures are sold at the first floor ticket office, signposted *Casă Internationale*. Advance tickets sold 24 hours or more before departure are sold at the *Casă Prealabil* on the 2nd floor, open daily, except Sunday, from 8 am to 6 pm. The ticket hall for local trains is on the ground floor. For ticket bookings by telephone call ☎ 250 071 (Russian and Moldovan only). The station also operates a 24 hour enquiry hotline (☎ 252 735/36/37).

Moldova's main train line heads east from Chişinău into Ukraine and then north through Belarus into Russia. Another line originates in Tiraspol, passing through Chişinău on its northbound route to Cernăuţi (Chernivtsi) and Ivan Francovsk in Ukraine. There are numerous trains from Chişinău to Ukraine, Belarus and onto Russia. West-bound, there are nightly trains to Romania and beyond.

There is one daily local train from Chişinău to Tighina and Tiraspol. Tighina is always listed on train timetables by its Russian name, Bendery. In addition, the twice-weekly Bucharest-Moscow *România Expres* passes through Chişinău at 1.30 pm then continues to Tighina (1¾ hours) and Tiraspol (2¼ hours).

There are four local trains daily to Ungheni on the Moldova-Romania border.

Getting Around

To/From the Airport Bus No 65 departs every 30 minutes between 5 am and 10 pm from the Central bus station to the airport. Microbus No 65a departs from the Wam fast food outlet, on the corner of Blvd Ştefan cel Mare and Str Ismail. Tickets costing US$0.20 can be bought from the driver.

Bus & Trolleybus Bus No 45 and microbus No 45a runs from the Central bus station to the South-western bus station. Bus No 1 goes from the train station to Blvd Ştefan cel Mare.

Most bus routes in town and to many outlying villages are served by nippy microbuses. These small, 15-seat buses are faster and more expensive than regular buses. Tickets are not issued: just give US$0.25 to the passenger in front who will in turn pass it on to the next passenger. It eventually reaches the driver. Microbuses depart from the main road at the start of the microbus route. They run every 15 minutes, between 7 am and 11 pm.

Trolleybus Nos 1, 2, 19, 22, 45 and bus Nos 13 and 19 go to the train station from the city centre. Bus Nos 2, 10, 16 and 37 go to Autogară Sud-vest. Tickets costing US$0.10 are sold at kiosks or direct from the driver. Don't let the *kopek* price printed on the ticket confuse you – it's simply a leftover from an obviously massive batch of tickets printed during the days of the USSR!

Car & Motorcycle Car rental does not exist in Moldova as, by law, motorists have to own the vehicle they drive. At the time of writing it was not even possible to hire a car in Romania and drive it into Moldova.

There is a 24 hour petrol station, Zimbru, east of Autogară Centrală on the corner of Str Sfante Gheorge and Blvd Avram Iancu. A-95 octane petrol (best for western vehicles) is US$0.50 a litre. Lower grade A-92/A-76 (OK for Ladas) is US$0.40/0.36.

Taxi The main taxi stand is in front of the Hotel Naţional. Drivers here will rip you off. Calling a taxi (☎ 616 565, 626 565, 626 720) is cheaper. The official rate is US$0.30 per kilometre.

CRICOVA

Cricova, some 15km north of Chişinău, is an underground wine town. The vast cellars are accessed by a labyrinth of underground streets stretching for more than 60km. Streets along which special vehicles drive are appropriately named Str Cabernet, Str Pinot and the like. More than one million bottles of fine white wines – 648 types – are stored in the cellars which are kept at a constant 12°C.

In Soviet times, Cricova wines and champagnes were considered among the top wines produced in the USSR. Its sparkling white wine was sold under the label 'Soviet Champagne'. Today, demand for its dry white sauvignon, muscadet and sweeter muscats remains high. Some five million bottles are produced each year, 25% of which are exported worldwide. Unique to the Cricova cellars is its sparkling red wine, called *kodrinskoie-sparkling*, which is made from cabernet-sauvignon stocks and marketed as having a 'rich velvet texture' and a 'blackcurrant and cherry' taste.

Buy Cricova wine on the cheap at the factory outlet shop, opposite the main bus stop in the centre of the village. The 'Soviet Champagne' – in reality simply white sparkling wine – costs US$2 a bottle. Note that *demi-dulce* is semi-sweet, *dulce* is sweet, and *brut* is dry. The shop is open daily, except Sunday, from 11 am to 2 pm, and then from 4 to 8 pm.

Next to the bus stop is a **memorial** to local victims of the 1992 Moldova-Transdniestr conflict

Getting There & Away

Unfortunately, you can only visit Cricova as part of an organised tour. The wine factory has its own excursion bureau (☎ 221 419; fax 225 339) in Chişinău at Str Mitropoli G Banulescu Bodoni 45 which arranges day trips to the cellars for a staggering US$55 per person (the bureau also arranges 'bodyguards and escorts' for an additional fee!). This includes transport to/from Chişinău, wine tasting, as well as two souvenir bottles of wine and a bottle of champagne. Tours have to be booked in advance. The Cricova-Tur office is open on weekdays from 9 am to 6 pm.

The entrance to the wine factory (☎ 2-444 035, 581 960 in Cricova is at Str Ungureanu 1. From the bus stop walk up the hill along Str 31 August then bear right to the factory. For an individual tour apply in writing (Moldovan or Russian only) to the director. Don't expect a speedy response.

From Chişinău bus No 2 runs every 15 minutes from Str Hîncești (Str Vasile Alexandri) to Cricova.

COJUŞNA

Cricova's competitors operate 25km northwest of Chişinău in the village of Cojuşna. Sales have likewise dropped since its fabulous distribution network collapsed along with the USSR, but its figures are still impressive – two million bottles of wine a month, 98% of which are exported to Russia, the CIS, Germany and the UK. Mainstays include 13 different red and white table wines including common stocks such as cabernet, sauvignon and riesling. Cojuşna also produces vodka for Moldova's diehards as well as heavier, port wines (*xeres*).

Cojuşna is geared for tourists. Those expecting an idyllic French-style chateau amid rolling acres of vineyards will leave disappointed. The winery has no land, having reaped the harvests of smaller wineries for the past 30 years. Organised tours take in the cellars and various wine-tasting halls decked out in different themes. A statue of Bahus, the god of wine, welcomes visitors at the entrance.

Buy wines from the Cojuşna shop on the complex. Expect to pay around US$4 for a 1982 bottle of Cabernet or US$0.87 for a bottle of regular 1994 plonk (still excellent).

Getting There & Away

Call the Cojuşna wine factory (Fabrica de Vinuri Cojuşna; ☎ 2-624 820, 628 436; fax 2-639 706) in advance to book a tour. It costs US$22 per person and includes a two hour tasting session of six collection wines. Tours in English are only available in the afternoon. The office is open weekdays from 8 am to 6 pm.

In Chişinău don't let the Cricova excursion bureau con you into paying US$45.50 for a tour to Cojuşna. Expensive perks include transport to/from Cojuşna from Chişinău, plus two souvenir bottles of wine and champagne.

Bus No 2 runs every 15 minutes from Str Hînceşti (Str Vasile Alexandri) in Chişinău to Cricova. Get off at the Cojuşna stop. Ignore the turning on the left marked Cojuşna and walk or hitch the remaining 2km along the main road to the winery entrance, marked by a tall, totem-pole-style pillar. You can also take bus No 37 from the bus stop opposite the circus in Chişinău to Stauceni where you can pick up any Cricova-bound bus.

STRĂŞENI, RECEA & ROMANEŞTI

Străşeni, 12km north-east of Chişinău is renowned for fine sparkling white wines which have been produced in the village for the past 35 years. The **Străşeni Wine Factory** (Fabrica de Vinuri Străşeni; ☎ 2-235 94, 226 76) produces around 1,250,000 bottles (100,000 decalitres) of wine a year, 80% of which is exported to CIS countries. Vineyards sprawl for 10,000 hectares around the village.

Recea, 9km north of Străşeni, is a small, family run wine cellar. The 2000 decalitres of sauvignon wine it yields is bottled,

labelled and prepared for export at the local cooperative.

The last of the trio is Romaneşti (☎ 2-40 478, 40 230), one of the largest wineries in Moldova and once one of the USSR's leading wine producers. Organised tours flocked here in their droves to taste the red Bordeaux-type wines drunk by Russian Tsars. Since the collapse of the USSR however, annual production has plummeted from 600,000 decalitres to 100,000. Romaneşti is 7km north of Recea.

Seven kilometres south-west of Străşeni in the isolated village of **Căpriana** is a large 14th century monastery. Forty-two Orthodox monks live here today. Daily services have been held here since 1926. Căpriana was one of the few monasteries in Moldova to survive the wrath of the communist regime following WWII when most churches and monasteries were closed, looted and destroyed.

Getting There & Away

You can visit all three wineries on a factory tour and wine tasting session. At Recea visitors are welcome all hours; just turn up. At Străşeni and Romaneşti you have to book a tour/degustation in advance. Străşeni is in the village centre at Str Oreiului 36. From the bus stop at the northern end of the village, cross the footbridge over the Chişinău-Ungheni highway and continue for 1km until you reach a crossroad. Continue straight, following a dirt drive which leads to the factory. Străşeni train station is 200m south of the bus stop on the main road.

Eleven buses depart daily from Chişinău Central bus station to Străşeni (30 minutes) between 8.20 am and 5.40 pm. Nippy microbuses run every hour. There are 10 daily trains (30 minutes) to/from Chişinău between 5 am and 11 pm. Most Ungheni-bound trains stop at Străşeni, as does the daily Chişinău-Moscow train and the daily Chişinău-Odessa train.

From Chişinău there's a daily bus to Recea. From Străşeni, the only means of getting to Recea is by taxi (US$3). Romaneşti is not served by public transport.

Three buses leave daily from Chișinău to Căpriana. The bus makes its return journey immediately, making a day trip difficult. Forget hitching. Few cars or carts pass by.

IALOVENI, MILEȘTII MICI & HÎNCEȘTI

Moldova's wine road sprawls south of Chișinău too: Ialoveni, 10km south of the capital, is a predominantly sherry-making area. Its wine cellars (☎ 268-22 297; fax 268-737 838), Str Alexandru cel Bun 4, welcome visitors year-round.

More famed are the cellars at Mileștii Mici, 15km south of Chișinău, which specialise in white table wines. Wine-tasting trips including lunch are arranged by the Cricova excursion bureau in Chișinău (US$45). Individuals can call the cellars (☎ 268-68 383, 68 374) to arrange cheaper tours.

Hîncești, 35km south-west of Chișinău, is home to a large industrial winery (☎ 234-22 349), producing some 1.3 million decalitres of white table wines a year. Wine tasting is offered.

From Chișnău, take Bus No 35 from Autogară Sud-vest to Ialoveni. There are no buses between Ialoveni and Milești Mici but a local driver will take you there for US$2. There is one direct bus daily at 4.15 pm from Chișinău's Autogară Sud-vest to Mileștii Mici.

ORHEI

• *area code ☎ 235, pop 37,500*

The modern town of Orhei, not to be confused with Orheul Vechi (Old Orhei), is 45km north of Chișinău. It is Moldova's sixth-largest city and was settled on the ruins of 14th century Orheul Vechi. Orhei was practically bombed to death during WWII and has little to offer tourists today. It serves as a good stepping stone if you want to visit Orheul Vechi.

Information

The telephone office is close to the former Catholic Church at Vasile Mahu 121. The central post office is a few doors down at Vasile Mahu 129. You can change money inside the currency exchange at the bus station (open erratic hours).

Things to See

A **statue of Vasile Lupu**, reigning prince of Moldavia (1634-53) stands majestically at the entrance to the city in front of the **St Dimitru Church** (Biserica Sfântu Dimitru) (1637). The main street, Blvd Ștefan cel Mare, is dominated by **St Nicholas' Church** (Biserica Sfântu Nicolae), dating from the 1630s.

Behind the Catholic church, currently under renovation, is a **monument** to the Orhei soldiers killed on the front line during the 1992 Moldovan-Transdniestran conflict in Tighina (Bendery) and Dubașari. Head-shots of some of the soldiers are exhibited in the excellent **History & Ethnographic Museum** (Muzeul de Istorie și Etnografie) at Str Renașterii Naționale 23. The museum traces the city's history from Vasile Lupu's reign through to WWII and Moldova's declaration of independence on 31 August 1989. The text is in Moldovan and Russian but is well illustrated with photographs. The museum is open daily, except Monday, from 9 am to 5 pm.

Ten kilometres south of Orhei in **Ivancea** is a good **ethnograhic museum**, housed in a 19th century stately mansion. Its eight halls are filled with traditional Moldovan costumes, musical instruments, pottery and folk art. Traditional dress from the Gagauz region in southern Moldova and those worn by people in Moldova's predominantly Bulgarian villages are exhibited too. The museum is open daily, except Monday, from 8 am to 5 pm.

Places to Stay & Eat

The *Hotel Codru* (☎ 24 821), Str Vasile Lupu 36, has basic, unheated singles/doubles with shared bathroom and no hot water for US$7/10. Doubles with private bath – still no hot water – are US$18. The *Codru Restaurant* next door is the only restaurant in town. It is open daily from 10 to 1 am.

Getting There & Away

Daily buses depart every half hour from Chişinău's Autogară Centrală to Orhei (two hours) between 9.15 am and 10 pm. All northbound buses from Chişinău stop in Orhei too, including daily buses to Bălţi, Edineţ and Briceni. From Orhei, there is one daily bus at 12.45 pm to Orheul vechi (Orheul Vechi).

All Chişinău-Orhei buses stop 2km short of Ivancea. Get off on the main highway then walk or hitch.

ORHEUL VECHI

Ten kilometres south-east of Orhei lies Orheul Vechi (Old Orhei; marked on maps as Trebujeni). Ştefan cel Mare built a fortress here in the 14th century but it was destroyed by Tartars in 1499.

It is the fantastic **Orheul Vechi monastery** (Complexul muzeistic Orheul Vechi), carved in a cliff in this wild, rocky, remote spot that draws most visitors. The **Cave monastery** (Mănăstire în Peşteră) inside a limestone cliff, overlooking the Raut river, was dug by Orthodox monks in the 13th century. It remained inhabited until the 18th century, and in 1996 a handful of monks returned to this unique place of worship which is slowly being restored and returned to its original use.

The central hall of the underground monastery is open to visitors. This served as the main church in the 13th century. The narrow trenches dug in the stone floor are still clearly evident. Until the 17th century, the monks slept in stone bunks (*keilies*) in an adjacent cave. Each bunk was lined with reeds from the river then covered with a woven mat for added warmth. An earthquake in the 17th century forced the monks to retreat from these stone cells to smaller caves further south along the cliff. The 10cm-wide cracks in the stone floor of these living quarters can still be seen today.

During the 18th century the cave-church was taken over by villagers from neighbouring Butceni. In 1905 they built a church above ground dedicated to the Ascension of St Mary. The church was shut down by the Soviets in 1944 and remained abandoned throughout the communist regime. Since 1996 services have once more been held in this small, whitewashed church. The gatehouse next to the church entrance was traditionally used as a baptism house. Archaeologists have recently uncovered remnants of a defence wall surrounding the monastery complex from the 15th century.

A well presented **village museum** is also included on the monastery complex. The ethnographic exhibits include a traditional 14th century Moldovan house in which up to eight people would have lived. The winter cottage, adjoining summer house, and root cellar for storing vegetables, are all perfectly restored. The windows of the winter cottage, traditionally covered with cow lung, are now glass-covered instead.

The Monastery complex (☎ 235-94 242) is open daily, except Monday, from 9 am to 5 pm. Admission is US$0.20 and includes an excellent 1½ hour guided tour in Moldovan or Russian. The ticket office is at the foot of the cliff. Daily services are held at 10 am and 6 pm in the church. Shorts are forbidden and women must cover their heads (scarves provided).

Getting There & Away

Getting to Orheul Vechi by public transport is tough. From Orhei, a bus departs daily for Trebujeni at 12.45 pm. Ask the bus to drop you by the signposted entrance to the complex. There is a daily afternoon bus back to Orhei from Orheul vechi. A taxi from Orhei to Orheul vechi costs US$6.

BĂLŢI, REZINA & LALOVA

Bălţi (pop 182,000), 150km north of Chişinău, is Moldova's fourth-largest city. It is a major industrial area, hence predominantly Russian-speaking, and offers little to do or see beyond being a convenient stopover en route to Ukraine.

Some 60km east of Bălţi on the western banks of the Dniestr river is Rezina, a small town 7km south of which is the Orthodox **Saharna monastery**. From Lalova you can visit the underground **Ţipova monastery**, dating from the 13th century when it was fashionable to carve churches and houses in rock. Caves offered the best form of protection against tribal attacks. Rezina has one hotel, *Hotel Noroc* (☎ 254-228 33), in Str Păcii.

In Bălţi, there are basic, rock-bottom priced rooms at the *Hotel*, off the main square. A bed is US$2. Grotty bathrooms are in the corridor. The more upmarket *Hotel Drushba* has doubles with private bath for US$15 a night, including a fried egg breakfast. The hotel has a casino and bar. To get to the centre of town from Bălţi bus station, take trolleybus No 3 to Blvd Ştefan cel Mare.

Getting There & Away

Bălţi is well served by buses. Daily services include one to Tiraspol, two to Soroca and Ungheni, three to Edineţ, and five to Ribniţa. There are buses every half hour to/from Chişinău.

There are also two buses daily to Iaşi in Romania, departing at 8.30 am and 2 pm.

SOROCA

Soroca fortress was part of a medieval chain of military fortresses built by the Moldavian *voievodes* (princes) between the 14th and 16th centuries to defend Moldavia's boundaries. Only its ruins remain.

Strategically placed at Moldavia's most north-eastern tip on the banks of the Dniestr river, Soroca was one of the key military strongholds. The ruins today are from a fortress built by Petru Rareş (1527-38) on the site of an older one. The fortress's four 20m-high towers are surrounded by a 30m-round defensive wall, 3m thick.

Moldova Tur in Chişinău arrange tours to the fortress. From Bălţi there are two daily buses to Soroca..

Gagauzia

Gagauzia (Gagauz Yeri) is a self-governed republic covering 3000sq km in southern Moldova. It has its own legislative *başkani*

(assembly) which is autonomous in regional affairs. On a national level, Gagauzia is represented by the assembly's elected *başkan* (head), a member of the Gagauz Halki political party who holds a safe seat in the Moldovan parliament.

Comrat is Gagauzia's capital. The republic is divided into three districts – the Comrat, and Ceadâr-Linga and Vulcăneşti which embrace the south of the region. Wedged between these latter two is the predominantly Bulgarian-populated district of Taracilia which is not part of Gagauzia. Gagauz territory is further broken up by three Bulgarian villages in Ceadâr-Linga and a predominantly Moldovan village in Comrat district, all of which are part of 'mainland' Moldova too.

The Gagauz are a Turkic-speaking, Christian ethnic minority whose Muslim descendants fled the Russian-Turkish wars in the 18th century. They were allowed to settle in the region in exchange for their conversion to Christianity. Their language is a dialect of Turkish, with vocabulary influenced by Russian Orthodoxy as opposed to the Islamic influences inherent in Turkish.

The Gagauz today (population 153,000) comprise 3.5% of Moldova's population. The republic has its own flag, its own police force, its own weekly journals – *Ana sözu* and *Cârlangaci* – written in Gagauz, and its own university partly funded by the Turkish government. Students are taught in Gagauz, Moldovan and Russian – the official languages of the republic. Gagauz is taught in 37 schools countrywide.

Gagauz autonomy was officially recognised by the Moldovan government in December 1994. Unlike their more militant separatists in Transdniestr, the Gagauz forfeited independence for large-scale autonomy.

Theirs is a predominantly agricultural region with little industry to sustain an independent economy

COMRAT

* *area code* ☎ *238 , pop 70,000*

Gagauzia's capital, 92km south of Chişinău,

is no more than a dusty, provincial town. In August 1990 it was the scene of violent clashes between Gagauz nationalists and Moldovan armed forces, pre-empted by calls from local leaders for the Moldovan government to hold a referendum on the issue of Gagauz sovereignty. Local protesters were joined by Transdniestran militia forces.

Comrat is home to the world's only Gagauz university. Most street signs are in Russian; some older ones are in Gagauz but in the Cyrillic script. Since 1989 however, Gagauzian, alongside Moldovan, has used the Latin alphabet. A few impoverished traders selling Soviet memorabilia, Turkish rugs or *kvas*, a locally made yeast drink, line the town's one main street – bare of pavement and lighting.

Orientation & Information

From the bus station, walk south along the main street, ulitsa Pobedy, past the market to ploshchad Pobedy (Victory Square). St John's Church stands on the western side of the square, behind which lies the central park. Prospekt Lenina runs parallel to ulitsa Pobedy Victory, west of the park.

Change money at the Moldovan Agrobank, ulitsa Pobedy 52, open weekdays from 8 am to 1 pm. A small currency exchange is inside the entrance to the market. The post office where you can make international calls via an operator is next to the bank at ulitsa Pobedy 55. It's open weekdays from 8 am to 6 pm, Saturday from 8 am to 5 pm.

Things to See

The regional **başkani** (assembly; ☎ 228 68) is on prospekt Lenina. A Gagauzian flag as well as a Moldovan flag flies from the roof. The Gagauzian flag, officially adopted on 3 October 1995, comprises three horizontal stripes coloured blue, white and red. Three white stars adorn the blue strips.

Next to the assembly is the **Gagauz Culture House**, in front of which stands a statue of Lenin. West of prospekt Lenina at ulitsa Galatsăna 17 is the **Gagauz University** (Komrat Devlet Üniversitesi; ☎ 23 508), founded in 1990 and home to 1500 students. Over 60% are Gagauz and study in their mother tongue. Mainstream courses are taught in Russian. The main foreign languages taught are English and Turkish. Unlike Moldovans, Gagauz lay no claim to any Latin roots or influences, but rather look to Turkey for cultural inspiration and heritage. The university has strong links with Turkish universities and in 1997 had received grants totalling US$50 million from the Turkish government.

Places to Stay & Eat

The *Hotel Medelean*, on the eastern side of ploshchad Pobedy at ulitsa Pobedy 117, is a fairly new, modern hotel, with nine double rooms for US$20 a night. It has two singles for US$7. Its in-house bar serves excellent şaşlik for US$1 and crisp, home-grown salads for US$0.50. It's open daily from 9 am to midnight.

Hotel Komfort (☎ 230 30) on ulitsa 31 August has nine basic rooms for US$2 per person a night. Home comforts are not included in the price.

Bop the night away at the *Freedom Disco & Bar* at Str Puşkina 44. Walk west along ulitsa Galatsăna, past the university. The bar is open daily from 4 pm to midnight and the disco rocks from 8 pm onwards.

Getting There & Away

There are five daily return buses from Chişinău to Comrat. The last return bus from Comrat departs at 7 pm. From Comrat there are two buses daily via Tighina to Tiraspol, departing at 6.20 and 9.05 am, and one only as far as Tighina.

Transdniestr

The self-declared republic of Transdniestr (population 700,000) incorporates the narrow strip of land on the eastern bank of the Dniestr river. A predominantly Russian-populated region, it declared independence from Moldova in 1991 sparking off a bloody civil war.

Travellers to Transdniestr will be stunned by a region which is very much an independent state in all but name. It has its own currency, police force, a 5000-strong army, and its own (unofficial) borders which are controlled by Transdniestran border guards. Local residents travel on the old Soviet passport issued by Transdniestran authorities as the republic's 'official' passport.

The two main towns in the region are Tiraspol, the capital, and Tighina (commonly known under its Russian name Bendery). Tighina is a security zone in which the peacekeeping forces are headquartered. The Transdniestran and Russian armies are based in Tiraspol. Western travellers can freely travel in the region. A curfew is still in force in some areas and empty shops testify to the region's devastated economy. Russian is the predominant language which can make getting around tough.

Despite all this, visiting Transdniestr provides visitors with a unique opportunity to witness the harsh realities of one of the world's few surviving communist bastions.

Government & Politics

Igor Smirnov was elected president of Transdniestr in December 1991 following the region's declaration of independence four months previously. In August 1994 the Moldovan parliament ratified a new constitution providing substantial autonomy to Transdniestr in regional affairs.

Smirnov, re-elected president in December 1996, is backed by Transdniestr's two main political organisations which dominate the Transdniestran parliament and district administrations: Working Transdniestr (WTD) emerged from the United Council of Workers' Collectives (OSTK) political party which was responsible for organising the armed uprising against Chişinău in 1992. The Bloc of Left Wing Forces (BLWF) backs a centrally planned economy, the revival of the USSR, and is opposed to all market reforms. Neither Smirnov's presidency or the Transdniestran parliament is recognised by the Moldovan government.

In 1993 six ethnic Moldovans were sentenced to life imprisonment for allegedly killing two Transdniestran officials. International human rights groups have since campaigned for their release, saying they were convicted for being members of the Christian Democratic Popular Front (CDPF), a political party which backs Moldovan reunification with Romania.

Economy

As a self-declared republic, Transdniestr's economy is disastrous despite the fact that 40% of Moldova's total potential industrial output is concentrated in Tiraspol. In late 1997, the rebels' republic owed US$241.3 million to the Russian Gazprom.

Inflation is rampant and the local currency, the Transdniestran rouble, is worthless. The average monthly salary is less than US$50 a month; the monthly pension between US$7 and US$14. State employers are not able to pay their workers, forcing many to earn a living at the flea market.

Population & People

Two-thirds of Transdniestr's 700,000-strong population is elderly, impoverished, and yearns for a return to the Soviet Union under which they had a better quality of life. Ethnic Russians comprise 25% of the population, ethnic Moldovans 40% and Ukrainians 28%.

Language

The official state languages in Transdniestr are Russian, Moldovan and Ukrainian. Students in schools and universities are taught in Russian, and local government and most official institutions operate almost solely in Russian. All street signs are written in Russian, Moldovan in the Cyrillic alphabet and sometimes Ukrainian.

Money

The Transdniestran rouble is a national joke – everyone's a millionaire yet everyone's broke. Most wealth dissolved into an oblivion of zeros long ago, persuading even the staunchest nationalist that *any* other currency is more stable than their own.

The only legal tender is the Transdniestran

MOLDOVA

rouble (NH). There are 50, 100, 200, 500, 1000, 5000, 10,000, 50,000 and 100,000 banknotes. The banknotes under 500 roubles have been rendered useless by inflation. There are two types of 50,000 notes – blue and brown. The brown ones featuring the drama theatre on their reverse are, in fact, worth 500,000 roubles – despite this being printed absolutely nowhere on the banknote.

Warning! Check when you get into town how many more zeros have been added to the face value of these notes.

Not surprisingly, hard currency is desperately sought after by most taxi drivers, shop keepers and market traders who will gladly accept payment in US$ – or even Moldovan lei or Ukrainian grivna. When changing money, don't change more than US$10 at a time. Even then you'll be left wondering how on earth you can safely conceal the hefty 2cm stack of rouble bills handed over in exchange for your dollars.

Currency Exchange At the time of going to press, the exchange rates were:

Germany	DM1	=	NH366,000
Moldova	L1	=	NH135,000
Ukraine	GV1	=	NH3342,000
USA	US$1	=	NH640,000
Russia	R1	=	NH109,000

Black Market Avoid changing money on the black market, even though this is the standard practise of locals and expats alike. If you are caught, you run the risk of being fined US$25.

Post & Communications
Transdniestran stamps featuring Suvorov can only be used for letters sent within the republic. These philatelic rarities are not recognised anywhere else. For letters to Moldova, Romania and the west, you have to use Moldovan stamps.

Funny Money

If a national currency is the symbol of statehood, Transdniestr has a long way to go before achieving real independence. Ever since the republic introduced its own currency, the printing presses have failed to keep up with the breakneck speed of hyperinflation, resulting in a mind-boggling set of unique numismatic specimens.

In 1992-93, following the collapse of the USSR, the Soviet rouble disintegrated into over 15 different currencies. Russia dumped its Soviet Lenin and hoisted the Russian tricolour on the Kremlin featured on its new rouble bills. Chişinău introduced its very own Moldovan leu on 29 November 1993.

Transdniestran separatists responded by immediately creating their own currency too. Lacking funding, they stuck a humble postage stamp of Suvorov, the local Russian war hero, on the Soviet rouble bills to create a currency they could proudly call their own. The new Lenin (formerly 1000 Soviet roubles) was worth 100 or 1000 Transdniestran roubles depending on the amount written on the little corner stamp.

In late August 1994 this makeshift currency was replaced by the first set of real Transdniestran rouble coupons, issued in denominations of 50, 100, 200, 500, 1000 and 5000. The bills featured Suvorov on one side and the parliament building on the reverse. Smaller denominations of 1, 5 and 10 rouble notes had also been printed at the Moscow press, but they were never circulated: inflation had outpaced the presses.

But they weren't defeated. In 1996, to catch up with galloping inflation the presses printed four additional zeros on their defunct 1, 5 and 10 rouble notes, upping their face values to 10,000, 50,000 and 100,000 roubles. For some bizarre reason, some fivers missed out on the zero treatment: a flashy silver hologram is stuck on their corners instead to indicate their true 50,000 worth.

The same year, a new brown 50,000 rouble note featuring Chmelnistki and the Chişinău Drama theatre were printed – only to be traded as half a million rouble notes (less than US$1) on their release in 1997.

The Transdniestran rouble stood 1:1 with the Russian rouble in 1994. In mid-1997, it equalled 109,000 Russian roubles. Ask the staunchest Transdniestran nationalist to trade you a wad of his funny money for a single greenback and he'll happily agree. ∎

Rationing

Some staple items, notably bread, are rationed. Locals are allocated a personal number, enabling them to buy one loaf of bread a day from an assigned state-run shop. Foreigners are not allowed to buy bread there, but must go to the market, where loaf prices are three or four times higher.

Curfew

The curfew imposed in Tighina during the 1992 military conflict is still enforced. You are not allowed to walk in the streets in Tighina between 11 pm and 5 am. You risk being fined by the local police if you do. Since no restaurants or bars are open after 10 pm, this restriction is not too much of a hardship.

Media

The predominantly Russian Transdniestran TV is broadcast in the republic between 4 pm and 2 am. Transdniestran Radio is on air for a couple of hours morning and evening.

The two local newspapers are in Russian. The *Transdniestra* is a purely nationalist affair advocating the virtues of an independent state; *N Pravda* is marginally more liberal. A handful of military newspapers spout the virtues of the local Transdniestran army.

TIRASPOL

• *area code ☎ 233 , pop 204,000*

Tiraspol, 70km east of Chişinău, is the second-largest city in Moldova. Its population is predominantly Russian (41%) with ethnic Moldovans comprising 18% and ethnic Ukrainians 32% of the city's population.

The city was founded in 1792 following Russian domination of the region. From 1929 onwards, Tiraspol served as the capital of the Moldovan Autonomous Soviet Socialist Republic (MASSR). Prior to Tiraspol's accession, the MASSR capital was in Balta in present-day Ukraine.

Today it is the capital of Transdniestr.

Orientation & Information

The train and bus stations are next to each other at the end of ulitsa Lenina. Exit the train station and walk up ulitsa Lenina, past Kirov park, to Str 25 October (the main street).

The central telephone office from which international calls can be booked is on ulitsa 25 Oktober. When the recipient answers, dial ☎ 3. The office is open daily from 7 am to 8.30 pm.

Change money next door at the Transdniestr Savings Bank, open weekdays from 8 am to 1 pm, 2 to 6 pm. There's a currency exchange in the central post office, ulitsa Lenina 17a (open weekdays 8 am to 6 pm).

City maps, regarded as military objects, are not available to humble tourists.

Registering with OVIR

All foreign visitors are required to register with the Tiraspol Militia Passport office (☎ 34 169), ulitsa Rosa Luxembourg 2. You have to state which hotel you are staying at, how many nights you intend to stay, and the purpose of your visit. You cannot check into any hotel until you have the scrap of paper dished out by the passport office in return for this information.

If you intend staying in Tiraspol longer than three days, you also have to register with OVIR (Otdel Viz I Registratsii; ☎ 61 200), Pereulok Rayevskaya 10. If you fail to do so, getting out of Transdniestr could be a costly exercise.

Note: Tighina's special security zone status enables foreign tourists to stay in the city without having to register with the local militia.

Water & Heating

Between 1 April and 30 October there is no heating or hot water in Tiraspol.

Things to See

Tiraspol has no history museum but the illustrated panels outside the city administration building, **House of Soviets** (Dom Sovetov) trace the city's history from 1792 when it became part of the Russian empire, through to the 1990s.

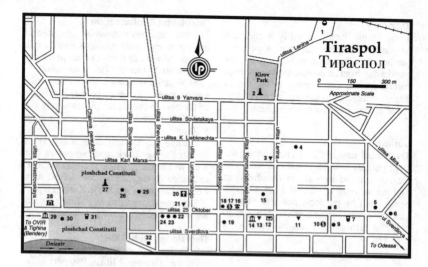

A **statue of Lenin** stands in front of the House of Soviets. Inside the building, there's a **memorial** to those who died in the 1992 military conflict, with a black and white portrait of each victim adorned with flowers.

Close by at ulitsa Kommunisticheskaya 34 is the **Museum of Headquarters**, where GI Kotovskovo, hero of the civil war, died in February 1920. The museum is open daily, except Thursday, from 10 am to 6 pm.

On ulitsa 25 Oktober stands a Soviet armoured tank from which the Transdniestran flag flies today. Behind is the **tomb of the Unknown Soldier**, flanked by an eternal flame in memory of those who died on 3 March 1992 during the first outbreak of fighting. The inscription in Russian reads 'You don't have a name but your deeds are eternal'. Eleven named soldiers killed prior to the civil war are buried here too. At the time of their burial, local authorities did not expect a further 500 people to be killed in what, until then, had been a relatively non-violent conflict. Those who died in the subsequent war are buried in the **city cemetery**, north of the centre, where a special alley has been allocated to the 1992 war victims.

Close by at ulitsa 25 Oktober 42, is the **house museum** of Nicolai Dimitriovich Zelinskogo. The poet (1866-1953) founded the first Soviet school of chemistry. The museum is open daily, except Tuesday, from 9 am to 5 pm. Opposite, is the **Presidential Palace** where Igor Smirnov rules his self-proclaimed republic.

Daily performances in Russian can be seen at 6 pm at the **Drama theatre**, ulitsa 25 Oktober, pictured on the 50,000 rouble bill. Close by is the **university**, founded in 1930. In front is a **statue of Chmelnistki**, pictured on the reverse side of the same bill.

At ulitsa Lenina 38, there is an outlet of the local **Kvint Brandy & Cognac factory** which still manages to function despite its sharp drop in sales since the collapse of the USSR. The shop is open daily, except Sunday, from 9 am to 2 pm, 3 pm to 7 pm. To the side of the Kino Cinema on ulitsa Lenina is a 1918 October Revolution **memorial**, erected to mark the 50th anniversary of the Russian revolution. Big plans are being made to celebrate its 100th birthday in 2017.

Places to Stay

Thanks to its two-tier pricing system, the

PLACES TO STAY

8	Hotel Drushba	Гостиница Дружба
32	Hotel Aist	Гостиница Аист

PLACES TO EAT

3	Astra	Кафе Астра
11	Plezinte Café	Кафе Плэчинте
13	Terasa Capital	
21	Bar Umbra	Умбра Бар

OTHER

1	Bus & Train Stations	Железнодорожны Воксал
2	Kirov Statue	
4	Lux Supermarket	Люкс
5	University	
6	Drama Theatre	
7	Eden	Едем Бар
9	House of Soviets	Дом Советов
10	Currency Exchange	
12	Post Office	
14	Museum of Headquarters	Музеи Штаба Навбригады Г.И. Котовского
15	Militia Passport Office	Паспортное Отделение
16	Central Telephone Office	Центральны Переговорный Пункт
17	Prisbank (Transdniestr Savings Bank)	Приднестровский Сберегательный Банк
18	Bukinist Bookshop	Букинист
19	Train & Airline Booking Office	Железнодорожная & Авиа Касса
20	Church	
22	Kvint Vodka Shop	Квинт
23	Artists' Salon	Художественный Салон
24	Travel Agency Aist	Агенство Аист
25	Kino	Кино
26	Disco & Music School	
27	Suvorov Statue	
28	Presidential Palace	
29	House Museum of ND Zelinskogo	Дом Музеи Н.Д. Зелинского
30	Heroes' Cemetery	
31	Prikhlada	

Hotel Drushba (☎ 34 131, 34 266), ulitsa 25 Oktober 118, is expensive. Doubles are US$18 for locals, and US$56 for foreigners. Rooms have private bath, TV and fridge, but bedsheets are grubby, toilet paper is not supplied and a hot bath is mission impossible.

Places to Eat

Considered the best of a bad bunch is the privately run *Astra* restaurant at ulitsa Karl Marxa 149. Cabbage, mushroom and mayonnaise salad is US$1.50, Armenian dried meat is US$2, and 100g of pelmeni is US$1.50. Avoid the ham and cheese omelette unless you're into hunks of fat.

At ulitsa 25 Oktober 116 is the small *Plezinte Café* which serves a small selection of lukewarm drinks, fresh cakes and savoury buns. The cheerier *Terasa Capital*, easily identifiable by its huge Caribbean-style Sprite and Coke umbrellas outside, is close by at ulitsa 25 Oktober 108.

Kiosks with tables and chairs stand outside the Kino Cinema on ulitsa Lenina.

Entertainment

The Astra has a billiard room and bar and is open daily from 11 am to 11 pm. A cooler bet is the underground bar-disco *Prikhlada* (☎ 34 642), opposite the presidential palace at ulitsa 25 Oktober 50. According to the sign outside you are not allowed to take in hand-grenades, guns, gas bottles or alcohol, while doormen adhere to a strict face control policy. It is a flashy place and is open daily from 11 to 3 am.

MOLDOVA

Entrance to the nightly teenage disco which kicks off inside the cinema at 8 pm is US$1. The dimly lit, green cellar bar, *Eden*, next to the Hotel Drushba at ulitsa 25 Oktober 126 gets good reports.

Getting There & Away

Bus Tickets for all buses are sold in the main ticket hall. You can only pay for tickets to other destinations in Transdniestr in the local currency. Bus tickets to Moldova/Ukraine are only sold in Moldovan lei/Ukrainian grivna. You can change money in the currency exchange in the central ticket hall.

Some additional buses not listed on the official timetable depart for Chişinău from outside the train station. These nippy microbuses leave every hour – or when they're full. Tickets are sold at the bus station or direct from the driver.

From Tiraspol there is one bus daily to Bălţi, two buses daily to Comrat, and three daily to Chişinău. There are also daily buses to Odessa in Ukraine. If you miss all three direct buses to Chişinău, hop on a trolleybus to Tighina from where numerous buses depart for the Moldovan capital.

Train The train station is on ulitsa Lenina. Tickets for same-day departures are sold in the main train station ticket hall. There is also an information booth – a question about national train services costs US$0.05, a question about services to CIS countries costs US$0.10, and a print-out of the correct timetable is US$0.12. Advance tickets (24 hours or more before departure) are sold in the ticket office on the second floor.

All Bucharest-Moscow and Chişinău-St Petersburg trains stop in Tiraspol. Most other eastbound trains from Chişinău to Ukraine and Russia stop in Tiraspol too (see Getting There & Away at the front of this book). There is one daily local train from Tiraspol and Chişinău.

Getting Around

Bus Nos 1 and 3, and microbuses Nos 1 and 3, run between the bus and train station, and the city centre. Tickets for regular buses

costing US$0.04 are sold by the driver. Tickets for microbuses cost US$0.30.

Trolleybus Nos 1 and 19 cross the bridge over the Dniestr to Tighina. Microbus Nos 1 and 19 also make the 20-minute journey but tickets are more expensive.

TIGHINA

- *area code ☎ 233 , pop 140,000*

Traditionally Tighina (Bendery in Russian), on the western banks of the Dniestr river, has always been an important military stronghold. Today it is home to the Russian-led peacekeeping force which has assured a fragile peace in the region since 1992.

During the 16th century Moldavian prince Ştefan cel Mare built a large defensive fortress here on the ruins of a fortified Roman camp. In 1538 the Ottoman sultan, Suleiman the Magnificent, conquered the fortress and transformed Tighina into a Turkish *raia* (colony), renaming the city Bender meaning 'belonging to the Turks'. Following the decisive Russian defeat of Sweden's Charles XII and Ukrainian Cossack leader Ivan Mazepa by Peter the Great at Poltava in 1709, it was to Tighina that the Swedish king and Cossack leader fled for refuge. Mazepa consequently died in Tighina fortress.

During the Russo-Turkish wars in the 18th century, Tighina was seized from the Turks by Russian troops who then massacred 30,000 Turkish Muslims in the city. In 1812 Tighina fell permanently into Russian hands and the fortress became occupied by Russian troops. USSR forces remained stationed here until 1992 when Tighina was made off-limits to armed forces. Theoretically the fortress has been empty since. Nevertheless it is not open to visitors.

The bloodiest fighting during the 1992 military conflict took place in Tighina and many walls of buildings in the centre remain badly bullet-pocked. The city today is protected as a security zone by peacekeeping forces who have various military installations and camouflaged personnel carriers at strategic points in the town. A pale blue flag with the letters MC written in pale yellow fly from these military points.

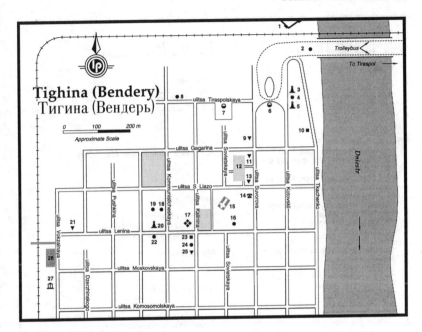

Tighina (Bendery)
Тигина (Вендерь)

0   100   200 m
Approximate Scale

ulitsa Tiraspolskaya
ulitsa Gagarina
ulitsa S Liazo
ulitsa Lenina
ulitsa Moskovskaya
ulitsa Komosomolskaya
ulitsa Sovetskaya
ulitsa Kommunisticheskaya
ulitsa Pushkina
ulitsa Vokzalnaya
ulitsa Dzerzhinskogo
ulitsa Kalinina
ulitsa Suvorova
ulitsa Kotovski
ulitsa Tkachenko
ulitsa Sovetskaya

Dniestr

Trolleybus
To Tiraspol
To Tiraspol

Orientation & Information

The left-luggage room in the bus station ticket hall is open daily from 6.30 to 11 am and 11.30 am to 4.30 pm. Change money at the currency exchange next to the central market on Str Sovetskaya. International telephone calls can be booked from the telephone office (open daily, except Sunday, from 7 am to 7.45 pm) on the corner of Str Lazlo and Str Suvorova. There is a Kodak Express outlet opposite the City Council building on ulitsa Lenina. The central department store is opposite the Hotel Dniestr on the corner of ulitsa Lenina and Str Kalinina.

Curfew

A curfew applies between 11 pm and 5 am.

Things to See

At the entrance to the city, close to the famous **Tighina-Tiraspol bridge**, is a **memorial park** dedicated to Tighina's 1992 war victims. An eternal flame burns in front of an armoured tank, from which flies the Transdniestran flag. Behind the tank is an eight-edged pyramid topped with an Orthodox cross. At the far end of the park, the names of 247 people killed in 1992 are engraved on a large memorial board. The park was opened in 1996.

Haunting **memorials** to those shot dead during the civil war are evident throughout many of the main streets in the centre.

The **City Council** building is at Lenina 17. Bullet holes are still evident in the wall. During the 1992 conflict, the immediate area in front of the council which witnessed the bloodiest fighting.

Next to the train station is a **Train Museum**, staged inside an old Russian CY 06-71 steam locomotive. It is open weekdays from 10 am to 5 pm. Running alongside Tiraspol's only museum is a typically Soviet, oversized granite mural in memory of the train workers who died in the 1918 revolution.

MOLDOVA

PLACES TO STAY

| 10 | Hotel Dniestr | Гостиница Днестр |
| 23 | Hotel Dniestr (branch) | Гостиница Днестр (Филиал) |

PLACES TO EAT

9	Bar Krom	Кром Бар
11	Café Minutka	Кафе Минутка
13	Café Jessica	Кафе Джесска
21	Tighina Café	Кафе Тигина
25	Terraced Café	

OTHER

1	Tighina Fortress	
2	Peacekeeping Force Post	М.С. Пост (Миротворческие Силы)
3	Flame to the Unknown Soldier	
4	Tank	
5	Memorial Monument 1992 Victims	
6	Trolleybus to Tiraspol	
7	Bus Station	Автовоксал
8	Peacekeeping Force Barracks	
12	Kolkhoz Market	Колхозны Рынок
14	Telephone Centre	Междугородны Телефон
15	Church	Преображенский Собор
16	City Council	
17	Floritchinka Department Store	Флоричика
18	Tennis Courts	
19	Fountain	
20	Lenin Statue	
22	Gorky Cinema	Кинотеатр Горкого
24	Cabaret Club	
26	Train Station	Железнодорожны Воксал
27	Train Museum	Музеи Революционной Боевои и Трудовои Славы Железнодорожников

Places to Stay & Eat

A three-tier pricing system is firmly intact at the central branch of the *Hotel Dniestr*, Str Kalinina 50. Foreigners pay US$10/33 for singles/doubles with shared bath. A luxury room with fridge, TV and private bathtub is US$58. Next door is the *Cabaret Club*. The terrace café at Str Kalinina 52 is also worth a nibble.

Overlooking the Dniestr river at Str Ktachenka 10 is the hotel's main branch. The *Hotel Dniestr* (☎ 29 478, 29 480) has 102 rooms. Singles/doubles with TV, fridge and private bath cost US$15/20 for foreigners. The café-bar on an old boat moored close by on the river is fine for an early nightcap.

The *Café Jessica*, opposite the telephone office on Str Liazo is the best place to eat in town. Lifesize statues of penguins stand outside the funky wooden exterior. The inside is not quite so fun but it's about the only place to get a real meal in town. The outside *Tighina Café* near the train station at Str Liazo 7 is OK.

Getting There & Away

The train station is at Privokzalnaya ploshchad. The information desk in the ticket hall is open daily from 8 am to 6 pm. Questions cost US$0.05 each. There is also a currency exchange here. Printed train timetables in Russian are sold from most news kiosks for US$0.15.

There are 16 buses daily to Chişinău and one daily to Comrat. Tickets for Chişinău can only be paid in Moldovan lei.

Trolleybus Nos 1 and 19 for Tiraspol depart from the bus stop next to the main roundabout at the entrance to Tighina. Tickets cost US$0.07. Microbuses Nos 1 and 19 also make the 20-minute journey but tickets are more expensive at US$0.23.

Glossary

These handy Romanian words can also be used in Moldova. Hungarian (Hun) is included for key words.

Agenţie de Voiaj CFR – train ticket office (Hun: vasúti jegyiroda)
Agenţie de Teatrală – theatre ticket office (Hun: színház jegyiroda)
autogară – bus station (Hun: távolsági autóbusz pályaudvar)
apă caldă – hot water (Hun: meleg víz)
apă reche – cold water (Hun: hideg víz)

bagage de mâna – left-luggage office (Hun: csomagmegőrző)
bandă roşie – red stripe (hiking)
barcă cu motor – motor boat
barcă cu rame – rowing boat
berărie – beer house
biserica – church (Hun: templom)
biserica de lemn – wooden church

cameră cu apă curentă – room with running water
cameră matrimonal – double room with a real double bed
casă de bilete – ticket office (Hun: jegyiroda)
cascadă – waterfall
căsuţe – wooden hut
cazare – room
cheile – gorge
cobalb – white-tailed eagle
crap – carp
cruce albastră – blue cross (hiking)

de jos – at the bottom
deschis – open (Hun: nyitva)
de sus – at the top
dispecerat cazare – accommodation office

egretă mică/mare – little/great egret
en detail – retail (shopping)
en gros – wholesale (shopping)

floare de colt – edelweiss

gara – train station (Hun: vasútállomás)
gâsca cu gât roşu – red-breasted goose
grădină de vară – summer garden
grinduri – sand dune

închis – closed (Hun: zárva)
ieşie – exit (Hun: kijárat)

intrare – entrance (Hun: bejárat)
intrare interzisa – no entry (Hun: tilos belépni)
joseni – lower

lebădă – swan
listă – menu
luptă – day

mănăstire – monastery (Hun: kolostor)
muzeul – museum (Hun: múzeum)

noapte – night
notă de plată – bill (Hun: számla)

orar – timetable (Hun: menetrend)

păduri – forest
pâine – bread
pelican comun – white pelican
piaţa – square (Hun: főtér) or market (Hun: piac)
popas – campsite (Hun: kemping)
plecare – departure: (Hun: indulás)
punct galbenă – yellow circle (hiking)

şalăul – pike perch
sală de concert – concert hall (Hun: hangversenyterem)
schimb valutar – currency exchange
scrumbie de Dunăre – Danube herring
sosire – arrival (Hun: érkezés)
spălătorie – launderette (Hun: patyolat)
spălătorie auto – car wash
stufăriş – reed bed
suseni – upper

telecabin – cable car
teleferic – collective term for all ski services
telescaun – chair lift
teleski – drag lift
terasa – terrace
ţigănuş – glossy Ibis
toaleta – toilet (Hun: toalett)
trasee – hiking trail
triunghi roşu – red triangle (hiking)

vamă – customs (Hun: vámkezelés)
vin albă – white wine (Hun: bor fehér)
vin roşu – red wine (Hun: bor vörös)

zone strict protejate – strictly protected zone

Language Guide

Romanian is much closer to classical Latin than the other Romance languages and the grammatical structure and basic word stock of the parent language are well preserved. Some Slavic words were incorporated in the 7th to 10th centuries as the Romanian language took definite shape. Speakers of French, Italian and Spanish won't be able to understand much spoken Romanian but will find written Romanian more or less comprehensible. Moldovan is a dialect of Romanian.

A few useful terms for getting around are *aleea*, 'avenue', *bulevardul*, 'boulevard', *calea*, 'road', *piaţa*, 'square', *şoseaua*, 'highway' and *strada*, 'street'. In Romania you can use the French *merci* to say 'thank you' – many locals do.

Lonely Planet's *Eastern Europe phrasebook* is very handy, with plenty of useful words and phrases translated into Romanian. In a sometimes difficult country such as Romania, the value of such a resource should not be underestimated.

Pronunciation

Until the mid-19th century, Romanian was written in the Cyrillic script, and between 1953 and 1994 its orthography was altered by the communists in an attempt to deny its Latin roots.

Today Romanian employs 28 Latin letters, some of which bear accents. It is spelt phonetically, so once you learn a few simple rules you should have no trouble with its pronunciation. Vowels without accents are pronounced as they are in Spanish or Italian. In Romanian there are no long and short vowels, but 'e', 'i', 'o' and 'u' form a diphthong or triphthong with adjacent vowels. At the beginning of a word, 'e' and 'i' are pronounced 'ye' and 'yi', while at the end of a word an 'i' is almost silent. At the end of a word 'ii' is pronounced 'ee'. The stress is usually on the penultimate syllable.

ă	as the 'ea' in 'pearl'
â	as the 'i' in 'river'
c	as in 'kit' (before 'a','o' and 'u')
c	as in church (before 'e' and 'i')
ch	as the 'k' in 'kit' (before 'e' and 'i')
g	as in 'good'
g	as in 'gentle' (before 'e' and 'i')
gh	as in 'good'
ş	'sh'
ţ	'tz'

Greetings & Civilities

Hello.	*Bună.*
Goodbye.	*La revedere.*
Good morning.	*Bună dimineaţa.*
Good day.	*Bună ziua.*
Good evening.	*Bună seara.*
Please.	*Vă rog.*
Thank you.	*Mulţumesc.*
I'm sorry/Forgive me.	*Iertaţi-mă.*
Excuse me.	*Scuzaţi-mă.*
Yes.	*Da.*
No.	*Nu.*

Small Talk

I don't understand.	*Nu înţeleg.*
Could you write it down?	*Puteţi să notaţi?*
What's it called?	*Cum se cheamă?*
Where do you live?	*De unde sânteţi?*
What work do you do?	*Cu ce vă ocupaţi?*
I'm a student.	*Sânt student.*

Accommodation

How much is it?	*Cât costă?*
Is that the price per person?	*Preţul acesta este per persoană?*
Is that the total price?	*Acesta este preţul total?*
Are there any extra charges?	*Mai este ceva de plătit?*
Do I pay extra for showers?	*Trebuie să plătesc în plus pentru duş?*

482

Where is there a cheaper hotel?	Unde este un hotel mai ieftin?
Should I make a reservation?	Pot face o rezervare?
It's very noisy.	Este foarte zgomotos.
Where is the toilet?	Unde este toaleta?

youth hostel	camin studentesc
camping ground	camping
private room	cameră particulară
single room	cameră de (pentru) o persoană
double room	cameră dublă

Getting Around

When is the ... bus?	Când este ... autobuz?
first	primul
last	ultimul
next	următorul

What time does it leave?	La ce oră este plecarea?
When is the next one after that?	Când este următorul după acesta?
How long does the trip take?	Cât timp durează excursia?
Where is the bus stop?	Unde este staţia de autobuz?
Where is the train station?	Unde este gara?
Where is the left-luggage room?	Unde este biroul pentru bagaje de mână?

arrival	sosire
departure	plecare
timetable	mersul/orar

Around Town

Where is ...?	Unde este ...?
the bank	banca
the museum	muzeu
the post office	poşta
the tourist information office	biroul de informatii turistice

Where are you going?	Unde mergeti?
I'm going to ...	Merg la ...
Where is it?	Unde este?
I can't find it.	Nu pot să găsesc.
Is it far?	Este departe?
Please show me on the map.	Vă rog arătaţi-mi pe hartă.
I want ...	Vreau ...
Do I need permission?	Am nevoie de aprobare?

left	stânga
right	dreapta
straight ahead	drept înainte

Entertainment

Where can I hear live music?	Unde pot asculta muzică ân concert?
Where can I buy a ticket?	Unde pot cumpăra un bilet?
I'm looking for a ticket.	Nu aveţi un bilet ân plus?
Is this a good seat?	Este un loc bun?

at the front	în primele rânduri
ticket	bilet

Food

I don't eat meat.	Nu consum carne.
beer	bere
bread	pâine
coffee	cafe
fish	peşte
fresh vegetables	legume proaspete
grocery store	băcănie
hot/cold	cald/rece
ice cream	înghețată
milk	lapte
mineral water	apă minerală
pork	porc
salad	salată
self-service cafeteria	autoservire
soup	supă
sugar	zahăr
tea	ceai
wine	vin

Shopping

Where can I buy one?	*Unde aş putea cumpăra?*
How much does it cost?	*Cât costă?*
That's (much) too expensive.	*Este (mult) prea scump.*
Is there a cheaper one?	*Pot găsi ceva mai ieftin?*
There is.	*Există.*
There isn't.	*Nu există.*

Time & Dates

When?	*Când?*
today	*azi*
tonight	*diseară*
tomorrow	*mâine*
in the morning	*dimineaţa*
in the evening	*seară*
every day	*în fiecare zi*
the day after tomorrow	*poimâine*
At what time?	*La ce oră?*
What time does it open?	*La ce oră se deschide?*
What time does it close?	*La ce oră se închide?*
open	*deschis*
closed	*închis*
Monday	*luni*
Tuesday	*marţi*
Wednesday	*miercuri*
Thursday	*joi*
Friday	*vineri*
Saturday	*sâmbătă*
Sunday	*duminică*
January	*ianuarie*
February	*februarie*
March	*martie*
April	*aprilie*
May	*mai*
June	*iunie*
July	*iulie*
August	*august*
September	*septembrie*
October	*octombrie*
November	*noiembrie*
December	*decembrie*

Numbers

1	*unu*
2	*doi*
3	*trei*
4	*patru*
5	*cinci*
6	*şase*
7	*şapte*
8	*opt*
9	*nouă*
10	*zece*
11	*unsprezece*
12	*doisprezece*
13	*treisprezece*
14	*patrusprezece*
15	*cincisprezece*
16	*şaisprezece*
17	*şaptesprezece*
18	*optsprezece*
19	*nouăsprezece*
20	*douăzeci*
21	*douăzeci şi unu*
22	*douăzeci şi doi*
23	*douăzeci şi trei*
30	*treizeci*
40	*patruzeci*
50	*cincizeci*
60	*şaizeci*
70	*şaptezeci*
80	*optzeci*
90	*nouăzeci*
100	*o sută*
1000	*o mie*
10,000	*zece mii*
one million	*un milion*

Index

LONELY PLANET JOURNEYS

JOURNEYS is a unique collection of travel writing – published by the company that understands travel better than anyone else. It is a series for anyone who has ever experienced – or dreamed of – the magical moment when they encountered a strange culture or saw a place for the first time. They are tales to read while you're planning a trip, while you're on the road or while you're in an armchair, in front of a fire.

JOURNEYS books catch the spirit of a place, illuminate a culture, recount a crazy adventure, or introduce a fascinating way of life. They always entertain, and always enrich the experience of travel.

THE GATES OF DAMASCUS
Lieve Joris

Translated by Sam Garrett

This best-selling book is a beautifully drawn portrait of day-to-day life in modern Syria. Through her intimate contact with local people, Lieve Joris draws us into the fascinating world that lies behind the gates of Damascus. Hala's husband is a political prisoner, jailed for his opposition to the Assad regime; through the author's friendship with Hala we see how Syrian politics impacts on the lives of ordinary people.

Lieve Joris, who was born in Belgium, is one of Europe's leading travel writers. In addition to an award-winning book on Hungary, she has published widely acclaimed accounts of her journeys to the Middle East and Africa. *The Gates of Damascus* is her fifth book.

'Expands the boundaries of travel writing' – **Times Literary Supplement**

KINGDOM OF THE FILM STARS
Journey into Jordan
Annie Caulfield

Kingdom of the Film Stars is a travel book and a love story. With honesty and humour, Annie Caulfield writes of travelling in Jordan and falling in love with a Bedouin. Her book offers fascinating insights into the country – from the traditional tent life of nomadic tribes to the first woman MP's battle with fundamentalist colleagues. *Kingdom of the Film Stars* unpicks some of the tight-woven Western myths about the Arab world, presenting cultural and political issues within the intimate framework of a compelling love story.

Annie Caulfield, who was born in Ireland and currently lives in London, is an award-winning playwright and journalist. She has travelled widely in the Middle East.

'Annie Caulfield is a remarkable traveller. Her story is fresh, courageous, moving, witty and sexy!' – **Dawn French**

LONELY PLANET TRAVEL ATLASES

Lonely Planet has long been famous for the number and quality of its guidebook maps. Now we've gone one step further and in conjunction with Steinhart Katzir Publishers produced a handy companion series: Lonely Planet travel atlases – maps of a country produced in book form.

Unlike other maps, which look good but lead travellers astray, our travel atlases have been researched on the road by Lonely Planet's experienced team of writers. All details are carefully checked to ensure the atlas corresponds with the equivalent Lonely Planet guidebook.

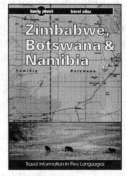

The handy atlas format means no holes, wrinkles, torn sections or constant folding and unfolding. These atlases can survive long periods on the road, unlike cumbersome fold-out maps. The comprehensive index ensures easy reference.

- full-colour throughout
- maps researched and checked by Lonely Planet authors
- place names correspond with Lonely Planet guidebooks
  – no confusing spelling differences
- legend and travelling information in English, French, German, Japanese and Spanish
- size: 230 x 160 mm

Available now:
Chile & Easter Island • Egypt • India & Bangladesh • Israel & the Palestinian Territories •Jordan, Syria & Lebanon • Kenya • Laos • Portugal • South Africa, Lesotho & Swaziland • Thailand • Turkey • Vietnam • Zimbabwe, Botswana & Namibia

---

LONELY PLANET TV SERIES & VIDEOS

Lonely Planet travel guides have been brought to life on television screens around the world. Like our guides, the programmes are based on the joy of independent travel, and look honestly at some of the most exciting, picturesque and frustrating places in the world. Each show is presented by one of three travellers from Australia, England or the USA and combines an innovative mixture of video, Super-8 film, atmospheric soundscapes and original music.

Videos of each episode – containing additional footage not shown on television – are available from good book and video shops, but the availability of individual videos varies with regional screening schedules.

Video destinations include: Alaska • American Rockies • Australia – The South-East • Baja California & the Copper Canyon • Brazil • Central Asia • Chile & Easter Island • Corsica, Sicily & Sardinia – The Mediterranean Islands • East Africa (Tanzania & Zanzibar) • Ecuador & the Galapagos Islands • Greenland & Iceland • Indonesia • Israel & the Sinai Desert • Jamaica • Japan • La Ruta Maya • Morocco • New York • North India • Pacific Islands (Fiji, Solomon Islands & Vanuatu) • South India • South West China • Turkey • Vietnam • West Africa • Zimbabwe, Botswana & Namibia

The Lonely Planet TV series is produced by:
Pilot Productions
The Old Studio
18 Middle Row
London W10 5AT UK

For video availability and ordering information contact your nearest Lonely Planet office.

Music from the TV series is available on CD & cassette.

PLANET TALK

Lonely Planet's FREE quarterly newsletter

We love hearing from you and think you'd like to hear from us.

*When...*is the right time to see reindeer in Finland?
*Where...*can you hear the best palm-wine music in Ghana?
*How...*do you get from Asunción to Areguá by steam train?
*What...*is the best way to see India?

For the answer to these and many other questions read PLANET TALK.

Every issue is packed with up-to-date travel news and advice including:

- a letter from Lonely Planet co-founders Tony and Maureen Wheeler
- go behind the scenes on the road with a Lonely Planet author
- feature article on an important and topical travel issue
- a selection of recent letters from travellers
- details on forthcoming Lonely Planet promotions
- complete list of Lonely Planet products

To join our mailing list contact any Lonely Planet office.

Also available: Lonely Planet T-shirts. 100% heavyweight cotton.

LONELY PLANET ONLINE

Get the latest travel information before you leave or while you're on the road

Whether you've just begun planning your next trip, or you're chasing down specific info on currency regulations or visa requirements, check out Lonely Planet Online for up-to-the minute travel information.

As well as travel profiles of your favourite destinations (including maps and photos), you'll find current reports from our researchers and other travellers, updates on health and visas, travel advisories, and discussion of the ecological and political issues you need to be aware of as you travel.

There's also an online travellers' forum where you can share your experience of life on the road, meet travel companions and ask other travellers for their recommendations and advice. We also have plenty of links to other online sites useful to independent travellers.

And of course we have a complete and up-to-date list of all Lonely Planet travel products including guides, phrasebooks, atlases, Journeys and videos and a simple online ordering facility if you can't find the book you want elsewhere.

www.lonelyplanet.com
or
AOL keyword: lp

LONELY PLANET

Guides by Region

Lonely Planet is known worldwide for publishing practical, reliable and no-nonsense travel information in our guides and on our Web site. The Lonely Planet list covers just about every accessible part of the world. Currently there are nine series: travel guides, shoe-string guides, walking guides, city guides, phrasebooks, audio packs, travel atlases, diving and snorkeling guides and travel literature.

AFRICA Africa – the South • Africa on a shoestring • Arabic (Egyptian) phrasebook • Arabic (Moroccan) phrasebook • Cairo • Cape Town • Central Africa • East Africa • Egypt • Egypt travel atlas • Ethiopian (Amharic) phrasebook • The Gambia & Senegal • Kenya • Kenya travel atlas • Malawi, Mozambique & Zambia • Morocco • North Africa • South Africa, Lesotho & Swaziland • South Africa, Lesotho & Swazi-land travel atlas • Swahili phrasebook • Tanzania, Zanzibar & Pemba • Trekking in East Africa • Tunisia • West Africa • Zimbabwe, Botswana & Namibia • Zimbabwe, Botswana & Namibia travel atlas
Travel Literature: The Rainbird: A Central African Journey • Songs to an African Sunset: A Zimbabwean Story • Mali Blues: Traveling to an African Beat

AUSTRALIA & THE PACIFIC Australia • Australian phrasebook • Bushwalking in Australia • Bush-walking in Papua New Guinea • Fiji • Fijian phrasebook • Islands of Australia's Great Barrier Reef • Melbourne • Micronesia • New Caledonia • New South Wales & the ACT • New Zealand • Northern Ter-ritory • Outback Australia • Papua New Guinea • Papua New Guinea (Pidgin) phrasebook • Queensland • Rarotonga & the Cook Islands • Samoa • Solomon Islands • South Australia • South Pacific Languages phrasebook • Sydney • Tahiti & French Polynesia • Tasmania • Tonga • Tramping in New Zealand • Vanuatu • Victoria • Western Australia
Travel Literature: Islands in the Clouds • Sean & David's Long Drive

CENTRAL AMERICA & THE CARIBBEAN Bahamas and Turks & Caicos • Barcelona • Bermuda • Central America on a shoestring • Costa Rica • Cuba • Dominican Republic & Haiti • Eastern Caribbean • Guatemala, Belize & Yucatán: La Ruta Maya • Jamaica • Mexico • Mexico City • Panama
Travel Literature: Green Dreams: Travels in Central America

EUROPE Amsterdam • Andalucía • Austria • Baltic States phrasebook • Barcelona • Berlin • Britain • British phrasebook • Canary Islands • Central Europe • Central Europe phrasebook • Corsica • Croatia • Czech & Slovak Republics • Denmark • Dublin • Eastern Europe • Eastern Europe phrase-book • Edinburgh • Estonia, Latvia & Lithuania • Europe • Finland • France • French phrasebook • Germany • German phrasebook • Greece • Greek phrasebook • Hungary • Iceland, Greenland & the Faroe Islands • Ireland • Italian phrasebook • Italy • Lisbon • London • Mediterranean Europe • Mediterranean Europe phrasebook • Norway • Paris • Poland • Portugal • Portugal travel atlas • Prague • Provence & the Côte d'Azur • Romania & Moldova • Rome • Russia, Ukraine & Belarus • Russian phrasebook • Scandinavian & Baltic Europe • Scandinavian Europe phrasebook • Scotland • Slovenia • Spain • Spanish phrasebook • St Petersburg • Switzerland • Trekking in Spain • Ukrainian phrasebook • Vienna • Walking in Britain • Walking in Italy • Walking in Ireland • Walking in Switzer-land • Western Europe • Western Europe phrasebook
Travel Literature: The Olive Grove: Travels in Greece

INDIAN SUBCONTINENT Bangladesh • Bengali phrasebook • Bhutan • Delhi • Goa • Hindi/Urdu phrasebook • India • India & Bangladesh travel atlas • Indian Himalaya • Karakoram Highway • Nepal • Nepali phrasebook • Pakistan • Rajasthan • South India • Sri Lanka • Sri Lanka phrasebook • Trekking in the Indian Himalaya • Trekking in the Karakoram & Hindukush • Trekking in the Nepal Himalaya
Travel Literature: In Rajasthan • Shopping for Buddhas

LONELY PLANET

Mail Order

Lonely Planet products are distributed worldwide. They are also available by mail order from Lonely Planet, so if you have difficulty finding a title please write to us. North and South American residents should write to 150 Linden St, Oakland, CA 94607, USA; European and African residents should write to 10a Spring Place, London NW5 3BH, UK; and residents of other countries to PO Box 617, Hawthorn, Victoria 3122, Australia.

ISLANDS OF THE INDIAN OCEAN Madagascar & Comoros ● Maldives ● Mauritius, Réunion & Seychelles

MIDDLE EAST & CENTRAL ASIA Arab Gulf States ● Central Asia ● Central Asia phrasebook ● Iran ● Israel & the Palestinian Territories ● Israel & the Palestinian Territories travel atlas ● Istanbul ● Jerusalem ● Jordan & Syria ● Jordan, Syria & Lebanon travel atlas ● Lebanon ● Middle East on a shoestring ● Turkey ● Turkish phrasebook ● Turkey travel atlas ● Yemen
Travel Literature: The Gates of Damascus ● Kingdom of the Film Stars: Journey into Jordan

NORTH AMERICA Alaska ● Backpacking in Alaska ● Baja California ● California & Nevada ● Canada ● Chicago ● Florida ● Hawaii ● Honolulu ● Los Angeles ● Louisiana ● Miami ● New England USA ● New Orleans ● New York City ● New York, New Jersey & Pennsylvania ● Pacific Northwest USA ● Puerto Rico ● Rocky Mountain States ● San Francisco ● Seattle ● Southwest USA ● Texas ● USA ● USA phrasebook ● Vancouver ● Washington, DC & the Capital Region
Travel Literature: Drive Thru America

NORTH-EAST ASIA Beijing ● Cantonese phrasebook ● China ● Hong Kong ● Hong Kong, Macau & Guangzhou ● Japan ● Japanese phrasebook ● Japanese audio pack ● Korea ● Korean phrasebook ● Kyoto ● Mandarin phrasebook ● Mongolia ● Mongolian phrasebook ● North-East Asia on a shoestring ● Seoul ● South-West China ● Taiwan ● Tibet ● Tibetan phrasebook ● Tokyo
Travel Literature: Lost Japan

SOUTH AMERICA Argentina, Uruguay & Paraguay ● Bolivia ● Brazil ● Brazilian phrasebook ● Buenos Aires ● Chile & Easter Island ● Chile & Easter Island travel atlas ● Colombia ● Ecuador & the Galapagos Islands ● Latin American Spanish phrasebook ● Peru ● Quechua phrasebook ● Rio de Janeiro ● South America on a shoestring ● Trekking in the Patagonian Andes ● Venezuela
Travel Literature: Full Circle: A South American Journey

SOUTH-EAST ASIA Bali & Lombok ● Bangkok ● Burmese phrasebook ● Cambodia ● Hanoi ● Hill Tribes phrasebook ● Ho Chi Minh City ● Indonesia ● Indonesia's Eastern Islands ● Indonesian phrasebook ● Indonesian audio pack ● Jakarta ● Java ● Laos ● Lao phrasebook ● Laos travel atlas ● Malay phrasebook ● Malaysia, Singapore & Brunei ● Myanmar (Burma) ● Philippines ● Pilipino (Tagalog) phrasebook ● Singapore ● South-East Asia on a shoestring ● South-East Asia phrasebook ● Thailand ● Thailand's Islands & Beaches ● Thailand travel atlas ● Thai phrasebook ● Thai audio pack ● Vietnam ● Vietnamese phrasebook ● Vietnam travel atlas

ALSO AVAILABLE: Antarctica ● Brief Encounters: Stories of Love, Sex & Travel ● Chasing Rickshaws ● Not the Only Planet: Travel Stories from Science Fiction ● Travel with Children ● Traveller's Tales

The Lonely Planet Story

Lonely Planet published its first book in 1973 in response to the numerous 'How did you do it?' questions Maureen and Tony Wheeler were asked after driving, bussing, hitching, sailing and railing their way from England to Australia.

Written at a kitchen table and hand collated, trimmed and stapled, *Across Asia on the Cheap* became an instant local bestseller, inspiring thoughts of another book.

Eighteen months in South-East Asia resulted in their second guide, *South-East Asia on a shoestring*, which they put together in a backstreet Chinese hotel in Singapore in 1975. The 'yellow bible', as it quickly became known to backpackers around the world, soon became *the* guide to the region. It has sold well over half a million copies and is now in its 9th edition, still retaining its familiar yellow cover.

Today there are over 350 titles, including travel guides, walking guides, language kits & phrasebooks, travel atlases, diving guides and travel literature. The company is the largest independent travel publisher in the world. Although Lonely Planet initially specialised in guides to Asia, today there are few corners of the globe that have not been covered.

The emphasis continues to be on travel for independent travellers. Tony and Maureen still travel for several months of each year and play an active part in the writing, updating and quality control of Lonely Planet's guides.

They have been joined by over 120 authors and 280 staff at our offices in Melbourne (Australia), Oakland (USA), London (UK) and Paris (France). Travellers themselves also make a valuable contribution to the guides through the feedback we receive in thousands of letters each year and on our web site.

The people at Lonely Planet strongly believe that travellers can make a positive contribution to the countries they visit, both through their appreciation of the countries' culture, wildlife and natural features, and through the money they spend. In addition, the company makes a direct contribution to the countries and regions it covers. Since 1986 a percentage of the income from each book has been donated to ventures such as famine relief in Africa; aid projects in India; agricultural projects in Central America; Greenpeace's efforts to halt French nuclear testing in the Pacific; and Amnesty International.

LONELY PLANET OFFICES

Australia
PO Box 617, Hawthorn, Victoria 3122
☎ (03) 9819 1877 fax (03) 9819 6459
email: talk2us@lonelyplanet.com.au

USA
150 Linden St, Oakland, CA 94607
☎ (510) 893 8555 TOLL FREE: 800 275 8555
fax (510) 893 8572
email: info@lonelyplanet.com

UK
10a Spring Place, London NW5 3BH
☎ (0171) 428 4800 fax (0171) 428 4828
email: go@lonelyplanet.co.uk

France
1 rue du Dahomey, 75011 Paris
☎ 01 55 25 33 00 fax 01 55 25 33 01
email: bip@lonelyplanet.fr
minitel: 3615 lonelyplanet *(1,29 F TTC/min)*

World Wide Web: www.lonelyplanet.com *or* AOL keyword: lp
Lonely Planet Images: lpi@lonelyplanet.com.au